Epistemology: the Big Questions

# Philosophy: The Big Questions

*Series Editor: James P. Sterba, University of Notre Dame, Indiana*

Designed to elicit a philosophical response in the mind of the student, this distinctive series of anthologies provides essential classical and contemporary readings that serve to make the central questions of philosophy come alive for today's students. It presents complete coverage of the Anglo-American tradition of philosophy, as well as the kinds of questions and challenges that it confronts today, both from other cultural traditions and from theoretical movements such as feminism and postmodernism.

*Aesthetics: the Big Questions*
Edited by Carolyn Korsmeyer

*Epistemology: the Big Questions*
Edited by Linda Martín Alcoff

*Ethics: the Big Questions*
Edited by James P. Sterba

*Metaphysics: the Big Questions*
Edited by Peter van Inwagen and Dean W. Zimmerman

*Philosophy of Language: the Big Questions*
Edited by Andrea Nye

*Philosophy of Religion: the Big Questions*
Edited by Eleonore Stump and Michael J. Murray

*Race, Class, Gender, and Sexuality: the Big Questions*
Edited by Naomi Zack, Laurie Shrage, and Crispin Sartwell

# EPISTEMOLOGY:

## *The Big Questions*

### EDITED BY LINDA MARTÍN ALCOFF

BLACKWELL
*Publishers*

Copyright © Blackwell Publishers Ltd, 1998

First published 1998

2 4 6 8 10 9 7 5 3 1

Blackwell Publishers Inc.
350 Main Street
Malden, Massachusetts 02148
USA

Blackwell Publishers Ltd
108 Cowley Road
Oxford OX4 1JF
UK

*Library of Congress Cataloging-in-Publication Data*
Epistemology : the big questions / edited by Linda Martín Alcoff.
      p.    cm. — (Philosophy, the big questions ; 3)
  Includes bibliographical references and index.
  ISBN 0-631-20579-9 — ISBN 0-631-20580-2 (pbk.)
  1. Knowledge, Theory of.   I. Alcoff, Linda.   II. Series.
BD161.E63  1998
121—dc21                           97-51452
                                        CIP

*British Library Cataloguing in Publication Data*
A CIP catalogue record for this book is available from the British Library.

Typeset in 10½ on 12½ pt Galliard
by Ace Filmsetting Ltd, Frome, Somerset
Printed in Great Britain by T.J. International, Padstow, Cornwall

This book is printed on acid-free paper

# CONTENTS

# CONTENTS

# PREFACE

Epistemology is a philosophical inquiry into the nature of knowledge, what justifies a belief, and what we mean when we say that a claim is true. As such, epistemology may seem daunting, but actually epistemological questions face us everyday. If I read something in the newspaper and believe what I have read, can I then be said to "know" it? Am I justified in believing what a teacher tells me, or what I remember of a past event, or only that which I can "see with my own eyes"? Is the most recently accepted scientific theory "true," even though it is likely to be modified or rejected in the future? If we cannot rely on science for the truth, how do we know we know anything at all?

Epistemology in the context of western philosophy is often thought to have begun with Plato, especially in the *Theaetetus*, where knowledge is first formulated as justified true belief; but as a self-conscious area of inquiry and as a coherent, developing conversation, it is usually dated from René Descartes' *Meditations*, a section of which opens this volume. Descartes initiated a radical challenge to tradition, and thus was a major influence on later Enlightenment philosophers, by calling all of his beliefs into doubt. Taking their lead from Descartes, many epistemologists since have been preoccupied with refuting skepticism and establishing both the possibility as well as the limits of human knowledge. For the last hundred years or so, however, epistemologists have shifted away from such ambitions toward more delimited questions, particularly those concerned with problems of justification, the organizational structure of knowledge, the meanings of epistemic terms, and the psychology of belief formation.

The twentieth-century linguistic turn, which translated traditional philosophical problems into questions about language, had a significant impact on epistemology as well as other fields, suggesting that the problem of knowledge was at bottom a problem concerning how to use the verb "to know" correctly, and that a close analysis of linguistic practice could answer most if not all of our epistemological questions. Perhaps most dramatic was the impact on accounts of truth, which came to be widely understood as a sort of exclamation point on a sentence without substantive meaning. Alternative to the focus on language was a focus on psychology and the scientific study of cognition, instigated by

W. V. O. Quine's argument that epistemology could find its answers by simply studying how believers actually justify their beliefs. This development, known today as the naturalized approach to epistemology, is also included in this volume.

These two twentieth-century trends in epistemology – the trend toward linguistic analysis and the trend toward a naturalistic approach – drove a broad wedge between the conversations about knowledge that were occurring mostly among Anglo-American philosophers and those occurring mostly among other European philosophers. Within the latter conversation, represented in this volume by Hans-Georg Gadamer, Ian Hacking, and Mary and Jim Tiles, the problem of history looms large for knowledge. That is, if our processes of knowing (or, as Hacking puts it, "styles of reasoning") evolve historically, and if we as knowers are historically conditioned by the available modes of perception and self-reflection present in our cultural era, then how can we rely on even our best methods as routes to truth? Actually, such a skeptical conclusion as this rhetorical question might seem to invite is not the general European (or "continental") response to the problem of history in relation to knowledge, but rather a reconfigured metaphysical account of what our claims to truth in reality entail.

The differences between Anglo-American and continental approaches to philosophy sometimes divert attention from the significant differences that exist within Anglo-American philosophy itself. The centrality of the problem of skepticism to epistemology is a case in point. Some have thought that epistemology is fundamentally or at least unavoidably concerned with skepticism. David Hume believed, for example, that sustained reflection about knowledge will eventually generate a skeptical attitude toward any claims to certainty. This reminds us of the adage about Socrates, that he knew enough to know that he didn't really know much at all. If Hume is correct, and epistemology is understood to be a sustained reflection about knowledge, then the need to consider and refute skepticism would seem to be its necessary core project. One result of this approach is that some proposed theories of knowledge, such as coherentism, will be rejected on the grounds that they cannot supply such a refutation. Coherentists hold that beliefs are justified on the basis of their ability to cohere with our web of beliefs, but what if the whole web is itself false? Unless coherentism can justify the web of beliefs as a whole, the coherentist procedure does not guarantee epistemic justification at all.

However, not all Anglo-American epistemologists agree about the centrality of skepticism in this way. Some hold that we *know* that we know at least some things, and the best way to ascertain the features of knowledge is then to explore what it is about the knowledge we do have that makes it knowledge. Going more on the offensive, others have argued that the concept of skepticism does not *make sense*, that it is incoherent in itself or self-refuting, since it requires some beliefs to generate a skeptical doubt in the first place, or because the skeptic is forced into a performative contradiction between the doxastic requirements of everyday life ("there is a truck barreling towards me") and their putative philosophical commitments. More recently, in this century, some have argued that the project to refute skepticism presupposes the possibility of characterizing all of our beliefs in one totalizing heap, of standing back from them as it were and assessing their status as a group. Thus, if sustained reflection on knowledge leads one to entertain general skeptical doubts, perhaps we should reflect, as Wittgenstein suggests, on how we are going about the process of reflection itself, and with what questions, concepts, and methodological commitments we begin.

For this volume, essays are collected from a wide range of philosophical starting points in order to generate a more comprehensive exploration of epistemological problems. My eye has been toward the future, and for that reason I have not included essays dealing with the Gettier problem, a chapter of epistemology that looks (thankfully) to be closing. It is my hope that in the future, twentieth-century impediments to conversations across diverse approaches in epistemology can be overcome. The fruitful results of this new dialogue will likely invigorate the field and resolve some stalemated debates. My graduate students at Syracuse University, to whom I dedicate this book, have inspired me to think creatively and optimistically about the future of philosophy. I would like especially to thank Heather Battaly, Marc Hight, and Eric Ramirez-Weaver for their invaluable editorial assistance. I am also very grateful to William Alston and Nancy Tuana for their helpful advice.

# ACKNOWLEDGMENTS

The editor and publishers gratefully acknowledge the following for permission to reproduce copyright material:

Cambridge University Press: for "Meditations" in *Descartes: Philosophical Writings, Vol. 2*, translated by John Cottingham, Robert Stoothoff, and Dugald Murdoch. Reprinted with the permission of Cambridge University Press; for Ernest Sosa, "The Raft and the Pyramid: Coherence versus Foundations in the Theory of Knowledge," pp. 165–91 in *Knowledge in Perspective* (Cambridge: Cambridge University Press, 1991). Copyright © 1991, Cambridge University Press, reprinted with the permission of Cambridge University Press;

Blackwell Publishers: for Ludwig Wittgenstein, "On Certainty;" for Paul Horwich, "The Minimal Theory," pp. 1–14 in *Truth* (Oxford: Blackwell, 1990); for Mary Tiles and Jim Tiles, "Idols of the Cave," pp. 1–6 and 169–212 in *An Introduction to Historical Epistemology: The Authority of Knowledge* (Oxford: Blackwell, 1993);

The Estate of A. J. Ayer: for "The Right to Be Sure," pp. 25–6, 31–5, and 41–4 in *The Problem of Knowledge* by A. J. Ayer (London: Penguin Books Ltd., 1956);

Princeton University Press: for Catherine Elgin, "Epistemology's End," pp. 3–20 in *Considered Judgment* (1996). Copyright © 1996 by Princeton University Press, reprinted by permission of Princeton University Press;

*Philosophical Topics*: for William P. Alston, "Internalism and Externalism in Epistemology from *Philosophical Topics*, 14, No. 1 (1986), pp. 185–226;

Kluwer Academic Publishers: for Carl Ginet, "The General Conditions of Knowledge: Justification," pp. 28–39 and 63–4 in *Knowledge, Perception, and Memory* (D. Reidel, 1975). Reproduced with kind permission from Kluwer Academic Publishers; for Alvin Goldman, "What is Justified Belief?" pp. 1–23 in *Justifica-*

ACKNOWLEDGMENTS

*tion and Knowledge*, edited by George Pappas (D. Reidel, 1979). Reprinted with kind permission from Kluwer Academic Publishers;

*Philosophy and Phenomenological Research*: for Keith DeRose, "Contextualism and Knowledge Attributions" in *Philosophy and Phenomenological Research*, 52 (December 1992), pp. 913–29. Reprinted by kind permission of the publishers;

Routledge, Inc.: for Lorraine Code, "Taking Subjectivity into Account," pp. 23–57 in *Rhetorical Spaces* (Routledge, 1993). Copyright © 1993. Reproduced by permission of Routledge, Inc.;

Alessandra Tanesini: for "The Practices of Justification;"

The Trustees of Princeton University: for Roderick Chisholm, "The Myth of the Given" in *The Foundations of Knowing*. Copyright © 1983 The Trustees of Princeton University. Reprinted with the permission of the Trustees of Princeton University;

Harvard University Press: for Laurence BonJour, "The Elements of Coherentism," pp. 87–110 in *Structure of Empirical Knowledge* (Cambridge, Mass.: Harvard University Press, 1985). Copyright © 1985 by the President and Fellows of Harvard University. Reprinted by permission of the publisher;

The Continuum Publishing Company: for Hans-Georg Gadamer, "The Hermeneutic Circle and the Problem of Prejudices," pp. 265–85 in *Truth and Method* (1989). English translation copyright © 1975 by Sheed and Ward Ltd, second revised edition copyright © 1989 by The Continuum Publishing Company, reprinted by permission of The Continuum Publishing Company;

Columbia University Press: for W. V. O. Quine, "Epistemology Naturalized," pp. 69–90 in *Ontological Relativity and Other Essays*. Copyright © 1969 by Columbia University Press. Reprinted with permission of the publisher;

Ridgeview Publishing Company: for Jaegwon Kim, "What is 'Naturalized Epistemology'?" pp. 381–405 in *Philosophical Perspectives, 2, Epistemology, 1988*, edited by James E. Tomberlin (copyright by Ridgeview Publishing Co., Atascadero, CA). Reprinted by permission of Ridgeview Publishing Company;

Phyllis Rooney: for "Putting Naturalized Epistemology to Work;"

MIT Press: for Ian Hacking, "Language, Truth and Reason," pp. 48–66 in *Rationality and Relativism*, edited by Hollis (MIT Press). Reprinted by permission of the publisher;

American Philosophical Association: for Richard Rorty, "Pragmatism, Relativism, and Irrationalism" in *Proceedings and Addresses*, Vol. 50, No. 6, pp. 719–38, reprinted by kind permission of the American Philosophical Association and the author;

*The Journal of Philosophy*: for Jonathan Vogel, "Cartesian Skepticism and Inference to the Best Explanation" in *The Journal of Philosophy*, LXXXVII, 11, (November 1990), pp. 658–66, reprinted by kind permission of the publishers and the author;

*The Journal of Philosophy*: for Barry Stroud, "Skepticism and the Possibility of Knowledge" in *The Journal of Philosophy*, LXXXI, 11, (October 1984), pp. 545–51, reprinted by kind permission of the publishers;

Academic Printing and Publishing: for Naomi Scheman, "Othello's Doubt/Desdemona's Death: The Engendering of Scepticism," pp. 57–74 in *Power, Gender, Values*, edited by Judith Genova (Edmonton, AB: Academic Printing and Publishing, 1987). Reprinted by kind permission of Academic Printing and Publishing;

University of Minnesota Press: for Genevieve Lloyd, "The 'Maleness' of Reason," pp. 103–10 and p. 122 in *The Man of Reason: "Male" and "Female" in Western Philosophy* (Minneapolis: University of Minnesota Press, 1984). Reprinted by kind permission of the University of Minnesota Press;

*Social Theory and Practice*: for Charles W. Mills, "Alternative Epistemologies" in *Social Theory and Practice*, Vol. 14, No. 3, (Fall 1988), pp. 237–63, reprinted by kind permission of the publisher and the author;

Every effort has been made to trace the copyright holders but if any have been inadvertently overlooked the publishers will be pleased to make the necessary arrangements at the first opportunity. The publishers apologize for any errors or omissions in the above list and would be grateful to be notified of any corrections that should be incorporated in the next edition or reprint of this book.

# PART ONE

# WHAT IS KNOWLEDGE?

# Introduction

René Descartes (1596–1650) was a French philosopher, mathematician, and scientist who, although writing well before the Enlightenment, had the courage and audacity to challenge the validity of all his beliefs, including his belief in God. Ironically, in pursuing the farthest reaches of what can be doubted, Descartes found the basis of knowledge itself. Descartes' meditations upon which of his beliefs might survive the test of rational doubt created a legacy that emphasized the need to justify our beliefs through tests of reason, logic, and clarity. Thus, for Descartes, only those beliefs which have survived the rigor of such tests can be called knowledge.

The two essays following the section taken from Descartes' *Meditations* offer representative twentieth-century approaches to knowledge through considerations of how and when we use the verb "to know." A. J. Ayer (1910–89) understands the question of knowledge as a question of meaning, since knowledge must be expressed in meaningful sentences before its status can be evaluated. Ayer then uses the norms of everyday language to flesh out and ultimately support the classical definition of knowledge as justified true belief. One's "right to be sure," or to be confident in making knowledge claims, can best be elucidated through an account of the rules of language.

Ludwig Wittgenstein (1889–1951), writing before Ayer, was actually the instigator behind this linguistic approach to philosophical problems. However, in this excerpt from his late work, *On Certainty*, Wittgenstein suggests some rather different conclusions to Ayer. It is not so much that philosophical problems can be *solved* through a turn toward linguistic practice, but that they can thereby be revealed as *specious*. He suggests we ask, when does doubt arise in the course of everyday knowledge, and when does it *not* arise. Wittgenstein seems to be mischievously suggesting that sustained philosophical reflections have only confused our understanding of what is necessary in order to have the "right to be sure."

Catherine Elgin's essay elegantly distinguishes between three types of epistemological approach, thus introducing the range of contemporary positions running from forms of foundationalism and positivism on the one hand all the way toward forms of idealism and postmodernism on the other. She organizes this range of options into three general conceptions of what knowledge is, and contrasts these with regard to their real-world applicability and whether they avoid relativism or skepticism. Taking issue with Ayer and Wittgenstein, Elgin argues that our choice between these approaches will be largely based on, not just linguistic rules, but our metaphysical intuitions and accounts of the real.

What, then, is knowledge? Perhaps this term itself admits of more than one valid definition, depending on what project one is engaged in. Below is a range of such projects.

### Further Reading

Cottingham, John. *Descartes*. Oxford: Basil Blackwell, 1986.

Dancy, Jonathan. *An Introduction to Contemporary Epistemology*. Oxford: Basil Blackwell, 1985.

Hacker, P. M. S. *Insight and Illusion: Themes in the Philosophy of Wittgenstein*. Revised edition. Oxford: Clarendon Press, 1986.

Russell, Bertrand. *The Problems of Philosophy*. Oxford: Oxford University Press, 1912.

# 1  Meditations

## *René Descartes*

MEDITATIONS ON FIRST PHILOSOPHY
*in which are demonstrated the existence of God and the distinction between
the human soul and the body*

### First Meditation

#### *What can be called into doubt*

Some years ago I was struck by the large number of falsehoods that I had accepted as true in my childhood, and by the highly doubtful nature of the whole
edifice that I had subsequently based on them. I realized that it was necessary,
once in the course of my life, to demolish everything completely and start again
right from the foundations if I wanted to establish anything at all in the sciences
that was stable and likely to last. But the task looked an enormous one, and I
began to wait until I should reach a mature enough age to ensure that no
subsequent time of life would be more suitable for tackling such inquiries. This
led me to put the project off for so long that I would now be to blame if by
pondering over it any further I wasted the time still left for carrying it out. So
today I have expressly rid my mind of all worries and arranged for myself a clear
stretch of free time. I am here quite alone, and at last I will devote myself
sincerely and without reservation to the general demolition of my opinions.

But to accomplish this, it will not be necessary for me to show that all my
opinions are false, which is something I could perhaps never manage. Reason
now leads me to think that I should hold back my assent from opinions which
are not completely certain and indubitable just as carefully as I do from those
which are patently false. So, for the purpose of rejecting all my opinions, it will
be enough if I find in each of them at least some reason for doubt. And to do
this I will not need to run through them all individually, which would be an
endless task. Once the foundations of a building are undermined, anything
built on them collapses of its own accord; so I will go straight for the basic
principles on which all my former beliefs rested.

Whatever I have up till now accepted as most true I have acquired either from
the senses or through the senses. But from time to time I have found that the
senses deceive, and it is prudent never to trust completely those who have deceived us even once.

Yet although the senses occasionally deceive us with respect to objects which
are very small or in the distance, there are many other beliefs about which doubt

is quite impossible, even though they are derived from the senses – for example, that I am here, sitting by the fire, wearing a winter dressing-gown, holding this piece of paper in my hands, and so on. Again, how could it be denied that these hands or this whole body are mine? Unless perhaps I were to liken myself to madmen, whose brains are so damaged by the persistent vapours of melancholia that they firmly maintain they are kings when they are paupers, or say they are dressed in purple when they are naked, or that their heads are made of earthenware, or that they are pumpkins, or made of glass. But such people are insane, and I would be thought equally mad if I took anything from them as a model for myself.

A brilliant piece of reasoning! As if I were not a man who sleeps at night, and regularly has all the same experiences[1] while asleep as madmen do when awake – indeed sometimes even more improbable ones. How often, asleep at night, am I convinced of just such familiar events – that I am here in my dressing-gown, sitting by the fire – when in fact I am lying undressed in bed! Yet at the moment my eyes are certainly wide awake when I look at this piece of paper; I shake my head and it is not asleep; as I stretch out and feel my hand I do so deliberately, and I know what I am doing. All this would not happen with such distinctness to someone asleep. Indeed! As if I did not remember other occasions when I have been tricked by exactly similar thoughts while asleep! As I think about this more carefully, I see plainly that there are never any sure signs by means of which being awake can be distinguished from being asleep. The result is that I begin to feel dazed, and this very feeling only reinforces the notion that I may be asleep.

Suppose then that I am dreaming, and that these particulars – that my eyes are open, that I am moving my head and stretching out my hands – are not true. Perhaps, indeed, I do not even have such hands or such a body at all. Nonetheless, it must surely be admitted that the visions which come in sleep are like paintings, which must have been fashioned in the likeness of things that are real, and hence that at least these general kinds of things – eyes, head, hands and the body as a whole – are things which are not imaginary but are real and exist. For even when painters try to create sirens and satyrs with the most extraordinary bodies, they cannot give them natures which are new in all respects; they simply jumble up the limbs of different animals. Or if perhaps they manage to think up something so new that nothing remotely similar has ever been seen before – something which is therefore completely fictitious and unreal – at least the colours used in the composition must be real. By similar reasoning, although these general kinds of things – eyes, head, hands and so on – could be imaginary, it must at least be admitted that certain other even simpler and more universal things are real. These are as it were the real colours from which we form all the images of things, whether true or false, that occur in our thought.

This class appears to include corporeal nature in general, and its extension; the shape of extended things; the quantity, or size and number of these things; the place in which they may exist, the time through which they may endure,[2] and so on.

So a reasonable conclusion from this might be that physics, astronomy, medicine, and all other disciplines which depend on the study of composite things, are doubtful; while arithmetic, geometry and other subjects of this kind, which deal only with the simplest and most general things, regardless of whether they really exist in nature or not, contain something certain and indubitable. For whether I am awake or asleep, two and three added together are five, and a square has no more than four sides. It seems impossible that such transparent truths should incur any suspicion of being false.

And yet firmly rooted in my mind is the long-standing opinion that there is an omnipotent God who made me the kind of creature that I am. How do I know that he has not brought it about that there is no earth, no sky, no extended thing, no shape, no size, no place, while at the same time ensuring that all these things appear to me to exist just as they do now? What is more, since I sometimes believe that others go astray in cases where they think they have the most perfect knowledge, may I not similarly go wrong every time I add two and three or count the sides of a square, or in some even simpler matter, if that is imaginable? But perhaps God would not have allowed me to be deceived in this way, since he is said to be supremely good. But if it were inconsistent with his goodness to have created me such that I am deceived all the time, it would seem equally foreign to his goodness to allow me to be deceived even occasionally; yet this last assertion cannot be made.[3]

Perhaps there may be some who would prefer to deny the existence of so powerful a God rather than believe that everything else is uncertain. Let us not argue with them, but grant them that everything said about God is a fiction. According to their supposition, then, I have arrived at my present state by fate or chance or a continuous chain of events, or by some other means; yet since deception and error seem to be imperfections, the less powerful they make my original cause, the more likely it is that I am so imperfect as to be deceived all the time. I have no answer to these arguments, but am finally compelled to admit that there is not one of my former beliefs about which a doubt may not properly be raised; and this is not a flippant or ill-considered conclusion, but is based on powerful and well thought-out reasons. So in future I must withhold my assent from these former beliefs just as carefully as I would from obvious falsehoods, if I want to discover any certainty.[4]

But it is not enough merely to have noticed this; I must make an effort to remember it. My habitual opinions keep coming back, and, despite my wishes, they capture my belief, which is as it were bound over to them as a result of long occupation and the law of custom. I shall never get out of the habit of confidently assenting to these opinions, so long as I suppose them to be what in fact they are, namely highly probable opinions – opinions which, despite the fact that they are in a sense doubtful, as has just been shown, it is still much more reasonable to believe than to deny. In view of this, I think it will be a good plan to turn my will in completely the opposite direction and deceive myself, by pretending for a time that these former opinions are utterly false and imaginary. I shall do this until the weight of preconceived opinion is counter-balanced and the distorting influence of habit no longer prevents my judgement from perceiving things correctly. In the meantime, I know that no danger or error will result from my plan, and that I cannot possibly go too far in my distrustful attitude. This is because the task now in hand does not involve action but merely the acquisition of knowledge.

I will suppose therefore that not God, who is supremely good and the source of truth, but rather some malicious demon of the utmost power and cunning has employed all his energies in order to deceive me. I shall think that the sky, the air, the earth, colours, shapes, sounds and all external things are merely the delusions of dreams which he has devised to ensnare my judgement. I shall consider myself as not having hands or eyes, or flesh, or blood or senses, but as falsely believing that I have all these things. I shall stubbornly and firmly persist in this meditation; and, even if it is not in my power to know any truth, I shall at least do what is in my power,[5] that is, resolutely guard against assenting to any falsehoods, so that the deceiver, however powerful and cunning he may be, will be unable to impose on me in the slightest degree. But this is an arduous undertaking, and a kind of laziness brings me back to normal life. I am like a prisoner who is enjoying an imaginary freedom while asleep; as he begins to suspect that he is asleep, he dreads being woken up, and goes along with the pleasant illusion as long as he can. In the same way, I happily slide back into my old opinions and dread being shaken out of them, for fear that my peaceful sleep may be followed by hard labour when I wake, and that I shall have to toil not in the light, but amid the inextricable darkness of the problems I have now raised.

## Second Meditation

*The nature of the human mind, and how it is better known than the body*

So serious are the doubts into which I have been thrown as a result of yesterday's meditation that I can neither put them out of my mind nor see any way of resolving them. It feels as if I have fallen unexpectedly into a deep whirlpool which tumbles me around so that I can neither stand on the bottom nor swim up to the top. Nevertheless I will make an effort and once more attempt the same path which I started on yesterday. Anything which admits of the slightest doubt I will set aside just as if I had found it to be wholly false; and I will proceed in this way until I recognize something certain, or, if nothing else, until I at least recognize for certain that there is no certainty. Archimedes used to demand just one firm and immovable point in order to shift the entire earth; so I too can hope for great things if I manage to find just one thing, however slight, that is certain and unshakeable.

I will suppose then, that everything I see is spurious. I will believe that my memory tells me lies, and that none of the things that it reports ever happened. I have no senses. Body, shape, extension, movement and place are chimeras. So what remains true? Perhaps just the one fact that nothing is certain.

Yet apart from everything I have just listed, how do I know that there is not something else which does not allow even the slightest occasion for doubt? Is there not a God, or whatever I may call him, who puts into me[6] the thoughts I am now having? But why do I think this, since I myself may perhaps be the author of these thoughts? In that case am not I, at least, something? But I have just said that I have no senses and no body. This is the sticking point: what follows from this? Am I not so bound up with a body and with senses that I cannot exist without them? But I have convinced myself that there is absolutely nothing in the world, no sky, no earth, no minds, no bodies. Does it now follow that I too do not exist? No: if I convinced myself of something[7] then I certainly existed. But there is a deceiver of supreme power and cunning who is deliberately and constantly deceiving me. In that case I too undoubtedly exist, if he is deceiving me; and let him deceive me as much as he can, he will never bring it about that I am nothing so long as I think that I am something. So after considering everything very thoroughly, I must finally conclude that this proposition, *I am, I exist*, is necessarily true whenever it is put forward by me or conceived in my mind.

But I do not yet have a sufficient understanding of what this "I" is, that now necessarily exists. So I must be on my guard against carelessly taking something else to be this "I", and so making a mistake in the very item of knowledge that I maintain is the most certain and evident of all. I will therefore go back and meditate on what I originally believed myself to be, before I embarked on this present train of thought. I will then subtract anything capable of being weakened, even minimally, by the arguments now introduced, so that what is left at the end may be exactly and only what is certain and unshakeable.

What then did I formerly think I was? A man. But what is a man? Shall I say "a rational animal"? No; for then I should have to inquire what an animal is, what rationality is, and in this way one question would lead me down the slope to other harder ones, and I do not now have the time to waste on subtleties of this kind. Instead I propose to concentrate on what came into my thoughts spontaneously and quite naturally whenever I used to consider what I was. Well, the first thought to come to mind was that I had a face, hands, arms and the whole mechanical structure of limbs which can be seen in a corpse, and which I called the body. The next thought was that I was nourished, that I moved about, and that I engaged in sense-perception and thinking; and these actions I attributed to the soul. But as to the nature of this soul, either I did not think about this or else I imagined it to be something tenuous, like a wind or fire or ether, which permeated my more solid parts. As to the body, however, I had no doubts about it, but thought I knew its nature distinctly. If I had tried to describe the mental conception I had of it, I would have expressed it as follows: by a body I understand whatever has a determinable shape and a definable location and can occupy a space in such a way as to exclude any other body; it can be perceived by touch, sight, hearing, taste or smell, and can be moved in various ways, not by itself but by whatever else comes into contact with it. For, according to my judgement, the power of self-movement, like the power of sensation or of thought, was quite foreign to the nature of a body; indeed, it was a source of wonder to me that certain bodies were found to contain faculties of this kind.

But what shall I now say that I am, when I am supposing that there is some supremely powerful and, if it is permissible to say so, malicious deceiver, who is deliberately trying to trick me in every way he can? Can I now assert that I possess even the most insignificant of all the attributes which I have just said belong to the nature of a body? I scrutinize them, think about them, go over them again, but nothing suggests itself; it is tiresome and pointless to go through the list once more. But what about the attributes I assigned to the soul? Nutrition or movement? Since now I do not have a body, these are mere fabrications. Sense-perception? This surely does not occur without a body, and besides, when asleep I have appeared to perceive through the senses many things which I afterwards realized I did not perceive through the senses at all. Thinking? At last I have discovered it – thought; this alone is inseparable from me. I am, I exist – that is certain. But for how long? For as long as I am thinking. For it could be that were I totally to cease from thinking, I should totally cease to exist. At present I am not admitting anything except what is necessarily true. I am, then, in the strict sense only a thing that thinks;[8] that is, I am a mind, or intelligence, or intellect, or reason – words whose meaning I have been ignorant of until now. But for all that I am a thing which is real and which truly exists. But what kind of a thing? As I have just said – *a thinking thing*.

What else am I? I will use my imagination.[9] I am not that structure of limbs which is called a human body. I am not even some thin vapour which permeates the limbs – a wind, fire, air, breath, or whatever I depict in my imagination; for these are things which I have supposed to be nothing. Let this supposition stand,[10] for all that I am still something. And yet may it not perhaps be the case that these very things which I am supposing to be nothing, because they are unknown to me, are in reality identical with the "I" of which I am aware? I do not know, and for the moment I shall not argue the point, since I can make judgements only about things which are known to me. I know that I exist; the question is, what is this "I" that I know? If the "I" is understood strictly as we have been taking it, then it is quite certain that knowledge of it does not depend on things of whose existence I am as yet unaware; so it cannot depend on any of the things which I invent in my imagination. And this very word "invent" shows me my mistake. It would indeed be a case of fictitious invention if I used my imagination to establish that I was something or other; for imagining is simply contemplating the shape or image of a corporeal thing. Yet now I know for certain both that I exist and at the same time that all such images and, in general, everything relating to the nature of body, could be mere dreams [and chimeras]. Once this point has been grasped, to say "I will use my imagination to get to know more distinctly what I am" would seem to be as silly as saying "I am now awake, and see some truth; but since my vision is not yet clear enough, I will deliberately fall asleep so that my dreams may provide a truer and clearer representation." I thus realize that none of the things that the imagination enables me to grasp is at all relevant to this knowledge of myself which I possess, and that the mind must therefore be most carefully diverted from such things[11] if it is to perceive its own nature as distinctly as possible.

But what then am I? A thing that thinks. What is that? A thing that doubts, understands, affirms, denies, is willing, is unwilling, and also imagines and has sensory perceptions.

This is a considerable list, if everything on it belongs to me. But does it? Is it not one and the same "I" who is now doubting almost everything, who nonetheless understands some things, who affirms that this one thing is true, denies everything else, desires to know more, is unwilling to be deceived, imagines many things even involuntarily, and is aware of many things which apparently come from the senses? Are not all these things just as true as the fact that I exist, even if I am asleep all the time, and even if he who created me is doing all he can to deceive me? Which of all these activities is distinct from my thinking? Which of them can be said to be separate from myself? The fact that it is I who am doubting and understanding and willing is so evident that I see no way of making it any clearer. But it is also the case that the "I" who imagines is the same "I". For even if, as I have supposed, none of the objects of imagination are real, the power of imagination is something which really exists and is part of my thinking. Lastly, it is also the same "I" who has sensory perceptions, or is aware of bodily things as it were through the senses. For example, I am now seeing light, hearing a noise, feeling heat. But I am asleep, so all this is false. Yet I certainly *seem* to see, to hear, and to be warmed. This cannot be false; what is called "having a sensory perception" is strictly just this, and in this restricted sense of the term it is simply thinking.

From all this I am beginning to have a rather better understanding of what I am. But it still appears – and I cannot stop thinking this – that the corporeal things of which images are formed in my thought, and which the senses investigate, are known with much more distinctness than this puzzling "I" which cannot be pictured in the imagination. And yet it is surely surprising that I should have a more distinct grasp of things which I realize are doubtful, unknown and foreign to me, than I have of that which is true and known – my own self. But I see what it is: my mind enjoys wandering off and will not yet submit to being restrained within the bounds of truth. Very well then; just this once let us give it a completely free rein, so that after a while, when it is time to tighten the reins, it may more readily submit to being curbed.

Let us consider the things which people commonly think they understand most distinctly of all; that is, the bodies which we touch and see. I do not mean bodies in general – for general perceptions are apt to be somewhat more confused – but one particular body. Let us take, for example, this piece of wax. It has just been taken from the honeycomb; it has not yet quite lost the taste of the honey; it retains some of the scent of the flowers from which it was gathered; its colour, shape and size are plain to see; it is hard, cold and can be handled without difficulty; if you rap it with your knuckle it makes a sound. In short, it has everything which appears necessary to enable a body to be known as distinctly as possible. But even as I speak, I put the wax by the fire, and look: the residual taste is eliminated, the smell goes away, the colour changes, the shape is lost, the size increases; it becomes liquid and hot; you can hardly touch it, and if you strike it, it no longer makes a sound. But does the same wax remain? It must be admitted that it does; no one denies it, no one thinks otherwise. So what was it in the wax that I understood with such distinctness? Evidently none of the features which I arrived at by means of the senses; for whatever came under taste, smell, sight, touch or hearing has now altered – yet the wax remains.

Perhaps the answer lies in the thought which now comes to my mind; namely, the wax was not after all the sweetness of the honey, or the fragrance of the flowers, or the whiteness, or the shape, or the sound, but was rather a body which presented itself to me in these various forms a little while ago, but which now exhibits different ones. But what exactly is it that I am now imagining? Let us concentrate, take away everything which does not belong to the wax, and see what is left: merely something extended, flexible and changeable. But what is meant here by "flexible" and "changeable"? Is it what I picture in my imagination: that this piece of wax is capable of changing from a round shape to a square shape, or from a square shape to a triangular shape? Not at all; for I can grasp that the wax is capable of countless changes of this kind, yet I am unable to run through this immeasurable number of changes in my imagination, from which it follows that it is not the faculty of imagination that gives me my grasp of the wax as flexible and changeable. And what is meant by "extended"? Is the extension of the wax also unknown? For it increases if the wax melts, increases again if it boils, and is greater still if the heat is increased. I would not be making a correct judgement about the nature of wax unless I believed it capable of being extended in many more different ways than I will ever encompass in my imagination. I must therefore admit that the nature of this piece of wax is in no way revealed by my imagination, but is perceived by the mind alone. (I am speaking of this particular piece of wax; the point is even clearer with regard to wax in general.) But what is this wax which is perceived by the mind alone?[12] It is of course the same wax which I see, which I touch, which I picture in my imagination, in short the same wax which I thought it to be from the start. And yet, and here is the point, the perception I have of it[13] is a case not of vision or touch or imagination – nor has it ever been, despite previous appearances – but of purely mental scrutiny; and this can be imperfect and confused, as it was before, or clear and distinct as it is now, depending on how carefully I concentrate on what the wax consists in.

But as I reach this conclusion I am amazed at how [weak and] prone to error my mind is. For although I am thinking about these matters within myself, silently and without speaking, nonetheless the actual words bring me up short, and I am almost tricked by ordinary ways of talking. We say that we see the wax itself, if it is there before us, not that we judge it to be there from its colour or shape; and this might lead me to conclude without more ado that knowledge of the wax comes from what the eye sees, and not from the scrutiny of the mind alone. But then if I look out of the window and see men crossing the square, as I just happen to have done, I normally say that I see the men themselves, just as I say that I see the wax. Yet do I see any more than hats and coats which could conceal automatons? I *judge* that they are men. And so something which I thought I was seeing with my eyes is in fact grasped solely by the faculty of judgement which is in my mind.

However, one who wants to achieve knowledge above the ordinary level should feel ashamed at having taken ordinary ways of talking as a basis for doubt. So let us proceed, and consider on which occasion my perception of the nature of the wax was more perfect and evident. Was it when I first looked at it, and believed I knew it by my external senses, or at least by what they call the "common" sense – that is, the power of imagination? Or is my knowledge more perfect now, after a more careful investigation of the nature of the wax and of the means by which it is known? Any doubt on this issue would clearly be foolish; for what distinctness was there in my earlier perception? Was there anything in it which an animal could not possess? But when I distinguish the wax from its outward forms – take the clothes off, as it were, and consider it naked – then although my judgement may still contain errors, at least my perception now requires a human mind.

But what am I to say about this mind, or about myself? (So far, remember, I am not admitting that there is anything else in me except a mind.) What, I ask, is this "I" which seems to perceive the wax so distinctly? Surely my awareness of my own self is not merely much truer and more certain than my awareness of the wax, but also much more distinct and evident. For if I judge that the wax exists from the fact that I see it, clearly this same fact entails much more evidently that I myself also exist. It is possible that what I see is not really the wax; it is possible that I do not even have eyes with which to see anything. But when I see, or think I see (I am not here distinguishing the two), it is simply not possible that I who am now thinking am not something. By the same token, if I judge that the wax exists from the fact that I touch it, the same result follows, namely that I exist. If I judge that it exists from the fact that I imagine it, or for any other reason, exactly the same thing follows. And the result that I have grasped in the case of the wax may be applied to everything else located outside me. Moreover, if my perception of the wax seemed more distinct[14] after it was established not just by sight or touch but by many other considerations, it must be admitted that I now know myself even more distinctly. This is because every consideration whatsoever which contributes to my perception of the wax, or of any other body, cannot but establish even more effectively the nature of my own mind. But besides this, there is so much else in the mind itself which can serve to make my knowledge of it more distinct, that it scarcely seems worth going through the contributions made by considering bodily things.

I see that without any effort I have now finally got back to where I wanted. I now know that even bodies are not strictly perceived by the senses or the faculty of imagination but by the intellect alone, and that this perception derives not from their being touched or seen but from their being understood; and in view of this I know plainly that I can achieve an easier and more evident perception of my own mind than of anything else. But since the habit of holding on to old opinions cannot be set aside so quickly, I should like to stop here and meditate for some time on this new knowledge I have gained, so as to fix it more deeply in my memory.

**Notes**

1 "... and in my dreams regularly represent to myself the same things" (French version).
2 "... the place where they are, the time which measures their duration" (French version).
3 "... yet I cannot doubt that he does allow this" (French version).
4 "... in the sciences" (added in French version).
5 "... nevertheless it is in my power to suspend my judgement" (French version).
6 "... puts into my mind" (French version).
7 "... or thought anything at all" (French version).
8 The word "only" is most naturally taken as going with "a thing that thinks," and this interpretation is followed in the French version. When discussing this passage with Gassendi, however, Descartes suggests that he meant the "only" to govern "in the strict sense."
9 "... to see if I am not something more" (added in French version).
10 Lat. *maneat* ("let it stand"), first edition. The second edition has the indicative *manet*: "The proposition still stands, *viz.* that I am nonetheless something." The French version reads: "without changing this supposition, I find that I am still certain that I am something."
11 "... from this manner of conceiving things" (French version).
12 "... which can only be conceived by the understanding or the mind" (French version).
13 "... or rather the act whereby it is perceived" (added in French version).
14 The French version has "more clear and distinct" and, at the end of this sentence, "more evidently, distinctly and clearly."

---

# 2  On Certainty

---

## *Ludwig Wittgenstein*

1    If you do know that *here is one hand*,[1] we'll grant you all the rest. When one says that such and such a proposition can't be proved, of course that does not mean that it can't be derived from other propositions; any proposition can be derived from other ones. But they may be no more certain than it is itself. (On this a curious remark by H. Newman.)

2    From its *seeming* to me – or to everyone – to be so, it doesn't follow that it *is* so. What we can ask is whether it can make sense to doubt it.

5    Whether a proposition can turn out false after all depends on what I make count as determinants for that proposition.

7    My life shews that I know or am certain that there is a chair over there, or a door, and so on. – I tell a friend, e.g. "Take that chair over there," "Shut the door," etc. etc.

10   I know that a sick man is lying here? Nonsense! I am sitting at his bedside, I am looking attentively into his face. – So I don't know, then, that there is a sick man lying here? Neither the question nor the assertion makes sense. Any more than the assertion "I am here," which I might yet use at any moment, if suitable occasion presented itself. – Then is "$2 \times 2 = 4$" nonsense in the same way, and not a proposition of arithmetic, apart from particular occasions? "$2 \times 2 = 4$" is a true proposition of arithmetic– not "on particular occasions" nor "always" – but the spoken or written sentence "$2 \times 2 = 4$" in Chinese might have a different meaning or be out and out nonsense, and from this is seen that it is only in use that the proposition has its sense. And "I know that there's a sick man lying here," used in an *unsuitable* situation, seems not to be nonsense but rather seems matter-of-course, only because one can fairly easily imagine a situation to fit it, and one thinks that the words "I know that . . . " are always in place where there is no doubt, and hence even where the expression of doubt would be unintelligible.

20   "Doubting the existence of the external world" does not mean for example doubting the existence of a planet, which later observations proved to exist. – Or does Moore want to say that knowing that here is his hand is different in kind from knowing the existence of the planet Saturn? Otherwise it would be possible to point out the discovery of the planet Saturn to the doubters and say that its existence has been proved, and hence the existence of the external world as well.

24   The idealist's question would be something like: "What right have I not to doubt the existence of my hands?" (And to that the answer can't be: I *know* that they exist.) But someone who asks such a question is overlooking the fact that a doubt about existence only works in a language-game. Hence, that we should first have to ask: what would such a doubt be like?, and don't understand this straight off.

31   The propositions which one comes back to again and again as if bewitched – these I should like to expunge from philosophical language.

33   Thus we expunge the sentences that don't get us any further.

45   We got to know the *nature* of calculating by learning to calculate.

46   But then can't it be described how we satisfy ourselves of the reliability of a calculation? O yes! Yet no rule emerges when we do so. – But the most important thing is: The rule is not needed. Nothing is lacking. We do calculate according to a rule, and that is enough.

47   *This* is how one calculates. Calculating is *this*. What we learn at school, for example. Forget this transcendent certainty, which is connected with your concept of spirit.

48   However, out of a host of calculations certain ones might be designated as reliable once for all, others as not yet fixed. And now, is this a *logical* distinction?

49   But remember: even when the calculation is something fixed for me, this is only a decision for a practical purpose.

74   Can we say: a *mistake* doesn't only have a cause, it also has a ground? I.e., roughly: when someone makes a mistake, this can be fitted into what he knows aright.

83   The truth of certain empirical propositions belongs to our frame of reference.

90   "I know" has a primitive meaning similar to and related to "I see" ("wissen," "videre"). And "I knew he was in the room, but he wasn't in the room" is like "I saw him in the room, but he wasn't there." "I know" is supposed to express a relation, not between me and the sense of a proposition (like "I believe") but between me and a fact. So that the *fact* is taken into my consciousness. (Here is the reason why one wants to say that nothing that goes on in the outer world is really known, but only what happens in the domain of what are called sense-data.) This would give us a picture of knowing as the perception of an outer event through visual rays which project it as it is into the eye and the consciousness. Only then the question at once arises whether one can be *certain* of this projection. And this picture does indeed show how our *imagination* presents knowledge, but not what lies at the bottom of this presentation.

94   But I did not get my picture of the world by satisfying myself of its correctness; nor do I have it because I am satisfied of its correctness. No: it is the inherited background against which I distinguish between true and false.

95   The propositions describing this world-picture might be part of a kind of mythology. And their role is like that of rules of a game; and the game can be learned purely practically, without learning any explicit rules.

109   "An empirical proposition can be *tested*" (we say). But how? and through what?

110   What *counts* as its test? – "But is this an adequate test? And, if so, must it not be recognizable as such in logic?" – As if giving grounds did not come to an end sometime. But the end is not an ungrounded presupposition: it is an ungrounded way of acting.

117   Why is it not possible for me to doubt that I have never been on the moon? And how could I try to doubt it?

First and foremost, the supposition that perhaps I have been there would strike me as *idle*. Nothing would follow from it, nothing be explained by it. It would not tie in with anything in my life.

When I say "Nothing speaks for, everything against it," this presupposes a principle of speaking for and against. That is, I must be able to say what *would* speak for it.

141   When we first begin to *believe* anything, what we believe is not a single proposition, it is a whole system of propositions. (Light dawns gradually over the whole.)

142   It is not single axioms that strike me as obvious, it is a system in which consequences and premises give one another *mutual* support.

160   The child learns by believing the adult. Doubt comes *after* belief.

166   The difficulty is to realize the groundlessness of our believing.

191   Well, if everything speaks for an hypothesis and nothing against it – is it then certainly true? One may designate it as such. – But does it certainly agree with reality, with the facts? – With this question you are already going round in a circle.

192    To be sure there is justification; but justification comes to an end.

193    What does this mean: the truth of a proposition is *certain*?

194    With the word "certain" we express complete conviction, the total absence of doubt, and thereby we seek to convince other people. That is *subjective* certainty.

But when is something objectively certain? When a mistake is not possible. But what kind of possibility is that? Mustn't mistake be *logically* excluded?

195    If I believe that I am sitting in my room when I am not, then I shall not be said to have *made a mistake*. But what is the essential difference between this case and a mistake?

196    Sure evidence is what we *accept* as sure, it is evidence that we go by in *acting* surely, acting without any doubt.

What we call "a mistake" plays a quite special part in our language games, and so too does what we regard as certain evidence.

199    The reason why the use of the expression "true or false" has something misleading about it is that it is like saying "it tallies with the facts or it doesn't," and the very thing that is in question is what "tallying" is here.

200    Really "The proposition is either true or false" only means that it must be possible to decide for or against it. But this does not say what the ground for such a decision is like.

203    [Everything² that we regard as evidence indicates that the earth already existed long before my birth. The contrary hypothesis has *nothing* to confirm it at all.

If everything speaks *for* an hypothesis and nothing against it, is it objectively *certain*? One can *call* it that. But does it *necessarily* agree with the world of facts? At the very best it shows us what "agreement" means. We find it difficult to imagine it to be false, but also difficult to make use of it.]

What does this agreement consist in, if not in the fact that what is evidence in these language games speaks for our proposition? (*Tractatus Logico-Philosophicus*)

204    Giving grounds, however, justifying the evidence, comes to an end; – but the end is not certain propositions striking us immediately as true, i.e. it is not a kind of seeing on our part; it is our *acting*, which lies at the bottom of the language-game.

205    If the true is what is grounded, then the ground is not *true*, nor yet false.

209    The existence of the earth is rather part of the whole *picture* which forms the starting-point of belief for me.

211    Now it gives our way of looking at things, and our researches, their form. Perhaps it was once disputed. But perhaps, for unthinkable ages, it has belonged to the *scaffolding* of our thoughts. (Every human being has parents.)

214    What prevents me from supposing that this table either vanishes or alters its shape and colour when no one is observing it, and then when someone looks at it again changes back to its old condition? – "But who is going to suppose such a thing!" – one would feel like saying.

215    Here we see that the idea of "agreement with reality" does not have any clear application.

217    If someone supposed that *all* our calculations were uncertain and that we could rely on none of them (justifying himself by saying that mistakes are always possible) perhaps we would say he was crazy. But can we say he is in error? Does he not just react differently? We rely on calculations, he doesn't; we are sure, he isn't.

221    Can I be in doubt at *will*?

225    What I hold fast to is not *one* proposition but a nest of propositions.

226    Can I give the supposition that I have ever been on the moon any serious consideration at all?

229    Our talk gets its meaning from the rest of our proceedings.

230    We are asking ourselves: what do we do with a statement "I *know* . . ."? For it is not a question of mental processes or mental states.

And *that* is how one must decide whether something is knowledge or not.

231    If someone doubted whether the earth had existed a hundred years ago, I should not understand, for *this* reason: I would not know what such a person would still allow to be counted as evidence and what not.

232    "We could doubt every single one of these facts, but we could not doubt them *all*." Wouldn't it be more correct to say: "we do not doubt them *all*." Our not doubting them all is simply our manner of judging, and therefore of acting.

243    One says "I know" when one is ready to give compelling grounds. "I know" relates to a possibility of demonstrating the truth. Whether someone knows something can come to light, assuming that he is convinced of it.

But if what he believes is of such a kind that the grounds that he can give are no surer than his assertion, then he cannot say that he knows what he believes.

247    What would it be like to doubt now whether I have two hands? Why can't I imagine it all? What would I believe if I didn't believe that? So far I have no system at all within which this doubt might exist.

248    I have arrived at the rock bottom of my convictions.

And one might almost say that these foundation-walls are carried by the whole house.

250    My having two hands is, in normal circumstances, as certain as anything that I could produce in evidence for it.

That is why I am not in a position to take the sight of my hand as evidence for it.

253    At the foundation of well-founded belief lies belief that is not founded.

292    Further experiments cannot *give the lie* to our earlier ones, at most they may change our whole way of looking at things.

336    But what men consider reasonable or unreasonable alters. At certain periods men find reasonable what at other periods they found unreasonable. And vice versa.

But is there no objective character here?

*Very* intelligent and well-educated people believe in the story of creation in the Bible, while others hold it as proven false, and the grounds of the latter are well known to the former.

341    That is to say, the *questions* that we raise and our *doubts* depend on the

fact that some propositions are exempt from doubt, are as it were like hinges on which those turn.

342   That is to say, it belongs to the logic of our scientific investigations that certain things are *in deed* not doubted.

343   But it isn't that the situation is like this: We just *can't* investigate everything, and for that reason we are forced to rest content with assumption. If I want the door to turn, the hinges must stay put.

344   My *life* consists in my being content to accept many things.

354   Doubting and non-doubting behaviour. There is the first only if there is the second.

357   One might say: "'I know' expresses *comfortable* certainty, not the certainty that is still struggling."

358   Now I would like to regard this certainty, not as something akin to hastiness or superficiality, but as a form of life. (That is very badly expressed and probably badly thought as well.)

359   But that means I want to conceive it as something that lies beyond being justified or unjustified; as it were, as something animal.

380   I might go on: "Nothing in the world will convince me of the opposite!" For me this fact is at the bottom of all knowledge. I shall give up other things but not this.

382   That is not to say that nothing in the world will in fact be able to convince me of anything else.

383   The argument "I may be dreaming" is senseless for this reason: if I am dreaming, this remark is being dreamed as well – and indeed it is also being dreamed that these words have any meaning.

418   Is my understanding only blindness to my own lack of understanding? It often seems so to me.

559   You must bear in mind that the language-game is so to say something unpredictable. I mean: it is not based on grounds. It is not reasonable (or unreasonable).

It is there – like our life.

## Notes

1   See G. E. Moore, "Proof of an External World", *Proceedings of the British Academy*, Vol XXV, 1939; also "A Defence of Common Sense" in *Contemporary British Philosophy, 2nd Series*, ed. J. H. Muirhead, 1925. Both papers are in Moore's *Philosophical Papers*, London, George Allen Unwin, 1959. (Editors.)
2   Passage crossed out in ms. (Editors.)

# 3　The Right to Be Sure

## A. J. Ayer

### Infallibility

The mistaken doctrine that knowing is an infallible state of mind may have contributed to the view, which is sometimes held, that the only statements that it is possible to know are those that are themselves in some way infallible. The ground for this opinion is that if one knows something to be true one cannot be mistaken. As we remarked when contrasting knowledge with belief, it is inconsistent to say "I know but I may be wrong." But the reason why this is inconsistent is that saying "I know" offers a guarantee which saying "I may be wrong" withdraws. It does not follow that for a fact to be known it must be such that no one could be mistaken about it or such that it could not have been otherwise. It is doubtful if there are any facts about which no one could be mistaken, and while there are facts which could not be otherwise, they are not the only ones that can be known. But how can this second point be reconciled with the fact that what is known must be true? The answer is that the statement that what is known must be true is ambiguous. It may mean that it is necessary that if something is known it is true; or it may mean that if something is known, then it is a necessary truth. The first of these propositions is correct; it restates the linguistic fact that what is not true cannot properly be said to be known. But the second is in general false. It would follow from the first only if all truths were necessary, which is not the case. To put it another way, there is a necessary transition from being known to being true; but that is not to say that what is true, and known to be true, is necessary or certain in itself.

　If we are not to be bound by ordinary usage, it is still open to us to make it a rule that only what is certain can be known. That is, we could decide, at least for the purposes of philosophical discourse, not to use the word "know" except with the implication that what was known was necessarily true, or, perhaps, certain in some other sense. The consequence would be that we could still speak of knowing the truth of a priori statements, such as those of logic and pure mathematics; and if there were any empirical statements, such as those describing the content of one's present experience, that were certain in themselves, they too might be included: but most of what we now correctly claim to know would not be knowable, in this allegedly strict sense. This proposal is feasible, but it does not appear to have anything much to recommend it. It is not as if a statement by being necessary became incapable of being doubted. Every schoolboy knows that it is possible to be unsure about a mathematical truth. Whether there are any empirical statements which are in any important sense indubitable is, as we shall see, a matter of dispute: if there are any they belong to a very narrow class. It is, indeed, important philosophically to distinguish between necessary and empirical statements, and in dealing with empirical statements to distinguish between different types and degrees of evidence. But there are better ways of bringing out these distinctions than by tampering with the meaning, or the application, of the verb "to know."

## The Right to Be Sure

The answers which we have found for the questions we have so far been discussing have not yet put us in a position to give a complete account of what it is to know that something is the case. The first requirement is that what is known should be true, but this is not sufficient; not even if we add to it the further condition that one must be completely sure of what one knows. For it is possible to be completely sure of something which is in fact true, but yet not to know it. The circumstances may be such that one is not entitled to be sure. For instance, a superstitious person who had inadvertently walked under a ladder might be convinced as a result that he was about to suffer some misfortune; and he might in fact be right. But it would not be correct to say that he knew that this was going to be so. He arrived at his belief by a process of reasoning which would not be generally reliable; so, although his prediction came true, it was not a case of knowledge. Again, if someone were fully persuaded of a mathematical proposition by a proof which could be shown to be invalid, he would not, without further evidence, be said to know the proposition, even though it was true. But while it is not hard to find examples of true and fully confident beliefs which in some ways fail to meet the standards required for knowledge, it is not at all easy to determine exactly what these standards are.

One way of trying to discover them would be to consider what would count as satisfactory answers to the question How do you know? Thus people may be credited with knowing truths of mathematics or logic if they are able to give a valid proof of them, or even if, without themselves being able to set out such a proof, they have obtained this information from someone who can. Claims to know empirical statements may be upheld by a reference to perception, or to memory, or to testimony, or to historical records, or to scientific laws. But such backing is not always strong enough for knowledge. Whether it is so or not depends upon the circumstances of the particular case. If I were asked how I knew that a physical object of a certain sort was in such and such a place, it would, in general, be a sufficient answer for me to say that I could see it; but if my eyesight were bad and the light were dim, this answer might not be sufficient. Even though I was right, it might still be said that I did not really know that the object was there. If I have a poor memory and the event which I claim to remember is remote, my memory of it may still not amount to knowledge, even though in this instance it does not fail me. If a witness is unreliable, his unsupported evidence may not enable us to know that what he says is true, even in a case where we completely trust him and he is not in fact deceiving us. In a given instance it is possible to decide whether the backing is strong enough to justify a claim to knowledge. But to say in general how strong it has to be would require our drawing up a list of the conditions under which perception, or memory, or testimony, or other forms of evidence are reliable. And this would be a very complicated matter, if indeed it could be done at all.

Moreover, we cannot assume that, even in particular instances, an answer to the question "How do you know?" will always be forthcoming. There may very well be cases in which one knows that something is so without its being possible to say how one knows it. I am not so much thinking now of claims to know facts of immediate experience, statements like "I know that I feel pain," which raise problems of their own into which we shall enter later on. In cases of this sort it may be argued that the question how one knows does not arise. But even when it clearly does arise, it may not find an answer. Suppose that someone were consistently successful in predicting events of a certain kind, events, let us say, which are not ordinarily thought to be predictable, like the results of a lottery. If his run of successes were sufficiently impressive, we might very well come to say that he knew which number would win, even though he did not reach this conclusion by any rational method, or indeed by any method at all. We might say that he knew it by intuition, but this would be to assert no more than that he did know it but that we could not say how. In the same way, if someone were consistently successful in reading the minds of others without having any of the usual sort of evidence, we might say that he knew these things telepathically. But in default of any further explanation this would come down to saying merely that he did know them, but not by any ordinary means. Words like "intuition" and "telepathy" are brought in just to disguise the fact that no explanation has been found.

But if we allow this sort of knowledge to be even theoretically possible, what becomes of the distinction between knowledge and true belief? How does our man who knows what the results of the lottery will be differ from one who only makes a series of lucky guesses? The answer is that, so far as the man himself is concerned, there need not be any difference. His procedure and his state of mind, when he is said to know what will happen, may be exactly the same as when it is said that he is only guessing. The difference is that to say that he knows is to concede to him the right to be sure, while to say that he is only guessing is to withhold it. Whether we make this concession will depend upon the view which we take of his performance. Normally we do not say that people know things unless they have followed one of the accredited routes to knowledge. If someone reaches a true conclusion without appearing to have any adequate basis for it, we are likely to say that he does not really know it. But if he were repeatedly successful in a given domain, we might very well come to say that he knew the facts in question, even though we could not explain how he knew them. We should grant him the right to be sure, simply on the basis of his success. This is, indeed, a point on which people's views might be expected to differ. Not everyone would regard a successful run of predictions, however long sustained, as being by itself a sufficient backing for a claim to knowledge. And here there can be no question of proving that this attitude is mistaken. Where there are recognized criteria for deciding when one has the right to be sure, anyone who insists that their being satisfied is still not enough for knowledge may be accused, for what the charge is worth, of misusing the verb "to know." But it is possible to find, or at any rate to devise, examples which are not covered in this respect by any established rule of usage. Whether they are to count as instances of knowledge is then a question which we are left free to decide.

It does not, however, matter very greatly which decision we take. The main problem is to state and assess the grounds on which these claims to knowledge are made, to settle, as it were, the candidate's marks. It is a relatively unimportant question what titles we then bestow upon them. So long as we agree about the marking, it is of no great consequence where we draw the line between pass and failure, or between the different levels of distinction. If we choose to set a very high standard, we may find ourselves committed to saying that some of what ordinarily passes for knowledge ought rather to be described as probable opinion. And some critics will then take us to task for flouting ordinary usage. But the question is purely one of terminology. It is to be decided, if at all, on grounds of practical convenience.

One must not confuse this case, where the markings are agreed upon, and what is in dispute is only the bestowal of honours, with the case where it is the markings themselves that are put in question. For this second case is philosophically important, in a way in which the other is not. The sceptic who asserts that we do not know all that we think we know, or even perhaps that we do not strictly know anything at all, is not suggesting that we are mistaken when we conclude that the recognized criteria for knowing have been satisfied. Nor is he primarily concerned with getting us to revise our usage of the verb "to know," any more than one who challenges our standards of value is trying to make us revise our usage of the word "good." The disagreement is about the application of the word, rather than its meaning. What the sceptic contends is that our markings are too high; that the grounds on which we are normally ready to concede the right to be sure are worth less than we think; he may even go so far as to say that they are not worth anything at all. The attack is directed, not against the way in which we apply our standards of proof, but against these standards themselves. It has, as we shall see, to be taken seriously because of the arguments by which it is supported.

I conclude then that the necessary and sufficient conditions for knowing that something is the case are first that what one is said to know be true, secondly that one be sure of it, and thirdly that one should have the right to be sure. This right may be earned in various ways; but even if one could give a complete description of them it would be a mistake to try to build it into the definition of knowledge, just as it would be a mistake to try to incorporate our actual standards of goodness into a definition of good. And this being so, it turns out that the questions which philosophers raise about the possibility of knowledge are not all to be settled by discovering what knowledge is. . . .

## The Quest for Certainty

The quest for certainty has played a considerable part in the history of philosophy: it has been assumed that without a basis of certainty all our claims to knowledge must be suspect. Unless some things are certain, it is held, nothing can be even probable. Unfortunately it has not been made clear exactly what is being sought. Sometimes the word "certain" is used as a synonym for "necessary" or for "a priori." It is said, for example, that no empirical statements are certain, and what is meant by this is that they are not necessary in the way that a priori statements are, that they can all be denied without self-contradiction. Accordingly, some philosophers take a priori statements as their ideal. They wish, like Leibniz, to put all true statements on a level with those of formal logic or pure mathematics; or, like the existentialists, they attach a tragic significance to the fact that this cannot be done. But it is perverse to see tragedy in what could not conceivably be otherwise; and the fact that all empirical statements are contingent, that even when true they can be denied without self-contradiction, is itself a matter of necessity. If empirical statements had the formal validity which makes the truths of logic unassailable they could not do the work that we expect of them; they would not be descriptive of anything that happens. In demanding for empirical statements the safeguard of logical necessity, these philosophers have failed to see that they would thereby rob them of their factual content.

Neither is this the only way in which their ideal of a priori statements fails them. Such statements are, indeed, unassailable, in the sense that, if they are true, there are no circumstances in which they could have been false. One may conceive of a world in which they had no useful application, but their being useless would not render them invalid: even if the physical processes of addition or subtraction could for some reason not be carried out, the laws of arithmetic would still hold good. But from the fact that a priori statements, if they are true, are unassailable in this sense, it does not follow that they are immune from doubt. For, as we have already remarked, it is possible to make mistakes in mathematics or in logic. It is possible to believe an a priori statement to be true when it is not. And we have seen that it is vain to look for an infallible state of intuition, which would provide a logical guarantee that no mistake was being made. Here too, it may be objected that the only reason that we have for concluding that any given a priori statement is false is that it contradicts some other which is true. That we can discover our errors shows that we have the power to correct them. The fact that we sometimes find ourselves to be mistaken in accepting an a priori statement, so far from lending favour to the suggestion that all those that we accept are false, is incompatible with it. But this still leaves it open for us to be at fault in any particular case. There is no special set of a priori statements of which it can be said that just these are beyond the reach of doubt. In very many instances the doubt would not, indeed, be serious. If the validity of some logical principle is put in question, one may be able to find a way of proving or disproving it. If it be suggested that the proof itself is suspect, one may obtain reassurance by going over it again. When one has gone over it again and satisfied oneself that there is nothing wrong with it, then to insist that it may still not be valid, that the conclusion may not really have been proved, is merely to pay lip service to human fallibility. The doubt is maintained indefinitely, because nothing is going to count as its being resolved. And just for this reason it is not serious. But to say that it is not serious is not logically to exclude it. There can be doubt so long as there is the possibility of error. And there must be the possibility of error with respect to any statement, whether empirical or a priori, which is such that from the fact that someone takes it to be so it does not follow logically that it is so. We have established this point in our discussion of knowledge, and we have seen that it is not vitiated by the fact that in the case of a priori statements there may be no other ground for accepting them than that one sees them to be true.

Philosophers have looked to a priori statements for security because they have assumed that inasmuch as these statements may themselves be certain, in the sense of being necessary, they can be certainly known. As we have seen, it may even be maintained that only what is certainly true can be certainly known. But this, it must again be remarked, is a confusion. A priori statements can, indeed, be known, not because they are necessary but because they are true and because we may be entitled to feel no doubt about their truth. And the reason why we are entitled to feel no doubt about their truth may be that we can prove them, or even just that we can see them to be valid; in either case there is an appeal to intuition, since we have at some point to claim to be able to see the validity of a proof. If the validity of every proof had to be proved in its turn, we should fall into an infinite regress. But to allow that there are times when we may justifiably claim the right to be sure of the truth of an a priori statement is not to allow that our intuitions are infallible. One is conceded the right to be sure when one is judged to have taken every reasonable step towards making sure: but this is still logically consistent with one's being in error. The discovery of the error refutes the claim to knowledge; but it does not prove that the claim was not, in the circumstances, legitimately made. The claim to know an a priori statement is satisfied only if the statement is true; but it is legitimate if it has the appropriate backing, which may, in certain cases, consist in nothing more than the statement's appearing to be self-evident. Even so, it may fail: but if such claims were legitimate only when there was no logical possibility of error, they could not properly be made at all.

Thus, if the quest for certainty is simply a quest for knowledge, if saying that a statement is known for certain amounts to no more than saying that it is known, it may find its object in a priori statements, though not indeed in them uniquely. If, on the other hand, it is a search for conditions which exclude not merely the fact, but even the possibility, of error, then knowledge of a priori statements does not satisfy it. In neither case is the fact that these a priori statements may themselves be certain, in the sense of being necessary, relevant to the issue. Or rather, as we have seen, it is relevant only if we arbitrarily decide to make it so.

# 4   Epistemology's End

## *Catherine Z. Elgin*

### Quarry

Unaccountable success, like inexplicable failure, disconcerts. Even when our undertakings achieve their avowed objectives, we endeavor to understand them. We wonder how our projects, practices, interests, and institutions fit into the greater scheme of things, what they contribute to and derive from it. Our curiosity extends beyond our limited forays into art and science, beyond our parochial concerns with commerce, politics, and law. We want to comprehend the interlocking systems that support or thwart our efforts. If we start out expecting thereby to gain fame, fortune, and the love of admirable people, many of us conclude that understanding itself is worth the candle. The epistemic quest need serve no further end.

What makes for an acceptable epistemic framework depends on the kind of excellence we are after and on the functions we expect it to perform in our cognitive economy. Agents adopt a variety of cognitive stances with different kinds and degrees of intellectual merit. In doing epistemology, we discriminate among such stances, segregating out those that are worthy of intellectual esteem. Different partitions of the cognitive realm underwrite different conceptions of epistemology's goals and vindicate the construction and employment of epistemic frameworks of different kinds.

Epistemological theories typically share an abstract characterization of their enterprise. They agree, for example, that epistemology is the study of the nature, scope, and utility of knowledge. But they disagree about how their shared characterization is concretely to be realized. So they differ over their subject's priorities and powers, resources and rewards, standards and criteria. To view them as supplying alternative answers to the same questions is an oversimplification. For they embody disagreements about what the real questions are and what counts as answering them. We cannot hope to decide among competing positions on the basis of point-by-point comparisons, for their respective merits and faults stubbornly refuse to line up. To understand a philosophical position and evaluate it fairly requires understanding the network of commitments that constitute it; for these commitments organize its domain, frame its problems, and supply standards for the solution of those problems.

John Rawls invokes a distinction between procedures[1] that extends to supply a useful classification of epistemological theories. A *perfect procedure* recognizes an independent criterion for a correct outcome and a method whose results – if any – are guaranteed to satisfy that criterion. Our independent criterion for the fair division of a cake, let us assume, is that a fair division is an equal one.[2] A cake-slicing procedure is perfect, then, just in case it yields an equal division when it yields any division. A finely calibrated electronic cake slicer that partitioned each cake it divided into equally large slices would provide a perfect procedure for fairly dividing cakes. The device would not have to be capable of dividing every cake. It might, for example, be inoperative on geometrically irregular cakes. But so long as every cake it divides is divided into equal sized slices, its use would be a perfect procedure for fairly dividing cakes. An *imperfect procedure* recognizes an independent criterion for a correct outcome but has no way to guarantee that the criterion is satisfied. The criterion for a correct outcome in a criminal trial is that the defendant is convicted if and only if he is guilty. Trial by jury, representation by counsel, the rules of evidence, and so on, are the means used to secure that result. But the means are not perfect. Sometimes a wrong verdict is reached. A *pure procedure* has no independent standard for a correct outcome. The procedure itself, when properly performed, determines what result is correct. And unless the procedure is actually performed, there is no fact of the matter as to which outcome is correct. A tournament is best construed as a pure procedure. Other construals are sometimes offered, but they are less satisfactory. If a tournament is construed as a perfect procedure for discovering the most able competitor, it is plainly defective. Anyone can have an off day or a bad series. Sometimes the best man doesn't win. And arguably, if it is construed as an imperfect procedure, it may be too imperfect. Consideration of how the parties fare overall may be a better indication of talent than hinging everything on their performance in a single game or series. But if the tournament is a pure procedure, such considerations are otiose. Winning the tournament is what makes a particular competitor the champion. The Celtics became the 1984 NBA champions by winning the playoffs. Nothing more was required; nothing less would do. A pure procedural interpretation of its function thus best explains how a tournament realizes the goal of an athletic competition: it incontrovertibly establishes a winner.

This tripartite division presents an attractive device for classifying epistemological theories. Extended to the epistemological realm, Rawls's division enables us to classify theories on the basis of differences in the sources and strength of epistemic justification they demand. *Very roughly* the difference is this: Perfect procedural epistemologies demand conclusive reasons, ones that guarantee the permanent acceptability of the judgments they vindicate. Imperfect procedural epistemologies require convincing reasons, but they recognize that convincing reasons need not be and typically are not conclusive. Pure procedural epistemologies construe reasons as constitutive. The reasons that, if true, would support a given claim, then, collectively amount to that claim. Plainly these criteria cry out for explication. It is far from obvious what makes for a reason, much less what makes for a conclusive, convincing, or constitutive reason. Moreover, each criterion admits of multiple, divergent explications. There is, for example, an array of perfect procedural theories whose members agree in their demand for conclusive reasons but disagree about what makes a reason conclusive. I do not want to enter into internecine squabbles here. Rather, I will sketch the considerations that tell in favor of each procedural stance. For present purposes, then, a rough characterization is enough.

One point should be emphasized. Epistemology is normative. It concerns what people ought to think and why. So recognizing the normativeness of central epistemological notions is crucial. A *reason* for $p$ is not just a consideration that, as a matter of brute psychological fact, prompts a subject to take it that $p$. It is a consideration that, ceteris paribus, confers some measure of obligation to do so. Other things being equal, given that reason $r$ obtains, $S$ would be (more or less) epistemically irresponsible if she failed to take it that $p$. Other things, of course, are not always equal. Reasons can be discredited or overridden. Even given $r$, $S$ would not be irresponsible if she failed to believe or suspect that $p$, in circumstances where $q$ also obtained. Thus, for example, symptoms that afford a prima facie obligation to think that a child has chicken pox are overridden by a blood test that discloses the absence of antibodies to the disease. Reasons, moreover, vary in strength. And reasons of differing strengths engender different epistemic obligations. A weak reason may confer an obligation to suspect that $p$; a weaker one, an obligation not to presume that $\sim p$. Thus red spots on a previously uninfected child's torso give a pediatrician an obligation to suspect, or at least not to exclude, that the child has chicken pox. But many other common conditions produce red spots, so it would be irresponsible to claim to know, on the basis of the spots alone, that he has the disease.

Weak reasons often persuade. That is a matter of psychological fact. But,

 – if reasons are conclusive, perfect procedural epistemology contends,
 – if they are convincing, imperfect procedural epistemology contends,
 – if they are constitutive of $p$, pure procedural epistemology contends,

$S$ ought to believe that $p$. Her reasons are good enough to secure the belief. Being measures of the goodness of reasons, then, 'conclusive', 'convincing', and 'constitutive' function normatively as well.


## Perfect Procedural Epistemology

If the truths it seeks are supposed to be antecedent and indifferent to our beliefs about them, and the test for truth affords a conclusive reason to accept its results, an epistemological theory construes itself as a perfect procedural position. The standard is rigorous. If $p$ is true and $p$ entails $q$, $q$ is also true. Still, $p$ may fail to be a conclusive reason for $q$. Suppose, for example, 'A calico cat swallowed the canary' is true; then, 'A cat swallowed the canary' is also true. But the mere truth of 'A calico cat swallowed the canary' does not convert Sam's belief that the cat is the culprit into knowledge. If Sam is ignorant of the truth in question, that truth is for him epistemically inert. Unless he has other reasons to fall back on, Sam's belief that a cat swallowed the canary is but a lucky guess. For all he knows, the canary could have been eaten by a hawk. According to perfect procedural epistemology, Sam does not know. For a perfect procedure provides a guarantee. Having satisfied its standard, the sentences it sanctions are immune to falsity and invulnerable to luck.

Both form and content have been thought to confer such immunity. Where form is the sole criterion, logic is supposed to be the guarantor of truth. Being a matter of form, the truth of

Either flamingos fly or flamingos do not fly

carries over to

Either molybdenum is malleable or molybdenum is not malleable.

Ornithological and metallurgical facts are irrelevant; logic alone decides. But logic's indifference to the way the world is invites the charge of vacuity. Such sentences, being about nothing, convey no information.

No such charge can be brought if content is involved. Sentences of a variety of kinds have been thought to owe their epistemic security to content.

*Analytic sentences.* 'Vixens are female foxes'; 'No bachelors are married.'

*Synthetic a priori sentences.* '7 + 5 = 12'; 'Every event has a cause.'

Some *fundamental laws.* 'Every integer has a successor'; 'You ought always act in such a way that you could will the maxim of your action to be a universal law'.

In these cases, epistemic standing seems to stem from, or to be intimately related to, necessity. Being necessarily true, the sentences in question could not have been false.

Some contingent sentences are also considered unimpeachable. For instance,

Some *self-ascriptions.* 'I am angry'; 'I seem to see a purple patch'; 'I think, therefore I am.'

Although contingent, these sentences are supposed so to relate to their objects that the conditions of their sincere utterance are the conditions of their truth. Incontrovertibility here attaches to tokens, not to types. Some assertions of 'I am elated' are true; others, false. The true ones, it is held, are certainly true; the false ones, lies. There is room for deception, but none for error. If I know what the sentence means, I know whether in asserting it I speak the truth.

Incontrovertibility is also claimed of

Some *sentences involving indexicals.* 'I am here now'; 'Yesterday's gone'; 'Tomorrow is another day.'

Such sentences are inevitably true; but different tokens of their indexical elements have different referents – Monday's tokens of 'yesterday' denote Sunday; Sunday's denote Saturday. So it is best to focus on tokens in these cases too.

I have culled the foregoing examples and the rationales for them from the history of philosophy. I do not contend that the categories are exclusive or exhaustive. Nor am I prepared to argue that every entry deserves its place on the list. Indeed, whether any sentence is genuinely unimpeachable remains to be seen. Still, there was traditionally a consensus that undeniable truth is a criterion of epistemic acceptability – a consensus that survived prolonged and bitter disagreements about how that criterion is to be satisfied.

Form and content are held jointly responsible for the unimpeachability of claims of a third kind – namely, the consequences of nonvacuous, unimpeachable truths. Perfect procedural epistemology contends that knowledge consists largely of claims of this kind. Unimpeachable claims are not all obvious. Some are revealed by explication and analysis; others are products of evidence and argument. Explication and analysis function archaeologically, uncovering claims that stand on their own. Rather than marshaling evidential support for a theory or practice, they articulate its presuppositions and commitments, dispel confusions in or about it, filter out what is false or untenable in it. By successive refinements, they hope to uncover the fundamental truths that underlie it. If the theory or practice in question is well-founded, the results of these processes are supposed to be obviously acceptable. In that case, we need only consider them to recognize that they are warranted. Manifestly, most of our knowledge is not obviously acceptable. But according to perfect procedural epistemology, it is unimpeachable; for its justification derives ultimately from obviously acceptable sentences.

Arguments function electronically, transmitting warrant from some sentences to others. Warrant-preserving inferences effect transmission without distortion. If our evidential base consists exclusively of warranted claims, and our methods prevent us from drawing unwarranted conclusions from warranted premises, our conclusions are secure. It follows that if knowledge is restricted to obviously acceptable claims and their consequences, and the methods for generating consequences are restricted to warrant-preserving inferences, knowledge meets the strictures of a perfect procedure: it obtains its justification in a way that no unwarranted sentence can, and its chain of justification serves as the test for warrant.

This picture of things is plainly foundationalist. Justification starts with sentences that are self-sustaining and is transmitted to other sentences by inferential chains. The conclusions require the support of the premises; without it, they are untenable. The premises, however, are epistemically autonomous; they derive no epistemological benefit from their relation to their consequences. Justification is a one-way street.

Austerity of resources and methods might seem to restrict knowledge unduly. But the matter is not altogether clear. To determine the scope of a perfect procedural theory, we must settle the criteria for obvious acceptability and for warrant-preserving inference. If only overtly incontrovertible sentences are obviously acceptable, and only first-order predicate calculus preserves warrant, our means are meager indeed. If, however, any initially credible sentence counts as obviously acceptable, and modal logic, inductive logic, and transformation rules of a language are valid inference tickets, our resources are greater. Still, once we set our sights on a specific cognitive goal, little choice remains. For a perfect procedure is characterized by a test that yields no false positives. If we seek truth, we have but one test that fits the bill: derivation by truth preserving means from known truths. To be sure, we can relax our objective and our standards in tandem. We might, for example, settle for plausibility, and evaluate candidates by a test that no implausible statement can pass. But we could assure that our test yielded no false positives only if we began with inherently plausible claims and inferred others from them in a way that does not dilute plausibility. So the structure of the positions is the same. Defects that are endemic to one are apt to have counterparts in the other.

Instead of considering defects here, however, I want to sketch what might be called the ideology of the program – the constellation of metaphysical and evaluative commitments that motivate perfect procedural epistemology and render its enterprise intelligible. Perfect procedural epistemologies doubtlessly differ over important details. What makes a sentence obviously acceptable and what inferences transmit acceptability are plainly subject to debate. But for present purposes, similarities are more significant than differences. If the procedure is vindicated, specific disagreements among perfect procedural positions become salient; if not, differences in detail hardly matter.

Metaphysically, perfect procedural epistemology is committed to the view that the facts are independent of anything we know or believe about them. Just what those facts are is, of course, hotly disputed. They may concern what is the case or what ought to be the case; they may consist of matter in motion, each of many monads reflecting the world from its own point of view, ideas in the mind of God. The crucial point is that because the identity and character of the facts is independent of what we think, we can be right or wrong about them; we can have true or false beliefs about the way the world is. The aim of perfect procedural epistemology is to learn those facts – not by chance, as Columbus happened on America, but in such a way that we are entitled to and secure in our beliefs about them. Otherwise, like Columbus, we might never realize what we have found, and so never stand to profit from it.

Perfect procedural epistemology demands cognitive security. To count as knowledge, a belief must be highly credible, and certifiable as such. Preferring ignorance to error, it excludes from knowledge anything that cannot pass its stringent tests. A variety of cognitive states, functions, and abilities fail to measure up. Being nonsentential, a painter's sense of color, a farmer's feel for the land, a poet's sensitivity to nuance can neither be evaluated in terms of truth nor justified by inference. Such sensibility is thus not knowledge. Nor is every truth bearer a candidate for knowledge. Those that are neither intrinsically credible nor susceptible of inferential justification are out of the running. Neither the insight an apt metaphor affords nor the understanding a great fiction engenders count as knowledge; for they are not backed by appropriate guarantees. And, of course, inadequately supported literal truths are excluded as well. A perfect procedure prevents falsehoods from passing for truths. It need not be, and is not, sensitive enough to discriminate truth from falsehood in every case.

Some truths (along with all falsehoods) fail its test and are thus denied the status of things known.

The justification for such severe constraints lies in the power of the system that results. Any claim that passes a perfect procedural test is secure. We need never look back; for new findings are impotent to undermine credibility.[3] This allows for the incremental growth of knowledge. A limited range of considerations is relevant to the evaluation of any hypothesis–namely, those that figure in its derivation from obviously acceptable claims. These being settled, the epistemic standing of the hypothesis is secure. As they pass the perfect procedural test, sentences are incorporated one by one into the body of knowledge. The position is absolutist. Acceptability is not relative to background information, available evidence, or other contextual factors. Whatever passes its test, and nothing else, is epistemically acceptable. And the test itself makes no concession to context. A perfect procedural epistemology guarantees that if a sentence satisfies its standards, that sentence is permanently credible. But it cannot guarantee that any sentence satisfies its standards. If none does, inquiry is abortive. Compromise being impermissible, the perfect proceduralist is then forced to skepticism.

Certain prima facie virtues of the position are plain. It respects what one might call the realist intuition – the view that the facts are independent of what we think about them, and that our beliefs and theories are right only if faithful to the facts. It respects Plato's conviction that knowledge differs from (mere) true opinion in having a tether – in being, that is, appropriately tied to the facts it concerns. And it respects the conviction, common among philosophers since Descartes, that its tether protects knowledge from hypothetical as well as actual counterexamples, that genuine knowledge is cognitively estimable come what may. Perfect procedural standards, then, echo a dominant theme in epistemology. Whether these convictions are consonant with our cognitive practice, of course, remains to be seen. And if they are not, whether we ought to reform theory or practice is not obvious. But before investigating the matter in detail, we should consider the conceptions of knowledge that pure procedures and imperfect procedures employ.

## Imperfect Procedural Epistemology

We can't, it seems, have everything. If objectives are settled independently of the mechanisms for realizing them, means may be exhausted before ends are reached. Should our methods prove grossly inadequate, we devise others or abandon the quest. Sometimes, however, we manage to design procedures that are generally successful, though not invariably so. Being imperfect, these procedures yield some defective products or sometimes fail to produce in circumstances where they should. Still, they get things right often enough to be worth using. Although we have reason to think that conscientious, impartial juries are usually right, they are not infallible. Some juries convict the innocent, some acquit the guilty, and some fail to reach a verdict. Plainly this state of affairs is unsatisfactory. Our only excuse for employing such a procedure is that we have no better. Society has a legitimate interest in fairly and accurately assigning criminal responsibility. Trial by jury, for all its defects, is the best way we know to make such assignments. We settle for an imperfect procedure for want of a better way to achieve a worthy end.

Induction is perhaps the most familiar imperfect epistemic procedure. Truth is its objective and ampliative inference its means. To draw the requisite inferences we marshal a large and varied body of evidence, describe that evidence in terms of projectible predicates, utilize refined statistical techniques, and so on. But the gap between premises and conclusions is not thereby bridged. The conclusion of a sound inductive argument may yet be false.

If the fallibility of induction is a manifestation of our general epistemological predicament, our best methods for securing knowledge are apt occasionally to fail. They may, like a hung jury, yield no verdict, leaving us in ignorance about the matter at hand. But sometimes they do worse. In counting undetected errors as knowledge, they yield false positives. Although there remains a presumption in favor of their products, these procedures, being fallible, are not intrinsically reliable. Still, the procedures we employ are the best ones available. So we have no way to differentiate their right answers from their wrong. On the principle that like cases should be treated alike, we ought to accord all products of the same procedure the same epistemic status. The problem is to decide what that status should be.

Impressed by a procedure's capacity to produce right answers (and acknowledging our inability to detect its errors), an epistemic fatalist might advocate accepting its products without reservation. We should treat our procedures as though they were perfect but recognize that in doing so we are vulnerable to epistemic misfortune. The fatalist then accepts the perfect procedural conception of the epistemic enterprise but concedes that without luck error is unavoidable. This is no small concession. To acknowledge the perennial possibility of error is to abandon hope of certainty. And certainty is the linchpin of the perfect procedural conception of knowledge. We are willing ruthlessly to restrict candidates for knowledge, forswear modes of justification, reorder epistemic priorities, and revise cognitive values, if by doing so we can achieve certainty. Security against error is a prize worth considerable epistemic sacrifice. The end of perfect procedural epistemology justifies the means.

But when the end is forsaken, the means lose their justification. Imperfect procedural philosophy must reform epistemology, legitimating both goals and methods. The considerations that led to perfect procedural stringency seem less compelling when certainty is not in the offing.

Instead of rejoicing in the general level of success of our epistemic ventures, and trusting luck to do the rest, the imperfect procedural stance I advocate adapts itself to the unfortunate propensity for error. Then even when a product appears unexceptionable, we do not accept it without reservation. Rather, we accord it provisional credibility, realizing that further findings may yet discredit it. Henceforth I shall use the phrase 'imperfect procedural epistemology' for such a position. Forced to admit fallibility, the imperfect procedural epistemologist demands corrigibility. Knowing that some well-founded conclusions are erroneous, she incorporates into her epistemology mechanisms for reviewing and revising or rejecting previously accepted claims.

Methods, too, are revisable. The best we could do yesterday need not be the best we can do today. So imperfect procedural epistemology is prepared to criticize, modify, reinterpret, and – if need be – renounce constituent ends and means.[4] If, for example, we discern a bias or limitation in inductive reasoning, we attempt to correct for it. There is, of course, no assurance of success. We might find no modification that does the trick. Or we might find one that does so only by creating more serious problems than it solves. Still, if we succeed, inductive reasoning improves. Although the procedure remains imperfect, it is less defective than it used to be. Imperfect procedural epistemology thus construes justification as inherently provisional. Reasons emerge from a self-monitoring, self-critical, self-correcting activity. Rather than deriving from a static system of uncompromising rules and rigid restrictions, they belong to and are vindicated by a fairly loose and flexible network of epistemic commitments, all accepted for the nonce as the best we can do, each subject to revision or revocation should defects emerge or improvements be found.

Perfect procedures confer permanent credibility. Nothing less than permanently credible claims can support their results, lest ineliminable error creep in. But imperfect procedures yield only provisional credibility. They are free to adduce a wider range of considerations to support their contentions, for both conclusions and arguments are subject to review. Being our best guesses as to how things stand, our considered judgments are initially credible. Should they prove inadequate, we round them out with hypotheses and hunches that we have less faith in. Clearly the method is risky, for considered judgments can be the repository of ancient error; unsupported hypotheses may be insupportable; hunches, wild. Still, the risk is bearable, since initial credibility is revocable. If our considered judgments lead to an untenable conclusion – if, for instance, it generates false predictions or conflicts with more highly warranted claims – we retrench, retool, and try again.

Since its results are revisable, imperfect procedural epistemology is free to use arguments, sources of evidence, and linguistic forms that perfect procedures cannot. An appreciation of the ways useful analogies, sensitive emotional responses, and apt metaphors enlighten might lead it to countenance some types of analogical, metaphorical, and emotive reasoning. Their acceptance is, of course, subject to revocation should they do more harm than good. But in this they do not differ from other modes of argument. Nor is there an order of absolute epistemic priority. Claims pertaining to physical objects may warrant or be warranted by sensation reports. Rules may be validated by yielding credible results, and results vindicated by being products of reasonable rules. Still, justification is not circular, since some elements possess a degree of initial credibility that does not derive from the rest. Justification is holistic. Support for a conclusion comes not from a single line of argument but from a host of considerations of varying degrees of strength and relevance. Indirect evidence and weak arguments, which alone would bear little weight, may be interwoven into a fabric that strongly supports a conclusion. Each element derives warrant from its place in the whole.

The aim of inquiry on the imperfect procedural model is a broad and deep understanding of its subject matter. And a measure of the adequacy of a new finding is its fit with what we think we already understand. If the finding is at all surprising, the background of accepted beliefs is apt to require modification to make room for it; and the finding may require revision to fit into place. So advancement of understanding is not an incremental growth of knowledge. A process of delicate adjustments takes place, its goal being a system in wide reflective equilibrium. Coherence alone will not suffice. A system is coherent if its components mesh. Reflective equilibrium requires more. The components of a system in reflective equilibrium must be reasonable in light of one another, and the system as a whole must be reasonable in light of our antecedent commitments about the subject at hand.

Considerations of cognitive value come into play in deciding what modifications to attempt. If, for example, science places a premium on repeatable results, a finding we cannot reproduce is given short shrift and one that is easily repeated may be weighted so heavily that it can undermine a substantial body of accepted theory. Equilibrium is not guaranteed. We may be unable to construct a system that accommodates our considered convictions and realizes our cognitive values. Considerable alteration may be necessary even to come close. Moreover, appearances can be deceiving. We may believe, with reason, that a system is in equilibrium when in fact it is not.

Imperfect procedural epistemology prefers error to ignorance. It risks error to achieve understanding. But it hedges its bets. Because accepted beliefs are corrigible, methods revisable, values subject to reappraisal, error is eliminable. Aware of its own inadequacies, imperfect procedural philosophy looks back as well as forward, reviewing, revoking, altering, and amending its previous conclusions, methods, and standards in light of later results. It considers nothing incontrovertible. What vindicates an individual statement, rule, method, or value is its incorporation into a network of cognitive commitments in wide reflective equilibrium. What vindicates such a network is its mesh with our prior understanding of the subject matter and the methods, rules, and values appropriate to it. Exact correspondence is neither needed nor wanted. Realizing that our previous position is incomplete, and suspecting that it is flawed, we would be unwise to take it as gospel. But we would be equally unwise to ignore it. We treat it as a touchstone, being the best independent source of information about its subject we have.

To go from a motley collection of convictions to a system of considered judgments in reflective equilibrium requires balancing competing claims against one another. There are likely to be several ways to achieve an acceptable balance. One system might, for example, sacrifice scope to achieve precision; another, trade precision for scope. Neither invalidates the other. Nor is there any reason to believe that a uniquely best system will emerge in the long run. So imperfect procedural epistemology is pluralistic, holding that the same constellation of cognitive objectives can be realized in several ways, and that several constellations of cognitive objectives may be worthy of realization. A sentence that is right according to one acceptable system may be wrong according to another. There is no straight and narrow path to truth.

Still, it does not follow that every statement, method, or value is right relative to some acceptable system. Among the considered judgments that guide our theorizing are convictions that certain things – for example, affirming a contradiction or exterminating a race – are just wrong. We are epistemically obliged to respect such convictions unless we find powerful reasons to revise them. There is no ground for thinking that such reasons are in the offing. So it does not follow from imperfect procedural philosophy that anything goes.

Nor does it follow that systems can be evaluated only by standards they acknowledge. An account that satisfies the standards it sets for itself might rightly be faulted for being blind to problems it ought to solve, for staking out a domain where there are only trivial problems, for setting too low standards for itself, and so forth. Sociobiology's fondness for 'just-so stories', for example, affords prima facie reason to doubt that its findings are epistemically estimable. An inquiry that succeeds by its own lights may yet be in the dark.

Imperfect procedural epistemology construes inquiry as a matter of pulling ourselves up by our bootstraps. The considered judgments that tether today's theory are the fruits of yesterday's theorizing. They are not held true come what may but accorded a degree of initial credibility because previous inquiry sanctioned them. We may subsequently revise or reject them, but they give us a place to start. Such an epistemological stance recognizes neither a beginning nor an end of inquiry. As epistemic agents, we are always in medias res.

Imperfect procedural epistemology finds a middle ground between the absolute and the arbitrary. Our convictions rarely if ever satisfy the standard for certainty or maximal credibility. But some are soundly backed by cognitively creditable reasons. Imperfect procedural epistemology gives such convictions their due. By denying that cognitive success requires anything like certainty, it avoids consigning well-founded convictions to the realm of ignorance. And by insisting that standards must be met, it avoids counting every conviction (or every widely held conviction) as knowledge. Moreover, in imperfect procedural epistemology, the perennial possibility of error leads to fallibilism, not to skepticism. It leads, that is, to the admission that any result is revocable, not to the conclusion that no result is tenable. Imperfect procedural epistemology affords no guarantees. It admits no criterion whose satisfaction assures that we could not be wrong. But it does offer a consolation: although our best efforts may fail, any failure can be regarded as a temporary setback. So a failure, should it occur, amounts not to a decisive defeat but to a challenge to do better next time.

## Pure Procedural Epistemology

Pure procedures do not purport to disclose what is already the case. They do not claim to generate correspondence to a mind-independent reality or to realize antecedently accepted values. What makes the outcome of a pure procedure right is simply its being a product of that procedure. Because it is a pure procedure, a footrace determines what it takes to win; the winner is (no more and no less than) the runner who has what it takes. A constellation of norms, conventions, rules, and objectives constitutes a practice and defines the pure procedures belonging to it. Together its components specify what counts as performing the procedures and what counts as doing so successfully. The criteria set the stage but do not identify the players. Only if the procedure is actually carried out are its performers and products determinate. For a pure procedure does not merely reveal its results; it generates them. That is what makes its products incontrovertible.

Perfect procedures and imperfect procedures are supposed to answer to something beyond themselves. So it is reasonable to ask whether they do what they claim – whether, that is, they are reliable. But pure procedures generate their results. Until the race is run, there is no winner. So we have no perspective from which to raise the question of reliability. For nothing more is required in the way of reliability than that the procedure be carried out in accordance with the rules it sets for itself. The result of that procedure, whatever it turns out to be, is ipso facto correct. Since there is nothing more to being right than being produced – and thereby certified – by the procedure, the product of a pure procedure is unimpeachable. One need only run a fair race and come in first in order to win. And standards of fairness and criteria of winning are internal to the practice of racing – the practice that produces winners.

One field of study that lends itself to a pure procedural construal is logic. All that it takes to be a theorem of a logical system is to be derivable from the system's axioms by the system's rules. To be sure, we can make mistakes in derivation, as in the performance of any other pure procedure. But if we do not, our results are unassailable. Any formula that satisfies the system's conditions for being a theorem is a theorem. Because its axioms and rules are explicitly codified, and because formal correctness seems not to involve correspondence with the independently real, logic is easily interpreted as a pure procedural inquiry. Logic's own seal of approval is all that is required for its derivations to count as valid.

Some philosophers – notably Thomas Kuhn, Richard Rorty, and the later Wittgenstein – take inquiry in general to be a pure procedural matter. Although most fields of study are not so strictly governed by explicit rules, all are, such philosophers contend, bound by implicit conventions – conventions powerful enough to fix the field's problems, methods, goals, and standards. By mastering the relevant conventions, we learn to play the language game, participate in the form of life, or work within the paradigm that they delimit. Moreover, if we look at what we do instead of at what we say, they maintain, we discover that the aim of inquiry is consensus, not correspondence. We design our practices and frame our conventions so that our procedures produce consensus. We consider something an outstanding problem for an intellectual community if its members seek, but have not yet achieved, agreement about it. And we do not worry that convictions everyone shares might fail to correspond to reality.

An inquiry, they urge, is constructed within a framework of tacit and explicit constraints. It is subject to publicly shared criteria and evaluated in terms of intersubjectively agreed-on norms. These organize the field into problems the discipline has the resources to solve, questions it has the capacity to answer. The conventions governing the discipline include devices for deflecting or disparaging embarrassing questions by, for example, pushing them off onto another field or discounting them as nonscientific, as pseudo-questions, or as what happens when language goes on holiday. Plainly a discipline's inability to answer such irrelevant or idle questions does not impugn its epistemic adequacy.

When consensus is achieved – when, that is, the community agrees that its objectives have been realized – a result becomes part of the corpus of knowledge. And, pure procedural philosophers contend, rightly so. For consensus is the product that inquiry is designed to produce. Because a result measures up to our standards for knowledge of its kind, that result – whatever it is – qualifies as knowledge. Since the criteria, standards, methods, and objectives are community property, and since the community expels inveterate naysayers, accord is bound to occur. To be sure, members of the community can disagree. But the scope of legitimate disagreement is restricted to disputes the practice has the mechanisms to resolve. Only those who share the community's standards and acknowledge the legitimacy of its objectives qualify as critics. Since the satisfaction of those standards and the realization of those objectives are publicly discernible matters, even the most carping of qualified critics will eventually come around. Objections by others are thought to be justifiably ignored. Not knowing the rules of the game, outsiders cannot tell winners from losers, fair plays from fouls. According to pure procedural epistemology then, community consensus is all we have and all we need for knowledge.

Justification of the fundamental elements of pure procedural knowledge is holistic.[5] To justify, say, the law of excluded middle is to reveal its role in the network of mutually supporting commitments that constitute classical logic. Moreover, the justification of methods, objectives, and beliefs is of a piece. Factual judgments have no epistemic primacy. By showing how each element contributes to the practice as a whole, we demonstrate that none is an idle wheel, that each is required for and involved in the working of the mechanism.

Plainly, such justification does not demonstrate truth – not, at least, if truth involves correspondence to a mind- and culture-independent realm. Nor does it claim to. What it does is show that a belief, method, value, or rule is an integral part of the practice. There is nothing more fundamental that can provide such a component with additional justification. The component is not self-justifying in the way that basic elements of perfect procedural knowledge are supposed to be. It does not stand on its own. Still, without that component, the mechanism would cease to function. The practice it belongs to would fall apart. And with the disintegration of the practice comes the dissolution of a shared form of life. So from the cognitive value of a pure procedure of inquiry and its associated form of life, the individual elements derive their justification.

Relativism results. Since the justification for fundamental beliefs, methods, objectives, and standards derives wholly from their place in a practice, they are justified only relative to that practice. Their warrant does not extend beyond the limits of the practice or survive the practice's demise. A law of excluded middle, for example, is justified relative to classical logic, unjustified relative to intuitionistic logic. It makes no sense to ask whether it is justified absolutely and independently of the specific logical systems it does, or does not, belong to. The highest scorer wins in tennis, loses in golf. But there is no saying absolutely whether high scores are better than low.

Although compatible with pure procedural epistemology, pluralism does not automatically follow from it. For such a position may be monopolistic. Thus Wittgenstein can be read as claiming that the conventions that underlie our form of life are constitutive of human rationality. For us, then, there are no alternatives. Kuhn contends that monopoly is required for, and is imposed by, mature science: only what accords with the conventions of the reigning paradigm counts as science. The relativism of pure procedural philosophy thus does not guarantee that an inquiry tolerates alternatives. To be sure, pure procedural philosophy may be pluralist. According to a version like Richard Rorty's,[6] each practice recognizes the optionality of (some of) its fundamental conventions and acknowledges that other practices result from choosing different options. A literary critic, while advancing one reading of a text, may concede the legitimacy of other interpretations. A set theorist appreciates that different axioms yield separate systems of equal interest and importance. The pure procedural pluralist like Rorty maintains that the fundamental elements of a system of thought, being conventional, are to some degree arbitrary. That being so, it would be arrogant to dismiss systems grounded in other, equally arbitrary conventions. Let a hundred flowers bloom.

Pure procedural pluralism carries no threat of inconsistency. Disagreements between communities of inquiry are spurious, since each community is responsible only to the standards it sets for itself. Since, for example, Newtonian and relativistic physicists assign different meanings and referents to the word 'mass', the Newtonian contention that mass is constant does not contradict the relativistic contention that mass is variable. And since relativistic physicists set standards that apply only to relativistic physics, the failure of Newtonian findings to satisfy them no more discredits Newtonian physics than the failure of a non-Euclidian geometry to respect the parallel postulate discredits its theorems.[7] The verdicts of one community of inquiry cannot impugn those of another, for their conclusions are mutually irrelevant. There is no perspective from which the verdicts of distinct communities can be compared.

The virtues of a pure procedural construal of knowledge stem from its interpretation of inquiries as social practices. It recognizes that by our own lights – which are, after all, the only lights we've got – our inquiries sometimes succeed. And it counts such success as knowledge. Moreover, a pure procedural construal preserves and justifies disciplinary autonomy. Each community of inquiry sets its own cognitive standards and, by satisfying them, achieves its own brand of knowledge.

Skepticism is avoided. A community poses problems or puzzles that it can solve. And any solution that satisfies its criteria for knowledge constitutes knowledge for it. Since pure procedural philosophy recognizes nothing more fundamental than basic conventions, it acknowledges nothing beyond those conventions for solutions to answer to. Correspondence is not necessary. Once we satisfy community standards, there is nothing left to be skeptical about. Nor should we be skeptical about whether the relevant standards have been satisfied, for that is a question we know how to answer. To be cognitively acceptable, a conclusion must be certified by the appropriate intellectual community. What I think is acceptable may turn out otherwise. But the consensus of the community cannot be mistaken. Whatever the community takes to satisfy its standards ipso facto does so. Nor need we worry that the community might wrongly credit a thesis that fails to satisfy its standards. For the standards at issue are the ones the community actually uses; these need not be the ones it explicitly avows. Actions speak louder than words. If the conclusions a community acts on diverge from the ones it avows, we take the actions to reveal its commitments and ignore the avowals. We look at what the members of a community do, not at what they say. So pure procedural knowledge is assured by the existence of communities that count some cognitive achievements as knowledge. And the limits of knowledge are the limits of what the communities count as knowledge. The conclusions of the community of inquiry are unimpeachable. For consensus is achieved; pure procedural knowledge requires nothing more.

## Notes

1 John Rawls, *A Theory of Justice* (Cambridge, Mass.: Harvard University Press, 1971), 85.
2 I modify Rawls's example slightly to bring out features that are important for my purposes but not for his.
3 Of course, new information can undermine the credibility of a contention we falsely believe has passed a perfect procedural test, but that is another matter.
4 See John Dewey, *Human Nature and Conduct* (New York: Random House, 1957), 25–35.
5 Some pure procedural philosophers, such as Richard Rorty, take justification to be holistic throughout. Others take only the fundamentals to be justified holistically. Nonfundamental claims are justified, as they are in perfect procedural knowledge, by their epistemic relation to fundamental claims.
6 Rorty denies that what he does is philosophy. For he takes genuine philosophy to be a perfect procedural matter. So he contends that he has abandoned philosophy and taken up cultural criticism. I see no reason to limit the scope of philosophy so narrowly and hence no reason to doubt that Rorty is doing philosophy. See Catherine Z. Elgin, 'Review: *Consequences of Pragmatism*', *Erkenntnis* 21 (1984): 423–31.
7 Thomas Kuhn, *The Structure of Scientific Revolutions* (Chicago: University of Chicago Press, 1970), 101.

# PART TWO

# HOW ARE BELIEFS JUSTIFIED?

# Introduction

Actually, the title of this section begs the question as to whether epistemology is pursuing the justification of *beliefs* or the justification of *believers*. Is it more important that *my belief* be justified, even if I am not fully aware of the reasons for its justification, or is it more central to the concept of justification that *I* be justified in holding my belief? So goes the current debate over "internalism" and "externalism", though more and more epistemologists are striving to incorporate both aspects in their theories of justication.

In the essays below, William P. Alston clarifies this distinction and presents challenges that an internalist account must overcome, while Carl Ginet and Alvin Goldman provide representative arguments for the two positions. For Ginet, to know that *p* one must evaluate the relevant reasons in a disinterested manner, and thus for him justification involves things that the knower must do. The concept of justification lays out epistemic procedures followed by reasonable, experienced people. It cannot demand absolute certainty or any requirements that are not practically possible. For Goldman, on the contrary, principles of justification must specify the truth conditions for belief, or under what conditions the belief is likely to be true, and not just when a reasonable agent is conventionally justified in holding a belief. Searching for such principles leads Goldman to develop a causal account of justification, an account that justifies beliefs when they are formed through a reliable belief-forming process.

Contextualist accounts of justification argue that the truth conditions of "*S* knows that *p*" vary according to context: not only the context of the belief but also the context of meaning in which the speaker is claiming to know. The essay by Keith DeRose provides a useful exposition and defense of this type of account, distinguishing it from the closely related "relevant alternatives" view of justification. DeRose's contextualism includes both internalist and externalist considerations.

The final two essays in this part offer different critiques of the way in which epistemologists have generally approached theories of justification, and then develop new alternatives. Lorraine Code argues that, internalism notwithstanding, epistemologists have taken the knowing subject too little into account on the grounds that the particular person who fills this role will make no difference. This may be the case, she allows, for the observation of everyday simple objects, but it is a mistake to take such cases as the paradigm for an analysis of epistemic practice. If we shift the paradigm cases of knowing, a very different set of questions about epistemic justification will emerge.

Alessandra Tanesini also urges a shift in the way we approach justification toward a fuller appreciation of the practice of justifying beliefs in a community. Philosophers usually attempt to abstract from the social practices of justification a general concept of justification with a closed set of properties. Tanesini argues that this project cannot succeed because the implicit norms embedded in actual epistemic practices cannot be codified. Moreover, we need to understand normative epistemology itself as an interventionist social practice rather than a mere elucidation of current norms. For Tanesini, as for Code, these points do not suggest that epistemic justification should not be the subject of philosophical analysis; rather, their suggestion is that attending to the specificity of individual knowers and the embeddedness of practices of justification within social and political contexts produces a different set of questions which an adequate account of justification must be able to address.

**Further Reading**

Alston, William P. *Epistemic Justification: Essays in the Theory of Knowledge*. Ithaca, NY: Cornell University Press, 1989.

Code, Lorraine. *What Can She Know? Feminist Theory and the Construction of Knowledge*. Ithaca, NY: Cornell University Press, 1991.

Goldman, Alvin. *Epistemology and Cognition*. Cambridge, MA: Harvard University Press, 1986.

Pappas, George and Marshall Swain (eds) *Essays on Knowledge and Justification*. Ithaca, NY: Cornell University Press, 1978.

# 5 Internalism and Externalism in Epistemology

## William P. Alston

One hears much these days of an epistemological distinction between "internal" and "external". It is often found in discussions of reliabilism in which the critic accuses the reliabilist of violating "internalist" restrictions on justification and of resting content with justification that is "external" to the subject's perspective.[1] But just what distinction is this (are these)? That is not so clear.

As just intimated, those who wield the distinction intend to be contrasting different views on what can confer justification or on what can convert mere true belief into knowledge. The main emphasis has been on justification, and we will continue that emphasis in this paper. In all these discussions it is the internalist position that lays down constraints; the externalist position *vis-à-vis* a given internalist position is simply the denial that the internalist constraint in question constitutes a necessary condition of justification. Thus our attempts at clarification can be confined to the internalist side.

As the name implies, an "internalist" position will restrict justifiers to items that are *within* something, more specifically, within the subject. But, of course, not everything that is "within" a knowing subject will be admitted as a possible justifier by an internalist. Physiological processes within the subject, of which the subject knows nothing, will not be allowed. Then just where, how, or in what sense, does something have to be "in the subject" in order to pass the internalist test?

Two quite different answers are given to this question in the literature. First there is the idea that in order to confer justification something must be within the subject's "perspective" or "viewpoint" on the world, in the sense of being something that the subject knows, believes, or justifiably believes. It must be something that falls within the subject's ken, something of which the subject has taken note. Second, there is the idea that in order to confer justification, something must be accessible to the subject in some special way, for example, directly accessible or infallibly inaccessible. We shall explore each of these versions in detail, noting alternative formulations of each, exposing unclarities and incoherences, and seeking to develop the strongest form of each position. We shall consider what can be said for and against each version, and we shall explore their interrelations. Finally we shall make some suggestions concerning the most reasonable position to take on these issues.

## I

Let's begin by considering the first form of internalism. In the essay already cited, Bonjour, in discussing the view that there are "basic beliefs", has this to say.

Thus if basic beliefs are to provide a suitable foundation for empirical knowledge, . . . then that feature, whatever it may be, in virtue of which an empirical belief qualifies as basic, must also constitute an adequate reason for thinking that the belief is true. And now if we assume, plausibly enough, that the person for whom a belief is basic must *himself* possess the justification for that belief if *his* acceptance of it is to be epistemically rational or responsible, and thus apparently that he must believe *with justification* both (a) that the belief has the feature in question and (b) that beliefs having that feature are likely to be true, then we get the result that this belief is not basic after all, since its justification depends on these other beliefs.[2]

The specific conclusion here is that there can be no basic beliefs, no beliefs that are justified otherwise than on the basis of other beliefs. But that is not our present concern. We are interested in the constraint on justification invoked by Bonjour to arrive at this result. That is the requirement that "that feature, whatever it may be, in virtue of which an empirical belief qualifies as basic", that is, that feature by virtue of which it is justified, must be justifiably believed by the subject to attach to that belief if the belief is to be thereby justified. That is, the justifying feature must be part of his "perspective on the world", must be known or justifiably believed by him to obtain if it is to do its justifying work.

Bonjour continues to employ this same understanding of internalism in characterizing the opposed externalist position.

But according to proponents of the view under discussion, the person for whom the belief is basic need not (and in general will not) have any cognitive grasp of any kind of this reason or of the relation that is the basis for it in order for this basic belief to be justified; all these matters may be entirely *external* to the person's subjective conception of the situation.[3]

When viewed from the general standpoint of the western epistemological tradition, externalism represents a very radical departure. It seems safe to say that until very recent times, no serious philosopher of knowledge would have dreamed of suggesting that a person's beliefs might be epistemically justified simply in virtue of facts or relations that were external to his subjective conception.[4]

Again, in "A Rationale for Reliabilism" Kent Bach writes as follows.

Internalism requires that a person have "cognitive grasp" of whatever makes his belief justified.[5]

And in "The Internalist Conception of Justification" Alvin Goldman writes:

Traditional epistemology has not adopted this externalist perspective. It has been predominantly *internalist*, or egocentric. On the latter perspective, epistemology's job is to construct a doxastic principle or procedure *from the inside*, from our own individual vantage point.[6]

All this would suggest the following formulation of internalism.

(1)   Only what is within the subject's "perspective" can determine the justi-
        fication of a belief.

Let's call this version of internalism "perspectival internalism" (henceforth 'PI').

PI needs some refinement before we are ready to consider what can be said
for and against it. First, we have been specifying the subject's "perspective"
disjunctively as what the subject "knows, believes, or justifiably believes". It will
make a considerable difference what choice we make from between these alternatives. For the present let's proceed in terms of justified belief. At a later stage
of the discussion we will explicitly consider the three alternatives and justify this
decision. This gives us the more specific formulation:

(2)   Only the justified beliefs of the subject can determine what further
        beliefs of that subject are justified.

(2) may seem to smell of circularity, but there can be no definitional circularity,
since the internalism we are discussing is not concerned with defining "justified"; it is merely laying down one constraint on the provision of justification.
There are, of course, well-known problems with making all justification depend
on other justified beliefs, and we shall attend to these in due course.

Next we need to consider the way in which the perspective *determines* the
justification of belief. But first a terminological matter. Bonjour's formulation is
in terms of a "feature" of the belief by which it is justified. Sometimes this is the
most natural construal, as when we think of beliefs about one's current conscious states as being justified by virtue of the fact that they, the beliefs, are
incorrigible, or by virtue of the fact that they, the beliefs, are "self-warranted".
However it is usually more natural to think of the justification of a belief as
stemming from its relation to some state of affairs other than itself, as when a
belief is justified by virtue of being based on adequate evidence or reasons, or by
virtue of arising from a certain sensory experience. To be sure, these ways of
talking are mutually translatable. By a well-known grammatical trick we can
always take a belief's relation to some external justifying state of affairs to be a
property of the belief. And, contrariwise, we can take the fact that belief B is
incorrigible to be the state of affairs that justifies it. Hence I shall feel free to use
now one construal, now the other, as seems most natural in the particular context. I will most often speak, however, in terms of justifying *facts* or *states of
affairs* and will refer to them as "justifiers".

Let's return to the issue concerning the way in which the perspective determines justification. In the first quotation from Bonjour he allows any sort of
fact, not just other justified beliefs of the subject, to be a justifier, provided the
subject has certain justified beliefs concerning it and its relation to the initial
belief. A justifier for a perceptual belief that there is a tree in front of one, can
be, for instance, a sensory experience from which that belief sprang. In that
case, the belief would be justified by the experience (or by its origin from the
experience) only if S justifiably believes that the belief sprang from that experience and that this origin is sufficient for justification. On this version the per-

spective determines justification by determining what can justify what; but it allows items outside the perspective (items other than justified beliefs of that subject) to function as justifiers.[7]

Here and elsewhere in the paper the following distinction will be useful. A belief is *mediately (indirectly)* justified provided it is justified by virtue of its relations to other justified beliefs of the subject that provide adequate support for it. In such cases the belief is justified by the *mediation* of those other beliefs. If it is justified in any other way it will be said to be *immediately (directly)* justified. In terms of this distinction, the view embodied in the first quotation from Bonjour rules out *purely* immediate justification, justification by something other than other justified beliefs of the subject *alone*, since it holds that an experience can justify a belief only if the subject has certain justified beliefs about the experience and its relation to the belief; but it is hospitable to mixed justification, in which both other justified beliefs *and* something else are required for justification.[8] There is or can be, however, a version of PI that is more radically opposed to immediate justification, one that would "perspectivize" justifiers more thoroughly, by holding that only justified beliefs can *be justifiers*. On this version what justifies a perceptual belief is not the experience itself, or actual origin from the experience, but the justified belief that the experience has occurred or that the belief originated from it.

We have made the distinction between these versions hang on what is allowed to count as "a justifier". In the perceptual case both versions require a justified belief that the relevant experience occurs, but they differ as to whether the experience itself can function in a justifying role. But this might be thought a trivial verbal difference, having to do only with where we draw the line between what is doing the justifying, and the conditions under which it is enabled to do so. What difference does it make where that line is drawn? On both views both "the justifier" and "the conditions that must obtain if it is to be a justifier" figure essentially in the conditions that are necessary for the belief in question to be justified. Why does it matter how we divide that set of conditions into what *does* the justifying and what *enables* it to do that justifying?

I agree that the division is not of any great importance. Nevertheless there is an important difference between the versions. For Bonjour's version, in allowing the experience itself into the necessary conditions for justification, under whatever rubric, is imposing a condition for the justification of the perceptual belief over and above those imposed by the more radical alternative. Put it this way. Both versions alike hold that S is justified in believing that *p* (that there is a tree in front of one) only if S is justified in believing that S has experience E. But Bonjour imposes the additional requirement that S *have* the experience; that is, he requires that the supporting belief be *true*. And this can be seen to mark a decisive superiority of the more radical alternative. We are dealing with a case in which S's belief that he or she has experience E provides him or her with an adequate reason for the perceptual belief. (If more justified beliefs on S's part, about normality or other background conditions, are required for this, let them be included also.) Otherwise the case would fall short of justification by reason of the insufficiency of the alleged ground and we would never get to the problems raised by the internalism-externalism distinction. But if I do justi-fiably believe that I am having E, and if that constitutes a sufficient reason for my supposing that $p$, that is surely enough for my being justified in believing that $p$. To require that my supporting beliefs be *true* might be appropriate it we were laying down requirements for knowledge, but it is clearly too strong a requirement for justification. If, for example, I am justified, to as high degree as you like, in supposing that my car is in my garage, then I am surely *justified* in denying that it is parked in front of the bank, even if, unbeknownst to me, someone had removed it from my garage and parked it in front of the bank. Thus Bonjour's version represents something of an overkill.[9] Let's codify the preferred version.

(3) The only thing that can justify S's belief that $p$ is some other justified beliefs of S.

Next let's note a respect in which (3) needs broadening. Recall the important notion of prima facie justification. One is prima facie justified in believing that $p$ provided that one is so situated that one will be (unqualifiedly, all things con-sidered justified in believing that $p$, provided there are no sufficient "overrid-ing"[10] considerations. Thus in a normal perceptual situation in which I take myself to see a tree in front of me, I am thereby prima facie justified in believing that there is a tree in front of me; but this justification can be overridden by abnormalities in the situation, for instance, sensory malfunctioning of various sorts. Now consider what a PI internalist should say about the conditions under which a prima facie justification is overthrown. Does the mere existence of a sufficiently serious malfunctioning suffice? Or would the subject have to know or be justified in believing that this was the case? Clearly it is the second alterna-tive that is in the spirit of PI. Just as the mere fact that a belief was produced in a highly reliable manner cannot justify it, so the mere fact that a belief was generated in an unreliable fashion cannot serve to discredit the belief. In both cases justification, or the lack thereof, depends on how the situation appears within my perspective, that is, on what I know or justifiably believe about it. If and only if I have sufficient reason to think there to be something fishy about this case of perception, will prima facie justification be overthrown. And, in-deed, most epistemologists have taken this line about what overrides prima facie justification, even where they haven't also accepted (3) as a constraint on justification.[11] Thus we should add overriders to the scope of (3). In the interest of concise formulation let us introduce the term "epistemizer" to range over anything that affects the justification of a belief, positively or negatively. We can then reformulate (3) as:

(4) The only thing that can epistemize S's belief that $p$ is some other justified belief(s) of S.

Now we are in a position to return to the choice between knowledge, belief, and justified belief in the specification of the subject's perspective. To deal with this properly we must note that (4) places severe restrictions on a theory of justification by implying that only *mediate* justification is available. Let's call any theory of justification that recognizes only mediate justification a "discursive" theory. The most prominent discursive theory is coherentism; whether there are any other varieties depends on how narrowly the boundaries of coherentism are drawn, and there is wide variation on this. For the present let's think of coherentism widely, as ranging over any discursive theory.

Next let's distinguish between "positive" and "negative" coherence theories. John Pollock introduced the distinction as follows:

> There are two kinds of coherence theories. On the one hand, there are coherence theories which take all propositions to be prima facie justified. According to those theories, if one believes a proposition, P, one is automatically justified in doing so unless one has a reason for rejecting the belief. According to theories of this sort, reasons function primarily in a negative way, leading us to reject beliefs but not being required for the justified acquisition of belief. Let us call these negative coherence theories. The other kind of coherence theory (a positive coherence theory) demands positive support for all beliefs.[12]

In other words, on a positive coherence theory a belief is justified only if it stands in the right relation to justifiers. On a negative coherence theory a belief is justified unless it stands in the wrong relation with overriders. What makes them both coherence theories is that in both cases the epistemizers must be drawn from the subject's propositional attitudes.

Now let's go back to the various sorts of propositional attitudes that might be supposed by PI to make up the subject's perspective: beliefs, justified beliefs, knowledge. In formulations (2), (3), and (4) we chose *justified belief* without explaining or justifying that choice. I now turn to that task.

First, what about the decision between knowledge and justified belief? Here the point is that the more modest constraint is called for. Suppose that I am justified in believing that my car is in the garage, since I left it there this morning and have been away from the house since, no one else has a key to the house or garage, and the neighborhood is remarkably free of crime. In the afternoon I see a car that looks like mine in the parking lot of a bank but believe that it isn't mine, on the grounds of my car's being in my garage. Suppose further that my car has been stolen and this is my car, so I didn't *know* that my car was in the garage even though I was justified in believing this. I am surely justified in believing that the car in the parking lot is not mine, even though the basis for this belief is something I am justified in believing but do not know. Cases like this indicate that it is sufficient for a belief to be a justifier that it be justified; it is not also required that it count as knowledge.

But what about the alternative between any beliefs, on the one hand, and only justified beliefs, on the other? It may seem that we can settle this issue in the same way. Suppose I merely believe that my car is in the garage, just because that is where I normally expect it to be when I don't have it with me; but I am not justified in believing this. On the contrary, I took it to a repair shop to be worked on yesterday; when I believe that it is in my garage, I have temporarily forgotten about this incident, even though I am quite capable of remembering it and would have been remembering it except for this temporary lapse. Again I take my car's being in my garage as a reason for supposing that the car I see in the bank parking lot is not mine. Here it is quite clear that I am not justified in this latter belief by virtue of basing it on an unjustified belief. On the contrary, the fact that I am quite unjustified in supposing my car to be in my garage shows that I don't become justified in some further belief by virtue of basing it on that belief. More generally, it seems that beliefs cannot acquire justification by being brought into relation with unjustified beliefs. One belief cannot "transfer" to another belief a justification it does not possess.

This last argument is, I believe, conclusive for what we might call "local" mediate justification, justification of a particular belief by the evidential or other logical relations in which it stands to one, or a few, other beliefs. Justification can be transferred "locally" only by beliefs that already have it. But the more common sort of discursive theory is a "holistic" coherence theory, one which takes a given belief to be justified, at least in the last analysis, not by its relations to a very few other beliefs "in the vicinity", but by the way in which it fits into some very large system of beliefs. Since the term "coherence theory" derives from the idea that a belief is justified if and only if it "coheres" with such a total system, it will be most natural to restrict the term "coherence theory" to holistic theories. The obvious choice for the system with which a belief must cohere in order to be justified is the totality of the subject's current beliefs. Thus on the most usual sort of coherence theory the subject's "perspective" by reference to which the justification of any particular belief is to be assessed consists of the subject's beliefs, without any further restriction to justified beliefs. Indeed, there could not be such a restriction. For on the kind of (pure) coherence theory we are now considering, a belief is or is not justified just by its relations to the whole of the subject's beliefs. Apart from that coherence with *all* the subject's beliefs there are no justified beliefs to serve as a reference class. Hence by the time the totality of beliefs has been segregated into justified and unjustified it is too late to use the former class as a touchstone to determine whether a given belief is justified. That determination has already been made. Of course, if at a future time the subject has some new beliefs, we can at that time assess their justificatory status, and this determination will be made after the earlier demarcation of the justified from the unjustified beliefs. But that doesn't change the verdict. At that future time, by the terms of the theory, a given belief (new or old) is justified solely on the basis of its coherence with the total set of beliefs the subject has at that time. And so for a pure coherence theory PI should be formulated as follows.

(5) Only the total set of S's beliefs at $t$ can function as an epistemizer at $t$.[13]

Since I find pure coherence theories quite unsatisfactory for a variety of reasons, I might seek to rule out (5) on those grounds. But in this essay I did not want to get into *substantive* epistemological issues like those concerning the opposition between foundationalism and coherentism. This essay is designed to be restricted to meta-epistemological issues concerning basic epistemological concepts, their explication, interrelations, and suitability for one or another purpose. Thus I shall just point out that the internalism-externalism dispute is mostly carried on by thinkers who believe in local mediate justification. Hence we will ensure maximum contact with that debate if we focus on (4) rather than (5) in the ensuing discussion.

One more point must be laid on the table before we turn to the consideration of what can be said in support of PI. Go back to the initial quotation from Bonjour; we have not yet squeezed it dry. There Bonjour requires for the justification of S's putatively basic belief that S justifiably believe not only that the belief have the "feature" in question but also *that beliefs having that feature are likely to be true*. When we come to the main argument for PI we will see the rationale for this additional higher level requirement. For the moment we need only note its general character. It is clear that Bonjour imposes *this* requirement just because he takes truth conducivity to be required for, as we might say, *justificatory efficacy*. Earlier in the essay he had written that "the distinguishing characteristic" of epistemic justification is "its internal relation to the cognitive goal of truth" (p. 54). Elsewhere Bonjour has laid it down that it is essential to a justifier to be "truth conductive".[14] Thus this additional requirement is really a requirement to the effect that the subject be justified in supposing not only that the putative justifier obtains but also that it be efficacious, that it have what it takes to justify the belief. But he can't come right out and say that. Consider his situation if he were to try. Formulate the additional requirement as: *S justifiably believes that the possession of that feature suffices to justify the belief*. But Bonjour is committed to deny this; his specific contention is that no feature of a belief can be sufficient to justify the belief; the subject must also have certain justified beliefs about that feature.[15] Then how about requiring that the possession of that feature is part of what confers justification on this belief? But we want the requirement to be more specific than that. The two justified beliefs are also part of what confers justification on the belief in this situation, but a different part. We want to specify what part the feature is contributing to the justification. That is what Bonjour is attempting to do with his requirement that S be justified in believing that the feature is probabilifying, that by virtue of having this feature the belief is likely to be true. That will do the job, on the assumption that probabilification is just what it takes for justificatory efficacy. But this is controversial. In fact, other internalists have been in the forefront of denying just this claim.[16] Thus it appears that if we are to give an adequate formulation of this higher level requirement, we must commit ourselves to some highly controversial assumption as to what is required for justification, some highly controversial assumption in substantive epistemology.

Fortunately there is a coward's way out, since we are working with (4), which restricts us to purely mediate justification, rather than with Bonjour's versions. On (4) the only justifiers are other justified beliefs of the same subject. Hence the way in which any justifier has to be related to a belief in order to do its job is to provide "adequate support" or "adequate evidence"; it must be an "adequate reason". No doubt, it is both obscure and controversial what is required for one belief (or the propositional content thereof) to constitute an adequate reason or to provide adequate support for another. But leaving all this aside, and taking cover behind the criterion-neutral term 'adequate', we can put the additional, higher level requirement just by saying that S must justifiably believe that the justifying belief(s) provide adequate support for the justified belief.[17] Tacking this on to our canonical formulation, we get:

(6) Only S's justified beliefs can epistemize S's belief that $p$, and then only if S justifiably believes that the other justified beliefs in question provide adequate support for $p$ (or for something else, in the case of overriders).

## II

We have now explicated PI sufficiently to consider what can be said in its favor. That consideration will lead to further refinements. First let's consider what defense is offered by Bonjour in "Externalist Theories of Empirical Knowledge". The main effort there is devoted to an attack on reliability theories, utilizing an example of alleged clairvoyance. It is stipulated that the subject has a reliable capacity for determining the disposition of distant objects on no apparent basis. Bonjour first argues that if the person has adequate reason for supposing that a belief thus formed is false, or that her clairvoyance is not reliable, then she is not justified in the clairvoyant beliefs, even though they are formed reliably. But, as Bonjour acknowledges, this shows only that the subject's justified beliefs do have a bearing on what other beliefs are justified, not that they are the only thing that can have this bearing. Next, he more boldly argues that in the case in which the subject has no reasons for or against the reliability of her powers or the truth of the belief (whether or not she believes that the powers are reliable), she is not justified in holding the beliefs, however reliable her clairvoyant powers are in fact. However these "arguments" simply consist in Bonjour's displaying his intuitions in opposition to those of his opponent. A couple of quotations will give the flavor.

> We are now face-to-face with the fundamental – and seemingly obvious – intuitive problem with externalism: *why* should the mere fact that such an external relation (the reliability of the faculty) obtains mean that Norman's belief is epistemically justified, when the relation in question is entirely outside his ken?
> One reason why externalism may seem initially plausible is that if the external relation in question genuinely obtains, then Norman will in fact not go wrong in accepting the belief, and it is, *in a sense*, not an accident that this is so. But how is this supposed to justify Norman's belief? From his subjective perspective, it *is* an accident that the belief is true.[18]

This is more like an appeal to PI than a support for that restriction. There are, as we shall see, some germs of a more substantial argument in Bonjour, but they will need developing.

Nor are we helped by a rather common argument for PI that stems from a confusion between the *activity* of justifying a belief and the *state* of a belief's being justified. Here is a good sample.

> In whatever way a man might attempt to justify his beliefs, whether to himself or to another, he must always appeal to some belief. There is nothing other than one's belief to which one can appeal in the justification of belief. There is no exit from the circle of one's beliefs.[19]

Of course, if I am to carry out the *activity* of justifying a belief, I must provide an argument for it; I must say something as to why one should suppose it to be true. And to do this I must employ other beliefs of mine. In saying what reasons there are for supposing that *p*, I am expressing other beliefs of mine and contextually implying that I am justified in accepting them. But this all has to do with the activity of *justifying* a belief, *showing* it to be justified. From the fact that I can *justify* a belief only by relating it to other beliefs that constitute a support, it does not follow that a belief can *be justified* only by its relations to other beliefs. Analogously, from the fact that I cannot justify my expenses without saying something in support of my having made them, it does not follow that my expenses cannot *be justified* unless I say something in support of my having made them. Indeed, we all have innumerable beliefs that are commonly taken to be justified but for which we never so much as attempt to produce reasons. It might be argued with some show of plausibility that one can be justified in believing that *p* only if it is *possible* for one to justify that belief; but I cannot imagine any remotely plausible argument for the thesis that I can be justified in believing that *p* only if I *have justified* that belief. Hence the point made by Lehrer about justifying leaves completely intact the possibility that one might *be justified* in a belief by something other than one's other beliefs.

We will have to make the same judgment on an analogous argument from what is involved in *deciding* what to believe. Here is a version by Pollock.

> In deciding what to believe, we have only our own beliefs to which we can appeal. If our beliefs mutually support our believing P, then it would be irrational for us not to believe P and hence belief in P is justified. There is no way that one can break out of the circle of his own beliefs.[20]

Again, even if this shows that I can have no basis other than my own beliefs for a *decision* as to what to believe, it falls far short of showing that nothing can *justify* a belief except other beliefs. For there is no reason to suppose that the only justified beliefs are those the subject *decided* to adopt.

Even though, as will appear in the fullness of time, I am no advocate of PI, I feel that I can improve on the recommendations for that view that can be found in the writings of its supporters. Here is what I take to be the strongest argument for it. I have gleaned the basic idea for this line of argument from various sources, but the development of it is my own.[21]

"First let's note that the fact that *q* can enter into the justification for S's believing that *p* only in the guise of S's being justified in believing that *q*. Consider the popular idea that what justifies me in beliefs about my own current conscious states is that such beliefs are infallible, that is, are such that I couldn't mistakenly form such a belief. But how could that fact justify those beliefs unless I were cognizant of the infallibility? If I am unaware of their infallibility, and they have no other justification, am I not proceeding *irresponsibly* in forming such beliefs? Just as the mere fact that X is about to attack me will not justify my striking X unless I have good reason to suppose that he is about to attack me, so the mere fact that current feeling beliefs are infallible can't justify me in accepting them unless I at least have good reason to regard them as infallible. *Pari passu*, the mere fact that I am being appeared to treely cannot render me justified in believing that there is a tree in front of me, unless I am justified in believing that I am being appeared to treely. If I am unaware of the existence of the warrant-conferring fact then, for me, it is just as if it did not exist. How can a fact of which I take no account whatever have any bearing on what it is *permissible* for me to do, in the way of action or of belief? Thus it would seem that my being justified in believing that *q* is at least a *necessary* condition of *q*'s playing a role in justifying my belief that *p*.

But it is also a sufficient condition. Provided I am justified in believing that beliefs about current feelings of the subject are infallible, what more could be required to legitimate those beliefs? Even if they are not in fact infallible, how can that prevent its being *permissible* for me to accept them? If, so far as I can tell, there are facts that strongly support the supposition that *p*, then surely it is *all right* for me to give my assent to *p*. What more could be *demanded* of me? I have done all I can. What the actual facts are over and above what I am most justified in believing is something I cannot be held *responsible* for. Once I have marshaled all the cognitive resources available to me to determine the matter, I have, in my body of justified beliefs, the closest approximation I can make to the actual facts. That is the best I have to go on, and it would be quite unreasonable to suggest that I *ought* to be going on something else instead. What I am justified in believing provides sufficient as well as necessary conditions for the justification of further beliefs."[22]

How does this line of argument go beyond simply displaying internalist (PI) intuitions? It does so by grounding those intuitions in a particular conception of justification, one that makes epistemic justification a matter of the subject's normative situation, a matter of how the subject's believing that *p* stands vis-à-vis relevant intellectual norms, standards, obligations, duties, and the like. If S's believing that *p* is *not* in contravention of relevant intellectual obligations, then it is *permissible* for him to believe that *p*, he cannot be rightly *blamed* for doing so, it is *all right* for him to hold that belief, he is *in the clear* in so believing. Let's call this a "deontological" conception of epistemic justification. The argument just presented exhibits the PI constraint as flowing from *what justification is*, as thus conceived. Since whether I am justified in believing that *p* depends on whether I could rightfully be blamed or held to account for so believing, then what is crucial for whether I am justified is the way the relevant facts appear from my perspective; justification depends on what the relevant facts are like, *so far as I can tell*. For that is what is crucial for whether I can be blamed for my belief. If and only if my belief is adequately supported *so far as I can tell*, I cannot be blamed for the belief.[23]

Elsewhere I have explored the deontological conception and contrasted it with the very different "strong position" (SP) conception, as well as distinguishing various versions of each.[24] Roughly speaking, to be SP justified in believing that *p* is to believe that *p* in such a way as to be in a strong position thereby to attain the truth and avoid error. It is to believe that *p* in a "truth conducive" way. It is for one's belief to have been formed in such a way or on such a basis that one is thereby likely to be believing correctly. Note that each conception omits the crucial emphasis of the other, thereby implicitly denying it to be necessary for justification. Freedom from blameworthiness, being in the clear as far as one's intellectual duties are concerned, is totally ignored by the "strong position" theorist. So long as one forms one's belief in a way that is well calculated to get the truth, it is of no concern how well one is carrying out intellectual duties. Conversely, the deontologist has nothing to say about truth conducivity.[25] So long as I am not violating any intellectual duties, I am "in the clear" in believing that *p*, whatever my chances for truth. This is not to say that each side denies the importance of what is crucial for the other. The deontologist need not be indifferent to the truth, nor need the "strong position" theorist be uninterested in intellectual duties. But they differ on how these admittedly important matters relate to epistemic justification.

To get a properly rounded picture we should also note a way in which truth-conducivity does typically enter into deontological theories of justification. Even though truth-conducivity does not enter into the meaning of "justified" for the deontologist, he is likely to give it a prominent place when he comes to spell out the content of our most important intellectual obligations. Such theorists typically hold that our basic intellectual obligation is to so conduct our cognitive activities as to maximize the chances of believing the true and avoiding believing the false.[26] Thus even though one may be deontologically justified without thereby being in a favorable position to get the truth, if our basic intellectual obligation is to maximize truth and minimize falsity, one cannot be deontologically justified in a belief unless one is believing in such a way that, so far as one can tell, is well calculated to reach the truth.

Now we can see that just as the deontological conception supports a PI restriction, so an SP conception supports its denial. It is obviously not conceptually necessary that one comes to believe that *p* in a truth-conductive way only if that belief is well supported by other justified beliefs of the subject. It is clearly possible that there are ways of being in a strong position in one's beliefs other than by basing those beliefs on other justified beliefs. Plausible examples of such other ways are not far to seek. Perceptual beliefs about the physical environment, for example, that the lilies are blooming in the garden, are based on the subject's sensory experience, on the way in which things sensorily appear to one. Furthermore let's make the plausible supposition that one does not typically form beliefs about how one is being sensorily appeared to; the sensory appearance directly gives rise to the belief about the environment. It is not that one says to oneself, even rapidly, implicitly, or below the level of consciousness,

"I am having a visual experience of such and such a sort; therefore the lilies are blooming in the garden". No such inference typically takes place, for the premises for such inferences are rarely made objects of belief. Finally, let's make the plausible assumption that our perceptual belief-forming mechanisms are generally reliable, at least for the sorts of perceptual beliefs we typically form, in the sorts of situations we typically encounter. Granting all this, perceptual belief formation constitutes massive support for the thesis that one can form beliefs in a reliable, truth-conducive manner without basing them on other justified beliefs.

Beliefs about one's current conscious states provide even stronger support. It is very plausible to suppose that we have a highly reliable (some would even say infallible) mechanism for the formation of such beliefs. And yet it would be extremely implausible to suppose that these beliefs are formed or held on the basis of reasons. What would such reasons be? It may be suggested that my reason for supposing that I feel sleepy at the moment is that I do believe this and that such beliefs are infallible. But many persons who form such beliefs do not even have the relevant concept of infallibility, much less typically believe that such beliefs are infallible whenever they come to believe such things. Once again we have reason to suppose that beliefs can satisfy the SP conception of justification without satisfying the PI constraint on justification.

Next let's note that the argument we have given for PI supports both the lower level and the higher level requirement laid down in (6). The "lower level requirement" is that the justifier for the belief that $p$ consist of other justified beliefs of the subject, and the "higher level requirement" is that the subject justifiably *believe that* these other justified beliefs provide adequate support for the belief that $p$. We have been emphasizing the way in which the argument establishes the lower level requirement, but it also lends powerful support to the higher level requirement. For suppose that my belief that $p$ is based on other justified beliefs of mine and, let's suppose, these other justified beliefs provide adequate support for the belief that $p$. But suppose further that I do not justifiably believe that these other beliefs do provide adequate support. In that case, so far as I can tell, I do not have within my perspective adequate support for $p$. Would I not be proceeding irresponsibly in adopting the belief that $p$? Couldn't I properly be held accountable for a violation of intellectual obligations in giving my assent to $p$ under those conditions? Therefore if I am to be in the clear in believing that $p$, the belief must not only be based on other justified beliefs of mine; I must also be justified in supposing those beliefs to provide sufficient support for the belief that $p$.

That shows that the higher level justified belief is necessary for justification. We can now proceed to argue that it, together with the lower level requirement, is sufficient. The crucial question here is whether it is also necessary for justification that the other justified beliefs do in fact provide adequate support, that their propositional contents are indeed so related as to make the one an adequate reason for the other. A consideration of conditions of blame, being in the clear, etc., will support a negative answer. For if, going on what I know or justifiably believe about the world, it is clear to me that other justified beliefs of mine adequately support the belief that $p$, what more could be required of me? Even if I am mistaken in that judgment, I made it in the light of the best considerations available to me. I can't be held to blame if I proceed in the light of the best reading of the facts of which I am capable. Hence a *justified belief* that I have adequate support is all that can rightfully be imposed in the way of a higher level requirement.

Now that we have a two-level PI internalism-externalism contrast, there is the possibility of being an internalist on one level and an externalist on another. The two parties disagree both over what can be a justifier and over that by virtue of which a particular item justifies a particular belief. A particularly live possibility of a compromise is an internalism as to what can justify and an externalism as to what enables it to justify. One could be a PI internalist about justifiers by virtue of recognizing only mediate justification, but insist that my belief that $p$ is justified by its relations to my belief that $q$ if and only if $q$ does in fact provide adequate support for $p$. At the end of the paper we shall advocate a similar mediating position, though the internalist component will not be the PI brand.

Now let's consider a way in which what is supported by our argument for PI differs from the formulation of PI with which we have been working. We have represented the deontologist as maintaining that whether S is justified in believing that $p$ is solely a function of what other justified beliefs S has. But that cannot be the whole story. Consider a case in which, although the sum total of the justified beliefs I actually possess provides an adequate basis for the belief that $p$, that would not have been the case had I been conducting myself properly. If I had looked into the matter as thoroughly as I should have, I would be in possession of effective *overriders* for my evidence for $p$, and my total body of evidence would not have given sufficient support for the belief that $p$. Here the belief that $p$ *is* adequately supported by the perspective on the world that I actually have, and I justifiably believe that it is; but nevertheless I am not in the clear in believing that $p$, not justified in the deontological sense.

These considerations show that PI must be modified if it is to be supported by a deontological conception of justification. It must include a codicil to the effect that overriders that the subject does not possess, but would have possessed had she been conducting herself as she should have been, also can serve to epistemize beliefs.[27] PI now becomes:

(7)  Only S's justified beliefs can epistemize S's belief that $p$, and then only if S justifiably believes that those other justified beliefs provide adequate support for S's belief that $p$; but overriders that S should have had but didn't can cancel out justification provided by the preceding.[28]

Going back once more to our argument for PI, I now wish to point out that it utilizes a special form of a deontological conception of justification that is limited in ways that render it either totally inapplicable, or at least severely limited in application.

First, it utilizes a concept of justification that assumes beliefs to be under direct voluntary control. The argument takes it that one is justified in believing that *p* if and only if one is not to blame *for believing that p*, if and only if *in that situation this was a belief that one was permitted to choose*. All this talk has application only if one has direct voluntary control over whether one believes that *p* at a given moment. If I lack such control, if I cannot believe or refrain from believing that *p* at will, then it is futile to discuss whether I am *permitted* to believe that *p* at *t* or whether I would be *irresponsible* in choosing to believe that *p* at *t*. And it seems that we just don't have any such control, at least not in general. For the most part my beliefs are formed willy-nilly. When I see a truck coming down the street, I am hardly at liberty either to believe that a truck is coming down the street or to refrain from that belief. Even if there are special cases, such as moral or religious beliefs, where we do have pinpoint voluntary control (and even this may be doubted), it is clear that for the most part we lack such powers.[29]

Not only does the argument in question presuppose direct voluntary control of belief; it considers the requirements for justification only for those beliefs that are acquired by an explicit, deliberate choice. For it arrives at the PI constraint by pointing out that only what I am cognizant of can be taken account of in my *decision* as to whether to believe that *p*. "If I am unaware of their infallibility, . . . am I not proceeding irresponsibly in *forming* such beliefs?" "If, so far as I can tell, there are facts that strongly support the supposition that *p*, then surely it is all right for me to give my assent to *p*." But this fact, that only what I am cognizant of can affect the permissibility of my choice, will imply a *general* constraint on justification only if justification is confined to beliefs that are *chosen* by a deliberate voluntary act. But even if beliefs are *subject to* direct voluntary control, that control need not always be exercised. One can hold that it is always in principle possible to choose whether to believe a given proposition without thereby being committed to the grossly implausible supposition that all our beliefs are in fact acquired by an explicit choice. Even overt actions that are uncontroversially under voluntary control, such as tying one's shoelaces, can be, and often are, performed habitually. Likewise, even if beliefs are as subject to direct voluntary control as tying one's shoelaces, beliefs are often acquired willy-nilly. Hence a concept of epistemic justification that is confined to beliefs acquired by deliberate choice covers only a small part of the territory.

Third, it follows from the point just made that the argument utilizes a concept of justification that evaluates a belief solely in terms of its original acquisition, for the argument has to do with what can determine the permissibility of the *choice* of a belief. But it is often noted by epistemologists that the epistemic status of a belief may change after its acquisition, as the subject comes to acquire or lose support for it. Suppose that after coming to believe that Susie is quitting her job, on the basis of no evidence worthy of the name and hence unjustifiably, I come into possession of adequate evidence for this supposition; let us further suppose that this new evidence now functions as the basis for my belief. In this case my belief comes to be justified *after* its acquisition. Thus a concept of justifiably *acquired* belief is at best only a part of an adequate concept of justified belief.

To be sure, it is not difficult to modify this very restrictive concept, so as to make it more generally applicable. Let's begin by showing how the direct voluntary control assumption can be dropped. It is uncontroversial that our beliefs are under *indirect* voluntary control, or at least subject to influence from our voluntary actions. Even if I can't effectively decide at this moment to stop believing that Reagan is inept, I could embark on a regimen that is designed to improve my assessment of Reagan, and it might even succeed in time. With this possibility of indirect influence in mind, we can reconstrue "intellectual obligations" so that they no longer attach to believings and abstentions therefrom, but to actions that are designed to influence our believings and abstentions. Reinterpreted in this way the argument would be that whether we are justified in believing that $p$ at $t$ would depend on whether prior to $t$ we had done what could reasonably be expected of us to influence that belief. The difference between these two understandings may be illustrated as follows. Suppose that my belief that there is life outside our solar system is inadequately supported by the totality of my justified beliefs. On the direct voluntary control interpretation I have an effective choice, whenever I consider the matter, as to whether to keep believing that or not. It is my duty to refrain from believing it since it is not adequately supported by my "perspective"; since I continue to believe it in defiance of my duty, I am doing something that is not permitted; my belief is not justified. But the matter sorts out differently on the "indirect voluntary control" construal. It is recognized that I lack the capacity to discard that belief at will; at most I have the ability to make various moves that increase the chances of the belief's being abandoned. Hence so long as I am doing as much along that line as could reasonably be expected of me, I can't be faulted for continuing to have the belief; and so it is justified. On either of these interpretations, whether my belief is justified is a function of how things appear in my perspective rather than of how they are in actual fact. So long as life outside the solar system is improbable relative to what I am justified in believing, then my belief is unjustified unless (on the indirect control version) my best efforts have failed to dislodge it.

Next consider how we can lift the other restrictions. We can confine this discussion to the direct control version, since on the indirect control version there was no reason to impose them in the first place. Let's first take the restriction to explicitly chosen beliefs. On the direct control version we can say that the belief is justified provided that it was acquired on such a basis that if the agent had chosen to adopt the belief on that basis he could not have been blamed for doing so. In other words, where the belief, or its furtherance, was not explicitly chosen we can evaluate it, on the deontological conception, by considering whether its basis is such that if it or its furtherance was chosen on that basis the agent would have been in the clear in so choosing.

Now let's see how to lift the restriction to the original acquisition of the belief, and extend the concept to the evaluation of one's continuing to believe that $p$ at times after its original acquisition. Once again the crucial move is to consider what would be the case if we were to make a choice that we did not in fact make. For one thing, we can consider what the judgment would be on my coming to believe this if the belief were voluntarily adopted on the basis of this evidence I possess at present (and analogously for the indirect control version). Or, closer to home, we could consider the possibility that I should now explicitly raise the question of whether to retain the belief, in the light of the evidence I now possess, and should come to a decision to retain it. In that case would I be in the clear in making that decision? If so, I am now justified in retaining the belief.

It is time to take our bearings with respect to these increasingly proliferating variations in a deontological concept of justification. To keep complexity within manageable bounds, I shall formulate a version that is designed to take care both of habitually formed beliefs and post-acquisition influences on justification. I shall formulate this both in a direct control and an indirect control version.

(8)   Direct control version. One is justified in believing that $p$ at $t$ if and only if either (a) in choosing at $t$ to adopt or retain the belief that $p$ one was not violating any intellectual obligations, or (b) one's belief that $p$ at $t$ has such a basis that if one were to decide, in the light of that basis, to retain one's belief that $p$, one would not be violating any intellectual obligations in so doing.

(9)   Indirect control version. One is justified in believing that $p$ at $t$ if and only if one's believing that $p$ at $t$ does not stem from any violations of intellectual obligations.

Thus it is not difficult to concoct distinctively deontological conceptions of justification that avoid the severe limitations of the concept employed by the argument for PI. But what sort of argument for PI can be constructed on the basis of these alternative conceptions?

The first point is that no case at all can be made for PI on the basis of the indirect control version. According to (9), justification is a function of certain features of the causal history of the belief. Was that history such that if the subject had lived up to her intellectual obligations in the past then she would not have believed that $p$? This is not a "perspectival" matter. The justified beliefs of the subject do not play any crucial role in determining whether or not that condition was satisfied. It is matter of what actually went on, rather than a matter of how what went on is represented in the subject's viewpoint. Thus (9) supports an externalist position on justification; at least it supports the externalist contrast to PI. Of course we could try to "perspectivize" (9). Any condition for anything that is in terms of what the facts actually are can receive a "perspectival" modification, transforming it into a condition that the facts be represented in a certain way in the subject's perspective. So modified, (9) would become:

(10)   S is justified in believing that $p$ if and only if S's belief that $p$ did not, so far as S can tell, stem from S's violations of intellectual obligations.

But (10) is wildly permissive. We rarely have reason to think that one of our beliefs stems from intellectual transgressions. To know about the causal history of beliefs takes research, and we rarely engage in such research. Hence we have very few beliefs about the causal history of our beliefs. And so practically all beliefs, no matter how shoddy or disreputable, will be justified on this criterion. The prospects for support for PI from an indirect control version of a deontological conception are vanishingly small.

Things do not look much rosier from the perspective of (8). According to (8) a belief can be justified on the basis of anything whatsoever, not just other justified beliefs of the subject, provided that one would be in the clear, vis-à-vis one's intellectual obligations, if one were to consider whether to retain the belief in the light of that basis. If one were to engage in such a consideration, one would, of course, be choosing to retain the belief on the basis of other justified beliefs, in particular the belief that that basis obtains. That is the situation envisaged by the restrictive concept employed in the original argument for PI. But the extended concept differs from that precisely by not making the actual obtaining of such a situation necessary for justification. It recognizes that a belief can be justified even if one never does make any decision with respect to it on the basis of what one justifiably believes about its basis. Hence on this modified deontological concept a belief could be justified by being based on some experience, even if the subject in fact has no beliefs about that experience. What is supported by (8) is a denial rather than an affirmation of the PI constraint.

Thus it appears that we have a significant argument for PI only if we utilize a concept of justification that cannot be seriously defended as generally applicable, a concept according to which the justification of beliefs is solely a matter of whether a belief is *chosen* in such a way that this choice does not involve any dereliction of intellectual duty. But we cannot seriously suppose that justified beliefs are restricted to those that are *chosen* in that way, even if some are. Insofar as we are working with an even minimally defensible concept of justification, the argument for PI dissipates.

When we consider the higher level requirement embodied in (7), things look even worse. (7) implies that I will be justified in believing that $p$ on the basis of my justified belief that $q$ only if I am justified in supposing that the latter belief provides adequate support for the former. One reason this darkens the prospects for PI is that it is doubtful that we satisfy that condition very often. Just how often it is satisfied depends on what it takes to be justified in beliefs like that, and that is not at all clear. One thing that is clear for the PI advocate, however, is that to be justified such a belief will have to be mediately justified, since that is the only kind of justification PI recognizes. We will have to have sufficient reasons for supposing that *the belief that $q$ adequately supports the belief that $p$* if we are to be justified in that higher level belief. How often do we have such reasons? Not very often, I would suggest. Perhaps the following will suffice to indicate the difficulties. Consider perceptual beliefs. If my perceptual belief that it is raining outside is to be mediately justified, this will presumably be on the basis of a justified belief that I am having certain visual experiences, plus perhaps (depending on the requirements we adopt) justified beliefs about the normality of the situation.[30] Now to have adequate reasons for supposing that reasons like that are sufficient support for a perceptual belief about one's environment is to be in the position that many great philosophers have labored to get themselves into when they have wrestled with the problem of how to infer facts about the external world from facts about the sensory experiences of the individual percipient. And even if some philosophers have solved that problem, which I am strongly inclined to deny, it is quite clear that the overwhelming majority of the population is not in possession of any such solution. For a second illustration, consider the point that in order for some nondeductive evidence to be adequate support for a given belief (so that this latter belief is justifiably held), there must be no other justified beliefs of mine that serve to defeat the prima facie support provided by the first-mentioned evidence. Suppose that my reason for supposing that Ray will be in his office today is that today is Wednesday and Ray has a fixed disposition to work in his office on Wednesday. I have temporarily forgotten, however, that Ray told me last week that he will be out of town on Wednesday of this week. When that justified belief of mine is added to the picture, the total evidence no longer adequately supports the supposition that Ray will be in his office today. This means that I can be justified in supposing that my belief that $q$ renders my belief that $p$ justified only if I am justified in supposing that there is nothing else I am justified in believing such that when that is added to $q$ the conjunction does not adequately support $p$. And it is difficult to be justified in any claim concerning what is or is not present in the totality of one's justified beliefs.

Thus it is dubious that the higher level requirement of PI is very widely satisfied. If that is required for justification, not many people are justified in many beliefs. But there is an even more serious difficulty with the requirement. It engenders an infinite regress. If in order to be justified in believing that $p$, I must be justified in believing that my reason, $q$, adequately supports $p$, the justification of this later belief requires the justification of a still higher level belief. That is, if $r$ is my reason for supposing that $q$ adequately supports $p$, I can be justified in supposing that $q$ adequately supports $p$, only if I am justified in supposing that $r$ adequately supports q adequately supports p. And my justification for this last belief includes my being justified in a still higher level belief about adequate support. Given PI, I cannot be justified in any belief without simultaneously being justified in all the members of an infinite hierarchy of beliefs of ever-ascending level.

Let's make sure we fully appreciate the character of this difficulty. The view that all justification is mediate itself gives rise to a much more widely advertised regress, this one stemming from the lower level requirement that a given belief can be justified only by its relation to another justified belief. The same is true of the justification of this supporting belief; that is to say, it can be justified only by its relation to still another justified belief; and so on ad infinitum. The standard coherentist response to this difficulty is to opt for a circle of justification, rather than an infinite regress, and then to switch from local to holistic justification. I find this response quite inadequate, but this is not the place to go into that. Instead I want to stress the difference in the difficulty entailed by the higher level regress. The preference for a circle over an infinite set is of no avail here.

Since there is a regress of *levels*, we are foreclosed from doubling back. No adequate-support belief at an earlier stage will serve to do the job required at a later stage because it will have the wrong content. At each stage what is required is a justified belief to the effect that the "reason for" relationship *at the immediately previous stage* is an adequate one; and no earlier beliefs of that sort in the hierarchy will have been concerned with that particular "reason for" relationship. Hence there is no alternative here to an infinite regress. And, needless to say, it is highly doubtful that any of us is in possession of such an infinite hierarchy of "adequate support" beliefs.

# III

PI has not emerged in strong shape from our examination. Let's turn now to the second construal of an internalist constraint on justification, and see if it fares any better. This second construal has to do with the kind of access we can have to justifiers. The general idea is that possible justifiers are restricted to items to which we have a specially favored access. This special access is variously specified as direct, incorrigible, and obtainable just by reflecting. We have already seen Goldman, in "The Internalist Conception of Justification," identifying internalism with PI. Here is an formulation of the second construal from the same essay.

> The basic idea of internalism is that there should be guaranteed epistemic access to the correctness of a DDP. No condition of DDP-rightness is acceptable unless we have epistemic access to the DDP that in fact satisfies the condition, i.e., unless we can tell which DDP satisfies it. The internalist's objection to externalism's condition of rightness, i.e., actual optimality, is precisely that cognizers may have no way of telling which DDP satisfies it. Internalism's *own* condition of rightness must, therefore, be such that any cognizer *can tell* which DDP satisfies it.[31]

Another person we cited as a source of PI, Kent Bach, also brings the second version into the picture in "A Rationale for Reliabilism."

> Internalism . . . treats justifiedness as a purely internal matter: if p is justified for S, then S must be aware (or at least be immediately capable of being aware) of what makes it justified and why.[32]

I have found, however, the most elaborate developments of this conception in epistemologists who do not actually employ the "internalism" label. Thus, R. M. Chisholm, in a well-known passage, lays it down that whenever we are justified in a belief, we can determine by reflection what it is that so justifies us.

> We presuppose, second, that the things we know are justified for us in the following sense: *we* can know what it is, on any occasion, that constitutes our grounds, or reason, or evidence for thinking that we know.

In beginning with what we think we know to be true, or with what, after reflection, we would be willing to count as being evident, we are assuming that the truth we are seeking is "already implicit in the mind which seeks it, and needs only to be elicited and brought to clear reflection".[33]

Carl Ginet gives a more elaborate statement of this version of internalism.

Every one of every set of facts about S's position that minimally suffices to make S, at a given time, justified in being confident that p must be *directly recognizable* to S at that time. By "directly recognizable" I mean this: if a certain fact obtains, then it is directly recognizable to S at a given time if and only if, provided that S at that time has the concept of that sort of fact, S needs at that time only to reflect clear-headedly on the question of whether or not that fact obtains in order to know that it does.[34]

In the interest of securing a definite target let's focus on the version of special access internalism that requires *direct* access for justifiers, construed along Ginet's lines. I shall refer to this second construal of internalism as "access internalism" (hereinafter "AI").

Our next order of business should be to consider the relation between the two internalisms. Now that we have completed the laborious process of explicating and refining our conception of PI, we are at last in a position to do this. Are the two conceptions importantly different? Just how are they related? Can one be subsumed under the other? Does one imply the other?

First let's consider the possibility that PI is a special case of AI. Is the restriction of justifiers to the subject's viewpoint a special case of a restriction of justifiers to what is directly accessible? Only if one's own perspective is directly accessible, and this does not seem to be the case. The sum total of my justified beliefs cannot be depended on to spread themselves before my eyes on demand, not even that segment thereof that is relevant to a particular belief under consideration. I may know something that provides crucial evidence for *p* and yet fail to realize this even on careful reflection. We need not invoke Freudian blockages to illustrate this, though they are relevant. It may be that the sheer volume of what I know about, for example, ancient Greek philosophy, is too great for my powers of ready retrieval; or some of this material may be so deeply buried as to require special trains of association to dislodge it. We are all familiar with cases in which something we knew all along failed to put in an appearance when it was needed to advance a particular inquiry. And, remembering our last modification of PI, still less is it the case that *what I would be justified in believing had I been behaving as I ought* is readily available on reflection.

Thus an item may pass the PI test without passing the AI test. PI is not a special case of AI. How about the converse? Is the restriction to the directly accessible just a special case of the restriction to the subject's justified beliefs and knowledge? Only if nothing other than my knowledge and justified beliefs is directly accessible to me. But that is clearly not the case. My feelings and other conscious experiences are directly accessible if anything is. And even if it were true, as I see no reason to suppose it to be, that I cannot have a conscious experience without knowing that I do, still the experience is distinguishable from the knowledge of the experience. Hence an item can pass the AI test without passing the PI test. This is what makes it possible for partisans of AI like Chisholm and Ginet to recognize immediate justification and to escape coherentism.

Thus PI and AI look quite independent of one another. But surely they must be closely related in some way. Otherwise how can we understand the fact that they are so persistently lumped together under the "internalism" label? And in fact on closer inspection we can see an interesting connection. We can think of AI as a broadening of PI. Whereas PI restricts justifiers to what the subject already justifiably believes (or, in the modified version, to that plus some of what the subject would justifiably believe under ideal conditions), AI enlarges that to include what the subject *can* come to know just on reflection. It is clear that any item that passes the AI test is something that is readily assimilable into the subject's viewpoint, just on reflection. AI, we might say, enlarges the conception of the subject's perspective to include not only what does in fact occur in that perspective (and what should occur), but also what *could* be there if the subject were to turn his attention to it.

Next let's turn to what can be said in support of AI. We have seen that PI is most plausibly supported on a deontological conception of justification, and the AI constraint has also been defended on that conception. Here we are fortunate to have an explicit statement of the argument from Carl Ginet.

Assuming that S has the concept of justification for being confident that p, S *ought* always to possess or lack confidence that p according to whether or not he has such justification. At least he ought always to withhold confidence unless he has justification. This is simply what is meant by having or lacking *justification*. But if this is what S ought to do in any possible circumstance, then it is what S *can* do in any possible circumstance. That is, assuming that he has the relevant concepts, S can always tell whether or not he has justification for being confident that p. But this would not be so unless the difference between having such justification and not having it were always directly recognizable to S. And that would not be so if any fact contributing to a set that minimally constitutes S's having such justification were not either directly recognizable to S or entailed by something directly recognizable to S (so that its absence would have to make a directly recognizable difference). For suppose it were otherwise: suppose that some part of a condition minimally sufficient for S's being justified in being confident that p were *not* entailed by anything directly recognizable to S. Then S's position could change from having such justification to lacking it without there being any change at all in what is directly recognizable to S. But if there is no change in directly recognizable features of S's position, S cannot tell that his position has changed in other respects: no matter how clearheadedly and attentively he considers his position he will detect no change. If it seemed to S before that he had justification for being confident that p then it must still seem so to him. So this sort of justification would be such that it would not always be possible for its subject to tell whether or not he possessed it, which is contrary to what we noted is an obvious essential feature of justification. So there can be no such justification. That is, there can be no set of facts giving S justification for being confident that p that has an essential part that is neither directly recognizable to S nor entailed by something directly recognizable to S.[35]

Note that the conclusion of this argument is not quite the same as the AI thesis I previously quoted from Ginet. According to that thesis, every part of a justifier must be directly recognizable; but the argument purports to show only that a justifier must be either this or *entailed* by what is directly recognizable. Ginet may feel that the additional disjunct makes no significant difference, but this is not the case. One may not be able to spot everything that is entailed by what is directly recognizable; the disjunctive conclusion leaves open the possibility of justifiers that are not wholly identifiable from what is directly recognizable. I shall, however, suppress this difficulty in the ensuing discussion. For the sake of simplicity I shall consider the thesis in the simpler form, bringing in the second disjunct only where it is specially relevant to the point under consideration.

I have said that Ginet argues from a deontological conception of justification, but this may not be obvious from his formulation of the argument. I shall try to make it more obvious. But first let's note that Ginet explicitly lays out such a conception.

> One is *justified* in being confident that p if and only if it is not the case that one ought not to be confident that p: one could not be justly reproached for being confident that p.[36]

This concept does not explicitly appear in the argument, but it is just below the surface. Ginet uses this concept to define the concept of *having a justification* that he employs in the argument.

> I shall take "S has justification for being confident that p" . . . to mean S is in a position such that if he is, or were to be, confident that p then he is, or would be, justified in being so.[37]

We then get "is justified in being confident that *p*" defined deontologically, as in the previous quotation. Thus the concept used in the argument is, so to say, the first derivative of a deontological conception. It is the concept of having what it takes to be justified in the deontological sense if one will only make use of those resources.

Before entering onto a critical scrutiny of the argument, let's note some of its features, with special attention to the points we were making concerning the argument for PI. First, the argument should, by rights, apply to overriders of prima facie justification as well as to justifiers. Consider that done. Second, Ginet is obviously presupposing direct voluntary control of belief. Since "in any possible circumstance", "S *ought* always to possess or lack confidence that p according to whether or not he has such justification", this is something that "S *can* do in any possible circumstance". It is always possible for S to stop and consider any actual belief of his, or any candidate for belief, and bring it about then and there that he does or does not adopt or continue to hold the belief according as he has or lacks sufficient justification for it.[38] It is not so clear whether Ginet's concept of justification applies only to beliefs that are acquired by a deliberate choice, and then only in terms of what is true at the moment of acquisition. Let's suppose that he is only assuming the ever-present possibility of a deliberate choice between adopting (continuing) a belief and refraining from doing so, and that to be justified in believing that $p$ is to be so situated that if one were, in that situation, to choose to believe that $p$ (or continue to do so), one could not be blamed, on intellectual grounds, for that choice.

It will help us to critically evaluate Ginet's argument if we exhibit its skeleton.

(1)   S ought to withhold belief that $p$ if he lacks justification for $p$.[39]
(2)   What S ought to do S can do.
(3)   Therefore, S can withhold belief wherever S lacks justification.
(4)   S has this capacity only if S can tell, with respect to any proposed belief, whether or not S has justification for it.
(5)   S can always tell us this only if justification is always directly recognizable.
(6)   Therefore justification is always directly recognizable.

This bare bones rendition should make it apparent where the argument goes astray. It is at step (5). (5) claims that S can tell whether he has justification for a belief only if it is directly recognizable by him whether he does or not. But why should we suppose this? Ginet, in company with almost all contemporary epistemologists, wisely avoids holding that one can know only what is evident to one on simple reflection and what is entailed by that. We know many things only because we have reasons for them in the shape of other things we know, and these reasons are not always deductively related to what they support. Thus direct recognition is only one way to acquire knowledge. Why should we suppose that only this way is available for knowing about justification? That would have to be argued. In the absence of any such argument we are at liberty to deny that justification can always be spotted just by reflection. The argument leaves standing the possibility that S might, in various instances, come to know in some other way whether he has a justification for $p$.

Consider the ethical analogy that is inevitably suggested by Ginet's argument. There is an exactly parallel argument for the thesis that the justification of actions is always directly recognizable. But that is clearly false. Often I have to engage in considerable research to determine whether a proposed action is justified. If it is a question of whether I would be justified in making a certain decision as department chairman without consulting the executive committee or the department as a whole, I cannot ascertain this just by reflection, unless I have thoroughly internalized the relevant rules, regulations, by-laws, and so on. Most likely I will have to do some research. Would I be legally justified in deducting the cost of a computer on my income tax return? I had better look up the IRS regulations and not just engage in careful reflection. The situation is similar with respect to more strictly moral justification. Would I be morally justified in resigning my professorship as late as April 12 in order to accept a position elsewhere for the following fall? This depends, inter alia, on how much inconvenience this would cause my present department, what faculty resources there are already on hand for taking up the slack, how likely it is that a suitable temporary replacement could be secured for the coming fall, and so on. There is no guarantee that all these matters are available to me just on simple reflection. Why should we suppose, without being given reasons to do so, that the justification of beliefs is different in this respect?

Let's remember that in the argument we quoted Ginet supported his position by a *reduction* that runs as follows.

(1)  Suppose that some part of a justification were not entailed by what is directly recognizable to S.

(2)  Then S's position could change from having such justification to lacking it without there being any change in what is directly recognizable to S.

(3)  But then S cannot tell that his position *vis-à-vis* justification has changed.

(4)  Therefore if S can always tell what his justificatory situation is, no part of a justification can fail to be directly recognizable.

This argument, in step (3), presupposes a strong foundationalism according to which any knowledge I can have is based on what is directly recognizable to me, and this could well be contested. But even if we go along with this, the argument is unsound. The trouble is in (2), in the assumption that *anything* not entailed by the directly recognizable can change with no change in what is directly recognizable. To assume this is to assume that the nondirectly recognizable is effectively reflected in what is directly recognizable only if the former is entailed by the latter. For if there are other modes of reflection, then a change in the former will sometimes be mirrored in a change in the latter, even when the former is not *entailed* by the latter. For convenience of exposition, let's lump together everything that is not entailed by anything directly recognizable by me as "the world". It is certainly the better part of reason to recognize that much of the world is not adequately reflected in what *I* can directly recognize; if that were not the case, I would be in an immeasurably stronger epistemic position than is the lot of humanity. But to suppose that the world beyond my direct recognition *never* reveals itself in what I can directly recognize would be subversive of the very type of foundationalism this argument presupposes. For in that case the foundations would ground no knowledge of anything beyond themselves except by way of logical deduction. And I am sure that Ginet does not want that. If then a change in "the world" is sometimes reflected in changes in the directly recognizable, why suppose that this is not the case with respect to justification?

Put the matter another way. All that Ginet can extract from his strong foundationalist assumption, his deontological concept of justification, and the "ought implies can" principle, is that it is always possible to determine *from* what is directly recognizable to the subject whether the subject is justified in a certain belief. But that does *not* imply that what does the justifying is itself directly recognizable, or is entailed by what is directly recognizable. It only implies that either it has this status *or* it can be ascertained on the basis of what is directly recognizable.[40]

However, Ginet's argument can easily be transformed into an argument for a more moderate form of AI. To begin with the other extreme, suppose we formulate AI just as the view that to be a justifier an item must be epistemically accessible in some way to the subject. It is not *impossible* for the subject to acquire that bit of knowledge (or justified belief). It does seem that Ginet's argument would establish that much accessibility, granted his premises. If I ought to do something that requires knowing the answer to a certain question, it must be *possible* for me to get that answer.

But what is the significance of this result? What does this constraint exclude? It excludes factors that are in principle unknowable by human beings; but it is dubious that any of the parties to the discussion are disposed to suggest justifiers that satisfy that description. The putative justifiers that internalists typically wish to exclude are items other than beliefs and experiences of the subject. Bonjour's clairvoyant subject in "Externalist Theories of Empirical Knowledge" is representative of the disputed territory. This person in fact has clairvoyant powers but has neither any understanding of what is going on nor any good reasons for supposing that these powers are reliable. So far as he can tell, the beliefs simply occur to him, and he is, strangely enough, irresistibly constrained to accept them. What shall we fasten on as the strongest candidate for a justifier here? There are no beliefs or experiences on which the clairvoyant beliefs are based. Let's say that if anything justifies them, it is their resulting from the exercise of reliable clairvoyant powers. The subject knows nothing of such powers. But is it *impossible* that he should discover them and discover that they are reliable? I see no reason to suppose that. He might ascertain this just by discovering that these strange beliefs about distant places that apparently just popped into his mind out of nowhere are invariably true. It appears, then, that the requirement of being knowable somehow is too weak to be of much interest.

Perhaps there is a mean between the extremes that is both of some significance and still not too strong to be supportable. We might try requiring knowability, not just on reflection at the moment, but at least without a great deal of research. Admittedly this is quite vague. The vagueness may be reduced by bringing in the notion of what could reasonably be expected in the way of time and effort devoted to searching out the justifiers. These expectations might differ from case to case, depending on the kind of justifiers that would be required, the capacities and initial position of the subjects, and so on. If a belief is based on experience, we would naturally expect the subject to ascertain that right off the bat. If, on the other hand, a belief is based on a large and complex body of evidence, we would not expect the subject to be able to survey all that in a moment. And so on. We might dub this intermediate conception "reasonably immediate accessibility".[41] Although this may seem a more reasonable requirement than Ginet's, and although it obviously is less restrictive, this increase in modesty has not purchased any greater support by Ginet's line of argument. I can't see that an "ought implies can" principle supports a "reasonably immediate accessibility" any more than it supports a direct recognizability. In the absence of further reasons to the contrary, all that would seem to be required by the principle is knowability in some way or other.

Now let's turn to the question of a higher level extension of AI. It is clear that the AI constraint, like the PI constraint, can be imposed on various levels. We saw that the basic argument for PI equally supported the first and second level constraints. It supported both the claim that a justifier had to be a justified belief, and the claim that one justified belief can justify another only if the subject is justified in the higher level belief that the first belief does adequately support the second. What about the argument for AI? Ginet does not use his argument to support a higher level extension. As noted earlier, he does impose a higher level PI constraint on mediate justification, but he associates no higher level constraint of any kind with his AI position. He takes AI to require only that *justifiers* be directly recognizable, not that it be directly recognizable that they possess justificatory efficacy. And yet his argument supports a higher level AI requirement just as strongly, or weakly, as the lower level requirement. This can be seen as follows. Suppose that the sorts of things that can count as justifiers are always accessible to me, but that it is not always accessible to me which items of these sorts count as justifications for which beliefs. I have access to the justifiers but not to their justificatory efficacy. This will take away my ability to do what I am said to have an obligation to do just as surely as the lack of access to the justifiers themselves. To illustrate, let's suppose that experiences can function as justifiers, and that they are accessible to us. I can always tell what sensory experiences I am having at a given moment. Even so, if I am unable to tell what belief about the current physical environment is justified by a given sensory experience, I am thereby unable to regulate my perceptual beliefs according as they possess or lack experiential justification. Knowing what the facts are doesn't suffice for enabling me to regulate my behavior accordingly; I also have to know the significance of these facts for what I ought to do. Thus the "ought implies can" argument supports the higher level requirement to just the extent to which it supports the lower level requirement.

Thus AI, too, has higher level troubles. The trouble is not nearly as severe as its PI analogue. For one thing, what is required here is not actual higher level knowledge (justified belief) about justification, but only the capacity to obtain it. Thus we are not required to attribute to all subjects an absurdly inflated body of actual knowledge about the conditions of justification. Second, for the same reason we are not faced with nasty infinite regresses or hierarchies. Since to be justified in believing that $p$, S need not actually justifiably believe that the alleged justifier is fitted to do its job, but only be capable of ascertaining this, we are not committed to an actual infinite hierarchy of such justified beliefs. Nevertheless there are serious questions as to whether even a modest AI higher level requirement is not too severe. The requirement implies that a state of affairs, A, cannot justify me in believing that $p$ unless I am capable of determining that A is a genuine justification for a belief that $p$. But how many subjects are capable of this? Indeed, there are substantial grounds for skepticism about the possibility of anyone's having adequate reasons for claims about justification. The grounds I have in mind concern the specter of epistemic circularity, the danger that, for instance, any otherwise promising argument for a principle laying down conditions under which perceptual beliefs are justified will have to use perceptual beliefs among its premises. I have considered this problem elsewhere and have concluded that, despite the pervasive presence of epistemic circularity in such arguments, it is possible to be justified in beliefs about the conditions of justification.[42] But even if that rather optimistic conclusion is justified, it still seems that many subjects are not capable of acquiring adequately justified beliefs concerning what justifies what. To go into this properly we would have to decide what it takes for the justification of such beliefs, and there is no time for this lengthy investigation in this paper. Let me just say that it seems eminently plausible that beliefs about what justifies what would have to be justified by reasons (not directly justified), and it would seem that such reasons are directly accessible to few if any of us.

All this suggests limiting AI to the lower level. Something can function as a justifier only if it is (fairly readily) accessible, but in order to function as a justifier it is not necessary that its justificatory efficacy be likewise accessible. At some point we must rely on things just *being* a certain way, without its also being the case that we do or can assure ourselves that they are that way. And this would seem to be the proper place to draw that line. We shall return to this possibility in the last section. For now, let's sharpen the issue by recalling the fact that a reliability account of justification (S is justified in believing that *p* if and only if S's belief that *p* was reliably produced) is often attacked on the grounds that justification could not be lost by a loss of reliability, so long as the situation is the same, *so far as we can tell*. Consider a possible world that is indistinguishable from the actual world so far as we can tell, but in which a Cartesian demon has rigged things so that our perceptual beliefs concerning external physical objects are all false, since there are no such objects. Since such a world is indistinguishable (by us) from our world, we would have just as much justification for our perceptual beliefs there as we actually do. But *ex hypothesi* those beliefs would not be reliably formed. Hence reliability is not necessary for justification. Here are some snatches of such an argument from an essay by Richard Foley. (The demon world is called "w".)

> If we are willing to grant that in our world some of the propositions S perceptually believes are epistemically rational, then these same propositions would be epistemically rational for S in w as well. After all, world w by hypothesis is one which from S's viewpoint is indistinguishable from this world. So, if given S's situation in this world his perceptual belief p is rational, his belief p would be rational in w as well.
>
> Even if, contrary to what we believe, our world is world w, it still can be epistemically rational for us to believe many of the propositions we do, since the epistemic situation in world w is indistinguishable from the epistemic situation in a world which has the characteristics we take our world to have. The point here is a simple one. In effect, I am asking you: aren't some of the propositions you believe epistemically rational for you to believe? And wouldn't whatever it is that make those propositions epistemically rational for you also be present in a world where these propositions are regularly false, but where a demon hid this from you by making the world from your viewpoint indistinguishable from this world (so that what you believed, and what you would believe on

reflection, and what you seemed to remember, and what you experienced were identical to this world)?[43]

In each of these passages the fact that we cannot distinguish w from the actual world is taken to imply that whatever justifies a certain belief in the one world will ipso facto justify that same belief in the other world. This argument presupposes an AI internalist constraint on both levels. For suppose AI put constraints only on what can count as a justifier, not also on what has justificatory efficacy for which beliefs. In that case the reliabilist would remain free to claim that although the same putative justifiers (of perceptual beliefs) are present in the two worlds, they do justify perceptual beliefs in the actual world but not in w, since their production of perceptual beliefs is reliable in the actual world but not in w. If and only if justificatory efficacy were subject to an AI constraint would this be impossible, as Foley claims. If, on the other hand, one follows my suggestion that we adopt an accessibility constraint only on the lower level, we can recognize that a state of affairs, A, can justify a belief that $p$ in one possible world and not in another, even though we can't tell any difference between the two worlds.

## IV

The upshot of the essay is that existing forms of internalism are in serious trouble. Both PI and AI run into severe difficulties over their higher level component, but if we try shearing off that component we lose such support as has been provided them. That support is less than impressive in any case. The only arguments of any substance that have been advanced proceed from a deontological conception of justification and inherit any disabilities that attach to that conception. Indeed, PI gains significant support only from the most restrictive form of a direct voluntary control version of that conception, one that is, at best, of limited application to our beliefs. As for AI, the arguments in the literature that are designed to establish a direct recognizability version markedly fail to do so. And it is not clear that a more moderate form of AI can be developed that will be both well supported by these arguments and strong enough to have any cutting edge.

Thus internalism has not emerged in strong shape from this examination. It looks as if no sort of internalist constraint can be justified, and hence that an unrestricted externalism wins the day. I do not believe, however, that so extreme a conclusion is warranted. I am convinced that the considerations advanced in this essay show that existing versions of internalism are untenable, and that such arguments as have been advanced for them fail to establish any form of that position. And yet I am inclined to suppose that a suitably modest form of AI internalism can be supported, though in a very different way form any employed by the internalists we have been discussing. If any readers have persevered this far, I will not further test their patience by embarking on a full dress development and defense of this suggestion, but I will just indicate what I have in mind.

Earlier I indicated that what I called a strong position (SP) conception of justification does not support any sort of internalist restriction. One can believe that *p* in such a way as to be in a strong position to acquire the truth whether or not that belief is supported adequately by other of one's justified beliefs (PI), and whether or not one has strong epistemic access to the grounds for the belief. In my "Concepts of Epistemic Justification" I have argued for the superiority of the SP conception over any kind of deontological conception. Thus, so far as these options for a concept of justification are concerned, pure externalism reigns supreme. Nevertheless I do not take this to be the last word. Even if internalist intuitions cannot be supported by the most basic features of the concept of justification, they may have a certain validity on their own, as an independent contribution to the concept. Let's once more consider "out of the blue" reliable modes of belief formation. Let's say that when I am suddenly seized with apparently irrational convictions concerning the current weather in some distant spot, these convictions always turn out to be correct. If there is nothing to justification other than believing in such a way as to be in a strong position to acquire the truth, then we should say that I am justified in those convictions. And yet we are loath to admit this, at least before I become aware of the reliability of this mode of belief formation. (After I become aware of this, I have an adequate reason for the convictions, and this should satisfy any internalist scruples.) Why this reluctance? What is missing? What is missing, of course, is any basis or ground that S *has,* *possesses,* for his belief, anything that he can point to or specify as that which gives him *something to go on* in believing this, any *sign* or *indication* he has that the belief is true. Wherever nothing like this is involved, we feel uneasy in taking S's belief to be *justified.* Thus it looks as if there is a basic, irreducible, requirement of *epistemic accessibility of ground for the belief* that attaches to our concept of epistemic justification.[44] For reasons we have rehearsed at some length, let's take the accessibility required to be of the relatively modest sort that we earlier called "reasonably immediate accessibility".

Can this requirement be derived from other features of the concept? It certainly cannot be derived from an SP conception, and we have seen that such support as it gleans from a deontological conception would bring fatal difficulties with it, even if such a conception were viable for epistemology. I am inclined to think that the requirement is a fundamental constituent of our concept of epistemic justification, though I do not take that to imply that there can be no sort of explanation for its presence. I will conclude by briefly adumbrating what I take to be responsible for this internalist feature of the concept.

My suggestion is that the background against which the concept of epistemic justification has developed is the practice of critical reflection on our beliefs, the practice of the epistemic assessment of beliefs (with respect to the likelihood of their being true), the challenging of beliefs and responses to such challenges. To respond successfully to such a challenge one must specify an adequate ground of the belief, a ground that provides a sufficient indication of the truth of the belief. It would, of course, be absurd to suggest that in order to be epistemically respectable, laudatory, or acceptable (justified), a belief must have actually been put to such a test and have emerged victorious. In suggesting that the concept has developed against the background of such a practice the idea is rather that what it is for a belief to be justified is that the belief and its ground be such that it is in a position to pass such a test; that the subject has what it takes to respond successfully to such a challenge.[45] A justified belief is one that *could* survive a critical reflection. But then the justifier must be accessible to the subject. Otherwise the subject would be in no position to cite it as what provides a sufficient indication that the belief is true. This, baldly stated, is what I take to be the explanation of the presence of an AI internalist constraint in the concept of epistemic justification. Further development of this suggestion must await another occasion.

## Notes

1  See, e.g., Laurence Bonjour, "Externalist Theories of Empirical Knowledge," *Midwest Studies in Philosophy*, 5 (1980).

2  Ibid., p. 55.

3  Ibid.

4  Ibid., p. 56.

5  *The Monist*, 68 (April 1985), 247.

6  *Midwest Studies in Philosophy*, 5 (1980), 32. Later in this essay Goldman considers what conditions should be laid down for the acceptance of a *doxastic decision principle* (DDP). A DDP is a "function whose *inputs* are certain conditions of a cognizer – e.g., his beliefs, perceptual field, and ostensive memories – and whose *outputs* are prescriptions to adopt (or retain) this or that doxastic attitude . . ." (p. 29). Here is what he takes to be "the condition appropriate to *externalism*":

> (1)  DDP X is right if and only if: X is *actually* optimal.

Whereas the first shot at formulating an appropriate condition for internalism is the following.

> (2)  DDP X is right if and only if: we are *justified* in believing that X is optimal.
> (pp. 33–34)

7  Note that in the passage quoted above Kent Bach says that "internalism requires that a person have 'cognitive grasp' of whatever makes his belief justified". This too would seem to allow that what makes the belief justified could be an item of any (suitable) sort, provided the person has a "cognitive grasp" of it.

8  Thus although in that passage Bonjour is arguing against the existence of "basic beliefs", i.e., immediately justified beliefs, the argument, if successful, will rule out only *purely* basic beliefs. It will not rule out beliefs a part of whose justification consists in something other than justified beliefs of the same subject.

9  What I am calling "Bonjour's version" does not represent his considered position, which is more like the other version. The former, however, is suggested by the passage under discussion. Perhaps Bonjour was led into it there because he was arguing with a partisan of immediate knowledge who claims that a certain nonbelief is sufficient for the justification of a certain belief. Having no reason to deny that the nondoxastic state of affairs obtains, Bonjour simply confined himself to alleging that even if it does obtain, the subject will also have to be justified in believing that it obtains.

10  I shall use "overrider" for something that cancels out a prima facie justification. Unlike some theorists I shall refrain from using "defeater" for this purpose, saving

that term (though not using it in this essay) for a fact the mere holding of which prevents a true, overall justified belief from counting as knowledge.

11   Thus principle (B) in R. M. Chisholm, *Theory of Knowledge*, 2d ed. (Englewood Cliffs, N.J.: Prentice-Hall, 1977), runs as follows:

> (B) For any subject S, if S believes, without ground for doubt, that he is perceiving something to be F, then it is beyond reasonable doubt for S that he perceives something to be F.

And "ground for doubt" is explained as follows.

> (D4.3) S believes, *without ground for doubt*, that p = $_{df}$ (i) S believes that p and (ii) no conjunction of propositions that are acceptable for S tends to confirm the negation of the proposition that p. (p. 76)

The PI constraint comes in by requiring "grounds for doubt" that consists in propositions that are "acceptable" for the subject, in order that the prima facie justification of perceptual beliefs be overthrown.

12   "A Plethora of Epistemological Theories," in George S. Pappas, ed., *Justification and Knowledge* (Dordrecht: D. Reidel, 1979), p. 101.

13   To be sure, there are more alternatives than the ones we have mentioned. In his book *Knowledge* (Oxford: Clarendon Press, 1974), Keith Lehrer plumps for a coherence theory in which the test of justification is coherence, not with the actual set of beliefs of the subject but with what Lehrer calls the subject's "corrected doxastic system", that subset "resulting when every statement is deleted which describes S as believing something he would cease to believe as an impartial and disinterested truth-seeker" (p. 190).

14   "Can Empirical Knowledge Have a Foundation?", *American Philosophical Quarterly*, 15 (January 1978), 5.

15   Of course the "feature" could be so specified that it included the subject's justified beliefs about another feature. But then it would be this latter feature with respect to which Bonjour is requiring the justified beliefs, and the point would still hold.

16   See, e.g., Richard Foley, "What's Wrong with Reliabilism?", *The Monist*, 68 (April 1985).

17   This requirement for mediate justification is embraced by many epistemologists who do not advocate (4) with its denial of any immediate justification. See, e.g., Carl Ginet, *Knowledge, Perception, and Memory* (Dordrecht: D. Reidel, 1975), pp. 47–9.

18   "Externalist Theories of Empirical Knowledge," p. 63.

19   Keith Lehrer, *Knowledge*, pp. 187–8.

20   "A Plethora of Epistemological Theories," p. 106. This does not represent Pollock's overall view.

21   This argument may be thought of as a development of Bonjour's suggestion that the subject must "possess the justification" for the belief "if *his* acceptance of it is to be epistemically rational or responsible". ("Externalist Theories of Empirical Knowledge," p. 55.)

22   Note that what this argument supports is a *positive, local justification* version of PI. But precisely parallel arguments can be given for other versions. For the suggestion of such an argument for a *negative, local justification* version, see the quotation from Wolterstorff in the following footnote. For an argument for a mere belief version, whether local or holistic, see Pollock's "A Plethora of Epistemological Theories," p. 109.

23   Here are some adumbrations of this argument. ". . . on the externalist view, a person may be ever so irrational and irresponsible in accepting a belief, when judged in light of his own subjective conception of the situation, and may still turn out to satisfy Armstrong's general criterion of reliability. This belief may in fact be reliable, even though the person has no reason for thinking that it is reliable . . . But such a person seems nonetheless to be thoroughly irresponsible from an epistemic standpoint in accepting such a belief, and hence not justified, contrary to externalism." (Bonjour, "Externalist Theories of Empirical Knowledge," p. 59.) Here is another adumbration, this time from the standpoint of a negative coherence theory that holds a belief to be justified provided one has no sufficient reason for giving it up. "If a person does not have adequate reason to refrain from some belief of his, what could possibly oblige him to give it up? Conversely, if he surrenders some belief of his as soon as he has adequate reason to do so, what more can rightly be demanded of him? Is he not then using the capacities he has for governing his beliefs, with the goal of getting more amply in touch with reality, as well as can rightly be demanded of him?" (Nicholas Wolterstorff, "Can Belief in God Be Rational?", in Alvin Plantinga and Nicholas Wolterstorff, eds., *Faith and Rationality* [Notre Dame, Ind.: University of Notre Dame Press, 1983], p. 163). Note the crucial occurrence in these passages of terms like "irresponsible", "oblige", and "rightly demanded". Both these authors, as well as other PI internalists, note the parallel between what is required for epistemic and for ethical justification. In both cases, it is argued, what is required is that the belief or the action be the one to adopt, so far as one can tell from one's own viewpoint on the world.

24   Essays 4 (where the SP conception is called an "evaluative conception", evaluative from the "epistemic point of view") and 5. For other developments of the deontological conception see Ginet, *Knowledge, Perception, and Memory*; Wolterstorff, "Can Belief in God Be Rational?"; and Margery B. Naylor, "Epistemic Justification," *American Philosophical Quarterly*, 25 (January 1988), 49–58.

25   Bonjour is an exception in trying to combine features of the two conceptions. On the one hand, he argues for PI from a deontological conception of justification. On the other hand, as we have seen, he presupposes the truth-conductivity of justification in formulating his higher level requirement.

26   Thus Wolterstorff: "Locke assumes – rightly in my judgment – that we have an obligation to govern our assent with the goal in mind of getting more amply in touch with reality." "Can Belief in God Be Rational?", p. 145.

27   There are other ways in which a subject's epistemic situation might have been different from what it actually is had the subject been doing a better job of carrying out her intellectual obligations. In particular, the subject might have had justifiers that she does not actually possess. However it is not at all clear that this and other differences from the actual situation have the same bearing on justification as the lack of overriders that one should have had. Consider a case in which if I had been attending to the matter as I should have I would have had justified beliefs that adequately support the belief that Jones is untrustworthy. As things actually stand I do not have adequate reasons for supposing that. Here, going on the justified beliefs I actually have, we would have to say that I would not be justified in believing that Jones is untrustworthy. But nor does it seem that this judgment would be reversed by the consideration that I would have had adequate support had I been conducting myself properly. Surely we don't want to say that the thing for me to do is to adopt that belief *in the absence of sufficient reasons*, even if I would have had sufficient reasons had I been managing my cognitive activities better.

28 At a few points in the preceding exposition the need for this qualification was more or less evident. Thus at one point I represented the deontologist as saying that the justification of a given belief depends on the "best representation of the world of which I am currently capable". I have also used such phrases as "one's best judgment of the facts" and "so far as one can tell". All of these phrases point to the "ideal viewpoint" rather than to the actual viewpoint. The best representation of the world of which I am currently capable may not be the representation I actually have. There will be a discrepancy, provided, as is usually the case to some extent, I have not made full use of my opportunities for ascertaining relevant features of the world. The importance of overriders that a subject ought to have but doesn't is well brought out by Wolterstorff, "Can Belief in God Be Rational?", pp. 165–6.

29 For a discussion of this issue see "The Deontological Conception of Epistemic Justification," in William P. Alston, *Epistemic Justification: Essays in the Theory of Knowledge* (Ithaca, N. Y.: Cornell University Press, 1989).

30 If this latter sort of reason is required, that constitutes a serious stumbling block, for it seems that we are rarely justified in any such belief, unless the requirements for justification are set very low. But that is not our present concern.

31 P.35. Remember that a DDP is, roughly, a principle that declares certain beliefs to be justified under certain conditions. Therefore the requirement that there be maximal epistemic access to a DDP is an accessibility analogue of what we were calling the "higher level requirement" component of PI. Interestingly enough, when it comes to a high accessibility "lower level requirement" with respect to justifiers, "input to the DDP" in Goldman's lingo, Goldman lays this down on his own, with no hint that it is required by internalism as contrasted with externalism. "If a DDP is to be actually *usable* for making deliberate decisions the conditions that serve as inputs must be *accessible* or *available* to the decision-maker at the time of decision. The agent must be *able to tell*, with respect to any possible input condition, whether that condition holds at the time in question" (p. 30). He even spells this out in such a way that it is *infallible* access that is required. "But what exactly do we mean in saying that a person "can tell" with respect to a given condition whether or not that condition obtains? Here is a reasonable answer: "For any person S and time t, if S asks himself at t whether condition C obtains at the time in question,then S will believe that condition C obtains then if and only if it does obtain then" (p. 31).

32 P. 250. Cf. p. 252.

33 *Theory of Knowledge*, p. 17. The quotation is from C. I. Lewis, *Mind and the World Order*. It should be acknowledged that in a later essay Chisholm states this assumption only for "some of the things I am justified in believing". See "A Version of Foundationalism," *Midwest Studies in Philosophy*, 5 (1980), 546.

34 *Knowledge, Perception, and Memory*, p. 34.

35 Ibid., p. 36.

36 Ibid., p. 28.

37 Ibid., p. 28.

38 In "Contra Reliabilism," *The Monist*, 68 (April 1985), Ginet defends this assumption against objections from me. Note that Ginet's argument could easily be recast in an "indirect voluntary control" form. Instead of premising that it is always possible to decide whether or not to believe, or to continue believing, that *p* in the light of the presence or absence of a sufficient justification, one can hold instead that it is always possible to decide whether to do various things to encourage or discourage belief that *p*, in the light of the presence or absence of a sufficient justification. The direct recognizability of justifiers will be as strongly

supported by this version as by the original version.

39    Ginet recognizes that we are intellectually obligated to refrain from believing that
      $p$ in the absence of justification, but he wisely holds back from claiming that we are
      obligated to believe that $p$ wherever we have a justification. The presence of justifi-
      cation gives me a *right* to believe, but I am not obliged to exercise that right; I have
      a choice as to whether or not to do so. It seems plausible to hold, e.g., that I am
      justified in believing everything that is entailed by my justified beliefs. But an infi-
      nite set of beliefs is so entailed. Thus if I were obligated to believe everything for
      which I have a justification, I would be in a pretty pickle. Ginet's recognition of this
      point is evinced by his modifying "S *ought* always to possess or lack confidence that
      $p$ according to whether or not he has such justification" to "At least he ought
      always to withhold confidence unless he has justification".

40    We could also attack the direct accessibility form of AI by pointing to the fact that
      not all commonly recognized justifiers satisfy the constraint. Remember that when
      we were considering the relations of PI and AI we pointed out that one cannot, in
      general, retrieve all relevant justified beliefs of oneself just on reflection.

41    Note that all these accessibility requirements, of whatever degree of stringency, can
      be thought of as related to PI in the same way. Any item that is epistemically
      accessible to S can be thought of as potentially an item in S's perspective on the
      world. Hence any sort of AI can be thought of as a broadening of PI to include
      potential additions to the perspective, as well as its present constituents.

42    See "Epistemic Circularity," in Alston, *Epistemic Justification*.

43    Richard Foley, "What's Wrong with Reliabilism?", *The Monist*, 68 (April 1985).
      See also Carl Ginet, "Contra Reliabilism," ibid.

44    Since I do not find any like tendency to withhold the concept of justification when
      the justificatory efficacy of the ground is not readily accessible to the subject, I am
      not saddled with the burden of a higher level accessibility constraint.

45    One indication that this is the right way to think about justification is the fact that
      we find it incongruous to apply the concept to beings that are incapable of critical
      reflection on their beliefs. The question of whether a dog is *justified* in supposing
      that his master is at the door is one that does not seem to arise. There are, to be
      sure, problems as to just how this restriction is to be interpreted. It seems clearly all
      right to apply the concept to human beings that have little skill at the game of
      challenge and response. The applicability to small children is less clear. But note
      that in both these cases we are dealing with beings that belong to a species many
      members of which are capable of critical reflection in a full-blooded form.

---

# 6    The General Conditions of Knowledge: Justification

---

## *Carl Ginet*

1. To *know* that $p$ it is not enough to be sure that $p$ and happen to be right.
One's confidence must be *justified* and that justification must be *disinterested*.

I shall take '$S$ has justification for being confident that $p$' (or '$S$ is justified in being confident that $p$') to mean '$S$ is in a position such that if he is, or were to be, confident that $p$ then he is, or would be, justified in being so.' One is *justified* in being confident that $p$ if and only if it is not the case that one ought not to be confident that $p$: one could not be justly reproached for being confident that $p$.

If one is justified in being confident that $p$, is it the case that one *should be* confident that $p$? In general, from its being false that one ought not to do something it does not follow that one ought to do it. But in certain cases the gap between these amounts to very little. Accepting a gift is (perhaps) such a case: if it is not the case that one ought not to accept a gift one has been offered (there is no reason why one ought not to) then one ought to accept it; exceptions to this are going to be rather special cases. Being confident is perhaps similar. Circumstances that justify a person in being confident that something is the case are generally also enough to oblige him to be confident in the sense that he will be open to a certain sort of criticism if he is not confident. When a person is justified in being confident that $p$ but he is not so then he is being (at least a bit) unreasonable, unless there is some special explanation (perhaps he very much wants it not to be the case that $p$). A position is not generally considered to be such as to make it reasonable (to provide sufficient reason) to be confident that $p$ unless it is also thought to be such as to make it unreasonable (lacking in any acceptable reason) not to be confident that $p$. Generally we think that confidence is not quite fully justified as long as there remains something that can rightly be regarded as a reason for still hesitating. But there are exceptions.

One clear sort of case that falls between being justified in being confident and not being justified in not being confident (where a person may be said to be justified whichever he is, confident or not) is that for which the distinction between interested and disinterested justification is useful. By a *disinterested* justification for being confident that $p$ I mean one that does not involve wanting it to be the case that $p$. That is, $S$ has a disinterested justification for being confident that $p$ if and only if there is true a proposition that entails that $S$ is justified in being confident that $p$ but does not entail that $S$ has reason to desire that $p$. If one can have a justification for being confident that $p$ that is *not* a *dis*interested justification, then of such a case it could be appropriate to say that although one's special interest in $p$ may justify one in being confident that $p$ one is also, from a disinterested point of view, justified if one is not confident that $p$.

And one clearly can have (interested) justification for being confident that $p$ although one lacks disinterested justification. Consider the following possible case: $S$ regards $R$ as his only close friend in the world. $S$ is dismissed from his job by his boss who tells $S$ that $R$ has reported that $S$ has been lifting cash from the till, although $S$ has actually done no such thing. Now, if $S$ has no good reason to think that his boss would want to lie about this particular matter then $S$ has some reason to suspect that $R$ did tell the boss a malicious falsehood about him; $S$ now has some reason to doubt, to lack confidence, that $R$ would never do such a thing. Indeed, we may suppose that, apart from $S$'s strong desire that $R$ should not have done this most unfriendly thing, $S$ does not have sufficient reason for being sure that $R$ has not done it. $S$ does not have a case for confidence that will survive *impartial* scrutiny. Yet $S$'s strong desire that $R$ should be his trustworthy friend, and $S$'s reasons for having that desire (of a sort most of us have for wanting dependable friends), may *justify* $S$, in a perfectly good sense, in maintaining his confidence that $R$ would not do such a thing. As long as the case against $R$ is not too overwhelming, who can blame or reproach $S$ for this faith in $R$? One would not have to think $S$ unreasonable to think that he would need much stronger evidence against $R$ for his trust to waver. $S$'s natural and reasonable dependence on the conviction that $R$ is his friend makes it quite reasonable for $S$ to maintain his trust in the face of some contrary evidence.

But it does not make it correct to say, even supposing that $S$ is right in his belief that $R$ did not do the nefarious deed, that $S$ *knows* that $R$ did not do it. For we may suppose that another person who was not thus emotionally related to $R$ and who knew as much about $R$ that is relevant as $S$ does might well *not* be justified (in any way) in being confident that $R$ did not do it and thus certainly not justified in claiming to *know* that. A person who claims to *know* that $p$ purports to give his hearers a special sort of assurance that $p$, a sort that he does not purport to give if he asserts merely that he is confident that $p$ or even that he has reason sufficient *for him* to be confident that $p$. When I say of someone (whether myself or someone else) that person *knows* that $p$ I imply that that person's position is such that were my hearers (or anyone else) in such a position they too would be justified in being confident that $p$, regardless of whether or not they want it to be the case that $p$. In this way the assertion that someone knows that $p$ – if the audience can believe the assertion is justified – can transfer the subject's warrant for being confident that $p$ to that audience. It can transfer the subject's knowledge that $p$, provided that the receiver of the assertion knows that its maker asserts what he knows. But we can rely on another's justified confidence only if that person's justification for confidence is independent of his desires. $S$'s strong desire that $p$ may properly weigh *for S* as a reason for believing that $p$ but it cannot serve another person as a reason for doing that (unless, of course, this other person sympathizes with $S$); whereas, for example, $S$'s confidence that he has seen a certain thing can serve another (to whom this confidence is known) as well as $S$ as a reason for believing that $p$. This is why $S$'s special desire that $p$ (and $S$'s reasons for having that desire) cannot make the difference as to whether or not $S$ is justified in claiming to *know* that $p$, although it can make the difference as to whether $S$ is justified or to be reproached in being confident that $p$. If the disinterested person possessing all the same relevant evidence would not be justified in claiming to know that $p$, then neither would the interested person, despite the fact that the latter's special desire that $p$ may be reason enough in the circumstances for that person to be confident that $p$.

So justification for being confident that $p$ is justification for claiming to know that $p$ only if it is disinterested.[1] I shall take up the question whether the converse of this is true as well, after I've said a bit more about the nature of justification for confidence. Hereafter, in order to make the prose a little easier on the eye, I shall frequently use 'justification' and its cognates, unmodified, as short for 'disinterested justification' and its cognates; it will be clearly indicated when the more general understanding of 'justification' is intended.

2. Incidentally, the features of assertion that $S$ knows that $p$ to which I have just called attention in order to explain why such assertions entail that $S$ has a *disinterested* justification, are the features that have led some philosophers to say that 'I know that $p$' is like 'I promise that $p$' in being a performative utterance (roughly equivalent to 'I assure you, cross my heart and hope to die, that $p$'). To claim to know that $p$ is, as noted, to give one's hearers a special sort of strong assurance that $p$, different from what would be given by simply asserting that $p$ or that one is sure that $p$. But this is completely explained by the fact that to claim to know is to claim to have a disinterested justification for being confident that $p$, one that would justify that confidence whether or not a person has a special interest in its being the case that $p$. If one claims to know that $p$ without really recognizing one's position as one that thus disinterestedly justifies being confident that $p$ one is liable to special censure. For then, even if one is confident that $p$ and it happens to be the case that $p$, one is still being deceitful in implying that one is disinterestedly justified in one's confidence when one has not recognized this to be the case. This is to try to lead someone else into confidence that $p$ through misrepresentation, through implying, contrary to what one really thinks, that were anyone else in one's position he would (regardless of whether or not he desires that $p$) be justified in being confident too. Thus the act of *claiming to know* is an act of giving assurance that makes appropriate special censure should it be performed in the wrong conditions. In this it does resemble the act of *promising*, which is an act of giving special assurance that one will do something, making appropriate special censure should a promise be given in the wrong conditions (for example, without fully intending to do the thing or without being justifiedly confident that one will be able to do it). But from this similarity between claiming to know and promising it does not follow that 'know' is like 'promise' in being a performative verb, so that to say 'I know that $p$' is merely to perform an act of giving assurance. Promising and claiming to know are linguistic *acts*. But knowing is not an act (linguistic or otherwise); it is a condition or state that one comes into or achieves (perhaps by means of certain acts). 'I know that $p$' ascribes the same state to its subject as 'He knows that $p$', which clearly reports no act, ascribes to its subject. And, because knowing entails having disinterestedly justified confidence, the third-person report gives its hearers the same reason for being assured that $p$ as does the first-person report. But the act-reporting 'He promises that $p$', if it gives a hearer any reason at all for being sure that $p$, does not give him as much reason, or in the same way, as does 'I promise that $p$.' 'He promises . . .' differs from 'I promise . . .' with respect to purporting to give reason for assurance about as much, and in the same way, as 'He *claims* to know . . .' differs from 'He knows . . .'.[2]

3. Condition (3) resembles condition (2) in that loose uses of 'know' may, at first glance, seem to show that this condition is not necessary for knowing that *p*. Consider, for example, the case of the adulterous wife who overhears her husband express the suspicion that she is being unfaithful and hurries to tell her lover that her husband 'knows' of their affair. It must be admitted that it would be silly in such circumstances for the lover to object to her remark on the ground that, for all they know, the husband may not have evidence that disinterestedly justifies him in being sure that they are having an affair. For their purposes (we may suppose) the husband *as good as* knows it if he so much as suspects it and so it is quite natural for them to speak loosely of his knowing it. We can see that this is a loose use of 'know'. and that respect for condition (3) is required when 'know' is being used strictly, by considering the case of the friend of the husband who tries to restrain him from rash action by saying, 'You don't *know* that she has been unfaithful. All you really know is that that notoriously untrustworthy gossip down the street says that she has. You ought at least to have better evidence than that, to *know* that she is guilty, before you make up your mind to do something that you may later regret.'

Another sort of case that might be thought to show that being justified in one's confidence is not necessary to knowing is the case of creatures of whom we comfortably say that they know things but of whom it seems absurd to say that they are justified or unjustified in being confident of them. I may say of my dog, on the basis of her excited behavior as she sees me taking down her leash, that she knows that I am going to take her for a walk. But, since she altogether lacks, and is incapable of acquiring, the concept of being justified or not in believing such a thing and, so, the concept of being influenced in her belief by the consideration of justification, it makes no sense to raise the question whether or not she is justified in her belief, whether or not she merits reproach for having that confident belief. Owing to the limitations of her 'form of life' (in Wittgenstein's sense) the whole category of appraisal in terms of being justified or reasonable or not in having a belief is simply inapplicable to her (as is also the category of moral appraisal as honest or dishonest, selfish or unselfish, conscientious or not, etc.). But I am inclined to say that my application of 'know' to my dog is in an extended sense of the term, based on similarities of my dog's case to those human cases where the term has primary application. This extended sense just eliminates consideration of the dimension of justification in which the dog cannot participate, but this dimension must be considered in the primary application. (The extended application of 'know' to my dog is, of course, encouraged by a counterpart in the dog's case to justification in the human case, the similarity between the fact that my dog's belief results from her having had several experiences of seeing the leash taken down and immediately thereafter being taken out for a walk and human justifications for claims to know what is about to occur that involve the subject's remembering that there has been a certain correlation of phenomena in his experience.) My interest here is in the primary sense, or application,[3] of 'know' – to human beings in the context of the human form of life.

Must creatures who do possess the concept of justification, and so can be appraised in terms of being justified or not in their beliefs, also be ones able to use language, to express things in symbols? It is far from clear that there is a logically necessary tie here.[4] It is, however, very hard to see how a being intelligent enough to have the notion of being justified or not in one's beliefs, to make judgments on that sort of question, could fail to be capable of acquiring some sort of language of roughly the same order of sophistication as ours. So it seems extremely unlikely that there ever have been or will be creatures possessing the concept of justification but lacking anything that could be called language.

4. What features must a person's position have if it justifies him in being confident that *p*? Many and various, of course, are the specific sorts of positions that do this. The features they need to give them this power will partly depend on the nature of the proposition that *p*. Some of them I will detail later for particular classes of propositions. But there are two quite general points about the nature of positions that justify confidence. I will discuss the first of these in this section and consider the second in the section that follows.

The first general point to be made is this: Every one of every set of facts about *S*'s position that minimally suffices to make *S*, at a given time, justified in being confident that *p* must be *directly recognizable* to *S* at that time. By 'directly recognizable' I mean this: if a certain fact obtains, then it is directly recognizable to *S* at a given time if and only if, provided that *S* at that time has the concept of that sort of fact, *S* needs at that time only to reflect clear-headedly on the question of whether or not that fact obtains in order to know that it does. A fact can be part of what justifies *S* in being confident that *p* only if it is a fact that can *directly* influence *S*'s doxastic attitude towards that proposition. That is, *S*'s doxastic attitude at any given time towards any given proposition can be justified or unjustified only on the basis of what at that time requires only *S*'s effort of attention or consideration in order to influence his attitude. It is not the fact that *there is* smoke rising from the forest that justifies *S* in being confident that there is fire in the forest but rather such facts as that *S is confident that he sees* smoke, *S has no reason to mistrust* his sight on this particular matter at this particular time, and *S seems to remember* that he has come to know that virtually always when there is smoke of the sort he sees there is fire. It is not the fact that the sum of the angles of a triangle is always 180° that justifies a person at a particular time in being confident that if two of the angles of this particular triangle are 90° and 45° then the third must be 45°, but rather such a fact as that he then confidently remembers having learned in some way (perhaps by having proved it, perhaps from a reliable authority) that the angles of a triangle always sum to 180°. The first sort of fact mentioned in each case cannot possibly influence a person's doxastic attitude towards a proposition except through the influence of the second sort, to which the first sort may give rise. (Indeed it is not clear that an abstract, mathematical fact, such as that the angles of the triangle sum to 180°, can intelligibly be said to enter into the relation of *influencing* a person's doxastic attitude at all, directly or indirectly.) It is only what can directly influence a person's doxastic attitudes at a given time, through his then simply attending to it, that can be relevant to evaluating the reasonableness of his doxastic attitudes for him at that time.

This requirement of direct recognizability means that every fact belonging to a set that minimally suffices for $S$'s having justification for being confident that $p$ must be such that if it obtains then the only possible way in which $S$ could fail to know that it obtains would be through either (a) failure to consider sufficiently carefully the question whether or not it obtains or (b) failure to possess the concept of that sort of fact. A position that gives one justification for being confident of a proposition must be such that, given sufficient intelligence, one could acquire an ability to recognize that position whenever one is in it.

Thus, for example, the fact that $S$ once came to know that Harrison was President between Cleveland's terms is not now directly recognizable to $S$ because $S$ may now fail to know of this fact through failure of memory and, in that circumstance, no amount of understanding of that sort of fact and clear-headed reflection on the question of whether it obtains could bring him to know that it does. Or, for another example, the fact that $S$ now sees snow falling is one that $S$ could fail to know owing to having good reason to think that what he sees that looks like snow falling is actually something else or that he is hallucinating, circumstances that no amount of clear-headed reflection on his position or understanding of what it is to see snow falling could remedy.

On the other hand, such facts as that $S$ is now (at least in a way) confident that the President between Cleveland's terms was Harrison, or that it now seems to $S$ that he remembers having come to know that Harrison was President between Cleveland's terms or that $S$'s visual experience now is as if he were seeing snow falling *are* facts of a sort which $S$ must know if he understands them and reflects sufficiently on the question of whether or not they obtain; they are directly recognizable to $S$. Facts directly recognizable to $S$ will, pretty obviously, all be current mental states or occurrences of which $S$ is the subject. 'It seems to $S$ that he remembers . . .' and '$S$ is confident that . . .' express *dispositional* mental states of $S$ that are directly recognizable to him. It is now true of $S$ that he is confident that . . . (or seems to remember . . .) if and only if, were he now to consider carefully the question whether he is confident that . . . (or whether it seems to him that he remembers . . .) and try to answer it for himself, his answer would be 'yes'. (In light of the possibility noted earlier that a person's knowing and sincere action as if confident that . . . could be *in a way* misleading as to his actual dispositional state of confidence, 'confident' [or 'believes'] should be read here and in later chapters as 'at least *in a way* confident' ['at least in a way believes']. This reading makes no difference to the claims I make with respect to the relations among being confident, having justification for being confident, and knowing, if 'knows' is read similarly.)

The requirement of direct recognizability on justification for confidence (or justification for any other degree of belief) – that is, the requirement that any minimally sufficient condition for $S$'s having justification for being confident that $p$ be directly recognizable to $S$ – can be seen to hold by the following argument.

Assuming that $S$ has the concept of justification for being confident that $p$, $S$

*ought* always to possess or lack confidence that *p* according to whether or not he has such justification. At least he ought always to with-hold confidence unless he has justification. This is simply what is meant by having or lacking *justification*. But if this is what *S* ought to do in any possible circumstance, then it is what *S can* do in any possible circumstance. That is, assuming that he has the relevant concepts, *S* can always tell whether or not he has justification for being confident that *p*. But this would not be so unless the difference between having such justification and not having it were always directly recognizable to *S*. And that would not be so if any fact contributing to a set that minimally constitutes *S*'s having such justification were not either directly recognizable to *S* or entailed by something directly recognizable to *S* (so that its absence would have to make a directly recognizable difference). For suppose it were otherwise: suppose that some part of a condition minimally sufficient for *S*'s being justified in being confident that *p* were *not* entailed by anything directly recognizable to *S*. Then *S*'s position could change from having such justification to lacking it without there being any change at all in what is directly recognizable to *S*. But if there is no change in directly recognizable features of *S*'s position, *S* cannot tell that his position has changed in other respects: no matter how clear-headedly and attentively he considers his position he will detect no change. If it seemed to *S* before that he had justification for being confident that *p* then it must still seem so to him. So this sort of justification would be such that it would not always be possible for its subject to tell whether or not he possessed it, which is contrary to what we noted is an obvious essential feature of justification. So there can be no such justification. That is, there can be no set of facts giving *S* justification for being confident that *p* that has an essential part that is neither directly recognizable to *S* nor entailed by something directly recognizable to *S*.

The requirement on justification of direct recognizability does *not* mean that one who can recognize a certain sort of position as justifying confidence that *p* and discriminate it from any other sort of position that does not do so – who understands that such a position does justify confidence that *p* – must be able to describe all the features that go to make it a justifying position, or even that he must have concepts of them all. One can learn to recognize a characteristic complex of features without acquiring distinct conceptions of all the parts on which the overall characteristic depends. A child can learn to discriminate and identify square figures before he realizes that a square has to have four equal sides forming four equal angles, even before he has a concept of what an angle is. Similarly we can learn to recognize various sorts of positions that justify confidence in various sorts of propositions – to discriminate them and identify them as such, to back our confidence and our claims to know by appealing to the fact that we are in a position that puts to rest or prevents reasonable doubt – before we know (if we ever do) how to give any sort of interesting analysis of such positions.

5. Can we say anything interesting of a completely general nature as to what features make a directly recognizable position one that justifies its subject in being confident of a proposition? Just a little (and this is my other general point

about the nature of such justifying positions).

Insofar as positions directly recognizable to a person can be *objectively* ranked as to how strong a belief in a given proposition, $p$, they justify that person in having – that is, insofar as we have a concept and practice of objective justification of degrees of belief – the ultimate authority for this ranking must be the concurring judgments of reasonable, experienced people who have the notion of and an interest in the practice of rational, objective justification of degrees of belief and who give the positions in question their thoughtful consideration. If we say of two sorts of directly recognizable positions that one would clearly justify a stronger belief in $p$ than the other (or, as it may be, that clearly neither would justify a stronger belief in $p$ than the other) we are right if and only if this would be the overwhelming judgment of reasonable, experienced people who knew what they were considering (so that their judgment would not be changed by their attending better to the nature of the positions in question or their having more experience or more rational intelligence). Similarly, to say of a certain sort of position that it clearly justifies confidence that $p$ is to say that reasonable, experienced people when fully aware of the nature of the position will overwhelmingly agree in treating it as one in which lacking confidence that $p$ is practically silly in normal circumstances (for a person with no particular desire that $p$ be false). That is, aware and reasonable persons do, or would, share a policy of regarding such a position as offering no motive to hesitate about $p$, at any rate not normally, not unless, for example, far worse consequences than normal seem likely to ensue if one were to be confident that $p$ and it turned out to be false that $p$.

According to such a general criterion for positions that justify confidence, I am, for example, justified in being confident that I see my younger son when my position is (roughly) the following: I am confident that I remember having seen that son's face many times before and that on those occasions it looked closely like the face that I am confident that I now see; I have no beliefs or impressions about this particular occasion that would, despite my having the visual and memory impressions implied in the preceding statement, give me reason to doubt that I see my son; I am confident that I remember having never seen nor heard of anyone else who looks so closely like my son and that I re-member having come to know that such close look-alikes are very rare in gen-eral. Thus described, this position does not *entail* that I see my son, but it justifies me in being confident that I do. In the ordinary course of life, to lack confidence in a proposition of that sort when in that kind of position with respect to it – to follow a policy of hesitating over such propositions and pro-tecting oneself against the possibility that they may be false even in such cir-cumstances would seem to virtually anyone to involve an unreasonably great cost in inconvenience and unpleasantness. For a reasonable person could find no adequate motive to incur such costs. It would be *practically* absurd, indeed practically *impossible*; scarcely anyone *could* actually follow such a policy over a significant period.

This general criterion for positions that justify confidence – the criterion of the generally agreed judgment in practice of reaonable, experienced people who know what they are judging – is unquestionably a vague one. There are several ways in which cases can fail to fall clearly on one side or the other of the line it draws. Take the notion of general agreement. What proportion agreeing is enough to make agreement general? Who will count as reasonable, experienced persons? And some cases will be controversial or else generally agreed to be unclear (that is, not clearly ones where confidence is justified and not clearly ones where it is not justified). But we should not expect the concept of justification of confidence in a proposition, or the concept of knowing a truth, to be any less vague.

To reject this criterion in favor of some stricter or looser one is to make a recommendation that has no chance of being followed by reasonable, experienced people and one they could be given no motive to follow. For it would be a recommendation that they ought to respond to certain kinds of positions (those included by a looser criterion or excluded by a stricter one that are not included or excluded, respectively, by the criterion of general agreement among reasonable, experienced people) in a way different from that which in fact they are, or would be, led to respond to them by the fullest influence of their reason, experience, and attention to the nature of the positions. Such a recommendation cannot be taken seriously.

## Notes

1   It might be argued that an exception to this must be made for justified claims to know arising out of *intention*. It might be said that if S fully intends to do a certain thing in certain circumstances it follows that (a) he is confident, and justified in being confident and claiming to know, that he will try to do that thing in those circumstances if further circumstances then permit him to try to do it and also that (b) he *wants* it to be the case that he will try . . . etc. So we seem to have a condition that both justifies a claim to know a certain proposition and also involves the subject's wanting that proposition to be true and, so, is not disinterested.

It may be correct to answer this by saying that a proper analysis of *fully intending* to do a thing will show that it is one part of this state that entails that its subject is confident with justification that he will try to do it . . . etc. and another independent part that entails that he wants it to be the case that he will try . . . etc.; so that the *minimally* sufficient condition here for being justified in claiming to know that one will try . . . does *not* entail the subject's wanting it to be the case that one will try . . . (I heard such an analysis proposed by H. P. Grice in a paper read at the University of Washington in Spring 1970, according to which fully intending to do a thing is broken down into something called *willing* to do it and confidence that one's willing will issue in one's trying to do it if circumstances permit. I am doubtful, however, that willing can be distinguished from mere wanting or desiring – as it must be if willing, in conjunction with the other condition, is to be necessary and sufficient for intending – except by importing into willing confidence or belief that one will (or would) try to do the thing if . . .) If, however, such an analysis is not correct and it must be allowed that there is a special *intentional* mode of confidence, and of being justified in being confident and claiming to know, that one will try to do a thing if . . ., then we seem to have a choice of two alternatives. We might just allow this sort of case to be an exception to the principle that disinterestedness in necessary for a justification for confidence to be also a justification for a claim to know; or we might amplify the explanation of interestedness so as to exclude this sort of case, by saying that in that explanation I mean by '*wanting* it to be the case that $p$' something stronger than the sense of 'wanting' implied by intending: I mean 'wanting' in that sense in which it makes sense to say 'Although he intends to do it, he does not *want* to do it'. Since in this work I am not much interested in this special sort of intentional confidence or knowledge it makes little difference here which alternative I choose.

2  Harrison (1962) gives a sound critique of the performative treatment of 'I know that $p$'.

3  There may be good reason to object to talk of an 'extended sense' here and to think it better to use 'sense' in such a way that 'know' does not have a different sense when applied to my dog. If so, I would put my point by saying that I am interested in the necessary conditions of knowing in those cases of the appropriate application of 'know' where the question of the subject's being justified or not in his confidence is also appropriate, and in such cases justification is necessary for knowing. A somewhat analogous case: 'wants' & 'desires' do not, we are very much inclined to say, apply in a different sense to a dog; nevertheless, their application to a mature human being differs from their application to a dog in the respect that the question of what the mature human being would *say* if giving an honest answer to the question whether he desires $X$ or not is applicable and, necessarily, relevant: that he would give an affirmative answer is, necessarily, some reason to think (although not necessary for its being the case) that he does desire $X$. Here would seem to be a clear example of a term such that, although it is true *a priori* that certain considerations are relevant to its application in certain sorts of cases and also true that they cannot be relevant in other sorts of cases where it is sensibly applied, it does not follow that the term has a different sense in its application to the two sorts of cases. 'Knows' and the consideration of whether or not the subject is justified in being confident may be like that.

4  For argument that there is see Bennett (1964). For what looks to me like an effective effort to describe what would be counter-examples see Kirk (1967).

**Works Cited**

Bennett, J. (1964) *Rationality*. London: Routledge and Kegan Paul.
Harrison, J. (1962). 'Knowing and Promising.' *Mind* 71, 443–57.
Kirk, R. (1967). 'Rationality without Language.' *Mind* 76, 369–486.

# 7  What is Justified Belief?

## *Alvin Goldman*

The aim of this paper is to sketch a theory of justified belief. What I have in mind is an explanatory theory, one that explains in a general way why certain beliefs are counted as justified and others as unjustified. Unlike some traditional approaches, I do not try to prescribe standards for justification that differ from, or improve upon, our ordinary standards. I merely try to explicate the ordinary standards, which are, I believe, quite different from those of many classical, e.g., 'Cartesian', accounts.

Many epistemologists have been interested in justification because of its presumed close relationship to knowledge. This relationship is intended to be preserved in the conception of justified belief presented here. In previous papers on knowledge (Goldman 1975), I have denied that justification is necessary for knowing, but there I had in mind 'Cartesian' accounts of justification. On the account of justified belief suggested here, it *is* necessary for knowing, and closely related to it.

The term 'justified', I presume, is an evaluative term, a term of appraisal. Any correct definition or synonym of it would also feature evaluative terms. I assume that such definitions or synonyms might be given, but I am not interested in them. I want a set of substantive conditions that specify when a belief is justified. Compare the moral term 'right'. This might be defined in other ethical terms or phrases, a task appropriate to meta-ethics. The task of normative ethics, by contrast, is to state substantive conditions for the rightness of actions. Normative ethics tries to specify non-ethical conditions that determine when an action is right. A familiar example is act-utilitarianism, which says an action is right if and only if it produces, or would produce, at least as much net happiness as any alternative open to the agent. These necessary and sufficient conditions clearly involve no ethical notions. Analogously, I want a theory of justified belief to specify in non-epistemic terms when a belief is justified. This is not the only kind of theory of justifiedness one might seek, but it is one important kind of theory and the kind sought here.

In order to avoid epistemic terms in our theory, we must know which terms are epistemic. Obviously, an exhaustive list cannot be given, but here are some examples: 'justified', 'warranted', 'has (good) grounds', has reason (to believe)', 'knows that', 'sees that', 'apprehends that', 'is probable' (in an epistemic or inductive sense), 'shows that', 'establishes that', and 'ascertains that'. By contrast, here are some sample non-epistemic expressions: 'believes that', 'is true', 'causes', 'it is necessary that', 'implies', 'is deducible from', and 'is probable' (either in the frequency sense or the propensity sense). In general, (purely) doxastic, metaphysical, modal, semantic, or syntactic expressions are not epistemic.

There is another constraint I wish to place on a theory of justified belief, in addition to the constraint that it be couched in non-epistemic language. Since I seek an explanatory theory, i.e., one that clarifies the underlying source of justificational status, it is not enough for a theory to state 'correct' necessary and sufficient conditions. Its conditions must also be appropriately deep or revelatory. Suppose, for example, that the following sufficient condition of justified belief is offered: 'If $S$ senses redly at $t$ and $S$ believes at $t$ that he is sensing redly, then $S$'s belief at $t$ that he is sensing redly is justified.' This is not the kind of principle I seek; for, even if it is correct, it leaves unexplained *why* a person who senses redly and believes that he does, believes this justifiably. Not every state is such that if one is in it and believes one is in it, this belief is justified. What is distinctive about the state of sensing redly, or 'phenomenal' states in general? A theory of justified belief of the kind I seek must answer this question, and hence it must be couched at a suitably deep, general, or abstract level.

A few introductory words about my *explicandum* are appropriate at this juncture. It is often assumed that whenever a person has a justified belief, he knows that it is justified and knows what the justification is. It is further assumed that the person can state or explain what his justification is. On this view, a justification is an argument, defense, or set of reasons that can be given in support of a belief. Thus, one studies the nature of justified belief by considering what a person might *say* if asked to defend, or justify, his belief. I make none of these sorts of assumptions here. I leave it an open question whether, when a belief *is* justified, the believer *knows* it is justified. I also leave it an open question whether, when a belief is justified, the believer can *state* or *give* a justification for it. I do not even assume that when a belief is justified there is something 'possessed' by the believer which can be called a 'justification'. I do assume that a justified belief gets its status of being justified from some processes or properties that make it justified. In short, there must be some justification-conferring processes or properties. But this does not imply that there must be an argument, or reason, or anything else, 'possessed' at the time of belief by the believer.

# I

A theory of justified belief will be a set of principles that specify truth-conditions for the schema ⌜S's belief in $p$ at time $t$ is justified⌝, i.e., conditions for the satisfaction of this schema in all possible cases. It will be convenient to formulate candidate theories in a recursive or inductive format, which would include (A) one or more base clauses, (B) a set of recursive clauses (possibly null), and (C) a closure clause. In such a format, it is permissible for the predicate 'is a justified belief' to appear in recursive clauses. But neither this predicate, nor any other epistemic predicate, may appear in (the antecedent of) any base clause.[1]

Before turning to my own theory, I want to survey some other possible approaches to justified belief. Identification of problems associated with other attempts will provide some motivation for the theory I shall offer. Obviously, I cannot examine all, or even very many, alternative attempts. But a few sample attempts will be instructive.

Let us concentrate on the attempt to formulate one or more adequate base-clause principles.[2] Here is a classical candidate:

(1) If $S$ believes $p$ at $t$, and $p$ is indubitable for $S$ (at $t$), then $S$'s belief in $p$ at $t$ is justified.

To evaluate this principle, we need to know what 'indubitable' means. It can be understood in at least two ways. First, '$p$ is indubitable for $S$' might mean: '$S$ has

no *grounds* for doubting *p*'. Since 'ground' is an epistemic term, however, principle (1) would be inadmissible on this reading, for epistemic terms may not
legitimately appear in the antecedent of a base clause. A second interpretation
would avoid this difficulty. One might interpret '*p* is indubitable for *S* psychologically, i.e., as meaning '*S* is psychologically incapable of doubting *p*'. This
would make principle (1) admissible, but would it be correct? Surely not. A
religious fanatic may be psychologically incapable of doubting the tenets of his
faith, but that doesn't make his belief in them justified. Similarly, during the
Watergate affair, someone may have been so blinded by the aura of the presidency that even after the most damaging evidence against Nixon had emerged
he was still incapable of doubting Nixon's veracity. It doesn't follow that his
belief in Nixon's veracity was justified.

A second candidate base-clause principle is this:

(2)   If *S* believes *p* at *t*, and *p* is self-evident, then *S*'s belief in *p* at *t* is justified.

To evaluate this principle, we again need an interpretation of its crucial term, in
this case 'self-evident'. On one standard reading, 'evident' is a synonym for
'justified'. '*Self*-evident' would therefore mean something like 'directly justified', 'intuitively justified', or 'nonderivatively justified'. On this reading 'self-
evident' is an epistemic phrase, and principle (2) would be disqualified as a
base-clause principle.

However, there are other possible readings of '*p* is self-evident' on which it
isn't an epistemic phrase. One such reading is: 'It is impossible to understand *p*
without believing it'.[3] According to this interpretation, trivial analytic and logical truths might turn out to be self-evident. Hence, any belief in such a truth
would be a justified belief, according to (2).

What does 'it is *impossible* to understand *p* without believing it' mean? Does
it mean '*humanly* impossible'? That reading would probably make (2) an unacceptable principle. There may well be propositions which humans have an innate and irrepressible disposition to believe, e.g., 'Some events have causes'.
But it seems unlikely that people's inability to refrain from believing such a
proposition makes every belief in it justified.

Should we then understand 'impossible' to mean 'impossible in principle', or
'logically impossible'? If that is the reading given, I suspect that (2) is a vacuous
principle. I doubt that even trivial logical or analytic truths will satisfy this definition of 'self-evident'. Any proposition, we may assume, has two or more components that are somehow organized or juxtaposed. To understand the
proposition one must 'grasp' the components and their juxtaposition. Now in
the case of *complex* logical truths, there are (human) psychological operations
that suffice to grasp the components and their juxtaposition but do not suffice
to produce a belief that the proposition is true. But can't we at least *conceive* of
an analogous set of psychological operations even for simple logical truths, operations which perhaps are not in the repertoire of human cognizers but which
might be in the repertoire of some conceivable beings? That is, can't we con-

ceive of psychological operations that would suffice to grasp the components and componential-juxtaposition of these simple propositions but do not suffice to produce *belief* in the propositions? I think we can conceive of such operations. Hence, for any proposition you choose, it will possible for it to be understood without being believed.

Finally, even if we set these two objections aside, we must note that self-evidence can at best confer justificational status on relatively few beliefs, and the only plausible group are beliefs in necessary truths. Thus, other base-clause principles will be needed to explain the justificational status of beliefs in contingent propositions.

The notion of a base-clause principle is naturally associated with the idea of 'direct' justifiedness, and in the realm of contingent propositions first-person-current-mental-state propositions have often been assigned this role. In Roderick Chisholm's terminology, this conception is expressed by the notion of a '*self-presenting*' state or proposition. The sentence 'I am thinking', for example, expresses a self-presenting proposition. (At least I shall *call* this sort of content a 'proposition', though it only has a truth value given some assignment of a subject who utters or entertains the content and a time of entertaining.) When such a proposition is true for person S at time t, S is justified in believing it at t: in Chisholm's terminology, the proposition is 'evident' for S at t. This suggests the following base-clause principle.

(3)   If p is a self-presenting proposition, and p is true for S at t, and S believes p at t, then S's belief in p at t is justified.

What, exactly, does 'self-presenting' mean? Chisholm (1977, p. 22) offers this definition: '*h* is self-presenting for S at t = $_{df.}$ *h* is true at t; and necessarily, if *h* is true at t, then *h* is evident for S at t.' Unfortunately, since 'evident' is an epistemic term, 'self-presenting' also becomes an epistemic term on this definition, thereby disqualifying (3) as a legitimate base clause. Some other definition of self-presentingness must be offered if (3) is to be a suitable base-clause principle.

Another definition of self-presentation readily comes to mind. 'Self-presentation' is an approximate synonym of 'self-intimation', and a proposition may be said to be self-intimating if and only if whenever it is true of a person that person believes it. More precisely, we may give the following definition.

(SP)   Proposition p is self-presenting if and only if: necessarily, for any S and any t, if p is true for S at t, then S believes p at t.

On this definition, 'self-presenting' is clearly not an epistemic predicate, so (3) would be an admissible principle. Moreover, there is initial plausibility in the suggestion that it is *this* feature of first-person-current-mental-state proposition – viz., their truth guarantees their being believed – that makes beliefs in them justified.

Employing this definition of self-presentation, is principle (3) correct? This cannot be decided until we define self-presentation more precisely. Since the operator 'necessarily' can be read in different ways, there are different forms of self-presentation and correspondingly different versions of principle (3). Let us focus on two of these readings: a '*nomological*' reading and a 'logical' reading. Consider first the nomological reading. On this definition a proposition is self-presenting just in case it is nomological necessary that if $p$ is true for $S$ at $t$, then $S$ believes $p$ at $t$.[4]

Is the nomological version of principle (3) – call it '$(3_N)$' – correct? Not at all. We can imagine cases in which the antecedent of $(3_N)$ is satisfied but we would not say that the belief is justified. Suppose, for example, that $p$ is the proposition expressed by the sentence 'I am in brain-state $B$', where '$B$' is shorthand for a certain highly specific neural state description. Further suppose it is a nomological truth that anyone in brain-state $B$ will ipso facto *believe* he is in brain-state $B$. In other words, imagine that an occurrent belief with the content 'I am in brain-state $B$' is realized whenever one is in brain-state $B$.[5] According to $(3_N)$, any such belief is justified. But that is clearly false. We can readily imagine circumstances in which a person goes into brain-state $B$ and therefore has the belief in question, though this belief is by no means justified. For example, we can imagine that a brain surgeon operating on $S$ artifically induces brain-state $B$. This results, phenomenologically, in $S$'s suddenly believing – out of the blue – that he is in brain-state $B$, without any relevant antecedent beliefs. We would hardly say, in such a case, that $S$'s belief that he is in brain-state $B$ is justified.

Let us turn next to the logical version of (3) – call it '$(3_L)$' – in which a proposition is defined as self-presenting just in case it is logically necessary that if $p$ is true for $S$ at $t$, then $S$ believes $p$ at $t$. This stronger version of principle (3) might seem more promising. In fact, however, it is no more successful than $(3_N)$. Let $p$ be the proposition 'I am awake' and assume that it is logically necessary that if this proposition is true for some person $S$ and time $t$, then $S$ believes $p$ at $t$. This assumption is consistent with the further assumption that $S$ frequently believes $p$ when it is false, e.g., when he is dreaming. Under these circumstances, we would hardly accept the contention that $S$'s belief in this proposition is always justified. But nor should we accept the contention that the belief is justified when it is *true*. The truth of the proposition logically guarantees that the belief is *held*, but why should it guarantee that the belief is *justified*?

The foregoing criticism suggests that we have things backwards. The idea of self-presentation is that truth guarantees belief. This fails to confer justification because it is compatible with there being belief without truth. So what seems necessary – or at least sufficient – for justification is that belief should guarantee truth. Such a notion has usually gone under the label of '*infallibility*', or '*incorrigibility*'. It may be defined as follows.

(INC)  Proposition $p$ is incorrigible if and only if: necessarily, for any $S$ and any $t$, if $S$ believes $p$ at $t$, then $p$ is true for $S$ at $t$.

Using the notion of incorrigibility, we may propose principle (4).

(4)  If $p$ is an incorrigible proposition, and $S$ believes $p$ at $t$, then $S$'s belief in $p$ at $t$ is justified.

As was true of self-presentation, there are different varieties of incorrigibility, corresponding to different interpretations of 'necessarily'. Accordingly, we have different versions of principle (4). Once again, let us concentrate on a nomological and a logical version, $(4_N)$ and $(4_L)$ respectively.

We can easily construct a counterexample to $(4_N)$ along the lines of the belief-state/brain-state counterexample that refuted $(3_N)$. Suppose it is nomologically necessary that if anyone believes he is in brain-state $B$ then it is true that he is in brain-state $B$, for the only way this belief-state is realized is through brain-state $B$ itself. It follows that 'I am in brain-state $B$' is a nomologically incorrigible proposition. Therefore, according to $(4_N)$, whenever anyone believes this proposition at any time, that belief is justified. But we may again construct a brain surgeon example in which someone comes to have such a belief but the belief isn't justified.

Apart from this counterexample, the general point is this. Why should the fact that $S$'s believing $p$ guarantees the truth of $p$ imply that $S$'s belief is justified? The nature of the guarantee might be wholly fortuitous, as the belief-state/brain-state example is intended to illustrate. To appreciate the point, consider the following related possibility. A person's mental structure might be such that whenever he believes that $p$ will be true (of him) a split second later, then $p$ is true (of him) a split second later. This is because, we may suppose, his believing it brings it about. But surely we would not be compelled in such a circumstance to say that a belief of this sort is justified. So why should the fact that $S$'s believing $p$ guarantees the truth of $p$ *precisely at the time of belief* imply that the belief is justified? There is no intuitive plausibility in this supposition.

The notion of logical incorrigibility has a more honored place in the history of conceptions of justification. But even principle $(4_L)$, I believe, suffers from defects similar to those of $(4_N)$. The mere fact that belief in $p$ logically guarantees its truth does not confer justificational status on such a belief.

The first difficulty with $(4_L)$ arises from logical or mathematical truths. Any true proposition of logic or mathematics is logically necessary. Hence, any such proposition $p$ is logically incorrigible, since it is logically necessary that, for any $S$ and any $t$, if $S$ believes $p$ at $t$ then $p$ is true (for $S$ at $t$). Now assume that Nelson believes a certain very complex mathematical truth at time $t$. Since such a proposition is logically incorrigible, $(4_L)$ implies that Nelson's belief in this truth at $t$ is justified. But we may easily suppose that this belief of Nelson is not at all the result of proper mathematical reasoning, or even the result of appeal to trustworthy authority. Perhaps Nelson believes this complex truth because of utterly confused reasoning, or because of hasty and ill-founded conjecture. Then his belief is not justified, contrary to what $(4_L)$ implies.

The case of logical or mathematical truths is admittedly peculiar, since the truth of these propositions is assured independently of any beliefs. It might seem, therefore, that we can better capture the idea of 'belief logically guaranteeing truth' in cases where the propositions in question are *contingent*. With this in mind, we might restrict ($4_L$) to *contingent* incorrigible propositions. Even this amendment cannot save ($4_L$), however, since there are counterexamples to it involving purely contingent propositions.

Suppose that Humperdink has been studying logic – or, rather, pseudo-logic – from Elmer Fraud, whom Humperdink has no reason to trust as a logician. Fraud has enunciated the principle that any disjunctive proposition consisting of at least forty distinct disjuncts is very probably true. Humperdink now encounters the proposition $p$, a contingent proposition with forty disjuncts, the seventh disjunct being 'I exist'. Although Humperdink grasps the proposition fully, he doesn't notice that it is entailed by 'I exist'. Rather, he is struck by the fact that it falls under the disjunction rule Fraud has enunciated (a rule I assume Humperdink is not *justified* in believing). Bearing this rule in mind, Humperdink forms a belief in $p$. Now notice that $p$ is logically incorrigible. It is logically necessary that if anyone believes $p$, then $p$ is true (of him at that time). This simply follows from the fact that, first, a person's believing anything entails that he exists, and second, 'I exist' entails $p$. Since $p$ is logically incorrigible, principle ($4_L$) implies that Humperdink's belief in $p$ is justified. But surely, given our example, that conclusion is false. Humperdink's belief in $p$ is not at all justified.

One thing that goes wrong in this example is that while Humperdink's belief in $p$ logically implies its truth, Humperdink doesn't *recognize* that his believing it implies its truth. This might move a theorist to revise ($4_L$) by adding the requirement that $S$ 'recognize' that $p$ is logically incorrigible. But this, of course, won't do. The term 'recognize' is obviously an epistemic term, so the suggested revision of ($4_L$) would result in an inadmissible base clause.

## II

Let us try to diagnose what has gone wrong with these attempts to produce an acceptable base-clause principle. Notice that each of the foregoing attempts confers the status of 'justified' on a belief without restriction on *why* the belief is held, i.e., on what *causally initiates* the belief or *causally sustains* it. The logical versions of principles (3) and (4), for example, clearly place no restriction on causes of belief. The same is true of the nomological versions of (3) and (4), since nomological requirements can be satisfied by simultaneity or cross-sectional laws, as illustrated by our brain-state/belief-state examples. I suggest that the absence of causal requirements accounts for the failure of the foregoing principles. Many of our counterexamples are ones in which the belief is caused in some strange or unacceptable way, e.g., by the accidental movement of a brain surgeon's hand, by reliance on an illicit, pseudo-logical principle, or by the blinding aura of the presidency. In general, a strategy for defeating a noncausal principle of justifiedness is to find a case in which the principle's antecedent is satisfied but the belief is caused by some faulty belief-forming process. The faultiness of the belief-forming process will incline us, intuitively, to regard the belief as unjustified. Thus, correct principles of justified belief must be principles that make causal requirements, where 'cause' is construed broadly to include sustainers as well as initiators of belief (i.e., processes that determine, or help to overdetermine, a belief's continuing to be held.)[6]

The need for causal requirements is not restricted to base-clause principles. Recursive principles will also need a causal component. One might initially suppose that the following is a good recursive principle: 'If $S$ justifiably believes $q$ at $t$, and $q$ entails $p$, and $S$ believes $p$ at $t$, then $S$'s belief in $p$ at $t$ is justified'. But this principle is unacceptable. $S$'s belief in $p$ doesn't receive justificational status simply from the fact that $p$ is entailed by $q$ and $S$ justifiably believes $q$. If what causes $S$ to believe $p$ at $t$ is entirely different, $S$'s belief in $p$ may well not be justified. Nor can the situation be remedied by adding to the antecedent the condition that $S$ justifiably believes that $q$ entails $p$. Even if he believes this, and believes $q$ as well, he might not put these beliefs together. He might believe $p$ as a result of some other, wholly extraneous, considerations. So once again, conditions that fail to require appropriate causes of a belief don't guarantee justifiedness.

Granted that principles of justified belief must make reference to causes of belief, what kinds of causes confer justifiedness? We can gain insight into this problem by reviewing some faulty processes of belief-formation, i.e., processes whose belief-outputs would be classed as unjustified. Here are some examples: confused reasoning, wishful thinking, reliance on emotional attachment, mere hunch or guesswork, and hasty generalization. What do these faulty processes have in common? They share the feature of *unreliability*: they tend to produce *error* a large proportion of the time. By contrast, which species of belief-forming (or belief-sustaining) processes are intuitively justification-conferring? They include standard perceptual processes, remembering, good reasoning, and introspection. What these processes seem to have in common in *reliability*: the beliefs they produce are generally true. My positive proposal, then, is this. The justificational status of a belief is a function of the reliability of the process or processes that cause it, where (as a first approximation) reliability consists in the tendency of a process to produce beliefs that are true rather than false.

To test this thesis further, notice that justifiedness is not a purely categorical concept, although I treat it here as categorical in the interest of simplicity. We can and do regard certain beliefs as more justified than others. Furthermore, our intuitions of comparative justifiedness go along with our beliefs about the comparative reliability of the belief-causing processes.

Consider perceptual beliefs. Suppose Jones believes he has just seen a mountain goat. Our assessment of the belief's justifiedness is determined by whether he caught a brief glimpse of the creature at a great distance, or whether he had a good look at the thing only thirty yards away. His belief in the latter sort of case is (ceteris paribus) more justified than in the former sort of case. And, if his belief is true, we are more prepared to say he *knows* in the latter case than in the former. The difference between the two cases seems to be this. Visual beliefs formed from brief and hasty scanning, or where the perceptual object is a long distance off, tend to be wrong more often than visual beliefs formed from detailed and leisurely scanning, or where the object is in reasonable proximity. In short, the visual processes in the former category are less reliable than those in the latter category. A similar point holds for memory beliefs. A belief that results from a hazy and indistinct memory impression is counted as less justified than a belief that arises from a distinct memory impression, and our inclination to classify those beliefs as '*knowledge*' varies in the same way. Again, the reason is associated with the comparative reliability of the processes. Hazy and indistinct memory impressions are generally less reliable indicators of what actually happened; so beliefs formed from such impressions are less likely to be true than beliefs formed from distinct impressions. Further, consider beliefs based on inference from observed samples. A belief about a population that is based on random sampling, or on instances that exhibit great variety, is intuitively more justified than a belief based on biased sampling, or on instances from a narrow sector of the population. Again, the degree of justifiedness seems to be a function of reliability. Inferences based on random or varied samples will tend to produce less error or inaccuracy than inferences based on nonrandom or nonvaried samples.

Returning to a categorical concept of justifiedness, we might ask just *how* reliable a belief-forming process must be in order that its resultant beliefs be justified. A precise answer to this question should not be expected. Our conception of justification is *vague* in this respect. It does seem clear, however, that *perfect* reliability isn't required. Belief-forming processes that *sometimes* produce error still confer justification. It follows that there can be justified beliefs that are false.

I have characterized justification-conferring processes as ones that have a 'tendency' to produce beliefs that are true rather than false. The term 'tendency' could refer either to *actual* long-run frequency, or to a 'propensity', i.e., outcomes that would occur in merely *possible* realizations of the process. Which of these is intended? Unfortunately, I think our ordinary conception of justifiedness is vague on this dimension too. For the most part, we simply assume that the 'observed' frequency of truth versus error would be approximately replicated in the actual long run, and also in relevant counterfactual situations, i.e., ones that are highly 'realistic', or conform closely to the circumstances of the actual world. Since we ordinarily assume these frequencies to be roughly the same, we make no concerted effort to distinguish them. Since the purpose of my present theorizing is to capture our ordinary conception of justifiedness, and since our ordinary conception is vague on this matter, it is appropriate to leave the theory vague in the same respect.

We need to say more about the notion of a belief-forming '*process*'. Let us mean by a 'process' a *functional operation* or procedure, i.e., something that generates a *mapping* from certain states – 'inputs' – into other states – 'outputs'. The outputs in the present case are states of believing this or that proposition at a given moment. On this interpretation, a process is a *type* as opposed to a *token*. This is fully appropriate, since it is only types that have statistical properties such as producing truth 80 percent of the time; and it is precisely such statistical properties that determine the reliability of a process. Of course, we also want to speak of a process as *causing* a belief, and it looks as if types are incapable of being causes. But when we say that a belief is caused by a given process, understood as a functional procedure, we may interpret this to mean that it is caused by the particular *inputs* to the process (and by the intervening events 'through which' the functional procedure carries the inputs into the output) on the occasion in question.

What are some examples of belief-forming 'processes' construed as functional operations? One example is reasoning processes, where the inputs include antecedent beliefs and entertained hypotheses. Another example is functional procedures whose inputs include desires, hopes, or emotional states of various sorts (together with antecedent beliefs). A third example is a memory process, which takes as input beliefs or experiences at an earlier time and generates as output beliefs at a later time. For example, a memory process might take as input a belief at $t_1$ that Lincoln was born in 1809 and generate as output a belief at $t_n$ that Lincoln was born in 1809. A fourth example is perceptual processes. Here it isn't clear whether inputs should include states of the environment, such as the distance of the stimulus from the cognizer, or only events within or on the surface of the organism, e.g., receptor stimulations. I shall return to this point in a moment.

A critical problem concerning our analysis is the degree of generality of the process-types in question. Input-output relations can be specified very broadly or very narrowly, and the degree of generality will partly determine the degree of reliability. A process-type might be selected so narrowly that only one instance of it ever occurs, and hence the type is either completely reliable or completely unreliable. (This assumes that reliability is a function of *actual* frequency only.) If such narrow process-types were selected, beliefs that are intuitively unjustified might be said to result from perfectly reliable processes; and beliefs that are intuitively justified might be said to result from perfectly unreliable processes.

It is clear that our ordinary thought about process-types slices them broadly, but I cannot at present give a precise explication of our intuitive principles. One plausible suggestion, though, is that the relevant processes are *content-neutral*. It might be argued, for example, that the process of *inferring p whenever the Pope asserts p* could pose problems for our theory. If the Pope is infallible, this process will be perfectly reliable; yet we would not regard the belief-outputs of this process as justified. The content-neutral restriction would avert this difficulty. If relevant processes are required to admit as input beliefs (or other states) with *any* content, the aforementioned process will not count, for its input beliefs have a restricted propositioned content, viz., '*the Pope asserts p*'.

In addition to the problem of 'generality' or 'abstractness' there is the previously mentioned problem of the '*extent*' of belief-forming processes. Clearly, the causal ancestry of beliefs often includes events outside the organism. Are such events to be included among the 'inputs' of belief-forming processes? Or should we restrict the extent of belief-forming processes to '*cognitive*' events, i.e., events within the organism's nervous system? I shall choose the latter course, though with some hesitation. My general grounds for this decision are roughly as follows. Justifiedness seems to be a function of how a cognizer deals with his environmental input, i.e., with the goodness or badness of the operations that register and transform the stimulation that reaches him. ('Deal with', of course, does not mean *purposeful* action; nor is it restricted to *conscious* activity.) A justified belief is, roughly speaking, one that results from cognitive operations that are, generally speaking, good or successful. But '*cognitive*' operations are most plausibly construed as operations of the cognitive faculties, i.e., 'information-processing' equipment *internal* to the organism.

With these points in mind, we may now advance the following base-clause principle for justified belief.

(5)   If $S$'s believing $p$ at $t$ results from a reliable cognitive belief-forming process (or set of processes), then $S$'s belief in $p$ at $t$ is justified.

Since 'reliable belief-forming process' has been defined in terms of such notions as belief, truth, statistical frequency, and the like, it is not an epistemic term. Hence, (5) is an admissible base clause.

It might seem as if (5) promises to be not only a successful base clause, but the only principle needed whatever, apart from a closure clause. In other words, it might seem as if it is a necessary as well as a sufficient condition of justifiedness that a belief be produced by reliable cognitive belief-forming processes. But this is not quite correct, given our provisional definition of 'reliability'.

Our provisional definition implies that a reasoning process is reliable only if it generally produces beliefs that are true, and similarly, that a memory process is reliable only if it generally yields beliefs that are true. But these requirements are too strong. A reasoning procedure cannot be expected to produce true belief if it is applied to false premises. And memory cannot be expected to yield a true belief if the original belief it attempts to retain is false. What we need for reasoning and memory, then, is a notion of '*conditional reliability*'. A process is conditionally reliable when a sufficient proportion of its output-beliefs are true *given that its input-beliefs are true*.

With this point in mind, let us distinguish *belief-dependent* and *belief-independent* cognitive processes. The former are processes some of whose inputs are belief-states.[7] The latter are processes *none* of whose inputs are belief-states. We may then replace principle (5) with the following two principles, the first a base-clause principle and the second a recursive-clause principle.

(6$_A$)   If $S$'s belief in $p$ at $t$ results ('immediately') from a belief-independent process that is (unconditionally) reliable, then $S$'s belief in $p$ at $t$ is justified.

(6$_B$)   If $S$'s belief in $p$ at $t$ results ('immediately') from a belief-dependent process that is (at least) conditionally reliable, and if the beliefs (if any) on which this process operates in producing $S$'s belief in $p$ at $t$ are themselves justified, then $S$'s belief in $p$ at $t$ is justified.[8]

If we add to (6$_A$) and (6$_B$) the standard closure clause, we have a complete theory of justified belief. The theory says, in effect, that a belief is justified if and only it is '*well formed*', i.e., it has an ancestry of reliable and/or conditionally reliable cognitive operations. (Since a dated belief may be over-determined, it may have a number of distinct ancestral trees. These need not all be full of reliable or conditionally reliable processes. But at least one ancestral tree must have reliable or conditionally reliable processes throughout.)

The theory of justified belief proposed here, then, is an *historical or genetic* theory. It contrasts with the dominant approach to justified belief, an approach that generates what we may call (borrowing a phrase from Robert Nozick) '*current time-slice*' theories. A current time-slice theory makes the justificational status of a belief wholly a function of what is true of the cognizer *at the time* of belief. An historical theory makes the justificational status of a belief depend on its prior history. Since my historical theory emphasizes the reliability of the belief-generating processes, it may be called '*historical reliabilism*'.

The most obvious examples of current time-slice theories are 'Cartesian' foundationalist theories, which trace all justificational status (at least of contingent propositions) to current mental states. The usual varieties of coherence theories, however, are equally current time-slice views, since they too make the justificational status of a belief wholly a function of *current* states of affairs. For coherence theories, however, these current states include all other beliefs of the cognizer, which would not be considered relevant by Cartesian foundationalism. Have there been other historical theories of justified belief? Among contemporary writers, Quine and Popper have historical epistemologies, though the notion of 'justification' is not their avowed *explicandum*. Among historical writers, it might seem that Locke and Hume had genetic theories of sorts. But I think that their genetic theories were only theories of ideas, not of knowledge or justification. Plato's theory of recollection, however, is a good example of a genetic theory of knowing.[9] And it might be argued that Hegel and Dewey had genetic epistemologies (if Hegel can be said to have had a clear epistemology at all).

The theory articulated by $(6_A)$ and $(6_B)$ might be viewed as a kind of 'foundationalism', because of its recursive structure. I have no objection to this label, as long as one keeps in mind how different this 'diachronic' form of foundationalism is from Cartesian, or other 'synchronic' varieties of, foundationalism.

Current time-slice theories characteristically assume that the justificational status of a belief is something which the cognizer is able to know or determine at the time of belief. This is made explicit, for example, by Chisholm (1977, pp. 17, 114–16). The historical theory I endorse makes no such assumption. There are many facts about a cognizer to which he lacks 'privileged access', and I regard the justificational status of his beliefs as one of those things. This is not to say that a cognizer is necessarily ignorant, at any given moment, of the justificational status of his current beliefs. It is only to deny that he necessarily has, or can get, knowledge or true belief about this status. Just as a person can know without knowing that he knows, so he can have justified belief without knowing that it is justified (or believing justifiably that it is justified).

A characteristic case in which a belief is justified though the cognizer doesn't know that it's justified is where the original evidence for the belief has long since been forgotten. If the original evidence was compelling, the cognizer's original belief may have been justified; and this justificational status may have been preserved through memory. But since the cognizer no longer remembers how or why he came to believe, he may not know that the belief is justified. If asked now to justify his belief, he may be at a loss. Still, the belief is justified, though the cognizer can't demonstrate or establish this.

The historical theory of justified belief I advocate is connected in spirit with the causal theory of knowing presented in chapter 4.[10] I had this in mind when I remarked near the outset of the paper that my theory of justified belief makes justifiedness come out closely related to knowledge. Justified beliefs, like pieces of knowledge, have appropriate histories; but they may fail to be knowledge either because they are false or because they founder on some other requirement for knowing of the kind discussed in the post-Gettier knowledge-trade.

There is a variant of the historical conception of justified belief that is worth mentioning in this context. It may be introduced as follows. Suppose $S$ has a set $B$ of beliefs at time $t_0$, and some of these beliefs are *unjustified*. Between $t_0$ and $t_1$ he reasons from the entire set $B$ to the conclusion $p$, which he then accepts at $t_1$. The reasoning procedure he uses is a very sound one, i.e., one that is conditionally reliable. There is a sense or respect in which we are tempted to say that $S$'s belief in $p$ at $t_1$ is 'justified'. At any rate, it is tempting to say that the *person* is justified in believing $p$ at $t$. Relative to his antecedent cognitive state, he did as well as could be expected: the *transition* from his cognitive state at $t_0$ to his cognitive state at $t_1$ was entirely sound. Although we may acknowledge this brand of justifiedness – it might be called '*terminal-phase reliabilism*' – it is not a kind of justifiedness so closely related to knowing. For a person to know proposition $p$, it is not enough that the *final phase* of the process that leads to his belief in $p$ be sound. It is also necessary that some entire history of the process be sound (i.e., reliable or conditionally reliable).

Let us return now to the historical theory. In the next section of the paper, I shall adduce reasons for strengthening it a bit. Before looking at these reasons, however, I wish to review two quite different objections to the theory.

First, a critic might argue that *some* justified beliefs do not derive their justificational status from their causal ancestry. In particular, it might be argued that beliefs about one's current phenomenal states and intuitive beliefs about elementary logical or conceptual relationships do not derive their justificational status in this way. I am not persuaded by either of these examples. Introspection, I believe, should be regarded as a form of retrospection. Thus, a justified belief that I am 'now' in pain gets its justificational status from a relevant, though brief, causal history.[11] The apprehension of logical or conceptual relationships is also a cognitive process that occupies time. The psychological process of 'seeing' or 'intuiting' a simple logical truth is very fast, and we cannot introspectively dissect it into constituent parts. Nonetheless, there are mental operations going on, just as there are mental operations that occur in idiots savants, who are unable to report the computational processes they in fact employ.

A second objection to historical reliabilism focuses on the reliability element rather than the causal or historical element. Since the theory is intended to cover all possible cases, it seems to imply that for any cognitive process $C$, if $C$ is reliable in possible world $W$, then any belief in $W$ that results from $C$ is justified. But doesn't this permit easy counter-examples? Surely we can imagine a possible world in which wishful thinking is reliable. We can imagine a possible world where a benevolent demon so arranges things that beliefs formed by wishful thinking usually come true. This would make wishful thinking a reliable process in that possible world, but surely we don't want to regard beliefs that result from wishful thinking as justified.

There are several possible ways to respond to this case and I am unsure which response is best, partly because my own intuitions (and those of other people I have consulted) are not entirely clear. One possibility is to say that in the possible world imagined, beliefs that result from wishful thinking *are* justified. In other words we reject the claim that wishful thinking could never, intuitively, confer justifiedness.[12]

However, for those who feel that wishful thinking couldn't confer justifiedness, even in the world imagined, there are two ways out. First, it may be suggested that the proper criterion of justifiedness is the propensity of a process to generate beliefs that are true in a *nonmanipulated environment*, i.e., an environment in which there is no purposeful arrangement of the world either to accord or conflict with the beliefs that are formed. In other words, the suitability of a belief forming process is only a function of its success in '*natural*' situations, not situations of the sort involving benevolent or malevolent demons, or any other such manipulative creatures. If we reformulate the theory to include this qualification, the counterexample in question will be averted.

Alternatively, we may reformulate our theory, or reinterpret it, as follows. Instead of construing the theory as saying that a belief in possible world $W$ is justified if and only if it results from a cognitive process that is reliable in $W$, we may construe it as saying that a belief in possible world $W$ is justified if and only if it results from a cognitive process that is reliable *in our world*. In short, our conception of justifiedness is derived as follows. We note certain cognitive processes in the actual world, and form beliefs about which of these are reliable. The ones we believe to be reliable are then regarded as justification-conferring processes. In reflecting on hypothetical beliefs, we deem them justified if and only if they result from processes already picked out as justification-conferring, or processes very similar to those. Since wishful thinking is not among these processes, a belief formed in a possible world $W$ by wishful thinking would not be deemed justified, even if wishful thinking is reliable in $W$. I am not sure that this is a correct reconstruction of our intuitive conceptual scheme, but it would accommodate the benevolent demon case, at least if the proper thing to say in that case is that the wishful-thinking-caused beliefs are unjustified.

Even if we adopt this strategy, however, a problem still remains. Suppose that wishful thinking turns out to be reliable *in the actual world*![13] This might be because, unbeknownst to us at present, there is a benevolent demon who, lazy until now, will shortly start arranging things so that our wishes come true. The long-run performance of wishful thinking will be very good, and hence even the new construal of the theory will imply that beliefs resulting from wishful thinking (in *our* world) are justified. Yet this surely contravenes our intuitive judgement on the matter.

Perhaps the moral of the case is that the standard format of a 'conceptual analysis' has its shortcomings. Let me depart from that format and try to give a better rendering of our aims and the theory that tries to achieve that aim. What we really want is an explanation of why we count, or would count, certain beliefs as justified and others as unjustified. Such an explanation must refer to our beliefs about reliability, not to the actual facts. The reason we count beliefs as justified is that they are formed by what we believe to be reliable belief-forming processes. Our beliefs about which belief-forming processes are reliable may be erroneous, but that does not affect the adequacy of the explanation. Since we believe that wishful thinking is an unreliable belief-forming process, we regard beliefs formed by wishful thinking as unjustified. What matters, then, is what we believe about wishful thinking, not what is true (in the long run) about wishful thinking. I am not sure how to express this point in the standard format of conceptual analysis, but it identifies an important point in understanding our theory.

## III

Let us return, however, to the standard format of conceptual analysis, and let us consider a new objection that will require some revisions in the theory advanced until now. According to our theory, a belief is justified in case it is caused by a process that is in fact reliable, or by one we generally believe to be reliable. But suppose that although one of $S$'s beliefs satisfies this condition, $S$ has no reason to believe that it does. Worse yet, suppose $S$ has reason to believe that his belief is caused by an *unreliable* process (although *in fact* its causal ancestry is fully reliable). Wouldn't we deny in such circumstances that $S$'s belief is justified? This seems to show that our analysis, as presently formulated, is mistaken.

Suppose that Jones is told on fully reliable authority that a certain class of his memory beliefs are almost all mistaken. His parents fabricate a wholly false story that Jones suffered from amnesia when he was seven but later developed *pseudo-memories* of that period. Though Jones listens to what his parents say and has excellent reason to trust them, he persists in believing the ostensible memories from his seven-year-old past. Are these memory beliefs justified? Intuitively, they are not justified. But since these beliefs result from genuine memory and original perceptions, which are adequately reliable processes, our theory says that these beliefs are justified.

Can the theory be revised to meet this difficulty? One natural suggestion is that the actual reliability of a belief's ancestry is not enough for justifiedness; in addition, the cognizer must be *justified in believing* that the ancestry of his belief is reliable. Thus one might think of replacing $(6_A)$, for example, with (7). (For simplicity, I neglect some of the details of the earlier analysis.)

(7)   If $S$'s belief in $p$ at $t$ is caused by a reliable cognitive process, and $S$ justifiably believes at $t$ that his $p$-belief is so caused, then $S$'s belief in $p$ at $t$ is justified.

It is evident, however, that (7) will not do as a base clause, for it contains the epistemic term 'justifiably' in its antecedent.

A slightly weaker revision, without this problematic feature, might next be suggested, viz.,

(8)   If $S$'s belief in $p$ at $t$ is caused by a reliable cognitive process, and $S$ believes at $t$ that his $p$-belief is so caused, then $S$'s belief in $p$ at $t$ is justified.

But this won't do the job. Suppose that Jones believes that his memory beliefs are reliably caused despite all the (trustworthy) contrary testimony of his parents. Principle (8) would be satisfied, yet we wouldn't say that these beliefs are justified.

Next, we might try (9), which is stronger than (8) and, unlike (7), formally admissible as a base clause.

(9)   If $S$'s belief in $p$ at $t$ is caused by a reliable cognitive process, and $S$ believes at $t$ that his $p$-belief is so caused, and this meta-belief is caused by a reliable cognitive process, then $S$'s belief in $p$ at $t$ is justified.

A first objection to (9) is that it wrongly precludes unreflective creatures – creatures like animals or young children, who have no beliefs about the genesis of their beliefs – from having justified beliefs. If one shares my view that justified belief is, at least roughly, *well-formed* belief, surely animals and young children can have justified beliefs.

A second problem with (9) concerns its underlying rationale. Since (9) is proposed as a substitute for $(6_A)$, it is implied that the reliability of a belief's own cognitive ancestry does not make it justified. But, the suggestion seems to be, the reliability of a *meta-belief*'s ancestry confers justifiedness on the first-order belief. Why should that be so? Perhaps one is attracted by the idea of a 'trickle-down' effect: if an n + 1-level belief is justified, its justification trickles down to an n-level belief. But even if the trickle-down theory is correct, it doesn't help here. There is no assurance from the satisfaction of (9)'s antecedent that the meta-belief itself is *justified*.

To obtain a better revision of our theory, let us reexamine the Jones case. Jones has strong evidence against certain propositions concerning his past. He doesn't *use* this evidence, but if he were to use it properly, he would stop believing these propositions. Now the proper use of evidence would be an instance of a (conditionally) reliable process. So what we can say about Jones is that he fails to use a certain (conditionally) reliable process that he could and should have used. Admittedly, had he used this process, he would have 'worsened' his doxastic states: he would have replaced some true beliefs with suspension of judgement.

Still, he couldn't have known this in the case in question. So, he failed to do something which, epistemically, he should have done. This diagnosis suggests a fundamental change in our theory. The justificational status of a belief is not only a function of the cognitive processes *actually* employed in producing it: it is also a function of processes that could and should be employed.

With these points in mind, we may tentatively propose the following revision of our theory, where we again focus on a base-clause principle but omit certain details in the interest of clarity.

> (10)   If $S$'s belief in $p$ at $t$ results from a reliable cognitive process, and there is no reliable or conditionally reliable process available to $S$ which, had it been used by $S$ in addition to the process actually used, would have resulted in $S$'s not believing $p$ at $t$, then $S$'s belief in $p$ at $t$ is justified.

There are several problems with this proposal. First, there is a technical problem. One cannot use an additional belief-forming (or doxastic-state-forming) process *as well as* the original process if the additional one would result in a different doxastic state. One wouldn't be using the original process at all. So we need a slightly different formulation of the relevant counterfactual. Since the basic idea is reasonably clear, however, I won't try to improve on the formulation here. A second problem concerns the notion of '*available*' belief-forming (or doxastic-state-forming) processes. What is it for a process to be 'available' to a cognizer? Were scientific procedures 'available' to people who lived in prescientific ages? Furthermore, it seems implausible to say that all 'available' processes ought to be used, at least if we include such processes as gathering *new* evidence. Surely a belief can sometimes be justified even if additional evidence gathering would yield a different doxastic attitude. What I think we should have in mind here are such additional processes as calling previously acquired evidence to mind, assessing the implications of that evidence, etc. This is admittedly somewhat vague, but here again our ordinary notion of justifiedness is vague, so it is appropriate for our analysans to display the same sort of vagueness.

This completes the sketch of my account of justified belief. Before concluding, however, it is essential to point out that there is an important use of 'justified' that is not captured by this account but can be captured by a closely related one.

There is a use of 'justified' in which it is not implied or presupposed that there is a *belief* that is justified. For example, if $S$ is trying to decide whether to believe $p$ and asks our advice, we may tell him that he is 'justified' in believing it. We do not thereby imply that he *has* a justified *belief*, since we know he is still suspending judgement. What we mean, roughly, is that he *would* or *could* be justified if he were to believe $p$. The justificational status we ascribe here cannot be a function of the causes of $S$'s believing $p$, for there is no belief by $S$ in $p$. Thus, the account of justifiedness we have given thus far cannot explicate *this* use of 'justified'. (It doesn't follow that this use of 'justified' has no connection with causal ancestries. Its proper use may depend on the causal ancestry of the cognizer's cognitive state, though not on the causal ancestry of his believing *p*.)

Let us distinguish two uses of 'justified': an *ex post* use and an *ex ante* use. The *ex post* use occurs when there exists a belief, and we say of *that belief* that it is (or isn't) justified. The *ex ante* use occurs when no such belief exists, or when we wish to ignore the question of whether such a belief exists. Here we say of the *person*, independent of his doxastic state *vis-à-vis p*, that *p* is (or isn't) suitable for him to believe.[14]

Since we have given an account of *ex post* justifiedness, it will suffice if we can analyze *ex ante* justifiedness in terms of it. Such an analysis, I believe, is ready at hand. *S* is *ex ante* justified in believing *p* at *t* just in case his total cognitive state at *t* is such that from that state he could come to believe *p* in such a way that this belief would be *ex post* justified. More precisely, he is *ex ante* justified in believing *p* at *t* just in case a reliable belief-forming operation is available to him such that the application of that operation to his total cognitive state at *t* would result, more or less immediately, in his believing *p* and this belief would be *ex post* justified. Stated formally, we have the following:

(11)   Person *S* is *ex ante* justified in believing *p* at *t* if and only if there is a reliable belief-forming operation available to *S* which is such that if *S* applied that operation to his total cognitive state at *t*, *S* would believe *p* at *t*-plus-delta (for a suitably small delta) and that belief would be *ex post* justified.

For the analysans of (11) to be satisfied, the total cognitive state at *t* must have a suitable causal ancestry. Hence, (11) is implicitly an historical account of *ex ante* justifiedness.

As indicated, the bulk of this paper was addressed to *ex post* justifiedness. This is the appropriate analysandum if one is interested in the connection between justifiedness and knowledge, since what is crucial to whether a person *knows* a proposition is whether he has an actual *belief* in the proposition that is justified. However, since many epistemologists are interested in *ex ante* justifiedness, it is proper for a general theory of justification to try to provide an account of that concept as well. Our theory does this quite naturally, for the account of *ex ante* justifiedness falls out directly from our account of *ex post* justifiedness.

### Notes

Research on this paper was begun while the author was a fellow of the John Simon Guggenheim Memorial Foundation and of the Center for Advanced Study in the Behavioral Sciences. I am grateful for their support. I have received helpful comments and criticism from Holly Smith, Mark Kaplan, Fred Schmitt, Stephen Stich, and many others at several universities where earlier drafts of the paper were read.

1   Notice that the choice of a recursive format does not prejudice the case for or against any particular theory. A recursive format is perfectly general. Specifically, an

explicit set of necessary and sufficient conditions is just a special case of a recursive format, i.e., one in which there is no recursive clause.

2   Many of the attempts I shall consider are suggested by material in William Alston 1971.

3   Such a definition (though without the modal term) is given, for example, by W. V. O. Quine and J. S. Ullian (1970, p. 21). Statements are said to be self-evident just in case 'to understand them is to believe them'.

4   I assume, of course, that 'nomologically necessary' is *de re* with respect to '*S*' and '*t*' in this construction. I shall not focus on problems that may arise in this regard, since my primary concerns are with different issues.

5   This assumption violates the thesis that Davidson calls 'The Anomalism of the Mental'. Cf. Davidson 1970. But it is unclear that this thesis is a necessary truth. Thus, it seems fair to assume its falsity in order to produce a counterexample. The example neither entails nor precludes the mental-physical identity theory.

6   Keith Lehrer's example of the gypsy lawyer is intended to show the inappropriateness of a causal requirement. (See Lehrer 1974, pp. 124–125.) But I find this example unconvincing. To the extent that I clearly imagine that the lawyer fixes his belief solely as a result of the cards, it seems intuitively wrong to say that he *knows* – or has a *justified belief* – that his client is innocent.

7   This definition is not exactly what we need for the purposes at hand. As Ernest Sosa points out, introspection will turn out to be a belief-dependent process since sometimes the input into the process will be a belief (when the introspected content is a belief). Intuitively, however, introspection is not the sort of process which may be merely conditionally reliable. I do not know how to refine the definition so as to avoid this difficulty, but it is a small and isolated point.

8   It may be objected that principles $(6_A)$ and $(6_B)$ are jointly open to analogues of the lottery paradox. A series of processes composed of reliable but less-than-perfectly-reliable processes may be extremely unreliable. Yet applications of $(6_A)$ and $(6_B)$ would confer justifiedness on a belief that is caused by such a series. In reply to this objection, we might simply indicate that the theory is intended to capture our ordinary notion of justifiedness, and this ordinary notion has been formed without recognition of this kind of problem. The theory is not wrong *as* a theory of the ordinary (naive) conception of justifiedness. On the other hand, if we want a theory to do more than capture the ordinary conception of justifiedness, it might be possible to strengthen the principles to avoid lottery-paradox analogues.

9   I am indebted to Mark Pastin for this point.

10  The reliability aspect of the theory also has its precursors in my earlier papers on knowing: Goldman 1975.

11  The view that introspection is retrospection was taken by Ryle, and before him (as Charles Hartshorne points out to me) by Hobbes, Whitehead, and possibly Husserl.

12  Of course, if people in world W learn *inductively* that wishful thinking is reliable, and regularly base their beliefs on this inductive inference, it is quite unproblematic and straightforward that their beliefs are justified. The only interesting case is where their beliefs are formed *purely* by wishful thinking, without using inductive inference. The suggestion contemplated in this paragraph of the text is that, in the world imagined, even pure wishful thinking would confer justifiedness.

13  I am indebted here to Mark Kaplan.

14  The distinction between *ex post* and *ex ante* justifiedness is similar to Roderick Firth's distinction between *doxastic* and *propositional* warrant. See Firth 1978.

**Works Cited**

Alston, William P. (1971) 'Varieties of Privileged Access.' *American Philosophical Quarterly* 8, 223–41.

Davidson, D. (1970) 'Mental Events.' In L. Foster and J. Swanson (eds), *Experience and Theory*. Amherst, MA: University of Massachusetts Press.

Firth, R. (1978) 'Are Epistemic Concepts Reducible to Ethical Concepts?' In A. Goldman and J. Kim (eds), *Values and Morals*. Dordrecht: D. Reidel.

Goldman, A. I. (1975) 'Innate Knowledge.' In S. Stitch, (ed.), *Innate Ideas*. Berkeley: University of California Press.

Lehrer, K. (1974) *Knowledge*. Oxford: Oxford University Press.

Quine W. V. O. and J. Ullian. (1970) *The Web of Belief*. New York: Random House.

---

# 8 Contextualism and Knowledge Attributions

---

## Keith DeRose

## I Contextualism: Initial Exposition

Consider the following cases.

> *Bank Case A*. My wife and I are driving home on a Friday afternoon. We plan to stop at the bank on the way home to deposit our paychecks. But as we drive past the bank, we notice that the lines inside are very long, as they often are on Friday afternoons. Although we generally like to deposit our paychecks as soon as possible, it is not especially important in this case that they be deposited right away, so I suggest that we drive straight home and deposit our paychecks on Saturday morning. My wife says, "Maybe the bank won't be open tomorrow. Lots of banks are closed on Saturdays." I reply, "No, I know it'll be open. I was just there two weeks ago on Saturday. It's open until noon."

> *Bank Case B*. My wife and I drive past the bank on a Friday afternoon, as in Case A, and notice the long lines. I again suggest that we deposit our paychecks on Saturday morning, explaining that I was at the bank on Saturday morning only two weeks ago and discovered that it was open until noon. But in this case, we have just written a very large and very important check. If our paychecks are not deposited into our checking account before Monday morning, the important check we wrote will bounce, leaving us in a *very* bad situation. And, of course, the bank is not open on Sunday. My wife reminds me of these facts. She then says, "Banks do change their hours. Do you know the bank will be open tomorrow?" Remaining as confident as I was before that the bank will be open then, still, I reply, "Well, no. I'd better go in and make sure."

Assume that in both cases the bank *will* be open on Saturday and that there is nothing unusual about either case that has not been included in my description of it. It seems to me that (1) when I claim to know that the bank will be open on Saturday in case A, I am saying something true. But it also seems that (2) I am saying something true in Case B when I concede that I *don't* know that the bank will be open on Saturday. Yet I seem to be in no better position to know in Case A than in Case B. It is quite natural to say that (3) If I know that the bank will be open on Saturday in Case A, then I also know that it will be in Case B.

Is there any conflict here among (1), (2), and (3)? I hope not, because I want to investigate and defend a view according to which all three of them are true. Of course, it would be inconsistent to claim that (1) and (2) are true, and also hold that (4) If what I say in Case A in claiming to know that the bank will be open on Saturday is true, then what I say in Case B in conceding that I don't know that the bank will be open on Saturday is false. But there is a big difference between (3) and (4), and this difference is crucial to the view I want to investigate and defend.

We may, following Peter Unger, call the view I want to investigate a "contextual"[1] theory of knowledge attributions: it is a theory according to which the truth conditions of sentences of the form "S knows that p" or "S does not know that p" vary in certain ways according to the context in which the sentences are uttered.[2] The contextualist can deny (4) even while admitting that I am in no better position to know in Case A than in Case B. The contexts of my utterances in the two cases make it easier for a knowledge attribution to be true in Case A than in Case B.

There are important contextual differences between Case A and Case B which one might think are relevant. First, there is the importance of being right. In Case B, a lot hinges on whether or not the bank will be open on Saturday, while in Case A it is not nearly as important that I be right. One might think that requirements for making a knowledge attribution true go up as the stakes go up.[3]

Second, there is the *mentioning* of a possibility. In Case B my wife raises the possibility that the bank may have changed its hours in the last two weeks. One might think that if this possibility has been mentioned, I cannot truly claim to know that the bank will be open on Saturday on the ground that two weeks ago it was open on Saturday unless I can rule out the possibility that the bank's hours have changed since then. On the other hand, perhaps I don't have to be able to rule out this possibility in order to truly say I know if, as in Case A, no such possibility has not been suggested.[4]

Third, there is the *consideration* of a possibility. Since my wife raised the possibility of the bank changing its hours in Case B, I have that possibility in mind when I utter my sentence. Perhaps, since I am considering this possibility, I must be able to rule it out in order to truthfully claim to know that the bank will be open on Saturday. On the other hand, in Case A I am not considering the possibility, so perhaps I do not have to be able to rule it out in order to truthfully say that I know that the bank will be open on Saturday.[5] (Of course, it must still be *true* that the bank will be open on Saturday in order for me to know that it will be.)

Again following Unger, we may call someone who denies that the types of contextual factors we have just looked at affect the truth conditions of knowledge attributions an "invariantist." According to the invariantist, such features of an utterance of a knowledge attribution do not affect how good an epistemic position the putative knower must be in for the attribution to be true. In considering the Bank Cases, for instance, the invariantist will assert (4), which seems very plausible, and will therefore deny either (1) or (2). Typically, the invariantist will deny (1). In fact, Unger uses the term "invariantism" to denote the position that the standards for true knowledge attributions remain constant *and very high* – as high as they can possibly be. This position I will call "sceptical invariantism," leaving the more general term "invariantism" to denote any position according to which the truth conditions for knowledge attribution do not vary in the way the contextualist claims they do, whether or not the standards are said to be very high. I will then use "non-sceptical invariantism" to refer to a position according to which the standards are held to be constant but relatively low.[6] The *sceptical* invariantist will deny (1). She may admit that I am *warranted in asserting* that I know in Case A or that it is *useful for me to say* that I know, but will insist that what I say in claiming that I know is, strictly speaking, false. On the other hand, similar maneuvers can be used by the *non-sceptical* invariantist to deny (2). A non-sceptical invariantist may admit that I *should not say* that I know in Case B, because my wife mistakenly thinks that I must be able to rule out the possibility that the bank has changed its hours in order to know that the bank will be open on Saturday, and saying that I know will lead her to believe that I can rule out that possibility. Still, my wife *is* mistaken about this requirement, and if I were to say that I knew, I would be saying something that is, though misleading, true. Thus, it is *useful for me to assert* that I *don't* know. But for all its usefulness, my assertion is, strictly speaking, false.

Contextualists, of course, can disagree about what types of features of the context of utterance really do affect the truth conditions of knowledge attributions and to what extent they do so. I will not here enter into this thorny issue, although I have a preference for the more "objective" features – like the importance of being right and what has been said in the conversation – and tend to discount as relevant to truth conditions such "subjective" features as what possibilities the speaker is considering.[7] In this paper I address some *general* issues that confront any contextualist. In Part II, I distinguish between contextualism and a very prominent theory of knowledge which has been called the "relevant alternatives" theory (RA), and in Part III, I respond to an important objection to which *any* form of contextualism seems vulnerable.

By thus isolating and defending contextualism, I will do much to clear the way for contextualist resolutions to sceptical arguments. Contextual theories of knowledge attributions have almost invariably been developed with an eye towards providing some kind of answer to philosophical scepticism. For some sceptical arguments threaten to show, not only that we fail to meet very high requirements for knowledge of interest to philosophers seeking absolute certainty, but also that we don't meet the truth conditions of ordinary, out-on-the-street claims to know. They thus threaten to establish the startling result that we never, or almost never, truly ascribe knowledge to ourselves or to other human beings. According to contextual analysis, when the sceptic presents her arguments, she manipulates various conversational mechanisms that raise the semantic standards for knowledge, and thereby creates a context in which she can truly say that we know nothing or very little. But the fact that the sceptic can thus install very high standards which we don't live up to has no tendency to show that we don't satisfy the more relaxed standards that are in place in ordinary conversations. Thus, it is hoped, our ordinary claims to know will be safeguarded from the apparently powerful attacks of the sceptic, while, at the same time, the persuasiveness of the sceptical arguments is explained.[8]

Many find such contextualist resolutions of sceptical arguments very attractive, especially since their main competition is the sceptical invariantist resolutions according to which the persuasiveness of various sceptical arguments is explained in a way as alarming as it is simple: They seem persuasive because they are indeed sound and successfully establish the startling conclusion that we never or almost never truly ascribe knowledge.[9] But many, while finding the contextualist resolutions a preferable alternative to an unacceptably radical form of scepticism, at the same time feel an initial resistance, closely related to the appeal of (4), to the thought that contextual factors of the types I've mentioned can really affect whether or not a subject knows.[10] While many are willing to accept this thought in order to avoid the sceptical conclusion, there remains a feeling that the contextualist is asking them to swallow pretty hard – although perhaps not quite so hard as the sceptical invariantist would have them swallow. As contextualists have rushed to apply their theories to the problem of scepticism, this initial resistance has not yet been adequately addressed. I will address this resistance, as well as some explicit objections to contextualism that have been raised in the philosophical literature and which are based on the source of this resistance, in Part III below. But first, in Part II, we must carefully distinguish contextualism from RA.

## II Contextualism and "Relevant Alternatives"

The most popular form of contextualism, I think it is fair to say, is what has been called the "relevant alternatives" view of knowledge (RA). But we must be careful here. As we shall see, it is a bit tricky to say just in what sense RA is a contextualist view. According to RA, a claim to know that p is made within a certain framework of relevant alternatives which are incompatible with p. To know that p is to be able to distinguish p from these relevant alternatives, to be able to rule out these relevant alternatives to p. But not every contrary of or alternative to p is a *relevant* alternative.[11] In an ordinary case of, say, claiming to know that some animals in a zoo are zebras, to borrow an example introduced by Fred Dretske,[12] the alternative that they are cleverly painted mules is *not* a relevant alternative, and one need not be able to rule it out in order truly to claim to know that the animals are zebras. But in an extraordinary case, that alternative might be relevant. How can it become relevant?

In one of the standard presentations of RA, Alvin Goldman (1976) presents various factors which can affect the range of relevant alternatives. These factors may be divided into two groups. First, there are features of the putative knower's situation; these I will call "subject factors."[13] A subject in an ordinary situation can be truly said to know that what he sees up ahead is a barn even if he cannot rule out the possibility that it is just a barn facade. But, Goldman points out, if there are a lot of such facades in the putative knower's vicinity, then the possibility that what the person is seeing is just a facade *is* a relevant alternative, and the person does not know that he is seeing a barn, even if what he sees happens to be an actual barn (pp. 772–73).

Second, there are features of the speaker's situation, which I will call "attributor factors." Goldman writes, "It is not only the circumstances of the putative knower's situation, however, that influence the choice of alternatives. The speaker's own linguistic and psychological context are also important." Goldman suggests that "if the speaker is in a class where Descartes's evil demon has just been discussed," then certain alternatives may be relevant which ordinarily are not (p. 776).

Insofar as a relevant alternatives theorist allows attributor factors to influence which alternatives are relevant, he is a contextualist. An invariantist can be a relevant alternatives theorist if he allows only subject factors to influence which alternatives are relevant.[14] Consider two situations in which Henry has a good, clear look at what he takes to be – and what, in fact, is – a barn. In Case C there are no barn facades around, but in Case D the area Henry finds himself in is (unbeknownst to him) teeming with barn facades, although Henry is luckily looking at the only actual barn in the area. This does not seem to be a pair of cases in which Henry is in equally good positions to know that what he is seeing is a barn; the conditional, *If Henry knows in Case C, then he knows in Case D* does not seem to be true, so the invariantist can agree that a sentence attributing knowledge to Henry in Case C can be true, while one attributing knowledge to him in Case D is false. And he can use the idea of "relevant alternatives" to explain the difference. Thus, although most versions of RA allow attributor factors to be relevant and are therefore contextualist views, an RA theorist need not be a contextualist.

Of course, in first-person present tense knowledge claims, the attributor of knowledge and the putative subject of knowledge are in the same situation (they are the same person at the same time). If Henry says, "I know that that's a barn," there is no difference between the speaker and the putative knower. In this situation the invariantist RA theorist will allow only factors that attach to Henry qua putative knower (e.g. the presence or lack of facades in his vicinity) to matter in evaluating his claim for truth, while the contextualist will also allow factors that attach to Henry qua attributor of knowledge (such as whether or not the issue of facades has been raised in the conversation) to matter.[15]

Although Goldman draws the distinction between what I am calling subject factors and attributor factors, he does not explain the importance of this distinction. I am stressing it because it is crucial to some of the important claims RA theorists have wanted to make about the *meanings* of knowledge attributions.[16] Gail Stine, for example, writes:

> In Dretske's zoo example, the animal's being a mule painted to look like a zebra is not a relevant alternative. So what one means when one says that John knows the animal is a zebra, is that he knows it is a zebra, as opposed to a gazelle, an antelope, or other animals one would normally expect to find in a zoo. If, however, being a mule painted to look like a zebra became a relevant alternative, then one would literally mean something different in saying that John knows that the animal is a zebra from what one meant originally and that something else may well be false. (Stine (1976), p. 255)

But here we must be very careful. Much depends on *how* the animal's being a painted mule has become a relevant alternative. Suppose that it has become a relevant alternative due to a change in subject factors: There has been a zebra shortage and many zoos (even reputable zoos) *have* been using painted mules in an attempt to fool the zoo-going public. This could come about without the speaker's knowing it. Would one then *mean* something different by saying that John knows that the animal is a zebra? I think not.

The meaning of "meaning," of course, is difficult to get hold of. But there seems to be a fairly straightforward and important sense in which one *does* mean something different if the range of relevant alternatives has been changed by attributor factors but does *not* mean something different if the range of relevant alternatives has been changed only by subject factors. Stewart Cohen, whose version of RA clearly is a contextualist one, writes that he

> construes "knowledge" as an indexical. As such, one speaker may attribute knowledge to a subject while another speaker denies knowledge to that same subject, without contradiction. (Cohen (1988), p. 97)

This lack of contradiction is the key to the sense in which the knowledge attributor and the knowledge denier mean something different by "know." It is similar to the sense in which two people who think they are in the same room but are in fact in different rooms and are talking to each over an intercom mean something different by "this room" when one claims, "Frank is not in this room" and the other insists, "Frank is in this room – I can see him!" There is an important sense in which both do mean the same thing by this room," in which they are using the phrase in the same sense. But there is also an important sense in which they do not mean the same thing by the phrase; this is the sense by which we can explain the lack of contradiction between what the two people are saying. To use David Kaplan's terminology, the phrase is being used with the same *character*, but with different *content*.[17] Similarly, in Bank Case B from Part I of this paper, when, in the face of my wife's doubt, I admit that I don't know that the bank will be open on Saturday, I don't contradict an earlier claim to know that I might have made before the doubt was raised and before the issue was so important because, in an important sense, I don't mean the same thing by "know" as I meant in the earlier claim: While "know" is being used with the same *character*, it is *not* being used with the same *content*. Or so the contextualist will claim.

But if the range of relevant alternatives is changed by subject factors, the meaning of "know" is not in the same way changed. If very many nearby banks *have* discontinued their Saturday hours in the last two weeks, then it seems that my original claim to know may well have been false, and if I admit that I did not know after this surprising fact about local banks is called to my attention, I will be taking back and contradicting my earlier claim to have known.

Recall the two cases in which Henry has a good, clear look at what he takes to be a barn. (In Case C, there are no barn facades around, but in Case D, the fields are filled with barn facades, but Henry is luckily looking at the only actual barn in the area.) In each case, insert two people in the back seat of the car Henry is driving, and have the first say to the second, "Henry knows that that is a barn." It seems that, in the sense under discussion, what the first person *means* by "knows" in each of the two cases is the same. In Case C what she is saying is true, while in Case D it is false. The presence of the barn facades has changed the *truth value*, but not the *truth conditions* or the meaning (content), of the first person's knowledge attribution.

So attributor factors affect the truth values of knowledge attributions *in a different way* than do subject factors: attributor factors working in such a way that they affect the content of the attribution, but subject factors working in a different way that does not affect its content. These different ways can be explained as follows. Attributor factors set a certain standard the putative subject of knowledge must live up to in order to make the knowledge attribution true: They affect *how good an epistemic position the putative knower must be in to count as knowing*. They thereby affect the truth conditions and the content or meaning of the attribution. Subject factors, on the other hand, determine whether or not the putative subject lives up to the standards that have been set, and thereby can affect the truth value of the attribution *without* affecting its content: They affect *how good an epistemic position the putative knower actually is in*.[18]

To make use of the character/content distinction, the "character" of "S knows that p" is, roughly, that S has a true belief that p and is in a *good enough* epistemic position with respect to p; this remains constant from attribution to attribution. But how good is good enough? This is what varies with context. What the context fixes in determining the "content" of a knowledge attribution is how good an epistemic position S must be in to count as knowing that p. The mentioning of alternatives like painted mules, or barn facades, or changes in banking hours, when there is no special reason for thinking such possibilities likely, can be seen as raising the strength and changing the content of "know" because the ability to rule out such alternatives would only be relevant if one were after a strong form of knowledge (if one were requiring the putative knower to be in a very good position in order to count as knowing).

Subject factors, then, are best construed, not as affecting the truth conditions of knowledge attributions, but rather as affecting whether those truth condi-

tions are satisfied. This fact severely limits RA's prospects for explaining variations in the content of knowledge attributions. RA, for all I've said, may be a
helpful tool for determining or explaining why certain attributions of knowledge have the *truth values* they have.[19] Note, however, that for RA to be successful in this capacity, it *must* allow subject factors to affect the range of relevant
alternatives, for, as Goldman's barn cases (cases C and D) clearly show and as is
evident in any case, subject factors can affect these truth values.

But RA theorists have wanted to make claims about the *meaning* of knowledge attributions:[20] Many of them have thought that the meaning of knowledge attributions changes from case to case depending upon various factors,
and they have thought that this change in meaning *amounts to* a change in the
range of alternatives that are relevant.[21] But we can now see that the content of
a given knowledge attribution cannot be specified by citing what the range of
relevant alternatives is, because that range is a function of subject factors (which
do not affect the content of the attribution) as well as attributor factors (which
do). There can be a drastic change in the range of relevant alternatives from one
attribution to another without there being any change in meaning between the
two attributions, then, because the change in the range of relevant alternatives
can, and often will, be the result of differences in subject factors, which will not
have any affect on the meaning of the attribution.[22]

## III The Objection to Contextualism

Having distinguished contextualism from RA, I will now seek to defend
contextualism from a certain type of important objection. The obvious attraction of contextualism, besides (and closely related to) the resolution of sceptical
arguments it purportedly provides, is that it seems to have the result that very
many of the knowledge attributions and denials uttered by speakers of English
are true – more than any form of invariantism can allow for, and certainly more
than sceptical invariantism can allow for. Thus, recalling the Bank Cases,
contextualism allows us to assert both (1) and (2), and many of us will find both
(1) and (2) compelling. Unfortunately, contextualism seems to be vulnerable
to a certain type of powerful objection which is closely related to the appeal of
(4). Suppose, to recall an example we've already considered, that two people
see some zebras in a zoo. Palle Yourgrau constructs the following conversation,
and claims that "something is amiss" in it:

 *A:* Is that a zebra?
 *B:* Yes, it is a zebra.
 *A:* But can you rule out its being merely a cleverly painted mule?
 *B:* No, I can't.
 *A:* So, you admit you didn't know it was a zebra?
 *B:* No, I did know then that it was a zebra. But after your question, I no longer
   know.[23]

This absurd dialogue is aimed at contextualists who think that the mentioning of a possibility incompatible with what one claims to know is enough to require that one rule the possibility out before one can truly claim to know. But this type of attack can work against other contextualists, also. Dialogues much like the above dialogue but with the following last lines seem equally absurd:

B′: No, I did know then that it was a zebra. But now that it has become so important that it be a zebra, I no longer know.

B″: No, I did know then that it was a zebra. But now that the possibility of its being a painted mule has occurred to me, I no longer know.

The general point of the objection is that whether we know something or not cannot depend on, to use Peter Unger's words, "the contextual interests of those happening to use the terms on a particular occasion" (Unger (1984), p. 37).

How shall the contextualist respond? The objection as I have put it forward, though it explains much of the initial resistance many feel toward contextualism, is based on a mistake. The contextualist believes that certain aspects of the context of an attribution or denial of knowledge attribution affect its content. Knowledge claims, then, can be compared to other sentences containing other context-sensitive words, like "here." One hour ago, I was in my office. Suppose I truly said, "I am here." Now I am in the word processing room. How can I truly say where I was an hour ago? I cannot truly say, "I was here," because I wasn't here; I was there. The meaning of "here", is fixed by the relevant contextual factors (in this case, my location) *of the utterance*, not by my location at the time being talked about.

Similarly, the contextualist may admit that the mentioning of the painted mules possibility affects the conditions under which one can truthfully say that one knows an animal to be a zebra: one now must be able to rule out that possibility, perhaps. But the contextualist need not, and should not, countenance the above dialogue. If in the context of the conversation the possibility of painted mules has been mentioned, and *if* the mere mention of this possibility has an effect on the conditions under which someone can be truly said to "know," then any use of "know" (or its past tense) is so affected, even a use in which one describes one's past condition. B cannot truly say, "I did know then that it was a zebra"; that would be like my saying, "I was here." B *can* say, "My previous knowledge claim was true," just as I can say, "My previous location claim was true." Or so I believe. But saying these things would have a point only if one were interested in the truth value of the earlier claim, rather than in the question of whether in the *present* contextually determined sense one knew and knows, or didn't and doesn't.

Yourgrau writes of the zebra case, "Typically, when someone poses a question regarding whether we really know that P obtains rather than some alternative to P, if we cannot satisfactorily answer the question, we conclude that our earlier claim to know was faulty" (p. 183). But do we? We do not stubbornly repeat ourselves, to be sure: "Still, I know that it is a zebra!" We *might* even say,

"I don't know" or "I didn't know." All of this the contextualist can handle. But do we (or should we) admit that our *earlier* claim was *false*? I am on the witness stand being questioned.

| | |
|---|---|
| *Lawyer:* | Were there any zebras in the zoo on April 23? |
| *Me:* | Yes. |
| *L:* | Do you know that? |
| *M:* | Yes. |
| *L:* | How do you know? |
| *M:* | I saw some there. |
| *L:* | So, you knew that they were zebras? |
| *M:* | Yes. |
| *L:* | Could you rule out the possibility that they were only cleverly painted mules? |
| *M:* | No, I suppose not. |
| *L:* | So, did you really know that they were zebras? |
| *M:* | Is there any reason to think that they were painted mules, of all things? |
| *L:* | Just answer the question! |

Well, how should I answer the question? If there is no special reason to think they were painted mules then *I* certainly wouldn't want to admit that I didn't know they were zebras, but maybe I'm just being stubborn, Suppose I do admit it:

| | |
|---|---|
| *M:* | I guess I didn't *know* that they were zebras. |
| *L:* | Aha! The witness has contradicted his earlier claim. First he says that he knew; now he says he didn't. Now which is it, Mr. DeRose? |

Surely something is amiss in *this* dialogue; my lawyer should object. I haven't contradicted my earlier claim, as much as it looks as if I have. It would be as if the following had occurred. While standing in a bright yellow room, I said, "This room is yellow." The lawyer then dragged me by the ear into a room in which all was grey and got me to say, "This room is grey," and now he is jumping all over me: "First he says, 'This room is yellow,' then he says, 'This room is grey.' Which is it?" The contextualist maintains that something very much like this has happened in my original dialogue with the lawyer. Of course, there is room for the invariantist to deny this contextualist claim. But it is *far* from clear that in cases like the one Yourgrau brings to our attention, we should admit that our earlier claim was false or that our later claim contradicts it.

So, the objection that whether we know something or not does not depend on contextual factors of the type we have been considering is based on a mistake. But Unger does not make this mistake when he raises an objection similar to the one we have been considering.[24] He writes of "our belief that the semantics of these expressions ["know" is one of the expressions being considered] is appropriately *independent*, that the conditions do not depend on the contextual interests of those happening to use the terms on a particular occasion" (Unger (1984), p. 37). Insofar as we do have *this* belief, that the conditions *for truly saying* that someone knows do not depend on the sorts of contextual factors we have been discussing, then contextualism goes against at least one of our beliefs. But it seems that much of the appeal of this belief derives from the plausibility of the thesis (with which the contextualist can agree) that whether *we know* something or not does not depend on such factors. The answer to the question, "Does she know?", in whatever context it is asked, including a philosophy paper, is determined by facts independent of contextual factors (or what I have been calling attributor factors). These contextual or attributor factors affect the content of the question, but once the question is asked with a specific content, its answer is determined by subject factors, which are precisely the kinds of factors which *can* very plausibly be thought to affect whether or not the subject knows. Going back to our opening examples, the contextualist can affirm (3) *in any context in which it is uttered*: If I know in Case A, then I know in Case B. Of course, the contextualist must deny (4), and (4) sounds very plausible, but much of the appeal of (4) comes from the plausibility of (3). And since we *must* give up either (1), (2), or (4), those who, like me, find (1) and (2) *very* plausible will be well-motivated to give up (4), especially since (3) can still be affirmed.

In general, then, when it looks as if the contextualist has to say something strongly counter-intuitive, what he must say turns out to be, on the contrary, something fairly theoretical concerning the truth conditions of certain sentences. Do we really have strong intuitions about such things? At any rate, the contextualist can go along with the simple facts that we all recognize: that if I know in Case A, then I know in Case B, and that whether we know something or not does not typically depend on our current interests or on other such contextual factors.

### Notes

I am indebted to Robert M. Adams, Rogers Albritton, Peter Unger, and an anonymous referee for *Philosophy and Phenomenological Research* for comments on previous drafts of this paper.

1  I take the terms "contextualism" and "invariantism" from Unger (1984).
2  The importance of this theory will not be confined to knowledge attributions. For instance, in DeRose (1991) I argue that S's assertion, "It is possible that P," where the embedded P is in the indicative mood, is true if and only if (1) no member of the relevant community *knows* that P is false and (2) there is no relevant way by which members of the relevant community can come to *know* that P is false. As I there argue, there is a great deal of flexibility in the matter of who is and is not to be counted as a member of the relevant community and what is and is not to be counted as a relevant way of coming to know: That these matters are determined by aspects of the contexts in which the statement is made. If, as I am here defending, there is a contextually-determined variation on how good an epistemic position one must be in to count as knowing, then – since epistemic possibilities have entirely to do with what is and is not known and what can and cannot come to be known in certain ways – this variation will affect the content of epistemic modal

statements as well: As the standards for knowledge go up, and it becomes harder and harder for a knowledge attribution to be true, it will become easier and easier for an assertion of epistemic possibility to be true.

3    That the importance of being right is an important contextual factor is suggested in Austin (1961), p. 76, fn. 1. Dretske denies the importance of this factor in (1981a), pp. 375–6.

4    David Lewis (1979) stresses this contextual factor, presenting an interesting account of how the mentioning of sceptical possibilities can affect the range of relevant alternatives by means of what he calls a "rule of accommodation." In Chapter 3 (see especially section I) of DeRose (1990), I argue that Lewis's account is not complete, and I locate an independent mechanism of standard changing which, I now believe, is *at least* as important (and probably considerably more important) to the application of contextualism to the problem of scepticism as is the mechanism Lewis has located.

5    Alvin I. Goldman (1976) stresses the importance of what possibilities the speaker is considering.

6    While Unger does not even consider the view that the standards for true knowledge attributions don't change but are held constant at a fairly low level, non-sceptical invariantism is defended (at least conditionally) by Robert Hambourger (1987). Hambourger argues that *if* the standards are constant (Hambourger does not believe that this antecedent is true), then they must be fairly low (pp. 256–7). In the terminology I have introduced, Hambourger is arguing that if some form of invariantism is correct, it must be a form of *non-sceptical* invariantism.

7    My main reason for discounting as relevant to truth conditions the matter of what the speaker is thinking, at least with respect to spoken interactions between people, is that I don't think that one should be able, merely by a private act of one's own thought to drastically "strengthen" the content of "know" in such a way that one can truly say to someone who is quite certain that he is wearing pants, "You don't know you're wearing pants," without there having been anything in the conversation to indicate that the strength of "know" has been raised. There *might* yet be a fairly tight connection between what raises the truth condition standards and what speakers *tend to* think or perhaps what they *should* think of the standards as being. Perhaps the truth conditions standards are what a typical speaker would take them to be or should take them to be, given what has gone on in the conversation. But it seems unfair to one's interlocutor for the truth condition standards of a *public, spoken* knowledge attribution to be changed by an idiosyncratic, private decision. It is far more plausible to suppose that when one is *thinking to one's self* about what is or is not "known," the content of "know" is directly tied to the strength the thinker intends.

8    While, as I've said, contextualist theories (including contextualist versions of RA) are almost invariably developed with an eye towards philosophical scepticism, the most thoroughly worked out contextualist attempts to resolve the problem of scepticism that I am aware of are to be found in Unger (1986), Cohen (1988) (see also Cohen (1987)), and DeRose (1990), especially Chapter 3. Fred Dretske has also applied this type of theory of knowledge to the problem of scepticism in several places. See Dretske (1970), (1971), (1981a), and (1981b).

9    See Unger (1975).

10   A typical objection one meets in presenting contextualism, as I know from personal experience, is: "How can *our* context have anything to do with whether or not *Henry* knows?", where Henry is a character in an example and so is not present

in the room.

11  See Goldman (1976), p. 772; Stine (1976), p. 249; and Dretske (1970), p. 1022.

12  See Dretske (1970), pp. 1015–16.

13  Please note that by "subject factors" I do *not* mean *subjective* (as opposed to objective) factors. I rather mean factors having to do with the putative *subject* of knowledge and her surroundings (as opposed to the attributor of knowledge).

14  Thus, what Goldman calls the "first view" of RA, according to which "a complete specification" of the putative knower's situation determines "a unique set of relevant alternatives" (pp. 775–6), is an invariantist version of RA. Goldman does not endorse this view; he says he is "attracted by the second view" (p. 777), which clearly is a contextualist version of RA.

15  Some factors, I believe, will both affect how good an epistemic position the speaker/ putative knower is in *and* (at least according to the contextualist) how good a position he must be in to make his knowledge claims true. Thus, they will be both subject and attributor factors.

16  I further discuss the importance of this distinction between subject factors and attributor factors and the resulting contextualist view according to which content varies in response to attributor factors in Chapter 1 of DeRose (1990). In particular, I there discuss, in addition to the issues treated in the present paper, the advantages such a view according to which content varies over a *range* has over theories like that put forward in Malcolm (1952) according to which there are two distinct senses of 'know': a strong sense and a weak one.

17  See Kaplan (1989), esp. pp. 500–7.

18  Unger makes a similar division in (1986), where he distinguishes between the "profile of the context," which corresponds roughly to how good a position the putative knower must be in to count as knowing, and the "profile of the facts," which corresponds roughly to how good a position the putative knower actually is in (see esp. pp. 139–40). Unger does not there discuss RA, and so does not use the distinction to distinguish contextualism from RA. He does, however, introduce an important complication which I have ignored in this paper, since it has little effect on the points I'm making here. Unger points out that there are many different aspects of knowledge and that in different contexts, we may have different demands regarding various of these aspects. Thus, for example, in one context, we may demand a very high degree of confidence on the subject's part before we will count him as knowing while demanding *relatively* little in the way of his belief being non-accidentally true. In a different context, on the other hand, we may have very stringent standards for non-accidentality but relatively lax standards for subject confidence. As Unger points out, then, things are not quite as simple as I make them out to be: Our standards are not just a matter of how good an epistemic position the subject must be in, but rather of how good in which respects. Stewart Cohen also suggests a related division, his more closely aligned with the spirit of RA. See note 22 below.

19  Thus what I take to be RA's *basic idea* – that to know that P, one must be able to rule out all of the relevant alternatives to P – may be sound.

20  RA's *basic idea* (see note 19, above) is not about contextual *variations in meanings*. Indeed, as I've pointed out, an RA theorist can be an invariantist. It is, then, in going *beyond* this basic idea that RA theorists have, by my lights, gone wrong by tying the meaning of a given attribution too closely to what the range of relevant alternatives is.

21  In addition to the Stine passage we have looked at, see, for example, Goldman

(1976), pp. 775–7 (esp. p. 777), where Goldman seems to think that *what proposition is expressed* by a given knowledge attribution is specified by what the range of relevant alternatives is. Something similar seems to be suggested in Lewis (1979), esp. pp. 354–5. Lewis seems to think of the "conversational score" of a given context, with respect to knowledge attributions and epistemic modal statements, to be something that can be specified by giving the range of possibilities that are relevant in that context.

22   A different view which escapes this problem but is still well within the spirit of RA is that the character of "S knows that p" is that S has a true belief that p and can rule out all alternatives to p that are *sufficiently probable*. The context of utterance can then be seen as fixing the content by determining just how probable an alternative must be to count as being sufficiently probable. Something like this alternative view is suggested by Cohen (1988), according to whom context determines "how probable an alternative must be in order to be relevant" (p. 96). (This view is only *suggested* by Cohen because he never says that this probability level for alternative relevance is *all* that context fixes in determining the content of an attribution.) Expanding this idea, we might then take aspects of the putative knower's situation to affect how *probable a given alternative is*. Instead of the meaning being specified by the range of alternatives that are relevant, this view, more plausibly, has it specified by the standards (in terms of probability) alternatives must meet to count as relevant. This still seems more precise than my admittedly vague talk of *how good an epistemic position* one must be in to count as knowing. I fear, however, that this precisification will not work. Among other reasons for doubting that the notion of probability can do all the work assigned to it here is this: The complication Unger raises about the many different aspects of knowledge (see note 18 above) shows that no single measure like the probability an alternative must have to be relevant can capture all that context does in fixing the content of a knowledge attribution. This probability standard of alternative relevance can be, *at best*, one among several aspects of knowledge the standards for which are fixed by context.

23   Yourgrau (1983), p. 183. The absurdity of such a conversation, along with the worry that it causes problems for theories of knowledge attributions like the one I am investigating, was originally suggested to me by Rogers Albritton, who has been making such suggestions since well before Yourgrau's article came out.

24   Actually, Unger does make this mistake at one point, not about knowledge but about flatness. Throughout his epistemological writings, Unger compares knowledge attributions with claims about the flatness of objects. In (1984), Unger describes an invariantist semantics for "flat" according to which an object must be as flat as possible in order for a sentence like "That is flat" to be true of it, and a contextualist semantics for "flat" according to which how flat something must be in order for a sentence like "That is flat" to be true of it varies with context, and he claims that there is no determinate fact as to which semantics is correct. In attacking the contextualist semantics for "flat," Unger writes: "How can the matter of whether a given surface is *flat*, in contradistinction to, say, whether it is suitable for our croquet game, depend upon the interests in that surface taken by those who happen to converse about it? This appears to go against our better judgement" ((1984), p. 39). But the contextualist need not and should not claim that "the matter of whether or not a given surface is flat" depends "upon the interests in that surface taken by those who happen to converse about it," although the contextualist *will* say that the truth conditions *for the sentence* "That is flat" do depend upon such contextual interests. I believe that the above passage is just a slip on Unger's

part; he is usually more careful in making his attack on contextualism. But it is revealing that Unger makes this slip: It shows how easy it is to confuse the claim (a) that whether or not something is flat or is known does not depend on contextual interests with the claim (b) that the truth conditions for a sentence about flatness or about knowledge do not depend on contextual interests, which does not follow from (a).

## Works Cited

Austin, J. L., (1961) "Other Minds," in J. L. Austin, *Philosophical Papers* (Oxford University Press): 44–84.

Cohen, Stewart, (1987) "Knowledge, Context, and Social Standards," *Synthese* 73: 3–26.

——, (1988) "How to be a Fallibilist," *Philosophical Perspectives* 2: 91–123.

DeRose, Keith, (1990) "Knowledge, Epistemic Possibility, and Scepticism," UCLA doctoral dissertation.

——, (1991) "Epistemic Possibilities," *The Philosophical Review* 100: 581–605.

Dretske, Fred, (1970) "Epistemic Operators," *Journal of Philosophy* 67: 1007–23.

——, (1971) "Conclusive Reasons," *Australasian Journal of Philosophy* 49: 1–22.

——, (1981a) "The Pragmatic Dimension of Knowledge, *Philosophical Studies* 40: 363–78.

——, (1981b) *Knowledge and the Flow of Information* (Cambridge, Massachusetts: MIT Press/Bradford Books).

Goldman, Alvin I., (1976) "Discrimination and Perceptual Knowledge," *Journal of Philosophy* 73: 771–91.

Hambourger, Robert, (1987) "Justified Assertion and the Relativity of Knowledge," *Philosophical Studies* 51: 241–69.

Kaplan, David, (1989) "Demonstratives," in J. Almog, J. Perry, H. Wettstein, ed., *Themes from Kaplan* (Oxford University Press): 481–563.

Lewis, David, (1979) "Scorekeeping in a Language Game," *Journal of Philosophical Logic* 8: 339–59.

Malcolm, Norman, (1952) "Knowledge and Belief," *Mind* 51: 178–89.

Stine, Gail C., (1976) "Skepticism, Relevant Alternatives, and Deductive Closure," *Philosophical Studies* 29: 249–61.

Unger, Peter, (1975) *Ignorance: A Case for Scepticism* (Oxford University Press).

——, (1984) *Philosophical Relativity* (Minneapolis: University of Minnesota Press).

——, (1986) "The Cone Model of Knowledge," *Philosophical Topics* 14: 125–78.

Yourgrau, Palle, (1983) "Knowledge and Relevant Alternatives," *Synthese* 55: 175–90.

# 9 Taking Subjectivity into Account

## *Lorraine Code*

### 1 The Problem

Suppose epistemologists should succeed in determining a set of necessary and sufficient conditions for justifying claims that "$S$ knows that $p$" across a range of "typical" instances. Suppose, further, that these conditions could silence the skeptic who denies that human beings can have certain knowledge of the world. Would the epistemological project then be completed? I shall maintain that it would not.

There is no doubt that a discovery of necessary and sufficient conditions that offered a response to the skeptic would count as a major epistemological breakthrough, if such conditions could be found. But once one seriously entertains the hypothesis that knowledge is a *construct* produced by cognitive agents within social practices and acknowledges the variability of agents and practices across social groups, the possible scope even of "definitive" justificatory strategies for "$S$-knows-that-$p$" claims reveals itself to be very narrow indeed. My argument here is directed, in part, against the breadth of scope that many epistemologists accord to such claims. I am suggesting that necessary and sufficient conditions in the "received" sense – by which I mean conditions that hold for any knower, regardless of her or his identity, interests, and circumstances, in other words of her or his subjectivity – could conceivably be discovered only for a narrow range of artificially isolated and purified empirical knowledge claims, which might be paradigmatic by fiat, but are unlikely to be so "in fact."

In this essay, I focus on "$S$-knows-that-$p$" claims and refer to "$S$-knows-that-$p$ epistemologies" because of the emblematic nature of such claims in Anglo-American epistemology. My suggestion is not that discerning necessary and sufficient conditions for the justification of such claims is the sole, or even the central, epistemological preoccupation. Rather, I use this label, "$S$-knows-that-$p$," as a trope that permits easy reference to the epistemologies of the mainstream. I use it for three principal reasons. First, I want to mark the positivist-empiricist orientation of these epistemologies, which is both generated and enforced by appeals to such paradigms. Second, I want to show that these paradigms prompt and sustain a belief that universally necessary and sufficient conditions can indeed be found. Third – and perhaps most importantly – I want to distance this discussion from analyses that privilege scientific knowledge, as "$S$-knows-that-$p$" epistemologies implicitly, and often explicitly, do, and hence to locate my argument within an "epistemology of everyday lives."

Coincidentally – but only, I think, coincidentally – the dominant epistemologies of modernity, with their Enlightenment legacy and later infusion with positivist-empiricist principles, have defined themselves around ideals of pure objectivity and value-neutrality. These ideals are best suited to govern evaluations of the knowledge of knowers who can be considered capable of achieving a "view from nowhere"[1] that allows them, through the autonomous exercise of their reason, to transcend particularity and contingency. The ideals presuppose a universal, homogeneous, and essential human nature that allows knowers to be substitutable for one another. Indeed, for "S-knows-that-$p$" epistemologies, knowers worthy of that title can act as "surrogate knowers" who are able to put themselves in anyone else's place and know her or his circumstances and interests in just the same way as she or he would know them.[2] Hence those circumstances and interests are deemed epistemologically irrelevant. Moreover, by virtue of their professed disinterestedness, these ideals erase the possibility of analyzing the interplay between emotion and reason, and obscure connections between knowledge and power. Hence they lend support to the conviction that cognitive products are as neutral – as politically innocent – as the processes that allegedly produce them. Such epistemologies implicitly assert that if one cannot see "from nowhere" (or equivalently, from an ideal observation position that could be anywhere and everywhere) – if one cannot take up an epistemological position that mirrors the "original position" of "the moral point of view" – then one cannot *know* anything at all. If one cannot transcend subjectivity and the particularities of its "locations," then there is no knowledge worth analyzing.

The strong prescriptions and proscriptions that I have highlighted reveal that "S-knows-that-$p$" epistemologies work with a closely specified kind of knowing. That knowledge is by no means representative of "human knowledge," or "knowledge in general" (if such terms retain a legitimate reference in these postmodern times), either diachronically (across recorded history), or synchronically (across the late-twentieth-century epistemic terrain). Nor have *theories* of knowledge throughout the history of philosophy developed uniformly around these same exclusions and inclusions. Not Plato, Spinoza, nor Hume, for example, would have denied that there are interconnections between reason and "the passions"; not stoics, Marxists, phenomenologists, pragmatists, nor followers of the later Wittgenstein would represent knowledge-seeking as a disinterested pursuit, disconnected from everyday concerns. And these are but a few exceptions to the "rule" that has come to govern the epistemology of the Anglo-American mainstream.

The *positivism* of positivist-empiricist epistemologies has been instrumental in ensuring the paradigmatic status of "S-knows-that-$p$" claims, and all that is believed to follow from them.[3] For positivist epistemologists, sensory observation in ideal observation conditions is the privileged source of knowledge, offering the best promise of certainty. Knowers are detached, neutral spectators, and the objects of knowledge are separate from them, inert items in the observational knowledge-gathering process. Findings are presented in *propositions* ( $S$ knows that $p$ ), which are verifiable by appeals to the observational data. Each individual knowledge-seeker is singly and separately accountable to the evidence, though the belief is that *his* cognitive efforts are replicable by any other individual knower in the same circumstances. The aim of knowledge-seeking is to achieve the capacity to predict, manipulate, and control the behavior of the objects known.

The fact/value distinction that informs present-day epistemology owes its strictest formulation to the positivist legacy. For positivists, value statements are not verifiable and hence are meaningless; they must not be permitted to distort the facts. And it is in the writings of the logical positivists and their heirs that one finds the most definitive modern articulations of the supremacy of scientific knowledge (for which read: the knowledge attainable in physics). Hence, for example, Karl Popper writes: "Epistemology I take to be the theory of *scientific knowledge*."[4]

From a positivistically derived conception of scientific knowledge comes the ideal objectivity that is alleged to be achievable by any knower who deserves the label. Physical science is represented as the site of controlled and objective knowing at its best, its practitioners as knowers *par excellence*. The positivistic separation of the contexts of discovery and justification produces the conclusion that even though information gathering (discovery) may sometimes be contaminated by the circumstantial peculiarities of everyday life, justificatory procedures can effectively purify the final cognitive product – the knowledge – from any such taint. Under the aegis of positivism, attempts to give epistemological weight to the provenance of knowledge claims – to grant justificatory or explanatory significance to social- or personal-historical situations, for example – risk committing the "genetic fallacy." More specifically, claims that there is epistemological insight to be gained from understanding the psychology of knowers, or analyzing their socio-cultural locations, invite dismissal either as "psychologism" or as projects belonging to the sociology of knowledge. For epistemological purists, many of these pursuits can provide anecdotal information, but none contributes to the real business of epistemology.

In this sketch I have represented the positivist credo at its starkest because it is these stringent aspects of its program that have trickled down not just to produce the tacit ideals of the epistemological orthodoxy, but to inform even well-educated laypersons' conceptions of what it means to be objective, and of the authoritative status of modern science.[5] Given the spectacular successes of science and technology, it is no wonder that the scientific method should appear to offer the best available route to reliable, objective knowledge not just of matters scientific, but of everything one could want to know, from what makes a car run, to what makes a person happy. It is no wonder that reports to the effect that "Science has proved . . ." carry an immediate presumption of truth. Furthermore, the positivist program offered a methodology that would extend not just across the natural sciences, but to the human/social sciences as well. All scientific inquiry – including inquiry in the human sciences – was to be conducted on the model of natural scientific inquiry, especially as it is practiced in physics.[6] Knowing people, too, could be scientific to the extent that it could be based in empirical observations of predictable, manipulable patterns of behavior.

I have focused on features of mainstream epistemology that tend to sustain the belief that a discovery of necessary and sufficient conditions for justifying

"$S$-knows-that-$p$" claims could count as the last milestone on the epistemological journey. Such claims are distilled, simplified, observational knowledge claims, objectively derived, prepositionally formulable, and empirically testable. The detail of the role they play varies according to whether the position they figure in is foundational or coherentist; whether it is externalist or internalist. My intent is not to suggest that "$S$-knows-that-$p$" formulations capture the essence of these disparate epistemic orientations, nor reduce them to one common principle. Rather, I am contending that certain reasonably constant features of their diverse functions across a range of inquiries – features that derive at least indirectly from the residual prestige of positivism and its veneration of an idealized scientific methodology – produce epistemologies for which the places $S$ and $p$ can be indiscriminately filled across an inexhaustible range of subject matters. The legislated (not "found") context-independence of the model generates the conclusion that knowledge worthy of the name must transcend the particularities of experience to achieve objective purity and value neutrality. Within this model the issue of taking subjectivity into account simply does not arise.

Yet despite the disclaimers, hidden subjectivities produce these epistemologies, and sustain their hegemony in a curiously circular process. It is true that, in selecting examples, the context in which $S$ knows or $p$ occurs is rarely considered relevant, for the assumption is that only in abstraction from contextual confusion can clear, unequivocal knowledge claims be submitted for analysis. Yet those examples tend to be selected – whether by chance or by design – from the experiences of a privileged group of people, then to be presented as paradigmatic for knowledge as such. Hence a certain range of contexts is, in effect, presupposed. Historically, the philosopher arrogated that privilege to himself, maintaining that an investigation of his mental processes could reveal the workings of human thought. In Baconian and later positivist-empiricist thought, as I have suggested, paradigmatic privilege belongs more specifically to standardized, faceless observers, or to scientists. (The latter, at least, have usually been white and male.) Their ordinary observational experiences provide the "simples" of which knowledge is comprised: observational simples caused, almost invariably, by medium-sized physical objects such as apples, envelopes, coins, sticks, and colored patches. The tacit assumption is that such objects are part of the basic experiences of every putative knower, and that more complex knowledge – or scientific knowledge – consists in elaborated or scientifically controlled versions of such experiences. Rarely in the literature, either historical or modern, is there more than a passing reference to knowing other people, except occasionally to a recognition (observational information) that this is a man – whereas that is a door, or a robot. Neither with respect to material objects, nor to other people, is there any sense of how these "knowns" figure in a person's life.

Not only do these epistemic restrictions suppress the context in which objects are known, they also account for the fact that, apart from simple objects – and even there it is questionable – one cannot, on this model, know anything well enough to do very much with it. One can only *perceive* it, usually at a distance. In consequence, most of the more complex, contentious, and locationally variable aspects of cognitive practice are excluded from epistemological analysis. Hence the knowledge that epistemologists analyze is not of concrete or unique aspects of the physical/social world. It is of *instances* rather than particulars; the norms of formal sameness obscure practical and experiential differences to produce a picture of a homogeneous epistemic community, comprised of discrete individuals with uniform access to the stuff of which knowledge is made.

The project of remapping the epistemic terrain that I envisage is subversive, even anarchistic, in challenging and seeking to displace some of the most sacred principles of standard Anglo-American epistemologies. It abandons the search for – denies the possibility of – the disinterested and dislocated view from nowhere. More subversively, it asserts the political investedness of most knowledge-producing activity, and insists upon the accountability – the epistemic responsibilities – of knowing subjects to the community, not just to the evidence.[7]

Because my engagement in the project is prompted, specifically, by a conviction that *gender* must be put in place as a primary analytic category, I start by assuming that it is impossible to sustain the presumption of gender-neutrality that is central to standard epistemologies: the presumption that gender has nothing to do with knowledge, that the mind has no sex, that reason is alike in all men, and "man" embraces "woman."[8] But gender is not an enclosed category, for it is interwoven, always, with such other sociopolitical-historical locations as class, race, and ethnicity, to mention only a few. It is experienced differently, and plays differently into structures of power and dominance, at its diverse intersections with other specificities. From these multiply describable locations the world looks quite different from the way it might look "from nowhere." Homogenizing those differences under a range of standard or "typical" instances always invites the question "standard or typical for whom?"[9] Answers to that question must, necessarily, take subjectivity into account.

My thesis, then, is that a "variable construction" hypothesis[10] requires epistemologists to pay as much attention to the nature and situation – the location – of $S$ as they commonly pay to the content of $p$; that a constructivist reorientation requires epistemologists to take subjective factors – factors that pertain to the circumstances of the subject, $S$ – centrally into account in evaluative and justificatory procedures. Yet the socially located, critically dialogical nature of this reoriented epistemological project preserves a realist commitment which ensures that it will not slide into subjectivism. This caveat is vitally important. Although I shall conclude this essay with a plea for a hybrid breed of relativism, my contention will be that realism and relativism are by no means incompatible. Hence although I argue the need to excise the positivist side of the positivist-empiricist couple, I retain a modified commitment to the empiricist side, for several reasons.

I have suggested that the stark conception of objectivity that characterizes much contemporary epistemology derives from the infusion of empiricism with positivistic values. Jettison those values, and an empiricist core remains that urges the significance, for survival and emancipation, of achieving reliable knowledge of the physical and social world.[11] People need to be able to explain the world and their circumstances as part of it; hence they need to be able to assume its "reality" in some minimal sense. The fact of the world's intractability to intervention and to wishful thinking is the strongest evidence of its independence from human knowers. Earthquakes, trees, disease, attitudes, and social arrangements are *there*, requiring different kinds of reaction, and (sometimes) intervention. People cannot hope to transform their circumstances and hence to realize emancipatory goals if their explanations cannot at once account for the intractable dimensions of the world, and engage appropriately with its patently malleable features. Hence it is necessary to achieve some match between knowledge and "reality," even when the reality at issue consists primarily in social productions, such as racism or tolerance, oppression or equality of opportunity. A reconstructed epistemological project has to retain an empirical-realist core that can negotiate the fixities and the less stable constructs of the physical-social world, while refusing to endorse the objectivism of the positivist legacy, or the subjectivism of radical relativism.

## 2   Autonomous Solidarity

Feminist critiques of epistemology, of the philosophy of science, and of social science have demonstrated that the ideals of the autonomous reasoner – the dislocated, disinterested observer – and the epistemologies they inform are the artifacts of a small, privileged group of educated, usually prosperous, white men.[12] Their circumstances enable them to believe that they are materially and even affectively autonomous, and to imagine that they are nowhere or everywhere, even as they occupy an unmarked position of privilege. Moreover, the ideals of rationality and objectivity that have guided and inspired theorists of knowledge throughout the history of western philosophy have been constructed through processes of suppressing the attributes and experiences commonly associated with femaleness and underclass social status: emotion, connection, practicality, sensitivity, idiosyncracy.[13] These systematic excisions of "otherness" attest to a presumed – and willed – belief in the stability of a social order that the presumers have good reasons to believe that they can ensure, because they occupy the positions that determine the norms of conduct and inquiry. Yet all that these convictions demonstrate is that ideal objectivity is a tacit generalization from the *subjectivity* of quite a small social group, albeit a group that has the power, security, and prestige to believe that its experiences and normative ideals hold generally across the social order, thus producing a group of like-minded practitioners ("we") and dismissing "others" as deviant, aberrant ("they"). These groupings are generated more as a by-product of systematically ignoring concrete experiences, of working with an idealized conception of experience "in general," so to speak, than as a conscious and intentional practice of reifying experiences that are specifically *theirs*. The experiences that epistemologists tend to draw upon are usually no more "experiential" than the "individuals" to whom the experiences allegedly belong are individuated. These are the generic experiences of generic epistemic subjects. But the end result is to focus philosophical analysis on examples that draw upon the commonplaces of privileged, white, male lives, and to assume that everyone else's life will, unquestionably, be like theirs.

Richard Foley's book, *The Theory of Epistemic Rationality*, illustrates my point. Foley bases his theory on a criterion of first-person persuasiveness, which he calls a "subjective foundationalism." He presents exemplary knowledge claims in the standard "*S*-knows-that-*p*" rubric. Whether or not a propositional knowledge claim turns out to be warranted for any putative knower/believer will depend upon its being "uncontroversial," "argument-proof" *for that individual*, "in the sense that all possible arguments against it are implausible."[14] Foley is not concerned that his "subjective" appeal could force him into subjectivism or solipsism. His unconcern, I suggest, is a product, precisely, of the confidence with which he expands his references to *S* into "we." Foley's appeals to *S*'s normality – to his being "one of us," "just like the rest of us" – to his not having "crazy, bizarre [or] outlandish beliefs,"[15] or "weird goals," "weird perceptions,"[16] underpin his assumption that in speaking for *S* he is speaking for everyone – or at least for "all of *us*." Hence he refers to what "Any normal individual on reflection would be likely to think,"[17] without pausing to consider the presumptuousness of the terminology. There are no problems, no politics of "we-saying" visible here; this is an epistemology oblivious to its experiential and political specificity. Yet its appeals to a taken-for-granted normality, achieved through commonality, align it with all of the positions of power and privilege that unthinkingly consign to epistemic limbo people who profess "crazy, bizarre, or outlandish" beliefs, and negate their claims to the authority that knowledge confers. In its assumed political innocence it prepares the ground for the practices that make "knowledge" an honorific and ultimately exclusionary label, restricting it to the products of a narrow subset of the cognitive activities of a closely specified group. The histories of women, and of other "others," attempting to count as members of that group are justifiedly bitter. In short, the assumptions that accord "*S*-knows-that-*p*" propositions a paradigmatic place generate epistemologies that derive from a privileged subjective specificity to inform social-political structures of dominance and submission. Such epistemologies – and Foley's is just one example – mask the specificity of their origins beneath the putative neutrality of the rubric.

Hence although subjectivity does not figure in any explicit sense in the formulaic, purely place-holder status of *S* in Foley's theory, there is no doubt that the assumptions that allow him to presume *S*'s normality – and apolitical status – in effect work to install a very specific conception of subjectivity in the *S*-place: a conception that demands analysis if the full significance of the inclusions and exclusions it produces are to be understood. These "subjects" are interchangeable only across a narrow range of implicit group membership. And the group in question is the dominant social group in western capitalist societies: propertied, educated, white men. Its presumed political innocence needs to be challenged. Critics must ask who this epistemology is for, whose interests it serves, and whose it neglects or suppresses in the process.[18]

I am not suggesting that "*S*-knows-that-*p*" epistemologies are the only ones that rely on silent assumptions of solidarity, however. Issues about the implicit politics of "we-saying" infect even the work of such an anti-foundationalist, anti-objectivist, anti-individualist as Richard Rorty, whom many feminists are tempted to see as an ally in their successor-epistemology projects. Again, the manner in which these issues arise is instructive.

In that part of his work with which feminist and other revisionary episte-mologists rightly find an affinity,[19] Rorty develops a sustained argument to the effect that the "foundational" (for which read "empiricist/positivist, and ra-tionalist") projects of western philosophy have been unable to fulfill their promise. That is to say, they have not been successful in establishing their claims that knowledge must – and can – be grounded in absolute truth and that necessary and sufficient conditions can be ascertained. Rorty turns his back on the (in his view) ill-conceived project of seeking absolute epistemic foundations, to advo-cate a process of "continuing . . . conversation rather than . . . discovering truth."[20] The conversation will be informed and inspired by the work of such "edifying philosophers" as Dewey, Wittgenstein, Heidegger, and (latterly) Gadamer. It will move away from the search for foundations to look within communally created and communally available history, tradition, and culture for the only possible bases for truth claims. Relocating questions about knowl-edge and truth to positions within the conversations of humankind does seem to break the thrall of objectivist detachment and to create a forum for dialogic, cooperative debate of the epistemological issues of everyday, practical life. Yet the question is how open that forum would – or could – be; who would have a voice in Rorty's conversations? They are not likely, I suspect, to be those who fall under Foley's exclusions.

In his paper "Solidarity or Objectivity?" Rorty reaffirms his repudiation of objectivist epistemologies to argue that "For the pragmatist [i.e., for him, as pragmatist] . . . 'knowledge' is, like 'truth,' simply a compliment paid to the beliefs which *we* think so well justified that, for the moment, further justifica-tion is not needed."[21] He eschews epistemological analysis of truth, rationality, and knowledge to concentrate on questions about "what self-image our society should have of itself."[22] Contending that philosophy is a frankly ethnocentric project, and affirming that "there is only the dialogue, only *us*," he advocates throwing out "the last residues of 'trans-cultural rationality.'"[23] It is evidently his belief that communal solidarity, guided by principles of liberal tolerance – and of Nietzschean irony – will provide solace in this foundationless world, *and* will check the tendencies of ethnocentricity to oppress, marginalize, or colo-nize.

Yet as Nancy Fraser aptly observes: "Rorty homogenizes social space, assum-ing tendentiously that there are no deep social cleavages capable of generating conflicting solidarities and opposing 'we's.'"[24] Hence he can presume that there will be no disagreement about the best self-image for "our" society; he can fail to note – or at least to take seriously – the androcentricity, class-centricity, and all of the other centricities that his solidarity claims produce. The very goal of achieving "as much intersubjective agreement as possible," of extending "the reference of 'us' as far as we can,"[25] with the belief that tolerance will do the job when conflicts arise, is unlikely to convince members of groups who have never felt solidarity with the representers of the self-image of the society. The very promise of inclusion in the extension of that "we" is as likely to occasion anxiety as it is to offer hope. Naming ourselves as "we" empowers us, but it always risks disempowering others. The "we-saying," then, of assumed or negotiated solidarity must always be submitted to critical analysis.

Now, it is neither surprising nor outrageous that epistemologies should derive out of specific human interests. Indeed, it is much less plausible to contend that they do not; human cognitive agents, after all, have made them. Why would they not bear the marks of their makers? Nor does the implication of human interests in theories of knowledge, *prima facie*, invite censure. It does alert epistemologists to the need for case-by-case analysis and critique of the sources out of which claims to objectivity and neutrality are made.[26] More pointedly, it forces the conclusion that if the ideal of objectivity cannot pretend to have been established in accordance with its own demands, then it has no right to the theoretical hegemony to which it lays claim.

Central to the program of taking subjectivity into account that feminist epistemological inquiry demands, then, is a critical analysis of that very politics of "we-saying" that objectivist epistemologies conceal from view. Whenever an "S-knows-that-$p$" claim is declared paradigmatic, the first task is to analyze the constitution of the group(s) by whom and for whom it is accorded that status.

## 3 Subjects and Objects

I have noted that the positivist-empiricist influence on the principal epistemologies of the mainstream manifests itself in assumptions that verifiable knowledge – knowledge worthy of the name – can be analyzed into observational simples; that the methodology of the natural sciences, and especially physics, is a model for productive inquiry; and that the goal of developing a "unified science" translates into a "unity of knowledge" project where all knowledge – including everyday and social-scientific knowledge about people – would be modelled on the knowledge ideally obtainable in physics. Reliance upon "S-knows-that-$p$" paradigms sustains these convictions. In the preceding section I have shown that these paradigms, in practice, are problematic with respect to the subjects (= knowers) who occupy the $S$ position, whose subjectivity and accountability are effaced in the formal structure. In this section, I shall show that they are, ultimately, oppressive for subjects who come to occupy the $p$ position – who become objects of knowledge – for their subjectivity and specificity are reduced to interchangeable, observable variables. When more elaborated knowledge claims are at issue – theories and interpretations of human behaviors and institutions are the salient examples here – these paradigms generate a presumption in favor of apolitical epistemic postures that is at best deceptive, at worst dangerous, both politically and epistemologically.

This last claim requires some explanation. The purpose of singling out *para-*

*digmatic* knowledge claims is to establish exemplary instances that will map, feature by feature, onto knowledge that differs from the paradigm in content, across a wide range of possibilities. Strictly speaking, paradigms are meant to capture just the formal, structural character of legitimate (= appropriately verifiable) knowledge. But their paradigmatic status generates presumptions in favor of much wider resemblances across the epistemic terrain than the model, on its strictest reading, permits. Hence it looks as if many more of the paradigm's features than the purely formal ones are generalizable to knowledge that differs not just in complexity, but in kind, from the simplified, paradigmatic example. Of particular interest in the present context is the fact that paradigms are commonly selected from mundane experiences of virtually indubitable facticity ("Susan knows that the door is open"): of simple objects in the world that seem to be just neutrally *there*. There appear to be no political stakes in knowing such a fact. Moreover, it looks (at least from the vantage point of the epistemologist) as though the poorest, the most "weird," and the most marginalized of knowers would have access to and know about these things in exactly the same way. Hence the substitutionalist assumption that the paradigm relies on points to the conclusion that *all* knowing – knowing theories, institutions, practices, life forms *and* forms of life – is just as objective, transparent, and apolitical an exercise.

My contention that subjectivity has to be taken into account takes issue with the belief that epistemologists need only to understand the conditions for propositional, observationally derived knowledge, and all the rest will follow. It challenges the concommitant belief that epistemologists need only to understand how such knowledge claims are made and justified by individual, autonomous, self-reliant reasoners, and they will understand all the rest. Such beliefs derive from conceptions of detached and faceless cognitive agency that mask the variability of the experiences and practices from which knowledge is constructed.

Even if necessary and sufficient conditions cannot yet be established, say in the form of unassailable foundations or seamless coherence, there are urgent questions for epistemologists to address. They bear not primarily upon criteria of evidence, justification, and warrantability, but upon the "nature" of inquirers: upon their interests in the inquiry, their emotional involvement and background assumptions, their character; upon their material, historical, cultural circumstances. Answers to such questions will rarely offer definitive assessments of knowledge claims, and hence are not ordinarily open to the charge that they commit the genetic fallacy; but they can be instructive in debates about the worth of such claims. I am thinking of questions about how credibility is established, about connections between knowledge and power, about political agendas, about epistemic responsibilities, and about the place of knowledge in ethical and aesthetic judgments. These questions are concerned less with individual, monologic cognitive projects than with the workings of epistemic communities as they are manifested in structures of authority and expertise, and in the processes through which knowledge comes to inform public opinion. Such issues will occupy a central place in reconstructed epistemological projects that eschew formalism in order to engage with cognitive practices and to promote emancipatory goals.

The epistemic and moral/political ideals that govern inquiry in technological, capitalist, free-enterprise western societies are an amalgam of liberal-utilitarian moral values, and the empirical-positivist intellectual values that I have been discussing in this essay. These ideals and values shape both the intellectual enterprises that the society legitimates and the language of liberal individualism that maps out the rhetorical spaces where those enterprises are carried out. The ideal of tolerance, openness, is believed to be the right attitude from which, initially, to approach truth claims. It combines with the assumptions that objectivity and value-neutrality govern the rational conduct of scientific and social-scientific research to produce the philosophical commonplaces of late-twentieth-century Anglo-American societies, not just in "the academy," but in the public perception – the "common sense," in Gramsci's terms – that prevails about the academy and the scientific community.[27] (Recall that for Rorty, tolerance is to ensure that post-epistemological societies will sustain productive conversations.) I have noted that a conversational item introduced with the phrase "Science has proved . . ." carries a presumption in favor of its reliability *because of* its objectivity and value-neutrality – a presumption that these facts can stand up to scrutiny *because* they are products of an objective, disinterested process of inquiry. (It is ironic that this patently "genetic" appeal – to the genesis of cognitive products in a certain kind of process – is normally cited to discredit other genetic accounts!) Open and fair-minded consumers of science will recognize its claims to disinterested, tolerant consideration.

I want to suggest that these ideals are inadequate to guide epistemological debates about contentious issues, and hence that it is deceptive and dangerous to ignore questions about subjectivity in the name of objectivity and value-neutrality. (Again, this is why simple observational paradigms are so misleading.) To do so, I turn to an example that is now notorious, at least in Canada.

Psychologist Philippe Rushton claims to have demonstrated that "Orientals as a group are more intelligent, more family-oriented, more law-abiding and less sexually promiscuous than whites, and that whites are superior to blacks in all the same respects."[28] Presented as "facts" that "science [i.e., an allegedly scientific psychology] has proved . . ." using an objective, statistical methodology, Rushton's findings carry a presumption in favor of their reliability *because* they are products of objective research.[29] The "Science has proved . . ." rhetoric creates a public presumption in favor of taking them at face value, believing them true until they are proven false. It erects a screen, a blind, behind which the researcher, like any other occupant of the *S* place, can abdicate accountability to anything but "the facts"; can present himself as a neutral, infinitely replicable vehicle through which data pass *en route* to becoming knowledge. He can claim to have fulfilled his epistemic obligations if, "withdraw[ing] to . . . [his] professional self,"[30] he can argue that he has been "objective," detached, disinterested in his research. The rhetoric of objectivity and value-neutrality places the burden of proof on the challenger rather than the fact-finder, and judges her guilty of intolerance, dogmatism, or ideological excess if she cannot make her challenge good. That same rhetoric generates a conception of knowledge for its own sake that at once effaces accountability requirements and threatens the dissolution of viable intellectual and moral community.

I have noted that the "Science has proved . . ." rhetoric derives from the socio-political influence of the philosophies of science that incorporate and are underwritten by "*S*-knows-that-*p*" epistemologies. Presented as the findings of a purely neutral observer who "discovered" facts about racial inferiority and superiority in controlled observation conditions, so that he could not, rationally, withhold assent, Rushton's results ask the community to be equally objective and neutral in assessing them. These requirements are at once reasonable and troubling. They are reasonable because the empiricist-realist component that, I have urged, is vital to any emancipatory epistemology makes it a mark of competent, responsible inquiry to approach even the most unsavory truth claims seriously, albeit critically. But the requirements are troubling in their implicit appeal to a doxastic involuntarism that becomes an escape hatch from the demands of subjective accountability. The implicit claim is that empirical inquiry is not only a neutral and impersonal process, but also an inexorable one: it is compelling, even coercive, in what it turns up, to the extent that an inquirer *cannot*, rationally, withhold assent. He has no choice but to believe that *p*, however unpalatable it may be. The individualism and presumed disinterestedness of the paradigm reinforces this claim.

It is difficult, however, to believe in the *coincidence* of Rushton's discoveries; and they could only be compelling in that strong sense if they could be shown to be purely coincidental – brute fact – something he came upon as he might bump into a wall. Talk about his impartial reading of the data assumes such hard facticity: the facticity of a blizzard, or a hot sunny day. "Data" is the problematic term here, suggesting that facts presented themselves neutrally to Rushton's observing eye, as though they were literally given, not sought or made. Yet it is not easy, with Rushton, to conceive of his "data" in perfect independence from ongoing debates about race, sex, and class.

These difficulties are compounded when Rushton's research is juxtaposed against analogous projects in other places and times. In her book, *Sexual Science*,[31] Cynthia Russett documents the intellectual climate of the nineteenth century, when claims for racial and sexual equality were threatening upheavals in the social order. She notes that, just at that time, there was a concerted effort among scientists to produce studies that would demonstrate the "natural" sources of racial and sexual *in*equality. Given its aptness to the climate of the times, it is hard to believe that this research was "dislocated," prompted by a disinterested spirit of objective, neutral fact-finding. It is equally implausible, at a time when racial and sexual unrest is again threatening the complacency of the liberal dream – and meeting with strong conservative efforts to contain it – that it could be purely by coincidence that Rushton reaches the conclusions he does. Consider Rushton's contention that, evolutionarily, as the brain increases in size, the genitals shrink; blacks have larger genitals, ergo . . . Leaving elementary logical fallacies aside, it is impossible not to hear echoes of nineteenth-century medical science's "proofs" that, for women, excessive mental activity interferes with the proper functioning of the uterus; hence, permitting women to engage in higher intellectual activity impedes performance of their proper reproductive roles.

The connections Rushton draws between genital and brain size, and conformity to idealized patterns of good, liberal, democratic citizenship, trade upon analogous normative assumptions. The rhetoric of stable, conformist family structure as the site of controlled, utilitarian sexual expression is commonly enlisted to sort the "normal" from the "deviant" and to promote conservative conceptions of the self-image a society should have of itself.[32] The idea that the dissolution of "the family" (= the nuclear, two-parent, patriarchal family) threatens the destruction of civilized society has been deployed to perpetuate white male privilege and compulsory heterosexuality, especially for women. It has been invoked to preserve homogeneous WASP values from disruption by "unruly" (= not law-abiding; sexually promiscuous) elements. Rushton's contention that "naturally occurring" correlations can explain the demographic distribution of tendencies to unruliness leaves scant room for doubt about the appropriate route for a society concerned about its self-image to take: suppress unruliness. As Julian Henriques puts a similar point, by a neat reversal, the "black person becomes the cause of racism whereas the white person's prejudice is seen as a natural effect of the information-processing mechanisms."[33] The "facts" that Rushton produces are simply presented to the scholarly and lay communities so that they allegedly "speak for themselves" on two levels: both roughly, as data, and in more formal garb, as research findings. What urgently demands analysis is the process by which these "facts" are inserted into a public arena that is prepared to receive them, with the result that inquiry stops right where it should begin.[34]

My point is that it is not enough just to be more rigorously empirical in adjudicating such controversial knowledge claims with the expectation that biases that may have infected the "context of discovery" will be eradicated in the purifying processes of justification. Rather, the scope of epistemological investigation has to expand to merge with moral-political inquiry, acknowledging that "facts" are always infused with values, and that both facts and values are open to ongoing critical debate. It would be necessary to demonstrate the innocence of descriptions (their derivation from pure data) and to show the perfect congruence of descriptions with "the described" in order to argue that descriptive theories have no normative force. Their assumed innocence licenses an evasion of the accountability that socially concerned communities have to demand of their producers of knowledge. Only the most starkly positivistic epistemology merged with the instrumental rationality it presupposes could presume that inquirers are accountable only to the evidence. Evidence is *selected*, not found, and selection procedures are open to scrutiny. Nor can critical analysis stop there, for the funding and institutions that enable inquirers to pursue certain projects and not others explicitly legitimize the work.[35] So the lines of accountability are long and interwoven; only a genealogy of their multiple strands can begin to unravel the issues.

What, then, should occur within epistemic communities to ensure that scientists and other knowers cannot conceal bias and prejudice, cannot claim *a right not to know* about their background assumptions, and the significance of their locations?

The crux of my argument is that the phenomenon of the disinterested inquirer is the exception rather than the rule; that there are no dislocated truths, and that some facts about the locations and interests at the source of inquiry are always pertinent to questions about freedom and accountability. Hence I am arguing, in agreement with Naomi Scheman, that:

> Feminist epistemologists and philosophers of science *along with others who have been the objects of knowledge-as-control* [have to] understand and . . . pose alternatives to the epistemology of modernity. As it has been central to this epistemology to guard its products from contamination by connection to the particularities of its producers, it must be central to the work of its critics and to those who would create genuine alternatives to remember those connections. . . .[36]

There can be no doubt that research is – often imperceptibly – shaped by presuppositions and interests external to the inquiry itself, which cannot be filtered out by standard, objective, disinterested epistemological techniques.[37]

In seeking to explain what makes Rushton possible,[38] the point cannot be to exonerate him as a mere product of his circumstances and times. Rushton accepts grants and academic honors in his own name, speaks "for himself" in interviews with the press, and claims credit where credit is to be had. He upholds the validity of his findings. Moreover, he participates fully in the rhetoric of the autonomous, objective inquirer. Yet although Rushton is plainly accountable for the sources and motivations of his projects, he is not singly responsible. Such research is legitimated by the community and speaks in a discursive space that is made available, prepared for it. So scrutinizing Rushton's "scientific" knowledge claims demands an examination of the moral and intellectual health of a community that is infected by racial and sexual injustices at every level. Rushton may have had reasons to believe that his results would be welcome.

Equally central, then, to an epistemological program of taking subjectivity into account are case-by-case analyses of the political and other structural circumstances that generate projects and lines of inquiry. Feminist critique – with critiques that center on other marginalizing structures – needs to act as an "experimental control" in epistemic practice so that every inquiry, assumption, and discovery is analyzed for its place in, and implications for, the prevailing sex/gender system as it intersects with the systems that sustain racism, homophobia, ethnocentrism.[39] The burden of proof falls upon inquirers who claim neutrality. The positions and power relations of gendered, and otherwise located, subjectivity have to be submitted to scrutiny, piece by piece, and differently according to the field of research, in all "objective" inquiry. The task is intricate, because the subjectivity of the inquirer is always also implicated, and has to be taken into account. Hence such projects are at once critical and self-critical. But this is no monologic, self-sufficient enterprise. Conclusions are reached, immoderate subjective omissions and commissions become visible, in dialogic processes among inquirers and – in social science – between inquirers and the subjects of their research.

It emerges from this analysis that although the ideal objectivity of the universal knower is neither possible nor desirable, a realistic commitment to achieving empirical adequacy that engages in situated analyses of the subjectivities of both the knower and (where appropriate) the known is both desirable and possible. This exercise in supposing that the places in the "*S*-knows-that-*p*" formula could be filled by asserting "Rushton knows that blacks are inferior" shows that simple, propositional knowledge claims that represent inquirers as purely neutral observers of unignorable data cannot be permitted to count as paradigms of knowledge. Objectivity *requires* taking subjectivity into account.

## 4   Knowing Subjects

Women – and other "others" – are *produced* as "objects of knowledge-as-control" by "*S*-knows-that-*p*" epistemologies and by the philosophies of science/social science that they inform. When subjects become objects of knowledge, reliance upon simple observational paradigms has the consequence of assimilating those subjects to physical objects, reducing their subjectivity and specificity to interchangeable, observable features.

"*S*-knows-that-*p*" epistemologies take for granted that observational knowledge of everyday objects forms the basis from which all knowledge is constructed. *Prima facie*, this is a persuasive belief. Observations of childhood development (at least in materially advantaged, "normal," western families) suggest that simple observational truths are the first bits of knowledge an infant acquires in learning to recognize and manipulate everyday objects. Infants seem to be objective in this early knowing: they *come across* objects and learn to deal with them, apparently without preconceptions, and without altering the properties of the objects. Objects ordinarily remain independent of a child's knowing; and these same objects – cups, spoons, chairs, trees, and flowers – seem to be the simplest and surest things that every adult knows. They are *there* to be known, they are reasonably constant through change. In the search for examples of what standard knowers know "for sure," such knowledge claims are obvious candidates. So it is not surprising that they have counted as paradigmatic.

I want to suggest, however, that when one considers how basic and crucial *knowing other people* is in the production of human subjectivity, paradigms and objectivity take on a different aspect.[40] If epistemologists require paradigms, or other less formal exemplary knowledge claims, knowing other people in personal relationships is at least as worthy a contender as knowledge of everyday objects. Developmentally, learning what she or he can expect of other people is one of the first and most essential kinds of knowledge a child acquires. She or he learns to respond *cognitively* to the people who are a vital part of, and provide access to, her or his environment long before she/he can recognize the simplest physical objects. Other people are the point of origin of a child's entry into the material/physical environment both in providing or inhibiting access to that environment – in making it – and in fostering entry into the language with which children learn to name. Their initial induction into language generates a framework of presuppositions which prompts children, from the earliest stages, to construct their environments variously, according to the quality of their affective, intersubjective locations. Evidence about the effects of sensory and emotional deprivation on the development of cognitive agency shows that a child's capacity to make sense of the world, and the manner of engaging in that process, is intricately linked with her or his caregivers' construction of the environment.

Now, theories of knowledge tend, traditionally, to be derived from the experiences of uniformly educated, articulate, epistemically "positioned" adults who introspect to review what they must once have known most simply and clearly. Locke's *tabula rasa* is one model; Descartes's radical doubt is another. Yet this introspective process consistently bypasses the epistemic significance of early experiences with other people, with whom the relations of these philosophers must surely have been different from their relations to objects in their environment. As Seyla Benhabib wryly notes, it is a strange world from which this picture of knowledge is derived: a world in which "individuals are grown up before they have been born; in which boys are men before they have been children; a world where neither mother, nor sister, nor wife exist."[41] Whatever the historical variations in childraising practices, evidence implicit in (similarly evolving) theories of knowledge points to a noteworthy constancy. In separated adulthood, the knowledge that enables a knower to give or withhold trust as a child, and hence to survive, is passed over as unworthy of philosophical notice. It is tempting to conclude that theorists of knowledge must either be childless, or must be so disengaged from the rearing of children as to have minimal developmental awareness. Participators in childraising could not easily ignore the primacy of knowing and being known by other people in cognitive development, nor denigrate the role such knowledge plays throughout an epistemic history. In view of the fact that disengagement, throughout a changing history and across a range of class and racial boundaries, has been possible primarily for *men* in western societies, this aspect of the androcentricity of objectivist epistemologies is not surprising.

Knowing other people in relationships requires constant learning: how to be with them, respond to them, act toward them. In this respect it contrasts markedly with the immediacy of common, sense-perceptual paradigms. In fact, if exemplary "bits" of knowledge were drawn from situations where people have to *learn* to know, rather than from taken-for-granted adult expectations, the complexity of knowing even the simplest things would not so readily be masked, and the fact that knowledge is *qualitatively* variable would be more readily apparent. Consider the strangeness of travelling in a country and culture where one has to suspend judgment about how to identify and deal with things from simple artifacts, to flora and fauna, to customs and cultural phenomena. These experiences remind epistemologists of how tentative a process making everyday observations and judgments really is.

Knowledge of other people develops, operates, and is open to interpretation at various levels; it admits of degree in ways that knowing that "the book is red" does not. Such knowledge is not primarily propositional: I can know that Alice is clever, and not *know* her very well at all in a "thicker" sense. Knowing "facts"

(= the standard "*S*-knows-that-*p*" substitutions) is part of such knowing, but the knowledge involved is more than, and different from, its propositional parts. Nor is this knowledge reducible to the simple, observational knowledge of the traditional paradigms. The fact that it is acquired differently, interactively, relationally, differentiates it both as process and as product from standard propositional knowledge. Yet its status as knowledge disturbs the smooth surface of the paradigm structure. The contrast between its multi-dimensional, multi-perspectival character and the stark simplicity of standard paradigms requires philosophers to reexamine the practice of granting exemplary status to those paradigms. "Knowing how" and "knowing that" are implicated, but they do not begin to tell the whole story.

The contention that people are *knowable* may sit uneasily with psychoanalytic decenterings of conscious subjectivity and with postmodern critiques of the unified subject of Enlightenment humanism. But I think this is a tension that has, at once, to be acknowledged and maintained. In practice, people often know one another well enough to make good decisions about who can be counted on and who cannot, who makes a good ally and who does not. Yet precisely because of the fluctuations and contradictions of subjectivity, this process is ongoing, communicative, interpretive. It is never fixed or complete: any fixity claimed for "the self" will be a fixity in flux. Nonetheless, I am arguing, something must be fixed to "contain" the flux even enough to permit references to and ongoing relationships with "this person." Knowing people always occurs within the terms of this tension.

Problems about determining criteria for justifying claims to know another person – the utter unavailability of necessary and sufficient conditions, the complete inadequacy of "*S*-knows-that-*p*" paradigms – must account for philosophical reluctance to count this as knowledge that bears epistemological investigation. Yet my suggestion that such knowledge is a model for a wide range of knowledge, and is not merely inchoate and unmanageable, recommends itself the more strongly in view of the extent to which cognitive practice is grounded upon such knowledge. I am thinking not just of everyday interactions with other people, but of the specialized knowledge – such as Rushton's – that claims institutional authority. Educational theory and practice, psychology, sociology, anthropology, law, some aspects of medicine and philosophy, politics, history and economics, all depend for their credibility upon knowing people. Hence it is all the more curious that observation-based knowledge of material objects, and the methodology of the physical sciences, hold such relatively unchallenged sway as the paradigm – and paragon – of intellectual achievement. The results of according observational paradigms continued veneration are evident in the reductive approaches of behaviorist psychology. They are apparent in parochial impositions of meaning upon the practices of other cultures still characteristic of some areas of anthropology; and in the simple translation of present-day descriptions into past cultural contexts that characterizes some historical and archaeological practice. But feminist, hermeneutic, and postmodern critiques are slowly succeeding in requiring objectivist social scientists to reexamine their presuppositions and practices. In fact, it is methodological disputes within the social sciences – and the consequent unsettling of positivistic hegemony – that, according to Susan Hekman, have set the stage for the development of a productive, postmodern approach to epistemology for contemporary feminists.[42]

I am not proposing that knowing other people become *the* new epistemological paradigm, but rather that it has a strong claim to exemplary status in the epistemologies that feminist and other case-by-case analyses will produce. I am proposing further that, if epistemologists require a model drawn from "scientific" inquiry, then a reconstructed, interpretive social science, liberated from positivistic constraints, will be a better resource than natural science – or physics – for knowledge as such.

Social science of whatever stripe is constrained by the factual-informational details that constrain all attempts to know people: physical, historical, biographical, environmental, social-structural, and other *facts* constitute its "objects" of study. These facts are available for objective analysis, yet they also lend themselves to varying degrees of interpretation and ideological construction. Social science often focuses upon meanings, upon purposeful and learned behavior, preferences, and intentions, with the aim of explaining what Sandra Harding calls "the origins, forms and prevalence of apparently irrational but culturewide patterns of human belief and action."[43] Such phenomena cannot be measured and quantified to provide results comparable to the results of a controlled physics experiment. Yet this constraint neither precludes social-scientific objectivity, nor reclaims the methodology of physics as paradigmatic. Harding is right to maintain that "the totally reasonable exclusion of intentional and learned behaviors from the subject matter of physics is a good reason to regard inquiry in physics as atypical of scientific knowledge-seeking."[44] I am arguing that it is equally atypical of everyday knowledge-seeking. Interpretations of intentional and learned behavior are indeed subjectively variable; yet taking subjectivity into account does not entail abandoning objectivity. Rabinow and Sullivan put the point well: "Discourse being about something, one must understand the World in order to interpret it. . . . Human action and interpretation are subject to many *but not indefinitely many* constructions."[45] When theorists acknowledge the oddity and peculiar insularity of physics-derived paradigms with their suppression of subjectivity, it is clear that their application to areas of inquiry where subjectivities are the "objects" of study has to be contested.

The problem about claiming an exemplary role for personal-knowledge models is to show how the kinds of knowledge integral to human relationships could work in situations where the object of knowledge is inanimate. The case has to be made by analogy, not by requiring knowers to convert from being objective observers of, to being friends with, tables and chairs, chemicals, particles, cells, planets, rocks, trees and insects. There are obvious points of disanalogy, not the least of which derives from the fact that chairs and planets and rocks cannot reciprocate or answer back in the ways that people can. There will be none of the mutual recognition and affirmation between observer and observed that there is between people. But Heisenberg's "uncertainty principle" suggests that not even physical objects are inert in and untouched by observational processes. If there is any validity to this suggestion, then it is not so easy to draw rigid lines separating responsive from unresponsive objects. Taking knowledge of other people as a model does not, *per impossible*, require scientists to begin talking to their rocks and cells, or to admit that the process is not working when the rocks fail to respond. It calls, rather, for a recognition that rocks and cells, and scientists, are located in multiple relations to one another, all of which are open to analysis and critique. Singling out and privileging the asymmetrical observer-observed relation is but one possibility.

A more stubborn point of disanalogy may appear to attach to the belief that it is possible to know physical objects, whereas it is never possible really to know other people. But this apparent disanalogy appears to prevent the analogy from going through because of another feature of the core presuppositions of empiricist-objectivist theories.

According to the standard paradigms, empirical observation can produce knowledge that is established, universally and uncontrovertibly, for all time. Whether or not such perfect knowledge has ever been achieved is an open question; a belief in its possibility guides and regulates mainstream epistemologies and theories of science. The presumption that knowing other people is difficult to the point of near-impossibility is declared by contrast with those paradigms, whose realization may only be possible in contrived, attenuated instances. By *that* standard, knowing other people, however well, does look like as pale an approximation as it was for Descartes, by contrast with the "clear and distinct ideas" he was otherwise able to achieve. The question, again, is why *that* standard, which governs so miniscule a part of the epistemic lives even of members of the privileged professional class and gender, should regulate legitimate uses of the label "knowledge."

If the positivist-empiricist standard were displaced by more complex analyses, where knowledge claims are provisional and approximate, knowing other people might not seem to be so different. Current upheavals in epistemology point to the productivity of hermeneutic, interpretive, literary methods of analysis and explanation in the social sciences. The skills these approaches require are not so different from the interpretive skills that human relationships require. The extent of their usefulness for the natural sciences is not yet clear. But one point of the challenge is to argue that natural-scientific inquiry has to be located differently, where it can be recognized as a socio-political-historical activity in which knowing who the scientist is can reveal important epistemological dimensions of her or his inquiry.

A recognition of the space that needs to be kept open for reinterpretation, of the contextualizing that adequate knowledge requires, becomes clearer in the light of the "personal" analogy. Though the analogy is not perfect, it is certainly no more preposterous to argue that people should try to know physical objects in the nuanced way that they know their friends, than it is to argue that they should try to know people in the unsubtle way that they often claim to know physical objects.

Drawing upon such an interpretive approach across the epistemic terrain would guard against reductivism and rigidity. Knowing other people occurs in a persistent interplay between opacity and transparency, between attitudes and postures that elude a knower's grasp and patterns that are clear and relatively constant. Hence knowers are kept on their cognitive toes. In its need to accommodate change and growth, this knowledge contrasts further with traditional paradigms which deal, on the whole, with objects that can be treated as permanent. In knowing other people, a knower's subjectivity is implicated, from its earliest developmental stages; in such knowing her or his subjectivity is produced, and reproduced. Analogous reconstructions often occur in the subjectivity of the person(s) she or he knows. Hence such knowledge works from a conception of subject-object relations different from that implicit in simple empirical paradigms. Claims to know a person are open to negotiation between knower and known, where the "subject" and "object" positions are always, in principle, interchangeable. In the process, it is important to watch for discrepancies between a person's sense of her own subjectivity, and a would-be knower's conception of how things are for her; yet neither the self-conception nor the knower-conception can claim absolute authority, for the limits of self-consciousness constrain the process as closely as does the interiority of mental processes and of experiential constructs, and their resulting unavailability to observation.

That an agent's subjectivity is so clearly implicated may create the impression that this knowledge is, indeed, purely subjective. But such a conclusion would be unwarranted. There *are* facts that have to be respected: facts that constitute "the person one is," at any historical moment.[46] Only certain stories can accurately be told; others simply cannot. "External" facts are obvious constraints: facts about age, sex, place and date of birth, height, weight, and hair color; the information that appears on a passport. They would count as objective even on a fairly traditional understanding of the term. Other information is reasonably objective as well: facts about marriage or divorce, childbirth, siblings, skills, education, employment, abode, and travel. But the intriguing point about knowing people – and another reason why it is epistemologically instructive – is that even knowing all the facts about someone does not count as knowing her as the person she is. No more can knowing all the facts about oneself, past and present, guarantee self-knowledge. Yet none of these problems raise doubts that there is such a creature as the person I am, or the person she is, now. Nor do they indicate the impossibility of knowing other people. If the limitations of these accumulated factual claims were taken seriously with respect to empirical knowledge more generally, the limitations of an epistemology built from "S-knows-that-$p$" claims would be more clearly apparent.

That perfect, objective knowledge of other people is not possible gives no support to a contention *either* that "other minds" are radically unknowable, *or* that people's claims to know one another never merit the label "knowledge." Residual assumptions to the effect that people are opaque to one another may explain why this knowledge has had minimal epistemological attention. Knowledge, as the tradition defines it, is *of* objects; only by assimilating people to objects can one hope to know them. This long-standing assumption is challenged by my claim that knowing other people is an exemplary kind of knowing, and that subjectivity has always to be taken into account in making and assessing knowledge claims of any complexity.

## 5 Relativism After All

The project I am proposing, then, requires a new *geography* of the epistemic terrain: one that is no longer primarily a physical geography, but a population geography that develops qualitative analyses of subjective positions and identities and of the social-political structures that produce them. Because differing social positions generate variable constructions of reality, and afford different perspectives on the world, the revisionary stages of this project will consist in case-by-case analyses of the knowledge produced in specific social positions. These analyses derive from a recognition that knowers are always *somewhere* – and at once limited and enabled by the specificities of their locations.[47] It is an interpretive project, alert to the possibility of finding generalities, commonalities within particulars – hence of the explanatory potential that opens up when such commonalities can be delineated. But it is wary of the reductivism that results when commonalities are presupposed or forced. It has no ultimate foundation, but neither does it float free, for it is grounded in experiences and practices, in the efficacy of dialogic negotiation and of action.

All of this having been said, my argument in this essay points to the conclusion that necessary and sufficient conditions for establishing empirical knowledge claims cannot be found, at least where experientially significant knowledge is at issue. Hence it poses the question whether feminist epistemologists must, after all, "come out" as relativists. In view of what I have been arguing, the answer to that question will have to be a qualified "yes."[48] Yet the relativism that my argument generates, I am claiming, is sufficiently nuanced and sophisticated to escape the scorn – and the anxiety – that "relativism, after all" usually occasions. To begin with, it refuses to occupy the negative side of the traditional absolutism/relativism dichotomy. It is at once realist, rational, and significantly objective; hence it is not forced to define itself within or against the oppositions between realism and relativism, rationality and relativism, objectivism and relativism.[49] Moreover, it takes as its starting point a recognition that the "positive" sides of the dichotomies have been caricatured to affirm a certainty that was never rightfully theirs.

The opponents of relativism have been so hostile, so thoroughly scornful in their dismissals, that it is no wonder that feminists, well aware of the folk-historical identification of women with the forces of unreason, should resist the very thought that the logic of feminist emancipatory analyses points in that direction.[50] Feminists know, if they know anything at all, that they have to develop the best possible explanations – hence the "truest" explanations – of how things are, if they are to intervene effectively in social structures and institutions. The intransigence of material circumstances constantly reminds them that their possibilities of world-making are neither unconstrained nor infinite; that they have to be able to produce accurate, transformative analyses of things as they *are*. In fact, many feminists are vehement in their resistance to relativism precisely because they suspect – not without reason – that only the supremely powerful and privileged, the self-proclaimed sons of God, could believe that they can make the world up as they will, can practice that supreme tolerance in whose terms all possible constructions of reality are equally worthy. Their fears are persuasive. Yet even at the risk of speaking within the oppositional mode, it is worth thinking seriously about the alternative. For there is no doubt that only the supremely powerful and privileged could believe, in the face of all the evidence to the contrary, that there is only one true view, and it is theirs; that they alone have the resources to establish universal, incontrovertible, and absolute Truth. Donna Haraway aptly notes that: "Relativism is a way of being nowhere while claiming to be everywhere";[5] but absolutism is a way of being everywhere while pretending to be nowhere – and neither one, in its starkest articulation, will do. For this reason alone, it is clear that the absolutism/relativism dichotomy needs to be displaced for it does not, as a true dichotomy must, use up all of the alternatives.[52]

The position I am advocating is one for which knowledge is always *relative* to (a perspective *on*, a standpoint *in*) specifiable circumstances. Hence it is constrained by a realist, empiricist commitment according to which getting those circumstances as right as possible is vital to effective action. It may appear to be a question-begging position, for it does assume that the circumstances can be known, and it relies heavily upon pragmatic criteria to make good that assumption. It can usually avoid regress, for although the circumstances in question may have to be specified *relative* to other circumstances, prejudgments, and theories, it is never (as with Neurath's raft) necessary to take away all of the pieces – all of the props – at once. Inquiry grows out of and turns back to practice, action; inquirers are always *in media res*, and the *res* are both identifiable and constitutive of perspectives and possibilities for action. Practice will show, not once and for all, but case by case, whether conclusions are reasonable, workable. Hence the position allows both for the development of practical projects, and for their corrigibility.

This "mitigated relativism" has a skeptical component: a consequence many feminists will resist even more vigorously than they will resist my claim for relativism. Western philosophy is still in thrall to an Enlightenment legacy which equates skepticism and nihilism: to the belief that if no absolute foundations – no necessary and sufficient conditions–can be established, then there can be no knowledge.[53] Nothing is any more reasonable, rational than anything else; there is nothing to believe in. This is the skepticism that necessary and sufficient conditions are meant to forestall.

But there are other skepticisms which are resourceful, not defeatist. The ancient skepticisms of Pyrrho and Sextus Empiricus were declarations not of nihilism, but of the impossibility of certainty, of the need to withhold definitive judgment. They advocated continual searching in order to prevent error, by suspending judgment. They valued a readiness to reconsider, and warned against hasty conclusions. These were skepticisms about the possibility of definitive knowledge, but not about the existence of a (knowable?) reality. For Pyrrhonists, skepticism was a moral stance that was meant to ensure the inner quietude (*ataraxia*) that was essential to happiness.[54]

My suggestion that feminist epistemologists can find a resource in such skepticisms cannot be pushed to the point of urging that they take on the whole package. There is no question that the quietude of *ataraxia* could be the achievement that feminists are after. Nor could they take on a skepticism that would immobilize them by negating all possibilities for action: a quietism born of a theorized incapacity to choose, to take a stand. So the skepticism that flavors the position I am advocating is better characterized as a commonsense, practical skepticism of everyday life than as a technical, philosophers' skepticism. It resembles the "healthy skepticism" that parents teach their children about media advertising; the skepticism that marks cautiously informed attitudes to politicians' promises.

Above all, feminists cannot opt for a skepticism that would make it impossible to know that certain practices and institutions are *wrong*, and likely to remain so. The political ineffectiveness of universal tolerance no longer needs demonstrating: sexism is just one obvious example of an undoubted intolerable. (Seyla Benhabib notes that Rorty's "admirable demand . . . to 'let a hundred flowers bloom' is motivated by a desire to depoliticize philosophy."[55]) So even the skepticism that I am advocating is problematic in the sense that it has to be carefully measured and articulated if it is not to amount merely to "an apology for the existing order."[56] Its heuristic, productive dimensions are best captured by Denise Riley's observation that "an active skepticism about the integrity of the sacred category 'women' would be no merely philosophical doubt to be stifled in the name of effective political action in the world. On the contrary, it would be a condition *for* the latter."[57] It is in "making strange," loosening the hold of taken-for-granted values, ideals, categories, and theories that skepticism demonstrates its promise.

Michel Foucault is one of the most articulate late-twentieth-century successors of the ancient skeptics. A skeptic in his refusal of dogmatic unities, essences, labels, Foucault examines changing practices of knowledge rather than taking the standard epistemological route of assuming a unified rationality or science. He eschews totalizing, universalist assumptions in his search for what John Rajchman calls the "invention of specific forms of experience which are taken up and transformed again and again."[58] His is a skepticism about the certainty, the stability of systems of representation. Like the ancient skeptics, Foucault can be cast as a realist. He never doubts that there *are* things, institutions, and practices whose genealogies, archaeologies can be written. His position recommends itself for the freedom that its skeptical component offers. Hence he claims:

> All my analyses are against the idea of universal necessities in human existence. They show the arbitrariness of institutions and show which space of freedom we can still enjoy and how many changes can still be made.[59]

Yet this is by no means an absolute freedom; for Foucault also observes:

> My point is not that everything is bad, but that everything is dangerous, which is not exactly the same as bad. If everything is dangerous, then we always have some-

thing to do. So my position leads not to apathy but to a hyper-and pessimistic activism. . . . [T]he ethico-political choice we have to make . . . is to determine which is the main danger.⁶⁰

One of the most urgent tasks that Foucault has left undone is that of showing how "we" can *know* what is dangerous.

There are many tensions within the strands that my skeptical-relativist recommendations try to weave together. For these I do not apologize. At this critical juncture in the articulation of emancipatory epistemological projects it is impossible to have all of the answers, to resolve all of the tensions and paradoxes. I have exposed some ways in which "S-knows-that-*p*" epistemologies are dangerous and have proposed one route toward facing and disarming those dangers: taking subjectivity into account. The solutions that route affords, and the further dangers it reveals, will indicate the directions that the next stages of this inquiry must take.

## Notes

Earlier versions of this essay were presented at the American Philosophical Association conference at Los Angeles, and to the Departments of Philosophy at McMaster University and McGill University. I am grateful to participants in those discussions – especially to Susan Dwyer, Hilary Kornblith, and Doug Odegard – for their comments and to Linda Alcoff and Libby Potter for editorial suggestions.

1   I allude here to the title of Thomas Nagel's book, *The View From Nowhere*. New York: Oxford University Press, 1986.
2   I owe the phrase "surrogate knower" to Naomi Scheman, in the paper "Descartes and Gender" which she presented to the conference "Reason, Gender, and the Moderns," University of Toronto, February 1990. I draw on this idea to make a rather different set of points in "Who Cares? The Poverty of Objectivism for a Moral Epistemology," in *Rhetorical Spaces: Essays on Gendered Locations* (New York: Routledge, 1995).
3   For an account of the central tenets of logical positivism, a representative selection of articles, and an extensive bibliography, see A. J. Ayer, ed., *Logical Positivism*. New York: The Free Press, 1959.
4   Karl Popper, *Objective Knowledge*. Oxford: Clarendon Press, 1972, p. 108 (emphasis in original).
5   Mary Hesse advisedly notes that philosophers of science would now more readily assert than they would have done in the heyday of positivism that facts in both the natural and social sciences are "value-laden." (See Mary Hesse, *Revolutions and Reconstructions in the Philosophy of Science*. Bloomington: Indiana University Press, 1980, pp. 172–173.) I am claiming, however, that everyday conceptions of scientific authority are still significantly informed by a residual positivistic faith.
6   For classic statements of this aspect of the positivistic program, see, for example, Rudolf Carnap, "Psychology in Physical Language," and Otto Neurath, "Sociology and Physicalism," in A.J. Ayer, ed., *Logical Positivism*.
7   I discuss such responsibilities in my *Epistemic Responsibility* (Hanover, NH: University Press of New England, 1987).
8   See Joan Scott, "Is Gender a Useful Category of Historical Analysis?" in Joan Wallach

Scott, *Gender and the Politics of History*. New York: Columbia University Press, 1989, for an elaboration of what it means to see gender as an analytic category.

9   Paul Moser, in his review of *Epistemic Responsibility*, takes me to task for not announcing "the necessary and sufficient conditions for one's being epistemically responsible." He argues that even if, as I claim throughout the book, epistemic responsibility does not lend itself to analysis in those terms, "we might still provide necessary and sufficient conditions for the wide range of typical instances, and then handle the wayward cases independently." (Paul Moser, Review of *Epistemic Responsibility*, Philosophical Books, 29:3, 1988, p. 155.) Yet it is precisely their "typicality" that I contest. Moser's review is a salient example of the tendency of dominant epistemologies to claim as their own even positions that reject their central premises.

10  See p. 124, where I claim that knowledge is a construct.

11  These aims are continuous with some of the aims of recent projects to naturalize epistemology by drawing on the resources of cognitive psychology. See especially W. V. O. Quine, "Epistemology Naturalized," in *Ontological Relativity and Other Essays*, New York: Columbia University Press, 1969; Hilary Kornblith's edited volume, *Naturalizing Epistemology*, Cambridge: MIT Press, 1985, Second Edition 1994; and Alvin I. Goldman, *Epistemology and Cognition*, Cambridge: Harvard University Press, 1986. Feminist epistemologists who are developing this line of inquiry are Jane Duran, *Toward a Feminist Epistemology*, Savage, MD: Rowman and Littlefield, 1991; and Lynn Hankinson Nelson, *Who knows? From Quine to a Feminist Empiricism*, Philadelphia: Temple University Press, 1990. Feminists who find a resource in this work have to contend with the fact that the cognitive psychology that informs it presupposes a constancy in "human nature," exemplified in "representative selves" who have commonly been white, male, and middle class. They have also to remember the extent to which appeals to "nature" have oppressed women and other marginal groups. I discuss these issues in greater detail in my essay, "What Is Natural About Epistemology Naturalized?" forthcoming.

12  For an extensive bibliography of such critiques up to 1989, see Alison Wylie, Kathleen Okruhlik, Sandra Morton, and Leslie Thielen-Wilson, "Philosophical Feminism: A Bibliographic Guide to Critiques of Science" in *Resources for Feminist Research/ Documentation sur la Recherche Feministe*, 19, 2, June 1990, pp. 2–36.

13  For an analysis of the androcentricity, the "masculinity" of these ideals, and their "feminine" exclusions, in theories of knowledge see Genevieve Lloyd, *The Man of Reason: "Male" and "Female" in Western Philosophy*, Minneapolis: University of Minnesota Press, 1984, Second Edition, 1993; and Susan Bordo, *The Flight to Objectivity*, Albany: State University of New York Press, 1987. For discussions of the scientific context, see Evelyn Fox Keller, *Reflections on Gender and Science*, New Haven: Yale University Press, 1985; Sandra Harding, *The Science Question in Feminism*, Ithaca: Cornell University Press, 1986; and Nancy Tuana, ed., *Feminism and Science*, Bloomington: Indiana University Press, 1989.

14  Richard Foley, *The Theory of Epistemic Rationality*, Cambridge, MA: Harvard University Press, 1987, p. 48.

15  Ibid., p. 114.

16  Ibid., p. 140.

17  Ibid., p. 54.

18  I have singled out Foley's book because it is such a good example of the issues I am addressing. But he is by no means atypical. Space does not permit a catalogue of similar positions, but Lynn Nelson notes that "Quine apparently assumes that at a given time 'we' will agree about the questions worth asking and the standards by

which potential answers are to be judged, so he does not consider social arrangements as epistemological factors." (Lynn Hankinson Nelson, *Who Knows*, p. 170.) Quine assumes, further, that "in the relevant community . . . we will all . . . see the same thing" (p. 184).

19  Here I am thinking of Richard Rorty, *Philosophy and the Mirror of Nature*, Princeton: Princeton University Press, 1979; and *Consequences of Pragmatism*, Minneapolis: University of Minnesota Press, 1982.

20  *Philosophy and the Mirror of Nature*, p. 373.

21  Richard Rorty, "Solidarity or Objectivity?", in John Rajchman and Cornel West, eds., *Post-Analytic Philosophy*, New York: Columbia University Press, 1985, p. 7, emphasis added.

22  Ibid., p. 11.

23  Ibid., p. 15.

24  Nancy Fraser, "Solidarity or Singularity? Richard Rorty between Romanticism and Technocracy." In Nancy Fraser, *Unruly Practices: Power, Discourse and Gender in Contemporary Social Theory*, Minneapolis: University of Minnesota Press, 1989, p. 104.

25  Rorty, "Solidarity or Objectivity?" p. 5.

26  I borrow the idea, if not the detail, of the potential of case-by-case analysis from Roger A. Shiner, "From Epistemology to Romance Via Wisdom." In Ilham Dilman, ed., *Philosophy and Life: Essays on John Wisdom*, The Hague: Martinus Nijhoff, 1984, pp. 291–314.

27  See Antonio Gramsci, *Selections from the Prison Notebooks*, translated and edited by Quintin Hoare and Geoffrey Nowell Smith, New York: International Publishers, 1971.

28  Rudy Platiel and Stephen Strauss, Toronto: *The Globe and Mail*, February 4, 1989, p. A6. I cite the newspaper report because the media produce the public impact that concerns me here. I discuss neither the quality of Rushton's research practice, nor the questions his theories and pedagogical practice pose about academic freedom. My concern is with how structures of knowledge, power, and prejudice grant him an epistemic place.

29  Commenting on the psychology of occupational assessment, Wendy Hollway observes: "That psychology is a science and that psychological assessment is therefore objective is a belief which continues to be fostered in organizations." She notes: "The legacy of psychology as science is the belief that the individual can be understood through measurement." (Wendy Hollway, "Fitting work: psychological assessment in organizations," in Julian Henriques, Wendy Hollway, Cathy Urwin, Couze Venn, and Valerie Walkerdine, *Changing the Subject: Psychology, Social Regulation and Subjectivity*, London: Methuen, 1984, pp. 35, 55.)

30  The phrase is Richard Schmitt's, in "Murderous Objectivity: Reflections on Marxism and the Holocaust," in Roger S. Gottlieb, ed., *Thinking the Unthinkable: Meanings of the Holocaust*. New York: Paulist Press, 1990, p. 71. I am grateful to Richard Schmitt for helping me to think about the issues I discuss in this section.

31  Cynthia Eagle Russett, *Sexual Science: The Victorian Construction of Womanhood*, Cambridge, MA: Harvard University Press, 1989. In this connection, see also Lynda Birke, *Women, Feminism, and Biology*. Brighton: Harvester Press, 1986; and Janet Sayers, *Biological Politics*. London: Tavistock Publications, 1982.

32  The best-known contemporary discussion of utilitarian, controlled sexuality is in Michel Foucault, *The History of Sexuality Volume I: An Introduction*, translated by Robert Hurley, New York: Vintage Books, 1980. Sexuality, in Foucault's analysis,

is utilitarian both in reproducing the population, and in cementing the family bond.

33    Julian Henriques, "Social Psychology and the Politics of Racism," in Henriques et al., *Changing the Subject*, p. 74.

34    Clifford Geertz comments: "It is not . . . the validity of the sciences, real or would-be, that is at issue. What concerns me, and should concern us all, are the axes that, with an increasing determination bordering on the evangelical, are being busily ground with their assistance." In "Anti Anti-Relativism," in Michael Krausz, ed., *Relativism: Interpretation and Confrontation*, Notre Dame: University of Notre Dame Press, 1989, p. 20.

35    Philippe Rushton has received funding from the Social Sciences and Humanities Research Council of Canada, and the Guggenheim Foundation in the USA: agencies whose status, in the North American intellectual community, confers authority and credibility. He has also received funding from the Pioneer Fund, an organization with explicit white supremacist commitments.

36    Naomi Scheman, "Commentary," in the "Symposium on Sandra Harding's 'The Method Question'" *APA Feminism and Philosophy Newsletter*, 1989, p. 42. Emphasis in original.

37    Helen Longino observes: " . . . how one determines evidential relevance, why one takes some state of affairs as evidence for one hypothesis rather than for another, depends on one's other beliefs, which we can call background beliefs or assumptions" (p. 43). And "When, for instance, background assumptions are shared by all members of a community, they acquire an invisibility that renders them unavailable for criticism" (p. 80). In *Science as Social Knowledge: Values and Objectivity in Scientific Inquiry*, Princeton: Princeton University Press, 1990.

38    Here I am borrowing a turn of phrase from Michel Foucault, when he writes, in quite a different context: "And it was this network that made possible the individuals we term Hobbes, Berkeley, Hume, or Condillac." Michel Foucault, *The Order of Things: An Archaeology of the Human Sciences*, New York: Random House, 1971, p. 63.

39    I owe this point to the Biology and Gender Study Group, in "The Importance of Feminist Critique for Contemporary Cell Biology." In Nancy Tuana, ed., *Feminism and Science*, Bloomington: Indiana University Press, 1989, p. 173.

40    The argument about the primacy of knowing other people is central to the position I develop in my *What Can She Know? Feminist Theory and the Construction of Knowledge*, Ithaca, NY: Cornell University Press, 1991. Portions of this section of this essay are drawn, with modifications, from the book.

41    Seyla Benhabib, "The Generalized and the Concrete Other." In Seyla Benhabib and Drucilla Cornell, eds., *Feminism As Critique*. Minneapolis: University of Minnesota Press, 1987, p. 85.

42    See Susan Hekman, *Gender and Knowledge: Elements of a Postmodern Feminism*, Boston: Northeastern University Press, 1990, especially p. 3. For an introduction to these disputes, see Paul Rabinow and William M. Sullivan, eds., *Interpretive Social Science: A Second Look*. Berkeley: University of California Press, 1987. I discuss both of these texts at greater length in another context in chapter six of this book.

43    Sandra Harding, *The Science Question in Feminism*, p. 47. Harding contends that "a critical and self-reflective social science should be the model for all science, and . . . if there are any special requirements for adequate explanations in physics, they are just that – special." Ibid., p. 44.

44    Ibid., p. 46.

45    Introduction, "The Interpretive Turn," in Rabinow and Sullivan, op. cit., p. 13, emphasis added.

46   The phrase is Elizabeth V. Spelman's, in "On Treating Persons as Persons," *Ethics* Vol. 88, 1977–78, 150–161, p. 151. I draw upon this article to analyze a related set of experiences in chapter four of this book.

47   Here I borrow a phrase from Susan Bordo, "Feminism, Postmodernism, and Gender-Scepticism." In Linda Nicholson, ed., *Feminism/Postmodernism*, New York: Routledge, 1990, p. 145.

48   I elaborate this answer in greater detail in the essay "Must a Feminist Be a Relativist After All?" in *Rhetorical Spaces*. This final section of this essay amounts to a preview of the longer discussion.

49   I allude here to three now-classic treatments of the relativism question: Anne Seller, "Realism versus Relativism: Toward a Politically Adequate Epistemology." In Morwenna Griffiths and Margaret Whitford, eds., *Feminist Perspectives in Philosophy*, Bloomington: Indiana University Press, 1988; Martin Hollis and Steven Lukes, eds., *Rationality and Relativism*, Cambridge: MIT Press, 1982; and Richard Bernstein, *Beyond Objectivism and Relativism*, Philadelphia: University of Pennsylvania Press, 1983.

50   Sandra Harding resists endorsing relativism, even in her discussions of standpoint and postmodern epistemologies. In one of her essays she introduces the neologism "interpretationism" as a solution, noting that "relativism is a consequence, but not always the intent, of interpretationism." (See her "Feminism, Science, and the Anti-Enlightenment Critiques," in Linda Nicholson, ed., *Feminism/Postmodernism*, p. 102, n. 5.) By contrast, I am urging the value of endorsing a reconstructed relativism, shorn of its enfeebling implications.

51   Donna Haraway, "Situated Knowledges: The Science Question in Feminism and the Privilege of Partial Perspective," *Feminist Studies* 14, 3, Fall 1988, 575–599, p. 584.

52   See Nancy Jay, "Gender and Dichotomy," *Feminist Studies* 7:1 1981, pp. 38–56, for a discussion of the exclusiveness of dichotomies.

53   Peter Unger, in *Ignorance: A Case for Scepticism*, Oxford: Clarendon Press, 1975, argues that because no knowledge claim can meet the exacting standards of formulation in absolute terms, there is only conjecture, opinion, fantasy. People are doomed to ignorance, and should simply avow their skepticism.

54   In thinking about Pyrrhonian skepticism I am indebted to David R. Hiley, "The Deep Challenge of Pyrrhonian Scepticism." *Journal of the History of Philosophy* 25:2 April 1987, pp. 185–213.

55   Seyla Benhabib, "Epistemologies of Postmodernism: A Rejoinder to Jean-François Lyotard." In Linda Nicholson, ed., *Feminism/Postmodernism*, p. 124.

56   The phrase is Hiley's op. cit., p. 213.

57   Denise Riley, *"Am I That Name?" Feminism and the Category of Women in History*, Minneapolis: University of Minnesota Press, 1988, p. 113.

58   John Rajchman, *Michel Foucault: The Freedom of Philosophy*. New York: Columbia University Press, 1985, p. 3.

59   Rux Martin, "Truth, Power, Self: An Interview with Michel Foucault, October 25, 1982." In Luther H. Martin, Huck Gutman, and Patrick H. Hutton, eds., *Technologies of the Self: A Seminar with Michel Foucault*, Amherst: University of Massachusetts Press, 1988, p. 11.

60   Michel Foucault, "On the Genealogy of Ethics: An Overview of Work in Progress." Afterword, in Hubert L. Dreyfus and Paul Rabinow, *Michel Foucault: Beyond Structuralism and Hermeneutics*, Second Edition, Chicago: University of Chicago Press, 1983, p. 231.

*Normativity*

# 10 The Practices of Justification

## *Alessandra Tanesini*

When reading some of the work that is typical of twentieth-century analytic epistemology, I am reminded of the Ptolemaic model of the solar system. Astronomers kept adding spheres to square the model with observation, until the model became unbelievably complex with many *ad hoc* features. Similarly, many epistemologists keep adding conditions to their analyses of knowledge. Nevertheless, these conditions are never quite sufficient or necessary. As soon as somebody comes up with a new analysis, another epistemologist will Gettier her, or find a counter-example of a different kind.

Analytic epistemology also seems to have lost touch with ordinary concerns about knowledge. It is of little or no use when it comes to an evaluation of the conduct of inquiry and criticism.[1] Nevertheless, it would seem that the main point of epistemology is precisely to provide such evaluations. Descartes, for example, criticized the reliance on established authorities which was typical of his times, and developed a new method for the acquisition of knowledge. This consideration raises the suspicion that analytic epistemology might have misconceived the kind of philosophical problems generated by the notions of knowledge and justification. The endless tinkering with necessary and sufficient conditions suggests that a Copernican revolution is needed in the study of knowledge.

I would like to propose that we look at knowledge from a different angle. I suggest we stop searching for the set of properties that is defining of knowledge, and adopt instead a different approach. I want to focus my discussion on an epistemic notion that has always been central to epistemological inquiry: justification. I shall not endeavor to find out which property or properties justification might consist of. Instead, I will discuss the practice of "giving and asking for reasons" in a community. In this way, I hope to provide an account which is relevant to the conduct of inquiry and criticism.

In the first part of this paper I explicate the difference between the starting point which has been traditionally adopted in twentieth-century analytic epistemology, and the one I intend to pursue. In the second part I begin to develop an account of justification in terms of practices. In the third part I discuss the complex relations between justification, as I understand it, and power.

## I

It is assumed in epistemology that the right questions to ask are: "what is knowledge?," "what is justification?" To answer these questions requires that one finds out the properties which constitute justification, or upon which justification supervenes. Why assume, however, that these questions have an answer? Why assume that there are such properties? Maybe we are deceived by grammar to postulate that when we say that a claim is justified, we are attributing a property to that claim.

The idea that there is no such "thing" as justification is, perhaps, not a new one. One may find in Foucault's work indications that he felt attracted to this position. It is generally assumed, however, that if one denies the existence of justification as a property, one has relinquished normativity altogether. It would be a mistake to draw this conclusion. Eliminativism is not the only alternative to epistemic realism. It is possible, instead, to hold that the purpose of epistemic talk is not attributive. Although there are no properties to which claims about justification are responsive, talk of justification can be preserved if it is not in the business of attributing properties. There would be no answer to the questions that epistemologists traditionally ask. Nevertheless, epistemic discourse need not be abandoned as an eliminativist would advocate. The alternative to realism and eliminativism is one that has already been developed for other kinds of normative talk.

Consider the example of ethical discourse. Imagine asking a non-cognitivist the question: "what is wrongness?" This is not a question she would think appropriate. For a non-cognitivist, ethical talk does not have a descriptive function; it is not in the business of attributing properties. Traditionally non-cognitivism focuses on the nature of the mental states associated with moral claims, and on the truth-aptness of the claims themselves. Broadly speaking, most non-cognitivists about moral discourse subscribe to expressivism, i.e., the view that moral claims express moral judgments, and these judgments are mental states of a kind different from beliefs (Darwall, Gibbard, Railton, 1992: 148–9). For example, emotivism is the species of expressivism according to which moral judgments consist in feelings.[2]

Until recently non-cognitivism in ethics has received either a semantic or a psychological characterization. Such characterizations represented attempts to spell out the difference between the sort of talk which has a descriptive function and that which does not. The semantic characterization claims that only descriptive talk can be assessed as to its truth or falsity. This is the approach adopted by earlier expressivists. It has encountered severe objections since, for example, we ordinarily attribute truth or falsity to moral claims. The psychological characterization of the difference between descriptive and non-descriptive talk offers a solution to this objection. Non-cognitivists might agree that moral claims are in a minimal sense truth-apt, but hold nevertheless that they differ in important respects from factual claims. They could explain this difference in terms of the psychological states expressed by the claims in question. Non-cognitivists could hold that non factual claims cannot be used to give the content of a belief (Jackson, Oppy, and Smith, 1994: 294).

Neither of these characterizations of non-cognitivism seem particularly suited to epistemology. Epistemic claims appear to be truth-apt. There seems to be nothing wrong with saying that it is true, for example, that I am justified in believing that I am Italian. Similarly, epistemic claims appear to give the con-

153

*self-contained 'justification'?* [handwritten margin note]

tent of beliefs. For example, my claim that I am justified in believing that I am Italian gives the content of my belief that my belief that I am Italian is justified.

There is, however, a more general account of non-cognitivism which makes it applicable to epistemology. It takes the defining characteristic of non-cognitivism about any given area of discourse to be that of attributing to claims in that area a function different from those fulfilled by other parts of language. This functional characterization, as developed by John O'Leary-Hawthorne and Huw Price, seems to capture what is central to non-cognitivism as a philosophical position, namely its anti-reductionist character (1996: 276).

When functionally characterized, non-cognitivism about any given area of discourse has two aspects: a metaphysical position, and a linguistic one. It holds that there are no facts or properties to which talk in that area of discourse typically responds. In particular, it holds that there are no naturalist properties which could perform this function. There are two ways of understanding this claim. First, it can mean that there are no normative facts of a certain kind. Second, it can mean that, although there are facts of that kind, claims in the given area of discourse should not be seen as typically responding to them. I do not think that in the context of this paper anything much hangs on the difference between these interpretations. In what follows, I will claim that there are no epistemic facts or properties. However, I have no objections to saying that there are such facts or properties, but that they do not play any causal explanatory role. The second aspect of non-cognitivism is the claim that talk in the area of discourse in question is not totally out of sorts, since it does not have the linguistic function of stating facts or attributing properties.

*or Conditions?* [handwritten margin note]

So interpreted, non-cognitivism could be seen as an attempt to reconcile naturalism with anti-reductivism. It would be a way of subscribing to a materialist ontology, whilst maintaining the autonomy of normative talk. Non-cognitivism could be interpreted as an answer to the Moorean open question argument which is meant to prove the failure of any reductive strategy. What is at stake is the claim that no amount of naturalistic analysis can account for the normativity of certain areas of discourse. Non-cognitivism, when properly understood, is the view that normative discourse performs a different linguistic function from non-normative discourse, and that this difference is categorical in the sense that there is no complex non-normative claim which could be used to the same linguistic effect as a normative one.

Non-cognitivism in ethics has a distinguished history. In the last few years, however, philosophers have attempted to provide accounts of other normative areas along these lines. For example, Saul Kripke (1982) has argued that meaning attributions have a normative character. Meaning, he claims, is a matter of correct use. He also provides arguments, which he attributes to Wittgenstein, against any reductivist account of meaning. Finally, Kripke advances what he calls a skeptical solution to the problem of meaning. Crucial to this solution is the claim that there are no facts to which meaning attributions are responsive. What Kripke has developed is a sort of non-cognitivism about meaning. A similar position about the matter of modality has been developed by Simon Blackburn (1993: 54). He, too, holds that modal talk is not responsive to special modal properties, but that modal talk nevertheless serves an important function. In this paper I adopt a similar strategy with regard to epistemic talk, which like discourses about morals, modals, and meaning has a normative character.

There are, I believe, good arguments to show why the twentieth-century quest for the property of justification is misconceived. I shall not present them in any detail here. Suffice it to say that I believe that that quest has been motivated by a misunderstanding about the kind of philosophical problems generated by the notion of justification. A philosophical theory of this notion is needed, but it will be a theory that is formulated in terms which are very different from those adopted in recent analytic epistemology.

## II

The starting point of analytic epistemology is to investigate those facts and properties which make epistemic claims true.[3] Instead, I suggest we discuss what functions epistemic talk serves in our ways of life. I want to explain the purpose of talking about justification. My explanation will make no appeal to epistemic facts or properties to which such talk would be attuned.

There is a close connection between justification and the social practice of providing reasons to back up our claims. The practice of giving grounds in defense of our assertions provides the background against which the concept of justification has been developed.[4] I propose that we need to explore this connection in order to understand the functions served by epistemic discourse. In this manner we can develop an epistemology which is not irrelevant to everyday conduct in inquiry and criticism. Furthermore, since the starting point is an investigation of the practices adopted by a culture, the epistemology thus developed can be socially situated; it will not aspire to the role of first philosophy.

In what follows I first sketch a brief description of the practice of giving and asking for reasons. On the basis of this description I then develop an account of the purpose of epistemic talk in the context of this wider practice. First of all, however, I will offer some remarks about the notion of "practice" as I employ it in this paper. My discussion of practices finds me broadly in agreement with the account provided by Robert Brandom (1994), although I disagree with his suggestions about the functions served by normative talk. I will then provide an account of the relations between norms and power. This issue can be raised in the context of Brandom's approach, although he does not himself discuss it.

A social practice is a way of doing things which has a normative dimension.[5] There are, in other words, standards implicit in the practice. For example, consider the game of soccer. If a player picks up the ball and runs with it in his hands, he has stopped playing the game. He is not engaging in this practice any longer. However, by doing so, he might initiate a new practice.[6] Nevertheless, the standards implicit in a practice can change. For example, in soccer a goalkeeper used to be allowed to pick up the ball with his hands when he received a back pass from a defender, but this is no longer the case.

The idea that the normative dimension of our lives can be accounted for in terms of practices is not new. It can be found in Ludwig Wittgenstein, and it has been developed further by Wilfrid Sellars and more recently by John McDowell and Brandom.[7] The recourse to practices is motivated by the attempt to explain rule-following behavior which, it has been argued, cannot be accounted for either in purely dispositional terms or in terms of interpretations of rules.[8] Dispositional accounts fail to explain normative behavior because it is impossible to analyze correct performance in terms of regularities in patterns of behavior. Accounts in terms of explicit rules also fail because they generate a regress. If correct performance is understood as performance guided by an explicit rule, another rule must be supplied providing an interpretation of the first rule. The second rule, however, also stands in need of an interpretation, and so on.

The appeal to practices is intended to provide an alternative account of norms which distinguishes them both from mere regularities of behavior and from explicit rules governing behavior. Norms do not exist independently of human practices. Rather, they are understood as structures of appropriateness which are implicit in practices. These structures are instituted by the practical normative attitudes adopted by practitioners. Normative attitudes are instances of taking something to be a correct performance according to a practice. For example, I cross the road at a traffic light when the walk signal appears, this action manifests a normative attitude. Implicitly, I take the action to be correct in accordance with the practice of road behavior. Similarly, when I pay for my purchases, in practice I take this performance to be correct in accordance with several practices which include the practice of treating money as an object with exchange value, and practices concerning moral behavior.

There are no standards of correctness which exist independently of every normative attitude. Instead, standards emerge out of these attitudes. Whether an action has a given normative status, whether it is correct in accordance with the practice, will depend on some normative attitudes. The example of road-crossing helps to clarify this point. There is no sense in which the norms of road behavior exist independently of attitudes toward it. These are norms that have been created by our practices.

The example of moral action is different. Whilst it is implausible to hold that everybody might be wrong about when it is appropriate to cross the road at a traffic light, it is at the very least plausible to claim that we may all be wrong about the morality of an action. It does not follow, however, that the norms of morality are not instituted by normative attitudes. Instead, it must be acknowledged that what a group or an individual actually takes to be correct, needs not be correct. Such an acknowledgment should not be construed as an appeal to norms that exist independently of practices. Rather, it requires that normative attitudes themselves are subject to normative assessment. It is only if one takes correctly a performance to be correct in accordance with a practice, that the performance *is* correct. For instance, suppose that everybody took eating animals to be correct. We, might, nevertheless be mistaken. It is only if our attitude toward meat-eating is correct, that the performance of this action is also correct. However, whether people correctly take meat-eating to be acceptable depends on the practice of evaluating current normative attitudes about eating animals. Every time we try to settle whether someone correctly takes something to be correct, we exhibit further normative attitudes. What we have here is an account that resists the temptation to reduce normative vocabulary to a vocabulary which is not normative. It is an account that holds that it is possible to discuss the norms implicit in a practice only in terms of norms implicit in other practices. I will explain this point in more detail below when I discuss the functions served by epistemic talk.

The notion of a normative attitude plays a crucial role in this account of norms. The presence of these attitudes is the feature that distinguishes norm-governed from merely regular behavior. Attitudes make the difference between behavior which is subject to norms and behavior that is sensitive to them. Only the latter is governed by norms. Sensitivity to norms involves acknowledging them; it involves treating in practice some performance as correct in accordance with a practice. Often, these normative attitudes are practical because they do not consist in endorsing a proposition; rather, they are implicit in behavior. For example, I manifest a negative normative attitude toward an action by refraining to engage in it, by encouraging others to refrain from it, and by disapproving of those who do.

This account of practices must be supplemented with an explanation of two features which are at the intersection between power and norms. These features are: (i) the quasi-bodily nature of some practical normative attitudes, and (ii) the relevance of the social locations of the practitioners to the standards implicit in practices. It is to these two features that I would like to turn briefly; I shall return to them in the third section of this paper.

Practices like playing a game or a musical instrument require a "feel for the game." We are inducted into these practices, and by means of training we learn to act in accordance with the normative standards implicit in the practice. In other words, we become sensitive to new norms, we acquire new normative attitudes. The trained scientist, for example, knows how to go about making an experiment. She is sensitive to the norms implicit in experimental practice. Her sensitivity will be expressed by endorsements of propositions about rules of conduct, but it will also involve bodily "habits." These habits are dispositions to behave in particular ways, which exhibit normative assessments. They are dispositions which invest behavior with a normative significance.[9] It is this feature that distinguishes habits from the sort of reliable discriminatory dispositions of which even entities like thermometers are capable. When one acquires a new habit of this kind, one has acquired a new range of normative attitudes. The learning process does not have to be mediated by beliefs. Rather, one is tempted to say that, by means of training, embodied individuals become endowed with new normative responses.

The second aspect of practices I want to discuss is the relevance of the social locations of practitioners to the normative standards implicit in practices. Not everybody is granted the same cognitive authority in every area of inquiry. Instead, we recognize the existence of experts by giving more weight to their normative attitudes in the areas in which they are expert. "Cognitive authority" is a normative notion whose attribution to individuals will be a matter of the normative assessments that are manifested in the behavior of other practitioners. It is impossible to have authority unless one can be treated as authoritative. Nevertheless, it does not follow that whoever is treated as an authority is authoritative. Whether somebody has this status will depend on whether she is correctly taken to be authoritative. The issue of correctness, however, is always dependent on human normative assessments.

Presently, social factors, such as race and gender, have an effect on normative assessments concerning cognitive authority. For example, there is an ingrained resistance to the attribution of such an authority to women and individuals who are not of European descent. Feminist epistemologists have often argued that individuals occupying socially marginal positions should, instead, be granted some cognitive authority especially on the matter of their marginality. Further, they hold that some individuals who are currently taken to have cognitive authority should not be granted such privilege. These epistemologists, in other words, have undertaken an evaluation of some current normative attitudes toward expertise. They have also advanced a proposal for the introduction of new normative assessments of cognitive authority. The social location of individuals is relevant to whether they are taken to have authority, and whether this assessment is correct. Experts have an important role in shaping the normative attitudes of the communities to which they belong. They have an influence on what is actually treated as correct in practice, and on assessments of current normative attitudes. In this manner social factors are relevant to the norms developed by a community through its practices.

What I have said above applies to practices in general. It is now time to turn to a practice that is of special epistemological interest. This is the practice of giving and asking for reasons of which asserting is a fundamental component. The point of asserting is to claim knowledge for oneself. If I assert that Saint Mark's Cathedral is in Venice, I make a claim which I take at least to be correct. Assertions, more specifically, are the sort of thing which can stand as a reason and for which reasons might be needed. They are, therefore, crucial to the game of giving and asking for reasons.

Since assertion is the sort of thing which functions as a reason, it can provide entitlements to further claims. In other words, it issues a license to further entitlements. Assertion also involves commitments, because it is the sort of thing for which reasons might be needed. In making an assertion a speaker undertakes the commitment to answer appropriate challenges to her claims. If she answers these challenges satisfactorily, she has discharged her commitment and gained an entitlement to her claim.[10] For example, if I claim that the rate of inflation will increase in the next quarter, I commit myself to giving reasons in support of my claim if challenged. If I answer these challenges to the questioner's satisfaction I have discharged the commitment I undertook. I have thus become entitled to my claim. I can discharge my commitment by giving reasons in support of my claim. In the case of this example, I might assert that the increased cost of labor is causing inflationary tendencies. By doing this, I implicitly commit myself to the view that the reason I have provided is indeed a reason in support of my original claim. This commitment also might be challenged. I might, however, adopt a different strategy to support my original assertion. I might defer to the authority of another person, whom I take to be entitled to make the claim under consideration.[11] In other words, I might rely on the testimony of others. Finally, I might be entitled to my claim by default, if it is not challenged.

Assertions also involve a structure of responsibility and authority. When I undertake a commitment, I undertake a responsibility to discharge it. If I succeed, I have fulfilled my responsibility and I have thereby gained some cognitive authority. Others might defer to me when they attempt to gain entitlement to the same claim. Of course, unless I am entitled to the claim, the deferring strategy employed by others will be to no effect.

It is now time to turn to the connection between epistemic talk and the practice of giving and asking for reasons which I have described. The question I want to address concerns the purpose served by such talk. Why do we talk of justification at all? A first option would be to understand such talk as providing a description of the practice of giving and asking for reasons. One may then try to explain this practice in terms of communal dispositions of a certain sort. This would amount to a dispositional account of justification, one that understands justification by means of communal, rather than individual, dispositions. According to this view we can explain the structure of appropriateness implicit in the practice in terms of regularity of behavior of the majority of the members of a community. Such an account, I believe, is doomed to fail for the same reasons for which accounts in terms of individual dispositions fail.[12]

A second option would be to take the practice of talking about justification to be supervenient upon communal dispositions, whilst holding that it is only when we describe the practice as a practice that we have a structure appropriate for understanding justification. Social practices involve implicit standards about, for example, what counts as a reason or when one should provide a reason for one's claims. Hence, it could be claimed that, since a practice provides standards of appropriateness, justification could be explicated in terms of what is licensed by the epistemic norms implicit in current epistemic practices. The linguistic role of epistemic claims would be to explicitate the standards of appropriateness which are implicit in current epistemic practices. This is the option adopted by Brandom. However, also this second option is unsatisfactory, since it entails that, if one were to challenge the standards implicit in current practice whilst acknowledging what they are, that person would contradict herself.

A different account is, therefore, necessary. What I would like to keep from the second option explored above is the view that it is only if we start with social practices as structures of appropriateness of behavior that we can understand normative discourse. What I would like to reject is the claim that the linguistic role of epistemic discourse is to codify the structures of appropriateness implicit in the practices. An example might be of help here. Talk of epistemic justification is not very common in everyday practice. Usually, we provide reasons for our claims without mentioning justification. However, talk of justification might be employed when what is challenged is the relevance of those reasons. For instance, suppose that somebody claims that the sun goes around the earth, and backs up this claim by referring to what the Bible says. One might well reply that what the Bible says on these matters is not a justification. It would be a mistake to read this reply as stating that the norms implicit in current practice do not license using the Bible in this manner. A speaker who makes this claim asserts that the Bible is of no help here, no matter what common practice licenses.

Talk of justification, I hold, is employed either to suggest a modification of common practice or to adopt such a practice. In other words, it is used as an endorsement of some relations between assertions as relations that confer entitlement even if they might not figure as such in the current practice. This is a view that has been advanced by Mark Lance (1992) who holds that normative claims are explained as interventions upon, rather than descriptions of, the underlying current social practice.[13] These interventions are themselves understood as functioning against the background of the current practice. Hence, they involve undertakings of commitments to respond to challenges deemed to be appropriate in the underlying practice. If such undertakings are successfully discharged then one has secured entitlement to one's claim and to what that claim licenses.

The approach I have sketched above provides the framework for a conception of the subject matter of epistemology, and of the point of epistemology itself which is very different from the one adopted in contemporary analytic theory of knowledge. The latter takes itself to be a study of the properties underlying justification and knowledge. I have claimed that there are no such properties, or that in any case they play no explanatory role in epistemology. Instead, epistemology is concerned with a range of practices for which the practice of giving and asking for reasons is fundamental. Epistemology does not investigate properties but structures of appropriateness. These are structures which are implicit in practices, and are instituted by human normative attitudes. It is not, however, merely concerned with the explication of these structures. Instead, the use of epistemic discourse typical of epistemology is a motor for change in the underlying practices of giving and asking for reasons. Epistemology thus understood is engaged in criticism and in the evaluation of the conduct of inquiry. In this respect it is very different from standard analytic epistemology.

The approach, I have outlined, also shows how situated criticism is an important part of epistemology.[14] I have claimed that norms are implicit in practice. I have also claimed that the point of normative discourse is to advance proposals for the alteration or preservation of current norms. Epistemic discourse is something we do; it is a practice. This practice also functions against the background of current practices which it might attempt to amend. This practice of criticism is therefore situated. The situatedness of all our practices can be made more explicit by noticing other features attributed to them by the account I have outlined.

First, rationality is not primarily a matter of formal logical relations. The practice of supporting one's claims is the practice of giving reasons for them. These are reasons that are taken to entitle one to these claims. Whether these reasons succeed in conferring entitlement is a matter of inferential relations. These, however, will include material deductive inferences, examples of inductive reasoning, as well as other ways of supporting claims. These are inferential relations that might not be instances of valid formal argument forms.

Second, inferential relations are instituted by human normative attitudes. Therefore, reason thus conceived is historically situated. This is not to say, once again, that whatever the community takes to be a good way of reasoning is appropriate. It entails, however, that reasoning develops out of the context of what the members of a culture take to be a good way of supporting specific claims. Nevertheless, these normative attitudes can be challenged. If the challenge is successful, it licenses the claim that what the community takes to be an instance of good reasoning is not so. Finally, reason is not unrelated to issues pertaining to bodies. Reason is primarily implicit in practices, and in the habits we develop when we are inducted into them. Creatures whose daily lives differ from each other, or whose bodies differ from each other are likely to develop different habits. They are likely in some cases to acknowledge in practice different forms of reasoning. This is not an all or nothing affair; there might be substantial overlap. Furthermore, modes of reasoning implicit in practice are the sort of thing which can be brought up for challenge.

## III

The multifarious relations between practices and power must now be explored. In its basic sense, power is just the ability to do something. For example, because I am able to read, it is correct to say it is in my power to do so. Power over others is the ability to make them do something, perhaps even against their wish. Individuals acquire power, including power over others, by virtue of the social positions they occupy. For example, traffic wardens can give parking tickets. More precisely, there are practices that entitle some individuals to perform actions which others could not successfully perform. Because I am not a traffic warden I cannot give a ticket to a careless driver. The figure of the traffic warden is instituted by the practice, the social position, which bestows power on the individual that occupies it; it would not exist independently of the practice.

Similar considerations apply to the practice of giving and asking for reasons. Those speakers who have gained entitlement to a given claim have an authority which is denied to others. Whilst traffic wardens can issue tickets, these speakers can issue licenses to assert claims. When individuals are granted authority in a whole area of inquiry, they acquire a social position which grants them privilege in a variety of other practices including some that have a clear political dimension. For example, experts can influence governments' decisions. Hence, epistemic practices are instrumental in the institution of social position which are bestowed with special powers by the political practices of the community.

This much is not controversial. It merely amounts to the claim that knowledge is an instrument of power. More interesting is the converse claim according to which power is instrumental to knowledge. I limit my discussion to an analysis of social power, since it is quite obvious that other kinds of power are instrumental to knowledge. If I didn't have the power to read, I wouldn't know some of the things I know. The issue to be examined is the relevance of the social positions occupied by individuals to the practice of giving and asking for reasons. In this case also, we must distinguish between trivial and interesting ways in which social positions are relevant to epistemic practice. It is by virtue of my social position as an academic that I have had the opportunity to travel and to know things which I might not have known otherwise. This is obvious, and not very interesting. Instead, I examine the relevance of the social positions occupied by speakers to the ways in which they gain entitlement to their claims.

Individuals who occupy different social positions are likely to have very different lives. As a consequence they develop cognitive habits, and normative attitudes attuned to their circumstances. For example, carers of young children have cognitive habits that others have not acquired; these habits are not mere reliable discriminatory dispositions since they exhibit normative assessments. Carers of young children, for instance, will acknowledge in practice material inferences to which other individuals might not be sensitive. Of course, there will be extensive overlap in habits and attitudes among members of a community. Otherwise, they would not constitute one community.[15] The social position of individuals also influences attributions of cognitive authority. The opinion of persons who have social status is often given more weight than the opinion of others. For example, they are not challenged as often. Cognitive habits and attributions of cognitive authority affect how one gains entitlement for one's claims. Persons with different habits might not employ the same ways of supporting claims. Individuals who are not granted the same cognitive authority gain different entitlements by default.

The social organization of communities makes an epistemic difference. Social status is relevant to attributions of cognitive authority which, in turn, play an important role in shaping what members of a community take to be correct when it comes to supporting their claims. These social factors do not just influence what people take to be right, they also influence what is right, since what is right is what is correctly taken to be right. Evaluation of current practice is also a matter of practice, and it is responsive to the implicit structure of appropriateness of the underlying practice which is being evaluated. The influence of social factors thus pervades every practice including the practices of giving and asking for reasons. This influence cannot be rooted out.

Furthermore, from the viewpoint of the approach I have outlined there are no good reasons to believe that social influences always have an undesirable effect on epistemic practices. The social structure of a community influences what its members take to be good reasons in support for claims. It is one of the tasks of epistemology to evaluate these practices, and if necessary to propose others that should take their place. It is possible that the adoption of these alternative practices would be facilitated by social changes in the community. Such changes, therefore, would have a positive effect on epistemic practices.

However, whether any given social factors have a good or bad influence on a practice is something that must be assessed in each individual case.

## Notes

1  This point has been forcefully made by Mark Kaplan (1991).
2  This is the position adopted, for example, by C. L. Stevenson (1996).
3  Supporters of the standard approach to epistemology usually believe in the existence of truth-makers. What makes true a claim that a belief is justified is the fact that the belief in question has the property of being justified.
4  I believe that even analytic epistemologists would concur on this point. William Alston, for example, makes this point himself (1989: 237)
5  I take practices to be essentially social. Arguments in support of this claim have been provided by Brandom (1995: 902–904).
6  The game of rugby was invented in this way.
7  See Wittgenstein (1988), Sellars (1963), McDowell (1984), and Brandom (1994).
8  This point is forcefully made by McDowell (1984).
9  Brandom has described these responsive dispositions as dispositions to apply concepts (1995: 897). I find this terminology misleading since it runs the danger of being interpreted in an over-intellectualistic manner.
10  The structure of commitments and entitlements involved in asserting has been discussed in detail by Brandom (1994).
11  I have ignored in this paper a crucial aspect of Brandom's account which is the main focus of his discussion. He argues that the notion of propositional content can be explained in terms of the structure of normative statuses such as entitlements and commitments implicit in the practice of asserting. Content is explained in terms of the inferential relations that are implicitly acknowledged in practice. The account provided in this paper is an account of asserting, rather than assertion. However, I have left this further issue unexplored because I do not consider it particularly important for the account of epistemic practices that I am trying to develop.
12  Curiously, however, Kripke (1982) seems to have adopted this point of view about epistemic claims.
13  Since this is an account of epistemic discourse that does not take it to be responsive to epistemic facts, one must provide some sort of causal explanation of why this discourse has emerged. I believe an account can be given in terms of coordination of behaviour. I do not, however, discuss this issue in this paper.
14  For a discussion of situated criticism which can be read along these lines see Nancy Fraser (1995: 64).
15  Membership of a community is, as Brandom points out (1994: 39), a normative issue. I shall not discuss it in this paper.

## Works Cited

Alston, William (1989). "An Internalist Externalism" in *Epistemic Justification: Essays in the Theory of Knowledge*. Ithaca: Cornell University Press, pp. 227–45.
Blackburn, Simon (1993). *Essays in Quasi-Realism*, Oxford: Oxford University Press.
Brandom, Robert (1994). *Making it Explicit*, Cambridge: Harvard University Press.

Brandom, Robert (1995). "Knowledge and the Social Articulation of the Space of Reasons," *Philosophy and Phenomenological Research*, 60 (4): 895–908.

Darwall, Stephen, Gibbard, Allan, and Railton, Peter (1992). "Toward *Fin de siècle* Ethics: Some Trends," *Philosophical Review*, 101: 115–189.

Fraser, Nancy (1995). "False Antitheses: A Response to Seyla Benhabib and Judith Butler" in Seyla Benhabib, Judith Butler, Drucilla Cornell, Nancy Fraser, Linda Nicholson (eds), *Feminist Contentions: A Philosophical Exchange*. New York and London: Routledge, pp. 59–74.

Kaplan, Mark (1991). "Epistemology on Holiday," *Journal of Philosophy*, 88(3): 132–54.

Kripke, Saul (1982). *Wittgenstein: On Rules and Private Language*. Oxford: Blackwell.

Jackson, Frank, Oppy, Graham, and Smith, Michael (1994) "Minimalism and Truth Aptness," *Mind*, 103: 287–302.

Lance, Mark (1992). "Where do we go from here?," unpublished *ms.*

McDowell, John (1984). "Wittgenstein on Following a Rule," *Synthese*, 58: 325–63.

O'Leary-Hawthorne, John and Price, Huw (1996). "How To Stand Up for Non-Cognitivism," *Australasian Journal of Philosophy*, 74(2): 275–92.

Sellars, Wilfrid (1963). *Science, Perception and Reality*. London: Routledge.

Stevenson, C. L. (1966). "The Emotive Meaning of Ethical Terms" in Joseph Margolis (ed.), *Contemporary Ethical Theory*. New York: Random House, pp. 81–103.

Wittgenstein, Ludwig (1988). *Philosophical Investigations*, trans. by G. E. M. Anscombe. Oxford: Basil Blackwell.

# PART THREE

# WHAT IS THE STRUCTURE OF KNOWLEDGE?

# Introduction

The question of the structure of knowledge is closely related to the problem of epistemic justification; however, it may not become apparent when we only consider how to justify particular beliefs or even classes of beliefs. The question of structure arises when we consider our knowledge as a whole. If knowledge requires justification, then it would seem that every particular belief requires reasons, and these reasons themselves will require reasons, and so on ad infinitum.

This is the epistemological problem of infinite regress, first discussed by Aristotle, and it has led epistemologists to consider the structural relations between types of knowledge. Foundationalism and coherentism have been the primary contenders for a solution to this problem in contemporary epistemology, though there are always a few epistemologists who deny that the problem has any meaningfulness (pragmatists and some contextualists would fit here, arguing against the possibility of epistemically evaluating all knowledge). Foundationalists halt the regress at some foundational layer of knowledge which is self-evident or self-justifying and thus not in need of further reasoned explanation; theirs is a pyramid model of knowledge. Coherentists argue that the regress need not be vicious under certain conditions and that a holistic model of knowledge provides justification without a privileged, ultimate ground; their model has been described as a raft that must be repaired without coming to shore. The first three essays in this section provide explorations of this debate, highlighting the various advantages and disadvantages accruing to each position. The final essay, by the German philosopher Hans-Georg Gadamer, is not explicitly addressed to the analytic terms of debate, and so may need some explanation.

Gadamer developed a general account of knowledge based on a study of hermeneutics, which is an exploration of the problems of ascertaining meaning in works of translation and interpretation. When we interpret a text, we always bring to the process a set of prejudgments (what he calls fore-having or fore-knowledge) that involve our historical and cultural background as well as our individual experience. The process of interpretation proceeds by a back and forth movement between the text itself and these prejudgments, which yields a kind of regress of its own that has been called "the hermeneutic circle."

The epistemic question is: how can we ever know if our interpretation is correct given the ubiquitous presence of these prior prejudgments? Gadamer provides the sketch of an answer to this problem in this excerpt from his major work, *Truth and Method*. On his view, there is no completely successful method by which we might escape the horizon of our prejudgments. Although there are significant epistemic differences between the natural and the social (or, roughly, what he calls human) sciences, the problem of prejudgments is a problem for all attempts to understand the world, not just in relation to the interpretation of texts. The answer to this problem according to Gadamer lies in reassessing the epistemic role of our prejudgments.

**Further Reading**

Alston, William P. *Epistemic Justification*. Ithaca, NY: Cornell University Press, 1989.

Bender, J., ed. *The Current State of the Coherence Theory* Dordrecht: Kluwer, 1989.

Weinsheimer, Joel C. *Gadamer's Hermeneutics: A Reading of Truth and Method*. New Haven: Yale University Press, 1985.

Williams, Michael. *Unnatural Doubts: Epistemological Realism and the Basis of Scepticism*. Oxford: Blackwell, 1991.

# 11   The Myth of the Given

## Roderick Chisholm

### 1

The doctrine of "the given" involved two theses about our knowledge. We may introduce them by means of a traditional metaphor:

(A)   The knowledge that a person has at any time is a structure or edifice, many parts and stages of which help to support each other, but which as a whole is supported by its own foundation.

The second thesis is a specification of the first:

(B)   The foundation of one's knowledge consists (at least in part) of the apprehension of what have been called, variously, "sensations," "sense-impressions," "appearances," "sensa," "sense-qualia," and "phenomena."

These phenomenal entities, said to be at the base of the structure of knowledge, are what was called "the given." A third thesis is sometimes associated with the doctrine of the given, but the first two theses do not imply it. We may formulate it in terms of the same metaphor.

(C)   The *only* apprehension that is thus basic to the structure of knowledge is our apprehension of "appearances" (etc.) – our apprehension of the given.

Theses (A) and (B) constitute the "doctrine of the given"; thesis (C), if a label were necessary, might be called "the phenomenalistic version" of the doctrine. The first two theses are essential to the emprical tradition in Western philosophy. The third is problematic for traditional empiricism and depends in part, but only in part, on the way in which the metaphor of the edifice and its foundation is defined and elaborated.

I believe it is accurate to say that, at the time at which our study begins, most American epistemologists accepted the first two theses and thus accepted the doctrine of the given. The expression "the given" became a term of contemporary philosophical vocabulary partly because of its use by C. I. Lewis in his *Mind and the World-Order* (Scribner, 1929). Many of the philosophers who accepted the doctrine avoided the expression because of its association with other more controversial parts of Lewis's book – a book that might be taken (though mistakenly, I think) also to endorse thesis (C), the "phenomenalistic version" of the doctrine. The doctrine itself – theses (A) and (B) – became a matter of general controversy during the period of our survey.

Thesis (A) was criticized as being "absolute" and thesis (B) as being overly "subjective." Both criticisms may be found in some of the "instrumentalistic" writings of John Dewey and philosophers associated with him. They may also be found in the writings of those philosophers of science ("logical empiricists") writing in the tradition of the Vienna Circle. (At an early stage of this tradition, however, some of these same philosophers seem to have accepted all three theses.) Discussion became entangled in verbal confusions – especially in connection with the uses of such terms as "doubt," "certainty," "appearance," and "immediate experience." Philosophers, influenced by the work that Ludwig Wittgenstein had been doing in the 1930s, noted such confusions in detail, and some of them seem to have taken the existence of such confusions to indicate that (A) and (B) are false.[1] Many have rejected both theses as being inconsistent with a certain theory of thought and reference; among them, in addition to some of the critics just referred to, we find philosophers in the tradition of nineteenth century "idealism."

Philosophers of widely diverging schools now believe that "the myth of the given" has finally been dispelled.[2] I suggest, however, that, although thesis (C), "the phenomenalistic version," is false, the two theses, (A) and (B), that constitute the doctrine of the given are true.

The doctrine is not merely the consequence of a metaphor. We are led to it when we attempt to answer certain questions about *justification* – our justification for supposing, in connection with any one of the things that we know to be true, that it is something that we know to be true.

## 2

To the question "What justification do I have for thinking I know that *a* is true?" one may reply: "I know that *b* is true, and if I know that *b* is true then I also know that *a* is true." And to the question "What justification do I have for thinking I know that *b* is true?" one may reply: "I know that *c* is true, and if I know that *c* is true then I also know that *b* is true." Are we thus led, sooner or later, to something *n* of which one may say: "What justifies me in thinking I know that *n* is true is simply that *n* is true." If there is such an *n*, then the belief or statement that *n* is true may be thought of either as a belief or statement that "justifies itself" or as a belief or statement that is itself "neither justified nor unjustified." The distinction – unlike that between a Prime Mover that moves itself and a Prime Mover that is neither in motion nor at rest – is largely a verbal one; the essential thing, if there is such an *n*, is that it provides a stopping place in the process, or dialectic, of justification.

We may now reexpress, somewhat less metaphorically, the two theses I have called the "doctrine of the given." The first thesis, that our knowledge is an edifice or structure having its own foundation, becomes (A) "every statement, which we are justified in thinking that we know, is justified in part by some statement that justifies itself." The second thesis, that there are appearances ("the given") at the foundation of our knowledge, becomes (B) "there are statements about appearances that thus justify themselves." (The third thesis – the "phenomenalistic version" of the doctrine of the given – becomes (C) "there are no self-justifying statements that are not statements about appearances.")

Let us now turn to the first of the two theses constituting the doctrine of the given.

# 3

"Every justified statement is justified in part by some statement that justifies itself." Could it be that the question this thesis is supposed to answer is a question that arises only because of some mistaken assumption? If not, what are the alternative ways of answering it? And did any of the philosophers with whom we are concerned actually accept any of these alternatives? The first two questions are less difficult to answer than the third.

There are the following points of view to be considered, each of which *seems* to have been taken by some of the philosophers in the period of our survey.

(1) One may believe that the questions about justification that give rise to our problem are based on false assumptions and hence that they *should not be asked* at all.

(2) One may believe that no statement or claim is justified unless it is justified, at least in part, by some other justified statement or claim that it does not justify; this belief may suggest that one should continue the process of justifying *ad indefinitum*, justifying each claim by reference to some additional claim.

(3) One may believe that no statement or claim *a* is justified unless it is justified by some other justified statement or claim *b*, and that *b* is not justified unless it in turn is justified by *a*; this would suggest that the process of justifying is, or should be, *circular*.

(4) One may believe that at some particular claims *n* the process of justifying should stop, and one may then hold of any such claim *n* either: (a) *n* is justified by something – viz., *experience* or *observation* – that is not itself a claim and that therefore cannot be said itself either to be justified or unjustified; (b) *n* is itself *unjustified*; (c) *n justifies itself*; or (d) *n is neither justified nor unjustified*.

These possibilities, I think, exhaust the significant points of view; let us now consider them in turn.

# 4

"The questions about justification that give rise to the problem are based on false assumptions and therefore should not be asked at all."

The questions are *not* based on false assumptions; but most of the philosophers who discussed the questions put them in such a misleading way that one is very easily misled into supposing that they *are* based upon false assumptions.

Many philosophers, following Descartes, Russell, and Husserl, formulated the questions about justification by means of such terms as "doubt," "certainty," and "incorrigibility," and they used, or misused, these terms in such a way that, when their questions were taken in the way in which one would ordinarily take them, they could be shown to be based on false assumptions. One may note, for example, that the statement "There is a clock on the mantelpiece" is not self-justifying – for to the question "What is your justification for thinking you know that there is a clock on the mantelpiece?" the proper reply would be to make some other statement (e.g., "I saw it there this morning and no one would have taken it away" – and one may then go on to ask "But are there any statements that can be said to justify themselves?" If we express these facts, as many philosophers did, by saying that the statement "There is a clock on the mantelpiece" is one that is not "certain," or one that may be "doubted," and if we then go on to ask "Does this doubtful statement rest on other statements that are certain and incorrigible?" then we are using terms in an extraordinarily misleading way. The question "Does this doubtful statement rest on statements that are certain and incorrigible?" – if taken as one would ordinarily take it – does rest on a false assumption, for (we may assume) the statement that a clock is on the mantelpiece is one that is not doubtful at all.

John Dewey, and some of the philosophers whose views were very similar to his, tended to suppose, mistakenly, that the philosophers who asked themselves "What justification do I have for thinking I know this?" were asking the quite different question "What more can I do to verify or confirm that this is so?" and they rejected answers to the first question on the ground that they were unsatisfactory answers to the second.[3] Philosophers influenced by Wittgenstein tended to suppose, also mistakenly, but quite understandably, that the question "What justification do I have for thinking I know this?" contains an implicit challenge and presupposes that one does not have the knowledge concerned. They then pointed out, correctly, that in most of the cases where the question was raised (e.g., "What justifies me in thinking I know that this is a table?") there is no ground for challenging the claim to knowledge and that questions presupposing that the claim is false should not arise. But the question "What justifies me in thinking I know that this is a table?" does not challenge the claim to know that this is a table, much less presuppose that the claim is false.

The "critique of cogency," as Lewis described this concern of epistemology, presupposes that we *are* justified in thinking we know most of the things that we do think we know, and what it seeks to elicit is the nature of this justification. The enterprise is like that of ethics, logic, and aesthetics:

> The nature of the good can be learned from experience only if the content of experience be first classified into good and bad, or grades of better and worse. Such classification or grading already involves the legislative application of the same principle which is sought. In logic, principles can be elicited by generalization from examples only if cases of valid reasoning have first been segregated by some criterion. In esthetics, the laws of the beautiful may be derived from experience only if the criteria of beauty have first been correctly applied.[4]

When Aristotle considered an invalid mood of the syllogism and asked himself "What is wrong with this?" he was not suggesting to himself that perhaps nothing was wrong; he presupposed that the mood *was* invalid, just as he presupposed that others were not, and he attempted, successfully, to formulate criteria that would enable us to distinguish the two types of mood.

When we have answered the question, "What justification do I have for thinking I know this?" what we learn, as Socrates taught, is something about ourselves. We learn, of course, what the justification happens to be for the particular claim with which the question is concerned. But we also learn, more generally, what the criteria are, if any, in terms of which we believe ourselves justified in counting one thing as an instance of knowing and another thing not. The truth that the philosopher seeks, when he asks about justification, is "already implicit in the mind which seeks it, and needs only to be elicited and brought to clear expression."[5]

Let us turn, then to the other approaches to the problem of "the given."

## 5

"No statement or claim would be justified unless it were justified, at least in part, by some other justified claim or statement that it does not justify."

This regressive principle might be suggested by the figure of the building and its supports: no stage supports another unless it is itself supported by some other stage beneath it – a truth that holds not only of the upper portions of the building but also of what we call its foundation. And the principle follows if, as some of the philosophers in the tradition of logical empiricism seemed to believe, we should combine a frequency theory of probability with a probability theory of justification.

In *Experience and Prediction* (University of Chicago, 1938) and in other writings, Hans Reichenbach defended a "probability theory of knowledge" that seemed to involve the following contentions:

(1) To justify accepting a statement, it is necessary to show that the statement is probable.

(2) To say of a statement that it is probable is to say something about statistical frequencies. Somewhat more accurately, a statement of the form "It is *probable* that any particular a is b" may be explicated as saying "Most *ds* are *bs*." Or, still more accurately, to say "The probability is *n* that a particular *a* is a *b*" is to say "The limit of the relative frequency with the property of being a *b* occurs in the class of things having the property *a* is *n*."

(3) Hence, by (2), to show that a proposition is probable it is necessary to show that a certain statistical frequency obtains; and, by (1), to show that a certain statistical frequency obtains it is necessary to show that it is probable that the statistical frequency obtains; and therefore, by (2), to show that it is probable that a certain statistical frequency obtains, it is necessary to show that a certain frequency of frequencies obtains . . .

(4) And therefore "there is no Archimedean point of absolute certainty left to

which to attach our knowledge of the world; all we have is an elastic net of probability connections floating in open space" (p. 192).

This reasoning suggests that an infinite number of steps must be taken to justify acceptance of any statement. For, according to the reasoning, we cannot determine the probability of one statement until we have determined that of a second, and we can not determine that of the second until we have determined that of a third, and so on. Reichenbach does not leave the matter here, however. He suggests that there is a way of "descending" from this "open space" of probability connections, but, if I am not mistaken, we can make the descent only by letting go of the concept of justification.

He says that, if we are to avoid the regress of probabilities of probabilities of probabilities . . ., we must be willing at some point merely to make a guess; "there will always be some blind posits on which the whole concatenation is based" (p. 367). The view that knowledge is to be identified with certainty and that probable knowledge must be "imbedded in a framework of certainty" is "a remnant of rationalism. An empiricist theory of probability can be constructed only if we are willing to regard knowledge as a system of posits."[6]

But if we begin by assuming, as we do, that there is a distinction between knowledge, on the one hand, and a lucky guess, on the other, then we must reject at least one of the premises of any argument purporting to demonstrate that knowledge is a system of "blind posits." The unacceptable conclusion of Reichenbach's argument may be so construed as to follow from premises (1) and (2); and premise (2) may be accepted as a kind of definition (though there are many who believe that this definition is not adequate to all of the uses of the term "probable" in science and everyday life.) Premise (1), therefore is the one we should reject, and there are good reasons, I think, for rejecting (1), the thesis that "to justify accepting a proposition it is necessary to show that the proposition is probable." In fairness to Reichenbach, it should be added that he never explicitly affirms premise (1); but some such premise is essential to his argument.

# 6

"No statement or claim *a* would be justified unless it were justified by some other justified statement or claim *b* that would not be justified unless it were justified in turn by *a*."

The "coherence theory of truth," to which some philosophers committed themselves, is sometimes taken to imply that justification may thus be circular; I believe, however, that the theory does not have this implication. It does define "truth" as a kind of systematic consistency of beliefs or propositions. The truth of a proposition is said to consist, not in the fact that the proposition "corresponds" with something that is not itself a proposition, but in the fact that it fits consistently into a certain more general system of propositions. This view may even be suggested by the figure of the building and its foundations. There is no difference in principle between the way in which the upper stories are supported by the lower, and that in which the cellar is supported by the earth just below it, or the way in which the stratum of earth is supported by various substrata farther below; a good building appears to be a part of the terrain on which it stands and a good system of propositions is a part of the wider system that gives it its truth. But these metaphors do not solve philosophical problems.

The coherence theory did in fact appeal to something other than logical consistency; its proponents conceded that a system of false propositions may be internally consistent and hence that logical consistency alone is no guarantee of truth. Brand Blanshard, who defended the coherence theory in *The Nature of Thought*, said that a proposition is true provided it is a member of an internally consistent system of propositions and *provided further* this system is "the system in which everything real and possible is coherently included."[7] In one phase of the development of "logical empiricism" its proponents seem to have held a similar view: a proposition – or, in this case, a statement – is true provided it is a member of an internally consistent system of statements and *provided further* this system is "the system which is actually adopted by mankind, and especially by the scientists in our culture circle."[8]

A theory of truth is not, as such, a theory of justification. To say that a proposition is true is not to say that we are justified in accepting it as true, and to say that we are justified in accepting it as true is not to say that it is true. (I shall return to this point in the final section.) Whatever merits the coherence theory may have as an answer to certain questions about truth, it throws no light upon our present epistemological question. If we accept the coherence theory, we may still ask, concerning any proposition *a* that we think we know to be true, "What is my justification for thinking I know that *a* is a member of the system of propositions in which everything real and possible is coherently included, or that *a* is a member of the system of propositions that is actually adopted by mankind and by the scientists of our culture circle?" And when we ask such a question, we are confronted, once again, with our original alternatives.

7

If our questions about justification do have a proper stopping place, then, as I have said, there are still four significant possibilities to consider. We may stop with some particular claim and say of it that either:

(a) It is justified by something – by experience, or by observation – that is not itself a claim and that, therefore, cannot be said either to be justified or to be unjustified;

(b) It is justified by some claim that refers to our experience or observation, and the claim referring to our experience or observation has *no* justification;

(c) It justifies itself; or

(d) It is itself neither justified nor unjustified.

The first of these alternatives leads readily to the second, and the second to the third or to the fourth. The third and the fourth – which differ only verbally, I think – involve the doctrine of "the given."

Carnap wrote, in 1936, that the procedure of scientific testing involves two operations: the "confrontation of a statement with observation" and the "confrontation of a statement with previously accepted statements." He suggested that those logical empiricists who were attracted to the coherence theory of truth tended to lose sight of the first of these operations – the confrontation of a statement with observation. He proposed a way of formulating simple "acceptance rules" for such confrontation and he seemed to believe that, merely by applying such rules, we could avoid the epistemological questions with which the adherents of "the given" had become involved.

Carnap said this about his acceptance rules: "If no foreign language or introduction of new terms is involved, the rules are trivial. For example: 'If one is hungry, the statement 'I am hungry' may be accepted'; or: 'If one sees a key one may accept the statement "there lies a key." ' "[9] As we shall note later, the first of these rules differs in an important way from the second. Confining ourselves for the moment to rules of the second sort – "If one sees a key one may accept the statement 'there lies a key' " – let us ask ourselves whether the appeal to such rules enables us to solve our problem of the stopping place.

When we have made the statement "There lies a key," we can, of course, raise the question "What is my justification for thinking I know, or for believing, that there lies a key?" The answer would be "I see the key." We cannot ask "What is my justification for seeing a key?" But we *can* ask "What is my justification for thinking that it is a *key* that I see?" and, if we *do* see that the thing is a key, the question will have an answer. The answer might be "I see that it's shaped like a key and that it's in the lock, and I remember that a key is usually here." The possibility of this question, and its answer, indicates that we cannot stop our questions about justification merely by appealing to observation or experience. For, of the statement "I observe that that is an A," we can ask, and answer, the question "What is my justification for thinking that I observe that there is an A?"

It is relevant to note, moreover, that conditions may exist under which seeing a key does *not* justify one in accepting the statement "There is a key" or in believing that one sees a key. If the key were so disguised or concealed that the man who saw it did not recognize it to be a key, then he might not be justified in accepting the statement "There is a key." If Mr Jones unknown to anyone but himself is a thief, then the people who see him may be said to see a thief – but none of those who thus sees a thief is justified in accepting the statement "There is a thief."[10]

Some of the writings of logical empiricists suggest that, although some statements may be justified by reference to other statements, those statements involve "confrontation with observation" are not justified at all. C. G. Hempel, for example, wrote that "the acknowledgement of an experiential statement as true is psychologically motivated by certain experiences; but within the system of statements which express scientific knowledge or one's beliefs at a given time, they function in the manner of postulates for which no grounds are offered."[11] Hempel conceded, however, that this use of the term "postulate" is misleading and he added the following note of clarification: "When an experiential sentence is accepted 'on the basis of direct experiential evidence,' it is indeed not asserted arbitrarily; but to describe the evidence in question would simply mean to repeat the experiential statement itself. Hence, in the context of cognitive justification, the statement functions in the manner of a primitive sentence."[12]

When we reach a statement having the property just referred to – an experiential statement such that to describe its evidence "would simply mean to repeat the experiential statement itself" – we have reached a proper stopping place in the process of justification.

# 8

We are thus led to the concept of a belief, statement, claim, proposition, or hypothesis, that justifies itself. To be clear about the concept, let us note the way in which we would justify the statement that we have a certain belief. It is essential, of course, that we distinguish justifying the statement *that* we have a certain belief from justifying the belief itself.

Suppose, then, a man is led to say "I believe that Socrates is mortal" and we ask him "What is your justification for thinking that you believe, or for thinking that you know that you believe, that Socrates is mortal?" To this strange question, the only appropriate reply would be "My justification for thinking I believe, or for thinking that I know that I believe, that Socrates is mortal is simply that I *do* believe that Socrates is mortal." One justifies the statement simply by reiterating it; the statement's justification is what the statement says. Here, then, we have a case that satisfies Hempel's remark quoted above; we describe the evidence for a statement merely by repeating the statement. We could say, as C. J. Ducasse did, that "the occurrence of belief is its own evidence."[13]

Normally, as I have suggested, one cannot justify a statement merely by reiterating it. To the question "What justification do you have for thinking you know that there can be no life on the moon?" it would be inappropriate, and impertinent, to reply by saying simply "There *can* be no life on the moon," thus reiterating the fact at issue. An appropriate answer would be one referring to certain *other* facts – for example, that we know there is insufficient oxygen on the moon to support any kind of life. But to the question "What is your justification for thinking you know that you believe so and so?" there is nothing to say other than "I *do* believe so and so."

We may say, then, that some statements are self-justifying, or justify themselves. And we may say, analogously, that certain beliefs, claims, propositions, or hypotheses are self-justifying, or justify themselves. A statement, belief, claim, proposition, or hypothesis may be said to be self-justifying for a person, if the person's justification for thinking he knows it to be true is simply the fact that it *is* true.

Paradoxically, these things I have described by saying that they "justify themselves" may *also* be described by saying that they are "neither justified nor unjustified." The two modes of description are two different ways of saying the same thing.

If we are sensitive to ordinary usage, we may note that the expression "I believe that I believe" is ordinarily used, not to refer to a second-order belief about the speaker's own beliefs, but to indicate that the speaker has not yet made up his mind. "I *believe that I believe* that Johnson is a good president" might properly be taken to indicate that, if the speaker *does* believe that Johnson is a good president, he is not yet firm in that belief. Hence there is a temptation to infer that, if we say of a man who is firm in his belief that Socrates is mortal, that he is "justified in believing that he believes that Socrates is mortal," our statement "makes no sense." A temptation also arises to go on and say that it "makes no sense" even to say of such a man, that his *statement* "I believe that Socrates is mortal" is one which is "justified" for him.[14] After all, what would it mean to say of a man's statement about his own belief, that he is *not* justified in accepting it?[15]

The questions about what does or does not "make any sense" need not, however, be argued. We *may* say, if we prefer, that the statements about the beliefs in question are "neither justified nor unjustified." Whatever mode of description we use, the essential points are two. First, we may appeal to such statements in the process of justifying some *other* statement or belief. If they *have* no justification they may yet *be* a justification – for something other than themselves. ("What justifies me in thinking that he and I are not likely to agree? The fact that I believe that Socrates is mortal and he does not.") Second, the making of such a statement does provide what I have been calling a "stopping place" in the dialectic of justification; but now, instead of signaling the stopping place by reiterating the questioned statement, we do it by saying that the question of its justification is one that "should not arise."

It does not matter, then, whether we speak of certain statements that "justify themselves" or of certain statements that are "neither justified nor unjustified," for in either case we will be referring to the same set of statements. I shall continue to use the former phrase.

There are, then, statements about one's own beliefs ("I believe that Socrates is mortal") – and statements about many other psychological attitudes – that are self-justifying. "What justifies me in believing, or in thinking I know, that I *hope* to come tomorrow? Simply that I *do* hope to come tomorrow." Thinking, desiring, wondering, loving, hating, and other such attitudes are similar. Some, but by no means all, of the statements we can make about such attitudes, when the attitudes are our own, are self-justifying – as are statements containing such phrases as "I think I remember" or "I seem to remember" (as distinguished from "I remember"), and "I think that I see" and "I think that I perceive" (as distinguished from "I see" and "I perceive"). Thus, of the two examples Carnap introduced in connection with his "acceptance rules" discussed above viz., "I am hungry" and "I see a key," we may say that the first is self-justifying and the second is not.

The "doctrine of the given," it will be recalled, tells us (A) that every justified statement, about what we think we know, is justified in part by some statement that justifies itself and (B) that there are statements about appearances that thus justify themselves. The "phenomenalistic version" of the theory adds (C) that statements about appearances are the *only* statements that justify themselves. What we have been saying is that the first thesis, (A), of the doctrine of the given is true and that the "phenomenalistic version," (C), is false; let us turn now to thesis (B).

## 9

In addition to the self-justifying statements about psychological attitudes, are there self-justifying statements about "appearances"? Now we encounter difficulties involving the word "appearance" and its cognates.

Sometimes such words as "appears," "looks," and "seems" are used to convey what one might also convey by such terms as "believe." For example, if I say "It appears to me that General de Gaulle was successful," or "General de Gaulle seems to have been successful," I am likely to mean only that I believe, or incline to believe, that he has been successful; the words "appears" and "seems" serve as useful hedges, giving me an out, should I find out later that de Gaulle was not successful. When "appear"-words are used in this way, the statements in which they occur add nothing significant to the class of "self-justifying" statements we have just provided. Philosophers have traditionally assumed, however, that such terms as "appear" may also be used in a quite different way. If this assumption is correct, as I believe it is, then this additional use does lead us to another type of self-justifying statement.

In the final chapter we shall have occasion to note some of the confusions to which the substantival expression "appearance" gave rise. The philosophers who exposed these confusions were sometimes inclined to forget, I think, that things do appear to us in various ways.[16] We can alter the appearance of anything we like merely by doing something that will affect our sense organs or the conditions of observation. One of the important epistemological questions about appearance is "Are there self-justifying statements about the ways in which things appear?"

Augustine, refuting the skeptics of the late Platonic Academy, wrote: "I do not see how the Academician can refute him who says: 'I know that this appears white to me, I know that my hearing is delighted with this, I know this has an agreeable odor, I know this tastes sweet to me, I know that this feels cold to me.' . . . When a person tastes something, he can honestly swear that he knows it is sweet to his palate or the contrary, and that no trickery of the Greeks can dispossess him of that knowledge."[17] Suppose, now, one were to ask "What justification do you have for believing, or thinking you know, that this appears white to you, or that that tastes bitter to you?" Here, too, we can only reiterate the statement: "What justifies me in believing, or in thinking I know, that this appears white to me and that that tastes bitter to me is that this *does* appear white to me and that *does* taste bitter."

An advantage of the misleading substantive "appearance," as distinguished from the verb "appears," is that the former may be applied to those sensuous experiences which, though capable of being appearances of things, are actually not appearances of anything. Feelings, imagery, and the sensuous content of dreams and hallucination are very much like the appearances of things and they are such that, under some circumstances, they could be appearances of things. But if we do not wish to say that they are experiences wherein some external physical thing *appears* to us, we must use some expression other than "appear." For "appear," in its active voice, requires a grammatical subject and thus requires a term that refers, not merely to a way of appearing, but also to *something that appears.*

But we may avoid *both* the objective "*Something* appears blue to me," and the substantival "I sense a blue *appearance.*" We may use another verb, say "sense," in a technical way, as many philosophers did, and equate it in meaning with the passive voice of "appear," thus saying simply "I *sense* blue," or the like. Or better still, it seems to me, and at the expense only of a little awkwardness, we can use "appear" in its passive voice and say "I am *appeared* to blue."

Summing up, in our new vocabulary, we may say that the philosophers who talked of the "empirically given" were referring, not to "self-justifying" statements and beliefs generally, but only to those pertaining to certain "ways of being appeared to." And the philosophers who objected to the doctrine of the given, or some of them, argued that no statement about "a way of being appeared to" can be "self-justifying."

## 10

Why would one suppose that "This appears white" (or, more exactly, "I am now appeared white to") is not self-justifying? The most convincing argument was this: If I say "This appears white," then, as Reichenbach put it, I am making a "comparison between a present object and a formerly seen object."[18] What I am saying *could* have been expressed by "The present way of appearing is the way in which white objects, or objects that I believe to be white, ordinarily appear." And this new statement, clearly, is not self-justifying; to justify it, as Reichenbach intimated, I must go on and say something further – something about the way in which I remember white objects to have appeared.

"Appears white" *may* thus be used to abbreviate "appears the way in which white things normally appear." Or "white thing," on the other hand, *may* be used to abbreviate "thing having the color of things that ordinarily appear white." The phrase "appear white" as it is used in the second quoted expression cannot be spelled out in the manner of the first; for the point of the second can hardly be put by saying that "white thing" may be used to abbreviate "thing having the color of things that ordinarily appear the way in which *white things* normally appear." In the second expression, the point of "appears white" is not to *compare* a way of appearing with something else; the point is to say something about the way of appearing itself. It is in terms of this second sense of "appears white" – that in which one may say significantly and without redundancy "Things that are white may normally be expected to appear white" – that we are to interpret the quotation from Augustine above. And, more generally, when it was said that "appear"-statements constitute the foundation of the edifice of knowledge, it was not intended that the "appear"-statements be interpreted as statements asserting a comparison between a present object and any other object or set of objects.

The question now becomes "Can we formulate any significant 'appear'-statements *without* thus comparing the way in which some object appears with the way in which some other object appears, or with the way in which the object in question has appeared at some other time? Can we interpret 'This appears white' in such a way that it may be understood to refer to a present way of appearing *without* relating that way of appearing to any other object?" In *Experience and Prediction*, Reichenbach defended his own view (and that of a good many others) in this way:

> The objection may be raised that a comparison with formerly seen physical objects should be avoided, and that a basic statement is to concern the present fact only, as it is. But such a reduction would make the basic statement empty. Its content is just that there is a similarity between the present object and one formerly seen; it is by means of this relation that the present object is described. Otherwise the basic statement would consist in attaching an individual symbol, say a number, to the present object; but the introduction of such a symbol would help us in no way, since we could not make use of it to construct a comparison with other things. Only in attaching the same symbols to different objects, do we arrive at the possibility of constructing relations between the objects. (pp. 176–7)

It is true that, if an "appear"-statement is to be used successfully in communication, it must assert some comparison of objects. Clearly, if I wish *you* to know the way things are now appearing to me, I must relate these ways of appearing to something that is familiar to you. But our present question is not "Can you understand me if I predicate something of the way in which something now appears to me without relating that way of appearing to something that is familiar to you?" The question is, more simply, "Can I predicate anything of the way in which something now appears to me without thereby comparing that way of appearing with something else?" From the fact that the first of these two questions must be answered in the negative it does not follow that the second must also be answered in the negative.[19]

The issue is not one about communication, nor is it, strictly speaking, an issue about language; it concerns, rather, the nature of thought itself. Common to both "pragmatism" and "idealism," as traditions in American philosophy, is the view that to *think* about a thing, or to *interpret or conceptualize* it, and hence to have a *belief* about it, is essentially to relate the thing to *other* things, actual or possible, and therefore to "refer beyond it." It is this view – and not any view about language or communication – that we must oppose if we are to say of some statements about appearing, or of any other statements, that they "justify themselves."

To think about the way in which something is now appearing, according to the view in question, is to relate that way of appearing to something else, possibly to certain future experiences, possibly to the way in which things of a certain sort may be commonly expected to appear. According to the "conceptualistic pragmatism" of C. I. Lewis's *Mind and the World-Order* (1929), we grasp the present experience, any present way of appearing, only to the extent to which we relate it to some future experience.[20] According to one interpretation of John Dewey's "instrumentalistic" version of pragmatism, the present experience may be used to present or disclose something else but it does not present or disclose itself. And according to the idealistic view defended in Brand Blanshard's *The Nature of Thought*, we grasp our present experience only to the extent that we are able to include it in the one "intelligible system of universals" (vol. 1, p. 632).

This theory of reference, it should be noted, applies not only to statements and beliefs about "ways of being appeared to" but also to those other statements and beliefs I have called "self-justifying." If "This appears white," or "I am appeared white to," compares the present experience with something else, and thus depends for its justification on what we are justified in believing about the something else, then so, too, does "I believe that Socrates is mortal" and "I hope that the peace will continue." This general conception of thought, therefore, would seem to imply that no belief or statement can be said to justify itself. But according to what we have been saying, if there is no belief or statement that justifies itself, then it is problematic whether any belief or statement is justified at all. And therefore, as we might expect, this conception of thought and reference has been associated with skepticism.

Blanshard conceded that his theory of thought "does involve a degree of scepticism regarding our present knowledge and probably all future knowledge. In all likelihood there will never be a proposition of which we can say, 'This that I am asserting, with precisely the meaning I now attach to it, is absolutely true.'"[21] On Dewey's theory, or on one common interpretation of Dewey's theory, it is problematic whether anyone can now be said to *know* that Mr Jones is working in his garden. A. O. Lovejoy is reported to have said that, for Dewey, "I am about to have known" is as close as we ever get to "I know."[22] C. I. Lewis, in his *An Analysis of Knowledge and Valuation* (Open Court, 1946) conceded in effect that the conception of thought suggested by his earlier *Mind and the World-Order* does lead to a kind of skepticism; according to the later work there *are* "apprehensions of the given" (cf. pp. 182–3) – and thus beliefs that justify themselves.

What is the plausibility of a theory of thought and reference that seems to imply that no one knows anything?

Perhaps it is correct to say that when we think about a thing we think about it as having certain properties. But why should one go on to say that to think about a thing must always involve thinking about some *other* thing as well? Does thinking about the other thing then involve thinking about some third thing? Or can we think about one thing in relation to a second thing without thereby thinking of a third thing? And if we can, then why can we not think of one thing – of one thing as having certain properties – without thereby relating it to another thing?

The linguistic analogue of this view of thought is similar. Why should one suppose – as Reichenbach supposed in the passage cited above and as many others have also supposed – that to *refer* to a thing, in this instance to refer to a way of appearing, is necessarily to relate the thing to some *other* thing?

Some philosophers seem to have been led to such a view of reference as a result of such considerations as the following: We have imagined a man saying, in agreement with Augustine, "It just does appear white – and that is the end of the matter." Let us consider now the possible reply that "It is not the end of the matter. You are making certain assumptions about the language you are using; you are assuming, for example, that you are using the word 'white' or the phrase 'appears white,' in a way in which you have formerly used it, or in the way in which it is ordinarily used, or in the way in which it would ordinarily be understood. And if you state your justification for this assumption, you *will* refer to certain other things – to yourself and to other people, to the word 'white,' or to the phrase 'appears white,' and to what the word or phrase has referred to or might refer to on other occasions. And therefore, when you say 'This appears white' you are saying something, not only about your present experience, but also about all of these other things as well."

The conclusion of this argument – the part that follows the "therefore" – does not follow from the premises. In supposing that the argument is valid, one fails to distinguish between (1) *what* it is that a man means to say when he uses certain words and (2) his assumptions concerning the adequacy of these words for *expressing* what it is that he means to say; one supposes, mistakenly, that what justifies (2) must be included in what justifies (1). A Frenchwoman not yet sure of her English, may utter the words "There are apples in the basket," intending thereby to express her belief that there are potatoes in the basket. If we show her that she has used the word "apples" incorrectly, and hence that she is mistaken in her assumption about the ways in which English speaking people use and understand the word "apples," we have not shown her anything relevant to her *belief* that there are apples in the basket.

Logicians now take care to distinguish between the *use* and *mention* of language (e.g., the English word "Socrates" is mentioned in the sentence " 'Socrates' has eight letters" and is used but not mentioned, in "Socrates is a Greek.")[23] As we shall have occasion to note further in the next chapter, the distinction has not always been observed in writings on epistemology.


# 11


If we decide, then, that there is a class of beliefs or statements that are "self-justifying," and that this class is limited to certain beliefs or statements about our own psychological states and about the ways in which we are "appeared to," we may be tempted to return to the figure of the edifice: our knowledge of the world is a structure supported entirely by a foundation of such self-justifying statements or beliefs. We should recall, however, that the answers to our original Socratic questions had *two* parts. When asked "What is your justification for thinking that you know *a*?" one may reply "I am justified in thinking I know *a*, because (1) I know *b* and (2) if I know *b* then I know *a*." We considered our justification for the *first* part of this answer, saying "I am justified in thinking I know *b*, because (1) I know *c* and (2) if I know *c* then I know *b*." And then we considered our justification for the first part of the second answer, and continued in this fashion until we reach the point of self-justification. In thus moving toward "the given," we accumulated, step by step, a backlog of claims that we did not attempt to justify – those claims constituting the *second* part of each of our answers. Hence our original claim – "I know that *a* is true" – does not rest on "the given" alone; it also rests upon all of those other claims that we made en route. And it is not justified unless these other claims are justified.

A consideration of these other claims will lead us, I think, to at least three additional types of "stopping place," which we are concerned, respectively, with memory, perception, and what Kant called the a priori. I shall comment briefly on the first two.

It is difficult to think of any claim to empirical knowledge, other than the self-justifying statements we have just considered, that does not to some extent rest on an appeal to memory. But the appeal to memory – "I remember that A occurred" – is not self-justifying. One may ask "And what is your justification for thinking that you remember that A occurred?" and the question will have an answer – even if the answer is only the self-justifying "I think that I remember that A occurred." The statement "I remember that A occurred" does, of course, imply "A occurred"; but "I think that I remember that A occurred" does not imply "A occurred" and hence does not imply "I remember that A occurred." For we can remember occasions – at least we think we can remember them – when we learned, concerning some event we had thought we remembered, that the event had not occurred at all, and consequently that we had not really remembered it. When we thus find that one memory conflicts with another, or, more accurately, when we thus find that one thing that we think we remember conflicts with another thing that we think we remember, we may correct one or the other by making further inquiry; but the results of any such inquiry will always be justified in part by other memories, or by other things that we think that we remember. How then are we to choose between what seem to be conflicting memories? Under what conditions does "I think that I remember that A occurred" serve to justify "I remember that A occurred"?

The problem is one of formulating a rule of evidence – a rule specifying the conditions under which statements about what we think we remember can justify statements about what we do remember. A possible solution, in very general terms, is "When we think that we remember, then we are justified in believing that we do remember, provided that what we think we remember does not conflict with anything else that we think we remember; when what we think we remember does conflict with something else we think we remember, then, of the two conflicting memories (more accurately, ostensible memories) the one that is justified is the one that fits in better with the other things that we think we remember." Ledger Wood made the latter point by saying that the justified memory is the one that "coheres with the system of related memories"; C. I. Lewis used "congruence" instead of "coherence."[24] But we cannot say precisely what is meant by "fitting in," "coherence," or "congruence" until certain controversial questions of confirmation theory and the logic of probability have been answered. And it may be that the rule of evidence is too liberal; perhaps we should say, for example, that when two ostensible memories conflict neither one of them is justified. But these are questions that have not yet been satisfactorily answered.

If we substitute "perceive" for "remember" in the foregoing, we can formulate a similar set of problems about perception; these problems, too, must await solution.[25]

The problems involved in formulating such rules of evidence, and in determining the validity of these rules, do not differ in any significant way from those that arise in connection with the formulation, and validity, of the rules of logic. Nor do they differ from the problems posed by the moral and religious "cognitivists" (the "nonintuitionistic cognitivists") mentioned in the first section. The status of ostensible memories and perceptions, with respect to that experience which is their "source," is essentially like that which such "cognitivists" claim for judgments having an ethical or theological subject matter. Unfortunately, it is also like that which other "enthusiasts" claim for still other types of subject matter.

## Notes

1 Philosophers in other traditions also noted these confusions. See, for example, John Wild, "The Concept of the Given in Contemporary Philosophy," *Philosophy and Phenomenological Research*, 1 (1940), 70–82.

2 The expression "myth of the given" was used by Wilfrid Sellars in "Empiricism and the Philosophy of Mind," in Herbert Feigl and Michael Scriven, eds., *Foundations of Science and the Concepts of Psychology and Psychoanalysis*, Minnesota Studies in the Philosophy of Science, vol. 1 (U. of Minn., 1956), pp. 253–329.

3 Dewey also said that, instead of trying to provide "Foundations for knowledge," the philosopher should apply "what is known to intelligent conduct of the affairs of human life" to "the problems of men." John Dewey, *Problems of Men* (Philosophical, 1946), pp. 6–7.

4 C. I. Lewis, *Mind and the World-Order* (Scribner, 1929), p. 29.

5 *Ibid.*, p. 19. Cf. Hans Reichenbach, *Experience and Prediction* (University of Chicago, 1938), p. 6; C. J. Ducasse, "Some Observations Concerning the Nature of Probability, *Journal of Philosophy*, 38 (1941), esp. 400–1.

6 Hans Reichenbach, "Are Phenomenal Reports Absolutely Certain?" *Philosophical Review*, (1952), 147–59; the quotation is from p. 150.

7 Brand Blanshard, *The Nature of Thought*, vol. 2 (Macmillan, 1940), p. 276.

8 C. G. Hempel, "On the Logical Postivists' Theory of Truth," *Analysis*, 2 (1935), 49–59; the quotation is from p. 57.

9 Rudolf Carnap, "Truth and Confirmation," in Herbert Feigl and W. S. Sellars, eds., *Readings in Philosophical Analysis* (Appleton, 1949), p. 125. The portions of the article quoted above first appeared in "Wahrheit und Bewährung," *Actes du congrès internationale de philosophie scientifique*, 4 (Paris; 1936), 18–23.

10 Cf. Nelson Goodman, *The Structure of Appearance* (Harvard, 1951), p. 104. If Goodman's book, incidentally, is not discussed in his collection of essays, the fault is with our conventional classification of philosophical disciplines. The book, which

is concerned with an area falling between logic and metaphysics, is one of the most important philosophical works written by an American during the period being surveyed.

11 C. G. Hempel, "Some Theses on Empirical Certainty," *Review of Metaphysics*, (1952), 621–9; the quotation is from p. 621.

12 Ibid., p. 628. Hempel's remarks were made in an "Exploration" in which he set forth several theses about "empirical certainty" and then replied to objections by Paul Weiss, Roderick Firth, Wilfrid Sellars, and myself.

13 C. J. Ducasse, "Propositions, Truth, and the Ultimate Criterion of Truth," *Philosophy and Phenomenological Research*, 4 (1939), 317–40; the quotation is from p. 339.

14 Cf. Norman Malcolm, "Knowledge of Other Minds," *Journal of Philosophy*, 55 (1958), 969–78. Reprinted in Malcolm, *Knowledge and Certainty: Essays and Lectures* (Prentice-Hall, 1963).

15 The principle behind this way of looking at the matter is defended in detail by Max Black in *Language and Philosophy*, p. 116 ff.

16 One of the best criticisms of the "appearance" (or "sense-datum") terminology was O. K. Bouwsma's "Moore's Theory of Sense-Data," in *The Philosophy of G. E. Moore*, pp. 201–21. In *Perceiving: A Philosophical Study* (Cornell, 1957), I tried to call attention to certain facts about appearing which, I believe, Bouwsma may have overlooked.

17 Augustine, *Contra academicos*, xi, 26; translated by Sister Mary Patricia Garvey as *Saint Augustine Against the Academicians* (Marquette, 1942); the quotations are from pp. 68–9.

18 *Experience and Prediction*, p. 176.

19 It may follow, however, that "the vaunted incorrigibility of the sense-datum language can be achieved only at the cost of its perfect utility as a means of communication" (Max Black, *Problems of Analysis* p. 66), and doubtless, as Black added, it would be "misleading to say the least" to speak of a "language that cannot be communicated" – cf. Wilfrid Sellars, "Empiricism and the Philosophy of Mind" – but these points do affect the epistemological question at issue.

20 This doctrine was modified in Lewis's later *An Analysis of Knowledge and Valuation* (Open Court, 1946) in a way that enabled him to preserve the theory of the given.

21 *The Nature of Thought*, vol. 2, pp. 269–70. Blanshard added, however, that "for all the ordinary purposes of life" we *can* justify some beliefs by showing that they cohere "with the system of present knowledge"; and therefore, he said, his theory should not be described as being "simply sceptical" (vol. 2, p. 271). Cf. W. H. Werkmeister, *The Basis and Structure of Knowledge* (Harper, 1946), part II.

22 Quoted by A. E. Murphy in "Dewey's Epistemology and Metaphysics," in P. A. Schlipp, ed., *The Philosophy of John Dewey* (Northwestern, 1939), p. 203. Dewey's theory of inquiry, however, was not intended to be an epistemology and he did not directly address himself to the questions with which we are here concerned.

23 Cf. W. V. O. Quine, *Mathematical Logic* (Norton, 1940; rev. ed., Harvard, 1951), sec. 4.

24 Ledger Wood, *The Analysis of Knowledge* (Princeton, 1941), p. 81; C. I. Lewis, *An Analysis of Knowledge and Valuation*, p. 334.

25 Important steps toward solving them were taken by Nelson Goodman in "Sense and Certainty," *Philosophical Review*, 61 (1952), 160–7, and by Israel Scheffler in "On Justification and Commitment," *Journal of Philosophy*, 51 (1954), 180–90. The former paper is reprinted in Roland Houde and J. P. Mullally, eds., *Philosophy of Knowledge* (Lippincott, 1960), pp. 97–103.

# 12   The Raft and the Pyramid: Coherence versus Foundations in the Theory of Knowledge

## *Ernest Sosa*

Contemporary epistemology must choose between the solid security of the ancient foundationalist pyramid and the risky adventure of the new coherentist raft. Our main objective will be to understand, as deeply as we can, the nature of the controversy and the reasons for and against each of the two options. But first of all we take note of two underlying assumptions.

## 1   Two Assumptions

(A1)   Not everything believed is known, but nothing can be known without being at least believed (or accepted, presumed, taken for granted, or the like) in some broad sense. What additional requirements must a belief fill in order to be knowledge? There are surely at least the following two: (a) it must be true, and (b) it must be justified (or warranted, reasonable, correct, or the like).

(A2)   Let us assume, moreover, with respect to the second condition A1(b): first, that it involves a normative or evaluative property; and, second, that the relevant sort of justification is that which pertains to knowledge: epistemic (or theoretical) justification. Someone seriously ill may have two sorts of justification for believing he will recover: the practical justification that derives from the contribution such belief will make to his recovery and the theoretical justification provided by the lab results, the doctor's diagnosis and prognosis, and so on. Only the latter is relevant to the question whether he knows.

## 2   Knowledge and Criteria (or Canons, Methods, or the Like)

a.   There are two key questions of the theory of knowledge:

(i)   What do we know?
(ii)   How do we know?

The answer to the first would be a list of bits of knowledge or at least of types of knowledge: of the self, of the external world, of other minds, and so on. An answer to the second would give us criteria (or canons, methods, principles, or the like) that would explain how we know whatever it is that we do know.

b. In developing a theory of knowledge, we can begin either with a(i) or with a(ii). Particularism would have us begin with an answer to a(i) and only then take up a(ii) on the basis of that answer. Quite to the contrary, methodism would reverse that order. The particularist thus tends to be antiskeptical on principle. But the methodist is as such equally receptive to skepticism and to the contrary. Hume, for example, was no less a methodist than Descartes. Each accepted, in effect, that only the obvious and what is proved deductively on its basis can possibly be known.

c. What, then, is the obvious? For Descartes it is what we know by intuition, what is clear and distinct, what is indubitable and credible with no fear of error. Thus for Descartes basic knowledge is always an infallible belief in an indubitable truth. All other knowledge must stand on that basis through deductive proof. Starting from such criteria (canons, methods, etc.), Descartes concluded that knowledge extended about as far as his contemporaries believed.[1] Starting from similar criteria, however, Hume concluded that both science and common sense made claims far beyond their rightful limits.

d. Philosophical posterity has rejected Descartes's theory for one main reason: that it admits too easily as obvious what is nothing of the sort. Descartes's reasoning is beautifully simple: God exists; no omnipotent perfectly good being would descend to deceit; but if our common sense beliefs were radically false, that would represent deceit on His part. Therefore, our common sense beliefs must be true or at least cannot be radically false. But in order to buttress this line of reasoning and fill in details, Descartes appeals to various principles that appear something less than indubitable.

e. For his part, Hume rejects all but a miniscule portion of our supposed common sense knowledge. He establishes first that there is no way to prove such supposed knowledge on the basis of what is obvious at any given moment through reason or experience. And he concludes, in keeping with this methodism, that in point of fact there really is no such knowledge.

## 3   Two Metaphors: The Raft and the Pyramid

Both metaphors concern the body or system of knowledge in a given mind. But the mind is of course a more complex marvel than is sometimes supposed. Here I do not allude to the depths plumbed by Freud, nor even to Chomsky's. Nor need we recall the labyrinths inhabited by statesmen and diplomats, nor the rich patterns of some novels or theories. We need look no further than the most common, everyday beliefs. Take, for instance, the belief that driving tonight will be dangerous. Brief reflection should reveal that any of us with that belief will join to it several other closely related beliefs on which the given belief depends for its existence or (at least) its justification. Among such beliefs we could presumably find some or all of the following: that the road will be icy or snowy;

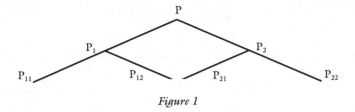

*Figure 1*

that driving on ice or snow is dangerous; that it will rain or snow tonight; that the temperature will be below freezing; appropriate beliefs about the forecast and its reliability; and so on.

How must such beliefs be interrelated in order to help justify my belief about the danger of driving tonight? Here foundationalism and coherentism disagree, each offering its own metaphor. Let us have a closer look at this dispute, starting with foundationalism.

Both Descartes and Hume attribute to human knowledge an architectonic structure. There is a nonsymmetric relation of physical support such that any two floors of a building are tied by that relation: one of the two supports (or at least helps support) the other. And there is, moreover, a part with a special status: the foundation, which is supported by none of the floors while supporting them all.

With respect to a body of knowledge K (in someone's possession), foundationalism implies that K can be divided into parts $K_1$, $K_2$, . . ., such that there is some nonsymmetric relation R (analogous to the relation of physical support) which orders those parts in such a way that there is one – call it F – that bears R to every other part while none of them bears R in turn to F.

According to foundationalism, each piece of knowledge lies on a pyramid like that in figure 1. The nodes of such a pyramid (for a proposition P relative to a subject S and a time t) must obey the following requirements:

a. The set of all nodes that succeed (directly) any given node must serve jointly as a base that properly supports that node (for S at t).
b. Each node must be a proposition that S is justified in believing at t.
c. If a node is not self-evident (for S at t), it must have successors (that serve jointly as a base that properly supports that node).
d. Each branch of an epistemic pyramid must terminate.

For the foundationalist Descartes, for instance, each terminating node must be an indubitable proposition that S believes at t with no possibility of error. As for the nonterminal nodes, each of them represents inferential knowledge, derived by deduction from more basic beliefs.

Such radical foundationalism suffers from a fatal weakness that is twofold:

(a) there are not so many perfectly obvious truths as Descartes thought; and
(b) once we restrict ourselves to what is truly obvious in any given context,

189

very little of one's supposed common sense knowledge can be proved on that basis.

If we adhere to such radical foundationalism, therefore, we are just wrong in thinking we know so much.

Note that in citing such a "fatal weakness" of radical foundationalism, we favor particularism as against the methodism of Descartes and Hume. For we reject the methods or criteria of Descartes and Hume when we realize that they plunge us in a deep skepticism. If such criteria are incompatible with our enjoyment of the rich body of knowledge that we commonly take for granted, then as good particularists we hold on to the knowledge and reject the criteria.

If we reject radical foundationalism, however, what are we to put in its place? Here epistemology faces a dilemma that different epistemologists resolve differently. Some reject radical foundationalism but retain some more moderate form of foundationalism. Others react more vigorously, however, by rejecting all forms of foundationalism in favor of a radically different coherentism. Coherentism is associated with idealism – of both the German and the British variety – and has recently acquired new vigor and interest.

The coherentists reject the metaphor of the pyramid in favor of one that they owe to the positivist Neurath, according to whom our body of knowledge is a raft that floats free of any anchor or tie. Repairs must be made afloat, and though no part is untouchable, we must stand on some in order to replace or repair others. Not every part can go at once.

According to the new metaphor, what justifies a belief is not that it can be an infallible belief with an indubitable object, nor that it have been proved deductively on such a basis, but that it cohere with a comprehensive system of beliefs.

## 4 A Coherentist Critique of Foundationalism

What reasons do coherentists offer for their total rejection of foundationalism? The argument that follows below summarizes much of what is alleged against foundationalism. But first we must distinguish between subjective states that incorporate a propositional attitude and those that do not. A propositional attitude is a mental state of someone with a proposition for its object: beliefs, hopes, and fears provide examples. By way of contrast, a headache does not incorporate any such attitude. One can of course be conscious of a headache, but the headache itself does not constitute or incorporate any attitude with a proposition for its object. With this distinction in the background, here is the antifoundationalist argument, which has two lemmas – a(iv) and b(iii) – and a principal conclusion.

a.    (i)   If a mental state incorporates a propositional attitude, then it does not give us direct contact with reality, e.g., with pure experience, unfiltered by concepts or beliefs.

      (ii)   If a mental state does not give us direct contact with reality, then it provides no guarantee against error.

(iii) If a mental state provides no guarantee against error, then it cannot serve as a foundation for knowledge.

(iv) Therefore, if a mental state incorporates a propositional attitude, then it cannot serve as a foundation for knowledge.

b. (i) If a mental state does not incorporate a propositional attitude, then it is an enigma how such a state can provide support for any hypothesis, raising its credibility selectively by contrast with its alternatives. (If the mental state has no conceptual or propositional content, then what logical relation can it possibly bear to any hypothesis? Belief in a hypothesis would be a propositional attitude with the hypothesis itself as object. How can one depend logically for such a belief on an experience with no propositional content?)

(ii) If a mental state has no propositional content and cannot provide logical support for any hypothesis, then it cannot serve as a foundation for knowledge.

(iii) Therefore, if a mental state does not incorporate a propositional attitude, then it cannot serve as a foundation for knowledge.

c. Every mental state either does or does not incorporate a propositional attitude.

d. Therefore, no mental state can serve as a foundation for knowledge. (From a(iv), b(iii), and c.)

According to the coherentist critic, foundationalism is run through by this dilemma. Let us take a closer look.[2]

In the first place, what reason is there to think, in accordance with premise b(i), that only propositional attitudes can give support to their own kind? Consider practices – e.g., broad policies or customs. Could not some person or group be justified in a practice because of its consequences: that is, could not the consequences of a practice make it a good practice? But among the consequences of a practice may surely be found, for example, a more just distribution of goods and less suffering than there would be under its alternatives. And neither the more just distribution nor the lower degree of suffering is a propositional attitude. This provides an example in which propositional attitudes (the intentions that sustain the practice) are justified by consequences that are not propositional attitudes. That being so, is it not conceivable that the justification of belief that matters for knowledge be analogous to the objective justification by consequences that we find in ethics?

Is it not possible, for instance, that a belief that there is something red before one be justified in part because it has its origin in one's visual experience of red when one looks at an apple in daylight? If we accept such examples, they show us a source of justification that serves as such without incorporating a propositional attitude.

As for premise a(iii), it is already under suspicion from our earlier exploration of premise b(i). A mental state M can be nonpropositional and hence not a candidate for so much as truth, much less infallibility, while it serves, in spite of that, as a foundation of knowledge. Leaving that aside, let us suppose that the relevant mental state is indeed propositional. Must it then be infallible in order to serve as a foundation of justification and knowledge? That is so far from being obvious that it seems more likely false when compared with an analogue in ethics. With respect to beliefs, we may distinguish between their being true and their being justified. Analogously, with respect to actions, we may distinguish between their being optimal (best of all alternatives, all things considered) and their being (subjectively) justified. In practical deliberation on alternatives for action, is it inconceivable that the most *eligible* alternative *not* be objectively the best, all things considered? Can there not be another alternative – perhaps a most repugnant one worth little if any consideration – that in point of fact would have a much better total set of consequences and would thus be better, all things considered? Take the physician attending to Frau Hitler at the birth of little Adolf. Is it not possible that if he had acted less morally, that would have proved better in the fullness of time? And if that is so in ethics, may not its likeness hold good in epistemology? Might there not be justified (reasonable, warranted) beliefs that are not even true, much less infallible? That seems to me not just a conceivable possibility, but indeed a familiar fact of everyday life, where observational beliefs too often prove illusory but no less reasonable for being false.

If the foregoing is on the right track, then the antifoundationalist is far astray. What has led him there?

As a diagnosis of the antifoundationalist argument before us, and more particularly of its second lemma, I would suggest that it rests on an Intellectualist Model of Justification.

According to such a model, the justification of belief (and psychological states generally) is parasitical on certain logical relations among propositions. For example, my belief (i) that the streets are wet is justified by my pair of beliefs (ii) that it is raining, and (iii) that if it is raining, the streets are wet. Thus we have a structure such as this:

$B(Q)$ is justified by the fact that $B(Q)$ is grounded on $(B(P), B(P \supset Q))$.

And according to an Intellectualist Model, this is parasitical on the fact that

$P$ and $(P \supset Q)$ together logically imply $Q$.

Concerning this attack on foundationalism I will argue (a) that it is useless to the coherentist, since if the antifoundationalist dilemma impales the foundationalist, a form of it can be turned against the coherentist to the same effect; (b) that the dilemma would be lethal not only to foundationalism and coherentism but also to the very possibility of substantive epistemology; and (c) that a form of it would have the same effect on normative ethics.

(a)　According to coherentism, what justifies a belief is its membership in a coherent and comprehensive set of beliefs. But whereas being grounded on B(P) and (B(P ⊃ Q) is a property of a belief B(Q) that yields immediately the logical implication of Q by [P and (P ⊃ Q)] as the logical source of that property's justificatory power, the property of being a member of a coherent set is not one that immediately yields any such implication.

It may be argued, nevertheless, (i) that the property of being a member of a coherent set would supervene in any actual instance on the property of being a member of a particular set *a* that is in fact coherent, and (ii) that this would enable us to preserve our Intellectualist Model, since (iii) the justification of the member belief B(Q) by its membership in *a* would then be parasitical on the logical relations among the beliefs in *a* which constitute the coherence of that set of beliefs, and (iv) the justification of B(Q) by the fact that it is part of a coherent set would then be *indirectly* parasitical on logical relations among propositions after all.

But if such an indirect form of parasitism is allowed, then the experience of pain may perhaps be said to justify belief in its existence parasitically on the fact that P logically implies P! The Intellectualist Model seems either so trivial as to be dull, or else sharp enough to cut equally against both foundationalism and coherentism.

(b)  If (i) only propositional attitudes can justify such propositional attitudes as belief, and if (ii) to do so they must in turn be justified by yet other propositional attitudes, it seems clear that (iii) there is no hope of constructing a complete epistemology, one which would give us, in theory, an account of what the justification of any justified belief would supervene on. For (i) and (ii) would rule out the possibility of a finite regress of justification.

(c)  If only propositional attitudes can justify propositional attitudes, and if to do so they must in turn be justified by yet other propositional attitudes, it seems clear that there is no hope of constructing a complete normative ethics, one which would give us, in theory, an account of what the justification of any possible justified action would supervene upon. For the justification of an action presumably depends on the intentions it embeds and the justification of these, and here we are already within the net of propositional attitudes from which, for the Intellectualist, there is no escape.

It seems fair to conclude that our coherentist takes his anti-foundationalist zeal too far. His antifoundationalist argument helps expose some valuable insights but falls short of its malicious intent. The foundationalist emerges showing no serious damage. Indeed, he now demands equal time for a positive brief in defense of his position.

## 5   The Regress Argument

a.   The regress argument in epistemology concludes that we must countenance beliefs that are justified in the absence of justification by other beliefs. But it reaches that conclusion only by rejecting the possibility in
principle of an infinite regress of justification. It thus opts for foundational
beliefs justified in some noninferential way by ruling out a chain or pyramid of justification that has justifiers, and justifiers of justifiers, and so on
*without end*. One may well find this too short a route to foundationalism,
however, and demand more compelling reasons for thus rejecting an infinite regress as vicious. We shall find indeed that it is not easy to meet this
demand.

b.   We have seen how even the most ordinary of everyday beliefs is the tip of
an iceberg. A closer look below the surface reveals a complex structure
that ramifies with no end in sight. Take again my belief that driving will
be dangerous tonight, at the tip of an iceberg, (I), that looks like figure 2.
The immediate cause of my belief that driving will be hazardous tonight
is the sound of raindrops on the windowpane. All but one or two members of the underlying iceberg are as far as they can be from my thoughts
at the time. In what sense, then, do they form an iceberg whose tip breaks
the calm surface of my consciousness?

Here I will assume that the members of (I) are beliefs of the subject,
even if unconscious or subconscious, that causally buttress and thus justify his prediction about the driving conditions.

Can the iceberg extend without end? It may appear obvious that it
cannot do so, and one may jump to the conclusion that any piece of
knowledge must be ultimately founded on beliefs that are *not* (inferentially) justified or warranted by other beliefs. This is a doctrine of *epistemic
foundationalism*.

Let us focus not so much on the *giving* of justification as on the *having*
of it. *Can* there be a belief that is justified in part by other beliefs, some of
which are in turn justified by yet other beliefs, and so on without end?
Can there be an endless regress of justification?

c.   There are several familiar objections to such a regress:

(i)    *Objection*: "It is incompatible with human limitations. No human
subject could harbor the required infinity of beliefs." *Reply*: It is
mere presumption to fathom with such assurance the depths of the
mind, and especially its unconscious and dispositional depths. Besides, our object here is the nature of epistemic justification in itself
and not only that of such justification as is accessible to humans.
Our question is not whether humans could harbor an infinite iceberg of justification. Our question is rather whether *any* mind, no
matter how deep, could do so. Or is it ruled out *in principle* by the
very nature of justification?

(ii)   *Objection*: "An infinite regress is indeed ruled out in principle, for if
justification were thus infinite how could it possibly end?"

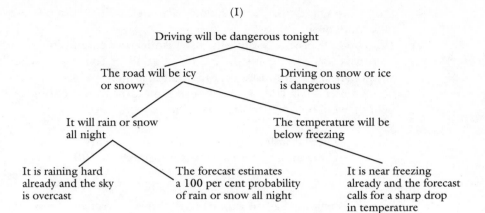

Figure 2

*Reply*: (i) If the end mentioned is *temporal*, then why must there be such an end? In the first place, the subject may be eternal. Even if he is not eternal, moreover, why must belief acquisition and justification occur seriatim? What precludes an infinite body of beliefs acquired at a single stroke? Human limitations may rule this out for humans, but we have yet to be shown that it is precluded in principle, by the very nature of justification. (ii) If the end mentioned is justificatory, on the other hand, then to ask how justification could possibly end is just to beg the question.

(iii)   *Objection*: "Let us make two assumptions: first, that S's belief of q justifies his belief of p only if it works together with a justified belief on his part that q provides good evidence for p; and, second, that if S is to be justified in believing p on the basis of his belief of q and is to be justified in believing q on the basis of his belief of r, then S must be justified in believing that r provides good evidence for p via q. These assumptions imply that an actual regress of justification requires belief in an infinite proposition. Since no one (or at least no human) can believe an infinite proposition, no one (no human) can be a subject of such an actual regress."[3]

*Reply*: Neither of the two assumptions is beyond question, but even granting them both, it may still be doubted that the conclusion follows. It is true that each finitely complex belief of the form "r provides good evidence for p via $q_1, \ldots q_n$" will *omit* how some members of the full infinite regress are epistemically tied to belief of p. But that seems irrelevant given the fact that for each member r of the regress, such that r is tied epistemically to belief of p, there *is* a finite belief of the required sort ("r provides good evidence for p via $q_1, \ldots q_n$") that ties the two together. Consequently, there is no apparent reason to suppose – even granted the two assumptions – that an infinite regress will require a single belief in an infinite proposition, and not just an infinity of beliefs in increasingly complex finite propositions.

(iv)   *Objection*: "But if it is allowed that justification extend infinitely, then it is too easy to justify any belief at all or too many beliefs altogether. Take, for instance, the belief that there are perfect numbers greater than 100. And suppose a mind powerful enough to believe every member of the following sequence:

($\sigma$1)   There is at least one perfect number > 100
There are at least two perfect numbers > 100
"              three       "              "

If such a believer has no other belief about perfect numbers save the belief that a perfect number is a whole number equal to the sum of its whole factors, then surely he is *not* justified in believing that there are perfect numbers greater than 100. He is quite unjustified in believing any of the members of sequence ($\sigma$1), in spite of the fact that a challenge to any can be met easily by appeal to its successor. Thus it cannot be allowed after all that justification extend infinitely, and an infinite regress is ruled out."

*Reply*: We must distinguish between regresses of justification that are actual and those that are merely potential. The difference is *not* simply that an actual regress is composed of actual beliefs. For even if all members of the regress are actual beliefs, the regress may still be *merely potential* in the following sense: while it is true that *if* any member *were* justified then its predecessors *would* be, still none is in fact justified. Anyone with our series of beliefs about perfect numbers in the absence of any further relevant information on such numbers would presumably be the subject of such a merely potential justificatory regress.

(v)   *Objection*: "But defenders of infinite justificatory regresses cannot distinguish thus between actual regresses and those that are merely potential. There is no real distinction to be drawn between the two. For if any regress ever justifies the belief at its head, then every regress must always do so. But obviously not every regress does so (as we have seen by examples), and hence no regress can do so."[4]

*Reply*: One can in fact distinguish between actual justificatory regresses and merely potential ones, and one can do so both abstractly and by examples.

What an actual regress has that a merely potential regress lacks is the property of containing only justified beliefs as members. What they both share is the property of containing no member without successors that would jointly justify it.

Recall our regress about perfect numbers greater than 100: i.e., there is at least one; there are at least two; there are at least three; and so on. Each member has a successor that would justify it, but no member is justified (in the absence of further information external to the regress). That is therefore a merely potential infinite regress. As for an actual regress, I see no compelling reason why someone (if not a human, then some more powerful mind) could not hold an infinite series of actually justified beliefs as follows:

(σ2)    There is at least one even number
         There are at least two even numbers
              "            three         "

It may be that no one could be the subject of such a series of justified beliefs unless he had a proof that there is a denumerable infinity of even numbers. But even if that should be so, it would not take away the fact of the infinite regress of potential justifiers, each of which is actually justified, and hence it would not take away the fact of the actual endless regress of justification.

The objection under discussion is confused, moreover, on the nature of the issue before us. Our question is *not* whether there can be an infinite potential regress, each member of which would be justified by its successors, such that the belief at its head is justified in virtue of its position there, at the head of such a regress. The existence and even the possibility of a single such regress with a belief at its head that was *not* justified in virtue of its position there would of course settle that question in the negative. Our question is, rather, whether there can be an actual infinite regress of justification, and the fact that a belief at the head of a potential regress might still fail to be justified despite its position does *not* settle this question. For even if there can be a merely potential regress with an unjustified belief at its head, that leaves open the possibility of an infinite regress, each member of which is justified by its immediate successors working jointly, where every member of the regress is in addition actually justified.

## 6  The Relation of Justification and Foundationalist Strategy

The foregoing discussion is predicated on a simple conception of justification such that a set of beliefs ß conditionally justifies (*would* justify) a belief X iff, necessarily, if all members of ß are justified then X is also justified (if it exists). The fact that on such a conception of justification actual endless regresses – such as (σ2) – seem quite possible blocks a straightforward regress argument in favor of foundations. For it shows that an actual infinite regress cannot be dismissed out of hand.

Perhaps the foundationalist could introduce some relation of justification – presumably more complex and yet to be explicated – with respect to which it could be argued more plausibly that an actual endless regress is out of the question.

There is, however, a more straightforward strategy open to the foundationalist. For he *need not* object to the possibility of an endless regress of justification. His essential creed is the more positive belief that every justified belief must be at the head of a terminating regress. Fortunately, to affirm the universal necessity of a terminating regress is *not* to deny the bare possibility of a nonterminating regress. For a single belief can trail at once regresses of both sorts: one terminating and one not. Thus the proof of the denumerably infinite cardinality of the set of evens may provide for a powerful enough intellect a *terminating* regress for each member of the *endless* series of justified beliefs:

(σ2)   There is at least one even number
       There are at least two even numbers
             "          three       "

At the same time, it is obvious that each member of (σ2) lies at the head of an actual endless regress of justification, on the assumption that each member is conditionally justified by its successor, which is in turn actually justified.

"Thank you so much," the foundationalist may sneer, "but I really do not need that kind of help. Nor do I need to be reminded of my essential creed, which I know as well as anyone. Indeed my rejection of endless regresses of justification is only a means of supporting my view that every justified belief must rest ultimately on foundations, on a terminating regress. You reject that strategy much too casually, in my view, but I will not object here. So we put that strategy aside. And now, my helpful friend, just what do we put in its place?"

Fair enough. How then could one show the need for foundations if an endless regress is not ruled out?

# 7   Two Levels of Foundationalism

a.  We need to distinguish, first, between two forms of foundationalism: one *formal*, the other *substantive*. A type of *formal foundationalism* with respect to a normative or evaluative property $\phi$ is the view that the conditions (actual and possible) within which $\phi$ would apply can be specified in general, perhaps recursively. *Substantive foundationalism* is only a particular way of doing so, and coherentism is another.

Simpleminded hedonism is the view that:
(i)   every instance of pleasure is good,
(ii)  everything that causes something good is itself good, and
(iii) everything that is good is so in virtue of (i) or (ii) above.
Simpleminded hedonism is a type of formal foundationalism with respect to the good.

Classical foundationalism in epistemology is the view that:
(i)   every infallible, indubitable belief is justified,
(ii)  every belief deductively inferred from justified beliefs is itself justified, and

(iii)   every belief that is justified is so in virtue of (i) or (ii) above. Classical foundationalism is a type of formal foundationalism with respect to epistemic justification.

Both of the foregoing theories – simpleminded hedonism in ethics, and classical foundationalism in epistemology – are of course flawed. But they both remain examples of formal foundationalist theories.

b.  One way of arguing in favor of formal foundationalism in epistemology is to formulate a convincing formal foundationalist theory of justification. But classical foundationalism in epistemology no longer has for many the attraction that it had for Descartes, nor has any other form of epistemic foundationalism won general acceptance. Indeed epistemic foundationalism has been generally abandoned and its advocates have been put on the defensive by the writings of Wittgenstein, Quine, Sellars, Rescher, Aune, Harman, Lehrer, and others. It is lamentable that in our headlong rush away from foundationalism we have lost sight of the different types of foundationalism (formal vs. substantive) and of the different grades of each type. Too many of us now see it as a blur to be decried and avoided. Thus our present attempt to bring it all into better focus.

c.  If we cannot argue from a generally accepted foundationalist theory, what reason is there to accept formal foundationalism? There is no reason to think that the conditions (actual and possible) within which an object is spherical are generally specifiable in non-geometric terms. Why should we think that the conditions (actual and possible) within which a belief is epistemically justified are generally specifiable in nonepistemic terms?

So far as I can see, the main reason for accepting formal foundationalism in the absence of an actual, convincing formal foundationalist theory is the very plausible idea that epistemic justification is subject to the supervenience that characterizes normative and evaluative properties generally. Thus, if a car is a good car, then any physical replica of that car must be just as good. If it is a good car in virtue of such properties as being economical, little prone to break down, etc., then surely any exact replica would share all such properties and would thus be equally good. Similarly, if a belief is epistemically justified, it is presumably so in virtue of its character and its basis in perception, memory, or inference (if any). Thus any belief exactly like it in its character and its basis must be equally well justified. Epistemic justification is supervenient. The justification of a belief supervenes on such properties of it as its content and its basis (if any) in perception, memory, or inference. Such a doctrine of supervenience may itself be considered, with considerable justice, a grade of foundationalism. For it entails that every instance of justified belief is founded on a number of its nonepistemic properties, such as its having a certain basis in perception, memory, and inference, or the like.

But there are higher grades of foundationalism as well. There is, for instance, the doctrine that the conditions (actual and possible) within which a belief would be epistemically justified *can be specified* in general, perhaps recursively (and by reference to such notions as perception, memory, and inference).

A higher grade yet of formal foundationalism requires not only that the conditions for justified belief be specifiable, in general, but that they be specifiable by a simple, comprehensive theory.

d. Simpleminded hedonism is a formal foundationalist theory of the highest grade. If it is true, then in every possible world goodness supervenes on pleasure and causation in a way that is recursively specifiable by means of a very simple theory.

Classical foundationalism in epistemology is also a formal foundationalist theory of the highest grade. If it is true, then in every possible world epistemic justification supervenes on infallibility-cum-indubitability and deductive inference in a way that is recursively specifiable by means of a very simple theory.

Surprisingly enough, coherentism may also turn out to be formal foundationalism of the highest grade, provided only that the concept of coherence is itself both simple enough and free of any normative or evaluative admixture. Given these provisos, coherentism explains how epistemic justification supervenes on the nonepistemic in a theory of remarkable simplicity: a belief is justified iff it has a place within a system of beliefs that is coherent and comprehensive.

It is a goal of ethics to explain how the ethical rightness of an action supervenes on what is not ethically evaluative or normative. Similarly, it is a goal of epistemology to explain how the epistemic justification of a belief supervenes on what is not epistemically evaluative or normative. If coherentism aims at this goal, that imposes restrictions on the notion of coherence, which must now be conceived innocent of epistemically evaluative or normative admixture. Its substance must therefore consist of such concepts as explanation, probability, and logical implication – with these conceived, in turn, innocent of normative or evaluative content.

e. We have found a surprising kinship between coherentism and substantive foundationalism, both of which turn out to be varieties of a deeper foundationalism. This deeper foundationalism is applicable to any normative or evaluative property $\phi$, and it comes in three grades. The *first* or lowest is simply the supervenience of $\phi$; the idea that whenever something has $\phi$ its having it is founded on certain others of its properties which fall into certain restricted sorts. The *second* is the explicable supervenience of $\phi$: the idea that there are formulable principles that explain in quite general terms the conditions (actual and possible) within which $\phi$ applies. The *third* and highest is the easily explicable supervenience of $\phi$: the idea that there is a *simple* theory that explains the conditions within which $\phi$ applies. We have found the coherentist and the substantive foundationalist sharing a primary goal: the development of a formal foundationalist theory of the highest grade. For they both want a simple theory that explains precisely how epistemic justification supervenes, in general, on the nonepistemic. This insight gives us an unusual viewpoint on some recent attacks against foundationalism. Let us now consider as an example a certain simple form of argument distilled from the recent antifoundationalist literature.[5]

## 8   Doxastic Ascent Arguments

Several attacks on foundationalism turn on á sort of "doxastic ascent" argument that calls for closer scrutiny.[6] Here are two examples:

A. A belief B is foundationally justified for S in virtue of having property F only if S is justified in believing (1) that most at least of his beliefs with property F are true, and (2) that B has property F. But this means that belief B is not foundational after all, and indeed that the very notion of (empirical) foundational belief is incoherent.

It is sometimes held, for example, that perceptual or observational beliefs are often justified through their origin in the exercise of one or more of our five senses in standard conditions of perception. The advocate of doxastic ascent would raise a vigorous protest, however, for in his view the mere fact of such sensory prompting is impotent to justify the belief prompted. Such prompting must be coupled with the further belief that one's senses work well in the circumstances, or the like. For we are dealing here with *knowledge*, which requires not blind faith but *reasoned* trust. But now surely the further belief about the reliability of one's senses itself cannot rest on blind faith but requires its own backing of reasons, and we are off on the regress.

B. A belief B of proposition P is foundationally justified for S only if S is justified in believing that there are no factors present that would cause him to make mistakes on the matter of the proposition P. But, again, this means that belief B is not foundational after all and indeed that the notion of (empirical) foundational belief is incoherent.

From the vantage point of formal foundationalism, neither of these arguments seems conclusive. In the first place, as we have seen, what makes a belief foundational (formally) is its having a property that is nonepistemic (not evaluative in the epistemic or cognitive mode), and does not involve inference from other beliefs, but guarantees, via a necessary principle, that the belief in question is justified. A belief B is made foundational by having some such nonepistemic property that yields its justification. Take my belief that I am in pain in a context where it is caused by my being in pain. The property that my belief then has, of being a self-attribution of pain caused by one's own pain, is, let us suppose, a nonepistemic property that yields the justification of any belief that has it. So my belief that I am in pain is in that context foundationally justified. Along with my belief that I am in pain, however, there come other beliefs that are equally well justified, such as my belief that someone is in pain. Thus I am foundationally justified in believing that I am in pain only if I am justified in believing that someone is in pain. Those who object to foundationalism as in A or B above are hence mistaken in thinking that their premises would refute foundationalism. The fact is that they would not touch it. For a belief is no less foundationally justified for having its justification yoked to that of another closely related belief.

The advocate of arguments like A and B must apparently strengthen his premises. He must apparently claim that the beliefs whose justification is entailed by the foundationally justified status of belief B must in some sense function as a *necessary source* of the justification of B. And this would of course preclude giving B foundationally justified status. For if the *being justified* of those beliefs is an *essential* part of the source of the justification of B, then it is ruled out that there be a wholly *nonepistemic* source of B's justification.

That brings us to a second point about A and B, for it should now be clear that these cannot be selectively aimed at foundationalism. In particular, they seem neither more nor less valid objections to coherentism than to foundationalism, or so I will now argue about each of them in turn.

> (A′)  A belief X is justified for S in virtue of membership in a coherent set only if S is justified in believing (1) that most at least of his beliefs with the property of thus cohering are true, and (2) that X has that property.

Any coherentist who accepts A seems bound to accept A′. For what could he possibly appeal to as a relevant difference? But A′ is a quicksand of endless depth. (How is he justified in believing A′(1)? Partly through justified belief that *it* coheres? And what would justify *this*? And so on. . . .)

> (B′)  A belief X is justified for S only if S is justified in believing that there are no factors present that would cause him to make mistakes on the subject matter of that belief.

Again, any coherentist who accepts B seems bound to accept B′. But this is just another road to the quicksand. (For S is justified in believing that there are no such factors only if . . . and so on.)

Why are such regresses vicious? The key is again, to my mind, the doctrine of supervenience. Such regresses are vicious because they would be logically incompatible with the supervenience of epistemic justification on such nonepistemic facts as the totality of a subject's beliefs, his cognitive and experiential history, and as many other nonepistemic facts as may seem at all relevant. The idea is that there is a set of such nonepistemic facts surrounding a justified belief such that no belief could possibly have been surrounded by those very facts without being justified. Advocates of A or B run afoul of such supervenience, since they are surely committed to the more general views derivable from either of A or B by deleting "foundationally" from its first sentence. In each case the more general view would then preclude the possibility of supervenience, since it would entail that the source of justification *always* includes an *epistemic* component.

## 9   Coherentism and Substantive Foundationalism

a.   The notions of coherentism and substantive foundationalism remain
     unexplicated. We have relied so far on our intuitive grasp of them. In this
     section we shall consider reasons for the view that substantive
     foundationalism is superior to coherentism. To assess these reasons, we
     need some more explicit account of the difference between the two.

     By coherentism we shall mean any view according to which the ulti-
     mate sources of justification for any belief lie in relations among that
     belief and other beliefs of the subject: explanatory relations, perhaps, or
     relations of probability or logic.

     According to substantive foundationalism, as it is to be understood
     here, there are ultimate sources of justification other than relations among
     beliefs. Traditionally these additional sources have pertained to the spe-
     cial content of the belief or its special relations to the subjective experi-
     ence of the believer.

b.   The view that justification is a matter of relations among beliefs is open
     to an objection from alternative coherent systems or detachment from
     reality, depending on one's perspective. From the latter perspective the
     body of beliefs is held constant and the surrounding world is allowed to
     vary; from the former it is the surrounding world that is held constant
     while the body of beliefs is allowed to vary. In either case, according to
     the coherentist, there could be no effect on the justification for any
     belief.

     Let us sharpen the question before us as follows. Is there reason to
     think that there is at least one system B′, alternative to our actual system
     of beliefs B, such that B′ contains a belief X with the following properties:

   (i)    in our present nonbelief circumstances we would not be justified in
          having belief X even if we accepted along with that belief (as our
          total system of beliefs) the entire belief system B′ in which it is
          embedded (no matter how acceptance of B′ were brought about);
          and

   (ii)   that is so despite the fact that belief X coheres within B′ at least as
          fully as does some actual justified belief of ours within our actual
          belief system B (where the justification of that actual justified belief
          is alleged by the coherentist to derive solely from its coherence
          within our actual body of beliefs B).

     The coherentist is vulnerable to counterexamples of this sort right at
     the surface of his body of beliefs, where we find beliefs with minimal
     coherence, whose detachment and replacement with contrary beliefs would
     have little effect on the coherence of the body. Thus take my belief that I
     have a headache when I do have a splitting headache, and let us suppose
     that this *does* cohere within my present body of beliefs. (Thus I have no
     reason to doubt my present introspective beliefs, and so on. And if my

belief does *not* cohere, so much the worse for coherentism, since my belief is surely justified.) Here then we have a perfectly justified or warranted belief. And yet such a belief may well have relevant relations of explanation, logic, or probability with at most a small set of other beliefs of mine at the time: say, that I am not free of headache, that I am in pain, that someone is in pain, and the like. If so, then an equally coherent alternative is not far to seek. Let everything remain constant, *including* the splitting headache, except for the following: replace the belief that I have a headache with the belief that I do *not* have a headache, the belief that I am in pain with the belief that I am *not* in pain, the belief that someone is in pain with the belief that someone is *not* in pain, and so on. I contend that my resulting hypothetical system of beliefs would cohere as fully as does my actual system of beliefs, and yet my hypothetical belief that I do *not* have a headache would not therefore be justified. What makes this difference concerning justification between my actual belief that I have a headache and the hypothetical belief that I am free of headache, each as coherent as the other within its own system, if not the actual splitting headache? But the headache is *not* itself a belief nor a relation among beliefs and is thus in no way constitutive of the internal coherence of my body of beliefs.

Some might be tempted to respond by alleging that one's belief about whether or not one has a headache is always *infallible*. But since we could devise similar examples for the various sensory modalities and propositional attitudes, the response given for the case of headache would have to be generalized. In effect, it would have to cover "peripheral" beliefs generally – beliefs at the periphery of one's body of beliefs, minimally coherent with the rest. These peripheral beliefs would all be said to be infallible. That is, again, a possible response, but it leads to a capitulation by the coherentist to the radical foundationalist on a crucial issue that has traditionally divided them: the infallibility of beliefs about one's own subjective states.

What is more, not all peripheral beliefs are about one's own subjective states. The direct realist is probably right that some beliefs about our surroundings are uninferred and yet justified. Consider my present belief that the table before me is oblong. This presumably coheres with such other beliefs of mine as that the table has the same shape as the piece of paper before me, which is oblong, and a different shape than the window frame here, which is square, and so on. So far as I can see, however, there is no insurmountable obstacle to replacing that whole set of coherent beliefs with an equally coherent set as follows: that the table before me is square, that the table has the same shape as the square window frame, and a different shape than the piece of paper, which is oblong, and so on. The important points are (a) that this replacement may be made without changing the rest of one's body of beliefs or any aspect of the world beyond, including one's present visual experience of something oblong, not square, as one looks at the table before one; and (b) that is so, in part, because of the fact (c) that the subject need not have any beliefs about his present sensory experience.

Some might be tempted to respond by alleging that one's present experience is *self-intimating*, i.e., always necessarily taken note of and reflected in one's beliefs. Thus if anyone has visual experience of something oblong, then he believes that he has such experience. But this would involve a further important concession by the coherentist to the radical foundationalist, who would have been granted two of his most cherished doctrines: the infallibility of introspective belief and the self-intimation of experience.

# 10   The Foundationalist's Dilemma

The antifoundationalist zeal of recent years has left several forms of foundationalism standing. These all share the conviction that a belief can be justified not only by its coherence within a comprehensive system but also by an appropriate combination of observational content and origin in the use of the senses in standard conditions. What follows presents a dilemma for any foundationalism based on any such idea.

a.   We may surely suppose that beings with observational mechanisms radically unlike ours might also have knowledge of their environment. (That seems possible even if the radical difference in observational mechanisms precludes overlap in substantive concepts and beliefs.)

b.   Let us suppose that there is such a being, for whom experience of type $\phi$ (of which we have no notion) has a role with respect to his beliefs of type $\phi$ analogous to the role that our visual experience has with respect to our visual beliefs. Thus we might have a schema such as the following:

| *Human* | *Extraterrestrial being* |
| --- | --- |
| Visual experience | $\phi$ experience |
| Experience of something red | Experience of something F |
| Belief that there is something red before one | Belief that there is something F before one |

c.   It is often recognized that our visual experience intervenes in two ways with respect to our visual beliefs: as cause and as justification. But these are not wholly independent. Presumably, the justification of the belief that something here is red derives at least in part from the fact that it originates in a visual experience of something red that takes place in normal circumstances.

d.   Analogously, the extraterrestrial belief that something here has the property of being F might be justified partly by the fact that it originates in a $\phi$ experience of something F that takes place in normal circumstances.

e.   A simple question presents the foundationalist's dilemma: regarding the epistemic principle that underlies our justification for believing that something here is red on the basis of our visual experience of something red, is it proposed as a fundamental principle or as a derived generalization? Let us compare the famous Principle of Utility of value theory, according to which it is best for that to happen which, of all the possible alternatives in the circumstances, would bring with it into the world the greatest balance of pleasure over pain, joy over sorrow, happiness over unhappiness, content over discontent, or the like. Upon this fundamental principle one may then base various generalizations, rules of thumb, and maxims of public health, nutrition, legislation, etiquette, hygiene, and so on. But these are all then derived generalizations which rest for their validity on the fundamental principle. Similarly, one may also ask, with respect to the generalizations advanced by our foundationalist, whether these are proposed as fundamental principles or as derived maxims or the like. This sets him face to face with a dilemma, each of whose alternatives is problematic. If his proposals are meant to have the status of secondary or derived maxims, for instance, then it would be quite unphilosophical to stop there. Let us turn, therefore, to the other alternative.

f.  On reflection it seems rather unlikely that epistemic principles for the justification of observational beliefs by their origin in sensory experience could have a status more fundamental than that of derived generalizations. For by granting such principles fundamental status we would open the door to a multitude of equally basic principles with no unifying factor. There would be some for vision, some for hearing, etc., without even mentioning the corresponding extraterrestrial principles.

g.  It may appear that there is after all an idea, however, that unifies our multitude of principles. For they all involve sensory experience and sensible characteristics. But what is a sensible characteristic? Aristotle's answer appeals to examples: colors, shapes, sounds, and so on. Such a notion might enable us to unify perceptual epistemic principles under some more fundamental principle such as the following:

> If $\sigma$ is a sensible characteristic, then the belief that there is something with $\sigma$ before one is (prima facie) justified if it is based on a visual experience of something with $\sigma$ in conditions that are normal with respect to $\sigma$.

h.  There are at least two difficulties with such a suggestion, however, and neither one can be brushed aside easily. First, it is not clear that we can have a viable notion of sensible characteristic on the basis of examples so diverse as colors, shapes, tones, odors, and so on. Second, the authority of such a principle apparently derives from contingent circumstances concerning the reliability of beliefs prompted by sensory experiences of certain sorts. According to the foundationalist, our visual beliefs are justified by their origin in our visual experience or the like. Would such beliefs be equally well justified in a world where beliefs with such an origin were nearly always false?

i.  In addition, finally, even if we had a viable notion of such characteristics, it is not obvious that fundamental knowledge of reality would have to derive causally or otherwise from sensory experience of such characteristics. How could one impose reasonable limits on extraterrestrial mechanisms for noninferential acquisition of beliefs? Is it not possible that such mechanisms need not always function through sensory experience of any sort? Would such beings necessarily be denied any knowledge of their surroundings and indeed of any contingent spatio-temporal fact? Let us suppose them to possess a complex system of true beliefs concerning their surroundings, the structures below the surface of things, exact details of history and geography, all constituted by concepts none of which corresponds to any of our sensible characteristics. What then? Is it not possible that their basic beliefs should all concern fields of force, waves, mathematical structures, and numerical assignments to variables in several dimensions? This is no doubt an exotic notion, but even so it still seems conceivable. And if it is in fact possible, what then shall we say of the noninferential beliefs of such beings? Would we have to concede the existence of special epistemic principles that can validate their noninferential beliefs? Would it not be preferable to formulate more abstract principles that can cover both human and extraterrestrial foundations? If such more abstract principles are in fact accessible, then the less general principles that define the human foundations and those that define the extraterrestrial foundations are both derived principles whose validity depends on that of the more abstract principles. In this the human and extraterrestrial epistemic principles would resemble rules of good nutrition for an infant and an adult. The infant's rules would of course be quite unlike those valid for the adult. But both would still be based on a more fundamental principle that postulates the ends of well-being and good health. What more fundamental principles might support both human and extraterrestrial knowledge in the way that those concerning good health and well-being support rules of nutrition for both the infant and the adult?

## 11  Reliabilism: An Ethics of Moral Virtues and an Epistemology of Intellectual Virtues

In what sense is the doctor attending Frau Hitler justified in performing an action that brings with it far less value than one of its accessible alternatives? According to one promising idea, the key is to be found in the rules that he embodies through stable dispositions. His action is the result of certain stable virtues, and there are no equally virtuous alternate *dispositions* that, given his cognitive limitations, he might have embodied with equal or better total consequences, and that would have led him to infanticide in the circumstances. The important move for our purpose is the stratification of justification. Primary justification attaches to virtues and other dispositions, to stable dispositions to act, through their greater contribution of value when compared with alternatives. Secondary justification attaches to particular acts in virtue of their source in virtues or other such justified dispositions.

The same strategy may also prove fruitful in epistemology. Here primary justification would apply to *intellectual* virtues, to stable dispositions for belief acquisition, through their greater contribution toward getting us to the truth. Secondary justification would then attach to particular beliefs in virtue of their source in intellectual virtues or other such justified dispositions.[7]

That raises parallel questions for ethics and epistemology. We need to consider more carefully the concept of a virtue and the distinction between moral and intellectual virtues. In epistemology, there is reason to think that the most useful and illuminating notion of intellectual virtue will prove broader than our tradition would suggest and must give due weight not only to the subject and his intrinsic nature but also to his environment and to his epistemic community. This is a large topic, however, to which I hope some of us will turn with more space, and insight, than I can now command.[8]

## 12 Summary

1  *Two assumptions.* (A1) that for a belief to constitute knowledge it must be (a) true and (b) justified; and (A2) that the justification relevant to whether or not one knows is a sort of epistemic or theoretical justification to be distinguished from its practical counterpart.

2  *Knowledge and criteria.* Particularism is distinguished from methodism: the first gives priority to particularly examples of knowledge over general methods of criteria, whereas the second reverses that order. The methodism of Descartes leads him to an elaborate dogmatism whereas that of Hume leads him to a very simple skepticism. The particularist is, of course, antiskeptical on principle.

3  *Two metaphors: the raft and the pyramid.* For the foundationalist every piece of knowledge stands at the apex of a pyramid that rests on stable and secure foundations whose stability and security does not derive from the upper stories or sections. For the coherentist a body of knowledge is a free-floating raft every plank of which helps directly or indirectly to keep all the others in place, and no plank of which would retain its status with no help from the others.

4  *A coherentist critique of foundationalism.* No mental state can provide a foundation for empirical knowledge. For if such a state is propositional, then it is fallible and hence no secure foundation. But if it is *not* propositional, then how can it possibly serve as a foundation for belief? How can one infer or justify anything on the basis of a state that, having no propositional content, must be logically dumb? An analogy with ethics suggests a reason to reject this dilemma. Other reasons are also advanced and discussed.

5  *The regress argument.* In defending his position, the foundationalist often attempts to rule out the very possibility of an infinite regress of justi-

fication (which leads him to the necessity for a foundation). Some of his arguments to that end are examined.

6  *The relation of justification and foundationalist strategy.* An alternative foundationalist strategy is exposed, one that does not require ruling out the possibility of an infinite regress of justification.

7  *Two levels of foundationalism.* Substantive foundationalism is distinguished from formal foundationalism, three grades of which are exposed: first, the supervenience of epistemic justification; second, its explicable supervenience; and, third, its supervenience explicable by means of a simple theory. There turns out to be a surprising kinship between coherentism and substantive foundationalism, both of which aim at a formal foundationalism of the highest grade, at a theory of the greatest simplicity that explains how epistemic justification supervenes on nonepistemic factors.

8  *Doxastic ascent arguments.* The distinction between formal and substantive foundationalism provides an unusual viewpoint on some recent attacks against foundationalism. We consider doxastic ascent arguments as an example.

9  *Coherentism and substantive foundationalism.* It is argued that substantive foundationalism is superior since coherentism is unable to account adequately for the epistemic status of beliefs at the "periphery" of a body of beliefs.

10  *The foundationalist's dilemma.* All foundationalism based on sense experience is subject to a fatal dilemma.

11  *Reliabilism.* An alternative to foundationalism of sense experience is sketched.

## Notes

1  But Descartes's methodism was at most partial. James Van Cleve has supplied the materials for a convincing argument that the way out of the Cartesian circle is through a particularism of basic knowledge. (See James Van Cleve, "Foundationalism, Epistemic Principles, and the Cartesian Circle," *Philosophical Review* 88 (1979): 55–91.) But this is, of course, compatible with methodism on inferred knowledge. Whether Descartes subscribed to such methodism is hard (perhaps impossible) to determine, since in the end he makes room for all the kinds of knowledge required by particularism. But his language when he introduces the method of hyperbolic doubt, and the order in which he proceeds, suggest that he did subscribe to such methodism.

2  Cf. Laurence Bonjour, "The Coherence Theory of Truth," *Philosophical Studies* 30 (1976): 281–312; and, especially, Michael Williams, *Groundless Belief* (New Haven: Yale University Press, 1977); and L. Bonjour, "Can Empirical Knowledge Have a Foundation?" *American Philosophical Quarterly* 15 (1978): 1–15.

3  Cf. Richard Foley, "Inferential Justification and the Infinite Regress," *American Philosophical Quarterly* 15 (1978): 311–16.

4  Cf. John Post, "Infinite Regresses of Justification and of Explanation," *Philosophical Studies* 38 (1980): 31–52.

5   The argument of this whole section is developed in greater detail in my paper "The Foundations of Foundationalism," *Nous* 14 (1980): 547–65.

6   For some examples of the influence of doxastic ascent arguments, see Wilfrid Sellars's writing in epistemology: e.g., "Empiricism and the Philosophy of Mind," in *Science, Perception and Reality* (London: Routledge & Kegan Paul, 1963), ch. 5, especially section VIII, and particularly p. 168. Also I. T. Oakley, "An Argument for Skepticism Concerning Justified Beliefs," *American Philosophical Quarterly* 13 (1976): 221–8; and Bonjour, "Can Empirical Knowledge Have a Foundation?"

7   This puts in a more traditional perspective the contemporary effort to develop a "causal theory of knowing." From our viewpoint, this effort is better understood not as an attempt to *define* propositional knowledge but as an attempt to formulate fundamental principles of justification.

    Cf. D. Armstrong, *Belief, Truth and Knowledge* (Cambridge, 1973); and that of F. Dretske, A. Goldman, and M. Swain, whose relevant already published work is included in *Essays on Knowledge and Justification*, ed. G. Pappas and M. Swain (Ithaca and London, 1978). But the theory is still under development by Goldman and Swain, who have reached general conclusions about it similar to those suggested here, though not necessarily – so far as I know – for the same reasons or in the same overall context.

8   The main ideas in this essay were first presented in a seminar of 1976–7 at the University of Texas. I am grateful to those who made that seminar a valuable stimulus.

---

# 13   The Elements of Coherentism

---

## *Laurence BonJour*

### 1   The Very Idea of a Coherence Theory

In light of the failure of foundationalism, it is time to look again at the apparent alternatives with regard to the structure of empirical justification which were distinguished in the discussion of the epistemic regress problem [in an earlier section]. If the regress of empirical justification does not terminate in basic empirical beliefs, then it must either (1) terminate in unjustified beliefs, (2) go on infinitely (without circularity), or (3) circle back upon itself in some way. As discussed earlier, alternative (1) is clearly a version of skepticism and as such may reasonably be set aside until all other alternatives have been seen to fail. Alternative (2) may also be a version of skepticism, though this is less clear. But the more basic problem with alternative (2) is that no one has ever succeeded in amplifying it into a developed position (indeed, it is not clear that anyone has even attempted to do so); nor do I see any plausible way in which this might be done. Failing any such elaboration which meets the objections tentatively developed earlier, alternative (2) may also reasonably be set aside. This then leaves alternative (3) as apparently the only remaining possibility for a nonskeptical account of empirical knowledge.

We are thus led to a reconsideration of the possibility of a coherence theory of empirical knowledge. If there is no way to justify empirical beliefs apart from an appeal to other justified empirical beliefs, and if an infinite sequence of distinct justified beliefs is ruled out, then the presumably finite system of justified empirical beliefs can only be justified from within, by virtue of the relations of its component beliefs to each other – if, that is, it is justified at all. And the idea of *coherence* should for the moment be taken merely to indicate whatever property (or complex set of properties) is requisite for the justification of such a system of beliefs.

Obviously this rather flimsy argument by elimination carries very little weight by itself. The analogous argument in the case of foundationalism lead to an untenable result; and that failure, when added to the already substantial problems with coherence theories which were briefly noted above, makes the present version even less compelling. At best it may motivate a more open-minded consideration of coherence theories than they have usually been accorded, such theories having usually been treated merely as dialectical bogeymen and only rarely as serious epistemological alternatives.

It will be useful to begin by specifying more precisely just what sort of coherence theory is at issue here. In the first place, our concern is with coherence theories of empirical justification and not coherence theories of truth; the latter hold that truth is to be simply identified with coherence (presumably coherence with some specified sort of system). The classical idealist proponents of coherence theories in fact generally held views of both these sorts and unfortunately failed for the most part to distinguish clearly between them. And this sort of confusion is abetted by views which use the phrase "theory of truth" to mean a theory of the criteria of truth, that is, a theory of the standards or rules which should be appealed to in deciding or judging whether or not something is true; if, as is virtually always the case, such a theory is meant to be an account of the criteria which can be used to arrive at a rational or warranted judgment of truth or falsity, then a coherence theory of truth in that sense would seem to be indiscernible from what is here called a coherence theory of justification, and quite, distinct from a coherence theory of the very nature or meaning of truth.[1] But if such confusions are avoided, it is clear that coherence theories of empirical justification are both distinct from and initially a good deal more plausible than coherence theories of empirical truth and moreover that there is no manifest absurdity in combining a coherence theory of justification with a correspondence theory of truth. Whether such a combination is in the end dialectically defensible is of course a further issue and one to which I will return in the final chapter of this book.

Second, it is also worth emphasizing at the outset that I am concerned here only with coherence theories which purport to provide a response to skepticism. My view thus differs from those of several recent coherence theorists, most notably Michael Williams but also, to a lesser extent, Gilbert Harman and Keith Lehrer, who depart from foundationalism not only in their account of the structure of empirical justification but also with regard to the goals or purposes of an epistemological theory, by holding that such a theory need not attempt to provide a "global" account of justification or to answer "global" varieties of skepticism.

Third, the dialectical motive for coherentism depends heavily on the unacceptability of the externalist position. It is thus crucially important that a coherentist view itself avoid tacitly slipping into a nonfoundationalist version of externalism. If coherentism is to be even a dialectically interesting alternative, the coherentist justfication must, in principle at least, be accessible to the believer himself.

The aim of this chapter is to begin the task of formulating a coherence theory which satisfied the foregoing structures by, first, considering in detail some of the main ingredients of such a view, including the idea of nonlinear or holistic justification, the concept of coherence itself, and the presumption concerning one's grasp of one's own system of beliefs; and, second, elaborating the leading objections which such a position must face. The upshot of the chapter will be the hardly surprising conclusion that a central, very likely decisive, issue with respect to coherence theories is whether they can somehow make room for a viable concept of *observation*.

## 2  Linear Versus Nonlinear Justification

The initial problem is whether and how a coherence theory constitutes even a *prima facie* solution to the epistemic regress problem. Having rejected both foundationalism and the actual-infinite-regress position, a coherentist must hold, as we have seen, that the regress of empirical justification moves in a circle – or, more plausibly, some more complicated and multidimensional variety of closed curve. But this response to the regress will seem obviously and utterly inadequate to one who approaches the issue with foundationalist preconceptions. Surely, his argument will go, such a resort to circularity fails to solve or even adequately confront the problem. Each step in the regress is a justificatory argument whose premises must be justified *before* they can confer justification on the conclusion. To say that the regress moves in a circle is to say that at some point one (or more) of the beliefs which figured earlier as a conclusion is now appealed to as a justifying premise. And this response, far from solving the problem, seems to yield the patently absurd result that the justification of such a belief depends, indirectly but still quite inescapably, on *its own* logically prior justification: it cannot be justified unless it is already justified. And thus, assuming that it is not justified in some independent way, neither it nor anything which depends upon it can be genuinely justified. Since empirical justification is always ultimately circular in this way according to coherence theories, there can on such a view be in the end no empirical justification and no empirical knowledge.

The crucial, though tacit, assumption which underlies this seemingly devastating line of argument is the idea that inferential justification is essentially *linear* in character, that it involves a one-dimensional sequence of beliefs, ordered by the relation of epistemic priority, along which epistemic justification is passed from the earlier to the later beliefs in the sequence via connections of inference. It is just this linear conception of justification which generates the regress problem in the first place. So long as it remains unchallenged, the idea that justification moves in a circle will seem obviously untenable, and only moderate or strong foundationalism will be left as an alternative: even weak foundationalism cannot accept a purely linear view of justification, since its initially credible beliefs are not sufficiently justified on that basis alone to serve as linear first premises for everything else. Thus the primary coherentist response to the regress problem cannot be merely the idea that justification moves in a circle, for this would be quite futile by itself; rather such a position must repudiate the linear conception of justification in its entirety.

But what is the alternative? What might a nonlinear conception of justification amount to? Briefly, the main idea is that inferential justification, despite its linear appearance, is essentially systematic or holistic in character: beliefs are justified by being inferentially related to other beliefs in the overall context of a coherent system.

The best way to clarify this view is to distinguish two importantly different levels at which issues of empirical justification can be raised. The epistemic issue on a particular occasion will usually be merely the justification of a single empirical belief, or small set of such beliefs, within the context of a cognitive system whose overall justification is (more or less) taken for granted; we may call this the *local* level of justification. But it is also possible, at least in principle, to raise the issue of the overall justification of the entire system of empirical beliefs; we may call this the *global* level of justification. For the sort of coherence theory which will be developed here – and indeed, I would argue, for any comprehensive, nonskeptical epistemology – it is the issue of justification as it arises at the latter, global, level which is in the final analysis decisive for the determination of empirical justification in general.[2] This tends to be obscured in practice, I suggest, because it is only issues of the former, local, sort which tend to be explicitly raised in actual cases. (Indeed, it may well be that completely global issues are never in fact raised outside the context of explicitly epistemological discussion; but I cannot see that this in any way shows that there is something illegitimate about them.)

It is at the local level of justification that inferential justification *appears* linear. A given justification belief is shown to be justified by citing other premise-beliefs from which it correctly follows via some acceptable pattern of inference. Such premise-beliefs may themselves be challenged, of course, with justification being offered for them in the same fashion. But there is no serious danger of an infinite regress at this level, since the justification of the overall system of empirical beliefs, and thus of most of its constituent beliefs, is *ex hypothesi* not at issue. One quickly reaches premise-beliefs which are dialectically acceptable in that particular context and which can thus function there rather like the foundationalist's basic beliefs. (But these *contextually basic beliefs*, as they might be called, are unlikely to be only or even primarily beliefs which would be classified as basic by any plausible version of foundationalism.)

If, on the other hand, no dialectically acceptable stopping point were reached, if the new premise-beliefs offered as justification continued to be challenged in turn, then (according to the sort of coherence theory with which I am concerned) the epistemic dialogue would if ideally continued eventually circle back upon itself, giving the appearance of a linear regress and in effect challenging the entire system of empirical beliefs. At this global level, however, the previously harmless illusion of linearity becomes a serious mistake. According to the envisaged coherence theory, the relation between the various particular beliefs is correctly to be conceived, not as one of linear dependence, but rather as one of mutual or reciprocal support. There is no ultimate relation of epistemic priority among the members of such a system and consequently no basis for a true regress. Rather the component beliefs of such a coherent system will ideally be so related that each can be justified in terms of the others, with the direction of argument on a particular occasion of local justification depending on which belief (or set of beliefs) has actually been challenged in the particular situation. And hence, a coherence theory wll claim, the apparent circle of justification is not in fact vicious *because* it is not *genuinely a circle*: the justification of a particular empirical belief finally depends, not on other particular beliefs as the linear conception of justification would have it, but instead on the overall system and its coherence.

According to this conception, the fully explicit justification of a particular empirical belief would involve four distinct main steps or stages of argument, as follows:

(1)   The inferability of that particular belief from other particular beliefs and further relations among particular empirical beliefs.
(2)   The coherence of the overall system of empirical beliefs.
(3)   The justification of the overall system of empirical beliefs.
(4)   The justification of the particular belief in question, by virtue of its membership in the system.

The claim of a coherence theory of empirical justification is that each of these steps depends on the ones which precede it. It is the neglecting of steps (2) and (3), the ones pertaining explicitly to the overall cognitive system, that lends plausibility to the linear conception of justification and thus generates the regress problem. And this is a very seductive mistake: since the very same inferential connections between particular empirical beliefs are involved in both step (1) and step (4), and since the issues involved in the intervening steps are very rarely (if ever) raised in practical contexts, it becomes much too easy to conflate steps (1) and (4), thus leaving out any explicit reference to the cognitive system and its coherence. The picture which results from such an omission is vastly more simple; but the price of this simplicity, according to coherence theories, is a radical distortion of the very concept of epistemic justification – and also, in the end, skepticism or something tantamount to it.

How tenable is such a nonlinear conception of empirical justification? Of the three crucial transitions represented in this obviously quite schematic account, only the third, from step (3) to step (4), is reasonably unproblematic, depending as it does on the inferential relations that obtain between the justificandum belief and the other beliefs of the system; in effect it is this transition which is made when an inferential justification is offered in an ordinary context of local justification, with the other steps being taken for granted. But the other two transitions are highly problematic, and the issues that they raise are crucial for understanding and assessing the very conception of a coherence theory.

The transition from step (1) to step (2), from the relations obtaining between particular beliefs to the attribution of the holistic property of coherence to the empirical system as a whole, is rendered problematic by the obscurity of the central concept of coherence itself. A fully adequate explication of coherence is unfortunately not possible within the scope of this book (nor, one may well suspect, within the scope of any work of manageable length). But I will attempt to render the concept manageably clear in the next section, where I will also suggest that the clarity of the concept of coherence is not, surprisingly enough, a very crucial issue in assessing the plausibility of coherence theories *vis-à-vis* their nonskeptical opponents.

The problems relating to the other problematic transition in the schematic account, that from step (2) to step (3), are, in contrast, more serious, indeed critical. What is at issue here is the question of the connection between coherence and epistemic justification: why, if a system of empirical beliefs is coherent (and more coherent than any rival system), is it thereby justified *in the epistemic sense*, that is, why is it thereby likely to be true? I will address this question in section 5, where the standard set of objections to coherence theories will be developed in further detail.

## 3   The Concept of Coherence

What, then, is coherence? Intuitively, coherence is a matter of how well a body of beliefs "hangs together": how well its component beliefs fit together, agree or dovetail with each other, so as to produce an organized, tightly structured system of beliefs, rather than either a helter-skelter collection or a set of conflicting subsystems. It is reasonably clear that this "hanging together" depends on the various sorts of inferential, evidential, and explanatory relations which obtain among the various members of a system of beliefs, and especially on the more holistic and systematic of these. Thus various detailed investigations by philosophers and logicians of such topics as explanation, confirmation, probability, and so on, may be reasonably taken to provide some of the ingredients for a general account of coherence. But the main work of giving such an account, and in particular one which will provide some relatively clear basis for *comparative* assessments of coherence, has scarcely been begun, despite the long history of the concept.

My response to this problem, for the moment at least, is a deliberate – though, I think, justified – evasion. It consists in pointing out that the task of giving an adequate explication of the concept of coherence is not uniquely or even primarily the job of coherence theories. This is so because coherence – or something resembling it so closely as to be subject to the same sort of problem – is, and seemingly must be, a basic ingredient of virtually all rival epistemological theories as well. We have already seen that weak foundationalism essentially involves an appeal to coherence. And it seems clear that even moderate and strong foundationalisms cannot avoid an appeal to something like coherence in giving an account of knowledge of the past, theoretical knowledge, and other types of knowledge which (on any view) go beyond direct experience. Thus it is not surprising that virtually all of the leading proponents of comprehensive foundationalist views, whether weak, moderate, or strong, employ the notion of coherence in their total epistemological accounts – though sometimes under other names, such as "congruence" (Lewis) or "concurrence" (Chisholm).[3] Even "contextualist" views, which attempt to repudiate the whole issue of global justification, make a similar appeal. The conclusion strongly suggested is that something like coherence is indispensable to any nonskeptical epistemological position which is even *prima facie* adequate. And if this is so, the absence of an adequate explication of coherence does not count against coherence theories any more than against their rivals.

The foregoing response is dialectically cogent in defending coherence theories against other, nonskeptical epistemologies, but it must be admitted that it is of little use *vis-à-vis* the skeptic, who may well argue that what it shows is that all nonskeptical epistemologies are fundamentally flawed by virtue of their dependence on this inadequately explicated concept. But although this challenge must be taken seriously, it is far from obvious that it is even close to being decisive. A better account of coherence is beyond any doubt something devoutly to be sought; but it is, I think, quite plausible to say, as Ewing does, that what proponents of coherence "are doing is to describe an ideal that has never yet been completely clarified but is none the less immanent in all our thinking,"[4] and to hold on this basis that our intuitive grasp of this notion, though surely not ideally satisfactory, will suffice so long as the only alternative is skepticism – which itself carries, after all, a significant burden of implausibility.

In any case, however, there is little point in talking at length about coherence without a somewhat clearer idea of what is involved. Thus I will attempt to provide in this section a reasonable outline of the concept of coherence, while recognizing that it falls far short of what would be ideal. The main points are: first, coherence is not to be equated with mere consistency; second, coherence, as already suggested, has to do with the mutual inferability of the beliefs in the system; third, relations of explanation are one central ingredient in coherence, though not the only one; and, fourth, coherence may be enhanced through conceptual change.

First. A serious and perennial mistake in discussing coherence, usually committed by critics but occasionally also by would-be proponents of coherence theories, is to assume that coherence means nothing more than logical consistency, the absence of explicit contradiction.[5] It is true that consistency is one requirement for coherence, that inconsistency is obviously a very serious sort of incoherence. But it is abundantly clear, as many coherentists have pointed out, that a system of beliefs might be perfectly consistent and yet have no appreciable degree of coherence.

There are at least two ways in which this might be so. The more obvious is what might be called *probabilistic inconsistency*. Suppose that my system of beliefs contains both the belief that P and also the belief that it is extremely improbable that P. Clearly such a system of beliefs may perfectly well be logically consistent. But it is equally clear from an intuitive standpoint that a system which contains two such beliefs is significantly less coherent than it would be without them and thus that probabilistic consistency is a second factor determining coherence.

Probabilistic consistency differs from straightforward logical consistency in two important respects. First, it is extremely doubtful that probabilistic inconsistency can be entirely avoided. Improbable things do, after all, sometimes happen, and sometimes one can avoid admitting them only by creating an even greater probabilistic inconsistency at another point.[6] Second, probabilistic consistency, unlike logical consistency, is plainly a matter of degree, depending on (a) just how many such conflicts the system contains and (b) the degree of improbability involved in each case. Thus we have two initial conditions for coherence, which we may formulate as follows:

(1)   A system of beliefs is coherent only if it is logically consistent.[7]
(2)   A system of beliefs is coherent in proportion to its degree of probabilistic consistency.

But these two requirements are still not enough. Imagine a set of beliefs, each member of which has simply no bearing at all on the subject matter of any of the others, so that they make no effective contact with each other. This lack of contact will of course assure that the set is both logically and probabilistically consistent by ruling out any possibility of conflict; but it will also assure that the members of the set fail to hang together in any very significant way. Thus consider the following two sets of propositions, A and B. A contains "this chair is brown," "electrons are negatively charged," and "today is Thursday." B contains "all ravens are black," "this bird is a raven," and "this bird is black." Clearly both sets of propositions are free of contradiction and are also probabilistically consistent. But in the case of A, this consistency results from the fact that its component propositions are almost entirely irrelevant to each other; though not in conflict, they also fail to be positively related in any significant way. And for this reason, set A possesses only a very low degree of coherence. In the case of set B, in contrast, consistency results from the fact that the component propositions, rather than being irrelevant to each other, fit together and reinforce each other in a significant way; from an epistemic standpoint, any two of them would lend a degree of positive support to the third (though only very weak support in two out of the three cases). Thus set B, though obviously much too small to have a really significant degree of coherence, is much more coherent than set A. As the classical proponents of coherence have always insisted, coherence must involve some sort of positive connection among the beliefs in question, not merely the absence of conflict.

Second. But what sort of positive connection is required and how strong must it be? The obvious answer to the first question is that the connections in question are inference relations namely, any sort of relation of content which would allow one belief or set of beliefs, if justified, to serve as the premise(s) of a cogent epistemic-justificatory argument for a further belief. The basic requirement for such an inference relation, as suggested in the earlier discussion of epistemic justification, is that it be to some degree truth-preserving; any sort of relation which meets this requirement will serve as an appropriate positive connection between beliefs, and no other sort of connection seems relevant here.

This much would be accepted by most, if not all, proponents of coherence theories. The main thing that divides them is the issue of how close and pervasive such inferential connections are required to be. One pole with regard to this issue is represented by the classical absolute idealists. Blanshard's formulation is typical:

> Fully coherent knowledge would be knowledge in which every judgment entailed, and was entailed by, the rest of the system.[8]

(In interpreting this formulation it is important to remember that Blanshard, like many others in this tradition, believes in synthetic entailments and indeed holds the admittedly dubious view that causal connections are one species of entailment.) The main problem with this view is that it is quite impossible even to imagine a system of beliefs which would satisfy such a requirement; as Blanshard himself admits, even such a system as Euclidean geometry, often appealed to as a paradigm of coherence, falls far short.[9] Thus it is plausible to weaken the requirement for coherence at least to the degree advocated by Ewing, who requires only that each proposition in a coherent system be entailed by the rest taken together, not that the reciprocal relation hold.[10] (We will see shortly that weakening the requirement in this way creates a problem which forces Ewing to add a further, related requirement.)

At the opposite extreme is Lewis's account of "congruence," a concept which plays a crucial role in his account of memory knowledge:

> A set of statements . . . will be said to be congruent if and only if they are so related that the antecedent probability of any one of them will be increased if the remainder of the set can be assumed as given premises.[11]

This is obviously an extremely weak requirement. A system of beliefs which satisfied it at only the most minimal level would possess a vastly lower degree of systematic interconnection than that envisaged by the idealists, in two significantly different respects. First, reducing the requirement from entailment to merely some increase in probability obviously allows a weakening of the inferential connections which constitute coherence. But this is no objection to Lewis's account, so long as it is understood that coherence is a matter of degree, and that a lower degree of inferential interconnection carries with it only a lower degree of coherence. Second, however, Lewis's account, and indeed Ewing's as well, by making the inferential connection between the individual belief in question and the rest of the system one-way rather than reciprocal, creates the possibility that a system of beliefs could count as coherent to as high a degree as one likes by being composed of two or more subsystems of beliefs, each internally connected by strong inference relations but none having any significant connection with the others. From an intuitive standpoint, however, it is clear that such a system, though coherent to some degree, would fall very far short of ideal coherence. Ideal coherence requires also that the entire system of beliefs form a unified structure, that there be laws and principles which underlie the various subsystems of beliefs and provide a significant degree of inferential connection between them. We are obviously very close here to the ideal of a "unified science," in which the laws and terms of various disparate disciplines are reduced to those of some single master discipline, perhaps physics; while such a specific result is not essential for coherence, it would represent one way in which a high degree of coherence could be achieved, and something in this general direction seems to be required.

Ewing attempts to meet this difficulty by adding as a separate requirement for coherence the condition that no set of beliefs smaller than the whole system be logically independent of the rest of the system,[12] and a similar requirement could be added to Lewis's account as well. It would be better, however, to make this further aspect of coherence also a matter of degree, since there are obviously many intermediate cases between a completely unified system and a system with completely isolated subsystems. Putting all of this together results in the following two additional conditions for coherence:

(3) The coherence of a system of beliefs is increased by the presence of inferential connections between its component beliefs and increased in proportion to the number and strength of such connections.

(4) The coherence of a system of beliefs is diminished to the extent to which it is divided into subsystems of beliefs which are relatively unconnected to each other by inferential connections.

It should be noted that condition (3), in addition to summarizing the preceding discussion, includes one important idea which did not emerge explicitly there: each individual belief can be involved in many different inferential relations, and the degree to which this is so is also a determinant of coherence.

Third. The foregoing account, though it seems to me to be on the right track, is obviously still extremely sketchy. One way to reduce this sketchiness somewhat is to consider the major role which the idea of *explanation* plays in the overall concept of coherence. As I have already suggested by mentioning the ideal of unified science, the coherence of a system of beliefs is enhanced by the presence of explanatory relations among its members.

Indeed, if we accept something like the familiar Hempelian account of explanation, this claim is to some extent a corollary of what has already been said.

According to that account, particular facts are explained by appeal to other facts and general laws from which a statement of the explanandum fact may be deductively or probabilistically inferred; and lower-level laws and theories are explained in an analogous fashion by showing them to be deducible from more general laws and theories.[13] Thus the presence of relations of explanation within a system of beliefs enhances the inferential interconnectedness of the system simply because explanatory relations *are* one species of inference relations.

Explanatory connections are not just additional inferential connections among the beliefs of a system, however; they are inferential connections of a particularly pervasive kind. This is so because the basic goal of scientific explanation is to exhibit events of widely differing kinds as manifestations of a relatively small number of basic explanatory principles. As Hempel remarks: "What scientific explanation, especially theoretical explanation, aims at is . . . an objective kind of insight that is achieved by a systematic unification, by exhibiting the phenomena as manifestations of common underlying structures and processes that conform to specific, testable, basic principles."[14] What Hempel calls "systematic unification" is extremely close to the concept of coherence.

One helpful way to elaborate this point is to focus on the concept of *anomaly*. For my purposes, an anomaly is a fact or event, especially one involving some sort of recurring pattern, which is claimed to obtain by one or more of the beliefs in the system of beliefs, but which is incapable of being explained (or would have been incapable of being predicted) by appeal to the other beliefs in the system.[15] (Obviously such a status is a matter of degree.) The presence of such anomalies detracts from the coherence of the system to an extent which cannot be accounted for merely by appeal to the fact that the belief in an anomalous fact or event has fewer inferential connections to the rest of the system than would be the case if an explanation were available. In the context of a coherentist position, such beliefs will have to be inferentially connected to the rest of the system in other, nonexplanatory ways if there is to be any justification for accepting them (see the discussion of observation in Chapter 6), and such connections may be very extensive. The distinctive significance of anomalies lies rather in the fact that they undermine the claim of the allegedly basic explanatory principles to be genuinely basic, and thus threaten the overall coherence of the system in a much more serious way. For this reason, it seems advisable to add one more condition to our list of conditions for coherence:

(5)    The coherence of a system of beliefs is decreased in proportion to the presence of unexplained anomalies in the believed content of the system.[16]

Having insisted on the close connection between coherence and explanation, we must nonetheless resist the idea that explanatory connections are all there is to coherence. Certain proponents of coherentist views, notably Sellars and Harman, have used phrases like "explanatory coherence" in speaking of coherence, seeming to suggest (though I doubt whether any of those using it really intend such a suggestion) that coherence depends *entirely* on explanatory connections.[17] One could of course adopt a conception of coherence which is restricted in this way, but there is no reason at all – from an epistemological standpoint – to do so. The epistemologically significant concept of coherence is bound up with the idea of *justification*, and thus any sort of inference relation which could yield some degree of justification also enhances coherence, whether or not such a relation has any explanatory force.

A simple example (borrowed from Lehrer who in turn borrowed it from Bromberger) may help to illustrate this point.[18] Suppose that I am standing three feet from a pole which is four feet high. Next to my foot is a mouse, and on top of the pole is perched an owl. From these conditions I may obviously infer, using the Pythagorean theorem, that the mouse is five feet from the owl. This inference is surely adequate to justify my believing that the mouse is five feet from the owl, assuming that I am justified in believing these other propositions. And intuitively speaking, this inferential connection means that the belief that the mouse is five feet from the owl coheres with the rest of my beliefs to quite a significant extent. But none of this has any apparent connection with explanation. In particular, as Lehrer points out, this inference does not in any way help to *explain* why the mouse is so close to the owl. Thus it is a mistake to tie coherence too closely to the idea of explanation. Of course, it is still true that the coherence of the system in question would be enhanced by adding an explanation for the presence of the mouse in such close proximity to the owl: given the usual behavior of mice around owls, the presence of the mouse at that distance is an explanatory and predictive anomaly. The point is simply that coherence is also enhanced by inferential connections of a nonexplanatory sort.

Fourth. The final point is really just a corollary of the one just made. To the extent that coherence is closely bound up with explanation and systematic unification, achieving a high degree of coherence may well involve significant conceptual change. This point is most clear in the area of theoretical science, though it has much broader application. A typical situation of theoretical explanation involves one or more anomalies at the "observational" level: apparently well-established facts formulated in the available system of concepts for which no adequate explanation seems to be available in those terms. By devising a new system of the oretical concepts the theoretician makes an explanation available and thus enhances the coherence of the system. In this way the progress of theoretical science may be plausibly viewed as a result of the search for greater coherence.[19]

The foregoing account of coherence is a long way from being as definitive as desirable. I submit, however, that it does indeed identify a concept which, in Ewing's phrase, is "immanent in all our thinking," including all our most advanced scientific thinking; and also that the concept thus identified, though vague and sketchy in many ways, is nonetheless clear enough to make it reasonable to use it, albeit with caution, in dealing with the sorts of epistemological issues under discussion here. In particular, it seems clear that the concept is not so vague as to be at all easy to satisfy.

## 4　The Doxastic Presumption

I have so far considered two of the elements which are arguably essential to a viable coherence theory: the idea of nonlinear justification and the concept of coherence itself. A third essential element is the presumption regarding one's grasp of one's own system of beliefs which I mentioned briefly at the end of the previous chapter; this is required, I will suggest, if our coherence theory is to avoid a relapse into externalism. (A fourth ingredient is the coherentist conception of observation; and a fifth, on a somewhat different level, is the metajustificatory argument for such a theory.)

It will be useful, before attempting to say in detail what the presumption in question amounts to and what it is supposed to do, to see more clearly why it is needed in the first place. According to a coherence theory of empirical justification, as so far characterized, the epistemic justification of an empirical belief derives entirely from its coherence with the believer's overall system of empirical beliefs and not at all from any sort of factor outside that system. What we must now ask is whether and how the fact that a belief coheres in this way is cognitively accessible to the believer himself, so that it can give *him* a reason for accepting the belief.

It would be possible, of course, to adopt an externalist version of coherentism. Such a view would hold that the person whose belief is justified need himself have no cognitive access to the fact of coherence, that his belief is justified if it in fact coheres with his system of beliefs, whether or not such coherence is cognitively accessible to him (or, presumably, to anyone). But such a view is unacceptable for essentially the same reasons which were offered against foundationalist versions of externalism and, as discussed earlier, seems to run counter to the whole rationale for coherence theories. (If externalism were acceptable in general, the foundationalist versions would obviously be far simpler and more plausible.) But if the fact of coherence is to be accessible to the believer, it follows that he must somehow have an adequate grasp of his total system of beliefs, since it is coherence with this system which is at issue. One problem which we will eventually have to confront is that it seems abundantly clear that no actual believer possesses an *explicit* grasp of his overall belief system; if such a grasp exists at all, it must be construed as tacit or implicit, which creates obvious problems for the claim that he is actually, as opposed to potentially, justified.

The problem at issue in this section is, however, more immediate and more serious. For whether the believer's grasp of his own system of beliefs is construed as explicit or implicit, of what can that grasp possibly consist except a set of empirical metabeliefs, *themselves in need of justification*, to the effect that he has such and such specific beliefs? How then are these metabeliefs themselves to be justified? If a return to foundationalism is to be avoided, the answer must apparently be that these metabeliefs too are justified by virtue of their coherence with the rest of my system of beliefs. And the problem is that it is absolutely clear that such an answer is unacceptable: it is beyond any doubt viciously circular to claim that the metabeliefs which constitute the believer's grasp of his system of beliefs are themselves justified by virtue of their coherence with that system – even if the nonlinear view of justification articulated earlier is accepted in its entirety. How can my metabelief $B_2$ that I have a certain other belief $B_1$ be justified for me by appeal to the fact that $B_2$ coheres with my total system of beliefs if my very grasp of that system depends on the justification of $B_2$ and other similar beliefs? How, that is, can my reason for accepting $B_2$ be its coherence with my total system of beliefs when I have no justification apart from the appeal to $B_2$ and similar beliefs for thinking that I even have that system of beliefs? The shift to holism is of no help here, since the very possibility of a nonexternalist holism depends on my having a cognitive grasp of my total system of beliefs and its coherence which is prior to the justification of the particular beliefs in the system. It is quite clear, therefore, that this grasp, upon which any nonexternalist appeal to coherence must depend, cannot itself be justified by appeal to coherence.[20] And thus the very idea of a coherence theory of empirical justification threatens to collapse.

Is there any solution to this problem? Most proponents of coherence theories seem, surprisingly enough, either to take the believer's grasp of his own system of beliefs entirely for granted, or simply to ignore the issue of whether their envisaged coherentist justification is accessible to the believer himself. And the obvious conclusion, suggested by some foundationalists in passing, is that this problem shows that even an intended coherence theory must involve an irreducibly foundationalist element, that one's grasp of one's own system of beliefs must be justified in a foundationalist manner, even if everything else depends on coherence. But if the antifoundationalist arguments offered in an earlier chapter are genuinely cogent, no such retreat to foundationalism is available here, and skepticism looms as the only conclusion unless a further alternative can be found.

It was suggested earlier that an a priorist version of foundationalism (or quasi-foundationalism) might attempt to solve the problem of how the empirical claim that I have a certain belief is to be justified by maintaining that the existence of the justificandum belief is *presupposed* by the very raising of the issue of justification, so that the metabelief in question is not in need of justification, while still being available as a justifying premise. The normal justificatory issue, on this view, is whether the believer is justified in holding a certain belief *which he does in fact hold*, not whether such a belief would be somehow justified in the abstract independently of whether he holds it, nor even the hypothetical issue of whether it would be justified *if* he held it (though these other questions can, of course, also be asked). But since the basic unit of justification for a coherence theory is an entire system of beliefs, the analogous claim within the context of such a position is that the raising of an issue of empirical justification *presupposes* the existence of some specifiable *system* of empirical beliefs – or rather, as I will explain below, of *approximately* that system; the primary justificatory issue is whether or not, under the presumption that I do indeed hold approximately the system of beliefs which I believe myself to hold, those beliefs are justified. And thus the suggested solution to the problem raised in this section is that the grasp of my system of beliefs which is required if I am to have cognitive access to the fact of coherence is dependent, in a sense yet to be adequately clarified, on this *Doxastic Presumption*, as I will call it, rather than requiring further justification.

But how exactly is this presumption to be understood? Three issues need to be considered: First, what is the significance of the qualifier "approximately" as it occurs in the above formulations of the presumption? Second, how exactly is this presumption supposed to function within the overall system of empirical knowledge? How exactly is it supposed to certify or secure (even the choice of word here is uncertain) one's grasp of one's system of beliefs? And third, what is the bearing of the Doxastic Presumption on issues pertaining to skepticism? – does it not amount to begging the question against a certain perhaps unusual, but nonetheless quite possible, version of skepticism? I will consider each of these questions in turn.

First. I have noted that the Doxastic Presumption is only that my representation of my overall system of beliefs is *approximately* correct. The point of the qualifier is that although assessments of coherence can be made only relative to a system of beliefs of which one has some prior grasp or representation, this does not mean that no aspect of that representation can be questioned. On the contrary, it is perfectly possible to raise the issue of whether I have a certain particular belief or reasonably small set of beliefs which I believe myself to have, and then to answer this question by appeal to the coherence or lack of coherence between the metabelief that I have the specific belief(s) in question and the rest of the system as I represent it – the existence of the rest of the system, but not of those particular beliefs, being presupposed. What is *not* possible is to question whether my grasp of my system of beliefs might be wholly or largely mistaken and then resolve *this* question by appeal to coherence: the raising of this issue would leave me with no sufficiently ample grasp of my system of beliefs which would not beg the question and relative to which coherence might be judged.

Second. It might seem plausible, at first glance, to construe the Doxastic Presumption as constituting a further *premise* to be employed in the justificatory arguments or at least as functioning like such a premise. But only a little reflection will show that such an interpretation is quite untenable. For what might such a premise say? The only apparent possibility is that it would say that my metabeliefs to the effect that I have certain beliefs may be presumed to be true, without requiring justification. And it is immediately obvious that such a premise would do me no good relative to the problem under discussion here. For to apply it in any useful fashion, I would need further premises to the effect that I do in fact believe myself to have such and such specific beliefs, and the justification of these further premises would obviously be just as problematic as before.

Thus the Doxastic Presumption, if it is to solve the problem, cannot function like a premise. It is rather a characterization of something which is, from the standpoint of a coherence theory, a basic and unavoidable feature of cognitive *practice*. Epistemic reflection, according to such a theory, *begins* from a (perhaps tacit) representation of myself as having (approximately) such and such a specific system of beliefs: only relative to such a representation can questions of justification be meaningfully raised and answered. This representation is presumably a product of something like ordinary introspection (as understood from within the system), but whereas most introspective beliefs can be justified by appeal to coherence, the metabeliefs which constitute this representation cannot be thus justified in general for the reasons already considered. The issue of their justification can be raised and answered in particular, relatively confined cases which are for some reason especially problematic. But apart from such cases, such metabeliefs must be presumed to be correct in order for the process of justification to even get started. And this is what the Doxastic Presumption says.

Thus the Doxastic Presumption does not, strictly speaking, function at all in the normal workings of the cognitive system. Rather it simply describes or formulates, from the outside, something that I unavoidably *do*: I assume that the beliefs constituting my overall grasp of my system of beliefs are, by and large, correct.

Third. But does not the Doxastic Presumption, or rather the aspect of cognitive practice which it reflects, amount to begging the question against a certain from of skepticism, namely, that form which would question whether my representation of my own system of beliefs is in fact accurate? The answer is that it would be begging the question if it purported to be an answer to such a skeptical challenge but that as proposed here no such answer is intended. It would be possible, of course, to argue that if it is correct that empirical justification is only possible relative to a specific system of beliefs whose existence is presumed, then it follows that skepticism of the sort in question simply makes no sense; the underlying idea would be that a question is meaningful only if there is some way, at least in principle, in which it can be answered. But I can see no reason to accept such a view, amounting as it does to a version of verificationism. What the discussion leading up to the Doxastic *Presumption* shows is precisely that a coherence theory of empirical justification cannot, in principle, answer this form of skepticism; and this seems to me to count in favor of the skeptic, not against him.

Thus the position advocated here holds that such a version of skepticism, though certainly unusual, is perfectly coherent (and thus that it would be desirable to be able to answer it) but also concedes that such an answer is unfortunately in principle not available for a coherence theory. However, the failure to answer one version of skepticism does not in any way mean that there is no point in attempting to answer others. The effect of the Doxastic Presumption is precisely to distinguish a version of skepticism which cannot be successfully answered from others which perhaps can. Even if it is not possible in general to justify my representation of my own system of beliefs, it may yet be possible to argue successfully relative to the presumption that this representation is (approximately) correct that the beliefs which I hold are justified in a sense which makes them genuinely likely to be true; and this would be a significant epistemological result, even if not quite the one which would be ideally desirable.

There is one more important point about the Doxastic Presumption to be noted here. Obviously a person's system of beliefs changes and develops over time as new beliefs are added and old ones abandoned or forgotten. And it is clear on reflection that one's grasp of these changes is just as incapable of being justified in general by appeal to coherence as is one's grasp of the system at a moment. Thus the Doxastic Presumption must be understood to include the presumption that one's grasp of this temporal dimension of one's system of beliefs is also approximately correct.

The foregoing will suffice for an initial discussion of the Doxastic Presumption. For the moment the central point is that something like this presumption seems to be unavoidable if a coherentist position is to even get started. Nothing like a justification for the presumption has been offered for the simple reason that if it is properly understood, none is required: there can obviously be no objection to asking what follows about the justification of the rest of my beliefs from the presumption that my representation of my own system of beliefs is approximately correct. The only questions needling to be asked are: first, whether it is possible to justify my representation of my own system of beliefs, rather than having to presume that it is correct (I have argued that it is not); and, second, whether the epistemological issue which results from this presumption is still worth bothering with (I have suggested that it is).

## 5   The Standard Objections

There is obviously much which is problematic in the very tentative and fragmentary picture of a coherence theory of empirical justification which has so far emerged in this chapter, and many important questions and problems remain to be considered. But even if the conception were otherwise acceptable, there would still remain the three standard and extremely forceful objections to coherence theories – objections which have usually been thought to destroy any plausibility which such a view might possess. As will become clear, these objections are not entirely independent of one another and indeed might be plausibly regarded as merely different facets of one basic point. But each of them possesses enough independent plausibility and intuitive force to warrant separate consideration.

(I) The alternative coherent systems objection. According to a coherence theory of empirical justification, at least as so far characterized, the system of beliefs which constitutes empirical knowledge is epistemically justified *solely* by virtue of its internal coherence. But such an appeal to coherence will never even begin to pick out one uniquely justified system of beliefs, since on any plausible conception of coherence, there will always be many, probably infinitely many, different and incompatible systems of belief which are equally coherent. No nonarbitrary choice between such systems can be made solely on the basis of coherence, and thus all such systems, and the beliefs they contain, will be equally justified. And this will mean in turn, since all or virtually all consistent beliefs will belong to some such system, that we have no more reason to think that the beliefs we actually hold are true than we have for thinking that any arbitrarily chosen alternative belief is true – a result which is surely tantamount to skepticism and which obviously vitiates entirely the concept of epistemic justification by destroying its capacity to discriminate between different empirical beliefs.

A clear conception of this objection requires that it not be exaggerated, as it frequently is. Sometimes it is said that if one has an appropriately coherent system, an alternative coherent system can be produced simply by negative all of the components of the first system. This would be so if coherence amounted simply to consistency; but once it is seen that such a conception of coherence is much too limited, there is no reason to accept such a claim. Nor is it even minimally plausible that, as is sometimes suggested, a "well written novel," or indeed anything remotely resembling an actual novel, would have the degree of coherence required to be a serious alternative to anyone's actual system of beliefs. What would be missing in both cases is the pervasive inferential and especially explanatory connections needed for a high degree of coherence.

But even without these exaggerations, the objection is obviously very forceful. One suggestive way to elaborate it is by appeal to the idea of alternative possible worlds. Without worrying about whether there are infinitely many possible worlds or whether all possible worlds are capable of being given equally coherent descriptions, it seems enormously obvious that there are at least very many possible worlds, differing in major ways from the actual world, which are capable of being described in equally coherent ways. But then a standard of justification which appeals only to internal coherence has no way of choosing among the various systems of beliefs which would correctly describe these various possible worlds; such a standard is apparently impotent to justify believing in one of these worlds as opposed to any of the others. The skeptic need ask for nothing more.

(II) The input objection. The second objection is somewhat more elusive, but also perhaps more fundamental. Coherence is purely a matter of the *internal* relations between the components of the belief system; it depends in no way on any sort of relation between the system of beliefs and anything external to that system. Hence if, as a coherence theory claims, coherence is the sole basis for empirical justification, it follows that a system of empirical beliefs might be adequately justified, indeed might constitute empirical knowledge, in spite of being utterly out of contact with the world that it purports to describe. Nothing about any requirement of coherence dictates that a coherent system of beliefs need receive any sort of *input* from the world or be in any way causally influenced by the world. But this is surely an absurd result. Such a self-enclosed system of beliefs, entirely immune from any external influence, cannot constitute empirical knowledge of an independent world, because the achievement of even minimal descriptive success in such a situation would have to be either an accident or a miracle, not something which anyone could possibly have any reason to expect – which would mean that the beliefs involved would not be epistemically justified, even if they should somehow happen to be true. This objection is most obviously forceful against a coherentist position, like my own, which adopts a realist conception of independent reality. But in fact it is cogent *vis-à-vis* any position, including at least most versions of idealism, which does not simply identify the individual believer's limited cognitive system with its object: how can a system of beliefs be justified in a sense which carries with it likelihood of truth, while at the same time being entirely isolated from the reality, however that be understood, which it purports to describe?

Though intuitively forceful, this objection is also rather vague – mainly because of the vagueness of the crucial notion of "input." It would, however, be a mistake to attempt too precise a specification here, prior to the development of a more specific theory. The rough idea is that some of the elements in the cognitive system must be somehow shaped or influenced by the world outside the system;[21] and that this must be not just something which might or might not happen to occur, but rather in some way an essential requirement for the justification of the system. But just what precise form such input might take is a matter to be specified by a particular theory.[22]

(III) The problem of truth. The final objection of the three is the most fundamental of all. Recall that one crucial part of the task of an adequate epistemological theory is to show that there is an appropriate connection between its proposed account of epistemic justification and the cognitive goal of *truth*. That is, it must be somehow shown that justification as conceived by the theory is *truth-conducive*, that one who seeks justified beliefs is at least likely to find true ones. All this is by now quite familiar. The objection is simply that a coherence theory will be unable to accomplish this part of the epistemological task unless it also adopts a coherence theory of truth and the idealistic metaphysics which goes along with it – an expedient which is both commonsensically absurd and also dialectically unsatisfactory.

Historically, the appeal to a coherence theory of truth was made by the absolute idealists and, in a slightly different but basically parallel way, by Peirce. These philosophers attempted to solve the problem of the relation between justification and truth by in effect construing truth as simply *identical* with justification-in-the-long-run. Thus an idealist, having adopted a coherence theory of epistemic justification, might argue that only by adopting a coherence theory of truth could the essential link between justification and truth be secured: obviously if truth is long-run, ideal coherence, it is plausible to suppose that it will be truth-conducive to seek a system of beliefs which is as coherent as one can manage to make it at the moment.[23] Something like this seems also to be the essential motivation behind Peirce's version of the pragmatic conception of truth in which truth is identified with the ideal, long-run outcome of scientific inquiry; whether this amounts to precisely a coherence theory of truth depends on just how Peirce's rather obscure account of justification is properly to be understood, but it is at least similar. The same underlying motivation also seems present, albeit less clearly, in other versions of pragmatism.

Obviously, given such a construal of truth, there will be no difficulty of principle in arguing successfully that one who accepts justified beliefs will in the long run be likely to find true ones. But such a gambit is nonetheless quite unsatisfactory in relation to the basic problem at issue, even if the intuitive and commonsensical objections to such accounts of truth are discounted. The whole point, after all, of seeking an argument connecting justification and truth is to provide a rationale or metajustification for the proposed standard of epistemic justification by showing that adopting it leads or is likely to lead to the attainment of truth. But the force of such a metajustification depends on the independent claim to acceptance of the concept of truth which is invoked. If – as seems to be the case both historically and dialectically with respect to the specific concepts of truth under discussion here – the only rationale for the chosen concept of truth is an appeal to the related standard of justification, then the proposed metajustification loses its force entirely. It is clearly circular to argue both (1) that a certain standard of epistemic justification is correct because it is conducive to finding truth, conceived in a certain way, and (2) that the conception of truth in question is correct because only such a conception can connect up in this way with the original standard of justification. Such a defense would obviously be available to the proponent of *any* proposed standard of epistemic justification, no matter how silly or counterintuitive or arbitrary it might be: all he has to do is adopt his own nonstandard conception of truth as justification-in-the-long-run (in his idiosyncratic sense of justification). The moral of the story is that although any adequate epistemological theory must confront the task of bridging the gap between justification and truth, the adoption of a nonstandard conception of truth, such as a coherence theory of truth, will do no good unless that conception is independently motivated.[24] Therefore, it seems that a coherence theory of justification has no acceptable way of establishing the essential connection with truth. A coherentist standard of justification, it is claimed, can be a good test only for a coherentist conception of truth, so that to reject the coherence theory of truth commits one also to the rejection of any such account of justification.[25]

Of these three objections, (III) is the most basic and (I) is the most familiar. It is (II), however, which must be dealt with first, since the answer to it turns out, not surprisingly, to be essential for answering the other two objections. My view is that the point advanced in (II) must in the end simply be accepted: a cognitive system which is to contain empirical knowledge must somehow receive input of some sort from the world. And this means that the purest sort of coherence theory turns out, as the objections claim, to be indeed unacceptable. I will argue, however, that this need not mean a return to foundationalism (which has already been shown to be hopeless), that a theory which is recognizably coherentist – and more important, which is free of any significant foundationalist ingredients – can allow for such input.

**Notes**

1   Rescher's "coherence theory of truth" in Rescher (1973) is a coherence theory of the criteria of truth, not of the nature of truth. Though leaving the connection with justification somewhat obscure, this book contains an excellent discussion of the distinction between the two sorts of theories of truth.

2   As already noted, some theories combine an appeal to coherence with a rejection of the global issue of justification. See, for example, Sklar (1975) and Williams (1980).

Because I see no warrant for dismissing the global issue in this way, such views seem to me to constitute merely complicated versions of skepticism.

3    See Lewis (1946, chap. II); and Chisholm (1977, chap. 4).

4    Ewing (1934, p. 231).

5    Perhaps the clearest example of this rather pervasive mistake is Scheffler (1967, chap. 5). Another interesting case is Rescher (1973): the "coherence criterion of truth" advocated there uses consistency to segregate propositions into maximally consistent subsets, and then chooses among those subsets on a variety of different bases, none of which have much to do with the standard idea of coherence. (Rescher's later development of the same view does, however, employ a more traditional notion of coherence, though in a different place.) See Rescher (1977), and also BonJour (1976).

6    One pervasive case of this sort is worth explicit notice: it often happens that my system of beliefs makes it extremely probable that an event of a certain general description will occur, while providing no guidance as to which of a very large number of alternative, more specific possibilities will realize this description. If there is nothing more to be said, each of the specific possibilities will be very improbable, simply because there are so many, while at the same time it will be highly probable that one of them will occur. In such a case, adding a new belief (arrived at through observation or in some other way) that one of the possible specific events has actually occurred will bring with it a measure of probabilistic inconsistency – but less than would result from excluding all such specific beliefs, thereby coming into conflict with the more general one.

7    It might be questioned whether it is not an oversimplification to make logical consistency in this way an absolutely necessary condition for coherence. In particular, some proponents of relevance logics may want to argue that in some cases a system of beliefs which was sufficiently rich and complex but which contained some trivial inconsistency might be preferable to a much less rich system which was totally consistent. And there are also worries such as the Preface Paradox. But while I think there may be something to be said for such views, the issues they raise are too complicated and remote to be entered into here.

8    Blanshard (1939, p. 264).

9    Ibid., p. 265.

10    Ewing (1934, p. 229).

11    Lewis (1946, p. 338), Chisholm's definition of "concurrence" in Chisholm (1977) is very similar.

12    Ewing (1934, pp. 229–30).

13    For refinements, see, e.g., the title essay in Hempel (1965).

14    Hempel (1967, p. 83).

15    On the Hempelian view, explanation and prediction involve the same sorts of inferential relations within the system of beliefs, differing only as to whether the fact in question is known prior to drawing the appropriate inference. Although this view is not uncontroversial, I will assume that it is at least approximately correct.

16    Such a situation of anomaly may of course involve probabilistic inconsistency in the sense explained above, but it need not do so in any very straightforward way; the set of basic explanatory principles does not normally include an explicit rider to the effect that anything which it cannot subsume is thereby rendered improbable.

17    For a version of such a position, see Lehrer (1974, chap. 7). (The position in question is one which Lehrer is criticizing, not one he wishes to advocate.)

18    Lehrer (1974, pp. 166–67).

19   For an elaboration of this view of scientific theories, see Wilfrid Sellars, "The Language of Theories," reprinted in Sellars (1963, pp. 106–26).

20   A coherence theory, at least as construed here, does not somehow reject any notion of epistemic priority. Its claim is rather that what look superficially like relations of epistemic priority and posteriority among individual beliefs turn out to be relations of reciprocal support in relation to a system of beliefs which is genuinely prior. Thus no appeal to the nonlinear conception of justification will help if it is the very existence of such a system which is in question.

21   I will ignore here the alternative possibility that a person's system of beliefs might be likely to be true because those beliefs shape reality rather than the other way around.

22   Many foundationalist views also fail to address this issue in any clear way, either by offering no real account of the status of the foundational beliefs or by merely appealing to the commonsensical belief that certain beliefs are somehow justified.

23   For the clearest version of this approach, see Blanshard (1939, chaps. 25 and 26).

24   A related objection also afflicts currently fashionable verificationist accounts of truth.

25   It is worth noting, however, that foundationalist views seem to face at least a somewhat analogous problem if it is true that they must appeal to coherence or something like it in their accounts of knowledge of the past, theoretical knowledge, and so on.

## Works Cited

Blanshard, Brand (1939). *The Nature of Thought*. London: Allen and Unwin.

BonJour, Laurence (1976). "Rescher's Idealistic Pragmatism." *Review of Metaphysics* 29: 702–26.

Chisholm, Roderick (1977). *Theory of Knowledge*, 2nd edn. Englewood Cliffs, NJ: Prentice-Hall.

Ewing, A. C. (1934). *Idealism*. London: Methuen.

Hempel, Carl G. (1965). *Aspects of Scientific Explanation*. New York: Free Press.

—— (1967). *Philosophy of Natural Science*. Englewood Cliffs, NJ: Prentice-Hall.

Lehrer, Keith (1974). *Knowledge*. Oxford: Oxford University Press.

Lewis, C. I. (1946). *An Analysis of Knowledge and Valuation*. La Salle, IL,: Open Court.

Rescher, Nicholas (1973). *The Coherence Theory of Truth*. Oxford: Oxford University Press.

—— (1977). *Methodological Pragmatism*. New York: New York University Press.

Scheffler, Israel (1967). *Science and Subjectivity*. New York: Bobbs-Merrill.

Sellars, Wilfred (1963). *Science, Perception and Reality*. London: Routledge and Kegan Paul.

Sklar, Lawrence (1975). "Methodological Conservatism." *Philosophical Review* 84: 374–400.

Williams, Michael (1980). "Coherence, Justification, and Truth." *Review of Metaphysics* 34: 243–72.

# 14   The Hermeneutic Circle

## Hans Georg Gadamer

THE ELEVATION OF THE HISTORICITY OF UNDERSTANDING TO THE STATUS
OF A HERMENEUTIC PRINCIPLE

## (A)   The Hermeneutic Circle and the Problem of Prejudices

### (i)   Heidegger's disclosure of the fore-structure of understanding

Heidegger entered into the problems of historical hermeneutics and critique
only in order to explicate the fore-structure of understanding for the purposes
of ontology.[1] Our question, by contrast, is how hermeneutics, once freed from
the ontological obstructions of the scientific concept of objectivity, can do justice to the historicity of understanding. Hermeneutics has traditionally understood itself as an art of technique.[2] This is true even of Dilthey's expansion of
hermeneutics into an organon of the human sciences. One might wonder whether
there is such an art or technique of understanding – we shall come back to the
point. But at any rate we can inquire into the consequences for the hermeneutics
of the human sciences of the fact that Heidegger derives the circular structure
of understanding from the temporality of Dasein. These consequences do not
need to be such that a theory is applied to practice so that the latter is performed differently – i.e., in a way that is technically correct. They could also
consist in correcting (and refining) the way in which constantly exercised understanding understands itself – a process that would benefit the art of understanding at most only indirectly.

Hence we will once more examine Heidegger's description of the hermeneutical circle in order to make its new fundamental significance fruitful for our
purposes. Heidegger writes, "It is not to be reduced to the level of a vicious
circle, or even of a circle which is merely tolerated. In the circle is hidden a
positive possibility of the most primordial kind of knowing, and we genuinely
grasp this possibility only when we have understood that our first, last, and
constant task in interpreting is never to allow our fore-having, fore-sight, and
fore-conception to be presented to us by fancies and popular conceptions, but
rather to make the scientific theme secure by working out these fore-structures
in terms of the things themselves" (*Being and Time*, p. 153).

What Heidegger is working out here is not primarily a prescription for the
practice of understanding, but a description of the way interpretive understanding is achieved. The point of Heidegger's hermeneutical reflection is not so
much to prove that there is a circle as to show that this circle possesses an
ontologically positive significance. The description as such will be obvious to

every interpreter who knows what he is about.[3] All correct interpretation must be on guard against arbitrary fancies and the limitations imposed by imperceptible habits of thought, and it must direct its gaze "on the things themselves" (which, in the case of the literary critic, are meaningful texts, which themselves are again concerned with objects). For the interpreter to let himself be guided by the things themselves is obviously not a matter of a single, "conscientious" decision, but is "the first, last, and constant task." For it is necessary to keep one's gaze fixed on the thing throughout all the constant distractions that originate in the interpreter himself. A person who is trying to understand a text is always projecting. He projects a meaning for the text as a whole as soon as some initial meaning emerges in the text. Again, the initial meaning emerges only because he is reading the text with particular expectations in regard to a certain meaning. Working out this fore-projection, which is constantly revised in terms of what emerges as he penetrates into the meaning, is understanding what is there.

This description is, of course, a rough abbreviation of the whole. The process that Heidegger describes is that every revision of the fore-projection is capable of projecting before itself a new projection of meaning; rival projects can emerge side by side until it becomes clearer what the unity of meaning is; interpretation begins with fore-conceptions that are replaced by more suitable ones. This constant process of new projection constitutes the movement of understanding and interpretation. A person who is trying to understand is exposed to distraction from fore-meanings that are not borne out by the things themselves. Working out appropriate projections, anticipatory in nature, to be confirmed "by the things" themselves, is the constant task of understanding. The only "objectivity" here is the confirmation of a fore-meaning in its being worked out. Indeed, what characterizes the arbitrariness of inappropriate fore-meanings if not that they come to nothing in being worked out? But understanding realizes its full potential only when the fore-meanings that it begins with are not arbitrary. Thus it is quite right for the interpreter not to approach the text directly, relying solely on the fore-meaning already available to him, but rather explicitly to examine the legitimacy – i.e., the origin and validity – of the fore-meanings dwelling within him.

This basic requirement must be seen as the radicalization of a procedure that we in fact exercise whenever we understand anything. Every text presents the task of not simply leaving our own linguistic usage unexamined – or in the case of a foreign language the usage that we are familiar with from writers or from daily intercourse. Rather, we regard our task as deriving our understanding of the text from the linguistic usage of the time or of the author. The question is, of course, how this general requirement can be fulfilled. Especially in the field of semantics we are confronted with the problem that our own use of language is unconscious. How do we discover that there is a difference between our own customary usage and that of the text?

I think we must say that generally we do so in the experience of being pulled up short by the text. Either it does not yield any meaning at all or its meaning is not compatible with what we had expected. This is what brings us up short and alerts us to a possible difference in usage. Someone who speaks the same language as I do uses the words in the sense familiar to me – this is a general presupposition that can be questioned only in particular cases. The same thing is true in the case of a foreign language: we all think we have a standard knowledge of it and assume this standard usage when we are reading a text.

What is true of fore-meanings that stem from usage, however, is equally true of the fore-meanings concerning content with which we read texts, and which make up our fore-understanding. Here too we may ask how we can break the spell of our own fore-meanings. There can, of course, be a general expectation that what the text says will fit perfectly with my own meanings and expectations. But what another person tells me, whether in conversation, letter, book, or whatever, is generally supposed to be his own and not my opinion; and this is what I am to take note of without necessarily having to share it. Yet this presupposition is not something that makes understanding easier, but harder, since the fore-meanings that determine my own understanding can go entirely unnoticed. If they give rise to misunderstandings, how can our misunderstandings of a text be perceived at all if there is nothing to contradict them? How can a text be protected against misunderstanding from the start?

If we examine the situation more closely, however, we find that meanings cannot be understood in an arbitrary way. Just as we cannot continually misunderstand the use of a word without its affecting the meaning of the whole, so we cannot stick blindly to our own fore-meaning about the thing if we want to understand the meaning of another. Of course this does not mean that when we listen to someone or read a book we must forget all our fore-meanings concerning the content and all our own ideas. All that is asked is that we remain open to the meaning of the other person or text. But this openness always includes our situating the other meaning in relation to the whole of our own meanings or ourselves in relation to it. Now, the fact is that meanings represent a fluid multiplicity of possibilities (in comparison to the agreement presented by a language and a vocabulary), but within this multiplicity of what can be thought – i.e., of what a reader can find meaningful and hence expect to find – not everything is possible; and if a person fails to hear what the other person is really saying, he will not be able to fit what he has misunderstood into the range of his own various expectations of meaning. Thus there is a criterion here also. *The hermeneutical task becomes of itself a questioning of things* and is always in part so defined. This places hermeneutical work on a firm basis. A person trying to understand something will not resign himself from the start to relying on his own accidental fore-meanings, ignoring as consistently and stubbornly as possible the actual meaning of the text until the latter becomes so persistently audible that it breaks through what the interpreter imagines it to be. Rather, a person trying to understand a text is prepared for it to tell him something. That is why a hermeneutically trained consciousness must be, from the start, sensitive to the text's alterity. But this kind of sensitivity involves neither "neutrality" with respect to content nor the extinction of one's self, but the foregrounding and appropriation of one's own fore-meanings and prejudices. The important thing is to be aware of one's own bias, so that the text can present itself in all its otherness and thus assert its own truth against one's own fore-meanings.

When Heidegger disclosed the fore-structure of understanding in what is considered merely "reading what is there," this was a completely correct phenomenological description. He also exemplified the task that follows from this. In *Being and Time* he gave the general hermeneutical problem a concrete form in the question of being.[4] In order to explain the hermeneutical situation of the question of being in terms of fore-having, fore-sight, and fore-conception, he critically tested his question, directed at metaphysics, on important turning points in the history of metaphysics. Here he was only doing what historical-hermeneutical consciousness requires in every case. Methodologically conscious understanding will be concerned not merely to form anticipatory ideas, but to make them conscious, so as to check them and thus acquire right understanding from the things themselves. This is what Heidegger means when he talks about making our scientific theme "secure" by deriving our fore-having, fore-sight and fore-conception from the things themselves.

It is not at all a matter of securing ourselves against the tradition that speaks out of the text then, but, on the contrary, of excluding everything that could hinder us from understanding it in terms of the subject matter. It is the tyranny of hidden prejudices that makes us deaf to what speaks to us in tradition. Heidegger's demonstration that the concept of consciousness in Descartes and of spirit in Hegel is still influenced by Greek substance ontology, which sees being in terms of what is present, undoubtedly surpasses the self-understanding of modern metaphysics, yet not in an arbitrary, willful way, but on the basis of a "fore-having" that in fact makes this tradition intelligible by revealing the ontological premises of the concept of subjectivity. On the other hand, Heidegger discovers in Kant's critique of "dogmatic" metaphysics the idea of a metaphysics of finitude which is a challenge to his own ontological scheme. Thus he "secures" the scientific theme by framing it within the understanding of tradition and so putting it, in a sense, at risk. All of this is a concretization of the historical consciousness involved in understanding.

The recognition that all understanding inevitably involves some prejudice gives the hermeneutical problem its real thrust. In light of this insight it appears that *historicism, despite its critique of rationalism and of natural law philosophy, is based on the modern Enlightenment and unwittingly shares its prejudices.* And there is one prejudice of the Enlightenment that defines its essence: the fundamental prejudice of the Enlightenment is the prejudice against prejudice itself, which denies tradition its power.

The history of ideas shows that not until the Enlightenment does *the concept of prejudice* acquire the negative connotation familiar today. Actually "prejudice" means a judgment that is rendered before all the elements that determine a situation have been finally examined. In German legal terminology a "prejudice" is a provisional legal verdict before the final verdict is reached. For someone involved in a legal dispute, this kind of judgment against him affects his chances adversely. Accordingly, the French préjudice, as well as the Latin praejudicium, means simply "adverse effect," "disadvantage," "harm." But this negative sense is only derivative. The negative consequence depends precisely on the positive validity, the value of the provisional decision as a prejudgment, like that of any precedent.

Thus "prejudice" certainly does not necessarily mean a false judgment, but part of the idea is that it can have either a positive or a negative value. This is clearly due to the influence of the Latin praejudicium. There are such things as préjugés légitimes. This seems a long way from our current use of the word. The German Vorurteil, like the English "prejudice" and even more than the French préjugé, seems to have been limited in its meaning by the Enlightenment critique of religion simply to the sense of an "unfounded judgment."[5] The only thing that gives a judgment dignity is its having a basis, a methodological justification (and not the fact that it may actually be correct). For the Enlightenment the absence of such a basis does not mean that there might be other kinds of certainty, but rather that the judgment has no foundation in the things themselves – i.e., that it is "unfounded." This conclusion follows only in the spirit of rationalism. It is the reason for discrediting prejudices and the reason scientific knowledge claims to exclude them completely.

In adopting this principle, modern science is following the rule of Cartesian doubt, accepting nothing as certain that can in any way be doubted, and adopting the idea of method that follows from this rule. In our introductory observations we have already pointed out how difficult it is to harmonize the historical knowledge that helps to shape our historical consciousness with this ideal and how difficult it is, for that reason, to comprehend its true nature on the basis of the modern conception of method. This is the place to turn those negative statements into positive ones. The concept of "prejudice" is where we can start.

## (ii)   The discrediting of prejudice by the enlightenment

If we consider the Enlightenment doctrine of prejudice, we find that it makes the following division: we must make a basic distinction between the prejudice due to human authority and that due to overhastiness.[6] This distinction is based on the origin of prejudices in the persons who have them. Either the respect we have for others and their authority leads us into error, or else an overhastiness in ourselves. That authority is a source of prejudices accords with the well-known principle of the Enlightenment that Kant formulated: Have the courage to make use of your *own* understanding.[7] Although this distinction is certainly not limited to the role that prejudices play in understanding texts, its chief application is still in the sphere of hermeneutics, for Enlightenment critique is primarily directed against the religious tradition of Christianity – i.e., the Bible. By treating the Bible as a historical document, biblical criticism endangers its own dogmatic claims. This is the real radicality of the modern Enlightenment compared to all other movements of enlightenment: it must assert itself against the Bible and dogmatic interpretation of it.[8] It is therefore particularly concerned with the hermeneutical problem. It wants to understand tradition correctly – i.e., rationally and without prejudice. But there is a special difficulty about this, since the sheer fact that something is written down gives it special authority. It is not altogether easy to realize that what is written down can be untrue. The written word has the tangible quality of something that can be demonstrated and is like a proof. It requires a special critical effort to free oneself from the prejudice in favor of what is written down and to distinguish here also, no less than in the case of oral assertions, between opinion and truth.[9] In general, the Enlightenment tends to accept no authority and to decide everything before the judgment seat of reason. Thus the written tradition of Scripture, like any other historical document, can claim no absolute validity; the possible truth of the tradition depends on the credibility that reason accords it. It is not tradition but reason that constitutes the ultimate source of all authority. What is written down is not necessarily true. We can know better: this is the maxim with which the modern Enlightenment approaches tradition and which ultimately leads it to undertake historical research.[10] It takes tradition as an object of critique, just as the natural sciences do with the evidence of the senses. This does not necessarily mean that the "prejudice against prejudices" was everywhere taken to the extremes of free thinking and atheism, as in England and France. On the contrary, the German Enlightenment recognized the "true prejudices" of the Christian religion. Since the human intellect is too weak to manage without prejudices, it is at least fortunate to have been educated with true prejudices.

It would be valuable to investigate to what extent this kind of modification and moderation of the Enlightenment[11] prepared the way for the rise of the romantic movement in Germany, as undoubtedly did the critique of the Enlightenment and the revolution by Edmund Burke. But none of this alters the fundamental fact. True prejudices must still finally be justified by rational knowledge, even though the task can never be fully completed.

Thus the criteria of the modern Enlightenment still determine the self-understanding of historicism. They do so not directly, but through a curious refraction caused by romanticism. This can be seen with particular clarity in the fundamental schema of the philosophy of history that romanticism shares with the Enlightenment and that precisely through the romantic reaction to the Enlightenment became an unshakable premise: the schema of the conquest of mythos by logos. What gives this schema its validity is the presupposition of the progressive retreat of magic in the world. It is supposed to represent progress in the history of the mind, and precisely because romanticism disparages this development, it takes over the schema itself as a self-evident truth. It shares the presupposition of the Enlightenment and only reverses its values, seeking to establish the validity of what is old simply on the fact that it is old: the "gothic" Middle Ages, the Christian European community of states, the permanent structure of society, but also the simplicity of peasant life and closeness to nature.

In contrast to the Enlightenment's faith in perfection, which thinks in terms of complete freedom from "superstition" and the prejudices of the past, we now find that olden times – the world of myth, unreflective life, not yet analyzed away by consciousness, in a "society close to nature," the world of Christian chivalry – all these acquire a romantic magic, even a priority over truth.[12] Reversing the Enlightenment's presupposition results in the paradoxical tendency toward restoration – i.e., the tendency to reconstruct the old because it is old, the conscious return to the unconscious, culminating in the recognition of the superior wisdom of the primeval age of myth. But the romantic reversal of the Enlightenment's criteria of value actually perpetuates the abstract contrast between myth and reason. All criticism of the Enlightenment now proceeds via this romantic mirror image of the Enlightenment. Belief in the perfectibility of reason suddenly changes into the perfection of the "mythical" consciousness and finds itself reflected in a paradisiacal primal state before the "fall" of thought.[13]

In fact the presupposition of a mysterious darkness in which there was a mythical collective consciousness that preceded all thought is just as dogmatic and abstract as that of a state of perfect enlightenment or of absolute knowledge. Primeval wisdom is only the counterimage of "primeval stupidity." All mythical consciousness is still knowledge, and if it knows about divine powers, then it has progressed beyond mere trembling before power (if this is to be regarded as the primeval state), but also beyond a collective life contained in magic rituals (as we find in the early Orient). It knows about itself, and in this knowledge it is no longer simply outside itself.[14]

There is the related point that even the contrast between genuine mythical thinking and pseudomythical poetic thinking is a romantic illusion based on a prejudice of the Enlightenment: namely that the poetic act no longer shares the binding quality of myth because it is a creation of the free imagination. It is the old quarrel between the poets and the philosophers in the modern garb appropriate to the age of belief in science. It is now said, not that poets tell lies, but that they are incapable of saying anything true; they have only an aesthetic effect and, through their imaginative creations, they merely seek to stimulate the imagination and vitality of their hearers or readers.

Another case of romantic refraction is probably to be found in the concept of an "organic society," which Ladendorf (217) says was introduced by H. Leo.[15] In Karl Marx it appears as a kind of relic of natural law that limits the validity of his socio-economic theory of the class struggle.[16] Does the idea go back to Rousseau's description of society before the division of labor and the introduction of property?[17] At any rate, Plato had already demonstrated the illusory nature of this political theory in his ironical account of a state of nature in the third book of the *Republic*.[18]

These romantic revaluations give rise to historical science in the nineteenth century. It no longer measures the past by the standards of the present, as if they were an absolute, but it ascribes to past ages a value of their own and can even acknowledge their superiority in one respect or another. The great achievements of romanticism – the revival of the past, the discovery of the voices of the peoples in their songs, the collecting of fairy tales and legends, the cultivation of ancient customs, the discovery of the worldviews implicit in languages, the study of the "religion and wisdom of India" – all contributed to the rise of historical research, which was slowly, step by step, transformed from intuitive revival into detached historical knowledge. The fact that it was romanticism that gave birth to the historical school confirms that the romantic retrieval of origins is itself based on the Enlightenment. Nineteenth-century historiography is its finest fruit and sees itself precisely as the fulfillment of the Enlightenment, as the last step in the liberation of the mind from the trammels of dogma, the step to objective knowledge of the historical world, which stands on a par with the knowledge of nature achieved by modern science.

The fact that the restorative tendency of romanticism could combine with the fundamental concerns of the Enlightenment to create the historical sciences simply indicates that the same break with the continuity of meaning in tradition lies behind both. If the Enlightenment considers it an established fact that all tradition that reason shows to be impossible (i.e., nonsense) can only be understood historically – i.e., by going back to the past's way of looking at things – then the historical consciousness that emerges in romanticism involves a radicalization of the Enlightenment. For nonsensical tradition, which had been the exception, has become the general rule for historical consciousness. Meaning that is generally accessible through reason is so little believed that the whole of the past – even, ultimately, all the thinking of one's contemporaries – is understood only "historically." Thus the romantic critique of the Enlightenment itself ends in Enlightenment, for it evolves as historical science and draws everything into the orbit of historicism. The basic discreditation of all prejudices, which unites the experimental fervor of the new natural sciences during the Enlightenment, is universalized and radicalized in the historical Enlightenment.

This is the point at which the attempt to critique historical hermeneutics has to start. The overcoming of all prejudices, this global demand of the Enlightenment, will itself prove to be a prejudice, and removing it opens the way to an appropriate understanding of the finitude which dominates not only our humanity but also our historical consciousness.

Does being situated within traditions really mean being subject to prejudices and limited in one's freedom? Is not, rather, all human existence, even the freest, limited and qualified in various ways? If this is true, the idea of an absolute reason is not a possibility for historical humanity. Reason exists for us only in concrete, historical terms – i.e., it is not its own master but remains constantly dependent on the given circumstances in which it operates. This is true not only in the sense in which Kant, under the influence of the skeptical critique of Hume, limited the claims of rationalism to the a priori element in the knowledge of nature; it is still truer of historical consciousness and the possibility of historical knowledge. For that man is concerned here with himself and his own creations (Vico) is only an apparent solution of the problem posed by historical knowledge. Man is alien to himself and his historical fate in a way quite different from the way nature, which knows nothing of him, is alien to him.

The epistemological question must be asked here in a fundamentally different way. We have shown above that Dilthey probably saw this, but he was not able to escape his entanglement in traditional epistemology. Since he started from the awareness of "experiences" (Erlebnisse), he was unable to build a bridge to the historical realities, because the great historical realities of society and state always have a predeterminate influence on any "experience." Self-reflection and autobiography – Dilthey's starting points – are not primary and are therefore not an adequate basis for the hermeneutical problem, because through them history is made private once more. In fact history does not belong to us; we belong to it. Long before we understand ourselves through the process of self-examination, we understand ourselves in a self-evident way in the family, society, and state in which we live. The focus of subjectivity is a distorting mirror. The self-awareness of the individual is only a flickering in the closed circuits of historical life. *That is why the prejudices of the individual, far more than his judgments, constitute the historical reality of his being.*

## (B)   Prejudices as Conditions of Understanding

### (i)   *The rehabilitation of authority and tradition*

Here is the point of departure for the hermeneutical problem. This is why we examined the Enlightnement's discreditation of the concept of "prejudice." What appears to be a limiting prejudice from the viewpoint of the absolute self-construction of reason in fact belongs to historical reality itself. If we want to do justice to man's finite, historical mode of being, it is necessary to fundamentally rehabilitate the concept of prejudice and acknowledge the fact that there are legitimate prejudices. Thus we can formulate the fundamental epistemological question for a truly historical hermeneutics as follows: what is the ground of the legitimacy of prejudices? What distinguishes legitimate prejudices from the countless others which it is the undeniable task of critical reason to overcome?

We can approach this question by taking the Enlightenment's critical theory of prejudices, as set out above, and giving it a positive value. The division of prejudices into those of "authority" and those of "overhastiness" is obviously based on the fundamental presupposition of the Enlightenment, namely that methodologically disciplined use of reason can safeguard us from all error. This was Descartes' idea of method. Overhastiness is the source of errors that arise in the use of one's own reason. Authority, however, is responsible for one's not using one's own reason at all. Thus the division is based on a mutually exclusive antithesis between authority and reason. The false prepossession in favor of what is old, in favor of authorities, is what has to be fought. Thus the Enlightenment attributes to Luther's reforms the fact that "the prejudice of human prestige, especially that of the philosophical [he means Aristotle] and the Roman pope, was greatly weakened."[19] The Reformation, then, gives rise to a flourishing hermeneutics which teaches the right use of reason in understanding traditionary texts. Neither the doctrinal authority of the pope nor the appeal to tradition can obviate the work of hermeneutics, which can safeguard the reasonable meaning of a text against all imposition.

This kind of hermeneutics need not lead to the radical critique of religion that we found, for example, in Spinoza. Rather, the possibility of supernatural truth can remain entirely open. Thus especially in the field of German popular philosophy, the Enlightenment limited the claims of reason and acknowledged the authority of Bible and church. We read in Walch, for example, that he distinguishes between the two classes of prejudice – authority and overhastiness – but considers them two extremes, between which it is necessary to find the right middle path, namely a mediation between reason and biblical authority. Accordingly, he regards prejudices deriving from overhastiness as prejudices in favor of the new, a predisposition to the overhasty rejection of truths simply because they are old and attested by authorities.[20] Thus he disputes the British free thinkers (such as Collins and others) and defends the historical faith against the norm of reason. Here the meaning of prejudice deriving from overhastiness is given a conservative reinterpretation.

There can be no doubt, however, that the real consequence of the Enlightenment is different: namely the subjection of all authority to reason. Accordingly, prejudice from overhastiness is to be understood as Descartes understood it – i.e., as the source of all error in the use of reason. This fits in with the fact that after the victory of the Enlightenment, when hermeneutics was freed from all dogmatic ties, the old division returns in a new guise. Thus Schleiermacher distinguishes between partiality and overhastiness as the causes of misunderstanding.[21] To the lasting prejudices due to partiality he contrasts the momentary ones due to overhastiness, but only the former are of interest to those concerned with scientific method. It no longer even occurs to Schleiermacher that among the prejudices in favor of authorities there might be some that are true – yet this was implied in the concept of authority in the first place. His alteration of the traditional division of prejudices documents the victory of the Enlightenment. Partiality now means only an individual limitation of understanding: "The one-sided preference for what is close to one's own sphere of ideas."

In fact, however, the decisive question is concealed behind the concept of partiality. That the prejudices determining what I think are due to my own partiality is a judgment based on the standpoint of their having been dissolved and enlightened, and it holds only for unjustified prejudices. If, on the other hand, there are justified prejudices productive of knowledge, then we are back to the problem of authority. Hence the radical consequences of the Enlightenment, which are still to be found in Schleiermacher's faith in method, are not tenable.

The Enlightenment's distinction between faith in authority and using one's own reason is, in itself, legitimate. If the prestige of authority displaces one's own judgment, then authority is in fact a source of prejudices. But this does not preclude its being a source of truth, and that is what the Enlightenment failed to see when it denigrated all authority. To be convinced of this, we need only consider one of the greatest forerunners of the European Enlightenment, namely Descartes. Despite the radicalness of his methodological thinking, we know that Descartes excluded morality from the total reconstruction of all truths by reason. This was what he meant by his provisional morality. It seems to me symptomatic that he did not in fact elaborate his definitive morality and that its principles, as far as we can judge from his letters to Elizabeth, contain hardly anything new. It is obviously unthinkable to defer morality until modern science has progressed enough to provide a new basis for it. In fact the denigration of authority is not the only prejudice established by the Enlightenment. It also distorted the very concept of authority. Based on the Enlightenment conception of reason and freedom, the concept of authority could be viewed as diametrically opposed to reason and freedom: to be, in fact, blind obedience. This is the meaning that we find in the language critical of modern dictatorships.

But this is not the essence of authority. Admittedly, it is primarily persons that have authority; but the authority of persons is ultimately based not on the subjection and abdication of reason but on an act of acknowledgment and knowledge – the knowledge, namely, that the other is superior to oneself in judgment and insight and that for this reason his judgment takes precedence – i.e., it has priority over one's own. This is connected with the fact that authority cannot actually be bestowed but is earned, and must be earned if someone is to lay claim to it. It rests on acknowledgment and hence on an act of reason itself which, aware of its own limitations, trusts to the better insight of others. Authority in this sense, properly understood, has nothing to do with blind obedience to commands. Indeed, authority has to do not with obedience but rather with knowledge. It is true that authority implies the capacity to command and be obeyed. But this proceeds only from the authority that a person has. Even the anonymous and impersonal authority of a superior which derives from his office is not ultimately based on this hierarchy, but is what makes it possible. Here also its true basis is an act of freedom and reason that grants the authority of a superior fundamentally because he has a wider view of things or is better informed – i.e., once again, because he knows more.[22] Thus, acknowledging authority is always connected with the idea that what the authority says is not irrational and arbitrary but can, in principle, be discovered to be true. This is the essence of the authority claimed by the teacher, the superior, the expert. The prejudices that they implant are legitimized by the person who presents them. But in this way they become prejudices not just in favor of a person but a content, since they effect the same disposition to believe something that can be brought about in other ways – e.g., by good reasons. Thus the essence of authority belongs in the context of a theory of prejudices free from the extremism of the Enlightenment.

Here we can find support in the romantic criticism of the Enlightenment; for there is one form of authority particularly defended by romanticism, namely tradition. That which has been sanctioned by tradition and custom has an authority that is nameless, and our finite historical being is marked by the fact that the authority of what has been handed down to us – and not just what is clearly grounded – always has power over our attitudes and behavior. All education depends on this, and even though, in the case of education, the educator loses his function when his charge comes of age and sets his own insight and decisions in the place of the authority of the educator, becoming mature does not mean that a person becomes his own master in the sense that he is freed from all tradition. The real force of morals, for example, is based on tradition. They are freely taken over but by no means created by a free insight or grounded on reasons. This is precisely what we call tradition: the ground of their validity. And in fact it is to romanticism that we owe this correction of the Enlightenment: that tradition has a justification that lies beyond rational grounding and in large measure determines our institutions and attitudes. What makes classical ethics superior to modern moral philosophy is that it grounds the transition from ethics to "politics," the art of right legislation, on the indispensability of tradition.[23] By comparison, the modern Enlightenment is abstract and revolutionary.

The concept of tradition, however, has become no less ambiguous than that of authority, and for the same reason – namely that what determines the romantic understanding of tradition is its abstract opposition to the principle of enlightenment. Romanticism conceives of tradition as an antithesis to the freedom of reason and regards it as something historically given, like nature. And whether one wants to be revolutionary and oppose it or preserve it, tradition is still viewed as the abstract opposite of free self-determination, since its validity does not require any reasons but conditions us without our questioning it. Of course, the romantic critique of the Enlightenment is not an instance of tradition's automatic dominance of tradition, of its persisting unaffected by doubt and criticism. Rather, a particular critical attitude again addresses itself to the truth of tradition and seeks to renew it. We can call it "traditionalism."

It seems to me, however, that there is no such unconditional antithesis between tradition and reason. However problematical the conscious restoration of old or the creation of new traditions may be, the romantic faith in the "growth of tradition," before which all reason must remain silent, is fundamentally like the Enlightenment, and just as prejudiced. The fact is that in tradition there is always an element of freedom and of history itself. Even the most genuine and pure tradition does not persist because of the inertia of what once existed. It needs to be affirmed, embraced, cultivated. It is, essentially, preservation, and it is active in all historical change. But preservation is an act of reason, though an inconspicuous one. For this reason, only innovation and planning appear to be the result of reason. But this is an illusion. Even where life changes violently, as in ages of revolution, far more of the old is preserved in the supposed transformation of everything than anyone knows, and it combines with the new to create a new value. At any rate, preservation is as much a freely chosen action as are revolution and renewal. That is why both the Enlightenment's critique of tradition and the romantic rehabilitation of it lag behind their true historical being.

These thoughts raise the question of whether in the hermeneutics of the human sciences the element of tradition should not be given its full value. Research in the human sciences cannot regard itself as in an absolute antithesis to the way in which we, as historical beings, relate to the past. At any rate, our usual relationship to the past is not characterized by distancing and freeing ourselves from tradition. Rather, we are always situated within traditions, and this is no objectifying process – i.e., we do not conceive of what tradition says as something other, something alien. It is always part of us, a model or exemplar, a kind of cognizance that our later historical judgment would hardly regard as a kind of knowledge but as the most ingenuous affinity with tradition.

Hence in regard to the dominant epistemological methodologism we must ask: has the rise of historical consciousness really divorced our scholarship from this natural relation to the past? Does understanding in the human sciences understand itself correctly when it relegates the whole of its own historicality to the position of prejudices from which we must free ourselves? Or does "unprejudiced scholarship" share more than it realizes with that naive openness and reflection in which traditions live and the past is present?

In any case, understanding in the human sciences shares one fundamental condition with the life of tradition: it lets itself be *addressed* by tradition. Is it not true of the objects that the human sciences investigate, just as for the contents of tradition, that what they are really about can be experienced only when one is addressed by them? However mediated this significance may be, and though it may proceed from a historical interest that appears to bear no relation to the present – even in the extreme case of "objective" historical research – the real fulfillment of the historical task is to determine anew the significance of what is examined. But the significance exists at the beginning of any such research as well as at the end: in choosing the theme to be investigated, awakening the desire to investigate, gaining a new problematic.

At the beginning of all historical hermeneutics, then, *the abstract antithesis between tradition and historical research, between history and the knowledge of it, must be discarded*. The effect (Wirkung) of a living tradition and the effect of historical study must constitute a unity of effect, the analysis of which would reveal only a texture of reciprocal effects.[24] Hence we would do well not to regard historical consciousness as something radically new – as it seems at first – but as a new element in what has always constituted the human relation to the past. In other words; we have to recognize the element of tradition in historical research and inquire into its hermeneutic productivity.

That an element of tradition affects the human sciences despite the methodological purity of their procedures, an element that constitutes their real nature and distinguishing mark, is immediately clear if we examine the history of research and note the difference between the human and natural sciences with regard to their history. Of course none of man's finite historical endeavors can completely erase the traces of this finitude. The history of mathematics or of the natural sciences is also a part of the history of the human spirit and reflects its destinies. Nevertheless, it is not just historical naivete when the natural scientist writes the history of his subject in terms of the present state of knowledge. For him errors and wrong turnings are of historical interest only, because the progress of research is the self-evident standard of examination. Thus it is only of secondary interest to see how advances in the natural sciences or in mathematics belong to the moment in history at which they took place. This interest does not affect the epistemic value of discoveries in those fields.

There is, then, no need to deny that elements of tradition can also affect the natural sciences – e.g., particular lines of research are preferred at particular places. But scientific research as such derives the law of its development not from these circumstances but from the law of the object it is investigating, which conceals its methodical efforts.[25]

It is clear that the human sciences cannot be adequately described in terms of this conception of research and progress. Of course it is possible to write a history of the solution of a problem – e.g., the deciphering of barely legible inscriptions – in which the only interest is in ultimately reaching the final result. Were this not so, it would have been impossible for the human sciences to have borrowed the methodology of the natural ones, as happened in the last century. But what the human sciences share with the natural is only a subordinate element of the work done in the human sciences.

This is shown by the fact that the great achievements in the human sciences almost never become outdated. A modern reader can easily make allowances for the fact that, a hundred years ago, less knowledge was available to a historian, and he therefore made judgments that were incorrect in some details. On the whole, he would still rather read Droysen or Mommsen than the latest account of the subject from the pen of a historian living today. What is the criterion here? Obviously the value and importance of research cannot be measured by a criterion based in the subject matter. Rather, the subject matter appears truly significant only when it is properly portrayed for us. Thus we are certainly interested in the subject matter, but it acquires its life only from the light in which it is presented to us. We accept the fact that the subject presents different aspects of itself at different times or from different standpoints. We accept the fact that these aspects do not simply cancel one another out as research proceeds, but are like mutually exclusive conditions that exist by themselves and combine only in us. Our historical consciousness is always filled with a variety of voices in which the echo of the past is heard. Only in the multifariousness of such voices does it exist: this constitutes the nature of the tradition in which we want to share and have a part. Modern historical research itself is not only research, but the handing down of tradition. We do not see it only in terms of progress and verified results; in it we have, as it were, a new experience of history whenever the past resounds in a new voice.

Why is this so? Obviously, in the human sciences we cannot speak of an object of research in the same sense as in the natural sciences, where research penetrates more and more deeply into nature. Rather, in the human sciences the particular research questions concerning tradition that we are interested in pursuing are motivated in a special way by the present and its interests. The theme and object of research are actually constituted by the motivation of the inquiry.[26] Hence historical research is carried along by the historical movement of life itself and cannot be understood teleologically in terms of the object into which it is inquiring. Such an "object in itself" clearly does not exist at all. This is precisely what distinguishes the human sciences from the natural sciences. Whereas the object of the natural sciences can be described idealiter as what would be known in the perfect knowledge of nature, it is senseless to speak of a perfect knowledge of history, and for this reason it is not possible to speak of an "object in itself" toward which its research is directed.[27]

## Notes

1   Heidegger, *Sein und Zeit*, pp. 312ff.
2   Cf. Schleiermacher's *Hermeneutik*, ed. Heinz Kimmerle in *Abhandlungen der Heidelberger Akademie*, (1959), 2nd *Abhandlung*, which is explicitly committed to the old ideal of an art formulated in rules (p. 127, n.: "I . . . hate it when theory does not go beyond nature and the bases of art, whose object it is").
3   Cf. Emil Staiger's description, which accords with that of Heidegger, in Die *Kunst*

*der Interpretation*, pp. 11ff. I do not, however, agree that the work of a literary critic begins only "when we are in the situation of a contemporary reader." This is something we never are, and yet we are capable of understanding, although we can never achieve a definite "personal or temporal identity" with the author. [See also my "Vom Zirkel des Verstehens," *Kleine Schriften*, IV, 54–61 (*GW*, II, 57–65) and the criticism of W. Stegmüller, *Der sogenannte Zirkel des Verstehens* (Darmstadt, 1974). The objection raised from a logical point of view against talk of the "hermeneutic circle" fails to recognize that this concept makes no claim to scientific proof, but presents a logical metaphor, known to rhetoric ever since Schleiermacher. Rightly opposed to this misunderstanding is Karl-Otto Apel, *Transformationen der Philosophie* (2 vols.; Frankfurt, 1973), II, 83, 89, 216 and passim.]

4  *Sein und Zeit*, pp. 312ff.

5  Cf. Leo Strauss, *Die Religionskritik Spinozas*, p. 163: "The word 'prejudice' is the most suitable expression for the great aim of the Enlightenment, the desire for free, untrammeled verification; the *Vorurteil* is the unambiguous polemical correlate of the very ambiguous word 'freedom.'"

6  *Praeiudicium auctoritatis et precipitantiae*, which we find as early as Christian Thomasius' *Lectiones de praeiudiciis* (1689/90) and his *Einleitung der Vernunftlehre*, ch. 13, §§39–40. Cf. the article in Walch, *Philosophisches Lexikon* (1726), pp. 2794ff.

7  At the beginning of his essay, "What Is Enlightenment?" (1784).

8  The enlightenment of the classical world, the fruit of which was Greek philosophy and its culmination in sophism, was quite different in nature and hence permitted a thinker like Plato to use philosophical myths to convey the religious tradition and the dialectical method of philosophizing. Cf. Erich Frank, *Philosophische Erkenntnis und religiöse Wahrheit*, pp. 31ff., and my review of it in the *Theologische Rundschau*, (1950), pp. 260–66. And see especially Gerhard Krüger, *Einsicht und Leidenschaft* (2nd ed., 1951).

9  A good example of this is the length of time it has taken for the authority of the historical writing of antiquity to be destroyed in historical studies and how slowly the study of archives and the research into sources have established themselves (cf. R. G. Collingwood, *Autobiography* [Oxford, 1939], ch. 11, where he more or less draws a parallel between turning to the study of sources and the Baconian revolution in the study of nature).

10  Cf. what we said earlier about Spinoza's *Theological-Political Treatise*.

11  As we find, for example, in G. F. Meier's *Beiträge zu der Lehre von den Vorurteilen des menschlichen Geschlechts* (1766).

12  I have analyzed an example of this process in a little study on Immermann's "Chiliastische Sonette," *Kleine Schriften*, II, 136–47 (*GW*, IX).

13  [See my "Mythos und Vernunft," *Kleine Schriften*, IV, 48–53 (*GW*, VIII) and "Mythos and Wissenschaft," *GW*, VIII.]

14  Horkheimer and Adorno seem to me right in their analysis of the "dialectic of the Enlightenment" (although I must regard the application of sociological concepts such as "bourgeois" to Odysseus as a failure of historical reflection, if not, indeed, a confusion of Homer with Johann Heinrich Voss [author of the standard German translation of Homer], who had already been criticized by Goethe.

15  H. Leo, *Studien und Skizzen zu einer Naturlehre des Staates* (1833).

16  Cf. the reflections on this important question by G. von Lukács in his *History and Class Consciousness*, tr. Rodney Livingstone (1923; Cambridge, Mass.: MIT Press, 1971).

17  Rousseau, *Discourse on the Origin of Inequality*.

18   Cf. my "Plato and the Poets," in *Dialogue and Dialectic: Eight Hermeneutical Studies on Plato*, tr. P. Christopher Smith (New Haven: Yale University Press, 1980), pp. 54f.

19   Walch, *Philosophisches Lexicon* (1726), p. 1013.

20   Walch, op. cit., pp. 1006ff. under the entry "Freiheit zu gedenken."

21   Schleiermacher, *Werke*, I, part 7, 31.

22   (It seems to me that the tendency to acknowledge authority, as for instance in Karl Jaspers, *Von der Wahrheit*, pp. 766ff., and Gerhard Krüger, *Freiheit und Weltverwaltung*, pp. 231ff., lacks an intelligible basis so long as this proposition is not acknowledged.) The notorious statement, "The party (or the Leader) is always right" is not wrong because it claims that a certain leadership is superior, but because it serves to shield the leadership, by a dictatorial decree, from any criticism that might be true. True authority does not have to be authoritarian. [This issue has meanwhile been much debated, particularly in my exchange with Jürgen Habermas. See *Hermeneutik und Ideologiekritik*, ed. Jürgen Habermas (Frankfurt, 1977) and my lecture at Solothurn, "Über den Zusammenhang von Autorität und kritischer Freiheit," *Schweizer Archiv für Neurologie, Neurochirurgie und Psychiatrie*, 133 (1983), 11–16. Arnold Gehlen especially has worked out the role of institutions.]

23   Cf. Aristotle, *Nichomachean Ethics*, X, 10.

24   I don't agree with Scheler that the preconscious pressure of tradition decreases as historical study proceeds (*Stellung des Menschen im Kosmos*, p. 37). The independence of historical study implied in this view seems to me a liberal fiction of a sort that Scheler is generally able to see through. (Cf. similarly in his *Nachlass*, I, 228ff., where he affirms his faith in enlightenment through historical study or sociology of knowledge.)

25   [The question appears much more complicated since Thomas Kuhn's *The Structure of Scientific Revolutions* (Chicago, 1963) and *The Essential Tension: Selected Studies in Scientific Tradition and Change* (Chicago, 1977).]

26   [That K. G. Faber in his thorough discussion in *Theorie der Geschichts-wissenschaft (2nd ed., Munich, 1972), p. 25, cannot quote this statement without placing an ironic exclamation mark after "constituted" obliges me to ask how else one defines a "historical fact"?*]

27   [Now, in the light of the part three decades of work in the philosophy of science, I willingly acknowledge that even this formulation is too undifferentiated.]

# PART FOUR

# WHAT IS NATURALIZED EPISTEMOLOGY?

# Introduction

In the Cartesian tradition, a general epistemological account of how we should arrive at our beliefs must precede a commitment to any substantive beliefs about the world around us. This apparently obvious methodological principle has guided epistemology since its inception. But the consequence of this view is that epistemology precedes science, and this claim has come to seem increasingly implausible. What seems obvious today is that epistemologists need to understand how human beings generate their beliefs, how perception works, and how the brain processes sensory input. In other words, epistemology should be based, not on ideal abstract conditions, or on how we *think* we know based merely on introspection, but on the real processes of human perceiving and knowing. W. V. O. Quine argues in his inaugurating essay for naturalized epistemology that this new approach makes epistemology a *branch* of the sciences rather than their judge and overseer.

Against Quine, epistemologists who are not so naturalistically inclined have argued that this approach guts epistemology of its unique task: to ascertain, not just how we do in fact form beliefs, but how we should. Thus, Jaegwon Kim argues that the concept of epistemic justification is a normative or evaluative concept. Although values and normative criteria must be consistent with the facts, and although reasons for believing are themselves non-valuational, the supervenience of values on facts neither entails nor even suggests the reducibility of values to facts. Thus, the normative task in epistemology must continue as an independent project.

Naturalized epistemology continues to have wide influence because most of its adherents do not follow Quine's apparent repudiation of normativity, and some argue that this is an inaccurate interpretation of his real intent. Naturalistic approaches, in more recent work, expand the significance of psychological processes and social context for epistemology without replacing normative concerns with mere description. Thus, naturalized epistemologies have encouraged new subfields in philosophy like social epistemology and feminist epistemology which are concerned with actually existing practices of justification. Phyllis Rooney's essay explores the links between feminist and naturalistic approaches to epistemology but ultimately argues that naturalized epistemology, as it is generally practiced, uncritically endorses individualistic assumptions about knowing processes. Even if naturalized epistemology can meet the objections of its normative-minded critics, then, there are more debates ahead concerning which sciences will prove most relevant for an adequate account of knowledge.

## Further Reading

Goldman, Alvin. *Epistemology and Cognition*. Cambridge, MA: Harvard University Press, 1986.
Kornblith, Hilary (ed.). *Naturalizing Epistemology*. Cambridge, MA: MIT Press, 1985.

Nelson, Lynn Hankinson. *Who Knows: From Quine to a Feminist Empiricism*. Philadelphia: Temple University Press, 1990.

Quine, W. V. O. *The Pursuit of Truth*. Cambridge, MA: Harvard University Press, 1990.

# 15 Epistemology Naturalized

## W. V. O. Quine

Epistemology is concerned with the foundations of science. Conceived thus broadly, epistemology includes the study of the foundations of mathematics as one of its departments. Specialists at the turn of the century thought that their efforts in this particular department were achieving notable success: mathematics seemed to reduce altogether to logic. In a more recent perspective this reduction is seen to be better describable as a reduction to logic and set theory. This correction is a disappointment epistemologically, since the firmness and obviousness that we associate with logic cannot be claimed for set theory. But still the success achieved in the foundations of mathematics remains exemplary by comparative standards, and we can illuminate the rest of epistemology somewhat by drawing parallels to this department.

Studies in the foundations of mathematics divide symmetrically into two sorts, conceptual and doctrinal. The conceptual studies are concerned with meaning, the doctrinal with truth. The conceptual studies are concerned with clarifying concepts by defining them, some in terms of others. The doctrinal studies are concerned with establishing laws by proving them, some on the basis of others. Ideally the obscurer concepts would be defined in terms of the clearer ones so as to maximize clarity, and the less obvious laws would be proved from the more obvious ones so as to maximize certainty. Ideally the definitions would generate all the concepts from clear and distinct ideas, and the proofs would generate all the theorems from self-evident truths.

The two ideals are linked. For, if you define all the concepts by use of some favored subset of them, you thereby show how to translate all theorems into these favored terms. The clearer these terms are, the likelier it is that the truths couched in them will be obviously true, or derivable from obvious truths. If in particular the concepts of mathematics were all reducible to the clear terms of logic, then all the truths of mathematics would go over into truths of logic; and surely the truths of logic are all obvious or at least potentially obvious, i.e., derivable from obvious truths by individually obvious steps.

This particular outcome is in fact denied us, however, since mathematics reduces only to set theory and not to logic proper. Such reduction still enhances clarity, but only because of the interrelations that emerge and not because the end terms of the analysis are clearer than others. As for the end truths, the axioms of set theory, these have less obviousness and certainty to recommend them than do most of the mathematical theorems that we would derive from them. Moreover, we know from Gödel's work that no consistent axiom system can cover mathematics even when we renounce self-evidence. Reduction in the foundations of mathematics remains mathematically and philosophically fascinating, but it does not do what the epistemologist would like of it: it does not reveal the ground of mathematical knowledge, it does not show how mathematical certainty is possible.

Still there remains a helpful thought, regarding epistemology generally, in that duality of structure which was especially conspicuous in the foundations of mathematics. I refer to the bifurcation into a theory of concepts, or meaning, and a theory of doctrine, or truth; for this applies to the epistemology of natural knowledge no less than to the foundations of mathematics. The parallel is as follows. Just as mathematics is to be reduced to logic, or logic and set theory, so natural knowledge is to be based somehow on sense experience. This means explaining the notion of body in sensory terms; here is the conceptual side. And it means justifying our knowledge of truths of nature in sensory terms; here is the doctrinal side of the bifurcation.

Hume pondered the epistemology of natural knowledge on both sides of the bifurcation, the conceptual and the doctrinal. His handling of the conceptual side of the problem, the explanation of body in sensory terms, was bold and simple: he identified bodies outright with the sense impressions. If common sense distinguishes between the material apple and our sense impressions of it on the ground that the apple is one and enduring while the impressions are many and fleeting, then, Hume held, so much the worse for common sense; the notion of its being the same apple on one occasion and another is a vulgar confusion.

Nearly a century after Hume's *Treatise*, the same view of bodies was espoused by the early American philosopher Alexander Bryan Johnson.[1] "The word iron names an associated sight and feel," Johnson wrote.

What then of the doctrinal side, the justification of our knowledge of truths about nature? Here, Hume despaired. By his identification of bodies with impressions he did succeed in construing some singular statements about bodies as indubitable truths, yes; as truths about impressions, directly known. But general statements, also singular statements about the future, gained no increment of certainty by being construed as about impressions.

On the doctrinal side, I do not see that we are farther along today than where Hume left us. The Humean predicament is the human predicament. But on the conceptual side there has been progress. There the crucial step forward was made already before Alexander Bryan Johnson's day, although Johnson did not emulate it. It was made by Bentham in his theory of fictions. Bentham's step was the recognition of contextual definition, or what he called paraphrasis. He recognized that to explain a term we do not need to specify an object for it to refer to, nor even specify a synonymous word or phrase; we need only show, by whatever means, how to translate all the whole sentences in which the term is to be used. Hume's and Johnson's desperate measure of identifying bodies with impressions ceased to be the only conceivable way of making sense of talk of bodies, even granted that impressions were the only reality. One could undertake to explain talk of bodies in terms of talk of impressions by translating one's whole sentences about bodies into whole sentences about impressions, without equating the bodies themselves to anything at all.

This idea of contextual definition, or recognition of the sentence as the primary vehicle of meaning, was indispensable to the ensuing developments in the foundations of mathematics. It was explicit in Frege, and it attained its full flower in Russell's doctrine of singular descriptions as incomplete symbols.

Contextual definition was one of two resorts that could be expected to have a liberating effect upon the conceptual side of the epistemology of natural knowledge. The other is resort to the resources of set theory as auxiliary concepts. The epistemologist who is willing to eke out his auster ontology of sense impressions with these set-theoretic auxiliaries is suddenly rich: he has not just his impressions to play with, but sets of them, and sets of sets, and so on up. Constructions in the foundations of mathematics have shown that such set-theoretic aids are a powerful addition; after all, the entire glossary of concepts of classical mathematics is constructible from them. Thus equipped, our epistemologist may not need either to identify bodies with impressions or to settle for contextual definition; he may hope to find in some subtle construction of sets upon sets of sense impressions a category of objects enjoying just the formula properties that he wants for bodies.

The two resorts are very unequal in epistemological status. Contextual definition is unassailable. Sentences that have been given meaning as wholes are undeniably meaningful, and the use they make of their component terms is therefore meaningful, regardless of whether any translations are offered for those terms in isolation. Surely Hume and A. B. Johnson would have used contextual definition with pleasure if they had thought of it. Recourse to sets, on the other hand, is a drastic ontological move, a retreat from the austere ontology of impressions. There are philosophers who would rather settle for bodies outright than accept all these sets, which amount, after all, to the whole abstract ontology of mathematics.

This issue has not always been clear, however, owing to deceptive hints of continuity between elementary logic and set theory. This is why mathematics was once believed to reduce to logic, that is, to an innocent and unquestionable logic, and to inherit these qualities. And this is probably why Russell was content to resort to sets as well as to contextual definition when in *Our Knowledge of the External World* and elsewhere he addressed himself to the epistemology of natural knowledge, on its conceptual side.

To account for the external world as a logical construct of sense data – such, in Russell's terms, was the program. It was Carnap, in his *Der logische Aufbau der Welt* of 1928, who came nearest to executing it.

This was the conceptual side of epistemology; what of the doctrinal? There the Humean predicament remained unaltered. Carnap's constructions, if carried successfully to completion, would have enable us to translate all sentences about the world into terms of sense data, or observation, plus logic and set theory. But the mere fact that a sentence is *couched* in terms of observation, logic, and set theory does not mean that it can be *proved* from observation sentences by logic and set theory. The most modest of generalizations about observable traits will cover more cases than its utterer can have had occasion actually to observe. The hopelessness of grounding natural science upon immediate experience in a firmly logical way was acknowledged. The Cartesian quest for certainty had been the remote motivation of epistemology, both on its conceptual and its doctrinal side; but that quest was seen as a lost cause. To endow the truths of nature with the full authority of immediate experience was as forlorn a hope as hoping to endow the truths of mathematics with the potential obviousness of elementary logic.

What then could have motivated Carnap's heroic efforts on the conceptual side of epistemology, when hope of certainty on the doctrinal side was abandoned? There were two good reasons still. One was that such constructions could be expected to elicit and clarify the sensory evidence for science, even if the inferential steps between sensory evidence and scientific doctrine must fall short of certainty. The other reason was that such constructions would deepen our understanding of our discourse about the world, even apart from questions of evidence; it would make all cognitive discourse as clear as observation terms and logic and, I must regretfully add, set theory.

It was sad for epistemologists, Hume and others, to have to acquiesce in the impossibility of strictly deriving the science of the external world from sensory evidence. Two cardinal tenets of empiricism remained unassailable, however, and so remain to this day. One is that whatever evidence there *is* for science *is* sensory evidence. The other, to which I shall recur, is that all inculcation of meanings of words must rest ultimately on sensory evidence. Hence the continuing attractiveness of the idea of a *logischer Aufbau* in which the sensory content of discourse would stand forth explicitly.

If Carnap had successfully carried such a construction through, how could he have told whether it was the right one? The question would have had no point. He was seeking what he called a *rational reconstruction*. Any construction of physicalistic discourse in terms of sense experience, logic, and set theory would have been seen as satisfactory if it made the physicalistic discourse come out right. If there is one way there are many, but any would be a great achievement.

But why all this creative reconstruction, all this make-believe? The stimulation of his sensory receptors is all the evidence anybody has had to go on, ultimately, in arriving at his picture of the world. Why not just see how this construction really proceeds? Why not settle for psychology? Such a surrender of the epistemological burden to psychology is a move that was disallowed in earlier times as circular reasoning. If the epistemologist's goal is validation of the grounds of empirical science, he defeats his purpose by using psychology or other empirical science in the validation. However, such scruples against circularity have little point once we have stopped dreaming of deducing science from observations. If we are out simply to understand the link between observation and science, we are well advised to use any available information, including that provided by the very science whose link with observation we are seeking to understand.

But there remains a different reason, unconnected with fears of circularity, for still favoring creative reconstruction. We should like to be able to *translate* science into logic and observation terms and set theory. This would be a great epistemological achievement, for it would show all the rest of the concepts of science to be theoretically superfluous. It would legitimize them – to whatever degree the concepts of set theory, logic, and observation are themselves legitimate – by showing that everything done with the one apparatus could in principle be done with the other. If psychology itself could deliver a truly translational reduction of this kind, we should welcome it; but certainly it cannot, for certainly we did not grow up learning definitions of physicalistic language in terms of a prior language of set theory, logic, and observation. Here, then, would be good reason for persisting in a rational reconstruction: we want to establish the essential innocence of physical concepts, by showing them to be theoretically dispensable.

The fact is, though, that the construction which Carnap outlined in *Der logische Aufbau Der Welt* does not give translational reduction either. It would not even if the outline were filled in. The crucial point comes where Carnap is explaining how to assign sense qualities to positions in physical space and time. These assignments are to be made in such a way as to fulfill, as well as possible, certain desiderata which he states, and with growth of experience the assignments are to be revised to suit. This plan, however illuminating, does not offer any key to *translating* the sentences of science into terms of observation, logic, and set theory.

We must despair of any such reduction. Carnap had despaired of it by 1936, when, in "Testability and meaning,"[2] he introduced so-called *reduction forms* of a type weaker than definition. Definitions had shown always how to translate sentences into equivalent sentences. Contextual definition of a term showed how to translate sentences containing the term into equivalent sentences lacking the term. Reduction forms of Carnap's liberalized kind, on the other hand, do not in general give equivalences; they give implications. They explain a new term, if only partially, by specifying some sentences which are implied by sentences containing the term, and other sentences which imply sentences containing the term.

It is tempting to suppose that the countenancing of reduction forms in this liberal sense is just one further step of liberalization comparable to the earlier one, taken by Bentham, of countenancing contextual definition. The former and sterner kind of rational reconstruction might have been represented as a fictitious history in which we imagined our ancestors introducing the terms of physicalistic discourse on a phenomenalistic and set-theoretic basis by a succession of contextual definitions. The new and more liberal kind of rational reconstruction is a fictitious history in which we imagine our ancestors introducing those terms by a succession rather of reduction forms of the weaker sort.

This, however, is a wrong comparison. The fact is rather that the former and sterner kind of rational reconstruction, where definition reigned, embodied no fictitious history at all. It was nothing more nor less than a set of directions – or would have been, if successful – for accomplishing everything in terms of phenomena and set theory that we now accomplish in terms of bodies. It would have been a true reduction by translation, a legitimation by elimination. *Definire est eliminare*. Rational reconstruction by Carnap's later and looser reduction forms does none of this.

To relax the demand for definition, and settle for a kind of reduction that does not eliminate, is to renounce the last remaining advantage that we supposed rational reconstruction to have over straight psychology; namely, the advantage of translational reduction. If all we hope for is a reconstruction that links science to experience in explicit ways short of translation, then it would seem more sensible to settle for psychology. Better to discover how science is in fact developed and learned than to fabricate a fictitious structure to a similar effect.

The empiricist made one major concession when he despaired of deducing the truths of nature from sensory evidence. In despairing now even of translating those truths into terms of observation and logico-mathematical auxiliaries, he makes another major concession. For suppose we hold, with the old empiricist Peirce, that the very meaning of a statement consists in the difference its truth would make to possible experience. Might we not formulate, in a chapter-length sentence in observational language, all the difference that the truth of a given statement might make to experience, and might we not then take all this as the translation? Even if the difference that the truth of the statement would make to experience ramifies indefinitely, we might still hope to embrace it all in the logical implications of our chapter-length formulation, just as we can axiomatize an infinity of theorems. In giving up hope of such translation, then, the empiricist is conceding that the empirical meanings of typical statements about the external world are inaccessible and ineffable.

How is this inaccessibility to be explained? Simply on the ground that the experiential implications of a typical statement about bodies are too complex for finite axiomatization, however lengthy? No; I have a different explanation. It is that the typical statement about bodies has no fund of experiential implications it can call its own. A substantial mass of theory, taken together, will commonly have experiential implications; this is how we make verifiable predictions. We may not be able to explain why we arrive at theories which make successful predictions, but we do arrive at such theories.

Sometimes also an experience implied by a theory fails to come off; and then, ideally, we declare the theory false. But the failure falsifies only a block of theory as a whole, a conjunction of many statements. The failure shows that one or more of those statements is false, but it does not show which. The predicted experiences, true and false, are not implied by any one of the component statements of the theory rather than another. The component statements simply do not have empirical meanings, by Peirce's standard; but a sufficiently inclusive portion of theory does. If we can aspire to a sort of *logischer Aufbau der Welt* at all, it must be to one in which the texts slated for translation into observational and logico-mathematical terms are mostly broad theories taken as wholes, rather than just terms or short sentences. The translation of a theory would be a ponderous axiomatization of all the experiential difference that the truth of the theory would make. It would be a queer translation, for it would translate the whole but none of the parts. We might better speak in such a case not of translation but simply of observational evidence for theories; and we may, following Peirce, still fairly call this the empirical meaning of the theories.

These considerations raise a philosophical question even about ordinary unphilosophical translation, such as from English into Arunta or Chinese. For, if the English sentences of a theory have their meaning only together as a body, then we can justify their translation into Arunta only together as a body. There will be no justification for pairing off the component English sentences with component Arunta sentences, except as these correlations make the translation of the theory as a whole come out right. Any translations of the English sentences into Arunta sentences will be as correct as any other, so long as the net empirical implications of the theory as a whole are preserved in translation. But it is to be expected that many different ways of translating the component sentences, essentially different individually, would deliver the same empirical implications for the theory as a whole; deviations in the translation of one component sentence could be compensated for in the translation of another component sentence. Insofar, there can be no ground for saying which of two glaringly unlike translations of individual sentences is right.[3]

For an uncritical mentalist, no such indeterminacy threatens. Every term and every sentence is a label attached to an idea, simple or complex, which is stored in the mind. When on the other hand we take a verification theory of meaning seriously, the indeterminacy would appear to be inescapable. The Vienna Circle espoused a verification theory of meaning but did not take it seriously enough. If we recognize with Peirce that the meaning of a sentence turns purely on what would count as evidence for its truth, and if we recognize with Duhem that theoretical sentences have their evidence not as single sentences but only as larger blocks of theory, then the indeterminacy of translation of theoretical sentences is the natural conclusion. And most sentences, apart from observation sentences, are theoretical. This conclusion, conversely, once it is embraced, seals the fate of any general notion of propositional meaning or, for that matter, state of affairs.

Should the unwelcomeness of the conclusion persuade us to abandon the verification theory of meaning? Certainly not. The sort of meaning that is basic to translation, and to the learning of one's own language, is necessarily empirical meaning and nothing more. A child learns his first words and sentences by hearing and using them in the presence of appropriate stimuli. These must be external stimuli, for they must act both on the child and on the speaker from whom he is learning.[4] Language is socially inculcated and controlled; the inculcation and control turn strictly on the keying of sentences to shared stimulation. Internal factors may vary *ad libitum* without prejudice to communication as long as the keying of language to external stimuli is undisturbed. Surely one has no choice but to be an empiricist so far as one's theory of linguistic meaning is concerned.

What I have said of infant learning applies equally to the linguist's learning of a new language in the field. If the linguist does not lean on related languages for which there are previously accepted translation practices, then obviously he has no data but the concomitances of native utterance and observable stimulus situation. No wonder there is indeterminacy of translation – for of course only a small fraction of our utterances report concurrent external stimulation. Granted, the linguist will end up with unequivocal translations of everything; but only by making many arbitrary choices – arbitrary even though unconscious – along the way. Arbitrary? By this I mean that different choices could still have made every-thing come out right that is susceptible in principle to any kind of check.

Let me link up, in a different order, some of the points I have made. The crucial consideration behind my argument for the indeterminacy of translation was that a statement about the world does not always or usually have a separable fund of empirical consequences that it can call its own. That consideration served also to account for the impossibility of an epistemological reduction of the sort where every sentence is equated to a sentence in observational and logico-math-ematical terms. And the impossibility of that sort of epistemological reduction dissipated the last advantage that rational reconstruction seemed to have over psychology.

Philosophers have rightly despaired of translating everything into observa-tional and logico-mathematical terms. They have despaired of this even when they have not recognized, as the reason for this irreducibility, that the state-ments largely do not have their private bundles of empirical consequences. And some philosophers have seen in this irreducibility the bankruptcy of epistemol-ogy. Carnap and the other logical positivists of the Vienna Circle had already pressed the term "metaphysics" into pejorative use, as connoting meaningless-ness; and the term "epistemology" was next. Wittgenstein and his followers, mainly at Oxford, found a residual philosophical vocation in therapy: in curing philosophers of the delusion that there were epistemological problems.

But I think that at this point it may be more useful to say rather that episte-mology still goes on, though in a new setting and a clarified status. Epistemol-ogy, or something like it, simply falls into place as a chapter of psychology and hence of natural science. It studies a natural phenomenon, viz., a physical hu-man subject. This human subject is accorded a certain experimentally control-led input – certain patterns of irradiation in assorted frequencies, for instance – and in the fullness of time the subject delivers as output a description of the three-dimensional external world and its history. The relation between the meager input and the torrential output is a relation that we are prompted to study for somewhat the same reasons that always prompted epistemology; namely, in order to see how evidence relates to theory, and in what ways one's theory of nature transcends any available evidence.

Such a study could still include, even, something like the old rational recon-struction, to whatever degree such reconstruction is practicable; for imaginative constructions can afford hints of actual psychological processes, in much the way that mechanical simulations can. But a conspicuous difference between old epistemology and the epistemological enterprise in this new psychological set-ting is that we can now make free use of empirical psychology.

The old epistemology aspired to contain, in a sense, natural science; it would construct it somehow from sense data. Epistemology in its new setting, con-versely, is contained in natural science, as a chapter of psychology. But the old containment remains valid too, in its way. We are studying how the human subject of our study posits bodies and projects his physics from his data, and we appreciate that our position in the world is just like his. Our very epistemologi-cal enterprise, therefore, and the psychology wherein it is a component chapter, and the whole of natural science wherein psychology is a component book – all this is our own construction or projection from stimulations like those we were meting out to our epistemological subject. There is thus reciprocal containment, though containment in different senses: epistemology in natural science and natural science in epistemology.

This interplay is reminiscent again of the old threat of circularity, but it is all right now that we have stopped dreaming of deducing science from sense data. We are after an understanding of science as an institution or process in the world, and we do not intend that understanding to be any better than the science which is its object. This attitude is indeed one that Neurath was already urging in Vienna Circle days, with his parable of the mariner who has to rebuild his boat while staying afloat in it.

One effect of seeing epistemology in a psychological setting is that it resolves a stubborn old enigma of epistemological priority. Our retinas are irradiated in two dimensions, yet we see things as three-dimensional without conscious inference. Which is to count as observation – the unconscious two-dimensional reception or the conscious three-dimensional apprehension. In the old epistemological context the conscious form had priority, for we were out to justify our knowledge of the external world by rational reconstruction, and that demands awareness. Awareness ceased to be demanded when we gave up trying to justify our knowledge of the external world by rational reconstruction. What to count as observation now can be settled in terms of the stimulation of sensory receptors, let consciousness fall where it may.

The Gestalt psychologists' challenge to sensory atomism, which seemed so relevant to epistemology forty years ago, is likewise deactivated. Regardless of whether sensory atoms or Gestalten are what favor the forefront of our consciousness, it is simply the stimulations of our sensory receptors that are best looked upon as the input to our cognitive mechanism. Old paradoxes about unconscious data and inference, old problems about chains of inference that would have to be completed too quickly – these no longer matter.

In the old anti-psychologistic days the question of epistemological priority was moot. What is epistemologically prior to what? Are Gestalten prior to sensory atoms because they are noticed, or should we favor sensory atoms on some more subtle ground? Now that we are permitted to appeal to physical stimulation, the problem dissolves; $A$ is epistemologically prior to $B$ if $A$ is causally nearer than $B$ to the sensory receptors. Or, what is in some ways better, just talk explicitly in terms of causal proximity to sensory receptors and drop the talk of epistemological priority.

Around 1932 there was debate in the Vienna Circle over what to count as observation sentences, or *Protokollsätze*.[5] One position was that they had the form of reports of sense impressions. Another was that they were statements of an elementary sort about the external world, e.g., "A red cube is standing on the table." Another, Neurath's, was that they had the form of reports of relations between percipients and external things: "Otto now sees a red cube on the table." The worst of it was that there seemed to be no objective way of settling the matter: no way of making real sense of the question.

Let us now try to view the matter unreservedly in the context of the external world. Vaguely speaking, what we want of observation sentences is that they be the ones in closest causal proximity to the sensory receptors. But how is such proximity to be gauged? The idea may be rephrased this way: observation sentences are sentences which, as we learn language, are most strongly conditioned to concurrent sensory stimulation rather than to stored collateral information. Thus let us imagine a sentence queried for our verdict as to whether it is true or false; queried for our assent or dissent. Then the sentence is an observation sentence if our verdict depends only on the sensory stimulation present at the time.

But a verdict cannot depend on present stimulation to the exclusion of stored information. The very fact of our having learned the language evinces much storing of information, and of information without which we should be in no position to give verdicts on sentences however observational. Evidently then we must relax our definition of observation sentence to read thus: a sentence is an observation sentence if all verdicts on it depend on present sensory stimulation and on no stored information beyond what goes into understanding the sentence.

This formulation raises another problem: how are we to distinguish between information that goes into understanding a sentence and information that goes beyond? This is the problem of distinguishing between analytic truth, which issues form the mere meanings of words, and synthetic truth, which depends on more than meanings. Now I have long maintained that this distinction is illusory. There is one step toward such a distinction, however, which does make sense: a sentence that is true by mere meanings of words should be expected, at least if it is simple, to be subscribed to by all fluent speakers in the community. Perhaps the controversial notion of analyticity can be dispensed with, in our definition of observation sentence, in favor of this straightforward attribute of community-wide acceptance.

This attribute is of course no explication of analyticity. The community would agree that there have been black dogs, yet none who talk of analyticity would call this analytic. My rejection of the analyticity notion just means drawing no line between what goes into the mere understanding of the sentences of a language and what else the community sees eye-to-eye on. I doubt that an objective distinction can be made between meaning and such collateral information as is community-wide.

Turning back then to our task of defining observation sentences, we get this: an observation sentence is one on which all speakers of the language give the same verdict when given the same concurrent stimulation. To put the point negatively, an observation sentence is one that is not sensitive to differences in past experience within the speech community.

This formulation accords perfectly with the traditional role of the observation sentence as the court of appeal of scientific theories. For by our definition the observation sentences are the sentences on which all members of the community will agree under uniform stimulation. And what is the criterion of membership in the same community? Simply general fluency of dialogue. This criterion

admits of degrees, and indeed we may usefully take the community more narrowly for some studies than for others. What count as observation sentences for
a community of specialists would not always so count for a larger community.

There is generally no subjectivity in the phrasing of observation sentences, as
we are now conceiving them; they will usually be about bodies. Since the distinguishing trait of an observation sentence is intersubjective agreement under
agreeing stimulation, a corporeal subject matter is likelier than not.

The old tendency to associate observation sentences with a subjective sensory
subject matter is rather an irony when we reflect that observation sentences are
also meant to be the intersubjective tribunal of scientific hypotheses. The old
tendency was due to the drive to base science on something firmer and prior in
the subject's experience; but we dropped that project.

The dislodging of epistemology from its old status of first philosophy loosed
a wave, we saw, of epistemological nihilism. This mood is reflected somewhat in
the tendency of Polányi, Kuhn, and the late Russell Hanson to belittle the role
of evidence and to accentuate cultural relativism. Hanson ventured even to
discredit the idea of observation, arguing that so-called observations vary from
observer to observer with the amount of knowledge that the observers bring
with them. The veteran physicist looks at some apparatus and sees an x-ray
tube. The neophyte, looking at the same place, observes rather "a glass metal
instrument replete with wires, reflectors, screws, lamps, and pushbuttons."[6] One
man's observation is another man's closed book or flight of fancy. The notion
of observation as the impartial and objective source of evidence for science is
bankrupt. Now my answer to the x-ray example was already hinted a little while
back: what counts as an observation sentence varies with the width of community considered. But we can also always get an absolute standard by taking in all
speakers of the language, or most.[7] It is ironical that philosophers, finding the
old epistemology untenable as a whole, should react by repudiating a part which
has only now moved into clear focus.

Clarification of the notion of observation sentence is a good thing, for the
notion is fundamental in two connections. These two correspond to the duality
that I remarked upon early in this lecture: the duality between concept and
doctrine, between knowing what a sentence means and knowing whether it is
true. The observation sentence is basic to both enterprises. Its relation to doctrine, to our knowledge of what is true, is very much the traditional one: observation sentences are the repository of evidence for scientific hypotheses. Its
relation to meaning is fundamental too, since observation sentences are the
ones we are in a position to learn to understand first, both as children and as
field linguists. For observation sentences are precisely the ones that we can correlate with observable circumstances of the occasion of utterance or assent, independently of variations in the past histories of individual informants. They
afford the only entry to a language.

The observation sentence is the cornerstone of semantics. For it is, as we just
saw, fundamental to the learning of meaning. Also, it is where meaning is firm-
est. Sentences higher up in theories have no empirical consequences they can
call their own; they confront the tribunal of sensory evidence only in more or

less inclusive aggregates. The observation sentence, situated at the sensory periphery of the body scientific, is the minimal verifiable aggregate; it has an empirical content all its own and wears it on its sleeve.

The predicament of the indeterminacy of translation has little bearing on observation sentences. The equating of an observation sentence of our language to an observation sentence of another language is mostly a matter of empirical generalization; it is a matter of identity between the range of stimulations that would prompt assent to the one sentence and the range of stimulations that would prompt assent to the other.[8]

It is no shock to the preconceptions of old Vienna to say that epistemology now becomes semantics. For epistemology remains centered as always on evidence, and meaning remains centered as always on verification; and evidence is verification. What is likelier to shock preconceptions is that meaning, once we get beyond observation sentences, ceases in general to have any clear applicability to single sentences; also that epistemology merges with psychology, as well as with linguistics.

This rubbing out of boundaries could contribute to progress, it seems to me, in philosophically interesting inquiries of a scientific nature. One possible area is perceptual norms. Consider, to begin with, the linguistic phenomenon of phonemes. We form the habit, in hearing the myriad variations of spoken sounds, of treating each as an approximation to one or another of a limited number of norms – around thirty altogether – constituting so to speak a spoken alphabet. All speech in our language can be treated in practice as sequences of just those thirty elements, thus rectifying small deviations. Now outside the realm of language also there is probably only a rather limited alphabet of perceptual norms altogether, toward which we tend unconsciously to rectify all perceptions. These, if experimentally identified, could be taken as epistemological building blocks, the working elements of experience. They might prove in part to be culturally variable, as phonemes are, and in part universal.

Again there is the area that the psychologist Donald T. Campbell calls evolutionary epistemology.[9] In this area there is work by Hüseyin Yilmaz, who shows how some structural traits of color perception could have been predicted from survival value.[10] And a more emphatically epistemological topic that evolution helps to clarify is induction, now that we are allowing epistemology the resources of natural science.[11]

## Notes

1 Johnson 1947.
2 Carnap 1936.
3 See Quine 1969, pp. 2 ff.
4 See Quine 1969, p. 28.
5 Carnap 1932; Neurath 1932.
6 N. R. Hanson 1966.
7 This qualification allows for occasional deviants such as the insane or the blind. Alternatively, such cases might be excluded by adjusting the level of fluency of dialogue whereby we define sameness of language. (For prompting this note and

influencing the development of this paper also in more substantial ways I am indebted to Burton Dreben.)
8   Cf. Quine 1960, pp. 31–46, 68.
9   D. T. Campbell 1959.
10  Huseyin Yilmaz 1962, 1967.
11  See Quine 1969b.

**Works Cited**

Campbell, D. T. (1959). "Methodological suggestions from a comparative psychology
of knowledge processes." *Inquiry* 2, 152–82.
Carnap, R (1932). "Protokollsätze." *Erkenntnis* 3, 215–28.
Carnap, R (1936–37). "Testability and Meaning." *Philosophy of Science* 3 (1936), 419–
71; 4 (1937), 1–40.
Hanson, N. R. (1966). "Observation and Interpretation." In S. Morgenbesser (ed.),
*Philosophy of Science Today*. New York: Basic Books.
Johnson, A. B. (1947). *A Treatise on Language*. Berkeley, CA: University of California
Press.
Neurath, O. (1932–33). "Protokollsätze." *Erkenntnis* 3, 204–14.
Quine, W. V. O. (1960). *Word and Object*. Cambridge, Mass: The MIT Press.
Quine, W. V. O. (1969). *Ontological Relativity and Other Essays*. New York: Columbia
University Press.
Yilmaz, Hüseyin (1962). "On color vision and a new approach to general perception."
In E.E.
Bernard and M. R. Kare (eds) (1962). *Biological Prototypes and Synthetic Systems*. New
York: Plenum Press.
Yilmaz, Hüseyin (1967). "Perceptual invariance and the psychophysical law." *Percep-
tion and Psychophysics* 2, 533–8.

# 16   What is "Naturalized Epistemology"?

## *Jaegwon Kim*

### 1   Epistemology as a Normative Inquiry

Descartes' epistemological inquiry in the *Meditations* begins with this question:
What propositions are worthy of belief? In the *First Meditation* Descartes can-
vasses beliefs of various kinds he had formerly held as true and finds himself
forced to conclude that he ought to reject them, that he ought not to accept
them as true. We can view Cartesian epistemology as consisting of the following
two projects: to identify the criteria by which we ought to regulate acceptance
and rejection of beliefs, and to determine what we may be said to know according to those criteria. Descartes' epistemological agenda has been the agenda of

Western epistemology to this day. The twin problems of identifying criteria of justified belief and coming to terms with the skeptical challenge to the possibility of knowledge have defined the central tasks of theory of knowledge since Descartes. This was as true of the empiricists, of Locke and Hume and Mill, as of those who more closely followed Descartes in the rationalist path.[1]

It is no wonder then that modern epistemology has been dominated by a single concept, that of *justification*, and two fundamental questions involving it: What conditions must a belief meet if we are justified in accepting it as true? and What beliefs are we in fact justified in accepting? Note that the first question does not ask for an "analysis" or "meaning" of the term "justified belief". And it is generally assumed, even if not always explicitly stated, that not just any statement of a necessary and sufficient condition for a belief to be justified will do. The implicit requirement has been that the stated conditions must constitute "criteria" of justified belief, and for this it is necessary that the conditions be stated *without the use of epistemic terms*. Thus, formulating conditions of justified belief in such terms as "adequate evidence", "sufficient ground", "good reason", "beyond a reasonable doubt", and so on, would be merely to issue a promissory note redeemable only when these epistemic terms are themselves explained in a way that accords with the requirement.[2]

This requirement, while it points in the right direction, does not go far enough. What is crucial is this: *the criteria of justified belief must be formulated on the basis of descriptive or naturalistic terms alone, without the use of any evaluative or normative ones, whether epistemic or of another kind*.[3] Thus, an analysis of justified belief that makes use of such terms as "intellectual requirement"[4] and "having a right to be sure"[5] would not satisfy this generalized condition; although such an analysis can be informative and enlightening about the inter-relationships of these normative concepts, it will not, on the present conception, count as a statement of *criteria* of justified belief, unless of course these terms are themselves provided with nonnormative criteria. What is problematic, therefore, about the use of epistemic terms in stating criteria of justified belief is not its possible circularity in the usual sense; rather it is the fact that these epistemic terms are themselves essentially normative. We shall later discuss the rationale of this strengthened requirement.

As many philosophers have observed,[6] the two questions we have set forth, one about the criteria of justified belief and the other about what we can be said to know according to those criteria, constrain each other. Although some philosophers have been willing to swallow skepticism just because what we regard as correct criteria of justified belief are seen to lead inexorably to the conclusion that none, or very few, of our beliefs are justified, the usual presumption is that our answer to the first question should leave our epistemic situation largely unchanged. That is to say, it is expected to turn out that according to the criteria of justified belief we come to accept, we know, or are justified in believing, pretty much what we reflectively think we know or are entitled to believe.

Whatever the exact history, it is evident that the concept of justification has come to take center stage in our reflections on the nature of knowledge. And apart from history, there is a simple reason for our preoccupation with justification: it is the only specifically epistemic component in the classic tripartite conception of knowledge. Neither belief nor truth is a specifically epistemic notion: belief is a psychological concept and truth a semantical-metaphysical one. These concepts may have an implicit epistemological dimension, but if they do, it is likely to be through their involvement with essentially normative epistemic notions like justification, evidence, and rationality. Moreover, justification is what makes knowledge itself a normative concept. On surface at least, neither truth nor belief is normative or evaluative (I shall argue below, though, that belief does have an essential normative dimension). But justification manifestly is normative. If a belief is justified for us, then it is *permissible* and *reasonable*, from the epistemic point of view, for us to hold it, and it would be *epistemically irresponsible* to hold beliefs that contradict it. If we consider believing or accepting a proposition to be an "action" in an appropriate sense, belief justification would then be a special case of justification of action, which in its broadest terms is the central concern of normative ethics. Just as it is the business of normative ethics to delineate the conditions under which acts and decisions are justified from the moral point of view, so it is the business of epistemology to identify and analyze the conditions under which beliefs, and perhaps other propositional attitudes, are justified from the epistemological point of view. It probably is only an historical accident that we standardly speak of "normative ethics" but not of "normative epistemology". Epistemology is a normative discipline as much as, and in the same sense as, normative ethics.

We can summarize our discussion thus far in the following points: that justification is a central concept of our epistemological tradition, that justification, as it is understood in this tradition, is a normative concept, and in consequence that epistemology itself is a normative inquiry whose principal aim is a systematic study of the conditions of justified belief. I take it that these points are uncontroversial, although of course there could be disagreement about the details – for example, about what it means to say a concept or theory is "normative" or "evaluative".

## 2   The Foundationalist Strategy

In order to identify the target of the naturalistic critique – in particular, Quine's – it will be useful to take a brief look at the classic response to the epistemological program set forth by Descartes. Descartes' approach to the problem of justification is a familiar story, at least as the textbook tells it: it takes the form of what is now commonly called "foundationalism". The foundationalist strategy is to divide the task of explaining justification into two stages: first, to identify a set of beliefs that are "directly" justified in that they are justified without deriving their justified status from that of any other belief, and then to explain how other beliefs may be "indirectly" or "inferentially" justified by standing in an appropriate relation to those already justified. Directly justified beliefs, or "basic beliefs", are to constitute the foundation upon which the superstructure of "nonbasic" or "derived" beliefs is to rest. What beliefs then are directly justified, according to Descartes? Subtleties aside, he claimed that beliefs about our own present conscious states are among them. In what does their justification consist? What is it about these beliefs that make them directly justified? Somewhat simplistically again, Descartes' answer is that they are justified because they are *indubitable*, that the attentive and reflective mind *cannot but assent* to them. How are nonbasic beliefs justified? By "deduction" – that is, by a series of inferential steps, or "intuitions", each of which is indubitable. If, therefore, we take Cartesian indubitability as a psychological notion, Descartes' epistemological theory can be said to meet the desideratum of providing nonepistemic, naturalistic criteria of justified belief.

Descartes' foundationalist program was inherited, in its essential outlines, by the empiricists. In particular, his "mentalism", that beliefs about one's own current mental state are epistemologically basic, went essentially unchallenged by the empiricists and positivists, until this century. Epistemologists have differed from one another chiefly in regard to two questions: first, what else belonged in our corpus of basic beliefs, and second, how the derivation of the nonbasic part of our knowledge was to proceed. Even the Logical Positivists were, by and large, foundationalists, although some of them came to renounce Cartesian mentalism in favor of a "physicalistic basis".[7] In fact, the Positivists were foundationalists twice over: for them "observation", whether phenomenological or physical, served not only as the foundation of knowledge but as the foundation of all "cognitive meaning" – that is, as both an epistemological and a semantic foundation.

## 3  Quine's Arguments

It has become customary for epistemologists who profess allegiance to a "naturalistic" conception of knowledge to pay homage to Quine as the chief contemporary provenance of their inspiration – especially to his influential paper "Epistemology Naturalized".[8] Quine's principal argument in this paper against traditional epistemology is based on the claim that the Cartesian foundationalist program has failed – that the Cartesian "quest for certainty" is "a lost cause". While this claim about the hopelessness of the Cartesian "quest for certainty" is nothing new, using it to discredit the very conception of normative epistemology is new, something that any serious student of epistemology must contend with.

Quine divides the classic epistemological program into two parts: *conceptual reduction* whereby physical terms, including those of theoretical science, are reduced, via definition, to terms referring to phenomenal features of sensory experience, and *doctrinal reduction* whereby truths about the physical world are appropriately obtained from truths about sensory experience. The "appropriateness" just alluded to refers to the requirement that the favored epistemic status ("certainty" for classic epistemologists, according to Quine) of our basic beliefs be transferred, essentially undiminished, to derived beliefs, a necessary requirement if the derivational process is to yield knowledge from knowledge.

What derivational methods have this property of preserving epistemic status? Perhaps there are none, given our proneness to err in framing derivations as in anything else, not to mention the possibility of lapses of attention and memory in following lengthy proofs. But logical deduction comes as close to being one as any; it can at least be relied on to transmit truth, if not epistemic status. It could perhaps be argued that no method can preserve certainty unless it preserves (or is known to preserve) truth; and if this is so, logical deduction is the only method worth considering. I do not know whether this was the attitude of most classic epistemologists; but Quine assumes that if deduction doesn't fill their bill, nothing will.

Quine sees the project of conceptual reduction as culminating in Carnap's *Der Logische Aufbau der Welt*. As Quine sees it, Carnap "came nearest to executing" the conceptual half of the classic epistemological project. But coming close is not good enough. Because of the holistic manner in which empirical meaning is generated by experience, no reduction of the sort Carnap and others so eagerly sought could in principle be completed. For definitional reduction requires point-to-point meaning relations[9] between physical terms and phenomenal terms, something that Quine's holism tells us cannot be had. The second half of the program, doctrinal reduction, is in no better shape; in fact, it was the one to stumble first, for, according to Quine, its impossibility was decisively demonstrated long before the *Aufbau*, by Hume in his celebrated discussion of induction. The "Humean predicament" shows that theory cannot be logically deduced from observation; there simply is no way of deriving theory from observation that will transmit the latter's epistemic status intact to the former.

I don't think anyone wants to disagree with Quine in these claims. It is not possible to "validate" science on the basis of sensory experience, if "validation" means justification through logical deduction. Quine of course does not deny that our theories depend on observation for evidential support; he has said that sensory evidence is the only evidence there is. To be sure, Quine's argument against the possibility of conceptual reduction has a new twist: the application of his "holism". But his conclusion is no surprise; "translational phenomenalism" has been moribund for many years.[10] And, as Quine himself notes, his argument against the doctrinal reduction, the "quest for certainty", is only a restatement of Hume's "skeptical" conclusions concerning induction: induction after all is not deduction. Most of use are inclined, I think, to view the situation Quine describes with no great alarm, and I rather doubt that these conclusions of Quine's came as news to most epistemologists when "Epistemology Naturalized" was first published. We are tempted to respond: of course we can't define physical concepts in terms of sense-data; of course observation "underdetermines" theory. That is why observation is observation and not theory.

So it is agreed on all hands that the classical epistemological project, conceived as one of deductively validating physical knowledge from indubitable sensory data, cannot succeed. But what is the moral of this failure? What should be its philosophical lesson to us? Having noted the failure of the Cartesian program, Quine goes on:[11]

The stimulation of his sensory receptors is all the evidence anybody has had to go on, ultimately, in arriving at his picture of the world. Why not just see how this construction really proceeds? Why not settle for psychology? Such a surrender of the epistemological burden to psychology is a move that was disallowed in earlier times as circular reasoning. If the epistemologist's goal is validation of the grounds of empirical science, he defeats his purpose by using psychology or other empirical science in the validation. However, such scruples against circularity have little point once we have stopped dreaming of deducing science from observation. If we are out simply to understand the link between observation and science, we are well advised to use any available information, including that provided by the very science whose link with observation we are seeking to understand.

And Quine has the following to say about the failure of Carnap's reductive program in the *Aufbau*:[12]

To relax the demand for definition, and settle for a kind of reduction that does not eliminate, is to renounce the last remaining advantage that we supposed rational reconstruction to have over straight psychology; namely, the advantage of translational reduction. If all we hope for is a reconstruction that links science to experience in explicit ways short of translation, then it would seem more sensible to settle for psychology. Better to discover how science is in fact developed and learned than to fabricate a fictitious structure to a similar effect.

If a task is entirely hopeless, if we know it cannot be executed, no doubt it is rational to abandon it; we would be better off doing something else that has some hope of success. We can agree with Quine that the "validation" – that is, logical deduction – of science on the basis of observation cannot be had; so it is rational to abandon this particular epistemological program, if indeed it ever was a program that anyone seriously undertook. But Quine's recommendations go further. In particular, there are two aspects of Quine's proposals that are of special interest to us: first, he is not only advising us to quit the program of "validating science", but urging us to take up another specific project, an empirical psychological study of our cognitive processes; second, he is also claiming that this new program replaces the old, that both programs are part of something appropriately called "epistemology". Naturalized epistemology is to be a kind of epistemology after all, a "successor subject"[13] to classical epistemology.

How should we react to Quine's urgings? What should be our response? The Cartesian project of validating science starting from the indubitable foundation of first-person psychological reports (perhaps with the help of certain indubitable first principles) is not the whole of classical epistemology – or so it would seem at first blush. In our characterization of classical epistemology, the Cartesian program was seen as one possible response to the problem of epistemic justification, the two-part project of identifying the criteria of epistemic justification and determining what beliefs are in fact justified according to those criteria. In urging "naturalized epistemology" on us, Quine is not suggesting that we give up the Cartesian foundationalist solution and explore others within the same framework[14] – perhaps, to adopt some sort of "coherentist" strategy, or to require of our basic beliefs only some degree of "initial credibility" rather than Cartesian certainty, or to permit some sort of probabilistic derivation in addition to deductive derivation of nonbasic knowledge, or to consider the use of special rules of evidence, like Chisholm's "principles of evidence",[15] or to give up the search for a derivational process that transmits undiminished certainty in favor of one that can transmit diminished but still useful degrees of justification. Quine's proposal is more radical than that. He is asking us to set aside the entire framework of justification-centered epistemology. That is what is new in Quine's proposals. Quine is asking us to put in its place a purely descriptive, causal-nomological science of human cognition.[16]

How should we characterize in general terms the difference between traditional epistemological programs, such as foundationalism and coherence theory, on the one hand and Quine's program of naturalized epistemology on the other? Quine's stress is on the *factual* and *descriptive* character of his program; he says, "Why not see how [the construction of theory from observation] *actually proceeds*? Why not settle for psychology?";[17] again, "Better to *discover how science is in fact developed and learned than* . . ."[18] We are given to understand that in contrast traditional epistemology is not a descriptive, factual inquiry. Rather, it is an attempt at a "validation" or "rational reconstruction" of science. Validation, according to Quine, proceeds via deduction, and rational reconstruction via definition. However, their *point* is justificatory – that is, to rationalize our sundry knowledge claims. So Quine is asking us to set aside what is "rational" in rational reconstruction.

Thus, it is normativity that Quine is asking us to repudiate. Although Quine does not explicitly characterize traditional epistemology as "normative" or "prescriptive", his meaning is unmistakable. Epistemology is to be "a chapter of psychology", a law-based predictive-explanatory theory, like any other theory within empirical science; its principal job is to see how human cognizers develop theories (their "picture of the world") from observation ("the stimulation of their sensory receptors"). Epistemology is to go out of the business of justification. We earlier characterized traditional epistemology as essentially normative; we see why Quine wants us to reject it. Quine is urging us to replace a normative theory of cognition with a descriptive science.

## 4   Losing Knowledge from Epistemology

If justification drops out of epistemology, knowledge itself drops out of epistemology. For our concept of knowledge is inseparably tied to that of justification. As earlier noted, knowledge itself is a normative notion. Quine's nonnormative, naturalized epistemology has no room for our concept of knowledge. It is not surprising that, in describing naturalized epistemology, Quine seldom talks about knowledge; instead, he talks about "science" and "theories" and "representations". Quine would have us investigate how sensory stimulation "leads" to "theories" and "representation" of the world. I take it that within the traditional scheme these "theories" and "representations" correspond to beliefs, or systems of beliefs; thus, what Quine would have us do is to investigate how sensory stimulation leads to the formation of beliefs about the world.

But in what sense of "lead"? I take it that Quine has in mind a causal or nomological sense. He is urging us to develop a theory, an empirical theory, that uncovers lawful regularities governing the processes through which organisms come to develop beliefs about their environment as a causal result of having their sensory receptors stimulated in certain ways. Quine says:[19]

> [Naturalized epistemology] studies a natural phenomenon, viz., a physical human subject. This human subject is accorded experimentally controlled input – certain patterns of irradiation in assorted frequencies, for instance – and in the fullness of time the subject delivers as output a description of the three-dimensional external world and its history. *The relation between the meager input and torrential output* is a relation that we are prompted to study for somewhat the same reasons that always prompted epistemology; namely, in order to see *how evidence relates to theory*, and in what ways one's theory of nature transcends any available evidence.

The relation Quine speaks of between "meager input" and "torrential output" is a causal relation; at least it is qua causal relation that the naturalized epistemologist investigates it. It is none of the naturalized epistemologist's business to assess whether, and to what degree, the input "justifies" the output, how a given irradiation of the subject's retinas makes it "reasonable" or "rational" for the subject to emit certain representational output. His interest is strictly causal and nomological: he wants us to look for patterns of lawlike dependencies characterizing the input-output relations for this particular organism and others of a like physical structure.

If this is right, it makes Quine's attempt to relate his naturalized epistemology to traditional epistemology look at best lame. For in what sense is the study of causal relationships between physical stimulation of sensory receptors and the resulting cognitive output a way of "seeing how evidence relates to theory" in an epistemologically relevant sense? The causal relation between sensory input and cognitive output is a relation between "evidence" and "theory"; however, it is not an *evidential relation*. This can be seen from the following consideration: the nomological patterns that Quine urges us to look for are certain to vary from species to species, depending on the particular way each biological (and possibly nonbiological) species processes information, but the evidential relation in its proper normative sense must abstract from such factors and concern itself only with the degree to which evidence supports hypothesis.

In any event, the concept of evidence is inseparable from that of justification. When we talk of "evidence" in an epistemological sense we are talking about justification: one thing is "evidence" for another just in case the first tends to enhance the reasonableness or justification of the second. And such evidential relations hold in part because of the "contents" of the items involved, not merely because of the causal or nomological connections between them. A strictly nonnormative concept of evidence is not our concept of evidence; it is something that we do not understand.[20]

None of us, I think, would want to quarrel with Quine about the interest or importance of the psychological study of how our sensory input causes our epistemic output. This is only to say that the study of human (or other kinds of) cognition is of interest. That isn't our difficulty; our difficulty is whether, and in what sense, pursuing Quine's "epistemology" is a way of doing epistemology – that is, a way of studying "how evidence relates to theory". Perhaps, Quine's recommendation that we discard justification-centered epistemology is worth pondering; and his exhortation to take up the study of psychology perhaps deserves to be heeded also. What is mysterious is why this recommendation has to be coupled with the rejection of normative epistemology (if normative epistemology is not a possible inquiry, why shouldn't the would-be epistemologist turn to, say, hydrodynamics or ornithology rather than psychology?). But of course Quine is saying more; he is saying that an understandable, if misguided, motivation (that is, seeing "how evidence relates to theory") does underlie our proclivities for indulgence in normative epistemology, but that we would be better served by a scientific study of human cognition than normative epistemology.

But it is difficult to see how an "epistemology" that has been purged of normativity, one that lacks an appropriate normative concept of justification or evidence, can have anything to do with the concerns of traditional epistemology. And unless naturalized epistemology and classical epistemology share some of their central concerns, it's difficult to see how one could *replace* the other, or be a way (a better way) of doing the other.[21] To be sure, they both investigate "how evidence relates to theory". But putting the matter this way can be misleading, and has perhaps misled Quine: the two disciplines do not investigate the same relation. As lately noted, normative epistemology is concerned with the evidential relation properly so-called – that is, the relation of justification – and Quine's naturalized epistemology is meant to study the causal-nomological relation. For epistemology to go out of the business of justification is for it to go of business.

## 5    Belief Attribution and Rationality

Perhaps we have said enough to persuade ourselves that Quine's naturalized epistemology, while it may be a legitimate scientific inquiry, is not a kind of epistemology, and, therefore, that the question whether it is a better kind of epistemology cannot arise. In reply, however, it might be said that there was a sense in which Quine's epistemology and traditional epistemology could be viewed as sharing a common subject matter, namely this: they both concern beliefs or "representations". The only difference is that the former investigates their causal histories and connections whereas the latter is concerned with their evidential or justificatory properties and relations. This difference, if Quine is right, leads to another (so continues the reply): the former is a feasible inquiry, the latter is not.

I now want to take my argument a step further: I shall argue that the concept of belief is itself an essentially normative one, and in consequence that if normativity is wholly excluded from naturalized epistemology it cannot even be thought of as being about beliefs. That is, if naturalized epistemology is to be a science of beliefs properly so called, it must presuppose a normative concept of belief.

Briefly, the argument is this. In order to implement Quine's program of naturalized epistemology, we shall need to identify, and individuate, the input and output of cognizers. The input, for Quine, consists of physical events ("the stimulation of sensory receptors") and the output is said to be a "theory" or "picture of the world" – that is, a set of "representations" of the cognizer's environment. Let us focus on the output. In order to study the sensory input-cognitive output relations for the given cognizer, therefore, we must find out what "representations" he has formed as a result of the particular stimulations that have been applied to his sensory transducers. Setting aside the jargon, what we need to be able to do is to attribute *beliefs*, and other contentful intentional states, to the cognizer. But belief attribution ultimately requires a "radical interpretation" of the cognizer, of his speech and intentional states; that is, we must construct an "interpretive theory" that simultaneously assigns meanings to his utterances and attributes to him beliefs and other propositional attitudes.[22]

Even a cursory consideration indicates that such an interpretation cannot begin – we cannot get a foothold in our subject's realm of meanings and intentional states – unless we assume his total system of beliefs and other propositional attitudes to be largely and essentially rational and coherent. As Davidson has emphasized, a given belief has the content it has in part because of its location in a network of other beliefs and propositional attitudes; and what at bottom grounds this network is the evidential relation, a relation that regulates what is reasonable to believe given other beliefs one holds. That is, unless our cognizer is a "rational being", a being whose cognitive "output" is regulated and constrained by norms of rationality – typically, these norms holistically constrain his propositional attitudes in virtue of their contents – we cannot intelligibly interpret his "output" as consisting of beliefs. Conversely, if we are unable to interpret our subject's meanings and propositional attitudes in a way that satisfies a minimal standard of rationality, there is little reason to regard him as a "cognizer", a being that forms representations and constructs theories. This means that there is a sense of "rational" in which the expression "rational belief" is redundant; every belief must be rational in certain minimal ways. It is not important for the purposes of the present argument what these minimal standards of rationality are; the only point that matters is that unless the output of our cognizer is subject to evaluation in accordance with norms of rationality, that output cannot be considered as consisting of beliefs and hence cannot be the object of an epistemological inquiry, whether plain or naturalized.

We can separate the core of these considerations from controversial issues involving the so-called "principle of charity", minimal rationality, and other matters in the theory of radical interpretation. What is crucial is this: for the interpretation and attribution of beliefs to be possible, not only must we assume the overall rationality of cognizers, but also we must continually evaluate and re-evaluate the putative beliefs of a cognizer in their evidential relationship to one another and other propositional attitudes. It is not merely that belief attribution requires the umbrella assumption about the overall rationality of cognizers. Rather, the point is that *belief attribution requires belief evaluation*, in accordance with normative standards of evidence and justification. If this is correct, rationality in its broad and fundamental sense is not an optional property of beliefs, a virtue that some beliefs may enjoy and others lack; it is a precondition of the attribution and individuation of belief – that is, a property without which the concept of belief would be unintelligible and pointless.

Two objections might be raised to counter these considerations. First, one might argue that at best they show only that the normativity of belief is an epistemological assumption – that we need to assume the rationality and coherence of belief systems when we are trying to *find out* what beliefs to attribute to a cognizer. It does not follow from this epistemological point, the objection continues, that the concept of belief is itself normative.[23] In replying to this objection, we can by-pass the entire issue of whether the rationality assumption concerns only the epistemology of belief attribution. Even if this premise (which I think is incorrect) is granted, the point has already been made. For it is an essential part of the business of naturalized epistemology, as a theory of how beliefs are formed as a result of sensory stimulation, to *find out* what particular beliefs the given cognizers have formed. But this is precisely what cannot be done, if our considerations show anything at all, unless the would-be naturalized epistemologist continually evaluates the putative beliefs of his subjects in regard to their rationality and coherence, subject to the overall constraint of the assumption that the cognizers are largely rational. The naturalized epistemologist cannot dispense with normative concepts or disengage himself from valuational activities.

Second, it might be thought that we could simply avoid these considerations stemming from belief attribution by refusing to think of cognitive output as consisting of "beliefs", namely as states having propositional contents. The "representations" Quine speaks of should be taken as appropriate neural states, and this means that all we need is to be able to discern neural states of organisms. This requires only neurophysiology and the like, not the normative theory of rational belief. My reply takes the form of a dilemma: either the "appropriate" neural states are identified by seeing how they correlate with beliefs,[24] in which case we still need to contend with the problem of radical interpretation, or beliefs are entirely by-passed. In the latter case, belief, along with justification, drops out of Quinean epistemology, and it is unclear in what sense we are left with an inquiry that has anything to do with knowledge.[25]

## 6  The "Psychologistic" Approach to Epistemology

Many philosophers now working in theory of knowledge have stressed the importance of systematic psychology to philosophical epistemology. Reasons proffered for this are various, and so are the conceptions of the proper relationship between psychology and epistemology.[26] But they are virtually unanimous in their rejection of what they take to be the epistemological tradition of Descartes and its modern embodiments in philosophers like Russell, C. I. Lewis, Roderick Chisholm, and A. J. Ayer; and they are united in their endorsement the naturalistic approach of Quine we have been considering. Traditional epistemology is often condemned as "aprioristic", and as having lost sight of human knowledge as a product of natural causal processes and its function in the survival of the organism and the species. Sometimes, the adherents of the traditional approach are taken to task for their implicit antiscientific bias or indifference to the new developments in psychology and related disciplines. Their own approach in contrast is hailed as "naturalistic" and "scientific", better attuned to significant advances in the relevant scientific fields such as "cognitive science" and "neuroscience", promising philosophical returns far richer than what the aprioristic method of traditional epistemology has been able to deliver. We shall here briefly consider how this new naturalism in epistemology is to be understood in relation to the classic epistemological program and Quine's naturalized epistemology.

Let us see how one articulate proponent of the new approach explains the distinctiveness of his position vis-à-vis that of the traditional epistemologists. According to Philip Kitcher, the approach he rejects is characterized by an "apsychologistic" attitude that takes the difference between knowledge and true belief – that is, justification – to consist in "ways which are independent of the causal antecedents of a subject's states".[27] Kitcher writes:[28]

> we can present the heart of [the apsychologistic approach] by considering the way in which it would tackle the question of whether a person's true belief that *p* counts as knowledge that *p*. The idea would be to disregard the psychological life of the subject, looking just at the various propositions she believes. If *p* is "connected in the right way" to other propositions which are believed, then we count the subject as knowing that *p*. Of course, apsychologisitc epistemology will have to supply a criterion for propositions to be "connected in the right way" . . . but proponents of this view of knowledge will emphasize that the criterion is to be given in *logical* terms. We are concerned with logical relations among propositions, not with psychological relations among mental states.

On the other hand, the psychologistic approach considers the crucial difference between knowledge and true belief – that is, epistemic justification – to turn on "the factors which produced the belief", focusing on "processes which produce belief, processes which will always contain, at their latter end, psychological events".[29]

It is not entirely clear from this characterization whether a psychologistic theory of justification is to be *prohibited* from making *any* reference to logical relations among belief contents (it is difficult to believe how a theory of justification respecting such a blanket prohibition could succeed); nor is it clear whether, conversely, an apsychologistic theory will be permitted to refer at all to beliefs qua psychological states, or exactly what it is for a theory to do so. But such points of detail are unimportant here; it is clear enough, for example, that

Goldman's proposal to explicate justified belief as belief generated by a reliable belief-forming process[30] nicely fits Kitcher's characterization of the psychologistic approach. This account, one form of the so-called "reliability theory" of justification, probably was what Kitcher had in mind when he was formulating his general characterization of epistemological naturalism. However, another influential form of the reliability theory does not qualify under Kitcher's characterization. This is Armstrong's proposal to explain the difference between knowledge and true belief, at least for noninferential knowledge, in terms of "a *law-like connection* between the state of affairs [of a subject's believing that *p*] and the state of affairs that makes "*p*" true such that, given the state of affairs [of the subject's believing that *p*], it must be the case that *p*."[31] There is here no reference to the causal *antecedents* of beliefs, something that Kitcher requires of apsychologistic theories.

Perhaps, Kitcher's preliminary characterization needs to be broadened and sharpened. However, a salient characteristic of the naturalistic approach has already emerged, which we can put as follows: justification is to be characterized in terms of *causal* or *nomological* connections involving beliefs as *psychological states* or *processes*, and not in terms of the *logical* properties or relations pertaining to the *contents* of these beliefs.[32]

If we understand current epistemological naturalism in this way, how closely is it related to Quine's conception of naturalized epistemology? The answer, I think, is obvious: not very closely at all. In fact, it seems a good deal closer to the Cartesian tradition than to Quine. For, as we saw, the difference that matters between Quine's epistemological program and the traditional program is the former's total renouncement of the latter's normativity, its rejection of epistemology as a normative inquiry. The talk of "replacing" epistemology with psychology is irrelevant and at best misleading, though it could give us a momentary relief from a sense of deprivation. When one abandons justification and other valuational concepts, one abandons the entire framework of normative epistemology. What remains is a descriptive empirical theory of human cognition which, if Quine has his way, will be entirely devoid of the notion of justification or any other evaluative concept.

As I take it, this is not what most advocates of epistemological naturalism are aiming at. By and large they are not Quinean eliminativists in regard to justification, and justification in its full-fledged normative sense continues to play a central role in their epistemological reflections. Where they differ from their nonnaturalist adversaries is the specific way in which criteria of justification are to be formulated. Naturalists and nonnaturalists ("apsychologists") can agree that these criteria must be stated in descriptive terms – that is, without the use of epistemic or any other kind of normative terms. According to Kitcher, an apsychologistic theory of justification would state them primarily in terms of *logical* properties and relations holding for propositional contents of beliefs, whereas the psychologistic approach advocates the exclusive use of *causal* properties and relations holding for beliefs as events or states. Many traditional epistemologists may prefer criteria that confer upon a cognizer a position of special privilege and responsibility with regard to the epistemic status of his beliefs, whereas most self-avowed naturalists prefer "objective" or "externalist" criteria with no such special privileges for the cognizer. But these differences are among those that arise within the familiar normative framework, and are consistent with the exclusion of normative terms in the statement of the criteria of justification.

Normative ethics can serve as a useful model here. To claim that basic ethical terms, like "good" and "right", are *definable* on the basic of descriptive or naturalistic terms is one thing; to insist that it is the business of normative ethics to provide *conditions* or *criteria* for "good" and "right" in descriptive or naturalistic terms is another. One may properly reject the former, the so-called "ethical naturalism", as many moral philosophers have done, and hold the latter; there is no obvious inconsistency here. G. E. Moore is a philosopher who did just that. As is well known, he was a powerful critic of ethical naturalism, holding that goodness is a "simple" and "nonnatural" property. At the same time, he held that a thing's being good "follows" from its possessing certain naturalistic properties. He wrote:[33]

> I should never have thought of suggesting that goodness was "non-natural", unless I had supposed that it was "derivative" in the sense that, whenever a thing is good (in the sense in question) its goodness ... "depends on the presence of certain non-ethical characteristics" possessed by the thing in question: I have always supposed that it did so "depend", in the sense that, if a thing is good (in my sense), then that it is so *follows* from the fact that it possesses certain natural intrinsic properties ...

It makes sense to think of these "natural intrinsic properties" from which a thing's being good is thought to follow as constituting naturalistic criteria of goodness, or at least pointing to the existence of such criteria. One can reject ethical naturalism, the doctrine that ethical concepts are definitionally eliminable in favor of naturalistic terms, and at the same time hold that ethical properties, or the ascription of ethical terms, must be governed by naturalistic criteria. It is clear, then, that we are here using "naturalism" ambiguously in "epistemological naturalism" and "ethical naturalism". In our present usage, epistemological naturalism does not include (nor does it necessarily exclude) the claim that epistemic terms are definitionally reducible to naturalistic terms. (Quine's naturalism is eliminative, though it is not a definitional eliminativism.)

If, therefore, we locate the split between Quine and traditional epistemology at the descriptive vs. normative divide, then currently influential naturalism in epistemology is not likely to fall on Quine's side. On this descriptive vs. normative issue, one can side with Quine in one of two ways: first, one rejects, with Quine, the entire justification-based epistemological program; or second, like ethical naturalists but unlike Quine, one believes that epistemic concepts are naturalistically definable. I doubt that very many epistemological naturalists will embrace either of these alternatives.[34]

## 7 Epistemic Supervenience – Or Why Normative Epistemology Is Possible

But why should we think that there *must be* naturalistic criteria of justified belief and other terms of epistemic appraisal? If we take the discovery and systematization of such criteria to be the central task of normative epistemology, is there any reason to think that this task can be fruitfully pursued, that normative epistemology is a possible field of inquiry? Quine's point is that it is not. We have already noted the limitation of Quine's negative arguments in "Epistemology Naturalized", but is there a positive reason for thinking that normative epistemology is a viable program? One could consider a similar question about the possibility of normative ethics.

I think there is a short and plausible initial answer, although a detailed defense of it would involve complex general issues about norms and values. The short answer is this: we believe in the supervenience of epistemic properties on naturalistic ones, and more generally, in the supervenience of all valuational and normative properties on naturalistic conditions. This comes out in various ways. We think, with R. M. Hare,[35] that if two persons or acts coincide in all descriptive or naturalistic details, they cannot differ in respect of being good or right, or any other valuational aspects. We also think that if something is "good" – a "good car", "good drop shot", "good argument" – then that must be so "in virtue of" its being a "certain way", that is, its having certain "factual properties". Being a good car, say, cannot be a brute and ultimate fact: a car is good *because* it has a certain contextually indicated set of properties having to do with performance, reliability, comfort, styling, economy, etc. The same goes for justified belief: if a belief is justified, that must be so *because* it has certain factual, nonepistemic properties, such as perhaps that it is "indubitable", that it is seen to be entailed by another belief that is independently justified, that it is appropriately caused by perceptual experience, or whatever. That it is a justified belief cannot be a brute fundamental fact unrelated to the kind of belief it is. There must be a *reason* for it, and this reason must be grounded in the factual descriptive properties of that particular belief. Something like this, I think, is what we believe.

Two important themes underlie these convictions: first, values, though perhaps not reducible to facts, must be "consistent" with them in that objects that are indiscernible in regard to fact must be indiscernible in regard to value; second, there must be nonvaluational "reasons" or "grounds" for the attribution of values, and these "reasons" or "grounds" must be *generalizable* – that is, they are covered by *rules* or *norms*. These two ideas correspond to "weak supervenience" and "strong supervenience" that I have discussed elsewhere.[36] Belief in the supervenience of value upon fact, arguably, is fundamental to the very concepts of value and valuation.[37] Any valuational concept, to be significant, must be governed by a set of criteria, and these criteria must ultimately rest on factual characteristics and relationships of objects and events being evaluated. There is something deeply incoherent about the idea of an infinitely descending series of valuational concepts, each depending on the one below it as its criterion of application.[38]

It seems to me, therefore, that epistemological supervenience is what underlies our belief in the possibility of normative epistemology, and that we do not need new inspirations from the sciences to acknowledge the existence of naturalistic criteria for epistemic and other valuational concepts. The case of normative ethics is entirely parallel: belief in the possibility of normative ethics is rooted in the belief that moral properties and relations are supervenient upon nonmoral ones. Unless we are prepared to disown normative ethics as a viable philosophical inquiry, we had better recognize normative epistemology as one, too.[39] We should note, too, that epistemology is likely to parallel normative ethics in regard to the degree to which scientific results are relevant or useful to its development.[40] Saying this of course leaves large room for disagreement concerning how relevant and useful, if at all, empirical psychology of human motivation and action can be to the development and confirmation of normative ethical theories.[41] In any event, once the normativity of epistemology is clearly taken note of, it is no surprise that epistemology and normative ethics share the same metaphilosophical fate. Naturalized epistemology makes no more, and no less, sense than naturalized normative ethics.

## Notes

An early version of this paper was read at a meeting of the Korean Society for Analytic Philosophy in 1984 in Seoul. An expanded version was presented at a symposium at the Western Division meetings of the American Philosophical Association in April, 1985, and at the epistemology conference at Brown University in honor of Roderick Chisholm in 1986. I am grateful to Richard Foley and Robert Audi who presented helpful comments at the APA session and the Chisholm Conference respectively. I am also indebted to Terence Horgan and Robert Meyers for helpful comments and suggestions.

1  In making these remarks I am only repeating the familiar textbook history of philosophy; however, what *our* textbooks say about the history of a philosophical concept has much to do with *our* understanding of that concept.

2  Alvin Goldman explicitly states this requirement as a desideratum of his own analysis of justified belief in "What is Justified Belief?", in George S. Pappas (ed.), *Justification and Knowledge* (Dordrecht: Reidel, 1979), p. 1. Roderick M. Chisholm's definition of "being evident" in his *Theory of Knowledge*, 2nd ed. (Englewood Cliffs, N. J.: Prentice-Hall, 1977) does not satisfy this requirement as it rests ultimately on an unanalyzed epistemic concept of one belief being *more reasonable than* another. What does the real "criteriological" work for Chisholm is his "principles of evidence". See especially (A) on p. 73 of *Theory of Knowledge*, which can usefully be regarded as an attempt to provide nonnormative, descriptive conditions for certain types of justified beliefs.

3  The basic idea of this stronger requirement seems implicit in Roderick Firth's notion of "warrant-increasing property" in his "Coherence, Certainty, and Epistemic Priority", *Journal of Philosophy* 61 (1964): 545–57. It seems that William P. Alston has something similar in mind when he says, ". . . like any evaluative property, epistemic justification is a supervenient property, the application of which is based

on more fundamental properties" (at this point Alston refers to Firth's paper cited above), in "Two Types of Foundationalism", *Journal of Philosophy* 73 (1976): 165–85 (the quoted remark occurs on p. 170). Although Alston doesn't further explain what he means by "more fundamental properties", the context makes it plausible to suppose that he has in mind nonnormative, descriptive properties. See Section 7 below for further discussion.

4   See Chisholm, ibid., p. 14. Here Chisholm refers to a "person's responsibility or duty *qua* intellectual being".

5   This term was used by A. J. Ayer to characterize the difference between lucky guessing and knowing; see *The Problem of Knowledge* (New York & London: Penguin Books, 1956), p. 33.

6   Notably by Chisholm in *Theory of Knowledge*, 1st ed., ch. 4.

7   See Rudolf Carnap, "Testability and Meaning", *Philosophy of Science* 3 (1936), and 4 (1937). We should also note the presence of a strong coherentist streak among some positivists; see, e.g., Carl G. Hempel, "On the Logical Positivists' Theory of Truth", *Analysis* 2 (1935): 49–59, and "Some Remarks on 'Facts' and Propositions", *Analysis* 2 (1935): 93–6.

8   In W. V. O. Quine, *Ontological Relativity and Other Essays* (New York: Columbia University Press, 1969). Also see his *Word and Object* (Cambridge. MIT Press, 1960); *The Roots of Reference* (La Salle, III.: Open Court, 1973); (with Joseph Ullian) *The Web of Belief* (New York: Random House, 1970); and especially "The Nature of Natural Knowledge" in Samuel Guttenplan (ed.), *Mind and Language* (Oxford: Clarendon Press, 1975). See Frederick F. Schmitt's excellent bibliography on naturalistic epistemology in Hilary Kornblith (ed.), *Naturalizing Epistemology* (Cambridge: MIT/Bradford, 1985).

9   Or confirmational relations, given the Positivists' verificationist theory of meaning.

10   I know of no serious defense of it since Ayer's *The Foundations of Empirical Knowledge* (London: Macmillan, 1940).

11   "Epistemology Naturalized", pp. 75–6.

12   Ibid., p. 78.

13   To use an expression of Richard Rorty's in *Philosophy and the Mirror of Nature* (Princeton: Princeton University Press, 1979), p. 11.

14   Elliott Sober makes a similar point: "And on the question of whether the failure of a foundationalist programme shows that questions of justification cannot be answered, it is worth noting that Quine's advice "Since Carnap's foundationalism failed, why not settle for psychology" carries weight only to the degree that Carnapian epistemology exhausts the possibilities of epistemology", in "Psychologism", *Journal of Theory of Social Behaviour* 8 (1978): 165–91.

15   See Chisholm, *Theory of Knowledge*, 2nd ed., ch. 4.

16   "If we are seeking only the causal mechanism of our knowledge of the external world, and not a justification of that knowledge in terms prior to science . . .", Quine, "Grades of Theoreticity", in L. Foster and J. W. Swanson (eds.), *Experience and Theory* (Amherst: University of Massachusetts Press, 1970), p. 2.

17   Ibid., p. 75. Emphasis added.

18   Ibid., p. 78. Emphasis added.

19   Ibid., p. 83. Emphasis added.

20   But aren't there those who advocate a "causal theory" of evidence or justification? I want to make two brief points about this. First, the nomological or causal input/output relations are not in themselves evidential relations, whether these latter are understood causally or otherwise. Second, a causal theory of evidence attempts to

state *criteria* for "e is evidence for h" in causal terms; even if this is successful, it does not necessarily give us a causal "definition" or "reduction" of the concept of evidence. For more details see section 6 below.

21  I am not saying that Quine is under any illusion on this point. My remarks are directed rather at those who endorse Quine without, it seems, a clear appreciation of what is involved.

22  Here I am drawing chiefly on Donald Davidson's writings on radical interpretation. See Essays 9, 10, and 11 in his *Inquiries into Truth and Interpretation* (Oxford: Clarendon Press, 1984). See also David Lewis, "Radical Interpretation", *Synthese* 27 (1974): 331–44.

23  Robert Audi suggested this as a possible objection.

24  For some considerations tending to show that these correlations cannot be lawlike see my "Psychophysical Laws", in Ernest LePore and Brian McLaughlin (eds.), *Actions and Events: Perspectives on the Philosophy of Donald Davidson* (Oxford: Blackwell, 1985).

25  For a more sympathetic account of Quine than mine, see Hilary Kornblith's introductory essay, "What is Naturalistic Epistemology?", in Kornblith (ed.), *Naturalizing Epistemology.*

26  See for more details Alvin I. Goldman, *Epistemology and Cognition* (Cambridge: Harvard University Press, 1986).

27  *The Nature of Mathematical Knowledge* (New York: Oxford University Press, 1983), p. 14.

28  Ibid.

29  Ibid., p. 13. I should note that Kitcher considers the apsychologistic approach to be an aberration of the twentieth century epistemology, as represented by philosophers like Russell, Moore, C. I. Lewis, and Chisholm, rather than an historical characteristic of the Cartesian tradition. In "The Psychological Turn", *Australasian Journal of Philosophy* 60 (1982): 238–53, Hilary Kornblith gives an analogous characterization of the two approaches to justification; he associates "justification-conferring processes" with the psychologistic approach and "epistemic rules" with the apsychologistic approach.

30  See Goldman, "What is Justified Belief?"

31  David M. Armstrong, *Truth, Belief and Knowledge* (London: Cambridge University Press, 1973), p. 166.

32  The aptness of this characterization of the "apsychologistic" approach for philosophers like Russell, Chisholm, Keith Lehrer, John Pollock, etc. can be debated. Also, there is the issue of "internalism" vs. "externalism" concerning justification, which I believe must be distinguished from the psychologistic vs. apsychologistic division.

33  Moore, "A Reply to My Critics", in P. A. Schilpp (ed.), *The Philosophy of G. E. Moore* (Chicago & Evanston: Open Court, 1942), p. 588.

34  Richard Rorty's claim, which plays a prominent role in his arguments against traditional epistemology in *Philosophy and the Mirror of Nature*, that Locke and other modern epistemologists conflated the normative concept of justification with causal-mechanical concepts is itself based, I believe, on a conflation of just the kind I am describing here. See Rorty, ibid., pp. 139ff. Again, the critical conflation consists in not seeing that the view, which I believe is correct, that epistemic justification, like any other normative concept, must have factual, naturalistic criteria, is entirely consistent with the rejection of the doctrine, which I think is incorrect, that justification itself *is*, or is *reducible* to, a naturalistic-nonnormative concept.

35   *The Language of Morals* (London: Oxford University Press, 1952), p. 145.
36   See "Concepts of Supervenience", *Philosophy and Phenomenological Research* 65 (1984): 153–76.
37   Ernest Sosa, too, considers epistemological supervenience as a special case of the supervenience of valuational properties on naturalistic conditions, in "The Foundation of Foundationalism", *Nous* 14 (1980): 547–64; especially p. 551. See also James Van Cleve's instructive discussion in his "Epistemic Supervenience and the Circle of Belief", The *Monist* 68 (1985): 90–104; especially, pp. 97–9.
38   Perhaps one could avoid this kind of criteriological regress by embracing directly apprehended valuational properties (as in ethical intuitionism) on the basis of which criteria for other valuational properties could be formulated. The denial of the supervenience of valuational concepts on factual characteristics, however, would sever the essential connection between value and fact on which, it seems, the whole point of our valuational activities depends. In the absence of such supervenience, the very notion of valuation would lose its significance and relevance. The elaboration of these points, however, would have to wait for another occasion; but see Van Cleve's paper cited in the preceding note for more details.
39   Quine will not disagree with this: he will "naturalize" them both. For his views on values see "The Nature of Moral Values" in Alvin I. Goldman and Jaegwon Kim (eds.), *Values and Morals* (Dordrecht: Reidel, 1978). For a discussion of the relationship between epistemic and ethical concepts see Roderick Firth, "Are Epistemic Concepts Reducible to Ethical Concepts?" in the same volume.
40   For discussions of this and related issues see Goldman, *Epistemology and Cognition*.
41   For a detailed development of a normative ethical theory that exemplifies the view that it is crucially relevant, see Richard B. Brandt, *A Theory of the Good and the Right* (Oxford: The Clarendon Press, 1979).

**Further Reading**

Alston, William P., "Two Types of Foundationalism" *Journal of Philosophy* 73 (1976): 165–85.

Armstrong, David M., *Truth, Belief and Knowledge* (London: Cambridge University Press, 1973).

Ayer, A. J., *The Foundations of Empirical Knowledge* (London: Macmillan, 1940).

Ayer, A. J., *The Problem of Knowledge* (New York & London: Penguin Books, 1956).

Brandt, Richard B., *A Theory of the Good and the Right* (Oxford: The Clarendon Press, 1979).

Carnap, Rudolf, "Testability and Meaning", *Philosophy of Science* 3 (1936), and 4 (1937).

Chisholm, Roderick M., *Theory of Knowledge*, 2nd ed. (Englewood Cliffs, N. J.: Prentice-Hall, 1977).

Davidson, Donald, *Inquiries into Truth and Interpretation* (Oxford: Clarendon Press, 1984).

Firth, Roderick, "Coherehce, Certainty, and Epistemic Priority", *Journal of Philosophy* 61 (1964): 545–57.

Firth, Roderick, "Are Epistemic Concepts Reducible to Ethical Concepts?" in Goldman, Alvin I. and Jaegwon Kim (eds.), *Values and Morals* (Dordrecht: Reidel, 1978).

Goldman, Alvin I., "What is Justified Belief?", In George S. Pappas (ed.), *Justification and Knowledge* (Dordrecht: Reldel, 1979).

Goldman, Alvin I., *Epistemology and Cognition* (Cambridge: Harvard University Press, 1986).

Hare, R. M., *The Language of Morals* (London: Oxford University Press, 1952).

Hempel, Carl G., "On the Logical Positivists' Theory of Truth", *Analysis* 2 (1935): 49–59.

Hempel, Carl G., "Some Remarks on 'Facts' and Propositions", *Analysis* 2 (1935): 93–96.

Kim, Jaegwon, "Concepts of Supervenience", *Philosophy and Phenomenological Research* 65 (1984): 153–76.

Kim, Jaegwon, "Psychophysical Laws", In Ernest LePore and Brian McLaughlin (eds.), *Actions and Events: Perspecties on the Philosophy of Donald Davidson* (Oxford: Blackwell, 1985).

Kitcher, Phillip, *The Nature of Mathematical Knowledge* (New York: Oxford University Press, 1983).

Kornblith, Hilary, "The Psychological Turn", *Australasian Journal of Philosophy* 60 (1982): 238–53.

Kornblith, Hilary, (ed.), *Naturalizing Epistemology* (Cambridge: MIT/Bradford, 1985).

Kornblith, Hilary, "What is Naturalistic Epistemology?", In Kornblith (ed.), *Naturalizing Epistemology*.

Lewis, David, "Radical Interpretation", *Synthese* 27 (1974): 331–44.

Moore, G. E., "A Reply to My Critics", in P. A. Schilpp (ed.), *The Philosophy of G. E. Moore* (Chicago & Evanston: Open Court, 1942).

Quine, W. V. O., *Word and Object* (Cambridge: MIT Press, 1960).

Quine, W. V. O., *Ontological Relativity and Other Essays* (New York: Columbia University Press, 1969).

Quine, W. V. O., (with Joseph Ullian), *The Web of Belief* (New York: Random House, 1970).

Quine, W. V. O., "Grades of Theoreticity", in L. Foster and J. W. Swanson (eds.), *Experience and Theory* (Amherst: University of Massachusetts Press, 1970).

Quine, W. V. O., *The Roots of Reference* (La Salle, IL,: Open Court, 1973); Quine, W. V. O., "The Nature of Natural Knowledge" in Samuel Guttenplan (ed.), *Mind and Language* (Oxford: Clarendon Press, 1975).

Quine, W. V. O., "The Nature of Moral Values" in Alvin I. Goldman and Jaegwon Kim (eds.), *Values and Morals* (Dordrecht: Reidel, 1978).

Rorty, Richard, *Philosophy and the Mirror of Nature* (Princeton: Princeton University Press, 1979).

Sober, Elliott, "Psychologism", *Journal of Theory of Social Behavior* 8 (1978): 165–91.

Sosa, Ernest, "The Foundation of Foundationalism", *Nous* 14 (1980): 547–64.

Van Cleve, James, "Epistemic Supervenience and the Circle of Belief", *The Monist* 68 (1985)" 90–104.

# 17 Putting Naturalized Epistemology to Work

*Phyllis Rooney*

## I Stranded between Descriptions and Prescriptions

This paper has emerged in significant part out of a peculiar kind of identity crisis. I was on a plane on my way to a conference to present a paper about philosophical reflections on cognition. Most of my references in this paper noted work by psychologists which had appeared in journals and books under the publishing rubric of psychology, and I had conversed with some psychologists in the process of working on the paper. Anticipating various questions that might be raised in the discussion, I was baffled by one such possible question: whether or not I would identify myself as a naturalist epistemologist. Initially it surely seemed that I should so identify myself, since I was exemplifying naturalized epistemology according to some basic understanding of that – I was referring to specific findings in psychology in my philosophical reflections on cognition. This seems to accord with James Maffie's initial characterization of "naturalists" in epistemology as "united by a shared commitment to the continuity of epistemology and science . . . [even though] they differ among themselves over what form this continuity should take" (1990: 281).

However, this characterization coupled with my predicament opened up a revealing discrepancy. Naturalist epistemologists are *committed* to a particular way of doing epistemology without in many cases actually doing it. An examination of most papers on naturalized epistemology reveals bibliographies with references mainly or exclusively to other philosophers published in philosophy journals and anthologies. In effect, these epistemologists are agreed that one *ought* to do epistemology in a certain way even if they are *not actually* doing it. I, on the other hand, was actually doing naturalized epistemology according to some minimal description of it, yet I was not sure I ought to be doing it in the way naturalist epistemologists construct that "ought," and to which, I surmised, I would need to subscribe in order to identify myself clearly as a naturalist epistemologist.

Much of the debate in naturalized epistemology has centered on the significance of descriptive accounts of knowing and knowledge production in what has traditionally been seen as purely or largely a normative philosophical endeavor concerned with norms of reasoning and justification. One of my main goals in this paper is to argue that this other descriptive/prescriptive distinction (between what epistemologists actually do and what they say epistemologists ought to do) also belongs centrally in the naturalized epistemology discussion; that the general debate about what naturalized epistemology is, how it ought to proceed, and whether we epistemologists ought to endorse it, cannot be undertaken at some distance from actual engagement with ongoing projects in science. My argument is thus not directed to work *in* naturalized epistemology like, for example, Miriam Solomon's discussion of scientific rationality (1992), which draws upon studies on the psychology of belief change and applies them to a particular episode in geology – the development and reception of continental drift theory, or Stephen Stich's work (1990), in which he seriously engages empirical studies about strategies in human reasoning in his philosophical reflections on rationality. My argument is directed to a substantial portion of the work that has generally fallen under the rubric "naturalized epistemology," which includes debates *about* naturalized epistemology among theorists with a range of views, from those who argue for a central role for science in epistemology to many of those, even, who argue against naturalized epistemology. Much of this work concerns itself with settling matters about epistemology, science, and especially the relationship between them, in what I shall maintain is a decidedly *non-naturalistic* way that significantly defeats the purpose of the whole endeavor at least to entertain seriously the possibility of a robust role for science in epistemology.

My argument also draws on a distinction between what I call a *verb-sense* and a *noun-sense* of epistemology. I am not presenting these as entirely distinct or oppositional ways of doing epistemology, but they represent a telling difference in emphasis and method that is especially borne out in naturalized epistemology. A noun-sense of epistemology is the one that has been more prominent in what is often identified as traditional epistemology. This approach to epistemology subscribes largely to the goal of arriving at a specific fixed theory of knowledge: specific claims about the nature and limits of knowledge, or about the structure of rational beliefs (where one might claim to have a foundationalist or a coherentist epistemology, for instance) normally stand as the focal points for discussion. For example, the claim that indeed there is knowledge that survives the skeptic, or the claim that knowledge is justified true belief (or alternatively that it is definitely not) are among the most visible traditional examples of such focal points of debate in epistemology. Such a noun-sense of epistemology typically projects (in a philosophical future, if not a historical one) *"final"* definitions, distinctions, claims, and theories about knowledge as the primary or only goal of epistemology, and, at any given time, normally subscribes to a reasonably well-defined set of philosophical methods with which to engage its central claims.

With a verb-sense of epistemology, on the other hand, we get more a sense of *doing* epistemology, of reflecting in a systematic way on knowledge and knowing while drawing ongoing critical attention to particular kinds of motivating concerns, questions, and methods in the way we do epistemology. A significant part of pragmatist epistemology, for example, which approaches both knowledge and epistemology as dynamic activities rather than as fixed givens falls more clearly within this verb-sense of epistemology. Many of the significant developments in feminist epistemology can be understood as subscribing more to this verb-sense of epistemology, as I argue elsewhere.[1] While not eschewing many of the traditional concerns with establishing specific claims about reason, certainty, and justification, an epistemologist with this approach also draws ongoing reflexive critical attention to the motivations and assumptions underlying these specific questions and projects in epistemology. One of my main aims in this paper is to argue that, even granting the diversity of views about *naturalizing* epistemology, theorists in this area still largely subscribe to a noun-sense of epistemology (which – for additional reasons that will be more apparent later – I will also refer to as *final*-philosophizing), and that they do so in a way that is fundamentally at odds with what I maintain are some of the significant impulses underlying the whole effort to naturalize epistemology. As I plan to show, a verb-sense of naturalized epistemology would foreground actual ongoing engagement with science and would not indulge its ought claims: that is, its claims about what epistemologists ought to do, at some theoretical distance from such engagement. In effect, what I am arguing is that naturalist epistemologists, who at least maintain that epistemologists should pay attention to descriptive (scientific) accounts of how people actually reason, cannot seriously promote this endeavor without carrying a similar prescription to the meta-level, that is, they cannot continue to speculate about what naturalized epistemology ought to be and what naturalist epistemologists ought to do independently of actual epistemological engagements with actual science.

In the following section of my paper I shall expand further on what I think is problematic – from a naturalist perspective – in much of the discussion about naturalized epistemology. In section III, I shall turn my attention to a specific area of ongoing research, which, I argue, provides an especially interesting case study highlighting many of the problems addressed in II. Scientific work on cognition and gender draws particular attention to the kinds of issues that are involved when cognitive scientists themselves incorporate critical reflection about their methodology into their discussion: this contrasts in an interesting way with the projections of ideal agreement concerning scientific findings that (as I argue in section II) naturalist epistemologists regularly appeal to. In this particular area of scientific research we are also encouraged to reflect on the division of the various cognitive sciences into the "individual" ones (cognitive psychology, neurophysiology, artificial intelligence, linguistics, and perhaps evolutionary biology) and the more "social" ones (sociology, social psychology, anthropology, communication studies, sociolinguistics, and history), and to reflect too on the uncritical endorsement of such a division that naturalist epistemologists often accept. In sections III and IV, I shall examine some of the implications for naturalized epistemology that I think result from a more critical appraisal of this "individual versus social" division. I will maintain that the issues raised here apply no less to naturalized epistemology projects that purport to take serious account of the social situatedness of knowers and knowledge and what the social-cognitive sciences tell us about such social epistemics.

I am using the term "naturalist epistemologist" to refer to those epistemologists who at least advocate naturalized epistemology even if they are not actually doing it – not even according to their own characterization of naturalized epistemology. Thus, like those it is attempting to pick out, this term is also stranded somewhere between a prescription and a description.

## II Non-naturalistic Dimensions of Naturalized Epistemology

I suggested above that we seek to identify more precisely what naturalized epistemology is, by asking *who* is identified or projected as *actually doing* naturalized epistemology and not just advocating it. Barry Stroud sees naturalized epistemology as "the scientific study of perception, learning, thought, language-acquisition, and the transmission and historical development of human knowledge – everything we can find out scientifically about how we come to know what we know" (1985: 71). This, however, picks out scientists as those engaged in naturalized epistemology, not philosophers who are not scientists which includes the vast majority of philosophers. In fact, this stipulation accords with Quine's original well-known assertion about naturalized epistemology – generally now known as the *eliminativist* position – that "epistemology, or something like it, simply falls into place as a chapter of psychology and hence of natural science" (1969:82). Yet, this presumably excludes Quine himself as one who does naturalized epistemology, as it also excluded me with my paper on the plane since I have never been in a psychology laboratory.

But perhaps this seems like quibbling. The findings of the cognitive sciences are just that, one might argue, whether apprehended by the scientists producing them, or by philosophers attending carefully to the scientists' reports and incorporating them into epistemological endeavors which, for non-eliminativist naturalists, still retain something of the a priori-normative. However, apart from the nontrivial reminder that the "findings" of the sciences are not necessarily unambiguously self-announcing – that is, beyond different scientific and philosophical interpretations and appropriations – other critical questions can be raised at this point. Of the potentially innumerable findings produced by all of the various cognitive sciences, how do we select those that we are to find epistemically significant to an epistemology that is to be a part of, or closely allied with, science? What exactly are we to do with these findings once we get them? What I am pressing here are questions that I think are in an important sense *prior to*, or at least fundamentally bound up with, questions about the justification of these scientific findings and whether or not there could be a non-circular justification of naturalized epistemology – these latter questions have garnered significant attention in the naturalized epistemology discussion that arose subsequent to Quine's original paper (Almeder, 1990; Amundson, 1983; Kornblith, 1985, 1994; Maffie, 1990; Quine, 1981; Stroud, 1985). When we pursue these kinds of "prior" questions we are led to a re-examination of fundamental assumptions about epistemology, science, and scientific findings that make it difficult, I shall argue, clearly to demarcate naturalized epistemology, much less naturalist epistemologists. We need to be on the lookout, especially for assumptions at work in the naturalized epistemology discussion (linked, I shall suggest, to a noun-sense of "final" philosophizing) that are somewhat at odds with what we might reasonably argue are significant impulses motivating the whole project to naturalize epistemology, assumptions that might thus be termed "non-naturalistic."

Hilary Kornblith stipulates that "the naturalistic approach to epistemology [consists] in this: question 1 [how ought we to arrive at our beliefs?] cannot be answered independently of question 2 [how do we arrive at our beliefs?] . . . descriptive questions about belief acquisition have an important bearing on normative questions about belief acquisition" (1994: 3 [1]). Kornblith then proceeds to discuss the "different camps within the naturalistic approach" which includes different views on "how direct a bearing psychology has on epistemology." His move here reflects a fairly common assumption among naturalist epistemologists that psychology (or cognitive science more generally) gives an accurate representation of how "we" (presumably regular folk engaged in our regular activities) actually arrive at our beliefs. Allied with this is the additional assumption that scientific descriptions of cognition form (or will form) a relatively coherent uniform account converging on, or reducible to, psychology or neuroscience (or perhaps a new favorite) as *the central* cognitive science. I also want to draw attention to a third assumption that emerges out of Kornblith's articulation: that knowledge and knowing, and hence epistemology, are paradigmatically about having and acquiring beliefs, and, specifically, beliefs held by individuals. Many might counter my suggestion here that this also needs to be argued by saying that this is set simply by our definition or general understanding of "knowledge" and "epistemology." However, such a (philosophical) definition is problematic for a naturalist, since it sets a prior constraint on what will be counted as epistemologically relevant information about knowing and knowledge drawn from the sciences. This is, in effect, a stipulation that simply begs the question against more robust forms of naturalized epistemology.

Additional assumptions emerge when we note that a significant part of the discussion in naturalized epistemology draws attention primarily or exclusively to scientific knowledge and what scientists themselves do in their epistemic practices in science (in cognitive and non-cognitive sciences), which is not necessarily the same as what "we" do in our non-scientific endeavors, or what cognitive science says "we" do. As was clearly present in Quine's formulation of naturalized epistemology also, there is the assumption here that scientific knowledge is the paradigm example of knowledge. This is partly – and I think not unreasonably – based on the view that scientific knowledge is more systematic, regulated, and documented, and thus it more readily lends itself to naturalistic scientific study. Yet, the privileging of scientific knowledge also regularly presumes that scientific knowledge is like knowledge generally, only better, in fact, the best we have, and thus it merits the status of paradigmatic knowledge. Thus, even though these discussions about scientific knowledge now comprise a distinct set of questions in *naturalized philosophy of science* (which might be understood as a sub-area of naturalized epistemology) there are unargued assumptions in the regular conflation of the two projects.

If we draw attention specifically to naturalized philosophy of science, concerns similar to those mentioned above emerge. Scientific knowledge is often portrayed as having some kind of uniformity and generality in its methods and epistemic practices, within a given science and even across different sciences, and, again, that cognitive science can or will present us with an accurate and uniform description of scientific knowledge and knowing. When we reflect on the use of cognitive science in the epistemological study of the methods and practices of science, we might note, as Ron Giere does, that there are at least "three disciplinary clusters" that naturalist philosophers of science appeal to: "(1) artificial intelligence (itself a branch of computer science), (2) cognitive psychology, and (3) cognitive neuroscience" (Giere 1992: xvi). However, Giere also notes that some question the emphasis resting solely on these three clusters by claiming that, as he articulates it, "the cognitive activities of scientists are embedded in a social fabric whose contribution to the course of scientific development may be as great as that of the cognitive interactions between scientists and the natural world" (xxv–xxvi). Thus, many argue, fields like sociology and social psychology also need to be included among the "cognitive" sciences that naturalist philosophers of science appeal to.[2]

In summary (and placing aside for now the much debated question about *what* naturalist epistemologists are to do with actual knowing and actual science), there are at least four things that naturalist epistemologists (variously) are claiming we epistemologists should take into account as a necessary part of our philosophical theorizing about knowledge: (i) what and how "we" actually know (and specifically acquire and justify beliefs); (ii) what cognitive science tells us about how we know; (iii) scientific knowledge and knowing; and (iv) what cognitive/social science tells us about scientific knowledge and knowing. We need to be more aware of the background assumptions about knowledge, epistemology, and science that are at work when various combinations of these – sometimes all four – are collapsed together. In addition, the promotion of each of these involves additional assumptions: (i) – and often (iii) also – assumes that knowledge is paradigmatically about beliefs held by individuals, and that general universal claims can be made or ought to be made about individual knowing or scientific knowledge (or that nothing else belongs to epistemology proper); (ii) and (iv) typically presuppose that the cognitive sciences (or even a specific cognitive science) presents or will eventually present a coherent uniform description of individual knowing and scientific knowledge.

I maintain that these kinds of assumptions, regularly deployed in philosophical arguments *about* naturalized epistemology, and especially by those normatively advocating it, are non-naturalistic in that they rest largely on understandings of epistemology and science that are problematic, not because they pay too much attention to science, but because they pay too little. The view that knowledge and epistemology are ideally concerned with beliefs held by individuals cannot readily accommodate naturalistic epistemological projects like those by Lynn Hankinson Nelson (1990, 1993), who examines particular episodes in science to argue that we gain a better understanding of important epistemological dimensions of science by taking communities rather than individuals as the locus of scientific knowledge. In the next section I shall argue that we may also be unnecessarily limiting our understanding of our "individual" epistemic realities with a particular focus on beliefs that are understood to be clearly distinguishable from other cognitive affects and attitudes, or, even if there are such beliefs, that they are the only ones worthy of epistemological analysis. (There are surely important dimensions of our epistemic realities that are more complex, and indeed more realistic and natural, than those envisaged by standard epistemological examples of putative propositional knowledge like "John Doe knows that the cat is on the mat," or "Smith believes that Jones owns a Ford.") In addition, even if there were naturalistic agreement about the distinguishing markers of beliefs, we cannot assume that science will present us with a uniform coherent general account of the development of beliefs. Many of these assumptions which naturalist epistemologists project onto science have a distinct ring of the kinds of a priori theorizing that naturalist epistemologists at least claim to subject to critique.

The work to date in naturalized *philosophy of science* tends to draw on a closer engagement with science than work in naturalized epistemology has done. This is largely due to the move in the last few decades to incorporate sociological and historical studies of science into the philosophy of science. Yet, even here, one still finds projections of science that rely more on pre-naturalist ideals of science than they do on actual studies of the diversity of epistemic practices and methods and subject areas in science – a diversity that does not, and need not, promise eventual convergence and uniformity. Science is nothing if not open-ended: it is not just the future that is open-ended, but so also is natural human ingenuity and creativity and human difference, not to mention the new empirical investigations and indeed new scientific disciplines that open-ended technological developments enable. Indeed, it could be argued that the dynamic development of science *requires* such open-endedness, and also *requires* the conflicting claims and theories (marking the push toward further investigation) that regularly circulate in particular areas of science.

The question then for naturalists is how to engage *now* with this real (often "messy") science, cognitive or otherwise. At the very least, I maintain, naturalists must have a verb-sense of naturalized epistemology that is more responsive to such a verb-sense of science – that is, science as a diversity of dynamic disciplines the concepts, questions, and findings of which are continually being modified in relation to changing conditions, including the changing conditions of empirical investigation and the changing social and political worlds within which such investigation is situated. Naturalist epistemologists must, in effect, bring a more critical and reflexive understanding of the assumptions and questions *they* bring to science, and a better understanding of the way in which some of the "prior" questions and expectations of the epistemological tradition might be ill-adapted to the very fields of science from which they now seek input. As argued above, we tend to get, instead, debates about naturalized epistemology that are framed largely by static "final" conceptions (or projected conceptions) of belief, knowledge, science, and epistemology that are characteristic of a noun-sense of epistemology. This is evident, perhaps most prominently, in the signature debate about what precise form(s) of continuity and connection between epistemology and science we can or ought to seek. Such debates have the sense of seeking now to settle where naturalized epistemology's final resting place will be in relation to science, given that epistemology has been unsettled (for naturalists at least) from its former pre-naturalist resting place: epistemology's projected location is still marked by final questions and claims – prominently still about the justification of beliefs – to which science will contribute its apportioned part of the final answers.

In pushing a verb-sense of naturalized epistemology I am not suggesting that epistemologists cannot start out with definite questions and projects – epistemology like any other inquiry cannot get started without some questions. Instead of claims and questions that seem to have arisen in a vacuum (or in the "epistemology" wing of a Platonic heaven, or even "in our tradition," which can be just as diffuse), I suggest we start with questions that are better identified and situated in terms of their traditional provenance (or lack of it) and their inherent assumptions. For example, the question "what is knowledge?" is meaningful if we understand knowledge to be the kind of thing that is expected to yield a certain kind of philosophical definition, or, among eliminativist naturalists, a philosophy-replacing scientific one. The question, "what does science tell us about how beliefs are formed?," simply invites further questions about why one would assume that scientists agree on the defining characteristics of belief, and even that if they did, they (in their many cognitive sciences or even within a specific cognitive science) can be expected to arrive at some consensus about their formation. Such questions are surely more properly directed to the tradition of epistemology than they are to science. I am not claiming that *epistemological* questions (however one might define such) cannot be brought to science or that they do not emerge from science, but that at least they must be better identified in terms of their normative and descriptive genealogies, and they must be more clearly directed to actual science (here and now) in its rich diversity of disciplinary and subdisciplinary projects – with full awareness of the often conflicting accounts of findings (and theoretical implications of findings) that are regularly in circulation among scientists themselves in specific areas of scientific research. We may well arrive at specific "final" claims and answers as a result of such questions and such engagement, but they too will be as situated as those questions and the particular forms of engagement with science that they elicit. I fail to see that such answers cannot be of interest to us as epistemologists, even if they are not the kinds of final answers we may have long dreamed about.

Despite differences among naturalists, it is regularly understood that they are at least in agreement on a certain minimal characterization of naturalized epistemology: that it is no longer "first philosophy," that it is not "transcendental" or "traditional" epistemology, that is, that it is no longer developing a priori norms of reasoning and justification independently of naturalistic attention to cognition and knowledge in action. This, it might be argued, is not a characterization endorsing "final" philosophizing. However, it has been argued that even such a characterization as this is problematic since it rests on unfair and perhaps overly simplistic views of "traditional" epistemology. Harvey Siegel has recently argued, for example, that the rejection of traditional epistemology – as forwarded by Quine and Gibson, in particular – rests on a straw version of traditional epistemology, and thus that it is unclear what the dispute between it and naturalized epistemology really is (Siegel, 1995: 49). If this dispute is somewhat murky then so is any characterization of naturalized philosophy that relies on it. What I have been arguing is that a much more useful characterization of naturalized epistemology, one that sincerely promotes an alliance with science, should be framed, instead, as a rejection of "final philosophy," that is, the project of starting out with such final projections and goals (typical of a noun-sense of epistemology) as the *sine qua non* of epistemology. I am, of course, granting that a *non-naturalist* might still want to argue for such a conception of episte- mology – I have been arguing that there are problems for naturalists in doing so.

## III  A Naturalist Excursion

I now turn to my specific naturalist excursion which significantly motivated these reflections on naturalized epistemology, and which provides further natu- ralistic support for many of the claims I make above. The particular area of scientific research I focus on, gender and cognition studies, proves to be an especially fruitful one within which to address at least two significant dimen- sions of the project to naturalize epistemology. On the one hand, as an area in the scientific study of cognition, this work provides a locus for specific naturalist epistemological reflection – where one can be said to be doing naturalized epis- temology. On the other hand, this particular area of active research in science provides helpful insight into the various conceptual, methodological, social, and political factors that are at work in any area of science (cognitive or other) that is the focus of ongoing scientific interest and change. It thus proves to be a good case study to direct attention to issues raised above about the (less-than- naturalist) characterizations of science that regularly inform the naturalized epis- temology debate more generally. Among scientists working in this field, differences emerge concerning the interpretation and significance of results; this is something that is not at all unique to this particular area of study, as philosophers of science, who attend carefully to the actual development of the sciences, are well aware. As we shall see, one cannot adequately discuss different methodological strategies in the scientific appropriation of cognition, of spe- cific cognitive capacities, and of gender without engaging in discussion about the political commitments involved in promoting particular areas of inquiry and particular models of cognition and of gender over other possible models. This, of course, furthers the important reminder that science does not develop in some kind of cognitive vacuum; it involves complex interrelationships among empirical findings, epistemological and methodological norms, and social and political values – interrelationships that naturalist epistemologists have too of- ten overlooked.

A significant moment in the last two decades of research on the psychology of gender came in 1974 with the publication of *The Psychology of Sex Differences*, in which Eleanor Maccoby and Carol Jacklin examined over 1400 studies on sex differences. They reported that studies (to that date) supported only four clear differences between male and females: with respect to cognition, male superiority in mathematical and visual – spatial abilities and female superiority in verbal ability; as regards social behavior, males were reported to be more aggressive (Maccoby and Jacklin, 1974). Subsequent work in this area has produced some revealing modifications and reservations concerning these findings. In addition to the overarching caution articulated by feminist psychologists about the difficulty of claiming anything about "inherent" (non-socialized) differences from these findings, other significant results have emerged. Newly developed methods of meta-analysis (which enable psychologists to synthesize quantitatively the results of many different studies in a particular area of research) have provided new tools for assessing the significance of sex difference findings. For example, they show that even in cases where sex differences seemed to appear with some regularity there is an upper limit of about 5 percent on the percentage of total variability in a given trait/behavior that can be predicted on the basis of sex (Deaux, 1984: 107). This clearly raises questions about the supposed explanatory relevance of sex as a "main effect" variable in scientific studies of social and cognitive behavior, and it comes under a critical light with the observation of the feminist psychologist, Rhoda Unger: "Although no adequate theoretical justification for what determines a relevant or irrelevant psychological category has ever been formulated, biological sex has long been an unquestioned psychological variable" (1990: 110). These criticisms also help to foreground the recurring concern with reports of findings from this area which tend to place greater emphasis on means (even when that is small) than on variance – this latter captures the often sizeable distribution for each gender and the significant overlap of genders.

However, the instability of sex-related differences across different studies has warranted special attention and has significantly contributed to the development of conceptions of gender which capture the *situational salience of gender*, a development which, as we shall see, also effects scientific appropriations of cognitive capacity in studies of gender and cognition. Experimental modifications changing the situational contexts of particular studies, specifically using different measuring instruments, providing different stimulus materials and test items, altering experimental settings, and so on, have yielded some revealing results. What had been considered relatively stable sex differences began to acquire a "now you see them, now you don't" quality (Unger 1990: 107). Among such results is the "discovery" that gender differences in public settings often do not hold up in private settings (generally supported by findings that people tend to conform more to gender roles and stereotypes in public settings); instructional formats that seem to draw differentially upon gender stereotypes and expectations yield different results with respect to sex differences; results differ when the experimenter is of a different sex; gender has been seen to interact fundamentally with other power and status differentials linked to the local salience of relations like race and class (or even specific status relations like employer/employee) as revealed in settings where group behavior and interaction were examined (Deaux, 1984; Deaux and Major, 1987; Hare-Mustin and Marecek, 1990).

In effect, gender emerges as significantly situational and interactive, as dynamic and performative, a dynamic that depends on the many ongoing situationally reinforced practices and institutions of gendering in specific social and cultural contexts. This focus on gender as situational draws attention to *proximal* factors in the expression and assessment of psychological behaviors and traits and marks a shift away from the traditional appraisal of such traits primarily or solely in terms of stable intrapsychic abilities which are the result of *distal* factors of biology and/or long-term socialization. Jeanne Marecek describes this move by feminist psychologists toward "alternative meanings of gender" in terms of critical assessments which "shift the focus of analysis away from matters internal to the individual to the interpersonal and institutional arenas . . . [where gender is seen] as neither stable, unitary, nor universal, but rather in flux, multiple, possibly fragmented, and local (i.e., defined in particular situations)" (1995: 162). Attention is thus drawn to uncovering the full impact of the deep commitment to the many social and cultural regulatory mechanisms of gendering, including, especially in this area of research, those that impact upon the organization of perception, judgment, and action. I shall return shortly to further reflection on the debate about the social and political dimensions of the development and presentation of the empirical results in this area of research, but first I want to draw attention to studies that more centrally address cognitive capacities.

While studies on gender and cognition that emphasize the situational salience of gender seem to apply most immediately to social cognition, they also have implications for the study of "individual-cognition," as we shall see shortly. When we think about the empirical psychological study of cognition we normally think about individual cognition as typically measured by what I call IISAP-cognition: isolated-individual-solving-a-puzzle-cognition. This has traditionally been the favored model, in philosophy, for projections of normative reasoning; social cognition is, at best, then reduced to a series of instances of such individual cognition. Psychology's long historical association with philosophy has strongly influenced the favoring of the IISAP model of individual cognition in psychology and also informs the relatively stubborn disciplinary division that still holds between (individual) psychology and social psychology – for example, practitioners typically identify themselves clearly in one or the other discipline. It is helpful at this point to remind ourselves of one of the recurring questions about specific delineations of naturalized epistemology which project the philosopher-epistemologist entertaining scientific findings as value-free empirical givens which, in particular, have not already incorporated earlier norms of epistemology. Ron Amundson's question, I think, applies to this larger discipline-specific question: "each theory [within the cognitive sciences] was generated, confirmed, and defended in association with specific methodological and epistemological commitments . . . how can [the epistemologist] be sure that she is not simply gazing on the reflected face of the cognitive theory's ancestor epistemology?" (Amundson, 1983: 335).

The situational salience of gender does seem to apply quite directly to contexts where *social* behavior and cognition are involved, and especially to what social psychologists call "gender-schematic contexts" where gender roles and expectations are functioning. Citing extensive work from social psychology, Kay Deaux and Brenda Major (1987) have developed a sophisticated experimental model designed to direct further study of "the degree to which gender-related behavior is variable, proximally caused, and context dependent" – though it is a model that is presented as a "supplement to existent models of sex differences" (1987: 369). While their emphasis here is on social *behavior* it is noteworthy that this behavior involves cognition at every turn since it takes account of the way people perceive, reflect, modify beliefs and attitudes: it is about how people can be said to know situations, themselves, and others in social interaction. Though the work that they examine largely focuses on gender stereotypes and expectations and their role in the cognitive and non-cognitive behavior of individuals in different situations, this work also has implications for a whole range of socially reinforced status and power relations among people. In particular, with this work our attention is drawn to the many less-than-fully-conscious/articulable modes of perception, behavior, identity-negotiation, and cognitive organization (how people go about organizing their perceptions and cognitions in given situations) that operate in a status-schematic society. In their recent collection of articles on work in the social psychology of interpersonal discrimination, Bernice Lott and Diane Maluso examine studies of sexism, racism, heterosexism, classism, and ageism, and they especially emphasize the "revealing commonalities in the ways that we tend to treat outgroup members – not just in extreme, destructive actions, but also in everyday, unnoticed patterns of distancing and avoidance" (1995: xii). These studies highlight the interrelationships among beliefs, attitudes, affects, and behaviors (distancing behaviors, for example) that sustain these kinds of discrimination. However, these studies also draw particular attention to the difficulty of clearly demarcating and assessing beliefs, feelings, and attitudes. Concerning efforts to define an attitude, for example, Lott and Maluso remark that "the investigation of relationships between attitude and behavior, or between attitude and affect, or between attitude and beliefs, becomes problematic because of the difficulty of assessing an attitude independently of its presumed components" (Lott and Maluso, 1995: 21). What is especially noteworthy about this research, particularly for naturalist and feminist epistemological projects promoting further study of the epistemic dimensions of social situatedness, is the inadequacy of philosophical models of cognition that rest largely on the analysis of discrete articulable beliefs held by individuals (that is, that do not take serious theoretical account of the complexity and range of beliefs and of the fundamental interconnections between beliefs, attitudes, and behaviors in our individual and social worlds).

These reflections about gender and cognition do not apply only to what has been characterized as "social cognition," and indeed they challenge the individual/social division itself. Experimental models that incorporate conceptions of gender as situational and dynamic have also been adapted to IISAP settings with individuals solving puzzles or dilemmas. For example, recent studies by Matthew Sharps and colleagues on gender and spatial cognition, which were designed to test the way in which "contextual variables" may differentially impact on women and men, are also clearly taking account of situational effect and challenging traditional models of gender and of cognition (Sharps et al., 1993, 1994). These studies examine the impact of specific changes in test formats in mental image rotation and spatial memory tasks, that is, changes that seem to trigger (or alternatively not trigger) gender-marked situational factors like gender stereotypes. In one experiment, women performed as well as the men when the spatial character of the task was de-emphasized in the initial instructions (but the "pure cognitive construct" or task remained the same). The authors of these studies conclude that experiments that indicate that men do better than women at spatial tasks need to be rethought in terms of the possible operation of contextual variable like the diminished motivational capacity of women in sociocultural contexts where they are subject to "implicit sociocultural stereotyping" that can promote "the negative feelings of women toward spatial cognitive capacities that may violate culturally mediated feminine self-concepts" (1994: 414). What we should note especially about these studies is the suggestion that self-concepts that are socioculturally encouraged and situated can also, it seems, operate in cognitive processing in experimental situations that are set up on the model of IISAP individual cognition. While the authors of these studies seem to distinguish between contextual factors (taken as "noncognitive factors" that can influence performance of a given task) and what they call "the pure cognitive construct alone," they also seem to waver in their projection of a pure core of cognition that can be realistically or theoretically distinguished from the contextual factors. They suggest that a relatively recent development in cognitive psychology, the concept of "situated cognition," could be more fully explored in the interpretation of their results. They add: "This viewpoint [stressed with situated cognition] holds that cognitive processes are not reifiable, disembodied functional entities operating in isolation. . . . The processes involved in spatial cognition do not operate in isolation, but instead function interactively with other situational and organismic variables, in attempts by individuals to solve problems posed by given situations or environments" (1993: 79; 1994: 422).

Experimental findings such as these clearly have implications for our understanding of cognition generally – they do not apply only to what might be called gender-significant contexts. The shift in conceptions of "gender" in gender and cognition studies is, as we see, also opening up a more critical appraisal of the specific conceptions of cognition that have informed studies in psychology generally. In particular, the development of the notion of situated cognition challenges the simplicity of philosophical and scientific models of cognition that posit and presume to measure distinct isolable "inner" entities, capacities, traits, and processes (beliefs, perceptions, spatial ability, verbal ability, processes of justification, and so on) – that is, "inner" traits and capacities that are theoretically distinguishable from the situational tasks that grant them meaning and measurement. In actuality, scientific studies tend to be much more modest – and situated – in their claims about specific cognitive abilities than scientists and philosophers might ideally project them to be. To my knowledge, no study claims to measure "spatial ability" as such: instead, good methodology requires clear descriptions of the particular test items that are used to measure "mental image rotation" or "spatial memory" or any others in a whole range of "spatial" tasks. In addition, these studies normally give specifics about the individual subjects tested – sex, age, race, class, occupation, and so on (not necessarily all of these in all studies). It is also very common for authors, in the concluding discursive sections of papers, to warn against generalizing beyond these specifics. The overall explanatory and interpretive frameworks discussed in these concluding sections are regularly presented with qualifying cautions, and they are often a matter of difference and debate among scientists working in the same area. In effect, fundamental conceptual and methodological criteria are continually being reassessed, discussed, and modified in specific areas of research, and the findings of those same areas are often presented with the appropriate qualifying and cautionary remarks.

Feminist reflection in sex differences research provides additional critical insight into the way in which different conceptual and methodological frameworks are influenced by the social and political values informing the contexts in which such research is undertaken. The March 1995 issue of the *American Psychologist* was largely devoted to this issue of "the science and politics of comparing women and men," and provides an up-to-date view of the discussion among feminist psychologists concerning both the findings and the significance of the whole project of sex differences research. There is some debate, for example, about what the quantitative meta-analytic techniques (which synthesize results from many different studies) say about the size of psychological sex differences (Eagly, 1995; Hyde and Plant, 1995). In this context, Alice Eagly notes, "even though quantitative synthesis is a rule-bound activity, it entails many subjective decisions, for example, in the selection of criteria for including and excluding studies from the sample and in the subsequent implementation of these criteria" (1995: 146). Such decisions can depend, for example, on whether one is developing an explanatory framework in sex differences research that addresses possible differences in biology, or early development, or more proximal factors like status, social roles, or gender-based expectancies, or various combinations of these. There is no uniform agreement among feminists that research programs exhibiting beta bias (a preference to minimize differences) provide insights into the effects of gendering and further the goals of feminism more effectively than those exhibiting alpha bias (a preference to exaggerate differences), though there is agreement that such preferences need to be the object of ongoing methodological and political critique.

Notable, also, among these different perspectives is that of Jeanne Marecek who argues that the different meanings of "gender" reflected in different methodological strategies is something that must also be central to critical debate in this area (Marecek, 1995; Rooney, 1995b). She discusses the different *conceptions of gender* emerging out of the shift away from the individual arena (where gender is treated as an individual difference or subject variable) to the interpersonal and institutional arenas. Among these new "alternative" conceptions of gender she includes: gender as a cultural accomplishment produced by a complex of social processes, gender as a set of principles that organize male – female relations, or as a marker of hierarchy that determines relations of power

(p. 162), or, again, as various combinations of these. She argues that such alternative conceptions provide a focused challenge to the tradition in sex differences research that has set out to measure stable "internal" properties of separate individuals: in treating "gender" as an unproblematic individual/psychological variable, the tradition has, she and others argue, reinforced the *status quo* view of "man" and "woman" as self-evident and unequivocal "natural" psychological categories. For those who might seek to dismiss feminist work in this area as politically motivated (and by implication not good science) she provides a critical reminder: "the agenda of preserving the *status quo* is as political and at least as formidable as the agenda of changing it" (p. 163). As this whole discussion effectively illustrates, what often distinguishes feminist work in science (from not-specifically-feminist work) is this additional critical awareness of the intricate relationships between science and culture: an awareness of the way in which seemingly straightforward and "neutral" methodological choices bear the mark of the social and political contexts within which science projects are developed and seen as relevant. Because feminist naturalists in epistemology and philosophy of science generally pay close attention to such levels of critique in science, they are thus less likely to make the kinds of generalized, overarching and ahistorical claims about science that (as noted in section II) not-specifically-feminist naturalists are inclined to make.

My discussion in this section has, then, involved a specific excursion into a particular area of science which proves to be a fruitful arena in which to challenge some of the non-naturalist assumptions regularly in circulation in discussions about naturalized epistemology. This excursion has elicited cautions about non-naturalist epistemological understandings of the nature and role of beliefs in cognition and knowledge that naturalists often attempt to carry over unwittingly into naturalized epistemology. I have also been challenging the ready assumption (by many naturalist epistemologists) that "science" (or even a specific scientific discipline) can be appropriated as something like a readily demarcated uniform endeavor that produces (or will produce) findings that are not the focus of ongoing debate – concerning interpretation, meaning, and so on – among scientists themselves. Such debate is apparent in an area like recent work on gender and cognition, which is undergoing significant change, but it is no less true of any of the many other projects in the cognitive sciences that are sites of active research and development. While in this section, I have been mainly drawing attention to the disciplinary division between (individual) cognitive psychology and social psychology, this attention can be extended to other disciplinary divisions in the cognitive sciences and to the ways in which such divisions both facilitate and constrain the kinds of findings that emerge from any given discipline. These divisions are sometimes the result of historical contingencies (specific technological developments – computers with artificial intelligence, for example – funding decisions, and so on); that is, they are not simply determined by "natural" differences in inherent subject matter. My discussion of the individual/social division in the cognitive sciences and my discussion of "situated cognition" (although short) both point to the need for greater critical appraisal of the individual/social division as it is used by both epistemologists and scientists. In my concluding section I turn to this issue of the social in knowledge, to its role in a naturalized epistemology that is put to work.

## IV  The Social in Naturalized Epistemology

It is important to note that the program to naturalize epistemology now includes projects that specifically emphasize the importance of social factors in cognition and knowledge (though one cannot assume that all those who stress the social are naturalists). Among such projects we can include Alvin Goldman's "social epistemics" (1986), Kornblith's attention to "some social features of cognition" (1987), Steve Fuller's "social epistemology" (1988), and Solomon's development of a "social empiricism" (1994). A whole range of projects in naturalized philosophy of science draw significantly from the sociology of knowledge. Frederick Schmitt's recent collection, titled "socializing epistemology" (1994), includes a range of arguments by epistemologists on the importance of taking account of the social in epistemology. Kornblith, in particular, argues that paying serious attention to the sociology of knowledge is "a straightforward extension of the naturalistic approach to epistemology" since, in effect, knowledge is also naturally a "socially mediated phenomenon" (Schmitt, 1994; 93, 97). While it may seem that such projects address my earlier concern about the limited role granted the social in naturalized epistemology, I shall argue that such projects do not "solve" my problems with the naturalized epistemology discussion generally, instead they simply shift those problems to another arena.

As noted earlier, much of the debate here (though again with a few exceptions) involves a conversation among epistemologists about what a social naturalized epistemology ought to include (or not include), rather than specific epistemological projects that engage with ongoing work in the social sciences. Among naturalists who push the sociology of scientific knowledge, for example, there is a tendency to assume that such studies can or will present general overarching accounts of the role of the social in the development of scientific knowledge. These kinds of assumption run foul of many of the problems I raised earlier. If we naturalists are to take account of what social scientists (sociologists, social psychologists, anthropologists and so on) tell us about knowledge, how are we to select among competing accounts across different fields, or among the different interpretations of the significance of findings within a given field? In addition, the meaningfulness and stability of terms like "social" and "sociological" in these discussions rely in part on an implicit endorsement of the disciplinary division between the individual cognitive and the social/cognitive sciences which in turn both relies on and reinforces an individual/social division that, as I argued in section III, really needs to be the focus of ongoing philosophical and scientific critique. In particular, studies of gender and cognition promoting the notion of "situated cognition" (as revealed even in IISAP experimental contexts) are clearly urging us to rethink the map of cognition which has too easily divided the potentially innumerable factors of cognitive context into "social" and "nonsocial" ones, and has thereby precluded the kinds of questions that feminists working in the cognitive sciences are now raising. While most of the studies I have referred to focus largely on gender as a marker of social situational regulation, they do so in a way that shows fundamental connections among gender and a whole range of social, status, and power relationships. Science and epistemology projects that do not seriously engage such axes of social situatedness run the risk of confining epistemic attention only to those who live and know outside of society and culture, and who, we might ask, are they?

It is helpful to see how these concerns with the appropriation of "the social" can be directed to specific programs in social naturalized epistemology. In his argument in "What is social about social epistemics?" Maffie takes Goldman to task for his somewhat limited conception of social cognition, and he adds: "class, race and gender affect cognitive performance in ways not fully captured in terms of information-based transactions between individuals" (1991: 107). His particular critique of the distinction between social and nonsocial cognition, as that distinction is deployed by Goldman and others, clearly connects with the kinds of critique that I have been advocating above. In a somewhat similar vein, Linda Alcoff notes that Fuller's "social epistemology" describes "the 'social turn' . . . without mentioning or citing a single feminist theorist working in this area and without raising any issues in regard to gender or race. 'Social' here evidently refers to the society of white men" (1996: 2).

This issue here is not simply about the amount of attention that is being given in these social epistemology programs to feminist work in science, epistemology, and philosophy of science. Though it is often characterized as such, neither do I think that feminist epistemology and philosophy of science can be simply described as particular forms of social epistemology or sociology of knowledge. It is certainly true that feminist philosophers of science have been particularly concerned with the role of contextual social and political values in the development of science and do not endorse science projects informed by sexist and racist values; yet, on the other hand, many feminists argue that social values can and do inform the cognitive development of good science (Code, 1996; Hankinson Nelson, 1990; Hankinson Nelson and Nelson, 1996; Harding, 1986, 1991; Longino, 1990, 1996; Potter, 1995; Rooney, 1992). It is in the debate that has emerged out of these tensions that feminists have been developing novel approaches to the science and values question, and, in particular, have been developing more nuanced understandings of "the social" rather than conceptions that simply pit it over and against "the rational" or characterize it as a readily circumscribed appendage to the rational. It is because many of the not-specifically-feminist projects that fall within the purview of "social epistemology" do not challenge the rational/social divide in the way that many feminist projects do, that the latter cannot readily be identified with the former. Joseph Rouse (1996) maintains, for example, that given important differences between feminist and sociological studies of science one cannot identify the former with the latter. In particular, he argues that sociologists of science still rely on a conception of *knowledge* as a relatively well-circumscribed totality and seek totalizing descriptions and explanations of science that involve a kind of theoretical detachment that feminists do not seek and often renounce. Feminist approaches point toward what Rouse argues is a "post-epistemological" conception of science and scientific knowledge that includes abandoning "the epistemological aspiration to a detached assessment of the totality of knowledge (or scientific knowledge). . . . The alternative is engaged and self-critical participation in the making and remaking of scientific knowledges of the world we live in" (1996: 211).

What Rouse challenges here in positing a "post-epistemological" conception of scientific knowledge, I would characterize as a "noun-sense" epistemology that seeks to assess knowledge generally, and science in particular, as a totality about which it is meaningful to project final definitions, claims and explanations. What I have been arguing is that such a noun-sense epistemology with a naturalist twist (that is, that seeks totalizing explanations in terms of the psychology of beliefs, or in terms of the sociology of epistemic practices, or whatever) largely misses the boat; that is, it fails to appreciate what an ongoing, two-way, and challenging conversation and engagement between epistemology and science might really look like, and even acts as a deterrent to a meaningful alliance with the sciences as ongoing activities that are responsive to all kinds of changing conditions and that invite or suggest any number of epistemological inquiries. A verb-sense of epistemology that encourages ongoing self-critical participation with knowledge and with epistemology also serves to remind us that as epistemologists, as putative knowers of knowledges, we too have individual/social identities, and that better knowledge of those identities (including the extent to which those identities may have been formed by "the tradition" in epistemology) can only add to our epistemological endeavors.

I started this inquiry by seeking to identify what it is to be a naturalist epistemologist, over and above advocating naturalized epistemology as a program – that is, seeking to identify what it is that a naturalist epistemologist would actually do, how she or he would actually engage with specific science projects. My difficulty in pinning down such epistemologists has had a parallel in my difficulty in pinning down a term to refer to them, a parallel that is surely telling. I have been using the term "naturalist epistemologist" throughout; however, this is not at all the norm – some use wording like "naturalists in epistemology" or "naturalistic epistemologists" or "those advocating naturalized epistemology." The term "naturalized epistemologist" is rarely used, presumably because that would pick out someone who has forsaken the ivory towers of the academy and has gone to live "in nature" (but still does epistemology!), or, alternatively, an epistemologist who has gone through a process of naturalization into citizenship. These are not, I gather, the specific activities and identities that proponents of naturalized epistemology are urging epistemologists to engage with and acquire, though, for now at least, they might well be much easier to actualize.

## Notes

1 See my "Feminist Epistemology and Naturalized Epistemology: An Uneasy Alliance," forthcoming in Lynn Hankinson Nelson and Jack Nelson (eds), *Feminist Interpretations of Quine* (eds), Penn State Press.
2 For more on these arguments about the importance of the social cognitive sciences in naturalizing philosophy of science see Downes, 1993, Fuller, 1988, and Solomon, 1994. Also see Hankinson Nelson, 1995, for a discussion of the significance of these debates for the development of a feminist naturalized philosophy of science. As Hankinson Nelson effectively shows with specific case studies, feminists are clearly interested in the communal and social aspects of scientific knowledge making, especially when they help to illuminate the sociopolitical dimensions of the background context which, it is argued by many feminists (see also Longino, 1990), inform the "internal" constitutive values, methods, and substantive claims of science.

# Works Cited

Alcoff, Linda Martín, 1996, *Real Knowing: New Versions of the Coherence Theory* (Ithaca, NY: Cornell University Press)

Almeder, Robert, 1990, "On Naturalizing Epistemology," *American Philosophical Quarterly*, vol. 27, no. 4, pp. 263–79.

Amundson, Ron, 1983, "The Epistemological Status of a Naturalized Epistemology," *Inquiry*, vol. 26, pp. 333–44.

Bohan, Janis S., 1993, "Regarding Gender: Essentialism, Constructionism, and Feminist Psychology," *Psychology of Women Quarterly*, 17, pp. 5–21.

Campbell, Richmond, 1994, "The Virtues of Feminist Empiricism," *Hypatia*, vol. 9, no. 1, pp. 90–115.

Code, Lorraine, 1996, "What is Natural about Epistemology Naturalized?," *American Philosophical Quarterly*, vol. 33, no. 1, pp. 1–22.

Deaux, Kay, 1984, "From Individual Differences to Social Categories: Analysis of a Decade's Research on Gender," *American Psychologist* vol. 39, no. 2, pp. 105–16.

Deaux, Kay, and Brenda Major, 1987, "Putting Gender into Context: an Interactive Model of Gender-Related Behavior" *Psychological Review* 94, vol., no. 3, pp. 369–89.

Downes, S., 1993, "Socializing Naturalized Philosophy of Science," *Philosophy of Science*, vol. 60, pp. 452–68.

Eagly, Alice H., 1995, "The Science and Politics of Comparing Women and Men," *American Psychologist*, vol. 50, no. 3, pp. 145–58.

Fuller, Steve, 1988, *Social Epistemology* (Bloomington, In: Indiana University Press).

Giere, Ronald N., 1992, "Introduction: Cognitive Models of Science," in *Cognitive Models of Science*, ed. Ronald N. Giere, *Minnesota Studies in the Philosophy of Science*, Vol. 15 (University of Minnesota Press).

Goldman, A., 1986, *Epistemology and Cognition* (Cambridge, MA: Harvard University Press)

Harding, Sandra, 1986, *The Science Question in Feminism* (Ithaca, NY: Cornell University Press).

——, 1991, *Whose Science? Whose Knowledge?: Thinking from Women's Lives* (Ithaca, NY: Cornell University Press).

Hare-Mustin, Rachel T. and Jeanne Marecek (eds), 1990, *Making A Difference: Psychology and the Construction of Gender* (New Haven, CT: Yale University Press)

Hyde, Janet Shilbey and Elizabeth Ashby Plant, 1995, "Magnitude of Psychological Gender Differences: Another Side to the Story," *American Psychologist*, vol. 50, no. 3, pp. 159–61.

Kornblith, Hilary (ed.), 1985, *Naturalizing Epistemology* (Cambridge, MA: MIT Press).

——, 1987, "Some Social Features of Cognition," *Synthese* 73: 27–42

Kornblith, Hilary (ed.), 1994, *Naturalizing Epistemology*, Second Edition (Cambridge, MA: MIT Press).

Longino, Helen, 1990, *Science as Social Knowledge: Values and Objectivity in Scientific Inquiry* (Princeton, NJ: Princeton University Press).

——, 1996, "Cognitive and Non-Cognitive Values in Science: Rethinking the Dichotomy," in Hankinson Nelson and Nelson (eds).

Lott, Bernice and Diane Maluso, 1995, *The Social Psychology of Interpersonal Discrimination* (New York: Guilford Press).

Maccoby, E. and C. Jacklin, 1974, *The Psychology of Sex Differences* (Stanford, CA: Stanford University Press).

Maffie, James, 1990, "Recent Work on Naturalized Epistemology," *American Philosophical Quarterly*, vol. 27, no. 4, pp. 281–93.

——, 1991, "What is Social about Social Epistemics?," *Social Epistemology*, vol. 5, no. 2, pp. 101–10.

Marecek, Jeanne, 1995, "Gender, Politics, and Psychology's Ways of Knowing," *American Psychologist*, vol. 50, no. 3, pp. 162–3.

Nelson, Lynn Hankinson. 1990, *Who Knows: From Quine to a Feminist Empiricism* (Philadelphia, PA: Temple University Press).

——, 1993, "Epistemological Communities," in Alcoff and Potter (eds), *Feminist Epistemologies* (New York: Routledge).

——, 1995, "A Feminist Naturalized Philosophy of Science," *Synthese*, vol. 104, pp. 399–421.

—— and Jack Nelson, (eds), 1996, *Feminism, Science, and the Philosophy of Science* (Kluwer Academic Publishers).

Potter, Elizabeth, 1995, "Methodological Norms in Traditional and Feminist Philosophy of Science," *PSA* 1994, Vol. 2, D. Hull, M. Forbes, and R. M. Burian (eds) (East Lansing, MI: Philosophy of Science Association), pp. 101–8.

Quine, W. V. O., 1969, "Epistemology Naturalized," in *Ontological Relativity and Other Essays* (New York: Columbia University Press).

——, 1981, "Reply to Stroud," in *Midwest Studies in Philosophy* vol. 6, P. French, E. Uehling, and H. Wettstein, (eds.), (Minneapolis: University of Minnesota Press, 1981).

Rooney, Phyllis. 1992, "On Values in Science: Is the Epistemic/Non-Epistemic Distinction Useful?," *PSA* 1992, vol. 1, pp. 13–22. David Hull, Micky Forbes, Kathleen Okruhlik (eds) (East Lansing, MI: Philosophy of Science Association).

——1995a "Rationality and the Politics of Gender Difference," *Metaphilosophy*, vol. 26, nos. 1 & 2, pp. 22–45.

——, 1995b, "Methodological Issues in the Construction of Gender as a Meaningful Variable in Scientific Studies of Cognition," *PSA* 1994, Vol. 2, D. Hull, M. Forbes, and R. M. Burian (eds) (East Lansing, MI: Philosophy of Science Association), pp. 109–19.

Rouse, Joseph, 1996, "Feminism and the Social Construction of Scientific Knowledge," in Hankinson Nelson and Nelson (eds).

Schmitt, Frederick F, 1994, *Socializing Epistemology: The Social Dimensions of Knowl-*

*edge* (Lanham, MD: Rowman & Littlefield).

Sharps, Matthew J., Angela L. Welton, and Jana L. Price, 1993, "Gender and Task in the Determination of Spatial Cognitive Performance," *Psychology of Women Quarterly*, vol. 17, pp. 71–83.

Sharps, Matthew J., Jana L. Price, and John K. Williams, 1994, "Spatial Cognition and Gender: Instructional and Stimulus Influences on Mental Image Rotation Performance," *Psychology of Women Quarterly*, vol. 18, pp. 413–25.

Siegel, Harvey, 1995, "Naturalized Epistemology and 'First Philosophy'," *Metaphilosophy* vol. 26, nos. 1 & 2, pp. 46–62.

Solomon, Miriam, 1992, "Scientific Rationality and Human Reasoning," *Philosophy of Science*, vol. 59, pp. 439–55.

——, 1994, "Social Empiricism," *Nous*, vol. 28, pp. 325–43.

Stich, Stephen, 1990, *The Fragmentation of Reason: Preface to a Pragmatic Theory of Cognitive Evaluation* (Cambridge, MA: MIT Press).

Stroud, Barry, 1985, "The Significance of Naturalized Epistemology," in Kornblith (ed).

Unger, Rhoda, 1990, "Imperfect Reflections of Reality: Psychology Constructs Gender," in Hare-Mustin and Marecek (eds).

# PART FIVE

# WHAT IS TRUTH?

# Introduction

Truth is one of the most complex and confusing topics in epistemology. Definitions and concepts of truth are often conflated with accounts of the criteria of truth, and the object of debate, or what counts as truth itself, proves to be an enigmatic creature.

It may seem odd, but for most epistemologists today truth is a non-issue. In the first place, although truth is a part of most definitions of knowledge, it is usually considered to belong within the provenance of metaphysics rather than epistemology, within the question of what there is rather than how we know. But second, it is often thought not to have even metaphysical interest, since its meaning can be wholly expressed in some version of Tarski's equivalence thesis as follows:

*p* is true if and only if *p*

Thus, one could claim that "*p* is true" more easily by simply claiming that "*p*." This is not to deny that there are circumstances in which truth assertions are substantively meaningful ("I am not kidding – the President is at the next table! It's true!"). But there is no extra *philosophical* sense added. Truth on this account is merely a kind of exclamation point.

Before such deflationary accounts of truth became the norm, the debate over truth centered on correspondence, coherence, verificationism, and pragmatist concepts. These debates moved between criterial accounts and definitions of truth, but in regard to definitions, correspondence accounts generally won out. Coherence or pragmatist theories may tell us how to get to the truth (though there is of course much debate over this), but the meaning of truth, as evident from both intuition and linguistic usage, is widely thought to be best captured in a correspondence account. The evolution of the correspondence theory of truth into the deflationary, mininal account, as in Tarski's schema above, largely explains the latter's wide acceptance. Paul Horwich's essay provides a representative rendition of a minimalist account.

In philosophy classrooms, as well as in other arenas of the academy, the spectre of truth often invokes concerns about relativism. After all, given the rapidity by which even the "mature" sciences correct their claims, what can we really rely on as "the truth" anymore? In an increasingly complex, multivocal world, can one culture or mode of inquiry plausibly assert an exclusive purchase on truth? If not, how are we to characterize these conflicts?

The essays by Ian Hacking and Richard Rorty take up this question, offering alternative solutions. Hacking suggests that the real difficulty is not over what is true, but what has a truth-value at all, that is, what can stand as a candidate for truth or falsehood. He calls *styles of reasoning* those modes of inquiry that set out the kinds of objects, models, and hypotheses that can be epistemically evaluated. Hacking's account has the virtue of explaining the prevalence of cognitive dissonance as well as the historicity (or ongoing evolution) of reason without entailing a self-refuting relativism: though the facts of the matter determine truth, they are not sufficient to determine or explain truth-value. We need an expanded account of truth that can take this complication into account.

Rorty offers a spirited defense of a pragmatic approach to truth. He argues that, although pragmatism offers no metaphilosophical antidote to relativism, contrary claims can be fought out on the usual grounds we always use when we disagree. In other words, for Rorty, metaphilosophical relativism has no more substantive impact than what deflationists claim for "is true." In fact, Rorty's anti-foundational, non-representational approach to epistemology brings us back full circle to minimalist, non-metaphysical accounts of truth.

Diverse positions on truth often talk past one another because they differ on antecedent issues concerning what a theory of truth is supposed to do. According to deflationists, accounts of truth have no metaphysical or non-semantic implications about the relation of human knowledge to the world independent of human practices, and thus the range of debates concerning this relation are simply philosophical false starts. For others, there are a number of perplexing philosophical problems associated with truth in regard to the ontological independence of scientific claims, the historical evolution of human knowledge, as well as cultural differences in traditions of rationality. Once again, then, epistemologists debate not just answers to the question of truth, but the proper formulation of the question itself.

**Further Reading**

Dummett, Michael. *Truth and Other Enigmas.* Oxford: Clarendon Press, 1978.

Putnam, Hilary. *Reason, Truth and History.* Cambridge: Cambridge University Press, 1981.

Quine, W. V. O. *The Pursuit of Truth.* Cambridge, MA: Harvard University Press, 1990.

Strawson, Peter. "Truth." *Proceedings of the Aristotelian Society*, supplemental vol. 24 (1950): 125–56.

Tarski, Alfred. "The Semantic Conception of Truth." *Philosophy and Phenomenological Research* 4(1943): 341–75.

# 18   The Minimal Theory

*Paul Horwich*

## A Sketch of the Minimalist Conception

'What is truth?' we sometimes ask – but the question tends to be rhetorical, conveying the somewhat defeatist idea that a good answer, if indeed there is such a thing, will be so subtle, so profound and so hard to find, that to look for one would surely be a waste of time. The daunting aura of depth and difficulty which surrounds this concept is perfectly understandable. For on the one hand the notion of truth pervades philosophical theorizing about the basic nature and norms of thought and action – e.g. '*truth* is the aim of science'; '*true* beliefs facilitate successful behaviour'; '*truth* is preserved in valid reasoning'; 'to understand a sentence is to know which circumstances would make it *true*'; 'evaluative assertions can be neither *true* nor false'. So insight into the underlying essence of truth promises, by helping us assess and explain such principles, to shed light on just about the whole of our conceptual scheme. But, on the other hand, this very depth can suggest that in inquiring into the nature of truth we have run up against the limits of analysis; and indeed it will be widely agreed that hardly any progress has been made towards achieving the insight we seem to need. The common-sense notion that truth is a kind of 'correspondence with the facts' has never been worked out to anyone's satisfaction. Even its advocates would concede that it remains little more than a vague, guiding intuition. But the traditional alternatives – equations of truth with 'membership in a coherent system of beliefs', or 'what would be verified in ideal conditions', or 'suitability as a basis for action' – have always looked unlikely to work, precisely because they don't accommodate the 'correspondence' intuition and this air of implausibility is substantiated in straightforward counterexamples. Hence the peculiarly enigmatic character of truth: a conception of its underlying nature appears to be at once necessary and impossible.

I believe that this impression is wholly wrong and that it grows out of two related misconceptions: first, that truth *has* some hidden structure awaiting our discovery; and, secondly, that hinging on this discovery is our ability to explain central philosophical principles such as those just mentioned, and thereby to solve a host of problems in logic, semantics and epistemology.

The main cause of these misconceptions, I suspect, is linguistic analogy. Just as the predicate, 'is magnetic', designates a feature of the world, *magnetism*, whose structure is revealed by quantum physics, and 'is diabetic' describes a group of phenomena, *diabetes*, characterizable in biology, so it seems that 'is true' attributes a complex property, *truth* – an ingredient of reality whose underlying essence will, it is hoped, one day be revealed by philosophical or scientific analysis. The trouble is that this conclusion – which we tend to presuppose in the question, 'What is truth?' – is unjustified and false. An expression might have a meaning that is somewhat disguised by its superficial form – tending, as Wittgenstein warned, to produce mistaken analogies, philosophical confusion, and insoluble pseudo-problems. The word, 'exists' provides a notorious example. And we are facing the same sort of thing here. Unlike most other predicates, 'is true' is not used to attribute to certain entities (i.e. statements, beliefs, etc.) an ordinary sort of property – a characteristic whose underlying nature will account for its relations to other ingredients of reality. Therefore, unlike most other predicates, 'is true' should not be expected to participate in some deep theory of that to which it refers – a theory that goes beyond a specification of what the word means. Thus its assimilation to superficially similar expressions is misleading. The role of truth is not what it seems.

In fact the truth predicate exists solely for the sake of a certain logical need. On occasion we wish to adopt some attitude towards a proposition – for example, believing it, assuming it for the sake of argument, or desiring that it be the case – but find ourselves thwarted by ignorance of what exactly the proposition is. We might know it only as 'what Oscar thinks' or 'Einstein's principle'; perhaps it was expressed, but not clearly or loudly enough, or in a language we don't understand; or – and this is especially common in logical and philosophical contexts – we may wish to cover infinitely many propositions (in the course of generalizing) and simply can't have all of them in mind. In such situations the concept of truth is invaluable. For it enables the construction of another proposition, intimately related to the one we can't identify, which is perfectly appropriate as the alternative object of our attitude.

Consider, for example

(1)   What Oscar said is true.

Here we have something of the form

(2)   x is F

whose meaning is such that, given further information about the identity of x – given a further premise of the form

(3) x = the proposition that p

– we are entitled to infer

(4)   p.

And it is from precisely this inferential property that propositions involving truth derive their utility. For it makes them, in certain circumstances, the only appropriate objects of our beliefs, suppositions, desires, etc. Suppose, for example, I have great confidence in Oscar's judgement about food; he has just asserted that eels are good but I didn't quite catch his remark. Which belief might I reasonably acquire? Well obviously not that eels are good. Rather what is needed is a proposition from which that one would follow, given identification of what Oscar said – a proposition equivalent to

(1*)   If what Oscar said is *that eels are good* then eels are good, and if he said *that milk is white* then milk is white . . . and so on;

and the *raison d'être* of the concept of truth is that it supplies us with a proposition: namely (1).

To take another example, suppose we wish to state the logical law of excluded middle:

(5)   Everything is red or not red, and happy or not happy, and cheap or not cheap . . . and so on.

Our problem is to find a single, finite proposition that has the intuitive logical power of the infinite conjunction of all these instances; and the concept of truth provides a solution.

(6)   Everything is red or not red,

is known to be equivalent to

(6*)   The proposition *that everything is red or not red* is true.

And similarly for the other instances. Thus the infinite series of universal disjunctions may be transformed into another infinite series of claims in which the same property, *truth*, is attributed to all the members of a class of structurally similar propositional objects. And in virtue of that form the sum of *these* claims may be captured in an ordinary universally quantified statement:

(5*)   Every proposition of the form ⟨everything is F or not F⟩ is true.

It is in just this role, and not as the name of some baffling ingredient of nature, that the concept of truth figures so pervasively in philosophical reflection.[1]

What permits the notion of truth to play that role is simply that, for any declarative sentence

(4)   p

our language guarantees an equivalent sentence

(4*) The proposition *that p* is true,

where the original sentence has been converted into a noun phrase, 'The proposition *that p*', occupying a position open to object variables, and where the truth predicate serves merely to restore the structure of a sentence: it acts simply as a *de-nominalizor*. In other words, in order for then truth predicate to fulfil its function we must acknowledge that

> (MT)    The proposition *that quarks really exist* is true if and only if quarks really exist, the proposition *that lying is bad* is true if and only if lying is bad, . . . and so on;

*but nothing more about truth need be assumed.* The entire conceptual and theoretical role of truth may be explained on this basis. This confirms our suspicion that the traditional attempt to discern the *essence* of truth – to analyse that special quality which all truths supposedly have in common – is just a pseudo-problem based on syntactic overgeneralization. Unlike most other properties, *being true* is insusceptible to conceptual or scientific analysis. No wonder that its 'underlying nature' has so stubbornly resisted philosophical elaboration; for there is simply no such thing.

This sort of deflationary picture is attractively demystifying.[2] Nevertheless, it has not been widely accepted, for it faces a formidable array of theoretical and intuitive objections. My aim in this book is to work out a form of the approach that is able to deal with all the alleged difficulties. Some of them expose genuine deficiencies in certain versions of the doctrine and reveal the need for a better formulation of the deflationary position. But most of the complaints have simply been given more weight than they deserve. Indeed I tend to think that the approach has been underrated more because of the sheer number of objections to it than because of their quality. Put in more positive terms, my plan is to provide a highly deflationary account of our concept of truth – but one that can nevertheless explain the role of the notion in scientific methodology and in science itself, and enable us to find answers to such questions as: In what does our grasp of truth consist? Why is it practically useful to believe the truth? Can there be, in addition, any purely intrinsic value to such beliefs? Does science aim and progress towards the truth? How does our conception of truth bear on the nature of various types of fact and on our capacity to discover them? Is truth an explanatorily vital concept in semantics or in any of the empirical sciences? – I shall start by giving what I believe is the best statement of the deflationary point of view. Because it contains no more than what is expressed by uncontroversial instances of the equivalence schema,

> (E) It is true *that p* if and only if p,

I shall call my theory of truth, '*the minimal theory*', and I shall refer to the surrounding remarks on behalf of its adequacy as '*the minimalist conception*'. With a good formulation in hand, I want to show that the standard criticisms of deflationary approaches are either irrelevant or surmountable, to display the virtues of the theory in comparison with alternatives, and, by answering the above questions, to draw out the implications of minimalism for issues in semantics, psychology and the philosophy of science. For the sake of simplicity and conformity with natural language I begin by developing the account of truth for *propositions*. However, I shall go on to argue that the minimalist conception applies equally well to the 'truth' of utterances, mental attitudes, and other types of entity.

It might be thought that minimalism is too obvious and too weak to have any significant philosophical implications. Let me try, in at least a preliminary manner, to quell this misgiving. The real proof, of course, will be in the execution of the project. We should start by distinguishing (very roughly) two types of 'philosophical implication'. First, there are general principles involving truth: for example, that verification indicates truth, and that true beliefs are conducive to successful action. And, secondly, there are solutions to philosophical problems: for example, the paradoxes of vagueness and the issue of scientific realism. According to the minimalist conception, the equivalence schema, despite its obviousness and weakness, is *not* too weak to have significant philosophical implications – at least within the first category. On the contrary, our thesis is that it is possible to explain *all* the facts involving truth on the basis of the minimal theory. This may indeed appear to be a rather tall order. But remember that most of the interesting facts to be explained concern relations between truth and certain other matters; and in such cases it is perfectly proper to make use of theories about these other matters, and not to expect that all the explanatory work be done by the theory of truth in isolation. When this methodological point is borne in mind it becomes more plausible to suppose that the explanatory duties of a theory of truth can be carried out by the minimal theory.

As for the second class of 'philosophical implication' – namely, solutions to problems – one would expect these to flow, not from the minimal theory as such (i.e. instances of the equivalence schema), but rather from the minimalist *conception* (i.e. the thesis that our theory of truth should contain nothing more than instances of the equivalence schema). Philosophical questions are typically based on confusion rather than simple ignorance. Therefore an account that makes plain the character of truth will permit a clearer view of any problems that are thought to involve truth. The account itself may well never entail, or even suggest, any solutions. But in so far as it elucidates one of the sources of confusion it will help us to untangle the conceptual knots that are generating the problems, and thereby facilitate their solution. In the limiting case, a conception of truth can achieve this result by enabling us to see that, contrary to what has been generally presupposed, the notion of truth is not even involved in the problem. The recognition that truth plays no role can be vital to achieving the clarity needed for a solution. Thus, to put the matter somewhat paradoxically, the *relevance* of a theory of truth may lie in its import regarding the *irrelevance* of truth. We shall see, I think, that this is very often the situation. Consider, for example, the debate surrounding scientific realism. It is commonly assumed that truth is an essential constituent of the problem; one sees reference to 'realist conceptions of truth' and to 'anti-realist conceptions of truth'; and questions about the meaning of theoretical assertions, our right to believe them, and what it would be for them to be true, are all lumped together as components of a single broad problem. This intertwining of philosophically crucial notions is why the realism issue has proved so slippery and tough. What I am claiming on behalf of the minimalist conception of truth is not that it, by itself, will engender realism or anti-realism; but rather that it will make it easier for us to see that the central aspects of the realism debate have nothing to do with truth. By providing this clarification of the main problems, minimalism will take us a long way toward being able to solve them.

## The Space of Alternative Theories

It will help us to focus on what is at stake in accepting the minimalist conception of truth if I contrast it with some of the well known alternatives.

### Correspondence

First there is the venerable notion that truth is the property of *corresponding with reality*. In its most sophisticated formulations this has been taken to mean that the truth of a statement depends on how its constituents are arranged with respect to one another and on which entities they stand for. One strategy along these lines (Wittgenstein, 1922) is to suppose that a statement as a whole *depicts* a possible fact whose constituents are referents of the statement's constituents, and that the statement is true if and only if such a fact exists. Another strategy (Austin, 1950; Tarski, 1958; Davidson, 1969) is to define truth in terms of reference and predicate-satisfaction without importing the notions of fact and structure. Either way, these correspondence theories further divide according to what is said about reference. For example, one might suppose, with Wittgenstein (1922), that it is simply indescribable; or, with Field (1972) and Devitt (1984), that reference is a naturalistic (causal) relation; or, with Quine (1970) and Leeds (1978), that it is merely a device for semantic ascent. From our minimalist point of view, the last of these ideas is along the right lines – reference and truth being parallel notions – although, as we shall argue, it is a mistake to explain truth in terms of reference.

### Coherence

The second most popular view of truth is known as the coherence theory. A system of beliefs is said to be coherent when its elements are consistent with one another and when it displays a certain overall simplicity. In that case, according to the coherence theory, the whole system and each of its elements are true. Thus truth is the property of *belonging to a harmonious system of beliefs*. This line was urged by the idealists, Bradley (1914) and Blanshard (1939), embraced by Hempel (1935), as the only alternative to what he regarded as the obnoxious metaphysics of *correspondence*, and resurrected for similar reasons by Dummett (1978) and Putnam (1981) (as the 'verificationist' or 'constructivist' theory) in their identification of truth with idealized justification. What has seemed wrong with this point of view is its refusal to endorse an apparently central feature of our conception of truth, namely the possibility of there being some discrepancy between what really *is* true and what we will (or should, given all possible evidence) *believe* to be true.

## Pragmatism

In the third place we have the so-called pragmatic theory of truth, devised by James (1909) and Dewey (1938), and recently elaborated by Rorty (1982) and Papineau (1987). Here truth is *utility*; true assumptions are those that work best – those which provoke actions with desirable results. From our perspective, although there is indeed an association between the truth of a belief and its tendency to facilitate successful activity, this fact is something to be *explained*, and not stipulated by the very definition of truth.

## Unanalysable quality

Fourthly – perhaps the least attractive conclusion – there is the one-time thesis of Moore (1899, 1910/11) and Russell (1904) that truth is an indefinable, inexplicable quality that some propositions simply have and others simply lack.[3] This gives a sense of impenetrable mysteriousness to the notion of truth and can be the resort only of those who feel that the decent alternatives have been exhausted.

These traditional approaches do not typically impugn the correctness of the equivalence schema,

(E)   $\langle p \rangle$ is true *iff* p,[4]

but question its completeness. They deny that it tells us about the *essential nature* of truth, and so they inflate it with additional content in ways that, I shall argue, are, at best, unnecessary and, at worst, mistaken. To explain this point a little further it is useful to imagine six dimensions on which alternative accounts of truth may be characterized – each dimension varying with respect to some form of theoretical commitment.

1   An account may or may not be compositional – it may or may not define the truth of an utterance or a proposition in terms of the semantic properties of its parts. For example, a theory inflated in this way might involve the principle,

(T/R)   'a is F' is true *iff* there exists an object x such that 'a' refers to x and 'F' is satisfied by x.

The minimalist policy is not to *deny* such principles relating truth, reference, and satisfaction, but to argue that our theory of truth should not contain them as *axioms*. Instead, they should be *derived* from a conjunction of the theory of truth and quite distinct minimalist theories of reference and satisfaction.

2   An account may or may not suppose that truth is a complex property – the property, for example, of *corresponding with reality*, or *being verified in ideal conditions*, or *facilitating successful behaviour*, or *having such-and-such naturalistically specified essence*. In the context of a compositional account, the parallel issue is whether *reference* and *satisfaction* are complex relational properties – according to some philosophers, reducible to *causal* notions. The minimalist denies that truth, reference, or satisfaction are complex or naturalistic properties.

3   One may or may not insist on a conceptual analysis of truth, a specification (in philosophically unproblematic terms) of the content of every statement employing the concept. Minimalism offers no such definition, and denies the need for one.

4   One may or may not attempt to formulate a non-trivial, finite theory of truth itself – a succinct body of statements about truth that can be tacked on to our other theories (in physics, mathematics, etc.) to enable the deduction of everything we believe about truth. According to minimalism, there is no such thing. We can say what is in the theory of truth – an infinity of biconditionals of the form, ⟨p⟩ is true *iff* p – but we cannot formulate it explicitly because there are too many axioms.

5   One may or may not propose an account which inextricably links truth with other matters: for example, assertion, verification, reference, meaning, success, or logical entailment. Minimalism involves the contention that truth has a certain purity – that our understanding of it is independent of other ideas.

6   In particular, an account of the truth of *utterances* may or may not invoke meaning-like entities such as propositions, beliefs, truth conditions, and possible states of affairs – as, for example, in

(U)   Utterance x is true *iff* x expresses the proposition *that p* and the proposition *that p* corresponds to a fact.

The minimalist view of utterances does not deny that there are such things as propositions, beliefs, truth conditions and possible states of affairs. It maintains only that our conception of truth for utterances does not presuppose them.

Thus my account will take the less theoretically loaded view with respect to each of these six dimensions of commitment. The theory of truth it proposes involves nothing more than the equivalence schema; its treatment of utterances does not invoke meaning-like entities; it is non-compositional; it denies that truth and reference are complex or naturalistic properties; and it does not insist on an eliminative account of truth attributions. In this way minimalism aims for a maximally deflationary theory of truth, which, though complete, has no extraneous content – a theory about truth, the whole of truth, and nothing but truth.

I should stress that our critique of the correspondence, coherence, constructivist, pragmatist, and primitivist accounts of truth is *not* that they are false. On the contrary, it seems quite likely that carefully qualified, true versions of each of them could be concocted. The main objection is rather that none can meet the *explanatory* demands on an adequate theory of truth. Specifically, none provides a good account of why it is that instances of the equivalence schema are true. Minimalism involves a reversal of that explanatory direction. We shall find that on the basis of the equivalence axioms it is easy to see why, and in what form, the traditional principles hold. Indeed every fact about truth can be naturally derived from those biconditionals. Therefore it is they that should constitute our basic theory of truth.

## Summary of Alleged Difficulties

Objections to deflationary approaches have concerned six related topics:

*The proper formulation:*   It has been no easy matter to provide even a *prima facie* plausible version of such a theory of truth – something that meets the normal methodological standards of fidelity to obvious fact, simplicity, explanatory power, etc., and that is not falsified by the 'liar' paradoxes.

*The explanatory role of the concept of truth:*   The concept of truth is apparently employed in certain forms of scientific explanation (e.g. to help account for the contribution of language use to the achievement of practical goals), and it has been argued on this basis that deflationism must be missing something – namely, the naturalistic character that provides truth with its causal properties.

*Methodology and scientific realism:*   A natural (realist) view of science is that it aims for, and gradually progresses towards, the truth – a goal that exists independently of our capacity to reach it, and that we value partly for its own sake, independently of any practical benefits that might accrue. This position would seem to require a substantial notion of truth – a conception of just the sort that the deflationary point of view eschews. In other words, any deflationary account of truth would seem to entail an antirealist perspective on science.

*Meaning and logic:*   A further body of objections concerns the role of truth in semantics, and the ability of any deflationary approach to explain this role. For example, it is usual to analyse *understanding* in terms of knowledge of truth conditions, to use the concepts of truth and reference to show how the meanings of sentences depend on the meanings of their parts, to suppose that truth must be a central concept in the appraisal of alternative rules of inference, and to treat various semantic phenomena (e.g. vagueness, empty names, expressive utterances) by exploiting the idea that a proposition might be neither true nor false. It is commonly assumed that deflationary theories of truth are precluded by these demands.

*Propositions and utterances:*   Propositions are regarded as such obscure and bizarre entities that it may seem undesirable to base an account of truth on the schematic principle,

(E)   The proposition ⟨p⟩ is true *iff* p,

which presupposes them. At the same time, the natural deflationary account of truth for *utterances*, the disquotational schema,

(D)   Any utterance of the sentence 'p' is true *iff* p

has difficulty with indexical expressions (try 'I am hungry'), foreign languages ('Schnee ist weiss'), and indeed with all sentence-tokens whose truth or falsity depends on the context in which they are produced.

*The 'correspondence' intuition:*   The idea that a representation is made true by its correspondence to reality has great intuitive appeal, yet there appears to be no room for any such conception within the deflationary picture.

## Notes

1   Notice that one could design an alternative way of putting the things that we actually express by means of the truth predicate. With the introduction of *sentence* variables, *predicate* variables and *substitutional* quantification our thoughts could be expressed as follows:

(1**)   For any sentence such that Oscar claimed that *it*, then *it*,

or in logical notation

(1***)   (p)((Oscar claimed that p) → p);

and

(5**)   Given any predicate, a thing is either *it* or not *it*,

or

(5***)   (F)(x)(Fx & – Fx).

However the variables '*it*', 'p', and 'F', are not the usual kind which replace *noun* phrases and refer to objects. Rather, 'F' must be construed as a 'pro-predicate', and 'p' as a 'pro-sentence'. Moreover, *generalization* with respect to these variables cannot be understood in the usual way as saying that every object has a certain property, but must be construed as asserting the truth of every legitimate substitution instance. Thus (1***) means intuitively that any result of substituting an English declarative sentence for 'p' in 'Oscar claimed *that p* → p' is true.

   The advantage of the truth predicate is that it allows us to say what we want without having to employ any new linguistic apparatus of this sort. It enables us to achieve the effect of generalizing substitutionally over sentences and predicates, but by means of ordinary variables (i.e. pronouns), which range over *objects*.

2 More or less deflationary views about truth are endorsed and defended (in various

forms and to various degrees) by Frege (1891, 1918), Ramsey (1927), Ayer (1935), Wittgenstein (1922, 1953), Strawson (1950) and Quine (1970). In recent years the idea has been developed by Grover, Camp and Belnap (1975), Leeds (1978), the present author (1982), A. Fine (1984), Soames (1984), Field (1986), M. J. Williams (1986), Lear (1987), Baldwin (1988) and Brandom (1988).

3  For an examination of this view as it appears in the early writings of Moore and Russell see Cartwright (1987).

4  I shall write '⟨p⟩' for 'the proposition that p', and 'iff' for 'if and only if'.

## Works Cited

Ayer, A. J. (1935). 'The Criterion of Truth.' *Analysis*, 3.

Baldwin, T. (1989). 'Can There Be a Substantive Theory of Truth?' *Récherche sur la philosophie et le language*, 10, Grenoble, Université des Sciences Sociales de Grenoble.

Brandom, R. (1988). 'Pramatism, Phenomenalism, and Truth Talk,' *Midwest Studies in Philosophy*, 12 ed. P. French, T. Uehling and H. Wettstein, Minneapolis, University of Minnesota Press.

Cartwright, R. (1987). 'A Neglected Theory of Truth,' *Philosophical Essays*, Cambridge, MA, MIT Press.

Field, H. (1986). 'The Deflationary Conception of Truth' *Fact, Science and Morality*, ed. G. MacDonald and C. Wright. Oxford: Blackwell.

Fine, A. (1984). 'The Natural Ontological Attitude.' *Scientific Realism*, ed. J. Leplin. Berkeley: University of California Press.

Frege, G. (1891). 'On Function and Concept,' in *Translations from the Philosophical Writings of G. Frege*. M. Black and P. Geach, trans. and ed. Oxford: Blackwell, 1960.

——. (1918). 'The Thought'. Trans. A. Quinton and M. Quinton. *Mind* 65: 1956.

Grover, D. Camp, J. And Belnap, N. (1975). 'A Prosentential Theory of Truth.' *Philosophical Studies*, 27.

Horwich, Paul (1982). *Probability and Evidence*. Cambridge: Cambridge University Press.

Leeds, S. (1978). 'Theories of Reference and Truth.' *Erkenntnis*, 13.

Lear, B. (1987). 'Truth Beyond All Verification.' *Michael Dummett*, ed. B. Taylor. Nijhoff, Dordrecht.

Quine, W. V. O. (1970). *Philosophy of Logic*. Englewood Cliffs, NJ: Prentice-Hall.

Ramsey, F. (1927). 'Facts and Propositions.' *Proceedings of the Aristotelian Society*. Arist. Supplementary vol. 7.

Soames, S. (1984). 'What is a Theory of Truth?' *Journal of Philosophy*, 81.

Strawson, P. (1950). 'Truth.' *Proceedings of the Aristotelian Society*. Supplementary vol. 24.

Williams, M. J. (1986). 'Do We (Epistemologists) Need a Theory of Truth?' *Philosophical Topics* 14.

Wittgenstein, L. (1922). *Tractatus Logico-Philosophicus*. London: Routledge and Kegan Paul.

—— (1953). *Philosophical Investigations*. Oxford: Oxford University Press.

# 19   Language, Truth and Reason

## *Ian Hacking*

I wish to pose a relativist question from within the heartland of rationality. It is not about the confrontation between science and alien cultures, for it comes out of our own scientific tradition. It does not rehearse the Kuhnian stories of revolution, replacement and incommensurability, but speaks chiefly of evolution and accumulation. Its sources are not hermeneutics but the canonical writings of positivism. Far from invoking 'the dogma of the dualism of scheme and reality' from which, according to Donald Davidson, 'we get conceptual relativity', it may well learn a trick from Davidson himself.[1]

I start from the fact that there have been different styles of scientific reasoning. The wisest of the Greeks admired Euclidean thought. The best minds of the seventeenth century held that the experimental method put knowledge on a new footing. At least part of every modern social science deploys some statistics. Such examples bring to mind different styles of reasoning with different domains. Each has surfaced and attained maturity in its own time, in its own way.

An inane subjectivism may say that whether $p$ is a reason for $q$ depends on whether people have got around to reasoning that way or not. I have the subtler worry that whether or not a proposition is as it were up for grabs, as a candidate for being true-or-false, depends on whether we have ways to reason about it. The style of thinking that befits the sentence helps fix its sense and determines the way in which it has a positive direction pointing to truth or to falsehood. If we continue in this vein, we may come to fear that the rationality of a style of reasoning is all too built-in. The propositions on which the reasoning bears mean what they do just because that way of reasoning can assign them a truth value. Is reason, in short, all too self-authenticating?

My worry is about truth-or-falsehood. Consider Hamlet's maxim, that nothing's either good or bad but thinking makes it so. If we transfer this to truth and falsehood, this is ambiguous between: (*a*) Nothing, which is true, is true, and nothing, which is false, is false, but thinking makes it so: (*b*) that preoccupies me. My relativist worry is, to repeat, that the sense of a proposition $p$, the way in which it points to truth or falsehood, hinges on the style of reasoning appropriate to $p$. Hence we cannot criticize that style of reasoning, as a way of getting to $p$, or to not-$p$, because $p$ simply is that proposition whose truth value is determined in this way.

The distinction between (*a*) and (*b*) furnishes a distinction between subjectivity and relativity. Let (*a*) be subjectivism: by thinking we might make something true, or make it false. Let (*b*) be the kind of relativity that I address in this paper: by thinking, new candidates for truth and falsehood may be brought into being. Many of the recent but already classical philosophical discussions of such topics as incommensurability, indeterminacy of translation, and conceptual schemes seem to me to discuss truth, where they ought to be considering truth-or-falsehood. Hence bystanders, hoping to learn from philosophers, have tended to discuss subjectivity rather than relativity. For my part, I have no doubt that our discoveries are 'objective', simply because the styles of reasoning that we employ determine what counts as objectivity. My worry is that the very candidates for truth or falsehood have no existence independent of the styles of reasoning that settle what it is to be true or false in their domain.

## Styles of Reasoning

It is not the case that *nothing's* either true or false but thinking makes it so. Plenty of things that we say need no reasons. That is the core of the discredited philosophical doctrine of observation sentences, the boring utterances that crop up in almost any language, and which make radical translation relatively easy. Translation is hard when one gets to whole new ranges of possibility that make no sense for the favoured styles of reasoning of another culture. It is there that ethnographers begin to have problems. Every people has generated its own peculiar styles. We are no different from others, except that we can see, more clearly from our own written record, the historical emergence of new styles of reasoning.

I take the word 'style' from the title of a forthcoming book by A. C. Crombie: *Styles of Scientific Thinking in the European Tradition*.[2] He concludes an anticipatory paper with the words:

> The active promotion and diversification of the scientific methods of late medieval and early modern Europe reflected the general growth of a research mentality in European society, a mentality conditioned and increasingly committed by its circumstances to expect and to look actively for problems to formulate and solve, rather than for an accepted consensus without argument. The varieties of scientific methods so brought in to play may be distinguished as,
>
> (1) the simple postulation established in the mathematical sciences,
> (2) the experimental exploration and measurement of more complex observable relations,
> (3) the hypothetical construction of analogical models,
> (4) the ordering of variety by comparison and taxonomy,
> (5) the statistical analysis of regularities of populations and the calculus of probabilities, and
> (6) the historical derivation of genetic development.
>
> The first three of these methods concern essentially the science of individual regularities, and the second three the science of the regularities of populations ordered in space and time.[3]

Coincidentally, at the same conference to which Crombie read these works, Winifred Wisan announced another forthcoming work, *Mathematics and the Study of Motion: Emergence of a New Scientific Style in the 17th Century*.[4] Both Crombie's and Wisan's papers were about Galileo, who has long been a favourite candidate for advancing a new style of thought. Sometimes words more dramatic than 'style' are used, as when Althusser writes of Thales opening up a new continent, that of mathematics, Galileo opening up the continent of dynamics and Marx that of history.[5] But often the word 'style' is chosen. It is to be found in Collingwood. Stephen Weinberg, the theoretical physicist, recalls Husserl speaking of a Galilean style for 'making abstract models of the universe to which at least the physicists give a higher degree of reality than they accord the ordinary world of sensation'.[6] Weinberg finds it remarkable that this style should work, 'for the universe does not seem to have been prepared with human beings in mind'. The linguist Noam Chomsky picks up this remark in his most recent book, urging that 'we have no present alternative to pursuing the 'Galilean style' in the natural sciences at least'.[7]

Like T.S. Kuhn's 'paradigm', the word 'style' serves my four contemporary authors to point to something general in the history of knowledge. There are new modes of reasoning that have specific beginnings and trajectories of development. Even these four will surely not agree in carving up histories into styles. The historian will find many styles where Chomsky sees only one. Doubtless the very word 'style' is suspect. It is cribbed from art critics and historians, who have not evolved a uniform connotation for the word. Nor would all their remarks about style tidily transfer to modes of reasoning. That is a problem that Wisan's paper begins to address. The success of the word 'style', as an analytic term for the history of science, may depend on the reception of Crombie's immensely learned historical analysis. Use of a borrowed word needs detailed examples to flush it out. Despite these reservations I shall take the fact that these recent writers employ the word in similar ways as an excuse for not attempting my own exegesis here.

## Arch-Rationalism

The existence of styles of reasoning does not immediately suggest relativism. Before elaborating the relativist worry sketched at the beginning of this paper, I shall first state a rationalist position informed by a proper respect both for history and for the idiosyncracies of ourselves and others. I shall call it arch-rationalism. (I, too, am an arch-rationalist most of the time).

The arch-rationalist believes what right-thinking people have known all along. There are good and bad reasons. It has taken millennia to evolve systems of reasoning. By and large our Western tradition has contributed more to this progress than any other. We have often been narrow, blinkered and insensitive to foreign insights. We have repressed our own deviant and original thinkers, condemning many to irretrievable oblivion. Some of our own once-favoured styles of reasoning have turned out to be dead ends and others are probably on the way. However, new styles of reasoning will continue to evolve. So we shall not only find out more about nature, but we shall also learn new ways to reason about it. Maybe Paul Feyerabend's advocacy of anarchy is right. To compel people to reason in approved ways is to limit us and our potentialities for novelty. Arch-rationalism is convinced that there are good and bad reasons, but since it does not commit us to any specific regimentation like that of formal logic or Sir Karl Popper, it is fairly receptive to Feyeraband's imitation anarchy.

My arch-rationalist thinks that there is a fairly sharp distinction between reasons and the propositions they support. Reasons merely help us find out what is the case. The arch-rationalist wants to know how the world is. There are good and bad reasons for propositions about nature. They are not relative to anything. They do not depend on context. The arch-rationalist is not an imperialist about reason. Maybe there could be people who never reason nor deliberate at all. They tell jokes, make and break promises, feign insults and so forth, but they never reason. Just as statistical reasons had no force for the Greeks, so one imagines a people for whom none of our reasons for belief have force. On the other hand the arch-rationalist is an optimist about human nature. We who value truth and reason do imagine that a truthless and unreasoning people would, if left alone, evolve truth and reason for themselves. They would in their own way acquire a taste for speculation about the diagonal of a square, for motion on the inclined plane, for the tracks of the planets, for the inner constitution of matter, the evolution of the species, the Oedipus complex and amino acids.

The arch-rationalist not only grants that our kinds of truth and reason may not play as great a role in the life of other peoples as in our own culture; he may also be a romantic, hankering after a simpler, less reason-impregnated life. He will grant that our values are not inevitable, nor perhaps the noblest to which our species can aspire. But he cannot escape his own past. His admission of the historicity of our own styles of reasoning in no way makes it less objective. Styles of reasoning have histories and some emerged sooner than others. Humankind has got better at reasoning. What ground for relativism could there be in all that?

Instead of challenging the assumptions of the arch-rationalist, I shall extract a hint of incoherence from his heartland, which is, in the end, positivism.

## Positivism

Positivism is commonly taken to be a hard-headed antagonism to all forms of relativism. I shall create a question for the arch-rationalist from three aspects of positivism itself. I draw them from Auguste Comte, Moritz Schlick and Michael Dummett, i.e. the original positivist of the 1840s, the leader of the Vienna Circle in 1930, and the most gifted present exponent of one among that family of doctrines.

*Comte.* He was an historicist. His epistemology is a massive and almost unreadable account of human knowledge, a narrative of the human mind in which each intellectual innovation finds its own niche. One of his ideas is that a branch of knowledge acquires a 'positivity' by the development of a new, positive, style of reasoning associated with it. He is none too clear what he means by 'positive'; he sometimes says he chose the word chiefly because it had overtones of moral uplift in all European languages. A positive proposition is one that is by some means befitting the branch of knowledge to which it belongs. We may pun on his word: a positive proposition is one that has a direction, a truth value. It is no distortion to say that for Comte a class of positive propositions is a class of propositions that are up for grabs as true-or-false.

There are many aspects of Comte's thought from which one hastily withdraws – I refer both to questions of ideology and to issues of interest to analytic philosophers of science (e.g. his analysis of causation) I draw attention only to the idea of a historical evolution of different styles of reasoning, each bringing in its train its own body of positive knowledge. Each finds its place in great tabular displays of the sciences that serve as pull-outs from his gigantic epistemological text, the *Cours de philosophie positive*. Comte did not think that the evolution of styles and of positive knowledges had come to an end. His life goal was the creation of a new positive science, sociology. This would require a new style of reasoning. He ill foresaw what this style would be, but his meta-conception of what he was doing was sound.

*Schlick*. One of the more memorable statements of logical positivism is Moritz Schlick's, 'the meaning of a sentence is its method of verification'.[8] Those words could not stand unmodified, because the Vienna Circle had succumbed to Gottlob Frege's dictum that meanings are definite, objective and fixed. Schlick's maxim would imply that a change or advance in a method of verification would change the meanings of a sentence. Rather than give up the idea of meanings handed down from generation to generation, tranquil and unmodified, logical positivists revised Schlick's maxim again and again, although with no satisfactory outcome.[9] But for Comte, or any other of those fortunate writers of 1840 not yet infected by Fregean theories of meaning, Schlick's statement would be just fine. It is precisely, for Comte, the methods of verification – the ways in which the positive truth values are to be established – that determine the content of a body of knowledge.

*Dummett*. In logic, a proposition that has a definite truth value, true, or false, is called *bivalent*. Dummett's work has made philosophers think closely about bivalence.[10] It was first inspired by a philosophical reconstruction of some of the thoughts behind intuitionist mathematics. In what is called a non-constructive proof, one cannot exhibit the mathematical objects that are proved to exist. (So one might have a step in which one asserts that there is a prime number with a certain property, but be unable to say which prime number it is.) Non-constructive proofs may also assume of a proposition that it is either true or false, without being able to show which truth value it has. Some philosophical mathematicians, including Dummett, have doubted whether such non-constructive proofs are admissible.

Dummett is attracted to the following basis of his doubt. Whether or not a proposition is bivalent must depend upon its meaning. He wonders how we can confer meanings on statements in nonconstructive mathematics – meanings in virtue of which the statements are bivalent, although there is no known way to settle the truth values. It is we who through our linguistic practices are the sole source of the meanings of what we say. How then can we confer a meaning on a statement, such that it is bivalent, when nothing we know how to do bears on the truth or the falsehood of the statement? Maybe statements of non-constructive mathematics acquire bivalence only as we perfect means of determining their truth values or exhibiting the mathematical objects of which they speak?

Although this subtle question arose in sharp form in the intuitionist critique of classical mathematics, Dummett extends it to other forms of discourse. Many statements about the past cannot now be settled by any practicable means. Are they bivalent? Might bivalence recede into the past as historical data become irrevocably erased? Dummett does not claim that his worries are conclusive, nor does he expect parallel answers for every kind of discourse. One might, on reflection, come out for bivalence in the case of history, but reject it for non-constructive mathematics.

*Positivity and bivalence.* I have spoken of being true-or-false, and have used Comte's word 'positive'. Is this the same idea as bivalence? Not as I shall use the words. Being positive is a less strong characteristic than bivalence. Outside mathematics I suspect that whether a statement is bivalent or not is an abstraction imposed by logicians to facilitate their analysis of deductive argument forms. It is a noble abstraction, but it is a consequence of art, not nature. In the speculative sciences that concern me in this paper, the interesting sentences are the ones that are up for grabs as true or false – ones for which we believe we have methods that will determine the truth values. The applications of these methods may require as yet unimagined technological innovation. Moreover we find out more about the world, we find out that many of our questions no longer make sense. Bivalence is not the right concept for science. Allow me a couple of examples to point to the distinction required.

At the time of Laplace it was very sensible to think that there are particles of caloric, the substance of heat, that have repulsive forces that decay rapidly with distance. On such an hypothesis Laplace solved many of the outstanding problems about sound. Propositions about the rate of extinction of the repulsive force of caloric were up for grabs as true or false and one knew how to obtain information bearing on the question. Laplace had an excellent estimate of the rate of extinction of the repulsive force, yet it turns out that the whole idea is wrongheaded. I would say that Laplace's sentences once were 'positive'. They were never bivalent. Conversely, Maxwell once said that some propositions about the relative velocity of light were intrinsically incapable of determination, yet a few years after he said that Michelson had invented the technology to give precise answers to Maxwell's questions. I would say that the sentences of interest to Maxwell had positivity when he uttered them, but were bivalent only after a transformation in technology – a transformation whose success depends on delicate experimental details about how the world works.

In short, Comte's 'positive' is drawing attention to a less demanding concept than Dummett's 'bivalent'. Yet the two are connected and so are the thoughts of both writers. Dummett says: not bivalent unless we have a proof of the truth value, or a known sure-fire method for generating the proof. Comte says: not positive, not in the running for being true-or-false, until there is some style of reasoning that will bear on the question.

Comte, Schlick and Dummett are no more relativist than Crombie or Chomsky. Yet a positivist train of thought, combined with an emphasis on styles of reasoning, has the germ of relativism. If positivity is consequent upon a style of reasoning, then a range of possibilities depends upon that style. They would not be possibilities, candidates for truth or falsehood, unless that style were in existence. The existence of the style arises from historical events. Hence although whichever propositions are true may depend on the data, the fact that they are candidates for being true is a consequence of an historical event. Conversely the rationality of a style of reasoning as a way of bearing on the truth of a class of propositions does not seem open for independent criticism, because the very sense of what can be established by that style depends upon the style itself.

Is that a nasty circle?

I shall proceed as follows. First, I observe that by reasoning I don't mean logic. I mean the very opposite, for logic is the preservation of truth, while a style of reasoning is what brings in the possibility of truth or falsehood. Then I separate my idea of style of reasoning from the incommensurability of Kuhn and Feyerabend, and from the indeterminacy of translation urged by Quine. Then I examine Davidson's fundamental objection to the supposition that there are alternative ways of thinking. He may refute subjectivity, as I understand stand it, but not relativity. The key distinction throughout the following discussion is the difference between truth-and-falsehood as opposed to truth. A second important idea is the looseness of fit between those propositions that have a sense for almost all human beings regardless of reasoning, and those that get a sense only within a style of reasoning.


## Induction, Deduction

Neither deductive logic nor induction occur on Crombie's list. How strange, for are they not said to be the basis of science? It is instructive that no list like Crombie's would include them. The absence reminds us that styles of reasoning create the possibility for truth and falsehood. Deduction and induction merely preserve it.

We now understand deduction as that mode of inference that preserves truth. It cannot pass from true premises to a false conclusion. The nature of induction is more controversial. The word has been used in many ways. There is an important tradition represented alike by the philospher C.S. Peirce and the statistician Jerzy Neyman: induction is that mode of argument that preserves truth most of the time.

Deduction and induction were important human discoveries. But they play little role in the scientific method, no more than the once revered syllogism. They are devices for jumping from truth to truth. Not only will they give us no original truth from which to jump, but also they take for granted the class of sentences that assert possibilities of truth or falsehood. That is why they do not occur in Crombie's list. In deduction and induction alike truth plays the purely formal role of a counter on an abacus. It matters not what truth is, when we employ the mechanics of the model theory of modern logicians. Their machine works well so long as we suppose that the class of sentences that have truth values is already given. (Or, in the case of intuitionist logic, one supposes that the class of sentences that may, through proof, acquire truth values is already given.) Induction equally assumes that the class of possible truths is predetermined. Styles of reasoning of the sort described by Crombie do something different. When they come into being they generate new classes of possibilities.

## Incommensurability and the Indeterminacy of Translation

Philosophers have recently given us two doctrines that pull in opposite directions. Both seem to use the idea of a conceptual scheme, a notion that goes back at least to Kant but whose modern nominalist version is due to Quine. He says that a conceptual scheme is a set of sentences held to be true. He uses the metaphor of core and periphery. Sentences at the core have a kind of permanence and are seldom relinquished, while those on the periphery are more empirical and more readily given up in the light of 'recalcitrant experience'.

My talk of styles of reasoning does not mesh well with Quine's idea of a conceptual scheme.[11] In his opinion two schemes differ when some substantial number of core sentences of one scheme are not held to be true in another scheme. A style of reasoning, in contrast, is concerned with truth-or-falsehood. Two parties, agreeing to the same styles of reasoning, may well totally disagree on the upshot, one party holding for true what the other party rejects. Styles of reasoning may determine possible truth values, but unlike Quine's schemes are not characterized by assignments of truth values. It is to be expected, then, that Quine's application of the idea of a conceptual scheme will not coincide with my idea of styles of reasoning.

Quine's most memorable thesis is the indeterminancy of translation. Let $L$ and $M$ be languages spoken by two truly disparate communities. Quine holds that there are indefinitely many possible but incompatible translations between $L$ and $M$. No matter how much speakers of $L$ and $M$ might converse, there is in principle no way of settling on a definitely right translation. This is not a matter of settling on nuances; Quine means that you could take a sentence $s$ of $L$ and translate it by one system of translation into $p$ of $M$, and translate it by another system into $q$ of $M$, and $p$ and $q$ would, in $M$, be held to be incompatible.

As we shall see in the next section, Donald Davidson has noticed that the notion of conceptual scheme does not ride well with the indeterminancy of translation. For how are we to say that speakers of $L$ have a scheme different from we who speak $M$? We must first pick out the true sentences from the core of the scheme of $L$, and show that many of these translate into sentences of $M$ that we who speak $M$ hold to be false. But what is to assure that this is the right translation? When translating there is a strong instinct to render central doctrines of $L$ as main truths of $M$. Once you focus on truth rather than truth-or-falsehood, you begin a chain of considerations that call in question the very idea of a conceptual scheme.

The thesis of indeterminacy of translation pulls in one direction and the idea of incommensurability pulls in another. We owe incommensurability to Kuhn and Feyerabend.[12] The idea is that disparate systems of thought are not mutually expressible. Kuhn has tended to make the idea fit commonplace situations while Feyerabend emphasizes the extreme. Thus Feyerabend's favourite example of incommensurability is the break between the cosmologies of archaic and classical Greece. Kuhn, in contrast, comes back to the idea of 'no common measure' in the original meaning of the word, and applies it to more everyday 'advances' in knowledge. When there has been a scientific revolution the new science may address new problems and employ new concepts. There is no way of settling whether the new science does its job better than the old one because they do different jobs. Kuhn finds this sort of incommensurability in all sorts of revolutions that strike the outsider as minor, while Feyerabend focuses on big shifts in human thought. Both writers once suggested that incommensurability should be understood in terms of schemes and translation. Incommensurability meant that there would simply be no way of translating from one scheme to another. Thus this idea pulls in a direction exactly opposite to Quine's. Indeterminancy says there are too many translations between schemes, while incommensurability says there are none at all.

Would either the Kuhnian or the Feyerabendian idea of incommensurability apply if styles of reasoning were to supersede each other? The Kuhnian 'no common measure' does not apply in any straightforward way because when we reason differently there is no expectation of common measure of the sort that successive Kuhnian paradigms invite. Hence it is to the more extreme, Feyerabendian, use of the term that we must look. That is surely the popular conception of incommensurability: the inability of one body of thought to understand another.

I do admit that there is a real phenomenon of disparate ways of *thinking*. Some styles of reasoning have been so firmly displaced that we cannot even recognize their objects. The renaissance medical, alchemical and astrological doctrines of resemblance and similitude are well-nigh incomprehensible. One does not find our modern notions of evidence deployed in those arcane pursuits. There is very little truth in all that hermetic writing, and to understand it one cannot search out the core of truth that meshes with our beliefs. Yet that stuff may not be best described as incommensurable with our modern chemistry, medicine and astronomy. It is not that the propositions match ill with our modern sciences, so much as that the way propositions are proposed and defended is entirely alien to us. You can perfectly well learn hermetic lore, and when you do so you end up talking the language of Paracelsus, possibly in translation. What you learn is not systems of translation but chains of reasoning which would have little sense if one were not re-creating the thought of one of those magi. What we have to learn is not what they took for true, but what they took for true-or-false. (For example, that mercury salve might be good for syphilis because mercury is signed by the planet Mercury which signs the marketplace, where syphilis is contracted.)

Understanding the sufficiently strange is a matter of recognizing new possibilities for truth-or-falsehood, and of learning how to conduct other styles of reasoning that bear on those new possibilities. The achievement of understanding is not exactly a difficulty of translation, although foreign styles will make translation difficult. It is certainly not a matter of designing translations which preserve as much truth as possible, because what is true-or-false in one way of talking may not make much sense in another until one has learned how to reason in a new way. Understanding is learning how to reason. When we encounter old or alien texts we have to translate them, but it is wrong to focus on that aspect of translation that merely produces sentences of English for sentences of the other language. With such a limited focus one thinks of charitably trying to get the old text to say as much truth as possible. But, even after Paracelsus is translated into modern German, one still has to learn how he reasoned in order to understand him. Since the idea of incommensurability has been so closely tied to translation rather than reasoning, I do not use it here.

The indeterminacy of translation is an equally wrong idea. It is empiricially empty, because we know that unequivocal translation evolves between any two communities in contact. It is the wrong theoretical notion because it starts from an idea of truth-preserving matching of sentences. In fact the possibilities available in one language are not there in the other. To get them into the second language one has to learn a way of reasoning and when that has been done there is no problem of translation at all, let alone indeterminacy.

There is perfect commensurability, and no indeterminacy of translation, in those boring domains of 'observations' that we share with all people as people. Where we as people have branches off from others as a people, we find new interests, and a looseness of fit between their and our commonplaces. Translation of truths is irrelevant. Communication of ways to think is what matters.

## Conceptual Schemes

In his famous paper, 'On the very idea of a conceptual scheme', Donald Davidson argues more against incommensurability than indeterminacy, but he is chiefly against the idea of a conceptual scheme that gives sense to either.[13] He provides 'an underlying methodology of interpretation' such that 'we could not be in a position' to judge 'that others had concepts or beliefs different from our own'. He makes plain that he does not reach this result by postulating 'a neutral ground, or a common coordinate system' between schemes. It is the notion of a scheme itself to which he is opposed. He rejects a 'dogma of dualism between scheme and reality' from which we derive the bogey of 'conceptual relativity, and of truth relative to a scheme'.

Davidson distinguishes two claims. Total translatability between schemes may be impossible, or there may be only partial untranslatability. Even if we do not follow the intricacies of his argument, nor even accept its premises, we can, like Davidson, dismiss the idea of total untranslatability. As a matter of brute fact all human languages are fairly easily partially translatable. The fact is closely connected with what I said earlier, that there is a common human core of verbal performances connected with what people tend to notice around them. But I said that there is a looseness of fit between that broad base of shared humanity and the interesting things that people like to talk about. That looseness leaves some space for incommensurability. It is not only the topics of discussion that may vary from group to group, but what counts as a point of saying something. Yet Davidson counters there too, and mounts a magnificent attack against even the notion of partial untranslatability between groups of people. Since in fact even partial untranslatability is chiefly a matter of coming to share the interest of another, and since lots of travellers are pretty sympathetic people, interests do get shared, so we should welcome an argument against partial untranslatability too. Yet since Davidson's argument may seem founded upon a lack of concern for alternative interests, we may fear his premises while we accept his conclusions. My diagnosis is that, like Quine, he assumes that a conceptual scheme is defined in terms of what counts as true, rather than of what counts as true-or-false.

## Truth versus Truth-or-Falsehood

Davidson concludes his argument against relativity with the words, 'Of course the truth of sentences remains relative to a language, but that is as objective as can be.' Earlier he rightly states what is wrong with the idea of making a sentence true:

> *Nothing*, makes sentences and theories true: not experience, not surface irritations [he there alluded to Quine], not the world . . . *That* experience takes a certain course, that our skin is warmed or punctured . . . these facts, if we like to talk that way, make sentences and theories true. But this point is better made without mention of facts. The sentence 'my skin is warm' is true if and only if my skin is warm. Hence there is no reference to a fact, a world, an experience, or a piece of evidence.[14]

Davidson's example, 'my skin is warm', serves me well. I urge a distinction between statements that may be made in any language, and which require no style of reasoning, and statements whose sense depends upon a style of reasoning. Davidson writes as if all sentences were of the former class. I agree that 'my skin is warm' is of that class. When I once looked for the best example of a sense-datum sentence to be actually published in the annals of real science, I hit upon precisely this sentence, or rather, 'my skin is warmed'. It begins Sir William Herschel's investigations of 1800 which are said to commence the theory of radiant heat. (He noticed that using filters of some colours his skin was warmed, while using other colours he had much light but little heat.)[15]

Herschel went on to pose a theory of invisible rays of heat, a theory that we now call correct, although his own experiments made him give it up. In the course of this reasoning he abandoned the following sentence, 'The heat which has the refrangibility of the red rays is occasioned by the light of those rays.' We can certainly write out a truth condition of the form '$s$ is true if and only if $p$' for this sentence. But there arises a problem for the sufficiently foreign translator. It is not that words like 'ray' and 'refrangible' are mildly theoretical and the translator may have no such notions in his vocabulary. If another culture has acquired the styles of reasoning enumerated by Crombie it can perfectly well learn Herschel's physics from the ground up – that is just what I do in making sense of Herschel's text. The problem is that the sufficiently foreign person will not have Herschel's kind of sentence as the sort of thing that can be true-or-false, because the ways of reasoning that bear on it are unknown. To exaggerate the case, say the translator is Archimedes. I do not choose him at random, for he wrote a great tract on burning mirrors and was a greater scientist than Herschel. Yet I say he would not be able to effect a translation until he had caught up on some scientific method.

I should repeat my opposition to usual versions of incommensurability. It is not that Herschel's science had some Newtonian principles about rays and refrangibility that determine the meaning of sentences in which those words occur, and so those sentences could not have the same meaning in another theory. On the contrary, Herschel's sentences were fairly immune to change in theory. They were up for grabs as true or false in 1800; Herschel thought first that a crucial sentence is true and later held it to be false; many years later the world agreed on the truth of the sentence. Herschel, then, first grabbed the right end of the stick and then grabbed the wrong one. My claim about a translator less well placed than Archimedes is that until he learns how to reason more like Herschel, there are no ends of a stick to grab.


## Schemes without Dogma

'Truth of sentences', writes Davidson, 'remains relative to a language, but that is as objective as can be.' I claim that for part of our language, and perhaps as part of any language, being true-or-false is a property of sentences only because we reason about those sentences in certain ways. Subjectivists put their worries in the form of saying that with different customs we could 'rightly' take some propositions for true while at present we take them for false. Davidson has dealt sharply with all such formulations. But he has left a space for a relativist fear. The relativist ought to say that there might be whole other categories of truth-or-falsehood than ours.

Perhaps I am proposing a version of the conceptual scheme idea. Quine's conceptual schemes are sets of sentences held for true. Mine would be sets of sentences that are candidates for truth or falsehood. Does such a notion fall into the 'dogma of scheme and reality' that Davidson resents? I do not think so. The idea of a style of reasoning is as internal to what we think and say as the

Davidsonian form, '*s* is true and only if *p*' is internal to a language. *A style is not a scheme that confronts reality.* I did speak earlier of styles of reasoning being applied to data and to the formation of data. But data are uttered and are subject to Davidsonian treatment. There is much to be said about the neglected field of study, experimental science, but it has nothing much to do with scheme/reality. My own present work on the subject tries to show how experiment has a life of its own unrelated to theories or schemes.

## Anarcho-Rationalism

This paper makes two assertions and draws some inferences from them. Each assertion and every inference is in need of clarification. To list them is to show how much more must be done.

(1) There are different styles of reasoning. Many of these are discernible in our own history. They emerge at definite points and have distinct trajectories of maturation. Some die out, others are still going strong.

(2) Propositions of the sort that necessarily require reasoning to be substantiated have a positivity, a being true-or-false, only in consequence of the styles of reasoning in which they occur.

(3) Hence many categories of possibility, of what may be true or false, are contingent upon historical events, namely the development of certain styles of reasoning.

(4) It may then be inferred that there are other categories of possibility than have emerged in our tradition.

(5) We cannot reason as to whether alternative systems of reasoning are better or worse than ours, because the propositions to which we reason get their sense only from the method of reasoning employed. The propositions have no existence independent of the ways of reasoning towards them.

This chain of reflections does not lead to subjectivity. It does not imply that some proposition, with a content independent of reasoning, could be held to be true, or to be false, according to the mode of reasoning we adopt. Yet this defeat of subjectivity seems hollow because the propositions that are objectively found to be true are determined as true by styles of reasoning for which in principle there can be no external justification. A justification would be an independent way of showing that the style gets at the truth, but there is no characterization of the truth over and above what is reached by the styles of reason itself.

Can there not be a meta-reason justifying a style of reason? Can one not, for example, appeal to success? It need not be success in generating technology, although that does matter. Nor is it to be success in getting at the truth, for that would be circular. There can, however, be non-circular successes in truth-related matters. For example, following Imre Lakatos, one might revamp Popper's method of conjecture and refutation, urging that a methodology of research programmes constantly opens up new things to think about.[16] I have quoted Chomsky giving a similar meta-reason. On his analysis of the Galilean style, it has not only worked remarkably well, but also, in the natural sciences, at least, we have no alternative but to go on using that style, although, of course, in the future it may not work. Although Chomsky does not make the distinction, his meta-reason is less that Galileo's style continues to find out the truth about the universe than that it poses new kinds of probing and answering. It has produced an open-ended dialogue. That might terminate in the face of a nature that ceased to participate in ways that the Galilean can make sense of. We know it might cease to cater to our interests, but at present (says Chomsky) we have no alternative.

Chomsky is saying that if we want to engage in certain pursuits (call them the natural sciences or even the pursuit of truth in our tradition), we must reason with our reasons. Other styles of reasoning may occur; some are current. Other people may have other interests. We ought at least to be cautious, in the social sciences, in looking for other styles of reasoning (that is the problem for other contributors to this collection). Such considerations may lead the arch-rationalist to be a stick-in-the-mud, but since relativity does not imply subjectivity, he can carry on doing what we do with few qualms.

Some arch-rationalists may even find themselves agreeing that an anarcho-rationalism I have learned from Feyerabend is appealing. Our overall interests in truth and reason may well be served by letting other styles of reason evolve in their own ways, unfettered by a more imperial kind of rationalism. But that does not mean to say that I, as anarcho-rationalist, will take up something so recently killed off in our own tradition as homoeopathic medicine and its appeal to similitudes. That is for others (though if they look healthier than me, I might join up). Anarcho-rationalism is tolerance for other people combined with the discipline of one's own standards of truth and reason. The anarcho-rationalist is at home with the sentiment expressed by Sartre in his last interview:

C'est ça ma tradition, je n'en ai pas d'autre.
Ni la tradition orientale, ni la tradition juive.
Elles me manquent par mon historicité.[17]


## Notes

1 Donald Davidson, 'On the very idea of a conceptual scheme', *Proceedings and Addresses of the American Philosophical Association*, 47 (1974), pp. 5–20.
2 London; Gerald Duckworth and Co., 1983.
3 A. C. Crombie, 'Philosophical presuppositions and shifting interpretations of Galileo' in J. Hintikka, D. Gruender and E. Agazzi (eds), *Theory Change, Ancient Axiomatics and Galileo's Methodology, Proceedings of the 1978 Pisa Conference on the History and Philosophy of Science* (Reidel, Dordrecht, 1981), vol. I, p. 284 [numerals (1)–(6) inserted].
4 W. L. Wisan, 'Galileo and the emergenece of a new scientific style', ibid., pp. 311–39.
5 Louis Althusser, *Politics and History* (New Left Books, London, 1972), p. 185.

6  Stephen Weinberg, 'The forces of nature', *Bulletin of the American Academy of Arts and Sciences*, 29 (1976), p. 28.

7  Noam Chomsky, *Rules and Representations* (Columbia University Press, New York, and Blackwell, Oxford, 1980), p. 9.

8  Moritz Schlick, 'Meaning and verification', *The Philosophical Review*, 46 (1936), p. 261.

9  For an account of repeated failures, see Ian Hacking, *Why Does Language Matter to Philosophy?* (Cambridge University Press, Cambridge, 1975), ch. 9.

10  Michael Dummett, *Truth and Other Enigmas* (Duckworth, London, 1976), *passim*.

11  W. V. O. Quine, *Word and Object* (Wiley, New York, 1960), ch. 2.

12  For one version of this famous idea, see Paul Feyerabend, *Science in a Free Society* (New Left Books, London, 1978), pp. 65–70, 1970–1.

13  Davidson, 'On the very idea of a conceptual scheme'. For a systematic explanation of Davidson's programme, see Ian Hacking, *Why Does Language Matter to Philosophy?* (Cambridge University Press, Cambridge, 1975), ch. 12.

14  Davidson, 'On the very idea of a conceptual scheme', p. 16.

15  For discussion and references, see Ian Hacking, 'Spekulation, Berechnung und die Erschaffung von Phänomenen' in P. Duerr (ed.), *Versuchungen: Aufsätze zur Philosophie Paul Feyerabends* (Suhrkamp, Frankfurt, 1981), pp. 126–58.

16  Imre Lakatos, *The Methodology of Scientific Research Programmes* (Cambridge University Press, Cambridge, 1978), chs 1 and 2.

17  *Le Nouvel Observateur*, 10 March 1980, p. 93.

---

# 20  Pragmatism, Relativism, and Irrationalism

---

## *Richard Rorty*

### Part I: Pragmatism

"Pragmatism" is a vague, ambiguous, and overworked word. Nevertheless, it names the chief glory of our country's intellectual tradition. No other American writers have offered so radical a suggestion for making our future different from our past, as have James and Dewey. At present, however, these two writers are neglected. Many philosophers think that everything important in pragmatism has been preserved and adapted to the needs of analytic philosophy. More specifically, they view pragmatism as having suggested various holistic corrections of the atomistic doctrines of the early logical empiricists. This way of looking at pragmatism is not wrong, as far as it goes. But it ignores what is most important in James and Dewey. Logical empiricism was one variety of standard, academic, neo-Kantian, epistemologically-centered philosophy. The great pragmatists should not be taken as suggesting an holistic variation of this variant, but rather as breaking with the Kantian epistemological tradition altogether. As long as we see James or Dewey as having "theories of truth" or "theories of knowledge" or "theories of morality" we shall get them wrong. We shall ignore their criticisms of the assumption that there ought to *be* theories about such matters. We shall not see how radical their thought was – how deep was their criticism of the attempt, common to Kant, Husserl, Russell, and C. I. Lewis, to make philosophy into a foundational discipline.

One symptom of this incorrect focus is a tendency to overpraise Peirce. Peirce is praised partly because he developed various logical notions and various technical problems (such as the counterfactual conditional) which were taken up by the logical empiricists. But the main reason for Peirce's undeserved apotheosis is that his talk about a general theory of signs looks like an early discovery of the importance of language. For all his genius, however, Peirce never made up his mind what he wanted a general theory of signs *for*, nor what it might look like, nor what its relation to either logic or epistemology was supposed to be. His contribution to pragmatism was merely to have given it a name, and to have stimulated James. Peirce himself remained the most Kantian of thinkers – the most convinced that philosophy gave us an all-embracing ahistorical context in which every other species of discourse could be assigned its proper place and rank. It was just this Kantian assumption that there was such a context, and that epistemology or semantics could discover it, against which James and Dewey reacted. We need to focus on this reaction if we are to recapture a proper sense of their importance.

This reaction is found in other philosophers who are currently more fashionable than James or Dewey – for example, Nietzsche and Heidegger. Unlike Nietzsche and Heidegger, however, the pragmatists did not make the mistake of turning against the community which takes the natural scientist as its moral hero – the community of secular intellectuals which came to self-consciousness in the Enlightenment. James and Dewey rejected neither the Enlightenment's choice of the scientist as moral example, nor the technological civilization which science had created. They wrote, as Nietzsche and Heidegger did not, in a spirit of social hope. They asked us to liberate our new civilization by giving up the notion of "grounding" our culture, our moral lives, our politics, our religious beliefs, upon "philosophical bases." They asked us to give up the neurotic Cartesian quest for certainty which had been one result of Galileo's frightening new cosmology, the quest for "enduring spiritual values" which had been one reaction to Darwin, and the aspiration of academic philosophy to form a tribunal of pure reason which had been the neo-Kantian response to Hegelian historicism. They asked us to think of the Kantian project of grounding thought or culture in a permanent ahistorical matrix as *reactionary*. They viewed Kant's idealization of Newton, and Spencer's of Darwin, as just as silly as Plato's idealization of Pythagoras, and Aquinas' of Aristotle.

Emphasizing this message of social hope and liberation, however, makes James and Dewey sound like prophets rather than thinkers. This would be misleading. They had things to say about truth, knowledge, and morality, even though they did not have *theories* of them, in the sense of sets of answers to the textbook problems. In what follows, I shall offer three brief sloganistic characterizations of what I take to be their central doctrine.

My first characterization of pragmatism is that it is simply antiessentialism applied to notions like "truth," "knowledge," "language," "morality," and similar objects of philosophical theorizing. Let me illustrate this by James's definition of "the true" as "what is good in the way of belief." This has struck his critics as not to the point, as unphilosophical, as like the suggestion that the essence of aspirin is that it is good for headaches. James's point, however, was that there *is* nothing deeper to be said: truth is not the sort of thing which *has* an essence. More specifically, his point was that it is no use being told that truth is "correspondence to reality." Given a language and a view of what the world is like, one can, to be sure, pair off bits of the language with bits of what one takes the world to be in such a way that the sentences one believes true have internal structures isomorphic to relations between things in the world. When we rap out routine undeliberated reports like "This is water," "That's red," "That's ugly," "That's immoral," our short categorical sentences can easily be thought of as pictures, or as symbols which fit together to make a map. Such reports do indeed pair little bits of language with little bits of the world. Once one gets to negative universal hypotheticals, and the like, such pairing will become messy and *ad hoc*, but perhaps it can be done. James's point was that carrying out this exercise will not enlighten us about why truths are good to believe, or offer any clues as to why or whether our present view of the world is, roughly, the one we should hold. Yet nobody would have asked for a "theory" of truth if they had not wanted answers to these latter questions. Those who want truth to have an essence want knowledge, or rationality, or inquiry, or the relation between thought and its object, to have an essence. Further, they want to be able to use their knowledge of such essences to criticize views they take to be false, and to point the direction of progress toward the discovery of more truths. James thinks these hopes are vain. There are no essences anywhere in the area. There is no wholesale, epistemological way to direct, or criticize, or underwrite, the course of inquiry.

Rather, the pragmatists tell us, it is the vocabulary of practice rather than of theory, of action rather than contemplation, in which one can say something useful about truth. Nobody engages in epistemology or semantics because he wants to know how "This is red" pictures the world. Rather, we want to know in what sense Pasteur's views of disease picture the world accurately and Paracelsus' inaccurately, or what exactly it is that Marx pictured more accurately than Machiavelli. But just here the vocabulary of "picturing" fails us. When we turn from individual sentences to vocabularies and theories, critical terminology naturally shifts from metaphors of isomorphism, symbolism, and mapping to talk of utility, convenience, and likelihood of getting what we want. To say that the parts of properly analyzed true sentences are arranged in a way isomorphic to the parts of the world paired with them sounds plausible if one thinks of a sentence like "Jupiter has moons." It sounds slightly less plausible for "The earth goes round the sun," less still for "There is no such thing as natural motion," and not plausible at all for "The universe is infinite." When we want to praise or blame assertions of the latter sort of sentence, we show how the deci-sion to assert them fits into a whole complex of decisions about what terminol-ogy to use, what books to read, what projects to engage in, what life to live. In this respect they resemble such sentences as "Love is the only law" and "His-tory is the story of class struggle." The whole vocabulary of isomorphism, pic-turing, and mapping is out of place here, as indeed is the notion of being true *of* *objects*. If we ask what objects these sentences claim to be true of, we get only unhelpful repetitions of the subject terms – "the universe," "the law," "his-tory." Or, even less helpfully, we get talk about "the facts," or "the way the world is." The natural approach to such sentences, Dewey tells us, is not "Do they get it right?", but more like "What would it be like to believe that? What would happen if I did? What would I be committing myself to?" The vocabu-lary of contemplation, looking, *theoria*, deserts us just when we deal with theory rather than observation, with programming rather than input. When the con-templative mind, isolated from the stimuli of the moment, takes large views, its activity is more like deciding what to *do* than deciding that a representation is accurate. James's dictum about truth says that the vocabulary of practice is unelimiable, that no distinction of kind separates the sciences from the crafts, from moral reflection, or from art.

So a second characterization of pragmatism might go like this: there is no epistemological difference between truth about what ought to be and truth about what is, nor any metaphysical difference between facts and values, nor any methodological difference between morality and science. Even nonpragmatists think Plato was wrong to think of moral philosophy as discov-ering the essence of goodness, and Mill and Kant wrong in trying to reduce moral choice to rule. But every reason for saying that they were wrong is a reason for thinking the epistemological tradition wrong in looking for the es-sence of science, and in trying to reduce rationality to rule. For the pragmatists, the pattern of all inquiry – scientific as well as moral – is deliberation concerning the relative attractions of various concrete alternatives. The idea that in science or philosophy we can substitute "method" for deliberation between alternative results of speculation is just wishful thinking. It is like the idea that the morally wise man resolves his dilemmas by consulting his memory of the Idea of the Good, or by looking up the relevant article of the moral law. It is the myth that rationality consists in being constrained by rule. According to this Platonic myth, the life of reason is not the life of Socratic conversation but an illuminated state of consciousness in which one never needs to ask if one has exhausted the pos-sible descriptions of, or explanations for, the situation. One simply arrives at true beliefs by obeying mechanical procedures.

Traditional, Platonic, epistemologically-centered philosophy is the search for such procedures. It is the search for a way in which one can avoid the need for conversation and deliberation and simply tick off the way things are. The idea is to acquire beliefs about interesting and important matters in a way as much like visual perception as possible – by confronting an object and responding to it as programmed. This urge to substitute *theoria* for *phronesis* is what lies behind the attempt to say that "There is no such thing as natural motion" pictures objects in the same way as does "The cat is on the mat." It also lies behind the hope that some arrangement of objects may be found which is pictured by the sentence "Love is better than hate," and the frustration which ensues when it is realized that there may be no such objects. The great fallacy of the tradition, the pragmatists tell us, is to think that the metaphors of vision, correspondence, mapping, picturing, and representation which apply to small, routine assertions will apply to large and debatable ones. This basic error be gets the notion that where there are no objects to correspond to we have no hope of rationality, but only taste, passion, and will. When the pragmatist attacks the notion of truth as accuracy of representation he is thus attacking the traditional distinctions between reason and desire, reason and appetite, reason and will. For none of these distinctions make sense unless reason is thought of on the model of vision, unless we persist in what Dewey called "the spectator theory of knowledge."

The pragmatist tells us that once we get rid of this model we see that the Platonic idea of the life of reason is impossible. A life spent representing objects accurately would be spent recording the results of calculations, reasoning through sorites, calling off the observable properties of things, construing cases according to unambiguous criteria, getting things right. Within what Kuhn calls "normal science," or any similar social context, one can, indeed, live such a life. But conformity to *social* norms is not good enough for the Platonist. He wants to be constrained not merely by the disciplines of the day, but by the ahistorical and nonhuman nature of reality itself. This impulse takes two forms – the original Platonic strategy of postulating novel *objects* for treasured propositions to correspond to, and the Kantian strategy of finding *principles* which are definatory of the essence of knowledge, or representation, or morality, or rationality. But this difference is unimportant compared to the common urge to escape the vocabulary and practices of one's own time and find something ahistorical and necessary to cling to. It is the urge to answer questions like "Why believe what I take to be true?" "Why do what I take to be right?" by appealing to something *more* than the ordinary, retail, detailed, concrete reasons which have brought one to one's present view. This urge is common to nineteenth-century idealists and contemporary scientific realists, to Russell and to Husserl; it is definatory of the Western philosophical tradition, and of the culture for which that tradition speaks. James and Dewey stand with Nietzsche and Heidegger in asking us to abandon that tradition, and that culture.

Let me sum up by offering a third and final characterization of pragmatism: it is the doctrine that there are no constraints on inquiry save conversational ones – no wholesale constraints derived from the nature of the objects, or of the mind, or of language, but only those retail constraints provided by the remarks of our fellow-inquirers. The way in which the properly-programmed speaker cannot help believing that the patch before him is red has *no* analogy for the more interesting and controversial beliefs which provoke epistemological reflection. The pragmatist tells us that it is useless to hope that objects will constrain us to believe the truth about them, if only they are approached with an unclouded mental eye, or a rigorous method, or a perspicuous language. He wants us to give up the notion that God, or evolution, or some other under-writer of our present world-picture, has programmed us as machines for accurate verbal picturing, and that philosophy brings self-knowledge by letting us read our own program. The only sense in which we are constrained to truth is that, as Peirce suggested, we can make no sense of the notion that the view which can survive all objections might be false. But objections – conversational constraints – cannot be anticipated. There is no method for knowing *when* one has reached the truth, or when one is closer to it than before.

I prefer this third way of characterizing pragmatism because it seems to me to focus on a fundamental choice which confronts the reflective mind: that between accepting the contingent character of starting-points, and attempting to evade this contingency. To accept the contingency of starting-points is to accept our inheritance from, and our conversation with, our fellow-humans as our only source of guidance. To attempt to evade this contingency is to hope to become a properly-programmed machine. This was the hope which Plato thought might be fulfilled at the top of the divided line, when we passed beyond hypotheses. Christians have hoped it might be attained by becoming attuned to the voice of God in the heart, and Cartesians that it might be fulfilled by emptying the mind and seeking the indubitable. Since Kant, philosophers have hoped that it might be fulfilled by finding the a priori structure of any possible inquiry, or language, or form of social life. If we give up this hope, we shall lose what Nietzsche called "metaphysical comfort," but we may gain a renewed sense of community. Our identification with our community – our society, our political tradition, our intellectual heritage – is heightened when we see this community as *ours* rather than *nature's*, *shaped* rather than *found*, one among many which men have made. In the end, the pragmatists tell us, what matters is our loyalty to other human beings clinging together against the dark, not our hope of getting things right. James, in arguing against realists and idealists that "the trail of the human serpent is over all," was reminding us that our glory is in our participation in fallible and transitory human projects, not in our obedience to permanent nonhuman constraints.

## Part II: Relativism

"Relativism" is the view that every belief on a certain topic, or perhaps about *any* topic, is as good as every other. No one holds this view. Except for the occasional cooperative freshman, one cannot find anybody who says that two incompatible opinions on an important topic are equally good. The philosophers who get *called* "relativists" are those who say that the grounds for choosing between such opinions are less algorithmic than had been thought. Thus one may be attacked as a relativist for holding that familiarity of terminology is a criterion of theory-choice in physical science, or that coherence with the institutions of the surviving parliamentary democracies is a criterion in social philosophy. When such criteria are invoked, critics say that the resulting philosophical position assumes an unjustified primacy for "our conceptual framework," or our purposes, or our institutions. The position in question is criticized for not having done what philosophers are employed to do: explain why our framework, or culture, or interests, or language, or whatever, is at last on the right track – in touch with physical reality, or the moral law, or the real numbers, or some other sort of object patiently waiting about to be copied. So the real issue is not between people who think one view as good as another and people who do not. It is between those who think our culture, or purpose, or intuitions cannot be supported except conversationally, and people who still hope for other sorts of support.

If there *were* any relativists, they would, of course, be easy to refute. One would merely use some variant of the self-referential arguments Socrates used against Protagoras. But such neat little dialectical strategies only work against lightly-sketched fictional characters. The relativist who says that we can break ties among serious and incompatible candidates for belief only by "nonrational" or "noncognitive" considerations is just one of the Platonist or Kantian philosopher's imaginary playmates, inhabiting the same realm of fantasy as the solipsist, the skeptic, and the moral nihilist. Disillusioned, or whimsical, Platonists and Kantians occasionally play at being one or another of these characters. But when they do they are never offering relativism or skepticism or nihilism as a serious suggestion about how we might do things differently. These positions are adopted to make *philosophical* points – that is, moves in a game played with fictitious opponents, rather than fellow-participants in a common project.

The association of pragmatism with relativism is a result of a confusion between the pragmatist's attitude toward *philosophical* theories with his attitude towards *real* theories. James and Dewey are, to be sure, metaphilosophical relativists, in a certain limited sense. Namely: they think there is no way to choose, and no point in choosing, between incompatible philosophical theories of the typical Platonic or Kantian type. Such theories are attempts to ground some element of our practices on something external to these practices. Pragmatists think that any such philosophical grounding is, apart from elegance of execution, pretty much as good or as bad as the practice it purports to ground. They regard the project of grounding as a wheel that plays no part in the mechanism. In this, I think, they are quite right. No sooner does one discover the categories of the pure understanding for a Newtonian age than somebody draws up another list that would do nicely for an Aristotelian or an Einsteinian one. No sooner does one draw up a categorical imperative for Christians than somebody draws up one which works for cannibals. No sooner does one develop an evolutionary epistemology which explains why our science is so good than somebody writes a science-fiction story about bug-eyed and monstrous evolutionary epistemologists praising bug-eyed and monstrous scientists for the survival value of their monstrous theories. The reason this game is so easy to play is that none of these philosophical theories have to do much hard work. The real work has been done by the scientists who developed the explanatory theories by patience and genius, or the societies which developed the moralities and institutions in struggle and pain. All the Platonic or Kantian philosopher does is to take the finished first-level product, jack it up a few levels of abstraction, invent a metaphysical or epistemological or semantical vocabulary into which to translate it, and announce that he has *grounded* it.

"Relativism" only seems to refer to a disturbing view, worthy of being refuted, if it concerns *real* theories, not just philosophical theories. Nobody really cares if there are incompatible alternative formulations of a categorical imperative, or incompatible sets of categories of the pure understanding. We *do* care about alternative, concrete, detailed cosmologies, or alternative concrete, detailed proposals for political change. When such an alternative is proposed, we debate it, not in terms of categories or principles but in terms of the various concrete advantages and disadvantages it has. The reason relativism is talked about so much among Platonic and Kantian philosophers is that they think being relativistic about philosophical theories – attempts to "ground" first-level theories – leads to being relativistic about the first-level theories themselves. If anyone really believed that the worth of a theory depends upon the worth of its philosophical grounding, then indeed they would be dubious about physics, or democracy, until relativism in respect to philosophical theories had been overcome. Fortunately, almost nobody believes anything of the sort.

What people do believe is that it would be good to hook up our views about democracy, mathematics, physics, God, and everything else, into a coherent story about how everything hangs together. Getting such a synoptic view often does require us to change radically our views on particular subjects. But this holistic process of readjustment is just muddling through on a large scale. It has nothing to do with the Platonic-Kantian notion of grounding. That notion involves finding constraints, demonstrating necessities, finding immutable principles to which to subordinate oneself. When it turns out that suggested constraints, necessities, and principles are as plentiful as blackberries, nothing changes except the attitude of the rest of culture towards the philosophers. Since the time of Kant, it has become more and more apparent to nonphilosophers that a really professional philosopher can supply a philosophical foundation for just about anything. This is one reason why philosophers have, in the course of our century, become increasingly isolated from the rest of culture. Our proposals to guarantee this and clarify that have come to strike our fellow-intellectuals as merely comic.

## Part III: Irrationalism

My discussion of relativism may seem to have ducked the real issues. Perhaps nobody is a relativist. Perhaps "relativism" is *not* the right name for what so many philosophers find so offensive in pragmatism. But surely there *is* an important issue around somewhere. There is indeed an issue, but it is not easily stated, nor easily made amenable to argument. I shall try to bring it into focus by developing it in two different contexts, one microcosmic and the other macrocosmic. The microcosmic issue concerns philosophy in one of its most parochial senses – namely, the activities of the American Philosophical Association. Our Association has traditionally been agitated by the question of whether we should be free-wheeling and edifying, or argumentative and professional. For my purposes, this boils down to an issue about whether we can be pragmatists and still be professionals. The macrocosmic issue concerns philosophy in the widest sense – the attempt to make everything hang together. This is the issue between Socrates on the one hand and the tyrants on the other – the issue between lovers of conversation and lovers of self-deceptive rhetoric. For my purposes, it is the issue about whether we can be pragmatists without betraying Socrates, without falling into irrationalism.

I discuss the unimportant microcosmic issue about professionalism first because it is sometimes confused with the important issue about irrationalism, and because it helps focus that latter issue. The question of whether philosophy professors should edify agitated our Association in its early decades. James thought they should, and was dubious about the growing professionalization of the discipline. Arthur Lovejoy, the great opponent of pragmatism, saw professionalization as an unmixed blessing. Echoing what was being said simultaneously by Russell in England and by Husserl in Germany, Lovejoy urged the sixteenth annual meeting of the APA to aim at making philosophy into a science. He wanted the APA to organize its program into well-structured controversies on sharply defined problems, so that at the end of each convention it would be agreed who had won.[1] Lovejoy insisted that philosophy could either be edifying and visionary *or* could produce "objective, verifiable, and clearly communicable truths," but not both. James would have agreed. He too thought that one could *not* be both a pragmatist and a professional. James, however, saw professionalization as a failure of nerve rather than as a triumph of rationality. He thought that the activity of making things hang together was *not* likely to produce "objective, verifiable, and clearly communicable truths," and that this did not greatly matter.

Lovejoy, of course, won this battle. If one shares his conviction that philosophers should be as much like scientists as possible, then one will be pleased at the outcome. If one does not, one will contemplate the APA in its seventy-sixth year mindful of Goethe's maxim that one should be careful what one wishes for when one is young, for one will get it when one is old. Which attitude one takes will depend upon whether one sees the problems we discuss today as permanent problems for human thought, continuous with those discussed by Plato, Kant, and Lovejoy – or as modern attempts to breathe life into dead issues. On the Lovejoyan account, the gap between philosophers and the rest of high culture is of the same sort as the gap between physicists and laymen. The gap is not created by the artificiality of the problems being discussed, but by the development of technical and precise ways of dealing with real problems. If one shares the pragmatists' anti-essentialism, however, one will tend to see the problems about which philosophers are now offering "objective, verifiable, and clearly communicable" solutions as historical relics, left over from the Enlightenment's misguided search for the hidden essences of knowledge and morality. This is the point of view adopted by many of our fellow-intellectuals, who see us philosophy professors as caught in a time-warp, trying to live the Enlightenment over again.

I have reminded you of the parochial issue about professionalization not in order to persuade you to one side or the other, but rather to exhibit the source of the anti-pragmatist's passion. This is his conviction that conversation necessarily aims at agreement and at rational consensus, that we converse in order to make further conversation unnecessary. The anti-pragmatist believes that conversation only makes sense if something like the Platonic theory of Recollection is right – if we all have natural starting-points of thought somewhere within us, and will recognize the vocabulary in which they are best formulated once we hear it. For only if something like that is true will conversation have a natural goal. The Enlightenment hoped to find such a vocabulary – nature's own vocabulary, so to speak. Lovejoy – who described himself as an "unredeemed *Aufklärer*" – wanted to continue the project. Only if we had agreement on such a vocabulary, indeed, could conversation be reduced to argumentation – to the search for "objective, verifiable, and clearly communicable" solutions to problems. So the anti-pragmatist sees the pragmatist's scorn for professionalism as scorn for consensus, for the Christian and democratic idea that every human has the seeds of truth within. The pragmatist's attitude seems to him elitist and dilettantish, reminiscent of Alcibiades rather than of Socrates.

Issues about relativism and about professionalization are awkward attempts to formulate this opposition. The real and passionate opposition is over the question of whether loyalty to our fellow-humans presupposes that there is something permanent and unhistorical which explains *why* we should continue to converse in the manner of Socrates, something which guarantees convergence to agreement. Because the anti-pragmatist believes that without such an essence and such a guarantee the Socratic life makes no sense, he sees the pragmatist as a cynic. Thus the microcosmic issue about how philosophy professors should converse leads us quickly to the macrocosmic issue: whether one can be a pragmatist without being an irrationalist, without abandoning one's loyalty to Socrates.

Questions about irrationalism have become acute in our century because the sullen resentment which sins against Socrates, which withdraws from conversation and community, has recently become articulate. Our European intellectual tradition is now abused as "merely conceptual" or "merely ontic" or as "committed to abstractions." Irrationalists propose such rubbishy pseudo-epistemological notions as "intuition" or "an inarticulate sense of tradition" or "thinking with the blood" or "expressing the will of the oppressed classes." Our tyrants and bandits are more hateful than those of earlier times because, invoking such self-deceptive rhetoric, they pose as intellectuals. Our tyrants write philosophy in the morning and torture in the afternoon; our bandits alternately read Hölderlin and bomb people into bloody scraps. So our culture clings, more than ever, to the hope of the Enlightenment, the hope that drove Kant to make philosophy formal and rigorous and professional. We hope that by formulating the *right* conceptions of reason, of science, of thought, of knowledge, of morality, the conceptions which express their *essence*, we shall have a shield against irrationalist resentment and hatred.

Pragmatists tell us that this hope is vain. On their view, the Socratic virtues –

willingness to talk, to listen to other people, to weigh the consequences of our actions upon other people – are *simply* moral virtues. They cannot be inculcated nor fortified by theoretical research into essence. Irrationalists who tell us to think with our blood cannot be rebutted by better accounts of the nature of thought, or knowledge, or logic. The pragmatists tell us that the conversation which it is our moral duty to continue is *merely* our project, the European intellectual's form of life. It has no metaphysical nor epistemological guarantee of success. Further (and this is the crucial point) *we do not know what "success" would mean except simply "continuance."* We are not conversing because we have a goal, but because Socratic conversation is an activity which is its *own* end. The antipragmatist who insists that agreement is its goal is like the basketball player who thinks that the reason for playing the game is to make baskets. He mistakes an essential moment in the course of an activity for the end of the activity. Worse yet, he is like a basketball fan who argues that all men by nature desire to play basketball, or that the nature of things is such that balls can go through hoops.

For the traditional, Platonic or Kantian philosopher, on the other hand, the possibility of *grounding* the European form of life – of showing it to be more than European, more than a contingent human project – seems the central task of philosophy. He wants to show that sinning against Socrates is sinning against our nature, not just against our community. So he sees the pragmatist as an irrationalist. The charge that pragmatism is "relativistic" is simply his first unthinking expression of disgust at a teaching which seems cynical about our deepest hopes. If the traditional philosopher gets beyond such epithets, however, he raises a question which the pragmatist must face up to: the *practical* question of whether the notion of "conversation" *can* substitute for that of "reason." "Reason," as the term is used in the Platonic and Kantian traditions, is interlocked with the notions of truth as correspondence, of knowledge as discovery of essence, of morality as obedience to principle, all the notions which the pragmatist tries to deconstruct. For better or worse, the Platonic and Kantian vocabularies are the ones in which Europe has described and praised the Socratic virtues. It is not clear that we know how to describe these virtues without those vocabularies. So the deep suspicion which the pragmatist inspires is that, like Alcibiades, he is essentially frivolous – that he is commending uncontroversial common goods while refusing to participate in the only activity which can preserve those goods. He seems to be sacrificing our common European project to the delights of purely negative criticism.

The issue about irrationalism can be sharpened by noting that when the pragmatist says "All that can be done to explicate 'truth', 'knowledge', 'mortality', 'virtue' is to refer us back to the concrete details of the culture in which these terms grew up and developed," the defender of the Enlightenment takes him to be saying "Truth and virtue are simply what a community agrees that they are." When the pragmatist says "We have to take truth and virtue as whatever emerges from the conversation of Europe," the traditional philosopher wants to know what is so special about Europe. Isn't the pragmatist saying, like the irrationalist, that *we* are in a privileged situation simply by being *us*? Further, isn't there something terribly dangerous about the notion that truth can only be characterized as "the outcome of doing more of what we are doing now"? What if the "we" is the Orwellian state? When tyrants employ Lenin's blood-curdling sense of "objective" to describe their lies as "objectively true," what is to prevent them from citing Peirce in Lenin's defense?[2]

The pragmatist's first line of defense against this criticism has been created by Habermas, who says that such a definition of truth works only for the outcome of *undistorted* conversation, and that the Orwellian state is the paradigm of distortion. But this is *only* a first line, for we need to know more about what counts as "undistorted." Here Habermas goes transcendental and offers principles. The pragmatist, however, must remain ethnocentric and offer examples. He can only say: "undistorted" means employing *our* criteria of relevance, where *we* are the people who have read and pondered Plato, Newton, Kant, Marx, Darwin, Freud, Dewey, etc. Milton's "free and open encounter," in which truth is bound to prevail, must itself be described in terms of examples rather than principles – it is to be more like the Athenian market-place than the council-chamber of the Great King, more like the twentieth century than the twelfth, more like the Prussian Academy in 1925 than in 1935. The pragmatist must avoid saying, with Peirce, that truth is *fated* to win. He must even avoid saying that truth *will* win. He can only say, with Hegel, that truth and justice lie in the direction marked by the successive stages of European thought. This is not because he knows some "necessary truths" and cites these examples as a result of this knowledge. It is simply that the pragmatist knows no better way to explain his convictions than to remind his interlocutor of the position they both are in, the contingent starting points they both share, the floating, ungrounded conversations of which they are both members. This means that the pragmatist cannot answer the question "What is so special about Europe?" save by saying "Do you have anything non-European to suggest which meets *our* European purposes better?" He cannot answer the question "What is so good about the Socratic virtues, about Miltonic free encounters, about undistorted communication?" save by saying "What else would better fulfill the purposes *we* share with Socrates, Milton, and Habermas?"

To decide whether this obviously circular response is enough is to decide whether Hegel or Plato had the proper picture of the progress of thought. Pragmatists follow Hegel in saying that "philosophy is its time grasped in thought." Anti-pragmatists follow Plato in striving for an escape from conversation to something atemporal which lies in the background of all possible conversations. I do not think one can decide between Hegel and Plato save by meditating on the past efforts of the philosophical tradition to escape from time and history. One can see these efforts as worthwhile, getting better, worth continuing. Or one can see them as doomed and perverse. I do not know what would count as a noncircular metaphysical or epistemological or semantical argument for seeing them in either way. So I think that the decision has to be made simply by reading the history of philosophy and drawing a moral.

Nothing that I have said, therefore, is an argument in favor of pragmatism. At best, I have merely answered various superficial criticisms which have been made of it. Nor have I dealt with the central issue about irrationalism. I have not answered the deep criticism of pragmatism which I mentioned a few minutes ago: the criticism that the Socratic virtues cannot, as a practical matter, be defended save by Platonic means, that without some sort of metaphysical comfort nobody will be able *not* to sin against Socrates. William James himself was not sure whether this criticism could be answered. Exercising his own right to believe, James wrote: "If this life be not a real fight in which something is eternally gained for the universe by success, it is no better than a game of private theatricals from which we may withdraw at will." "It *feels*," he said, "like a fight."

For us, footnotes to Plato that we are, it *does* feel that way. But if James's own pragmatism were taken seriously, if pragmatism became central to our culture and our self-image, then it would no longer feel that way. We do not know how it *would* feel. We do not even know whether, given such a change in tone, the conversation of Europe might not falter and die away. We just do not know. James and Dewey offered us no guarantees. They simply pointed to the situation we stand in, now that both the Age of Faith and the Enlightenment seem beyond recovery. They grasped our time in thought. We did not change the course of the conversation in the way they suggested we might. Perhaps we are still unable to do so; perhaps we never shall be able to. But we can nevertheless honor James and Dewey for having offered what very few philosophers have succeeded in giving us: a hint of how our lives might be changed.

## Notes

1   See A. O. Lovejoy, "On Some Conditions of Progress in Philosophical Inquiry," *The Philosophical Review*, XXVI (1917): 123–163 (especially the concluding pages). I owe the reference to Lovejoy's paper to Daniel J. Wilson's illuminating "Professionalization and Organized Discussion in the American Philosophical Association, 1900–1922," *Journal of the History of Philosophy*, XVII (1979): 53–69.
2   I am indebted to Michael Williams for making me see that pragmatists have to answer this question.

# PART SIX

# WHAT IF WE DON'T
# KNOW ANYTHING AT ALL?

# Introduction

Here is the problem: how do you know *for certain* that you are sitting here reading this page? How do you know that your brain is not suspended right now in a vat of chemicals with wires running into it that create the sensations you think you are experiencing? In such a case, every piece of empirical evidence you might rely on to prove that you really are here could be used to prove that really you are not.

David Hume, though writing well before such laboratory scenarios began to seem plausible, maintained that any sustained reflection on knowledge will lead to skeptical doubts that undermine our claim to certainty. We may have *some* reasons to believe that we are not brains in a vat, and even *good* reasons, but our reasons are not absolutely conclusive. We can generate skeptical doubts about specific beliefs, for example, concerning the existence of other minds, memory, induction, as well as the external world, or we can maintain a global skepticism about any sort of assertion. The apparent incoherence of such a position (the fact that global skepticism should undermine a belief in global skepticism as well) can be avoided if we make no positive claim but simply decline to make any claims at all.

Jonathan Vogel's essay provides a concise refutation of skepticism and defense of common sense based on explanatory value, not an argument that would convince a radical skeptic but one that accounts for why the skeptical hypothesis, though possible, is not epistemically warranted. Such refutations and the continuing debate over how (and whether) to avoid epistemological skepticism are not the only topics of debate, however, and the remaining two essays in this section provide samples of two other important problematics in epistemology concerning skepticism: (1) what role should skepticism play in epistemology generally? Barry Stroud argues that the importance of attending to skepticism does not lie in its possible validity but in how it can help to shape and focus our general thinking about knowledge; (2) in a different vein, why has skepticism, a position that no one really holds, persistently reappeared in the history of epistemology? What draws us to it, or alternatively, *who* is it that is moved by skeptical arguments? Naomi Scheman offers, not a refutation, but a therapeutic diagnosis of the source of skepticism's attraction. In the tradition of Wittgenstein's approach to philosophical puzzles, Scheman reformulates the skeptical question in order to ask: why do we *think* we do not know anything at all? Her provocative answer, developed through a rumination on *Othello*, suggests that there is more to epistemological skepticism than meets the eye.

## Further Reading

Burnyeat, Myles (ed). *The Sceptical Tradition*. Berkeley, CA: University of California Press, 1983.

Klein, Peter. *Certainty: A Refutation of Skepticism*. Minneapolis, MN: University of Minnesota Press, 1981.

Hume, David. *A Treatise of Human Nature* (1740). Ed. by L. A. Selby-Brigge. Revised edn, P. H. Nidditch. Oxford: Oxford University Press, 1978.

Unger, Peter. *Ignorance: A Case for Scepticism*. Oxford: Oxford University Press, 1975.

# 21    Cartesian Skepticism and Inference to the Best Explanation

## *Jonathan Vogel*

The problem of skepticism about the external world, or Cartesian skepticism, has its roots in the underdetermination of theory by evidence. We each adopt a body of common-sense beliefs about the world which answers to our sensory experience. In principle, however, the beliefs we base on that experience are subject to underdetermination, and we can devise radical alternatives to the common-sense account. Such alternatives take the form of skeptical hypotheses, like Descartes's fiction that his experiences are caused by an evil demon.

Certainly, when the choice arises, we hold to the common-sense view, and reject its skeptical competitors.[1] But what (epistemic) reasons can we have for doing so? In cases of underdetermination generally, principles of inference to the best explanation can license the choice of one theory over others. Accordingly, we would be justified in preferring the common-sense account to skeptical hypotheses, if the common-sense account provides better explanations of why our experience is the way it is.[2] My purpose here is to inquire into the explanatory advantages of the common-sense view, and to develop a response to skepticism along the lines just indicated.[3]

One obstacle to carrying out this project is that the standards by which explanations are evaluated are themselves difficult to identify and to make precise. In what follows, I shall be making some controversial assumptions about explanatory goodness, and I shall have to rely on largely unanalyzed notions of simplicity, ad-hoc-ness, and the like. To be explicit, I shall presuppose:

(a)    Ad hoc explanations should be avoided, i.e., very roughly, if *A* is offered as an explanation of *B*, *A* ought not to be isolated from other explanations and data (it ought to be independently testable, it must figure in the explanation of something other than *B*, etc.).

(b)    Other things being equal, a simpler explanation is superior to a more complicated one.

(c)    Where explanation is concerned, more is better, if you get something for it. In particular, it is desirable to be able to give higher-level explanations of lower-level ones.

Another methodological point requires some comment. In comparing skeptical hypotheses with our everyday account of the world. I shall exclude from the latter any advanced scientific beliefs. To be sure, science adds great power and coherence to our explanations of phenomena, and one might argue that no explanatory scheme the skeptic devises could seriously compete with our best scientific theories. But it seems implausible that, without such theories, we would lack adequate grounds for rejecting skeptical hypotheses. Accordingly, I shall try to show that even a scientifically unsophisticated common-sense view of the world provides more adequate explanations than its skeptical competitors.

# I

Our beliefs about the external world serve an explanatory function. A person's sensory experience exhibits patterns and regularities at many levels, and our common-sense beliefs account for these in ways that seem to be coherent and economical. I shall call the body of these beliefs the *real-world hypothesis* (RWH).[4]

The skeptic points out that there are alternative explanations of how a person's sensory experience arises. In principle, a great many ways of formulating and developing these counterhypotheses are open to the skeptic – for example, through various stories about evil demons and brains in vats. But elaborate (not to mention crazy) fantasies of deception may be only tenuously connected to the content of one's experiences and may lack cohesiveness. For instance, suppose that you seem to see some snow falling, and the skeptic suggests that this experience is being foisted on you by a demon. Then, to explain why the demon makes you have snow experience (rather than experience of some other kind), the skeptic tells you that there is a second demon that has put the first one up to it. Clearly, we are not getting anywhere; positing a second demon that directs the first on this occasion (and does only that) is explanatorily idle or ad hoc. The skeptic could try to escape such a result by refusing to say in any detail how your experiences come about. A hypothesis in this vein might specify only that your experiences are all caused by some deceptive spirit, and no more. The cure is as bad as the disease, however: the skeptic will succeed in avoiding ad hoc higher-level posits only by foregoing higher-level explanations altogether.

The RWH, by contrast, gives us a rich and well-integrated explanatory apparatus. We not only posit objects that cause our experiences, we are also able to explain why and how these objects behave as they do. If the explanations provided by a skeptical counterhypothesis are either ad hoc or impoverished in comparison with those of the RWH, then we have good grounds for preferring the latter to the former. According to the skeptic, we fail to know things because the RWH is faced with competitors that we have no reason to reject. But we have just seen that not any competitor will do. The skeptic's position will be empty unless he can provide us with reason to think that a *satisfactory* competitor exists (in particular, a sufficiently rich competitor that is not unduly burdened with ad hoc explanatory posits).

The lesson here is that the skeptic needs to frame an alternative that matches the RWH very closely. If a skeptical hypothesis can be made sufficiently similar in relevant respects to the RWH, then, one might expect, that skeptical hypothesis will match the RWH in explanatory adequacy. To the extent that explanatory virtues like coherence, depth, and simplicity are matters of theoretical structure, a skeptical hypothesis that is isomorphic to the RWH will explain things just as well as the RWH does. An improved skeptical hypothesis of this sort has to satisfy two principal constraints: (i) it should invoke items corresponding to the elements of the RWH; (ii) it should also posit, as holding of these items, a pattern of properties, relations, and explanatory generalizations mirroring those of the RWH.

As an example of how this would work, suppose you seem to see the wind blowing a piece of paper off your desk. According to the RWH, your visual impressions of the paper flying off your desk are caused by the paper. Similarly, your tactile sensations of the wind are caused by a real movement of air against your skin. And, finally, the wind stands in a relation of cause and effect to the movement of the paper. The skeptic's procedure will be to extract the explanatory skeleton or core from the RWH – that there are *some* entities bearing *some* properties that are related in ways exactly analogous to those specified by the RWH – and then to add that the entities and their properties are somehow different from the ones mentioned in the RWH.[5]

Thus, a skeptical hypothesis might present the following alternative explanation of your experiences. All that there is to the world is your brain in a vat, and a computer that is connected to your brain. Your tactile experiences are caused by the realization of a computer program that simulates wind, and your visual impressions are caused by the realization of another program that simulates a paper blowing off a desk. Also, the skeptical hypothesis can specify that the first routine calls the second, so that (as in the RWH) the cause of the wind experience would be the cause of the cause of the paper-blowing experience. This way of reconstructing the explanatory structure of a small fragment of the RWH might be extended to apply to all the entities and explanatory connections posited by the RWH. The result would be a skeptical hypothesis that was completely isomorphic to the RWH, with portions of the computer disk supposed to occupy the explanatory roles we normally assign to familiar objects.[6] I shall be calling this the *computer skeptical hypothesis* (CSH).

Of course, the CSH is an outlandish suggestion, and we are confident that it is false. Yet, in reflecting on this situation philosophically, it is possible to misread what has gone wrong. One proposal is that skeptical hypotheses are invariably burdened with more unexplained explainers than is the RWH.[7] The CSH will lack answers to questions like "Why does the computer operate the way it does?" or "Where did the computer come from in the first place?" But it is not at all clear that the RWH does any better in the face of analogous demands. Both the CSH and the RWH invoke ultimate regularities that are not themselves explained, and neither can account for the existence of the physical world as such. Generally, since the RWH and the CSH are meant to have the same structure, anywhere the RWH can explain a lower-level phenomenon by a higher-level regularity, the CSH should be able to do the same. The CSH will have unexplained explainers only insofar as the RWH has them also.

Another suggestion that enjoys some currency is that the RWH is, in a very straightforward way, simpler than the CSH, and hence to be preferred. The idea here is that there would be a one-one mapping from the objects posited by the RWH to their stand-ins in the computer's memory, where these are treated as discrete individuals. There are, though, items required (at least tacitly) by the CSH which escape this mapping, e.g., the computer's central processing unit and perhaps the brain in the vat itself. So, the argument runs, the CSH is committed to the existence of more items than the RWH, and is to be preferred on that account.

This line of thought is problematic in several respects. First, one could just as well argue that the CSH is simpler than the RWH, on the grounds that the CSH posits only two objects (the computer and one's brain), whereas the RWH is committed to the existence of a great many more things. Moreover, it is far from clear that, all by itself, positing fewer entities is a theoretical virtue.[8] And finally, if need be, the CSH could be revised to eliminate the role of the central processing unit altogether. The skeptic could suppose that the elements of the computer memory act directly on each other, and on the seat of consciousness, in causal patterns that mirror those of the RWH.

Now, as will emerge shortly, I think there is something right about the claims that the CSH is less coherent and less simple than the RWH. But if explanatory coherence and simplicity are treated solely in structural terms, it should not be surprising that these claims do not go through. After all, the causal-explanatory structures invoked by the RWH and the CSH are identical; the two differ only as to what entities bear the specified causal relations to one another.

The rejoinders just considered miss something important about the motivations behind the skeptic's argument. At root, the skeptic questions our ability to read off the "real" or intrinsic character of things from those things' causal behavior. This challenge emerges in its simplest form with the initial thought that one's experience of any familiar object might be caused by something other than that object (e.g., an evil demon). The point is that the known effect – namely, your experience – does not fix the character of its cause.[9]

On the face of it, the requirement that a skeptical hypothesis must have a more fully articulated structure – one that matches the RWH in various ways – seems insufficient to meet this problem. For, if we assume that causal relations are contingent and that there is in principle no obstacle to our positing whatever causal relations we like, what reason could there be why one set of entities is better suited than another to occupy the positions within the structure of the RWH itself? It would appear that, in principle, there should be skeptical hypotheses that will explain the contents of one's experience just as well as the RWH. The choice between such hypotheses and the RWH will then be arbitrary, giving the skeptic what he needs.

## II

To appreciate the superiority of the RWH over its skeptical competitors, we need to take into account the content, as well as the form, of the explanations the RWH provides. In particular, our ordinary view of things involves beliefs in the existence of objects with familiar spatial characteristics (e.g., we believe that there are bricks that are oblong and oranges that are round). The ascription of specific spatial properties to objects does explanatory work within the RWH (e.g., accounting for why oranges roll easily and bricks do not). Since the CSH posits objects with altogether different spatial characteristics – we are assuming that its objects are just portions of a computer disk – the CSH will have to account for the relevant phenomena in some other fashion. But by bringing in these additional explanations (whatever they may be), the CSH runs the risk of taking on a more elaborate explanatory apparatus than the RWH. To put the point I am trying to make more directly: niceties aside, the fact that something is spherical explains why it behaves like a sphere (in its interactions with us and with other things). If something that *is not* a sphere behaves like one, this will call for a more extended explanation.

This intuitive claim is bound to raise some philosophical qualms. Why must the fact that the CSH invokes *different* configurations of matter in its explanations mean that CSH has to be *more complicated* than the RWH? Again, setting niceties aside, why is the skeptic not free to stipulate that, in his account, it is certain magnetic patterns on a disk, not spheres, which behave like spheres (at least in terms of the experiences they bring about, directly and indirectly)?

Let us see just what would be involved in maintaining an explanatory parity between the CSH and RWH. To fix ideas, suppose that, according to the RWH, there is a hyacinth beside your doorway. For each RWH object, there has to be a CSH counterpart, which we can imagine to be the piece of the computer disk which stores the information about the object to be stimulated. So, the CSH would have it that there is a piece of the disk holding a file about a hyacinth beside your door, specifically. Moreover, wherever the RWH assigns a certain property to the hyacinth, the CSH must ascribe a corresponding, but different property to the hyacinth's CSH analog. According to the RWH, the hyacinth has a particular location, namely, that of being beside your door. The hyacinth counterpart will have some parallel feature, which we might call a "pseudo location." The pseudo location of the hyacinth counterpart is just that physical property in virtue of which the counterpart simulates being located near your door. In general, what the RWH explains by reference to genuine locations, the CSH will explain in terms of these pseudo locations.

Since we make reference to the locations of objects in giving various everyday explanations, location properties are part of the explanatory apparatus of the RWH. Now, we find that the (genuine) locations ascribed to any two objects at a time are invariably different. We do not need any empirical law or regularity to explain this; it is a necessary truth pertaining to the nature of physical objects that there cannot be two such objects at the same place at the same time.[10]

The explanatory structure of the CSH is meant to duplicate that of the RWH. Since the CSH is isomorphic to the RWH, and the RWH always ascribes different locations to the objects it posits, the CSH will invariably ascribe different pseudo locations to things it posits. This calls for an explanation, if possible. At this point, however, the CSH faces a loss in either simplicity or explanatory power. To make the issue more concrete, imagine that the way things work in the CSH computer is that each object's pseudo location is the physical realization of having coordinates $(x,y,z)$ written in its file.[11] There will have to be some explicit principle within the CSH that no two objects are to be assigned the same pseudo location, i.e., that no two objects are to have the same coordinates written in their files. Otherwise, the fact that no two objects have the same pseudo location remains unexplained. Of course, the CSH would include within it the necessary truth that two physical objects cannot occupy the same *genuine* location in space, but this is of no help to the CSH in explaining why two of its objects cannot have the same *pseudo* location. To achieve this, it would appear that the CSH has to add an extra empirical regularity, to which no regularity in the RWH corresponds. Such an addition will make the CSH inferior to the RWH on simplicity grounds, however.

The skeptic could escape this outcome if it could be guaranteed by some other necessary truth that different CSH objects will have different pseudo locations. In other words, the pseudo location of a CSH object would have to be encoded by some physical property $P$ (other than that of having some specified location), such that it is impossible for two physical objects to have $P$ at the same time. But it seems to me that there are no such physical properties. After all, if a given physical object with whatever properties exists at one place, it appears perfectly possible for there to be an absolutely similar object elsewhere, instantiating all the same properties at the same time – except location.[12]

Actually, the problem facing the skeptic is a general one, independent of the fact that CSH itself invokes physical objects (i.e., bits of computer disk) in its explanations. Suppose that the skeptic offers instead a quasi-Leibnizian hypothesis, according to which the world consists solely of minds and their properties. These minds and their states are supposed to act in ways that mirror the behavior of everyday things as specified by the RWH. Each mind that stands in for a RWH object must have a property corresponding to the genuine location the RWH ascribes to its object; this pseudo location will be a (partial) mental state. The question arises again as to why these pseudo locations are invariably different from one mind to another. Presumably (*pace* Leibniz), it is possible for two different minds to think exactly the same thing at the same time, so no necessary truth prevents them from having the same pseudo location. Once again, such an occurrence would have to be ruled out by some kind of extra "exclusion principle," for which no counterpart exists in the RWH.

I claimed earlier that our normal ascription of spatial properties to things does real explanatory work; furthermore, it seems plausible that you incur an added explanatory burden if you suppose that something lacking a particular spatial property still behaves as though it had it. What I have been saying about locations and pseudo locations makes this same point on a more abstract level. In skeptical hypotheses, some other property (e.g., a magnetic property or a mental property) is supposed to substitute for the spatial property of being located at particular place. As we have seen, further explanation is then needed to establish why these properties, which are not genuine location properties, behave as though they were. It seems that this sort of difficulty will attach to skeptical hypotheses generally, giving us good reasons to reject them.[13]

## III

I have presented some antiskeptical arguments based on explanatory considerations. But surely there is a world of familiar objects about us, and we have known that all along. So what, then, is the point of giving these arguments in the first place? This question deserves an extended response, but for now a very brief answer will have to do. I take it that the specious character of the explanations the skeptic offers is immediately apparent – they come across as contrived or unduly indirect – and this is a reason why we reject skepticism as a doctrine. Realizing that skeptical hypotheses are defective, however, is not the same thing as spelling out precisely what their defects are. To do this requires philosophical work – work of the sort I have undertaken here.

### Notes

1  Some philosophers, especially followers of Ludwig Wittgenstein, would deny that skeptical hypotheses can genuinely compete for acceptance with the body of our common-sense beliefs. See, for example, Stanley Cavell, *The Claim of Reason* (New York: Oxford, 1979), pp. 218–220.

2  This approach to skepticism has been advocated by Michael Slote, Frank Jackson, Jonathan Bennett, James Cornman, J. L. Mackie, and Alan Goldman, among others.

3  On certain views about skepticism and about inference to the best explanation, this approach to skepticism will seem ill-conceived. One might hold that it is simply constitutive of rationality to reject skeptical hypotheses out of hand; thus, it is unnecessary to enter into the relative explanatory merits of the common-sense view and its skeptical alternatives. From another point of view, the explanatory advantages of the common-sense view could never give us a reason to accept it as *true*, rather than as merely handy or to our taste. The issues that arise here are important, and they must be addressed at some point by anyone who bases an answer to skepticism on explanatory considerations. These very general objections will be moot, however, if the appeal to explanatory considerations does not even succeed on its own terms. Whether it does so is my present concern.

4  This way of putting things may seem unfortunate to those who reject the representative theory of perception. But the point could be recast as follows: we have a set of beliefs about the world, i.e., the RWH. Our having those beliefs admits of alternative explanations, including skeptical explanations and the RWH itself. The tenability of skepticism turns on whether the truth of the RWH provides a better explanation than do skeptical hypotheses of why we believe the RWH in the first place.

5  Basically, this amounts to something like forming the Ramsey sentence of the RWH and adding to it further specifications that, in each case, the object on property denoted by the bound variables is something other than the one posited by the RWH. The RWH itself can be construed as the "Ramsey sentence" plus the stipulation that the objects and properties called for by the "Ramsey sentence" are indeed the familiar ones. See here Grover Maxwell, "Theories, Perception, and Structural Realism," in R. Colodny, ed., *The Nature and Function of Scientific Thought* (Pittsburgh: University Press, 1970) and for some needed refinements,

David Lewis, "How to Define Theoretical Terms," *Philosophical Papers*, vol. I. (New York: Oxford, 1983). The possibility of framing skeptical hypotheses with the same structure as the RWH is noted by Lawrence Sklar in his "Saving the Noumena," *Philosophy and Spacetime Physics* (Berkeley: California University Press, 1985), pp. 59–60.

6   We need not suppose that the computer itself was built or programed by anyone. Rather, this hypothesis is to be understood simply as a description of an alternative way the (physical) world might be.

7   A claim of this sort is made by Alan Goldman, although it is directed at a fantastical skeptical story that postulates experimenters with deceptive motives. See Goldman, *Empirical Knowledge* (Berkeley: California University Press, 1989), p. 212.

8   It could be objected that what matters for explanatory adequacy is not economy with respect to the number of individuals posited, but rather in the number of different kinds invoked. But this does not appear to help – the skeptic can get by with just a few kinds of things (brain, vat, computer) while the RWH might be said to invoke these and many more.

9   This was the way Kant understood the situation. The skeptic, he says, "assumed that the only immediate experience is inner experience and that from it we can only *infer* outer things – and this, moreover, only in an untrustworthy manner, as in all cases where we are inferring from given effects to determinate causes"; *The Critique of Pure Reason*, N. K. Smith, trans. (New York: St Martin's, 1965), p. 245.

10   For a discussion of this principle, see Denis Robinson, "Re-identifying Matter," *The Philosophical Review*, XCI (1982): 317–341; on the role of necessary truths in explanations, see Clark Glymour, "Explanation and Realism," in J. Leplin, ed., *Scientific Realism* (Berkeley: California University Press, 1984), esp. pp. 184–6.

11   For purposes of exposition, I am pretending that an object is located at a point rather than a region.

12   Of course, there are characterizations like "the only building taller than 110 stories" or "identical to Socrates", which are satisfied by at most one object at a time. If these expressions involve reference to properties, they are properties of a different type than those with which I am concerned here.

13   One might, try to frame a skeptical hypothesis that avoids this difficulty by assigning to objects different locations (and spatial properties generally) in place of those specified by the RWH. Formulated this way, our problem becomes one of choosing a particular geometry of the world from among those logically compatible with the empirical data, and one might continue to defend the choice of the RWH by appeal to explanatory considerations. See here Lawrence Sklar, *Space, Time, and Spacetime* (Berkeley: California University Press, 1977), pp. 91–101, although Sklar himself is highly critical of such uses of inference to the best explanation. Sklar has a valuable discussion of the affinities between Cartesian skepticism and problems in the epistemology of geometry.

# 22   Skepticism and the Possibility of Knowledge

## *Barry Stroud*

Skepticism in recent and current philosophy represents a certain threat or challenge in the theory of knowledge. What is that threat? How serious is it? How, if at all, can it be met? What are the consequences if it cannot be met?

I obviously do not have time to go into all these questions, or into any of them thoroughly. I can only sketch a point of view in the hope of provoking some discussion.

The first question is clearly the place to start. I believe the true nature of the skeptical threat is still not properly understood, nor are the consequences of its not being met. That is one reason we have tended to give inadequate answers to the other questions. It is still widely felt that skepticism is not really worth taking seriously, so it hardly matters whether the challenge can be met or not. That kind of reaction seems to me to rest on a philosophical misconception.

Many would dismiss skepticism and defend not taking it seriously on the grounds that it is not a doctrine or theory any sensible person would contemplate adopting as the truth about our position in the world. It seems to them frivolous or perverse to concentrate on a view that is not even a conceivable candidate in the competition for the true or best theory as to how things are. I would grant – indeed insist – that philosophical skepticism is not something we should seriously consider adopting or accepting (whatever that means). But does that mean that it is silly to worry about skepticism? I think it does not. A line of thinking can be of deep significance and great importance in philosophy even if we never contemplate accepting a "theory" that claims to express it.

One reason that is so is that philosophy thrives on paradox, absurdity, dilemma, and difficulty. There are often what look like good arguments for surprising or outrageous conclusions. Taking the paradoxical reasonings seriously and re-examining the assumptions they rest on can be important and fruitful when there is no question at all of our ever contemplating adopting a "theory" or doctrine embodying the absurd conclusion.

The point is clearest in the case of antinomies – explicit contradictions. We know we cannot believe the conclusion; it couldn't possibly be true. To take The Liar, or Russell's paradox, seriously is not to hold open even the remote option of believing that someone who says he is lying speaks both truly and falsely, or that there is a set that both is and is not a member of itself. Such "theories" would be worse than outrageous as things to believe, but that in no way diminishes the need to take seriously the reasoning that leads to them.

The same is true even when the conclusion of the paradoxical or surprising reasoning falls short of explicit contradiction. The Eleatic doctrine that nothing moves, for example, need not be in any remote sense a live intellectual option for us in order for us to be rightly challenged, overwhelmed, perhaps even stumped, by Zeno's argument that Achilles can never overtake the Tortoise. The mere idea of something's being true at a time can seem to generate the absurd result that there is never any real alternative to what happens, that things are fated to happen as they do. We can be impelled to investigate that line of reasoning without thinking that otherwise we would have to adopt the "theory" that we have no control over what we do or what happens to us. Again, it seems undeniable that adding one more molecule to a table would not turn it into a non-table, any more than pulling one hair from a bushy head would make it bald. The discomfort I feel in the thought that an exactly similar step can be taken again, and again, does not show that I in any way consider accepting a "theory" according to which there could be a table the size and shape of the earth, or that a bushy head and a bald head are the same sort of thing.

Those modern philosophers most closely connected to the skeptical tradition and most impressed by skeptical reasoning – Descartes. Hume, and Russell, for example – do not hold that believing the conclusions of that reasoning is a real option for us. The ancient skeptics themselves seem not to have accepted, or to have contemplated accepting or declaring the truth of any "theory" either. They were highly anti-theoretical philosophers, and their strictures would have extended to any theoretical pronouncements put into their own mouths by their opponents as well. But none of that shows that skeptical ideas were not worth taking seriously or were not of great philosophical importance.

The importance of skepticism came always from the uses to which its ideas were put – different uses at different times. It is now widely understood to represent a certain threat or challenge in the theory of knowledge. That is not to say that everything in epistemology as we think of it today, or even in that challenge, can be traced back to the skeptical tradition alone. Exactly which skeptical ideas were important in defining the modern philosophical concern with human knowledge, how and to what extent they were used, and to what effect – all these are intriguing historical questions. Clearly, it is complicated. The role of sense-perception in our knowledge of the world became an important issue even for those apparently untouched by skepticism – by those in the atomist tradition, for example, from Galileo to Boyle and Locke, as well as by Descartes himself in his studies of optics and the physiology of perception. I want to concentrate for the moment on the problem or challenge itself. I think that, whatever its historical source, it has come to define, or perhaps even create, the philosophical concern with our knowledge of the world.

What do we want from a philosophical theory of knowledge? What is it supposed to do? It seems that we simply want to understand how we get the knowledge we have – to explain how it is possible. But I don't think that is enough to uniquely identify the philosophical problem.

Take what is usually called in philosophy "our knowledge of the world around us." Now it seems obvious, without any philosophical preconceptions, that there are countless ways of coming to know something about the world around us. I can find out that there is a bus-drivers' strike in Rome, for example, by waiting in vain for a bus or by reading a newspaper or by getting a letter from a friend.

How many different ways of finding out is that? Is reading a newspaper only one way, or possibly many? Is reading it in the *New York Times* a different way of finding it out from reading it in the *New York Post*? It seems hopeless to try counting. Obviously we do not just want a list of sources. What we seek in philosophy is not just anything that is true about how we get knowledge of the world around us.

The philosophical interest in knowledge is general, and in at least two different ways. We are interested in all of our knowledge of the world taken all together, or in some domain characterized in general terms. To ask only how we come to know some things in the domain, given that we already know certain other things in it, is not to ask about all knowledge of that kind in general. And we don't just want a heterogeneous list of ways of coming to know. We want to find a single way, or a small number of very general "ways of knowing." To explain how they work will be to explain, in general, how knowledge of the kind in question is possible.

Is that enough, then, to identify what we are interested in in the philosophy of knowledge? I don't think so. Suppose we eventually establish contact with some beings elsewhere in space. We receive some regular signals, we send back similar messages, and eventually find ourselves communicating with something somewhere. We take the opportunity to find out about them. We ask them where they are, what it is like there, what they are like, how they send out their signals, how they receive ours, and so on. Suppose they do the same with us. One day there appears on our receiving screen the question "How do you come to know of the things around you?" We send back the answer "We see them with our eyes, we touch them with parts of our bodies, we hear the noises they make . . ." That might be just what those beings want to know. Perhaps for them it's all a matter of sonar, or something we do not even understand. But even if that answer is just what the aliens want, is it what we want in philosophy?

I think we recognize that the philosophical question is not simply a request for information of this kind. What we want, rather, is some kind of *explanation* of our knowledge – some account of how it is possible. But what kind of explanation of its possibility? Our friends in space could send back a message pressing us for details. "Exactly how does seeing work?", they might ask. "What has to happen after light strikes your eye in order for you to know something about what is reflecting the light? How can you recognize the objects around you and pick them out from the background? Please send detailed explanation." We could send answers to some of their questions. We might even send them as much as we can of our science as it is and let them figure it out for themselves. Maybe they would send back better explanations than we've now got. That would be super naturalized epistemology, if not supernaturalized epistemology.

But would it be what we seek in philosophy? Sending them that information would be like sending them what we know about motion and acceleration, from which they could easily deduce that Achilles will have no trouble overtaking the Tortoise. Would that meet Zeno's challenge? What puzzles us in that case, if anything does, is how it is possible for Achilles to overtake the Tortoise *if* what Zeno relies on at each step of the argument is true. We want to know how overtaking is possible given those undeniable facts invoked by Zeno. That is how that challenge is to be met – not simply by reminding us of the obvious facts of motion and acceleration, or, worse still, by running off and overtaking a tortoise oneself.

The same is true in the case of our knowledge of the world. It is not enough simply to know something; and not just any explanation of how such knowledge is possible will do. It is true that we come to know of the things around us by seeing and touching them, but that is just the sort of information we could send to the aliens in space. Only they or others similarly removed from us would seek that kind of answer. The philosophical question has not yet been reached.

We want a general answer to the question. It should be expressed in terms of a general "way of knowing." And we find that general source in what we call "the senses" or "sense-perception." The problem then is to explain how we can get any knowledge at all of the world around us on the basis of sense-perception. But again, not just any explanations will do, any more than just any relevant information about motion and acceleration will answer Zeno's question. When our friends in space request such explanations we do not understand them to be asking a philosophical question about our knowledge. What *we* want is an explanation of how we could get any knowledge of things around us on the basis of sense-perception, given certain apparently undeniable facts about sense-perception.

The difficulty comes in philosophy when we try to see exactly how sense-perception works to give us knowledge of the world. We are led to think of seeing, or perceiving generally, in a certain way. What is in question is our knowledge of anything at all about the world, of any of the truths that are about things around us. The difficulty in understanding how sense-perception gives us knowledge of any such truths is that it seems at least possible to perceive what we do without thereby knowing something about the things around us. There have been many versions of that fundamental idea. But whether it is expressed in terms of "ideas" or "experiences" or "sense data" or "appearances" or "takings" or "sensory stimulations," or whatever it might be, the basic idea could be put by saying our knowledge of the world is "underdetermined" by whatever it is that we get through that source of knowledge known as "the senses" or "experience." Given the events or experiences or whatever they might be that serve as the sensory "basis" of our knowledge, it does not follow that something we believe about the world around us is true. The problem is then to explain how we nevertheless know that what we do believe about the world around us is in fact true. Given the apparent "obstacle," how is our knowledge possible?

It is an "obstacle" because it seems to make our knowledge impossible, just as the facts cited by Zeno seem to make overtaking impossible. If several different possibilities are all compatible with our perceiving what we do, the question is how we know that one of those possibilities involving the truth of our beliefs about the world does obtain and the others do not. That would seem to require an inference of some sort, some reasonable hypothesis or some form of reasoning that could take us from what we get in sense-perception to some proposition about the world around us. That hypothesis or principle of inference itself either will imply something about the world around us or it will not. If it does, it belongs among those propositions our knowledge of which has yet to be explained, so it cannot help explain that knowledge. If it does not, how can our acceptance of it lead to knowledge of the way things are around us? If it itself implies nothing about such things, and we could perceive what we do without knowing anything about such things, how is our knowledge to be explained? If we are in fact in that position, how is our knowledge of the world around us possible?

The problem is too familiar to need further elaboration here. I have wanted to stress only how very special a question it is about the possibility of knowledge, and what one must do to bring it before our minds in its proper philosophical form. That alone is thought to be enough to show that the question is frivolous or idle. The alleged "obstacle" to our knowledge is thought to be easily avoidable. Even if that quite special question cannot be answered satisfactorily, there is felt to be no good reason to ask it in the first place. The "assumptions" on which it is based are held to be wrong, misguided, and in any case not inevitable.

One familiar criticism is that the whole project is based on the mistaken assumption that there are or must be sensory "foundations" of our knowledge of the world which are in some way "epistemically prior" to the knowledge they serve to support. Abandon that assumption, it is suggested, and the whole problem, or the need to answer it as formulated, disappears. "Enlightened" epistemologists have accordingly moved beyond that quaint doctrine known as "foundationalism." They seek a "nonfoundational" theory of knowledge.

There is not time to go carefully into that complicated issue here. I think the suggestion does not penetrate very deeply into the sources of skepticism; it seems to me to get things almost exactly upside down. And regarding it as simply a matter of deciding to adopt or not to adopt a certain "assumption" is just another way of not taking skepticism seriously. But if we ignore or reject out of hand the familiar traditional question I have tried to identify, what is left?

Suppose we abandon, or never reach, the idea or hope that our knowledge of the world around us is to be explained as being derived from some knowledge or experience that is not itself knowledge of the world around us – something that is "prior to" or "underdetermines" the knowledge we are interested in. What would we then need a philosophical "theory of knowledge" for? It might seem that we would simply have liberated ourselves from an unrealistic restriction, and we could then go ahead and simply explain how our knowledge is possible. But if we are free to explain it in terms of sense-perception that *does* amount to knowledge of the things around us, can we ever properly understand *all* our knowledge of the world – how any of it is possible at all?

The "liberated" question can easily be answered by saying that we know of the things around us by perceiving them. We see them, we touch them, we hear them, and so on. We even read about them in the newspaper. But that was just the sort of information we could send to the aliens in space. Is that the sort of thing we want to find out about our knowledge of the world when we wonder, as we do in philosophy, how any of it is possible? Obviously not. We already know all that. If it were the job of a "nonfoundational theory of knowledge" to give us answers like that, it would be even more tedious than skeptical "foundational" theories are now widely held to be.

I do not say that such "enlightened" "theories" or explanations could never tell us anything we do not already know. Obviously, when they got down to the physiological details, they could. But I think there is something we aspire to in the philosophical theory of knowledge that such explanations would not give us. We want an account of our knowledge of the world that would make all of it intelligible to us all at once. We want to see how knowledge of the world could come to be out of something that is not knowledge of the world. Without that, we will not have the kind of doubly general explanation we seek. I think skepticism in epistemology now represents, and perhaps always did represent, the possibility that such an explanation is impossible; that we cannot consider all our knowledge of the world all at once and still see it as knowledge. Given that project, the threat is that skepticism will be the only answer. That alone would not straightforwardly imply that we can know nothing of the world around us – that we can never know whether there is a bus drivers' strike in Rome, for example. But it would suggest that a certain kind of understanding of our position in the world might be beyond us. Taking that possibility seriously, trying to see whether it is so, and if so why, would then be what taking skepticism seriously would amount to. To dismiss it simply on the grounds that we do know many things and that it would be ridiculous to believe we do not would be like assuring us that Achilles will overtake the Tortoise, and that it would be ridiculous to believe that he will not. And we will be in a position to dismiss it on the ground that it is absurd even to seek the kind of understanding philosophers have sought of our knowledge only when we understand better what that goal is, why we seek it, why it is unattainable, and what a philosophical "theory of knowledge" that did not aspire to it would look like.

---

# 23   Othello's Doubt/Desdemona's Death: The Engendering of Scepticism

---

*Naomi Scheman*

## I

Toward the end of *The Claim of Reason* Stanley Cavell gives a reading of *Othello* that is at the same time a reading of philosophical scepticism.[1] Upon first encountering these readings, I was struck by their aptness and by their mutual illumination. Doubting, for Othello or for the sceptic, responds to an unease at the heart of the experiences of immersion in the world and connectedness to others. The immersion and the connection are at the same time terrifying and tenuous and then terrifying in their tenuousness. Embodied human experiences, notably of sexuality, are central to Cavell's account;[2] gender is not: it figures only briefly and then as a symmetrical difference.[3]

In this essay I want to suggest a rereading of some of the texts that engage these questions, a rereading that places the asymmetries of gender at the crux of sixteenth-century Europe, a time and place that was profoundly and disturbingly disordered.[4] Shakespeare explored the disorder, attendant in part on the loss of centering authority, most notably in *King Lear*. Many of his other works continue this exploration, playing out a range of responses to the disorder of the world.

One such response is the "problem comedic."[5] It is, I think, best represented by *All's Well That Ends Well*. The philosophical analogue is the "mitigated scepticism" of Montaigne. Another response is tragically played out in *Othello*. I want to argue that the impulse Shakespeare is exploring in that play, which leads Othello to embrace Iago's view of the world, is the impulse that informs Descartes's *Meditations*[6] and the subsequent course of Western science and epistemology. It is a consequence of my argument that this impulse is as necessarily murderous and tragic in "real life" as it is in Shakespeare's play.

## II

As narrated by Richard Popkin,[7] sixteenth-century Europe underwent a threefold sceptical crisis: theological, sparked by the Reformation and fueled by fideistic defenses of Catholicism; humanistic, as a relativistic response to learning about the different ways of life in the recently discovered new world and recently rediscovered ancient world; and scientific, with the undermining of the bases of Aristotelian science and the debates about what, if anything, could replace them. Popkin situates Montaigne, especially *The Apology for Raymond Sebond*, in this context:

> By extending the implicit sceptical tendencies of the Reformation crisis, the humanistic crisis, and the scientific crisis, into a total *crise pyrrhonienne*, Montaigne's genial *Apologie* became the *coup de grâce* to an entire intellectual world. It was also to be the womb of modern thought, in that it led to the attempt either to refute the new Pyrrhonism, or to find a way of living with it.[8]

Montaigne himself chose to live with it, and his *Essays* are largely a record of the sort of life thereby chosen: forgiving of oneself and others, discursive, amused, literate, and nondogmatically conservative, a place from which the world is attentively observed, but never definitively known. Such a life and the world within which it is lived can be seen as the subjects of Shakespeare's problem comedies, at least one of which – *All's Well That Ends Well* – has been argued to be drawn in part directly from Montaigne.[9]

The accommodation to scepticism is historically uneasy, poised between nostalgia for a (mis)remembered world of unquestioned certainty and stability and the hope that scientific rationality will bring the world under our practical and epistemic control. This uneasiness has tinged many critical readings of the problem plays (so that the plays themselves *are* the problems – like problem children). E. K. Chambers, for example, writes of *All's Well*, *Troilus and Cressida*, and *Measure for Measure*: "They are all unpleasant plays, the utterances of a puzzled and disturbed spirit, full of questioning, sceptical of its own ideas, looking with new misgivings into the ambiguous shadows of a world over which a cloud has passed and made a goblin of the sun."[10]

Arthur Kirsch offers a more redemptive reading of *All's Well*.[11] He sees Bertram the way he suggests Montaigne would see him, as an adolescent boy, prey to "the nakedness of sexuality,"[12] in need of acceptance and, Kirsch argues, redemption into Pauline marriage through the agency of a virtuous heroine.[13] Kirsch, whose interpretive framework is Freudian and Christian, finds "the fabric of Montaigne's essay" ("On Some Verses of Virgil") in "the elegiac cast of *All's Well*, its pervasive opposition of age and youth, the association of that opposition with marriage and lust and with virtue and nobility, the depiction of Bertram as a 'princock boy . . . in season . . . in the age next unto infancy.' " The play and the essay have as "their common denominator, an unremitting focus upon erotic love and a consciousness of sexuality itself as a supreme instance of the mixed nature of our being."[14]

As a woman and a feminist I am ambivalent about the attitudes Kirsch finds in the play, as I am ambivalent about Montaigne. I am attracted by the epistemic modesty, the air of humane acceptance of embodied, sexual humanness, and the room in such a world, with such men, for women of strength, intelligence, and maturity. I am, however, at the same time, and prompted by many of the same words and images, disturbed by the central and structuring role of marriage as redemptive – for men – and the view of women as the natural agents of that redemption.[15]

Consider, for example, Helena's remarks to Diana and her mother after the bed-trick: "But, O, strange men,/That can such sweet use make of what they hate,/When saucy trusting of the cozen'd thoughts/Defiles the pitchy night;/so lust doth play/With what it loathes for that which is away."[16] The thought here is a perceptive, critical insight into a profoundly disturbing feature of male sexuality – the easy compatibility of desire and contempt. Such an insight might well ground feminist unease about that sexuality and about one's prescribed place as a woman in relation to it. But the lines are introduced by Helena's reassurance that all will turn out as it should: "Doubt not but heaven/Hath brought me up to be your daughter's dower,/As it hath fated her to be my motive/And helper to a husband."[17]

Thus, Helena embodies the humane acceptance of (male) human sexuality, even in one of its most distressing forms, with a sigh of "boys will be boys" and the confidence, or at least the hope, that marriage – "real" marriage, consummated and fecund – will make everything all right.[18] Men seem by this state of affairs to be spared the hard labor of maturity, having it done for them by virtuous and more than faintly maternal young women.

Connected, I think, to the historically uneasy accommodation to scepticism is *male* ambivalence about this picture. The cost of having one's sexual appetites indulged and then indulgently forgiven has typically been seen as exorbitant. Maternal female power is experienced as castrating, and the redemption of marriage is seen, like the redemption of socially proper religion, as a trap. As attractive as being forever a little boy may appear, the attendant (sense of) powerlessness usually evokes at least ambivalence.

Kirsch both captures and expresses this ambivalence when he writes of *All's Well* that "throughout the play Bertram is confronted by a conspiracy of women whose nurturing affections threaten to control and therefore deprive him of the energy of his aggressive sexual instincts, to bring him to what he calls 'the dark house and the detested wife'" (II. iii. 285).[19] Kirsch finds the resolution to the ambivalence in the bed-trick: Bertram is drawn into marriage through acting (so he believes) "freely" – i.e., out of aggressive and unlawful sexual instinct. As Kirsch puts it, "Bertram's freedom enables him to conquer Helena and discover her as a woman, a conquest that provides the basis for a marriage in which there can be desire as well as affection. . . ."[20]

Another locus of male ambivalence is the awareness that the voracious sexuality being humanely accepted is not one's own exclusive possession: one is in danger of being cuckolded by *other* naughty boys. Acknowledgement of *female* (hetero) sexual desire (as in *All's Well*), and of male desire for that desire, also raises the fear of cuckoldry. Genuine, autonomous desire – the only sort worth desiring – is uncontrollable by its object: "O curse of marriage!/That we can call these delicate creatures ours, / And not their appetites!"[21] As Coppelia Kahn notes, Touchstone and Lavatch, the clowns in *As You Like It* and *All's Well*, turn "shame to witty advantage by spurious logic": each "shows himself a wise fool by recognizing and accepting the folly that is inevitably his as a married man."[22] Needless to say, wise or not, such attitudes are not stable: (imagined) cuckoldry becomes in later plays, notably *Othello* and *The Winter's Tale*, the locus of real or narrowly and magically averted tragedy.[23]

## III

For the remainder of this essay I want to look at the other response to the pyrrhonian crisis, the one that Shakespeare explores in *Othello* and that finds its major philosophical expression in Descartes. It can arise either out of the ambivalence engendered by the problem comedic resolution or more directly out of the fears and threats to the ego presented by an apparently stabler (mis)remembered earlier world. The historical breaking apart of that world became the ground on which a new conception of the self emerged, a self whose definition rested on a violent repudiation of the presumed power of the earlier world to engulf and submerge the individual. The remembered experience of maternal power became in this process an intrapsychic trope for what had in historical fact been the nearly exclusively male power of feudalism.

Alongside the figure of the phallically powerful mother is a fantasy of exclusively possessing her from a position of omnipotence. The fantasy is, of course, itself unstable: the mother is desired *as* powerful, as the source of nurturance and life itself, but as such she is perceived as a threat not only to infantile omnipotence but to the self as independently existing. This fantasy, along with the ambivalence it engenders, rather than becoming integrated into a sexual economy that recognizes the otherness of the object of desire, remains intact as the basis of culturally normative male desire.

Ambivalence, and the violent warding off of ambivalence, are thus inevitable in a world in which men are expected to dominate, in part by the expression and evocation of sexual desire, women – whose bodily presence reawakens infantile experiences of dependency and symbiotic intimacy.[24] The playing out of these anxieties is evident in "Shakespeare's recurrent preoccupation with betrayal and with feminine powers to create and destroy *suddenly*, and in the repeated desire of his male characters both to be that all-powerful woman and to control the means of nurturance themselves, to the exclusion of the otherness of others."[25]

*Othello* and Descartes's *Meditations* are permeated by this anxiety. Descartes's world, as Popkin argues,[26] is in the throes of scepticism. Although we may read Descartes as self-confidently working toward the overthrow of Scholasticism and the institutionalization of the epistemology of modern science, he saw his project equally as one of warding off the threat of epistemic nihilism, a threat he perceived the Montaignean sceptic as posing. Similarly, although a number of critics have noted the resemblance of the plot and setting of *Othello* to comedy,[27] Othello, in his sense of himself and his love for Desdemona, is shown to be as antithetical to the comedic spirit as Descartes's epistemic desires are to Montaigne's humane scepticism.

One important reason why *Othello* seems like a comedy gone horribly wrong is that at the start Desdemona is a perfect comedic heroine: apparently and unremarkedly motherless and strongly attached to a powerful father,[28] perceptively and bawdily witty, strong-willed, passionate and unconventionally adventurous, realistic and mocking of Othello's extravagant romanticism, with an intimate female confidante and friend who is not her social peer (a relationship that counterpoints but never hinders the thematically central heterosexual one).

Othello loves her for her (their) conversation:[29] he is drawn by it into the comedic world, described by Susan Snyder as one of "multiple possibilities held in harmonious balance . . . anarchic dislocations of order and identity . . . the world where lovers always win, death always loses, and nothing is irrevocable . . . ."[30] In this world, Othello's military life becomes an adventure story to tell to Desdemona: "She lov'd me for the dangers I had pass'd,/And I loved her that she did pity them./This only is the witchcraft I have us'd."[31]

The "witchcraft" is, rather, Desdemona's: through her perception of Othello ("I saw Othello's visage in his mind")[32] she weaves from his own words, actions, and feelings a world of magical delight. And he comes to feel that his continued existence rests on the continued reality of this magical world – that is, on Desdemona's continued, faithful weaving of it. In railing about his horror that he can no longer believe in her, Othello speaks of Desdemona's love and fidelity as a *place* "where I have garner'd up my heart,/Where either I must live, or bear no life;/The fountain from the which my current runs/ Or else dries up. . . ."[33]

The dependency and vulnerability of living in a world magically constructed from lovers' conversation and of having one's sense of self mirrored in a woman's eyes pose a threat – to which Iago and his alternative metaphysics and epistemology are an answer. Iago offers Othello a place to stand, off to the side, hidden, eavesdropping, from which he can put Desdemona, their love, and the world they wove to the test. Stepping back, outside that world, he interrogates her and it, assembling evidence, demanding proofs, imaging, as he moves further into madness, that the movement is toward the greater clarity of dispassionate objectivity.

Proximity to Desdemona is epistemically dangerous: "I'll not expostulate with her, lest her body and beauty unprovide my mind again . . ."[34] It is because Othello comes to see his relationship to Desdemona as one of intolerable vulnerability and epistemic dependency (what, in better times, one would call trust or faith) that he manages *not* to see how vulnerable to and dependent upon Iago he eventually becomes. Male bonding, in this play as elsewhere, is not experienced as the threat to autonomy that connection to women is.[35]

Iago's perspective, the one he offers to Othello, has been described as scientific[36] or, with a slight shift of emphasis, as judicial.[37] Terence Hawkes describes Iago's method of reasoning as Baconian, based on what in scholastic terminology was called *ratio inferior*, to be distinguished from *ratio superior*, the faculty of wisdom – intuitive, inspired, and theological – represented in the play by the transcendence of Desdemona's love. Hawkes situates the play in the Elizabethan struggle between "lower" and "higher" reason, between those who would "observe, analyze, explain, define, and . . . interpret . . . with . . . validity, logical necessity, and rational certitude,"[38] and those like Montaigne who would chasten the ambitions of scientific reason.

Hawkes's point is that Iago's skillful manipulation of the appearances (he doesn't exactly *lie*) is not a perversion of scientific reason, but, in its power to seduce Othello, a demonstration both of the incapacity of such reason to comprehend aspects of the world that lie beyond it and of the defenseless inability of that world to provide a logical, rational proof of its own reality. It needs – demands – no proof, but pressed to give one, it will inevitably fail. Montaigne might be warning Othello: "take heed lest any man deceive you by Philosophie and vain seducement, according to the rudiments of the world."[39]

W. H. Auden sees Iago similarly as "a parabolic figure for the autonomous pursuit of scientific knowledge through experiment which we all [i.e., modern Westerners], whether we are scientists or not, take for granted as natural and right." He goes on to distinguish such knowledge by the ascetic disinterest of the investigator, the necessary absence of reciprocity (unlike the knowing of a friend, which requires reciprocity), and the having of power over the object of knowledge.[40]

Both Auden's and Hawkes's characterizations of scientific epistemology are as applicable to Cartesian rationalism as to Baconian empiricism. Although Bacon was more likely to have been in the air Shakespeare was breathing, the fundamental objectifying stance was common to both perspectives. If, as we shall see, nature is unlikely to survive the distancing tactics to which the empiricist subjects her, she fares no better with the rationalist, for whom she is an even less active epistemic partner.[41]

Auden argues that "Iago treats Othello as an analyst treats a patient . . . Everything he says is designed to bring to Othello's consciousness what he has already guessed is there. Accordingly, he has no need to tell lies."[42] But Auden attributes the *motivation* for this process solely to Iago: "the fall of Othello is the work of another human being; nothing he says or does originates with himself. In consequence, we feel pity for him but no respect; our aesthetic respect is reserved for Iago."[43] This final claim, and its consequence that *Othello* is not a proper tragedy, have been hotly debated. I want to argue against it by suggesting that we see Iago not just as exploiting what he finds in Othello, but as answering a need: if Iago hadn't been there, Othello would have had to invent him.[44]

Which is, of course, what Descartes did, with the evil genius of his first Meditation. The evil genius is invoked to steel Descartes's resolve not to be seduced into belief in a world that has presented itself to him through his sometimes deceptive senses, the "charm" of fables, the "power and beauty" of eloquence, the "ravishing delicacy and sweetness" of poetry, and the soberer delights of mathematics, philosophy, theology, morals, jurisprudence, and medicine.[45] He withdraws from the world – even, ultimately, from his own body – in order to put his relationship with it on a different footing: he aims to find and maintain himself in a position of epistemic control, knowing himself (i.e., his mind) while agnostic of all else, and admitting knowledge of the world only after it has been subjected to tests and proofs.

Descartes's doubt in the *Meditations* is clearly self-induced, and he confidently expects to regain the world he has willed away.[46] But, as Popkin argues, we need to take seriously the threat scepticism posed to Descartes. Epistemic dependency was both intolerable and increasingly unreliable, and his central interest in the growth of science demanded foundations more secure than the scepticism of Montaigne would allow. His response to doubt was very much Othello's: "Think'st thou I'ld make a life of jealousy? / To follow still the changes of the moon / With fresh suspicions? No, to be once in doubt / Is once to be resolv'd."[47]

Othello goes on to express the (increasingly desperate) hope that Desdemona will survive the tests he is putting her to, as though he could reconstruct the world of their love from a position outside of it, secure in the knowledge that it was really, "objectively," all that, while wrapped up in it, he had taken it to be. Descartes displays greater confidence, and the apparently comedic resolution to the *Meditations* presents the solemnized Baconian "chaste marriage" of the knowing mind with nature already pregnant with scientific possibility.[48]

Descartes's confident relation to the world is grounded in his confidence about God as his true and nondeceiving parent. Othello is, by contrast, radically unparented, a foreigner who is accepted and admired as a soldier but who is barred by racism from real connection to the world he moves in – except for the miracle of Desdemona's love. Descartes established the relationships the other way around: his untouchably certain existence as God's creature (his letters patent of noble lineage) licenses his establishing a relationship with nature in which his own identity and status are not at risk.

The shift that Descartes effects is a radical revisioning of what it is to be parented, one that replaces maternity with paternity as the relationship from which the self derives its identity. To be mothered is to find oneself helplessly in a situation over which one can initially exercise no conscious, rational control; one's mother and one's relationship to her are *given*, and the relationship grows and changes as one's self does. One's ability to affect consciously the nature of the bond grows along with one's emerging sense of self, rather than proceeding from that self.

Paternity, on the other hand, is notoriously uncertain. "Being fathered" refers most usually not to the sort of ongoing, evolving, interactive process that being mothered is, but to a discrete causal event whose particulars are shrouded in mystery and are the subject of speculation and attempts at scientific proof. To place oneself in the world as one's father's son is to claim a lineage, a heritage, a name. As Freud put it, the "turning from the mother to the father [the triumph of patriarchy over matriarchy] points . . . to a victory of intellectuality over sensuality – that is, an advance in civilization, since maternity is proved by the evidence of the senses while paternity is an hypothesis, based on an inference and a promise. Taking sides in this way with a thought-process in preference to a sense perception has proved to be a momentous step."[49]

Connected with the transformed meaning of parentage is the transformed meaning of nature and the natural. Descartes rejects nature as a seductive and misleading teacher, whose lessons can be genuinely profited from only when they are brought under the epistemic quality control of the individual knower. Strictly regulated laboratory science must replace common sense as the route to nature's secrets: we cannot trust what she chooses to show us but must force her to reveal herself to us. "Natural light," on the other hand, illuminates that which cannot be doubted: "I possess no other faculty whereby to distinguish truth from falsehood, which can teach me that what this light shows me to be true is not really true. . . . But as far as natural impulses are concerned . . . when I had to make active choice between virtue and vice . . . they have often enough led me to the part that was worse. . . ."[50]

The activity of self-induced doubt is used to split the self and its impulses into parts that are and that are not to be trusted, to be identified with. The self as mothered – desiring, sensual, embodied, interactive, continuously influenced, and dependent – must yield to the self as fathered – autonomous, related statically to the law, in a position to judge, armed, and vigilant.

Nature in *Othello* undergoes a similar transformation: it "appears to have changed sides. Love's ally is now love's enemy, partly because the angle of vision has changed: nature as instinctual rightness [at odds with reason, as in the comedies] gives way to nature as abstract concept, susceptible like all concepts to distortion and misapplication." Snyder's discussion focuses on the shift from the "particular" to the "general" sense of nature, from an appeal to "particular and personal . . . individual essence" to "common experience and prejudice" and "observed law(s) of nature."[51]

I want to draw the distinction slightly differently: between aspects of nature that emerge out of experience, whether they be someone's true desire, motivation, or character or the comedic force of nature that runs counter to all rational, judicious attempts to dam it up, and nature as the object of scientific – or pseudoscientific – generalization. In this latter sense, the concept of nature needn't be "distorted" or "misapplied" (by its *own* lights, anyway) radically to disorder a world of interdependency, trust, vulnerability, and epistemic reciprocity. Disordering that world is exactly what it's been invented to do, by being that from which the knowing self must be alienated and over which that self must learn to exercise control.

*Othello* and the *Meditations*, in passages that have posed enduring exegetical and critical difficulties, record the attempts of each of their protagonists to exercise this control over a representative "natural" object: Desdemona's handkerchief and Descartes's ball of wax. The natural world Othello is fleeing is the comedic one; hence, the associations of female, sexual magic with the handkerchief and its origins.[52] The handkerchief becomes a "free-floating signifier".[53] various characters attempt to fix and control its meaning – as love token, talisman, or hard evidence of adultery.

Initially the handkerchief symbolizes for Othello Desdemona's power over him, passed on to her by his mother, who got it from a sibyl. Losing it, he says, she would lose that power and face "such perdition / As nothing else could match."[54] She does, of course, lose it, in part because for her its sentimental value is overshadowed by what she hopes will be its usefulness in soothing Othello's headache: when he brusquely rejects it, and her attempts to comfort him, she lets it fall.

The juxtaposition here of Othello's romantic attitude with Desdemona's more quotidian view of love mirrors the interchange between them when, upon landing in Cyprus, Othello tells her, "If it were now to die, / 'Twere now to be most happy; for I fear / My soul hath her content so absolute / That not another comfort like to this / Succeeds in unknown fate," and she replies, "The heavens forbid / But that our loves and comforts should increase / Even as our days do grow."[55]

Appropriately, at the end of the play, when the handkerchief has fallen entirely into the world of ocular proofs and pieces of evidence, its origin also shifts: Othello describes it as "an antique token / My father gave my mother."[56] Part of the attempt to pin the handkerchief down, to make it hold fast with sufficient evidential weight to justify a murder, is recasting its lineage as patriarchal: it came from the father.

Descartes's ball of wax is a similarly free-floating signifier. He encounters it first through his senses: "that sweetness of honey, . . . that particular whiteness, . . . that figure, . . . that sound."[57] It is pleasantly, seductively, sensual, and it is particular: it is *that* ball of wax. But, he goes on to argue, it is as such unknowable; all those qualities are subject to change: "While I speak and approach the fire what remained of the taste is exhaled, the smell evaporates, the color alters, the figure is destroyed, the size increases, it becomes liquid, it heats, scarcely can one handle it, and when one strikes it, no sound is emitted . . . yet the same wax remains." Seduced immersion in the sensuous particularities of the wax is epistemically dangerous.

Descartes needs to step back, "abstracting from all that does not belong to the wax . . . [to] see what remains." The first step is from sensory engagement with the piece of wax to the imagination of its possible changes of state. Imagination, however, encompasses only finitely many such changes, while the wax can maintain its identity through a literal infinity of changes. "We must then grant that I could not even understand through the imagination what this piece of wax is, and that it is my mind alone which perceives it. . . . Its perception is neither an act of vision, nor of imagination, and has never been such although it may have appeared formerly to be so."

Othello's "knowledge" of Desdemona went through a similar process: from immediate, engaged perception of her particularity, through Iago-prompted pornographic imaging of her possible changes, to subsuming her under supposed general laws of female sexual behavior. Epistemically, the loss was a double one: of Othello's concrete engagement with her as a ground of his knowledge and of Desdemona's particularity. In practice, of course, the principal loss was of Desdemona's life.

Descartes claims to have achieved "a more evident and perfect conception of what the wax was." He claims for his new conception greater "distinctness," though not, of course, of *this* piece of wax as compared to all others: "nothing remains excepting a certain extended thing which is flexible and movable." But that is precisely to say that it has no particular size or shape nor, he argues, any particular smell, taste, color, or sound. There remains nothing in his final, trustworthy conception of the ball of wax to distinguish it from any other piece of wax or, for that matter, from any other relatively plastic physical object. Its identity consists essentially in its being subject to the laws of geometry and physics. Descartes describes how he has reached this point with the wax: "I distinguish the wax from its external forms, and . . . just as if I had taken from it its vestment, I consider it quite naked. . . ."

Although vision is for Descartes as fundamentally unreliable as any other sense, the *metaphor* of vision is central to the epistemology of modern science. As Evelyn Fox Keller and Christine Grontkowski argue,[58] vision played a central role in Greek epistemology as well, but with a difference. For the Greeks vision was an activity, analogous to illumination; it partook of the divine and was for Plato quite literally the philosopher's mode of apprehension of the Forms. For Descartes and his contemporaries, as for us, vision has been taken to be a relatively passive affair, involving the action of light on receptors in the eye. As such it is an unreliable ground for knowledge for an agent whose epistemic authority rests on his [*sic*] autonomous agency and his control over what he knows.

Vision does, however, as Keller and Grontkowski go on to show, provide an excellent *metaphor* for knowledge so conceived.[59] One sees best at some distance from the object, one can see without being seen and without affecting or being (otherwise) affected by the object, and seeing is spatial rather than temporal: one can take in "all at once" an array of objects, some changing and some static. Furthermore, one can, if one chooses, fix the object in one's gaze; as one cannot, for example, dominate someone by one's intensely focused *listening*.[60]

On Keller and Grontkowski's account, Descartes "enabled us to retain *both* the conception of knowledge as active and the use of the visual metaphor by severing the connection between the "seeing" of the intellect and physical seeing – by severing, finally, the mind from the body."[61] Thus, the "natural light of reason" and the "inborn light" reveal truths to us wholly independently of our senses, and by them we see with otherwise unattainable clarity – in our mind's (incorporeal) eye.[62]

Robert B. Heilman explores in detail the role of a "vocabulary of seeing" in Iago's manipulation of Othello's relation to Desdemona.[63] What Othello comes to believe he needs is the distanced, unaffected, objective view of Desdemona achieved by covert observation and conclusive pieces of evidence. Heilman contrasts with this stance Desdemona's practice of "a doctrine of sight more profound and veracious than Othello's system of ocular proof . . . [which] rests firmly on the imaginative perception of quality that may deny or transcend the visual evidence."[64]

A similar contrast is drawn by Keller and Grontkowski. They argue that neither literal nor metaphorical vision need carry implications of disembodiment and domination. Going back to Plato, they find another aspect of sight, namely that of communion, found in Plato's ideal relation to the Forms as well as in the common experience of "locking eyes." Fundamental to both is the eroticism of vision – the aspect most notably exorcized from its rational and scientific employment.[65]

The contrast between Iagoan and Desdemonean visual epistemology thus does not mirror that between natural (sensory) vision and the natural light of reason in Descartes, as a purely empiricist reading of Iago and his reliance on visual evidence might lead one to believe. Iago's stance is one essentially shared by empiricists and rationalists alike. Descartes distrusts the senses, and Iago gets Othello to (mis)place his faith in what they (can be made to) show, but what the two have in common is the adoption of a fundamentally paranoid alienation from a form of belief experienced as dangerously seductive in favor of a detached and controlling objectivity.

I want to argue, finally, that nature in the *Meditations* (and in the theory and practice of modern science) is, like Desdemona, murdered on the altar of this paranoid epistemology. Winifred Nowottny's account of Desdemona's murder as an execution, the final triumph of justice over love,[66] is helpfully supplemented by Madelon Sprengnether's argument that Othello fears Desdemona's power (which consists in his vulnerability to her) and feels humiliated by what he takes to be her betrayal of him: "it is the fear or pain of victimization on the part of the man that leads to his victimization of women. It is those who perceive themselves to be powerless who may be incited to the acts of greatest violence."[67]

That is, Othello embraces Iago's view of Desdemona for refuge against the fear induced by his vulnerability to her, by his need for her to be an autonomous, desiring other (loving him, showing him pure in her eyes) and his terror at his identity's being thus "garner'd up" in another. Embracing Iago's view has the result of bringing him to believe what he (thought) he most feared – that Desdemona was unfaithful to him; but, as awful as that belief was for him, it warded off one more awful yet: that Desdemona was not a "whore," that the world she wove by loving him was *real*, far more real than the one Iago offered, though (because) not in his control.

## IV

Francis Barker writes about the "metaphysics of death" at the heart of the discourse of modernity: his primary texts are Pepys's diary, *Hamlet*, Rembrandt's *Anatomy Lesson*, Marvell's "To His Coy Mistress," and Descartes's *Meditations* and *Discourse on Method*.[68] He remarks on the startling return of the body in Descartes's texts, but notes that it is a different body from the one banished in the First Meditation. The one that returns is the object of knowledge, to be anatomized, dissected, studied, scrutinized, and controlled – by the knowing subject, who knows himself quite apart from it. There are, however, two problems with this body: it is dead (or machine-like; anyway, its soul has fled), and it's on the other side of an epistemic divide – to which it has been banished in the name of epistemological hygiene, and where it is kept by a continuing paranoia. Consequently, knowledge of it is always uncertain. Discourse

> departs from itself in order to have something corporeal to represent – for in a positivist universe, without an object of knowledge there is strictly nothing to say – but in so far as it is constrained to operate this structure of separation it must set at a permanent distance the signs which are to be interpreted if meaning is to inhere. It founds itself on a gulf which is to a degree unbridgeable, and necessarily so for this discourse to function meaningfully at all.[69]

One of the distinctive marks of modernity is the importance of the individual, including individual sentiment in relation to marriage and individual certainty in relation to knowledge. We needn't be wishing our way back to an earlier time to note the costs of individualism, particularly those associated with gender: until quite recently – and in many, conceptual and practical ways, still – individuals are male, and maleness has had at its definitional heart a paranoid flight from femininity and a need for administrative structures to control and contain it, and, of course, us. The failure of those structures, or the fear, however ill-founded, that they might fail, has characteristically precipitated violence against women and against those aspects of men and of the world – most notably nature (herself) – that are associated with us.

Shakespearean problem comedy and Montaignean scepticism represent one response to the failure of the magically or religiously guaranteed conjunction of sexuality with marriage and certainty with knowledge. It's a response in which one's individual (male) agency is limited – in exchange for an acceptance of one's nature, which is precisely to be thus limited. Nothing will ever again be quite as it was, but high-spirited, intelligent virgin mother/wives will make it – almost – all right.

This response did not prevail. Rather, there has been an attempt – *per impossible* – to *force* the comedic ending, to bring about Bacon's "chaste and lawful marriage" of the knower with the known through the adoption of a distanced and controlling posture toward the world. The hope is for a sadistic encounter (chaste and lawful though it may be) in which nature is stripped bare and forced to reveal herself. Sadism's border with necrophilia is not, however, well marked: particularly when nature – or women – are desired *as* maternally powerful, they are likely to arouse murderous feelings of infantile impotence in those who in fact dominate them. Consequently, the prospects for this union are not good: though we are meant not to notice, the heroine was killed in the first act.[70]

## Notes

I am enormously indebted to the several feminist communities in which I have thought about the issues in this essay – notably, the Women's Studies Program and the Center for Advanced Feminist Studies at the University of Minnesota and the Midwestern and Eastern chapters of the Society for Women in Philosophy. Conversations with Michael Root have improved both my ideas and my writing style, though he would still quarrel with both.

1 Stanley Cavell, *The Claim of Reason: Wittgenstein, Skepticism, Morality, and Tragedy* (New York: Oxford University Press, 1979), pp. 433–96.
2 See Cavell's "Knowing and Acknowledging," and "The Avoidance of Love: A Reading of *King Lear*," in *Must We Mean What We Say?* (New York: Scribner's, 1969).
3 See Luce Irigary. "The Blind Spot of an Old Dream of Symmetry," Part 1 of *Speculum of the Other Woman*, trans. Gillian C. Gill (Ithaca: Cornell University Press, 1985), for a critical exploration of the (male) view of gender difference as symmetrical.
4 Questions about a possible "gender inflection" to scepticism are ones Cavell has addressed since the publication of *The Claim of Reason*. See, in particular, his essay, "Psychoanalysis and Cinema," in *Psychiatry and the Humanities* 10 (1986).
5 The term and its history are discussed by Carol Thomas Neely, *Broken Nuptials in Shakespeare's Plays* (New Haven: Yale University Press, 1985), pp. 58–65. I don't take it to be precise; my use of it should become clear and is strongly influenced by her discussion.
6 My reading of Descartes takes as its starting point an interpretation that is already controversial in its viewing scepticism for Descartes as a genuine threat, not just a philosophical tool. It is presented, with some variations, in Richard H. Popkin, *The History of Scepticism from Erasmus to Descartes* (New York: Harper and Row, 1964), and E. M. Curley, *Descartes against the Skeptics* (Cambridge: Harvard University Press, 1978). I don't want to argue the merits of this interpretation, although I do find it convincing. Rather, I would hope that the use to which I put it will lend it additional support.

7   Popkin, *The History of Scepticism*, esp. chaps. 1–3.

8   Ibid., p. 55.

9   In particular, from "On Some Verses of Virgil." See Arthur Kirsch, *Shakespeare and the Experience of Love* (Cambridge: Cambridge University Press, 1981), p. 38; and A. P. Rossiter, *Angel with Horns and Other Shakespeare Lectures*, ed. Graham Storey (London: Longmans, Green & Co. Ltd, 1961), p. 98.

10  E. K. Chambers, *Shakespeare: A Survey* (London: Sidgwick & Jackson, 1925), p. 210, quoted in Neely, p. 225 n. 4.

11  Kirsch, *Shakespeare and the Experience of Love*, pp. 37ff, 111–36.

12  Ibid., p. 118.

13  Ibid., p. 186 n. 8.

14  Ibid., p. 127. Kirsch is quoting from Montaigne, "On Some Verses of Virgil," and the elisions are his.

15  For an alternative, feminist view of marriage and institutionalized heterosexuality in women's lives, see Adrienne Rich, "Compulsory Heterosexuality and Lesbian Existence." *Signs* 5 (1980): 631–60.

16  *All's Well* IV. iv. 21–5. All references to plays of Shakespeare are from *The Riverside Shakespeare*, ed. G. Blakemore Evans (Boston: Houghton Mifflin, 1974).

17  Neely (*Broken Nuptials*, pp. 75ff) discusses the friendships between Shakespearean women as intimate, mutually sympathetic and helpful, and supportive and furthering of heterosexual, marital bonds. Although she goes on to argue that "comic action characteristically weakens or breaks old bonds to make way for new ones" (ibid., p. 77), she explicitly excludes bonds of female friendship from this fate. The argument that such bonds *do* succumb to the comedic ending has been made by Shirley Nelson Garner, "*A Midsummer Night's Dream*: 'Jack shall have Jill; / Nought shall go ill,'" *Women's Studies* 9 (1981): 47–63.

    The disagreement may reflect, in part, the choice of plays: the more the classic world of romantic comedy is intact, the more heterosexual romantic love may sweep away all other attachments and sentiments. But there is an additional issue of perspective: an explicitly nonheterosexist perspective, such as Garner's – one which does not accept heterosexuality as normative – is more likely to reveal the limitations, losses, and betrayals of female relationships exacted by the comedic marriage ending.

18  Kirsch (*Shakespeare and the Experience of Love*, p. 137) finds in Helena's words a "sense of paradoxical wonder," an attitude he takes to pervade the play as a whole. He argues that Rossiter is wrong to find "horror or revulsion" in Helena's words.

19  Ibid., p. 141.

20  Ibid., p. 142.

21  *Othello* III. iii. 268–70.

22  Coppelia Kahn, *Man's Estate: Masculine Identity in Shakespeare* (Berkeley: University of California Press, 1981), chap. 5, "'The Savage Yoke': Cuckoldry and Marriage," pp. 124ff.

23  Similar paths through Shakespeare are being traced by a number of feminist critics, such as Madelon Sprengnether, who reads "the development from the comedies through the problem plays and the major tragedies in terms of an explosion of the sexual tensions that threaten without rupturing the surface of the earlier plays." Published under Madelon Gohlke. "'I wooed thee with my sword': Shakespeare's Tragic Paradigms," in Carolyn Swift Lenz, Gayle Greene, and Carol Thomas Neely, eds., *The Woman's Part: Feminist Criticism of Shakespeare* (Urbana: University of Illinois Press, 1980), pp. 150–70; quotation, p. 154.

24  See Dorothy Dinnerstein, *The Mermaid and the Minotaur: Sexual Arrangements and Human Malaise* (New York: Harper & Row, 1976).

25  Murray Schwartz, "Shakespeare through Contemporary Psychoanalysis," *Hebrew University Studies in Literature* 5 (1977): 182–98, quoted in Kahn, p. 153, n. 4.

26  Popkin, *The History of Scepticism*, esp. chaps. 9, 10.

27  See Neely (*Broken Nuptials*, pp. 109ff), especially on the roles of sexuality and gender in comedic structure.

28  Cavell addresses this feature of the lives of the heroines of the '30s and '40s film comedies he discusses in *Pursuits of Happiness: The Hollywood Comedy of Remarriage* (Cambridge: Harvard University Press, 1981). For further discussion, see his essay in *Psychiatry and the Humanities* 10 (1986); also my "Missing Mothers/ Desiring Daughters: Framing the Sight of Women."

   My account of Desdemona and of the comedic elements in *Othello* owes much to Neely's (*Broken Nuptials*, pp. 109–17). For an illuminating account of why such a spirited Desdemona should respond so helplessly to Othello's jealous rages, see S. N. Garner, "Shakespeare's Desdemona," *Shakespeare Studies* 9 (1976): 233–52.

29  Conversation as a marital (and democratic) ideal is a topic throughout *Pursuits of Happiness* (a connection that leads me to suggest that the interpretation of *Othello* I'm urging is one we'd have seen had Katharine Hepburn Played Desdemona). The degeneration of Desdemona's language, its "increasing obliqueness" and opacity, and her becoming "the victim of her ambiguities" are explored in Madelon Gohlke, "'All that is spoke is marred': Language and Consciousness in *Othello*," *Women's Studies* 9 (1982): 157–76; quotations, 167.

30  Susan Snyder, *The Comic Matrix of Shakespeare's Tragedies* (Princeton: Princeton University Press, 1979). Although I find Snyder's readings perceptive and I draw on them extensively, I differ with her in attempting to locate the tragedy not – as she does – in "the tragic implications in any love relationship" (p. 84), but in a historically specific, and gendered, set of attitudes.

31  *Othello* I. iii. 167–69.

32  *Othello* I. iii. 252.

33  *Othello* IV. ii. 58–61.

34  *Othello* IV. i. 200–202.

35  Toni McNaron has drawn my attention to Othello's picking up Iago's speech patterns as he picks up his epistemic stance, and to the homoeroticism in the relationship between the two men, including a mock marriage in which they swear undying loyalty (III. iii. 460–80). Othello fails to perceive Iago's increasing possession of his soul in part because he thinks of eroticism and its attendant threats of dependency wholly in relation to women, and he regards the world of men and soldiering as a refuge from those threats.

36  See W. H. Auden, "The Joker in the Pack," in *The Dyer's Hand and Other Essays* (New York: Random House, 1948), pp. 246–72; and Terence Hawkes, "Iago's Use of Reason," *Studies in Philology* 58 (1961): 160–69.

37  See Winifred M. T. Nowottny, "Justice and Love in *Othello*," *University of Toronto Quarterly* 21 (1952): 330–44.

38  Hawkes, "Iago's Use of Reason," p. 165.

39  Quoted in ibid., p. 169.

40  Auden, "The Joker in the Pack," p. 270.

41  Kant's criticism of the sceptical consequences of both empiricism and rationalism makes a similar link: once the self imagines the "external world" as in need of proof, a proof that it is in a position to demand, search for, and recognize, it has

placed that world on the other side of a gulf nothing can span. See *Critique of Pure Reason*, trans. Norman Kemp Smith (New York: St Martin's Press, 1965), esp. "The Refutation of Idealism," B274–79, and "The Fourth Paralogism: Of Ideality," A366–80. Kant argues that the self cannot in fact coherently so imagine the world, since it can have no sense of itself apart from the world in which it finds itself.

42 Auden, "The Joker in the Pack," p. 266.

43 Ibid., p. 247. Hawkes also sees Iago as the active incarnation of scientific reason, with Othello torn between him and Desdemona.

44 For a related discussion of Othello's need to believe in Desdemona's infidelity, see Shirley Nelson Garner, "Male Bonding and the Myth of Women's Deception in Shakespeare's Plays," in Norman N. Holland and Sidney Homan, eds, *Shakespeare's Personality* (Berkeley: California University Press, 1989). Garner draws attention to the role such a belief plays in the maintenance of connections between men. Her argument has interesting implications about the nature and role of the (male) scientific community in the acquisition and validation of knowledge.

45 René Descartes, *Discourse on the Method*, in Elizabeth S. Haldane and G. R. T. Ross, eds, *The Philosophical Works of Descartes*, vol. 1 (Cambridge: Cambridge University Press, 1977); quotations, p. 84.

46 The psychological process of decathecting the world and "recreating" it under the control of the narcissistically aggrandized ego is at the heart of Freud's account of paranoia. See "Psycho-Analytic Notes upon an Autobiographical Account of a Case of Paranoia," *Standard Edition* 12 (London: Hogarth Press, 1958): 9–82.

47 *Othello* III. iii. 178–81.

48 For a discussion of the complicated sexual imagery in Bacon, see Evelyn Fox Keller, *Reflections on Gender and Science* (New Haven, Conn.: Yale University Press, 1985), esp. "Baconian Science: The Arts of Mastery and Obedience," pp. 33–42.

49 Sigmund Freud, *Moses and Monotheism* (London: Hogarth Press, 1949), pp. 23, 114. Quoted in Peggy Kamuf, "Writing like a Woman," Sally McConnell-Ginet, Ruth Borker, and Nelly Furman, eds, *Women and Language in Literature and Society* (New York: Praeger, 1980), p. 289. The insertion and elision are Kamuf's.

50 Meditation III, in Haldane and Ross, vol. 1, pp. 160ff.

51 Snyder, *The Comic Matrix*; all quotations in this paragraph are from p. 77.

52 *Othello* III. iv. 53–73. I am most persuaded by the account of the handkerchief in Neely, *Broken Nuptials*, pp. 128–31. See also her critical discussion of alternative readings, pp. 237f, n. 33.

53 The term is Timothy Murray's, from an unpublished paper entitled "*Othello*, An Index and Obscure Prologue to Foul Generic Thoughts," cited in Neely, *Broken Nuptials*, p. 234, n. 21, and p. 238, n. 33. Neely argues against Murray that, although characters do struggle over the symbolism of the handkerchief, it "like Desdemona, has an essence which is independent of the fantasies surrounding it" (p. 238, n. 33). The argument comes down to a tension at the heart of feminist theory: are *women* "free-floating signifiers" or do we "have an essence which is independent of the fantasies surrounding us"? It's not a tension I think we can – or should try to – resolve: we need both to explore the terrifying extent to which we have been reduced to men's dreams and theories of us *and* to hold on to our deeply felt, though perhaps unaccountable, untheorizable conviction that we are something other than those dreams and theories.

54 *Othello* III. iv. 67–68.

55 *Othello* II. i. 189–95. See Neely, *Broken Nuptials*, p. 116.

56 *Othello* V. ii. 217–18.

57   Meditation II, p. 154. Subsequent quotations from pp. 154–56.

58   Evelyn Fox Keller and Christine R. Grontkowski, "The Mind's Eye," in Sandra Harding and Merrill B. Hintikka, eds, *Discovering Reality: Feminist Perspectives on Epistemology, Metaphysics, Methodology, and Philosophy of Science* (Dordrecht: Reidel, 1983), pp. 207–24.

59   Keller and Grontkowski's account of the phenomenology of vision as a ground for its epistemological pre-eminence is drawn from Hans Jonas, "The Nobility of Sight," *Philosophy and Phenomenological Research* 14 (1954), esp. pp. 507, 513–18.

60   Note the centrality of the gaze to Sartre's characterization of the fundamental impulse toward the other as sadistically objectifying. *Being and Nothingness*, trans. Hazel E. Barnes (New York: Washington Square Press, 1966), pp. 441–504.

61   Keller and Grontowski, "The Mind's Eye," p. 215.

62   Vision itself reappears in Descartes's epistemology. Once knowledge is secured on a footing independent of the senses, properly controlled observation, vigilantly policed, is admitted as a necessary source of knowledge about the world, and vision is pre-eminently the observing sense. Descartes's extensive work in visual optics testifies to his concern to establish the conditions under which visual evidence is admissible testimony, ranking just below – and, of course, answerable to – sensorily unaided reason as a guide to the truth. Object-relations psychoanalytic theorists (such as Winnicott and Mahler) and Lacan, followed by feminist theorists influenced by them, have begun the development of an alternative epistemology that, as Keller and Grontkowski recommend, eroticizes vision (while perhaps also sharing the central metaphorical role with other senses). See, for example, Caroline Whitbeck, "A Different Reality: Feminist Ontology," in Carol Gould, ed., *Beyond Domination: New Perspectives on Women and Philosophy* (Totowa, N.J.: Rowman and Allanheld, 1983), and "Love, Knowledge and Transformation," *Hypatia* 2 (1984): 393–405. For a different but related approach to an erotics of vision, see Marilyn Frye, *The Politics of Reality: Essays in Feminist Theory* (Trumansburg, N.Y.: The Crossing Press, 1983), esp. "In and Out of Harm's Way: Arrogance and Love," and "To Be and Be Seen: The Politics of Reality."

63   Robert B. Heilman, *Magic in the Web: Action and Language in Othello* (Lexington: University of Kentucky Press, 1956), pp. 58–64.

64   Ibid., p. 62.

65   Another closely connected aspect of vision is the much-discussed mirroring phase of infant development, in which the reciprocal gaze of mother and child becomes the field in which the infant's sense of self initially takes root.

66   Nowottny, "Justice and Love," esp. p. 343.

67   Gohlke, "'I wooed thee with my sword'," p. 156.

68   Francis Barker, *The Tremulous Private Body* (London: Methuen, 1984), esp. pp. 95–112.

69   Ibid., p. 105.

# HOW IS EPISTEMOLOGY POLITICAL?

# Introduction

In keeping with the rules of good sportsmanship, this final section offers critics of epistemology the last word. However, none of the authors below argue for a true end to epistemology or to the philosophical analysis of knowledge. Rather, each argues for a renewed, and deeper, understanding about what epistemology is doing, how it is affected by its social context, and how it in turn produces political effects.

Genevieve Lloyd's essay is an excerpt from her influential study of the history of concepts of reason, *The Man of Reason: "Male" and "Female" in Western Philosophy*. Though we have not treated the topic of reason directly in this volume, it is closely associated with concepts of epistemic justification. Lloyd shows in her book that although rationality has been differently defined by the Greeks, by the moderns, and by more contemporary philosophers, an association between maleness and reason has persisted alongside an opposition between reason and femaleness. As the quotation marks in her title should suggest, however, hers is not an argument about innate characteristics or tendencies in men or in women, but about the culturally conditioned constructions of masculinity and femininity that have interpreted and influenced actual human behavior. Reason has been associated with men, not just in the sense that men were thought to have more of it, but also in that reason itself was defined in intrinsic relation to concepts and practices of masculinity.

This claim raises the troubling specter of relativism: is there, then, a male reason and a female reason, one form of rationality for those from Mars and another for those from Venus, as a popular book espousing gender differences would have it? Lloyd rejects such a view, but argues that, if there is to be a reason truly available to all, it is yet to be developed. Toward this very goal, a clearer assessment of the biased history of reason must surely be our first task.

Charles Mills' essay, "Alternative Epistemologies," usefully outlines and explains various epistemological projects that have arisen in the recent past, each concerned with epistemology's role in epistemic racial and sexual discrimination, or the denigration of the epistemic reliability of people of color and women. He suggests that both feminist epistemologies and the explorations of "black modes of cognition" are based on a social account of knowing which was best developed within the Marxist tradition. On this account, the social location of knowers is a constitutive feature of their epistemic reliability in regard to a significant range of topics. In particular, for Marxists, feminists, and black nationalists, there are three possible social sources of epistemic privilege: "the oppression subordinate groups suffer, their potentially universal character, their differential experience." Mills then summarizes and assesses the debates over such sources and concludes that, despite many difficulties yet to be overcome, adequate epistemologies should incorporate into their accounts of justification the impact of the differential cognitive access that is a structural feature of hierarchical societies.

The final essay offers a critique of traditional epistemology's general approach through a discussion of its development since the era of Bacon and Descartes.

Mary and Jim Tiles' contribution is taken from their book, *An Introduction to Historical Epistemology*, which offers a more complete account of the genealogy of contemporary epistemological dispositions through revealing the importance of such relatively neglected thinkers as Bacon, Vico, and Newton. The authors suggest that it is Bacon's vision of inquiry in particular that continues to frame epistemology, even though we have largely ignored Bacon's own awareness and treatment of the cultural, historical, and economic obstacles to improving our knowledge. However, where others such as Richard Rorty have concluded from their own critical assessment of modernist epistemology that we can only transcend its limitations by letting go of the epistemological quest, Mary and Jim Tiles argue that philosophical discussions about knowledge (which are disciplined rather than mere conversations) are as necessary as ever, precisely because of the unexamined social influences on knowing.

The future, then, in the eyes of each author in this section, needs to evolve beyond the present stymied non-interaction between traditionalist accounts that assume a universal knower capable of transcending their social embeddedness, and postmodern refusals to engage seriously with normative epistemic judgments or grounds for knowledge. Toward this, the big questions in epistemology perhaps need to get even bigger, or broader, than ever before.

## Further Reading

Alcoff, Linda and Elizabeth Potter (eds). *Feminist Epistemologies*. New York: Routledge, 1993.

Alcoff, Linda Martín. *Real Knowing: New Versions of the Coherence Theory*. Ithaca, NY: Cornell University Press, 1996.

Antony, Louise M. and Charlotte Witt (eds). *A Mind of One's Own: Feminist Essays on Reason and Objectivity* Boulder, CO: Westview Press, 1993.

Bernstein, Richard. *Beyond Objectivism and Relativism: Science, Hermeneutics and Praxis*. Philadelphia, PA: University of Pennsylvania Press, 1983.

Bordo, Susan. *The Flight to Objectivity: The Cartesian Masculinization of Culture*. Albany, NY: SUNY Press, 1987.

Harding, Sandra. *The Science Question in Feminism* Ithaca, NY: Cornell University Press, 1986.

——. *Whose Science? Whose Knowledge?* Ithaca, NY: Cornell University Press, 1991.

Rajchman, John and Cornel West (eds). *Post-Analytic Philosophy*. New York: Columbia University Press, 1985.

Schmitt, Frederick (ed.). *Socializing Epistemology: The Social Dimensions of Knowledge*. Boston, MA: Rowman & Littlefield, 1994.

# 24  The "Maleness" of Reason

*Genevieve Lloyd*

What exactly does the 'maleness' of Reason amount to? It is clear that what we have in the history of philosophical thought is no mere succession of surface misogynist attitudes, which can now be shed, while leaving intact the deeper structures of our ideals of Reason. There is more at stake than the fact that past philosophers believed there to be flaws in female character. Many of them did indeed believe that women are less rational than men; and they have formulated their ideals of rationality with male paradigms in mind. But the maleness of Reason goes deeper than this. Our ideas and ideals of maleness and femaleness have been formed within structures of dominance – of superiority and inferiority, 'norms' and 'difference', 'positive' and 'negative', the 'essential' and the 'complementary'. And the male – female distinction itself has operated not as a straightforwardly descriptive principle of classification, but as an expression of values. The equation of maleness with superiority goes back at least as far as the Pythagoreans. What is valued – whether it be odd as against even numbers, 'aggressive' as against 'nurturing' skills and capacities, or Reason as against emotion – has been readily identified with maleness. Within the context of this association of maleness with preferred traits, it is not just incidental to the feminine that female traits have been construed as inferior – or, more subtly, as 'complementary' – to male norms of human excellence. Rationality has been conceived as transcendence of the feminine; and the 'feminine' itself has been partly constituted by its occurrence within this structure.

It is a natural response to the discovery of unfair discrimination to affirm the positive value of what has been downgraded. But with the kind of bias we are confronting here the situation is complicated by the fact that femininity, as we have it, has been partly formed by relation to, and differentiation from, a male norm. We may, for example, want to insist against past philosophers that the sexes are equal in possession of Reason; and that women must now be admitted to full participation in its cultural manifestations. But, in the case of de Beauvoir's feminist appropriation of the ideal of transcendence, this approach is fraught with difficulty. Women cannot easily be accommodated into a cultural ideal which has defined itself in opposition to the feminine. To affirm women's equal possession of rational traits, and their right of access to the public spaces within which they are cultivated and manifested, is politically important. But it does not get to the heart of the conceptual complexities of gender difference. And in repudiating one kind of exclusion, de Beauvoir's mode of response can help reinforce another. For it seems implicitly to accept the downgrading of the excluded character traits traditionally associated with femininity, and to endorse the assumption that the only human excellences and virtues which deserve to be taken seriously are those exemplified in the range of activities and concerns that have been associated with maleness.

However, alternative responses are no less beset by conceptual complexities. For example, it may seem easy to affirm the value and strengths of distinctively 'feminine' traits without subscribing to any covertly assumed 'norm' – to have, as it were, a genuine version of Rousseau's idea that the female mind is equal, but different. But extricating concepts of femininity from the intellectual structures within which our understanding of sexual difference has been formed is more difficult than it seems. The idea that women have their own distinctive kind of intellectual or moral character has itself been partly formed within the philosophical tradition to which it may now appear to be a reaction. Unless the structural features of our concepts of gender are understood, any emphasis on a supposedly distinctive style of thought or morality is liable to be caught up in a deeper, older structure of male norms and female complementation. The affirmation of the value and importance of 'the feminine' cannot of itself be expected to shake the underlying normative structures, for, ironically, it will occur in a space already prepared for it by the intellectual tradition it seeks to reject.

Thus it is an understandable reaction to the polarizations of Kantian ethics to want to stress the moral value of 'feminine' concerns with the personal and particular, as against the universal and impartial; or the warmth of feeling as against the chillingly abstract character of Reason. But it is important to be aware that the 'exclusion' of the feminine has not been a straightforward repudiation. Subtle accommodations have been incorporated into the social organization of sexual division – based on, or rationalized by, philosophical thought – which allow 'feminine' traits and activities to be both preserved and downgraded. There has been no lack of male affirmation of the importance and attractiveness of 'feminine' traits – in women – or of gallant acknowledgement of the impoverishment of male Reason. Making good the lacks in male consciousness, providing it with a necessary complementation by the 'feminine', is a large part of what the suppression, and the correlative constitution, of 'womankind' has been all about. An affirmation of the strengths of female 'difference' which is unaware of this may be doomed to repeat some of the sadder subplots in the history of western thought.

The content of femininity, as we have it, no less than its subordinate status, has been formed within an intellectual tradition. What has happened has been not a simple exclusion of women, but a constitution of femininity through that exclusion. It is remarkable that Hegel, the notorious exponent of the 'nether world' of femininity, should have had such insight into the conceptual complexities of sexual difference. Hegel's diagnosis of 'womankind', as we have seen, occurs in a wider framework, which endorses the relegation of women to the private domain. But his understanding of the complexity, and the pathos, of gender difference in some ways transcends that. He saw that life in the nether world has conditioned the modes of female consciousness; that the distinctively 'feminine' is not a brute fact, but a structure largely constituted through suppression. To agree with this is not to deny that the 'feminine' has its own strengths and virtues. In the current climate of critical reflection on ideals of Reason, some of the strengths of female 'difference' can be seen as deriving from their very exclusion from 'male' thought-styles. To have been largely excluded from the dominant, and supposedly more 'advanced', forms of abstract thought or moral consciousness can be seen as a source of strength when their defects and impoverishment become apparent. But such strengths must be seen in relation to structural features of gender difference. They are strengths that derive from exclusion; and the merits of such 'minority consciousness' depend on avoiding asserting it as a rival norm.[1]

Attempting to identify or affirm anything distinctively 'feminine' has its hazards in a context of actual inequality. If the full range of human activities – both the nurturing tasks traditionally associated with the private domain and the activities which have hitherto occupied public space – were freely available to all, the exploration of sexual difference would be less fraught with the dangers of perpetuating norms and stereotypes which have mutilated men and women alike. But the task of exposing and criticizing the maleness of ideals of Reason need not wait upon the realization of such hopes; it may indeed be an important contribution to their realization.

The denigration of the 'feminine' is to feminists, understandably, the most salient aspect of the maleness of the philosophical tradition. But the issue is important for men, too. The lives of women incorporate the impoverishing restraints of Reason's transcended 'nether world'. But maleness, as we have inherited it, enacts, no less, the impoverishment and vulnerability of 'public' Reason. Understanding the contribution of past thought to 'male' and 'female' consciousness, as we now have them, can help make available a diversity of intellectual styles and characters to men and women alike. It need not involve a denial of all difference. Contemporary consciousness, male or female, reflects past philosophical ideals as well as past differences in the social organization of the lives of men and women. Such differences do not have to be taken as norms; and understanding them can be a source of richness and diversity in a human life whose full range of possibilities and experience is freely accessible to both men and women.

Can anything be salvaged of the ideal of a Reason which knows no sex? Much of past exultation in that ideal can be seen as a self-deceiving failure to acknowledge the differences between male and female minds, produced and played out in a social context of real inequalities. But it can also be seen as embodying a hope for the future. A similar ambiguity characterizes Hegel's own famous expression of faith in Reason, summed up in his slogan that the real is the rational and the rational the real. This has, not surprisingly, been seen by many as a dubious rationalization of the status quo. But it can also be taken as the expression of an ideal – as an affirmation of faith that the irrational will not prevail. Such a faith may well appear naive; but that does not mean it is bad faith. The confident affirmation that Reason 'knows no sex' may likewise be taking for reality something which, if valid at all, is so only as an ideal. Ideal equalities, here as elsewhere, can conceal actual inequalities. Notwithstanding many philosophers' hopes and aspirations to the contrary, our ideals of Reason are in fact male; and if there is a Reason genuinely common to all, it is something to be achieved in the future, not celebrated in the present. Past ideals of Reason, far from transcending sexual difference, have helped to constitute it. That ideas of maleness have developed under the guise of supposedly neutral ideals of Reason has been to the disadvantage of women and men alike.

Philosophers have defined their activity in terms of the pursuit of Reason, free of the conditioning effects of historical circumstance and social structures. But despite its professed transcendence of such contingencies, Philosophy has been deeply affected by, as well as deeply affecting, the social organization of sexual difference. The full dimensions of the maleness of Philosophy's past are only now becoming visible. Despite its aspirations to timeless truth, the History of Philosophy reflects the characteristic preoccupations and self-perceptions of the kinds of people who have at any time had access to the activity. Philosophers have at different periods been churchmen, men of letters, university professors. But there is one thing they have had in common throughout the history of the activity: they have been predominantly male; and the absence of women from the philosophical tradition has meant that the conceptualization of Reason has been done exclusively by men. It is not surprising that the results should reflect their sense of Philosophy as a male activity. There have of course been female philosophers throughout the western tradition. But, like Philo's or Augustine's women of Reason, they have been philosophers despite, rather than because of, their femaleness; there has been no input of femaleness into the formation of ideals of Reason.

As women begin to develop a presence in Philosophy, it is only to be expected that the maleness of Philosophy's past, and with it the maleness of ideals of Reason, should begin to come into focus; and that this should be accompanied by a sense of antagonism between feminism and Philosophy. We have seen that Philosophy has powerfully contributed to the exclusion of the feminine from cultural ideals, in ways that cannot be dismissed as minor aberrations of the philosophical imagination. But it is important that the tensions between feminism and Philosophy should not be misconstrued. The exclusion of the feminine has not resulted from a conspiracy by male philosophers. We have seen that in some cases it happened despite the conscious intent of the authors. Where it does appear explicitly in the texts, it is usually incidental to their main purposes; and often it emerges only in the conjunction of the text with surrounding social structures – a configuration which often is visible only in retrospect.

Feminist unease about ideals of Reason is sometimes expressed as a repudiation of allegedly male principles of rational thought. Such formulations of the point make it all too easy for professional philosophers to dismiss as confused all talk of the maleness of Reason. As I pointed out at the beginning, contemporary philosophical preoccupation with the requirements of rational belief, the objectivity of truth and the procedures of rational argument, can make it difficult for them to see the import of criticisms of broader cultural ideals associated with Reason. The claim that Reason is male need not at all involve sexual relativism about truth, or any suggestion that principles of logical thought valid for men do not hold also for female reasoners.

Philosophers can take seriously feminist dissatisfaction with the maleness of Reason without repudiating either Reason or Philosophy. Such criticisms of ideals of Reason can in fact be seen as continuous with a very old strand in the western philosophical tradition; it has been centrally concerned with bringing to reflective awareness the deeper structures of inherited ideals of Reason. Philosophy has defined ideals of Reason through exclusions of the feminine. But it also contains within it the resources for critical reflection on those ideals and on its own aspirations. Fortunately, Philosophy is not necessarily what it has in the past proudly claimed to be – a timeless rational representation of the real, free of the conditioning effects of history.

To study the History of Philosophy can be of itself to engage in a form of cultural critique. Few today share Hegel's vision of the History of Philosophy as the steady path of Reason's progress through human history. But it does reveal a succession of ways of construing Reason which have, for better or worse, had a formative influence on cultural ideals, and which still surface in contemporary consciousness. I have tried to bring out how these views of Reason have been connected with the male-female distinction. In doing so, I have of course often highlighted points which were not salient in the philosophers' own perceptions of what they were about. Bringing the male-female distinction to the centre of consideration of texts in this way may seem to misrepresent the History of Philosophy. But philosophers, when they tell the story of Philosophy's past, have always done so from the perspective of their own preoccupations, shared with their non-philosopher contemporaries – pressing questions which were not central to the philosophers they were explicating.

To highlight the male–female distinction in relation to philosophical texts is not to distort the History of Philosophy. It does, however, involve taking seriously the temporal distance that separates us from past thinkers. Taking temporal distance seriously demands also of course that we keep firmly in view what the thinkers themselves saw as central to their projects. This exercise involves a constant tension between the need to confront past ideals with perspectives drawn from the present and, on the other hand, an equally strong demand to present fairly what the authors took themselves to be doing. A constructive resolution of the tensions between contemporary feminism and past Philosophy requires that we do justice to both demands.

**Note**

1   The phrase 'minority consciousness' is from Deleuze, G. (1978) 'Philosophie et minorité', *Critique*, 369, 154–5.

# 25   Alternative Epistemologies

## *Charles W. Mills*

The presumption that epistemology as it has traditionally been defined is a neutral and universalist theory of cognitive norms and standards has come under increasing attack by feminist philosophers. Though there are significant divergences in the diagnoses offered of the deficiencies of orthodox epistemology, and corresponding variations in the positive proposals advanced for its improvement or supersession, a clear consensus has now been established that some kind of "feminist epistemology" is called for.[1] A parallel critique has also come from some black philosophers, who have argued that philosophy has not been immune to the racism that has pervaded so much of western thought about non-European peoples.[2] The literature here, however, is not remotely as extensive as that for the feminist case, reflecting the continuing under-representation of black scholars in the field.[3] Finally, there is, of course, the longstanding challenge of the Marxist political tradition, which some theorists at least have taken to be committed to the epistemic superiority of the "proletarian" to the "bourgeois" standpoint in comprehending the world.[4]

In all three cases, then, we have the advocacy of what could be termed alternative epistemologies, in that the processes of cognizing validated by the dominant perspective are being characterized as somehow inadequate.

What I want to do in this paper is to examine and elucidate some of the major arguments offered for and against the legitimacy of such epistemologies. But a preliminary clarification (and perhaps also a justification) is necessary for those readers not acquainted with the literature. The proponents of such views do not, for the most part, see themselves as offering, within the conventional framework, alternative analyses of such traditional epistemological topics as memory, perception, belief, and so on, or coming up with startling new solutions to the Gettier problem. Nor is their paradigmatic cognizer that familiar Cartesian figure, the abstract, disembodied individual knower, beset by skeptical and solipsistic hazards, trying to establish a reliable cognitive relationship with the basic furniture of the Universe.[5] Rather, the sentiment tends to be that this framework itself needs to be transcended, and that the standard, hallowed array of "problems" in the field should itself be seen as problematic. Thus a destructive genealogical inquiry underspins part of their recommended reconceptualization, the suggestion being that certain issues have historically been seen as problems in the first place only because of the privileged universalization of the experience and outlook of a very limited (particularistic) sector of humanity – largely white, male, and propertied.

It can readily be appreciated, therefore, that such arguments, or assertions, would be unlikely to impress the average subscriber to *Mind*. They would be seen as question-begging, as presupposing that all the important issues have been settled. And it might be felt that such epistemologies – if the title is even conceded to them – do not therefore deal with the really serious, basic philosophical questions: the existence of the external world and of other minds, the reliability of perception, the trustworthiness of memory.

But the following challenge could be mounted to orthodox dismissiveness: how serious is this seriousness really? If these alternative epistemologies admittedly focus on less fundamental beliefs, are they not redeemed by genuine rather than histrionic questioning? Hume pointed out long ago that, whatever skeptical iconoclasm with respect to everyday beliefs philosophers may indulge in privately (or with their colleagues), "immediately upon leaving their closets, [they] mingle with the rest of mankind in those exploded opinions." Nor is this necessarily just a matter of expedient conformity with the unenlightened herd, for he admits that in his own case when he tries to "return to these speculations" after a few hours at backgammon, "they appear so cold, and strain'd, and ridiculous, that I cannot find in my heart to enter into them any further."[6] So one could be forgiven for suggesting that much of mainstream epistemology's apparent intellectual radicalism and daring about foundational beliefs is purely ritualistic and (literally) academic, having no practical implications for the actual beliefs and behavior either of the non-philosophical population at large or even of the philosophers themselves. But if this diagnosis is correct, and mainstream epistemology is in fact just, or largely, a sterile conceptual game, then why should it be seen as intrinsically a more serious undertaking than the project of these alternative epistemologies: the genuine (not simulated) revolutionizing and reconstruction of our received, hegemonically commonsensical picture of social reality?

Such, at any rate, could be one possible line of defense for the validity of these epistemologies. Characteristically, then, their concerns will be not the problem of other minds, but the problem of why women were not thought to have minds; not an investigation of the conditions under which individual memory is reliable, but an investigation of the social conditions under which systematic historical amnesia about the achievements of African civilizations became possible; not puzzlement about whether or not physical objects exist, but puzzlement about the cognitive mechanisms that make relational social properties appear under capitalism as reified intrinsic natural properties. In what follows, I will try to clarify some of their crucial theoretical commonalities as well as their differences.

## 1   Arguments from Biological Causation

As Alan Soble has pointed out, two fundamentally different kinds of answer have been offered to the question why subordinate groups may have differential, and superior, insight into the structure of social reality: (i) There are biological differences in the cognizing equipment, or in the embodied interaction with the world, of the groups involved; and (ii) there are significant socially caused divergences in their situation that affect their perception.[7] Our main focus will be on the latter, more prominent, claim, but a few words on the biological answer would not be inappropriate, if only to establish it as a foil.

The basic notion here is that traditionally subordinated groups, such as women and blacks, have an innately superior cognizing apparatus, and so can better know the world than the dominant group of white males. (A democratized, "environmentalist" variation on this position would be that all humans have the potential for these capacities to develop, but the respective circumstances of subordination and domination have fostered their flourishing/atrophy.) What is involved, then, is a kind of "oppositional" biological determinism, which has been embraced both by radical feminists and by some sectors of the black nationalist movement.

Alison Jaggar, for example, cites the work of radical feminists who believe in female intuition, a female capacity to enter into a direct mystical connection with the world, and in specifically female parapsychological powers such as "lonth."[8] Similarly, Sandra Harding mentions the view that women's biological functions – menstruation, intercourse, pregnancy, nursing – afford them distinctive kinds of experiences that are physiologically based.[9] Along parallel lines, some adherents of the black philosophy of negritude, developed by Aimé Césaire and Léopold Senghor, have argued that there are characteristically black modes of cognition: "Senghor's theory of negritude . . . contains within it a theory of knowledge, indeed an epistemology. The key notion in Senghor's theory is that of *emotion*, which he virtually erects into a function of knowledge and attributes to the African as a cardinal principle of his racial disposition."[10] And Harding cites more recent claims of the same kind, for example, that varying quantities of melanin, different sorts of amino acid, and divergent brain patterns "underlie cultural differences between Africans and Europeans."[11]

There are familiar, post-Kuhnian problems in evaluating these claims, since any reference to the meagerness or non-existence of their scientific basis is likely to be met with the accusation of *petitio*. Yet if the usual distinction between belief and knowledge is not to be abandoned (and those who are expressly challenging traditional belief systems would seem to have a good reason for wanting to retain it), then claims to alternative and superior forms of noetic access would still have to be cashed out in fairly traditional ways to seem persuasive. It is not just a question here of convincing a white male audience (which might be dismissed as intellectually irredeemable anyway), but of winning over other women and blacks who do accept the standard paradigm, and with whom dialogue would presumably be seen as important. (Though perhaps some kind of direct approach to the awakening in others of these putatively dormant cognitive powers could render discursive proof unnecessary, the deed superseding the word.) Finally, it should be pointed out that these positions have often been criticized by other women and blacks as implicitly endorsing the oppressor's theoretical framework. Thus Abiola Irele, summarizing some of the criticisms made of Senghor, comments: "Negritude is presented in these objections as not only too static to account for the diversified forms of concrete life in African societies but also, because of its 'biologism,' as a form of acquiescence in the ideological presuppositions of European racism."[12]

A more mundane basis than parapsychology for male/female cognitive distinctness would be sexual dimorphism in brain structure, since there is some indication that spatial and linguistic skills are not symmetrically distributed between the sexes.[13] Both feminists and anti-feminists have taken these findings to establish innate cognitive differentiation, one side seeing female and the other male superiority in the data. As Lorraine Code has pointed out, though, the brain develops its functions by practice, so even if these differences can be unequivocally substantiated, the ultimate causes may still be social rather than biological. Pending the transformation of patriarchal structures, widespread and continuing stereotyping of gender roles for children makes it very difficult to separate what is truly innate from what is merely socialized.[14]

## 2 Arguments from Social Causation

We turn now to the major argument, that from social situation. This argument is best developed within the Marxist tradition, and the most influential version of the "feminist epistemology" claims (feminist standpoint theories) explicitly invokes that tradition, so this is the place to begin.[15] By now, of course, there are multitudinous Marxisms, not to mention post-Marxisms, but the variety that lends itself best to this project is the relatively old-fashioned (some would probably say, more harshly, discredited) "scientific realist" interpretation of Marx. In this interpretation, Marx's appearance/reality dichotomy in *Capital* is a statement of the anti-positivist, realist insistence on the necessity for distinguishing between naïvely spontaneous and methodologically adequate conceptualizations of empirical data.[16] Historical materialism would then be a theory of the workings of the capitalist system, which is – to cite some of the crucial scientific realist claims – objective, genuinely referential, and a better, more progressive approximation to truth than its predecessors.[17] It is within this framework that I think the most plausible defense can be given of the validity of "alternative epistemologies," a defense that avoids epistemological relativism.

The argument goes something like this. Marx's theorization of society includes a meta-theoretical element, in that his general claims about the social determination of belief commit him to genetic explanations both of other important competing theories and, reflexively, of the origins of Marxism itself. Thus, in this respect (though not, as I shall later contend, in others), he is in agreement with Barry Barnes and David Bloor when they insist on a "symmetry" of explanation-schemes both for theories deemed scientific and for those deemed unscientific.[18] The latter may, of course, have all kinds of causes, including idiosyncratic personal ones, but Marx's belief is that when it comes to the sociologically important patterns of long-term systematic error that affect significant sectors of the population, we should look for structurally generated misperceptions that arise out of the social system itself.

Now in *Capital*, there is a brief but illuminating passage where Marx argues that Aristotle was hindered, despite his great intellect, from seeing human labor as the foundation of all value because Greek slavery presumed "the inequality of men and of their labor-powers."[19] An implicit contrast with the later capitalist mode of production is involved here, for the suggestion seems to be that the low level of technological development, and the economic and ideological centrality of slavery, meant that there was no social group to whom the idea of human equality would "naturally" have occurred. So this particular societal illusion (innate human inequality) would have the whole society in its grip, with no countervailing ideational tendencies (or at least no materially based ones). By contrast, Marx believes that the illusory appearances of capitalism – though admittedly exerting a certain doxastic pull on everybody – can be at least partially "seen through" from a certain perspective, that of course being the perspective of the working class. The account Marx gives is of an ostensibly abstract, non-gendered and non-racialized, capitalism, so that his theoretical focus is on class-related illusions. But feminists and black nationalists can obviously argue that actually existing sexist and racist capitalism (which does include the capitalist systems Marx studied) also generates other illusory appearances, which are not reducible to class, and which are differentially penetrable cognitively by other social groups. So the key claim in all cases is that social causation can have both positive and negative epistemic effects.

This, then, is the central idea that has to be defended if the project of alternative epistemologies is to get off the ground: that social causation can be epistemologically beneficial. The next step is to clarify precisely what social characteristic is supposed to produce this superior insight. I think there are three main candidates, which are not always disentangled from one another: the oppression subordinate groups suffer, their potentially universal character, and their differential experience.

Let us begin with oppression. This term is broader than exploitation (in the technical Marxist sense) and, as such, can be extended to groups other than the working class. It is also harder to define. Alison Jaggar suggests the following analysis: "Oppression is the imposition of unjust constraints on the freedom of individuals or groups." She later goes on to argue that the suffering of oppressed groups is epistemically beneficial: "Their pain provides them with a motivation for finding out what is wrong, for criticizing accepted interpretations of reality and for developing new and less distorted ways of understanding the world."[20]

But even if this tendency exists, there is also, as Jon Elster has pointed out, "the tendency of the oppressed and exploited classes in a society to believe in the justice of the social order that oppresses them."[21] So one has to be careful not to put too much weight on this explanation: suffering itself is not necessarily cognitively illuminating. It is significant that Marx did not seem to think that the (clearly oppressed) slaves of ancient Greece were likely to make the cognitive leap to the notion of universal human equality. And it is a familiar fact that although several subordinate classes could be regarded as oppressed under capitalism – the petty bourgeoisie, the peasantry, the lumpenproletariat, and the working class – only in the last of these did Marx think a revolutionary consciousness was likely to develop. (For the lumpenproletariat, the condition of which could be regarded as most miserable, he had nothing but contempt, seeing them as most prone to sell out to capital.) Thus Alan Soble, who takes oppression to be the crucial factor in the feminist claim, argues against it on the grounds that "each oppressed group (women, workers, blacks, chicanos, the handicapped, etc.) can make a claim to epistemological superiority," so that "the result is that the Marx-based epistemological argument . . . collapses into trivial pluralism."[22]

I suggest, then, that the mere fact of oppression, though possibly producing an openness to alternate views, is not enough. Let us now look at universality. In Marx's early writings, the proletariat is characterized as "an estate which is the dissolution of all estates . . . which cannot emancipate itself without emancipating itself from all other spheres of society and thereby emancipating all other spheres of society."[23] Joseph McCarney draws on this vision of totality to argue that since the proletariat is the "universal class," "Marx was able to combine the necessity of social roots with the aspiration to the whole" because "the standpoint of the whole and that of the proletariat were identical in the historical circumstances of the time."[24]

But for a non-Hegelian Marxist, the seemingly teleological causality of this claim is not readily convincing. Why should the fact (if it is a fact) that a particular class will bring about a classless society in the future retroactively guarantee them a holistic perspective? Jon Elster has emphasized the necessity of providing "microfoundations," specific causal mechanisms, for teleological and functional claims.[25] The question then would be: what causal mechanisms could plausibly be suggested that would make this hypothetical causality operable? Moreover, even if it is conceded that the proletariat comes closest of all the classes of capitalism to a genuinely universalist viewpoint, this certainly does not exhaust the taxonomy of important social groups. The experiences of blacks and women with working-class racism and sexism, the frequently sectarian practices of vanguard Marxist groupings in relation to non-class struggles and issues, and the continuing under-representation of women in the upper echelons of the power structures of existing self-described "socialist" states, all cast doubt on the actual universality of the proletarian perspective. And if a good case cannot be made for the working class, then *a fortiori* it is hardly likely to be made for blacks or women.

What is left, then, is differential group experience, and it is on this foundation that I think the best case can be made for the cognitive superiority of alternative viewpoints. A metaphor that may be helpful is the idea of some kind of "experiential space," which is not homogeneous, but is full of structured heterogeneities and discontinuities, so that a social dimension is built in to its architecture from the start. As Bhikhu Parekh puts it:

> A society is not a collection of individuals, but a system of positions. . . . To be a member of a society is to occupy a prestructured social space and to find oneself already related to others in a certain manner. . . . Since [one's] relations with other positions are objectively structured in a determinate manner, so are [one's] social experiences. . . . Since [one's] social experiences are structured, [one's] forms of thought, the categories in terms of which [one] perceives and interprets the social world, are also structured.[26]

Far from its being the case, then, that an asocial Cartesian knower can move freely along all axes of this space, there will be certain resistances linked specifically to one's social characteristics and group membership, that will determine, at least tendentially, the kinds of experiences one is likely to have and the kinds of concepts one is accordingly likely to develop. In virtue of our common humanity there is obviously a common ("universal") zone that makes the Cartesian project plausible in the first place; one must avoid the absurd kind of hyperbole that suggests there is no overlap at all between the experiences of different groups. But there will also be areas of experience that lie outside the normal trajectory through the world of members of hegemonic groups. The claim that defenders of alternative epistemologies must make is that subordinate groups' access to these areas gives them a more veridical picture of the dynamics of the social system. If it doesn't strain the metaphor too much, a rough distinction could probably be made between experiences that are outside the hegemonic framework in the sense of involving an external geography (a muckraking Frederick Engels brings details of British slum conditions to the shocked attention of a middle-class audience) and experiences that are outside because they redraw the map of what was thought to be already explored territory (feminists put forward the claim that most "seductions" have a coercive element that makes them more like rapes).

Thus in the latter situation there is a double shock, that arises not merely from the simply alien but from the alienated familiar, the presentation of the old from a new angle. It is this kind of inversion of perspective that is most characteristic of alternative epistemologies. Given the initial scientific realist assumptions, the argument must be that these alternative sets of experiences are not epistemically indifferent *vis-à-vis* one another, but that hegemonic groups characteristically have experiences that foster illusory perceptions about society's functioning, whereas subordinate groups characteristically have experiences that (at least potentially) give rise to more adequate conceptualizations. It is a question not so much of simple oppression, then, but rather of an oppression so structured that epistemically enlightening experiences result from it.

At this stage, though, it may be argued that I have overstated the degree of epistemic divergence between different perspectives. Granted that people have differing views about things, there is no reason why we cannot learn, through communication, to understand other viewpoints, and so achieve a more balanced perspective; to exaggerate these admitted differences into alternative epistemologies is ridiculous.

One problem with this kind of liberal approach is that rival sets of experiences are often contradictory rather than complementary (as in perspective "inversion," for example), so a simple synthesis is not really possible. In addition, this approach underestimates the difficulty members of hegemonic groups have in accepting alternative descriptions of their experienced reality. Apart from the prima facie appearance of the situation, already mentioned, there is also the contributory role of background hegemonic ideologies, which helps to sustain a particular interpretation of what is happening, and to denigrate other viewpoints. Thus there will be a basic skepticism about conflicting reports. Sandra

Harding points to "the struggle we have had to get women's testimony about rape, wife battering, sexual harassment, and incest experiences accepted as reliable by police, the courts, employers, psychiatrists, other men and women, etc."[27]

Moreover, in many cases reports will not even be forthcoming, since members of subordinate groups may judge it imprudent, given the power relations involved, to give an honest account of how they feel about things. The oral and literary history of the black experience, for example, is full of stories and parables that emphasize the necessity of dissembling before even apparently sincere and concerned whites, the need to tell them what it is calculated they want to hear rather than the truth: the mask of the cheerful grin. Thus in a crucial episode at the beginning of Ralph Ellison's classic postwar novel, *The Invisible Man*, the nameless narrator overhears (and is at the time bewildered by) his grandfather's deathbed advice to his father: "Son, after I'm gone I want you to keep up the good fight. I never told you, but our life is a war. . . . I want you to overcome 'em with yeses, undermine 'em with grins, agree 'em to death and destruction."[28]

Finally, psychological obstacles ("hot" mechanisms) also stand in the way of acceptance of redescriptions that cast interpersonal transactions in terms of coercion and oppression, quite apart from the ("cold") skepticism that arises from the intrinsic incongruity of these reports with one's own hegemonic group experience.[29] It could be said that if there are things one needs to know, there are also things one needs not to know, and an interesting socio-psychological account could probably be constructed of mechanisms of societal blocking of unwanted information that would be the Marxist equivalent of the Freudian repression of unhappy memories. For all these reasons, then, members of hegemonic groups are in practice unlikely to be receptive to alternative viewpoints.

## 3   Some Criticisms

Let us now consider some criticisms of this kind of approach that have been made by Jon Elster. Elster's basically positivist account of Marx is hostile to the idea that a "working-class perspective" has any merit, and this hostility would presumably extend, *a fortiori*, to any similar claims made by women and blacks. He sees as Marx's "most original contribution" to the theory of cognitive distortion a particular version of the fallacy of composition, in this case the "idea that the economic agents tend to generalize locally valid views into invalid global statements."[30] But he finds "no basis in [Marx's] work for suggesting different sorts of biases, or different frequency of bias, among the members of different classes."[31] Thus Elster's reading seems to suggest that all members of society, regardless of class position, are equally subject to cognitive distortion. Working-class membership would not therefore confer any epistemic advantage.

Now I think that this claim can fairly easily be demonstrated to be a misreading of Marx. As I indicated earlier, Marx does believe that capitalism produces general "illusions," and that all classes are subject to them. To take a standard, frequently cited example from *Capital*, the voluntaristic character of the trans-action between worker and capitalist is an "illusory appearance" produced at the market level ("the sphere of simple circulation"), since here it seems that both parties to this transaction "are constrained only by their own free will." And this "phenomenal form," the wage-form, constitutes, according to Marx, "the basis of all the juridical notions of both laborer and capitalist," and all the corresponding "illusions as to liberty."[32]

Thus far one can agree with Elster: trans-class symmetry obtains. But the point is that this is only one doxastic tendency among others: Marx also delin-eates a countervailing, demystifying tendency that is class specific rather than general. For, in addition to the (common/"universal") experience of the de-ceptive equality of the market, workers also have the (class-determined/"par-ticular") experience of economic constraint arising from the *de facto* capitalist monopoly of society's means of production, and the *dis*illusioning experience of capitalist production itself. Thus workers have spontaneously and directly available to them a conflicting set of experiences, that dramatically undercuts the voluntaristic and egalitarian appearance of the transaction, and that would, if followed up conceptually, lead in quite a different theoretical direction.[33] Workers' divergent experiences, then, given them a cognitive advantage over capitalists in understanding the workings of the "hidden structure" of the sys-tem. Hence the experiential symmetry between them at the market level is ab-sent at the deeper level of production.

But this account is not readily accommodated by Elster's reading of Marx. Capitalists may tend to globalize the locally valid by assuming (or, perhaps more accurately, not caring to think too much about this idea) that workers enjoy the same material freedom to enter or not enter the contractual relationship, but it would surely not be accurate to claim that workers are as prone (if at all) to make the same assumption. For workers feel the material constraints directly – no speculation is needed. And the point is, of course, equally cogent for many other differences in their respective situations. It is not romanticizing the ca-pacities of the downtrodden to observe that throughout the history of the strug-gles of subordinate groups, those at the bottom of the social ladder have usually shown themselves to be quite well aware that the conditions of their social superiors differ from their own. Indeed, it is precisely the perception of this difference, and its assessment as unjust, that have often motivated such strug-gles in the first place.

Elster also offers a more general critique of the social causation of "epistemologies." He suggests that the epistemic norm for which we should strive is "rationally grounded beliefs." These beliefs will, of course, not neces-sarily be true, but they have a better chance of being true than non-rationally grounded beliefs, being evidentially based. The presumption is that to be ra-tionally grounded, the beliefs must be rationally caused, which means "(i) the causes of the belief are reasons for holding it and (ii) the reasons cause the beliefs *qua* reasons, not in some accidental manner." One could, through non-rational causes, arrive at rationally grounded beliefs, but this outcome would be fortuitous. Material interest and social position, however, are non-relevant causes: hence, Elster argues, "socially caused beliefs are not rationally caused."[34]

Why does Elster see this as so self-evidently true? I think it is because he has the following picture of social causation in mind. Someone comes to believe that *p*, not through an objective investigation of the evidence for *p*, but because *p* "corresponds" to his or her class interests. For example, some capitalists may be receptive to libertarianism not because they have actually read Ayn Rand, Robert Nozick, Milton Friedman, and the rest of the crew, and made some attempt to assess their arguments, but because they oppose further expansion of the social welfare system, and want a philosophy that supports such views. In this kind of case, the causes of the belief are independent of the state of affairs the belief is about, so that we have no reason to think the belief is rationally grounded.

But the category of socially caused beliefs is certainly not exhausted by such examples. If workers, on the basis of their experiences in the factory, at the bargaining table, or on the picket line, come to realize that the atomistic social ontology of liberalism is profoundly misleading and that society is really divided into opposing classes; if women, on the basis of their experiences at work, on dates, or on the streets at night, come to realize that the threat of rape by males is omnipresent and plays a major role in determining female behavior; if blacks, on the basis of their experiences with housing, the job market, and the police, come to realize how pervasive, despite official denials, white racism continues to be; then in all these cases their beliefs surely do have an evidential base. Yet the preceding causal chains can all meaningfully be described as "social," since these experiences are more likely to arise in the lives of one social group than in others. Elster's assumption seems to be that all social causal chains lack evidential links, but if this proposition is not demonstrated, it is merely a stipulative definition from which implications can be drawn only at the risk of circularity (social causation is causation that does not involve rational causation and so is unlikely to produce rationally grounded beliefs).

What is obviously called for, then, is the drawing of internal distinctions between different varieties of social causation, according to their likelihood of producing positive or negative epistemic consequences. Bloor and Barnes's "strong program" demands explanatory symmetry for both true and false beliefs, rejecting the notion that sociologists of belief should be restricted to the elucidation of genealogies of error. The conclusions they draw are epistemologically relativist ones, the ubiquity of social causation allegedly dissolving the pretensions of any belief set to epistemically privileged status. But as several critics have argued, one can accept symmetry about the *fact* of causation while still rejecting it with respect to the *nature* of causation and its probable differential consequences. W. H. Newton-Smith contrasts the cases of two people with particular beliefs about where they are sitting, only one of whom has operative perceptual faculties. In each case, belief is the result of causal processes, but this symmetry does not extend deeper: "In the case of a veridical perceptual belief the causal chain involved runs through the state of affairs that gives the belief its truth-value. With non-veridical perceptual beliefs the causal chain may have nothing to do with the state of affairs that gives the belief its truth-value."[35] In a parallel fashion, then, it can be argued that in the cases cited above, the actual state of affairs (differentially perceived) gives rise to the beliefs in particular social groups. Once we allow reasons to be causes, there is no contradiction in affirming that beliefs can be simultaneously socially and rationally caused.[36]

## 4   Naturalized Epistemology and Radical Theory

I suggest that work in so-called naturalized epistemology may be of value in establishing an empirical basis for the above claims about hegemonic and alternative belief systems. In his Introduction to *Naturalizing Epistemology*, Hilary Kornblith suggests that the inter-relations among three questions can be said to generate the project of naturalizing epistemology: "(1) How ought we to arrive at our beliefs? (2) How do we arrive at our beliefs? (3) Are the processes by which we do arrive at our beliefs the ones by which we ought to arrive at our beliefs?"[37] The strong version of what Kornblith calls "the replacement thesis" would simply dissolve question (1) into question (2). Since the advocates of alternative epistemologies want to challenge hegemonic but mystifying ideologies and belief systems, they would obviously not want to give up the normative dimension of epistemology. A weaker version, however, in which psychological findings about belief acquisition are deemed to be relevant to the erection of normative standards, would not necessarily have this drawback, and indeed could be valuable in several ways.

First of all, the explicit connecting of the epistemological project to the ways in which people actually do acquire beliefs about the world can only be a positive corrective to the solipsist figure of the Cartesian knower. As David Hillel-Ruben has emphasized in his book on the Marxist theory of knowledge, "Knowledge is irreducibly *social*."[38] Similarly, Lorraine Code has pointed out that the misleading image of the "autonomous epistemic agent" needs to be replaced by the idea of "a community of knowers":

> To a much greater extent than the examples commonly taken to illustrate epistemological points might lead one to believe, people are dependent, at a fundamental level, upon other people . . . for what they, often rightly, claim to know. . . .
>
> Far from being autonomous in the senses discussed above, knowledge is an interpersonal product that requires communal standards of affirmation, correction, and denial for its very existence. So a study of the workings of epistemic community is as important a focus of epistemological inquiry as in an analysis of perception- and memory-based knowledge claims.[39]

And such a study could, of course, legitimately investigate subjects currently excluded from mainstream epistemology, such as the transmission of hegemonic ideologies to new members of the community. Similarly, the contextualization of the process of acquiring knowledge within a social matrix opens a theoretical space for the consideration of socially generated illusions, in contrast to the wearying parade of elliptical coins, apparently broken sticks, afterimages, color-varying objects, and all the other bric-a-brac of putatively problematic perceptual phenomena marched back and forth across the epistemological stage for the past few centuries.

Finally, and linked to the preceding point, the findings of cognitive psychology about specific mechanisms of inferential distortion may be useful for translating into twentieth-century terminology Marx's somewhat musty vocabulary of "appearance," "phenomenal form," and so on, as well as for detailing cognitive mechanisms he would not have had the theory to analyze himself. This would have the virtue of presenting Marx's claims in a framework more accessible to (and taken more seriously by) a mainstream philosophical audience, a point of obvious importance if these ideas are ever to achieve de-ghettoization.

Although there is no space here to follow this program up, I want to give at least one concrete illustration. Richard Nisbett and Lee Ross argue that "people's understanding of the rapid flow of continuing social events" depends less on formal "judgmental procedures" than on "general knowledge [and – one wants to insert here – what is wrongly taken to be knowledge] of objects, people, events, and their characteristic relationships," which may be articulated as explicit propositional theory and as sub-propositional schematic cognitive structures, variously characterized as schemas, frames, scripts, nuclear scenes, and prototypes. These cognitive structures provide an "interpretative framework for the lay scientist" and "supplement" the information given with much "assumed" information.[40]

Work in the Marxist theory of ideology, particularly that resulting from the influence of Gramsci, has emphasized that perhaps even more important than ideologies at the explicit and articulated level (for example, libertarianism, biological determinism) are ideologies in the more primeval sense of underlying patterns and matrices of belief, or ideology as "common sense." The former are at least visible as ideologies, specific demarcated bodies of thought in contestation for people's belief, whereas the latter may seem to be mere neutral background, an ideational framework to be accepted by all, without political implications. Thus the latter may well be more influential and efficacious than the former simply by virtue of their ability to set the terms of the debate, to limit the options deemed worthy of consideration. (John McMurtry has argued that the "forms of social consciousness" Marx mentions in the 1859 Preface should be seen in this light, as the underpinnings of more explicit ideologies.[41]) What radicals must obviously do, then, is to establish a link between Nisbett and Ross's "schemas" and hegemonic ideological patterns, showing that in oppressive societies these schemas are often so structured as to convey misinformation. Thus the British authors of a book on understanding racism and sexism emphasize that these ideas should not be viewed as "abstract concepts" but as "lived experience":

> For the racist, beliefs are not only cognitive categories or stereotypes – they represent a way of making sense and reacting to a range of social experiences. Ideology, in this sense, is not simply imposed from the outside by some super-powerful

socialization agency; on the contrary, it is used by people to define their own lives and to understand the struggles and conflicts of the world they live in. In encountering Blacks, Jews, and other groups, the white worker . . . reproduces racism as a means of coping with the exigencies of the moment. It is easier to live with unemployment if you can account for it in terms of what appears to be an accessible explanation.[42]

Correspondingly, the argument would be that in such interactions, victims of racism and sexism have, because of their differential experience, a better chance of developing schemas that objectively reflect the situation.

Consider, in this light, one of the most important schemas cited by Nisbett and Ross:

The most general and encompassing lay theory of human behavior – so broadly applied that it might more aptly be termed a "metatheory" – is the assumption that behavior is caused primarily by the enduring and consistent dispositions of the actor, as opposed to the particular characteristics of the situation to which the actor responds. . . . [I]n large measure the error, we suspect, lies in a very broad proposition about human conduct, to wit, that people behave as they do because of a general disposition to behave in the way that they do. . . . The "dispositionalist" theory, in short, is thoroughly woven into the fabric of our culture.[43]

It may be argued that this general schema explains the propensity for what the left calls "blame-the-victim" theories.[44] Such theories come in conservative (naturalistic/biological) and liberal (culturalist/social) versions; in both cases, however, the focus is on the individual's alleged deficiencies, whether these are seen to be genetic or environmental (for example, the "culture of poverty") in origin. The importance of this kind of psychological research is that it demonstrates a plausible experiential base (Marx's "phenomenal forms") for such views, which can be established independently of any appeal to the role of hegemonic ideologies. On the one hand, oppressive social structures constrain people into certain roles, narrow their choices, and disable and restrict them in various ways, thereby creating apparent evidential support for negative dispositionalist accounts: low working-class IQ scores, the underrepresentation of women and blacks in intellectual fields, and the feminization and racialization of poverty. On the other hand, subordinated social groups that have actually tried to overcome the systemic roadblocks to their development will be (once again, as a result of social causation) in a better cognitive position to form true beliefs about the mechanisms of oppression and more receptive to "situationist" accounts than hegemonic groups, to whom these constraints will be less visible.

## 5  Objectivism and Alternative Epistemologies

Finally, I want to say a few words about the inter-relations between these different "epistemologies."

For an older Marxism, of course, this problem would not have arisen in the first place. The presumed causal centrality of the capitalist system to all structures of oppression implied that the working-class vision, the proletarian perspective, was sufficiently comprehensive to encompass the viewpoints of all other oppressed groups. The term that has come to be used to describe these universalist pretensions is "class reductionism," in this particular case the implication that the phenomenological specificities of women's and blacks' oppression can be assimilated to the working-class's experience of exploitation.[45]

In response, socialist feminists have pointed to rape, wife-beating, sexual harassment, prostitution, objectification of female sexuality, domestic labor, and so on as phenomena that resist such assimilation, and that are not readily theorizable in orthodox Marxist categories. They have argued that Marx's notion of alienation is impoverished, and that the analysis of women's alienation would have to be extended to include alienation from one's sexuality and one's control of motherhood.[46] Obviously, then, many important experiences do not, in the normal course of events, enter the phenomenological world of the working-class male. Perhaps the strongest piece of evidence supporting the inadequacy of this perspective is the fact that, as Sandra Harding points out, only now, after the re-emergence of the women's movement, has the "sex/gender system" become theoretically visible.[47]

Similarly, throughout most of the twentieth century, the black liberation movement has been engaged in a debate about the relationship between race and class, and the ability of Marxist concepts to explain black oppression.[48] The challenge to orthodox Marxist theory may be even stronger in this case, since there is no equivalent to Engels's book on the family. Thus more than one theorist has concluded that "essentially, Marxism has no theory of nationalism."[49] Moreover, Marx and Engels were influenced by Hegel's distinction between "world-historic" and "non-world-historic" peoples, "civilized" and "barbarian" nations, and they display a clear Eurocentricity in their writings about nonwhite peoples.[50] Accordingly, Cedric Robinson has argued that the racism that infects so much of western thought is present in Marxist theory also, so it would be a fundamental error to see Marxism as "a *total* theory of liberation."[51] *Black Marxism*, the title of Robinson's book, is apparently cognate with "socialist feminism," but whereas socialist feminist critiques of orthodox Marxism (such as Jaggar's) use the (reconstructed) theory to criticize existing Marxism's conceptual lacunae, Robinson suggests that the African critique of Marxism would be more of an external critique, challenging Marxism from a position outside western thought. For the black experience in this case starts from an ontological status of official non-personhood, and as such the alienation is more fundamental and far-reaching than anything that can be spun out of Marxist concepts of estrangement from one's product. In this spirit, the sociologist, Orlando Patterson, has proposed the notion of "natal alienation," that is "the definition of the slave, however recruited, as a socially dead person": "[I]t goes directly to the heart of what is critical in the slave's forced alienation, the loss of ties of birth in both ascending and descending generations. . . . The slave was the ultimate human tool, as imprintable and as disposable as the master wished."[52]

Even a reconstructed Marxism, then, may not have the theoretical resources to express this experience.

One reaction to the apparent failure of Marxism to live up to its promise of a genuinely unifying vision has been the post-Marxist embrace of a relativistic pluralism, the positing of multiple realities. This development is, of course, encouraged by a broader cultural trend towards a skeptical relativism. Thus in a discussion of Sandra Harding's book on feminist epistemology, Alison Wylie suggests that Harding displays a systematic ambivalence, vacillating between postmodernist pluralism and "a variant of the enlightenment ideal of producing a unitary, authoritative conception of reality."[53] That conception is now seen in some quarters as politically dangerous, the "totalizing" vision necessarily leading (though this sometimes seems to be less argued for than derived by a kind of conceptual onomatopoeia) to "totalitarianism," the suppression of difference in the monofocal eye.[54]

An obvious problem with this apparently democratic relativism is that if all viewpoints are equally validated, then there seems to be no reason why currently hegemonic perspectives (classist, sexist, racist) should not be treated similarly, and if a choice is then going to be made on non-evidential grounds, these perspectives will have the advantages of tradition, widespread acceptance, privileged media dissemination, and so on. Moreover, alternative viewpoints themselves are to a significant extent constructed out of phenomenological raw material by intellectuals: "Those who construct the standpoint of women must begin from women's experience as women describe it, but they must go beyond that experience theoretically and ultimately may require that women's experience be redescribed."[55] The decision to retain certain elements as theoretically significant while discarding others can be made only by appeal, implicit or explicit, to some set of normative criteria devised to guarantee objectivity and representativeness. Alternatively, if one wishes to invoke a democratic relativism here also, then what prevents the whole enterprise from degenerating into a multiplicity of individual viewpoints, so that the prized social dimension drops out, and we are left – as a *reductio* of the whole project – with those isolated Cartesian knowers again?

The temptations of relativism arise understandably out of the indubitable difficulty of trying to assemble class, race, and gender perspectives into a coherent syncretic outlook. Moreover, as is often pointed out, the positing of a "woman's perspective" (or a "working-class" or "black" perspective, for that matter) necessarily involves an artificial abstraction from other determinants: "[E]ven if one is always a man or a woman, one is never *just* a man or a woman. One is young or old, sick or healthy, married or unmarried, a parent or not a parent, employed or unemployed, middle class or working class, rich or poor, black or white, and so forth. . . . Experience does not come neatly in segments."[56] Thus some critics have suggested that the entire enterprise is doomed from the outset because of the fragmented and disjunctive character of what is being represented as unitary.[57] But even if a sufficient commonality of experience to justify the theoretical construction can be demonstrated, the daunting task remains of working out the epistemic implications of these overlaps and intersections of identity, for those who are oppressed in one context may be oppressors in another. Hence the retreat into a non-judgmental epistemic neutrality.

I would argue, though, that this very differentiation makes the retention of normativity all the more necessary. It is precisely because the working class Marx studied was not an abstraction, but a group composed largely of white males, that their subversive insight into the structure of social oppression (and the Marxist theory derived from it) was only partial. Women's perspective was required to uncover the significance of rape as a sustaining mechanism of patriarchal repression. But because the women who developed this analysis were themselves largely white, they in turn tended to miss the particular historical significance of rape accusations made against black men by white women. Again, therefore, a theoretical corrective was necessary, this time in the form of a critique of white, middle-class feminist theory by black women.[58] Putting all these analyses on the same epistemic plane, it seems to me, contradicts the evident truth that in each case a better approximation to the holistic reality of the situation is being achieved. An account of social subordination that does not draw on the experiences of women and blacks is simply theoretically weaker than one that does.

For the past century, Marxism has been the most powerful theory of the dialectic of social oppression. But it has become obvious that this oppression is multi-dimensional and that the historical forces that produced Marxism as a theory have now thrown up other perspectives, other visions, illuminating aspects of the structured darknesses of society that Marx failed to see. What is needed is a synthesis of these alternative epistemologies that recognizes both the multiplicity and the unity, the experiential subjectivity and the causal objectivity, of hierarchical class-, gender-, and race-divided society.

### Notes

This article is ten years old, so some of the references are now dated, although the issues are still very much alive. In one or two places, I have added some new sources, and made stylistic changes, but I decided that a radical revision would be pointless. The article reflects the debate at the time, and is thus useful in illustrating both what has and what has not changed.

1   For some discussions, see, for example: Lorraine B. Code, "Is the Sex of the Knower Epistemologically Significant?" *Metaphilosophy*, 12 (1981), 267–76; Alan Soble, "Feminist Epistemology and Women Scientists," *Metaphilosophy*, 14 (1983), 291–307; Sandra Harding and Merrill B. Hintikka, eds., *Discovering Reality: Feminist Perspectives on Epistemology, Metaphysics, Methodology, and Philosophy of Science* (Dordrecht: D. Reidel, 1983), esp. the essays by Jane Flax, Nancy Hartsock, and Sandra Harding; Alison M. Jaggar, *Feminist Politics and Human Nature* (Totowa, NJ: Rowman & Allanheld, 1983), esp. chap. 11; Jean Grimshaw, *Philosophy and Feminist Thinking* (Minneapolis: University of Minnesota Press, 1986); Sandra Harding, *The Science Question in Feminism* (Ithaca: Cornell University Press, 1986); Marsha Hanen and Kai Nielsen, eds., *Science, Morality and Feminist Theory*, supplement to *Canadian Journal of Philosophy* 13 (Calgary: University of Calgary Press,

1987). For a more recent overview, see Linda Alcoff and Elizabeth Potter, eds., *Feminist Epistemologies* (New York: Routledge, 1993).

2   See, for example, Leonard Harris, ed., *Philosophy Born of Struggle: Anthology of Afro-American Philosophy from 1917* (Dubuque, Iowa: Kendall/Hunt publishing Co., 1983) and Howard McGary Jr., "Teaching Black Philosophy," *Teaching Philosophy*, 7 (1984), 129–37. Happily, much more material is available now than there was at the time, for example: Lewis Gordon, *Bad Faith and Antiblack Racism* (Atlantic Highlands, NJ.: Humanities Press, 1995); John Pittman, ed., *African-American Perspectives and Philosophical Traditions* (New York: Routledge, 1996); Lucius T. Outlaw Jr., *On Race and Philosophy* (New York: Routledge, 1996); Lewis R. Gordon, ed., *Existence in Black: An Anthology of Black Existential Philosophy* (New York: Routledge, 1997)

3   In his 1986 statistical profile of the American Philosophical Association (APA) membership, compiled from responses on renewal notices, David Hoekema reports that of the 2961 philosophers who responded (a 48 percent response rate), only 35 identified themselves as black. He emphasizes that a substantial number of people (719) failed to answer the question on minority status, but the lowness of the figure seems significant nonetheless. Of those 35, only 3 were women. See *Proceedings and Addresses of the APA*, 59 (1986), 717–23. Similarly, an APA survey on member departments yielded the information that in 1985 blacks earned only 1 percent of the PhDs in philosophy, by comparison with a 3.3 percent rate for PhDs generally. See *Proceedings and Addresses of the APA*, 61 (1987), 357–60. As with any other complex social phenomenon, racism is sustained by a plurality of causes. Thus a past history of racist practices (like the response given to the black philosopher Broadus Butler in 1952 when he applied for a job at a "white" university: "Why don't you go where you will be among your own kind?" – cited in Harris, *Philosophy Born of Struggle*, p. ix) obviously has a "bleaching" effect on the discipline that tends to perpetuate itself in other ways, since traditional philosophy in the academy – the ivory tower's ivory tower – then seems completely remote from black concerns and interests, and thus fails to attract potential graduate students. It is clearly significant that both McGary's and Harris's bibliographies have so few listings for philosophy journals and that many of the most prominent black thinkers cited are not academic philosophers, at least as narrowly defined.

Since this article was written, the profile of blacks in the profession has improved significantly, as indicated by a number of books and anthologies published or forthcoming, the formal recognition of Africana Philosophy by the APA, the launching in 1991 of the *APA Newsletter on Philosophy and the Black Experience*, and the establishment of the *Journal of Africana Philosophy*. Obviously, however, since blacks constitute only about 1 percent of North American philosophers, a tremendous distance remains to be covered, both in numbers and in influence on the content of the discipline.

4   The classic example of such an interpretation is, of course, George Lukács's *History and Class Consciousness*, trans. Rodney Livingstone (1968; Cambridge: MIT Press, 1971). See esp. "Reification and the Consciousness of the Proletariat," 83–222.

5   See Jaggar, *Feminist Politics*, chap. 11.

6   David Hume, *A Treatise of Human Nature*, ed. L. A. Selby-Bigge (Oxford: Clarendon Press, 1888), 216, 269.

7   Soble, "Feminist Epistemology," 294.

8   Jaggar, *Feminist Politics*, 366–7.

9   Harding, *Science Question*, 179–82.

10 Abiola Irele, Introduction to Paulin J. Hountondji, *African Philosophy: Myth and Reality*, trans. Henri Evans and Jonathan Ree (1976; Bloomington: Indiana University Press, 1983), 18.

11 Harding, *Science Question*, 179.

12 Irele, *African Philosophy*, 21.

13 See Code, "Is the Sex," and also Steven Rose, Leon J. Kamin, and R. C. Lewontin, *Not in Our Genes: Biology, Ideology and Human Nature* (Harmondsworth, Middlesex: Penguin, 1984), chap. 6.

14 See Code, "Is the Sex," 270–1, and Rose et al., *Not in Our Genes*, chap. 6.

15 Harding, *Science Question*, chap. 6.

16 For a detailed account of such an interpretation, see Russell Keat and John Urry, *Social Theory as Science*, 2nd edn (1975; London: Routledge & Kegan Paul, 1982).

17 See the discussions in Jarrett Leplin, ed., *Scientific Realism* (Berkeley: University of California Press, 1984).

18 See, for example, Barry Barnes, *Scientific Knowledge and Sociological Theory* (London: Routledge & Kegan Paul, 1974), and David Bloor, *Knowledge and Social Imagery* (London: Routledge & Kegan Paul, 1976).

19 Karl Marx, *Capital*, vol. 1 (New York: International Publishers, 1967), 59–60.

20 Jaggar, *Feminist Politics*, 6, 370.

21 Jon Elster, "Belief, Bias and Ideology," in Martin Hollis and Steven Lukes, eds., *Rationality and Relativism* (Cambridge: MIT Press, 1982), 131.

22 Soble, "Feminist Epistemology," 302.

23 Karl Marx and Frederick Engels, *Collected Works*, vol. 3 (New York: International Publishers, 1975), 186.

24 Joseph McCarney, "Recent Interpretations of Ideology," *Economy and Society*, 14 (1985), 89–90.

25 Jon Elster, *Making Sense of Marx* (New York: Cambridge University Press, 1985).

26 Bhikhu Parekh, *Marx's Theory of Ideology* (Baltimore: Johns Hopkins University Press, 1982), 18–19.

27 Sandra Harding, "Ascetic Intellectual Opportunities: Reply to Alison Wylie," in Hanen and Nielsen, *Science, Morality, and Feminist Theory*, 77.

28 Ralph Ellison, *The Invisible Man* (1952; New York: Vintage, 1995), 16.

29 Elster discusses "hot" and "cold" mechanisms of cognitive distortion in *Making Sense of Marx*, 18–22.

30 Elster, *Making Sense of Marx*, 19.

31 Ibid., 19.

32 Marx, *Capital*, 1: 176, 539–40.

33 See, for example, G. A. Cohen, "The Structure of Proletarian Unfreedom," *Philosophy and Public Affairs*, 12 (1983), 3–33.

34 Elster, *Making Sense of Marx*, 474.

35 W. H. Newton-Smith, *The Rationality of Science* (Boston: Routledge & Kegan Paul, 1981), 253.

36 See the discussion of Warren Schmaus, "Reasons, Causes, and the 'Strong Programme' in the Sociology of Knowledge," *Philosophy of the Social Sciences*, 15 (1985), 189–96.

37 Hilary Kornblith, ed., *Naturalizing Epistemology* (Cambridge: MIT Press, 1987), 1.

38 David-Hillel Ruben, *Marxism and Materialism: A Study in Marxist Theory of Knowledge*, 2nd edn (1977; Atlantic Highlands: Humanities Press, 1979), 109.

39    Lorraine Code, "Second Persons," in Hanen and Nielsen, *Science, Morality and Feminist Theory*, 374–75, 377–78.

40    Richard Nisbett and Lee Ross, *Human Inference: Strategies and Shortcomings of Social Judgment* (Englewood Cliffs, NJ: Prentice-Hall, 1983), 28–9.

41    John McMurtry, *The Structure of Marx's World-View* (Princeton: Princeton University Press, 1978), chap. 6.

42    Arthur Brittan and Mary Maynard, *Sexism, Racism and Oppression* (Oxford: Basil Blackwell, 1984), 183.

43    Nisbett and Ross, *Human Inference*, 31.

44    William Ryan, *Blaming the Victim*, 2nd edn (1972; New York: Vintage, 1976).

45    For a good discussion, see Frank Cunningham, *Democratic Theory and Socialism* (New York: Cambridge University Press, 1987), chap. 9.

46    Jaggar, *Feminist Politics*, 307–17.

47    Sandra Harding, "Why Has the Sex/Gender System Become Visible Only Now?" in Harding and Hintikka, *Discovering Reality*, 311–24.

48    For some discussions, see, for example: Cedric J. Robinson, *Black Marxism: The Making of the Black Radical Tradition* (London: Zed Press, 1983); Manning Marable, "Black Studies: Marxism and the Black Intellectual Tradition," in Bertell Ollman and Edward Vernoff, eds, *The Left Academy: Marxist Scholarship on American Campuses*, vol. 3 (New York: Praeger, 1986), 35–66; Bernard R. Boxill, "The Race–Class Questions," and Lucius T. Outlaw Jr., "Race and Class in the Theory and Practice of Emancipatory Social Transformation," both in Harris, *Philosophy Born of Struggle*, 107–16 and 117–29.

49    Ronaldo Munck, *The Difficult Dialogue: Marxism and Nationalism* (London: Zed Books, 1986), 2. See also Ephraim Nimni, "Marxism and Nationalism," in Martin Shaw, ed., *Marxist Sociology Revisited: Critical Assessments* (London: Macmillan, 1985), 99–142.

50    See Nimni, "Marxism and Nationalism," and Munck, *Difficult Dialogue*, chap. 1.

51    Robinson, *Black Marxism*, 451.

52    Orlando Patterson, *Slavery and Social Death: A Comparative Study* (Cambridge, MA: Harvard University Press, 1982), 5–7.

53    Alison Wylie, "The Philosophy of Ambivalence: Sandra Harding on *The Science Question in Feminism*," in Hanen and Nielsen, *Science, Morality and Feminist Theory*, 65.

54    See, for example, Cary Nelson and Lawrence Grossberg, eds., *Marxism and the Interpretation of Culture* (Urbana: University of Illinois Press, 1988), where this connection seems to be taken for granted in several of the articles.

55    Jaggar, *Feminist Politics*, 384.

56    Grimshaw, *Philosophy and Feminist Thinking*, 84–5.

57    See Soble, "Feminist Epistemology."

58    See, for example: Angela Davis, *Women, Race and Class* (New York: Random House, 1981), esp. chap. 11, which discusses Susan Brownmiller's *Against Our Will: Men, Women and Rape* (New York: Simon & Schuster, 1975); bell hooks, *Ain't I a Woman: Black Women and Feminism* (Boston: South End Press, 1981); Gloria T. Hull, Patricia Bell Scott, and Barbara Smith, eds, *All the Women Are White, All the Blacks Are Men, But Some of Us Are Brave: Black Women's Studies* (Old Westbury, New York: The Feminist Press, 1982). For more recent work, see Patricia Hill Collins, *Black Feminist Thought: Knowledge, Consciousness, and the Politics of Empowerment* (1990; New York: Routledge, 1991).

# 26   Idols of the Cave

## *Mary Tiles and Jim Tiles*

*Idols of the Cave take their rise in the peculiar constitution, mental or bodily, of each individual; and also in education, habit and accident.*

*Novum Organum* I LIII

Philosophical conversation is not one conversation but an overlapping network of conversations; and there is no single fixed framework that governs all these discussions. One can feel the framework shift as one moves from discussions held within one tradition to those conducted within another. Within different traditions, issues and assumptions about knowledge have different degrees of importance. In the tradition broadly defined as "analytic," assumptions about what constitutes knowledge, and what can and cannot be known, influence discussions about almost every other issue. Discussions about knowledge, even when not seeming to get anywhere, reinforce a framework and serve to keep those assumptions in place.

Challenges to that framework of assumptions can take the form of challenging the importance of engaging in epistemology. Those disposed to make such challenges may try to appeal to the sense, which many people have, that discussions about knowledge appear to progress only in the direction of becoming increasingly remote from anything in non-academic life. The motive for challenging the very enterprise of epistemology may be the desire (more or less self-consciously articulated) to alter or replace what is perceived to be the dominant framework of discussion. It may also be a more diffuse hostility to any idea that one framework should dominate; the discussions carried out within epistemology would thus be able to pretend to special authority.

Recently, resistance to the idea that there should be any dominant framework dictating, for example, artistic style, has come to be called "postmodernism." It is not inappropriate to apply this term in philosophy, since it is common to conceive philosophy as taking its "modern" form early in the seventeenth century and the history of the issues, problems, and standards of relevance which now preoccupy "western" philosophers appears to have taken a decisive turn in the hands of Descartes. That turn not only made certain assumptions about knowledge integral to discussions of other philosophical issues. It also moved to sever the pursuit of knowledge – as well as discussions of what knowledge is, how to acquire it, and of how to justify claims to possess it – from the influence of practical concern, of beliefs supported by tradition and of any bias encouraged by the social, political, and economic interests of participants in discussions of knowledge. In other words, it encouraged participants in philosophical discussions to adopt an Olympian standpoint, which not only hid from them the possibility that the framework of their discussion was culturally limited, it made this suggestion appear positively impertinent. And it underwrote the assumption, particularly among those who sought knowledge of the natural world (natural philosophers, or "scientists" as they came to be called in the nineteenth century) that their efforts could be conducted in an atmosphere insulated from questions of practical consequences and narrow cultural perspectives.

So a move to dismantle wholesale the epistemology industry is a move against a form (however modest) of cultural hegemony. But it is both hazardous and unnecessary to leave in its place nothing but loose, undisciplined discussion ("edifying conversation" according to a gloss favored by Richard Rorty, a prime mover against epistemology). It is unnecessary because it is possible to open up the framework in which knowledge is discussed; epistemology (as opposed to one familiar way of conducting it) is not the creation of Descartes and does not require his framework to be sustained. It is hazardous because even if there were no epistemologists reinforcing through their practice the assumption that knowledge can be pursued and secured without reference to practical concerns or cultural biases, this assumption would not go away. Those (women and minorities), who feel their voices, their perspectives and their potential contributions have been unjustifiably ignored (and in some cases rejected as unworthy) by a special perspective masquerading as universal, will not find that the institutions which have ignored (and demeaned) them will suddenly open their ears. . . .

[Rather than] not engaging at all in epistemology as a discipline, [we] suggest that a wiser course would be to conduct it in a framework more comprehensive than is presently common. . . . To relocate the framework we have stepped back a generation from Descartes and made Francis Bacon a pivotal figure in our discussion. . . . Bacon is not only explicit about the kind of practical orientation which he desired for his new natural philosophy, but he was also mindful of the obstacles, the prejudices, the biases, the limitations of perspective and experience that stand in the way of improving our knowledge. He attempted a fourfold classification of these obstacles, which he designated "Idols" for rhetorical effect. . . . [A]ssociated with each class of Idols is an important source of obstacles to the improvement of knowledge, perception (Tribe), philosophic tradition (Theater), language (Market Place), and history (Cave). These are, we argue, obstacles that we cannot ever wholly transcend, in short because they are also the material out of which we are condemned (if that is the right word) to fashion ourselves, to remake our material and cognitive lives.

## 1   Human Nature and Human Knowledge

Whereas Idols of the Tribe are a product of what is universal in the human condition Idols of the Cave are a product of peculiar circumstances, which frequently play an important but unacknowledged rôle in shaping the way we think and what we are prepared to believe. Obstacles to the improvement of knowledge are generated by the way the light of nature is refracted and discolored as it passes through the private "cave or den" of the "lesser world" (*Novum*

*Organum* I XLII) created by individual predilections, regardless of whether they arise from some innate personal disposition or from acquired habits, from general education or even from special experience gained in the pursuit of science.

Bacon saw the last of these as the source of the errors of the alchemists and of his contemporary Gilbert, who had made a thorough study of the loadstone and was prone to find the principles of magnetism in everything. Aristotle, Bacon believed, had in a similar way exaggerated the importance of logic (I LIV). There are also several opposing thought styles which cut across intellectual party lines and disciplinary boundaries. People will insist that knowledge consists in whatever it is that satisfies their minds, whether it be broad resemblances between things or the subtle respects in which things differ (I LV). Some will insist that understanding requires analyzing things into their smallest constituents and explaining all in terms of the properties of the constituents; others will insist on seeking to explain things in terms of the comprehensive structures which they form (I LVII). Some have regard only for what has a lengthy history; others have faith only in novelty (I LVI).

The division between the Idols of the Tribe and the Idols of the Cave rests on the distinction between what is universal in, and what is peculiar to, the circumstances of human beings. Any attempt to say in advance which is which depends on something like Aristotle's distinction between what can be assigned to nature (in this case human nature) and what is accidental. But even in Aristotelian terms, the Idols of the Cave would be a doubtful topic for inclusion in any theoretical discussion of knowledge. Theories are designed to be general in application and for this reason Aristotle denied there could be *epistémé* of accidents (*Metaphysics* 1026b3), for accidents are precisely what we cannot say anything systematic and general about. We can perhaps offer rule-of-thumb advice such as Bacon's caution to "every student of nature" to be particularly suspicious of "whatever his mind seizes and dwells upon with particular satisfaction," and when dealing with such matters exercise much more care "to keep the understanding even and clear" (I LVIII). But we cannot offer any systematic treatment of such obstacles. An epistemology which looks for universal principles governing the justification of claims to know, or which seeks to discern the general scope and limits of human understanding, will not concern itself with Idols of the Cave.

But how then can any epistemology distinguish between what is contingent and what is universal as regards human capacities to acquire knowledge and the limitations to which they are subject? It seems that in order to proceed, any epistemology will either have to presume an account of human nature as its starting point, or will have to admit to some dependency on the sciences, such as psychology, sociology, anthropology and history, which study human beings. But shouldn't a theory of knowledge also incorporate an account of the nature and possible status of our knowledge of human nature, or of human beings? Here there is clearly a danger of circularity. This could be benign, if the accounts are all self-consistent, but if they work to undermine one another the position will be unstable. The only escape from this circularity would be to find some way of making the discussion of knowledge independent of any claims or presuppositions about the nature of human beings.

It was one of the strengths of Descartes' epistemology that he recognized the need for an account of knowledge to take on a reflexive character. He turned his proposed method (of analysis/synthesis) for acquiring all knowledge onto the problem of acquiring knowledge of himself and his own cognitive capacities (Haldane and Ross, 1955, I 24f.), arguing that it enabled him without difficulty to know his own nature. His consequent identification of himself with his mind, treating the body as not part of his essence, meant that as far as his knowledge was concerned such aspects of his material embodiment, as race, sex and social class were irrelevant. His confidence that he could know his mind better than his body or anything in the material world, meant that when he applied the method of doubt, he need have no fear about the success of his efforts to suspend his beliefs and to refrain from reaffirming any until they were properly grounded. A mind, a personal den or cave, could be purged once and for all by doubt and would then no longer discolor or distort its contents.

This Cartesian response to Idols in general (that is, to the need to recognize that our beliefs may not merely be inadequate but may stand in the way of the improvement of our knowledge and understanding) places the Idols of the Cave in a peculiar limbo. For the Cave becomes the center of the foundation of our claims to be able to know. Once he had the assurance of the existence of a benevolent God, Descartes could evade all the Idols in Bacon's cataloge; but even before he secured this assurance, he was in a position to rid himself of the contingent determinations which generate the Idols of the Cave. Unless, that is, like Gilbert, who saw magnetism in everything, and Aristotle, who imposed demonstration on everything, Descartes was the victim of an Idol of his own Cave. In other words, his belief that he could purge his Cave was, perhaps, no more than a fantasy based on mistaking his genuine achievements in mathematics for the key to all knowledge. Can one so easily break free of the perspective shaped by the contingencies of education, profession, or social standing? Are these influences so obvious that all it takes is a comprehensive vow to suspend one's beliefs in order to avoid those influences?

Being able to assure oneself that one has no prejudices is, after all, a good way to insulate one's prejudices. Unless Descartes' views of human nature and knowledge can themselves legitimately claim freedom from any contingent determinations, proponents of alternative conceptions would be justified in suspecting that these views and the epistemology which rests on them embody the kind of bias that arises when the perspective of one individual or group of individuals is over-generalized and claimed to be universal. This is the stance from which feminists, marxists and others have criticized epistemology in the Cartesian tradition.

Challenges of this sort to the validity of Cartesian epistemology face a strategic problem. Just as Bacon recognized that because he was challenging traditional conceptions of knowledge and of human dignity, to enter into detailed disputations with the Schoolmen would require participation in the framework he was challenging, critics of Cartesian epistemology have realized that they cannot argue with their opponents in terms those opponents would find convincing. By the same token those defending a broadly Cartesian, (and as they see it) strictly philosophical conception of epistemology, must treat as impertinent the suggestion that their standpoint is a limited perspective masquerading as universal. To acknowledge the dependence of their theories of knowledge on disputable conceptions of human nature or of knowledge would be to undermine the foundations of their own position. Unless, that is, they could achieve the kind of reflexive closure sought by Descartes and Kant and give, by their own criteria, solid *a priori* arguments for the exclusive correctness of these conceptions.

The possibility of this kind of closure depends upon being able to separate the object of knowledge of the empirical sciences (the natural world) from the system (the knowing subject, language, or culture) in which the knowledge is embodied, and to claim a more favorable epistemic access to the latter. The way of ideas was premised on taking the ideas of the knowing subject to be the system in which knowledge is embodied, assuming a universal human intellect whose nature was transparent to its own reflective introspection. What tended to discredit this (narrowly) Cartesian attempt to secure closure in the Cave was the (anti-psychologist) fear that, however thorough the applications of Descartes' method of doubt, each person's Cave might remain a grotto filled with Bacon's Idols. Reaction to the undercutting of this seventeenth and eighteenth century route to epistemology was, not surprisingly, different depending on whether the route from Descartes had been empiricist or rationalist. In fact both of these positions proved to be unstable, once their conception of knowledge was applied to knowledge of human beings. Consider first the empiricist alternative.

## 2   Epistemology as an Empirical Science of Human Nature

Although Hume rejected the way Aristotle treated the concept of human nature as a set of capacities and potentialities, he did not set out specifically to displace the concept of human nature. In fact he felt sufficiently confident about its applicability to write *A Treatise of Human Nature*, which set out to provide a foundation for the rest of the sciences.

> If therefore the sciences of Mathematics, Natural Philosophy and Natural Religion, have such a dependence on the knowledge of man, what may be expected in the other sciences, whose connexion with human nature is more close and intimate? The sole end of logic is to explain the principles and operations of our reasoning faculty, and the nature of our ideas: morals and criticism regard our tastes and sentiments: and politics consider men as united in society, and dependent on each other. . . . In pretending therefore to explain the principles of human nature, we in effect propose a compleat system of the sciences, built on a foundation almost entirely new, and the only one upon which they can stand with any security. (*Treatise*, Introduction)

What notion of nature could provide this new foundation? Simply the thought that in all people, at all times, a single set of principles govern the association of ideas, just as natural scientists take the universe to be governed by an unchanging set of natural laws. Hume did not hesitate to compare his project to the practice of the leading natural philosopher of his age, Newton.

> Astronomers had long contented themselves with proving, from the phaenomena, the true motions, order, and magnitude of the heavenly bodies: Till a philosopher, at last, arose, who seems, from the happiest reasoning, to have also determined the laws and forces by which the revolutions of the planets are governed and directed. And the like has been performed with regard to other parts of nature. And there is no reason to despair of equal success in our enquiries concerning the mental powers and economy, if prosecuted with equal capacity and caution. It is probable, that one operation and principle of the mind depends upon another, which again may be resolved into one more general and universal. (*Enquiries*, I I).

The method to be followed is that of experience and observation. Newton begins his *Principia* by setting down definitions of key terms followed by a list of axioms or laws of motion employing them. He says that these principles "have been received by mathematicians, and are confirmed by abundance of experiment" (*Principia*, I p. 21). Hume similarly begins by giving definitions and by setting down principles of the association of ideas. He goes on to give examples, claiming that people can confirm his principles by reference to their own experience. Here, like Descartes, he assumes that the mind is equipped to look into itself to gain at least the experience and observation necessary to conduct a self-study as an empirical science. In the *Enquiries* (I I) the task is described as creating a "mental geography, or delineation of the distinct parts and powers of the mind." The distinctions that need to be made will all be apparent to the (self) reflective consciousness.

Although this initially appears to put us in a position of privileged epistemic access with regard to acquiring knowledge of our own minds, Hume's own arguments work to undermine any right to claim this. Although he has twice been quoted immediately above as speaking of inquiring into the mind's "powers," it is a consequence of Hume's arguments that we cannot apply the concept of power to nature or to ourselves. We have no impression either from the operation of our own minds or from our observation of nature which can supply an idea of power (*Treatise* I III xiv). Likewise, Hume finds that there is no rational ground for the belief that nature is governed by unchanging laws.

But where does Hume find the standard, by reference to which he can judge that there is no rational legitimation for this belief? Hume's conception of reason is of a faculty of perceiving relations between ideas. He presumes that since ideas are in the mind and complex ideas are the product of associations made as the mind functions according to laws, the complexity of an idea will be something which can be known with certainty, since reflection gives us complete and accurate knowledge of our own ideas and hence a complete basis for perceiving any relations there may be between them. Here we have a vestige of Descartes' procedure; the epistemological asymmetry which affords Hume a rational standard is a product of the Cartesian transparency of the mind to its own reflective rational gaze.

Nevertheless, although Hume needs this absolute point of reference to be able to make his skeptical claims, the remainder of his account of the operation of the mind, and of causal reasoning in particular, works to undercut the assumption that standards of reasoning will be uniform across cultures and historical periods. Hume claims that because we habitually make inferences from effect to cause, and cause to effect, we tend to think that there is some necessary connection between them, a law which underwrites the validity of our inferences. We think that where there is smoke there must be fire, so it is correct to draw the conclusion that there is fire. But Hume claims that the habit of making the inference is prior, and it is this habit projected onto the world, which we suppose to be a connection between things, which matches that between our thoughts. Now if this is so, it follows that different peoples, in different settings developing different habits of thought in response to their experiences, will come to regard different patterns of inference as valid and different kinds of connections between events as possible, necessary or impossible.

Thus, for example, Galen and his followers formed a set of beliefs about disease and its causes according to which disease is the product of an imbalance amongst the four humours, blood, phlegm, black bile and yellow bile, and their experience would be interpreted within this framework. A Galenic physician would see fever as a symptom of too much blood and prescribe bleeding. Modern Western physicians would regard such a treatment as quite irrational and obviously harmful. Their beliefs about disease might lead them to suspect a bacteriological infection and they would prescribe antibiotics. These doctors approach patients with different mind-sets, which include different views about the human being, the relation between mind and body, as well as different views about what is evident in experience and how evidence should bear on their theories and their practices.

From Hume's standpoint the most that could be said is that both are equally wrong to be confident of the framework within which they reason; neither has any rational justification, even though both may think they do. This opens the way to an empirical study of belief formation and patterns of justification. In other words we could embark on a social-psychology of knowledge, where the goal would be to determine what occasioned people to come to think, in the way that they do, by reference to psychological, social, economic or political factors, i.e., factors which do not justify but which explain in terms of an assumed common psychology of motivating factors and non-rational mental principles (such as Hume's principles of association).

This is indeed the kind of account for which Hume himself offers a basis. His "mechanics of the mind" is an account of the psychology of belief; i.e., a framework for explaining why people come to have the beliefs they have, which does not offer any justification for those beliefs or portray the beliefs as justified. Hume's principles of the association of ideas are analogs of Newton's law of gravitational attraction. Hume claims that we believe those things which are presented to the mind with the most force and vivacity. Association transmits force and vivacity (much as impact transmits momentum) so that if a forceful and vivacious idea of smoke is present and this is associated with fire, the force and vivacity of the idea of smoke will be transmitted to that of fire and the result will be belief that there is a fire. This account describes the preservation of belief through a chain of inferences not as something justified by the truth preserving character of the rules of inference applied, but as a natural product of psychological laws.

It is also used to describe the "weighing of evidence" in cases where our experience, such as that of the association of a particular kind of weather with a particular time of year, has not been "uniform." People in Northern Europe will believe more strongly that there will be frost some time in January than those from more southern parts of Europe. This is because they have more experience of this being the case, so the force and vivacity of these experiences outweighs that of experiences of cases where there has been no frost (*Enquiries* I vi). Hume's psychology of belief thus gives a common set of evidentiary principles which will be found to be employed by everyone, but which does not justify the beliefs formed on that basis.

There is, however, a real problem with Hume's position. It is one which he himself to some extent acknowledged but did not resolve. It is possible to regard Hume's arguments as an amusing intellectual exercise, but what of their effects? Hume, like many philosophers of the period, is anti-dogmatic. He wants to undermine claims to absolute knowledge and so urge the cause of tolerance, especially religious tolerance. His arguments in other words should have the effect that (on the basis of self understanding) people change the way they think and should not, for example, believe unconditionally in the principle of the Uniformity of Nature, and should not treat associations of ideas as rational connections.

Suppose people did alter their behavior in this way. They would be people to whom Hume's psychology of belief would apply in an importantly different way. Assuming self-understanding has the desired effect, people would not associate ideas in the same casual manner as those who were not persuaded by Hume's arguments. There is even the possibility that by accepting this account of human nature people might start arranging the world and behaving in such as way as to make it correct. Skeptical arguments, which convince them of the ineffectiveness of any reasoning, might persuade them to pay no regard to reasoning, thus making it empirically true that reasoning has no effect, where it might well have had some before. In which case Hume's psychology of belief would have come to give a correct description because it was believed and only after it had been propounded and accepted. It would not be universally correct because it would not have been correct at the time of its proposal.

Suppose, on the other hand, as Hume did, that his views are descriptively correct at the time of writing. On the basis of his own psychology of belief Hume was able to see why as matters then stood people on the whole were not persuaded by lengthy reasoning such as that contained in his own arguments. Hume expressed both pessimism over the effectiveness of his efforts and perplexity over the rôle which norms ("what ought to have influence on us") have in his project.

Shall we, then, establish it for a general maxim, that no refin'd or elaborate reasoning is ever to be receiv'd? Consider well the consequences of such a principle. By this means you cut off entirely all science and philosophy . . . and you expressly contradict yourself; since this maxim must be built on the preceding reasoning, which will be allowed to be sufficiently refin'd and metaphysical . . . For my part I know not what ought to be done in the present case. I can only observe what is commonly done; which is that this difficulty is seldom if ever thought of; and even where it has once been present to the mind, it is quickly forgot, and leaves but a small impression behind it. Very refin'd reflections have little or no influence on us; and yet we do not, and cannot establish it for a rule, that they ought not to have any influence; which implies a manifest contradiction. (*Treatise* I IV vii)

In other words if what he said was right, he was not going to achieve anything by writing a book giving lengthy philosophical justifications for his views.

The paradox is that if Hume is right about belief formation, his arguments will have no effect, but if he is wrong they could possibly achieve the desired effect. If the point of undertaking a science of human nature was (as Hume suggested) to achieve a self-understanding, which would put all the sciences on a new and secure footing, then this science is (perhaps in spite of itself) part of a project of self-improvement. When we understand ourselves better we will be able to do things in new and better ways and will not repeat old mistakes, old habits of thought, including an over-reliance on reason and an unhealthy contempt for our natural inclinations. To be effective self-understanding has to have an impact on the beings who are the object of study. Hume cannot both treat human science as continuous with the natural sciences, viewed as capable only of giving empirically accurate descriptions, and as part of the project of making new ways of thinking and acting possible.

The project of the natural sciences, as reflected in the epistemology of representation, was founded on the presumption that improvements in our state of knowledge have no effect on the object that we are seeking to understand. The thing known is the way it is independently of our attempts to learn about it. This presumption is built into the principle of the Uniformity of Nature. Hume's epistemology transfers the presumption to human science. He himself argued that there is no sense in looking for a human nature in anything other than empirically established "laws" of behaviour. If coming to know those laws has the potential to modify the behavior they are supposed to describe, then the study of human behavior cannot be modelled on the natural sciences. Hume's position is thus problematic because he tries to base an epistemology on what can only, according to that very epistemology, be regarded as empirically established laws of human thought. But part of the project of that epistemology was to effect changes in the way people "reason" or form their beliefs. And if it is possible for behavior to be changed in that way, it is not possible to believe that human thought is entirely governed by empirically discoverable laws.

These problems reveal that a necessary condition for a universal, normative epistemology to be modelled on natural science, one which is conceived as aiming to yield descriptively correct laws, is that the system in which knowledge is embodied be something which can be treated by analogy with a natural object, i.e., as something which is not modified either by our attempts to come to understand it, or by the impact of the norms proposed. In other words, the system and its interconnections would have to be independent of human attempts to acquire knowledge and of their behavior. This rules out natural language and culture for both are highly dependent on human belief and behavior. It seems that to transcend the Cave and its Idols it will be necessary to reach for Plato's Forms (the project is after all in some respects analogous to Plato's. Thus in recent literature we find Popper's "third world" (Popper, 1973, chapter 3) and Armstrong's epistemology (Armstrong, 1983) based on real universals. For the empiricists, however, this creates another problem. How can we ever get knowledge of such a non-empirical realm? Here we have come full circle. The knowledge project seems to require the kind of old-fashioned metaphysics against which empiricism originally defined itself.

## 3   Epistemology as an Experimental Science of Human Nature

Empiricism is defined by its opposition to the claim that there can be any substantive knowledge that is not derived from experience; in Hume's terms, all knowledge takes the form either of relations of ideas (analytic, necessary, *a priori*) or of matters of fact (synthetic, contingent, *a posteriori*). This not only rules out metaphysics but it rules out the possibility of there being anything which might claim the status of synthetic *a priori* knowledge: something nontrivial not known by reference to experience but which applies necessarily within the realm of experience. This hostility to synthetic *a priori* knowledge is in turn due to pursuing rigorously something which appears to be involved in possessing objective knowledge.

Subjectivity is commonly the result of the subject's unwarranted contribution to whatever system (ideas, beliefs, theories) embodies knowledge. We consequently know (objectively) to the extent that we render ourselves passive and allow the system which embodies knowledge to be shaped by whatever will make it reflect accurately what it is we hope to know (cf. Descartes' quest for the point at which the will has to submit). Anything we might want, anticipate, or imagine must be excluded. It is this attitude which ultimately pressures empiricists to adopt toward their own practice the stance of someone observing and describing but not venturing to interfere. And it calls into question any privilege which subjects might claim for the access they have to the system which embodies knowledge.

In Decartes' epistemology, however, objective knowledge is not so relentlessly shaped by the idea that objective knowledge is the product of passive determination. For his method is also premised on the idea that objective knowledge can only be achieved through active critical reflection. The passive way in which we allow our beliefs to accumulate through everyday experience gives rise to conflicting beliefs, not to knowledge. Only active doubt, pushed to its limits, can reveal what must, objectively, in spite of our activity, be the case. Here Descartes has based his epistemology not on mere self observation in the detached sense of observing the normal course of his trains of thought – the observation to which Hume appeals for confirmation of his principles of the association of ideas. Instead, Descartes is inviting subjects to conduct an experiment, pushing their minds out of the normal course. The experiment is conducted to see whether there is a point at which doubt must stop. The point about experiments is that we can claim the special knowledge, which agents have of their own intentions, to relate what was done to the result obtained. To this extent Descartes can be read as basing his epistemology on the experimental method which he, like Bacon, advocated as the way to use experience to learn more about the natural world.

This element of agency in Descartes' conception of himself may well have contributed to his general confidence in the transparency of his mind, but he nowhere considers carefully the rôle of the mind's activity as an element in what is known, or whether he satisfactorily strikes a balance between the active and passive functions of the mind in knowing. His emphasis on method is an emphasis on knowledge as the product of activity, but its justification through the method of doubt provides a criterion in terms of passivity – genuine knowledge consists of the clear and distinct perceptions which force themselves on us, which we are incapable of doubting, no matter how hard we try. The separation between idea as neutral presentation of content and the attitude which we take toward it by an exercise of will, encourages a conception of intellect as passive and separate from the active will. Judgment is an exercise of the will. This does not fit easily with Descartes' discussion of what is required of reason in the implementation of method, where, for example, he says that one must go over chains of inference repeatedly in the mind to secure understanding of them.

There is a similar oscillation in Descartes' geometry, which is the source of his conception of a general method for acquiring knowledge Descartes linked geometry and algebra by considering a geometrical curve to be defined by the equation of the motion of a point that would trace out that curve. That is, definition describes a construction. Yet Descartes then takes the static contemplation of the equation as the paradigmatic state of knowledge – having a clear and distinct idea – something which is quite timeless and which can appear to stand outside time. This made it possible for both empiricists, who came to emphasize the passivity of the intellect, and the later rationalists, who emphasized intellectual activity, to take their cues from Descartes.

Where Hume read the success of Newtonian natural science as the success of empirical methods of induction from observation, Kant read it as the success of the merger of rational, mathematical methods with experimental methods. His critique of pure reason based its claims to scientific status, to yielding knowledge of reason and its system of representations, on its use of experimental method. Thus Kant says: "What we are adopting as our new method of thought, namely that we can know a priori of things only what we ourselves put into them" (*Critique of Pure Reason* B xviii). The footnote to this passage then begins, "This method, modelled on that of the student of nature, consists in looking for the elements of pure reason in what admits of confirmation or refutation by experiment." In the next footnote Kant draws an analogy between the "analysis of the metaphysician" and experiments in chemistry. Chemists start with naturally occurring substances which they regard as compounds of simpler substances and seek, by experiments, to analyze them into their components and to discern laws of chemical composition and interaction. A thorough understanding of the chemical composition of say, sugar, would be confirmed if it were possible to take the chemical components and from them manufacture synthetic or artificial sugar. Kant started from items of empirical knowledge (experience), which he presumed to be composite, sought to analyze them and by so doing to advance to a theory of knowledge in the same way that chemists advance to chemical theories.

The difference is that whereas naturally occurring chemical compounds have not been put together by us, so that we are ignorant of the principles of composition as well as of the nature of the ingredients, in the case of empirical knowledge it has been put together by the operation of our minds. Kant presumes, like Descartes, that the mind has privileged access to the principles of its own operation. Experience is a product of judgments which we make, and we have special access to the concepts and principles which structure our experience, because we may be assumed to know what form of judgment we are making when we make it. *A priori* knowledge is possible because we impose these forms on all that experts influence on our sensibility. *A priori* knowledge is justified because if we do not impose these forms, concepts and principles, experience is not possible.

Kant's account of how mathematical knowledge is possible forms a crucial bridge between his view of natural science as successful because experimental and his hopes for a philosophy which starts with a theory of knowledge. The basis of Kant's explanation of how mathematics can provide us with demonstrations of statements, which are not true solely in virtue of the concepts involved (are not analytic), is found in his account of the imagination. The forms of judgment are not the only respects in which mental activity makes a contribution to knowledge. There are in addition forms (of space and time) which are imposed on experience by our sensibility, that is by our capacity to have objects presented to us. These forms constrain not only what we can perceive but also what we can imagine.

But our imagination can function in such a way as to generate (construct) objects which have no properties other than those determined by these forms, i.e., it can construct, or create, without empirical material being given to it. When constructing "out of nothing" in this way the products only have properties which arise from their mode of construction. Since there are no component materials there can be no properties which derive from that source. Since we actively perform the construction in imagination we know the principle of construction (a general procedure) and have insight into how this procedure relates to the construct produced.

The syllogism, which demonstrates "All Greeks are mortal" from the premisses "All men are mortal" and "All Greeks are men," only shows us what is contained in our concept of being a Greek. Mathematics, Kant believed, could go beyond reasoning "from concepts;" it could reason "from the construction of concepts." For example, what makes geometry a science that can demonstrate that all triangles have interior angles equal to two right angles (in the traditional sense of showing why all triangles must have this property) is that it is possible to exhibit the universal principles embodied in a concept, such as a triangle, by using the imagination to "construct that concept."

By "constructing a concept" Kant had in mind the procedure by which mathematicians in the course of a proof will generate an example, in order to show what is embodied in the principles which govern the construction of any example of the concept under consideration. Thus, a line will be drawn through the apex of a triangle parallel to its base. That this may be done is not contained in the definition of a triangle but follows from the principles which permit the construction of a triangle; and these principles are taken by Kant to reflect a spatial structure which our sensible intuitions must have. The key, Kant believed, to understanding how there could be significant *a priori* knowledge in mathematics, was to be found in the mind's own activity.

Kant's emphasis on the respects in which the mind must be active in knowing thus not only provided an answer to Hume's attack on the possibility of nontrivial (synthetic) knowledge which was both necessary and universal (*a priori*), it breathed new life into the Cartesian project of an epistemology based on special insight which humans have into their own nature. However, Kant's epistemology, it must be noted, rests on some substantial assumptions about the universal and unchanging forms within which humans are able to think and articulate their knowledge. He assumes that we are all equipped with the same forms of intuition, space and time, and that our faculties of imagination, judgment and reason all function according to the same principles and employ the same forms. It is the assumption of fixed and universal forms of thought which allows Kant to offer a justification for the claim that reason can conduct a complete and exhaustive self-examination on the basis of which the scope and limits of human understanding can be set once and for all. Only thus can a critical examination of the forms, which our understanding must take, set these limits in such a way that *a priori* knowledge of substantive first principles of physics is possible.

But what happens to this enterprise if the assumptions about these universal and unchanging forms no longer appear secure? Consider, for example, the forms of sensibility. Since it was assumed in Kant's day that there was only one science of geometry, Kant was confident that our sensible intuitions have but one *a priori* spatial structure. Subsequent developments of alternative (non-Euclidean) geometries called into question the principle used in the example given above. One may assume there are no lines through the apex parallel to the base of the triangle, or one may assume there are many different lines through the apex parallel to the base. Each assumption generates a different geometry with a different answer to the question, "What is the sum of the internal angles of a triangle?"

There is a tradition some two millennia long based on the assumption, which governed not only geometrical demonstrations but also the practice of measurement, that the first principle (there is exactly one line parallel to the base of any triangle) is correct. The assumption was so strong that to conceive any other alternative was a singular mathematical achievement. Is this because of the way we naturally organize our sensory experience, and is it therefore an (inescapable) Idol of the Tribe, as Kant suggested? If it were, it would be not merely difficult but impossible to conceive these alternatives and give them application in the empirical world. Yet non-Euclidean geometry plays a crucial role in Einstein's theories of relativity. Acceptance of Einstein's theories in physics means that the conviction that Euclidean geometry was founded on self-evidently true first principles must now be regarded as a long standing Idol enshrined in the caves of those who pursued the science of geometry or based their physics on it.

If all Kant can establish is that there have to be forms, concepts and principles which structure experience, but cannot determine which, if any, are universal and unchanging, then his project will not be able to reach a standpoint free of the contingencies which generate Idols of the Cave. His transcendental philosophy cannot, any more than Descartes' method of doubt, claim to pave the way to a universal perspective. But it did not necessarily require the development of non-Euclidean geometry and non-Newtonian physics to make this apparent. Kant was aware enough of the possibility of change to have raised serious questions about the universality of the standpoint his epistemology tried to take up.

The conception of reason as a basis of action and a force for change led Kant to a view of reason as not merely a set of fixed capacities, which form part of the nature of each individual, but as something whose projects and development transcend individuals. By the eighteenth century it had become clear that the project on which the natural sciences had embarked required the cooperative work of many people and would require many generations of such work. The conception of a full understanding of the natural world as something which could be embodied in an individual (something still possible with Descartes and Leibniz) was already recognized to be unrealistic. This puts a strain on the Cartesian approach to epistemology which emphasizes and can provide a foundation only for individual knowledge. The lack of analogy between religious knowledge needing to be grounded in inner conviction and knowledge of the natural world as proposed by the Baconian project became clearer as the natural sciences developed.

Kant's route to externalizing the projects of theoretical reason was opened for him by the stress he placed on the importance of practical reason, which includes governing the activities of theoretical reason. It was widened by his arguments for a morality based on reason and the demands of living in a community whose other members are also recognized as rational beings. Once we recognize that a human lifetime is too short for the full development of human rational potential, we have to hope that the development achieved by one generation will be handed down to the next. Without believing in this cumulative progress, we would never be motivated to work on or contribute to projects which we know we are as individuals incapable of completing. The projects of natural science make sense only for individuals in the context of an enduring community of rational beings. Thus Kant says, "In man (as the only rational creature on earth) these natural capacities which are directed to the use of his reason are to be fully developed only in the race, not in the individual" (*On History*, p. 13).

But how can Kant or any individual philosopher, writing from within history, be assured that their rational powers are developed to the full extent necessary to be able to discern the scope and limits of human understanding? How can any philosopher pretend to stand outside history? The difficulty is that Kant seems to have made reason both historical and outside time, both relative to individuals and their historical contexts, and universal. Time for Kant was, after all, like space, only a form of intuition; it formed the frame of the empirical world of appearances not of the unknowable world of things in themselves. It is this division, replacing Descartes' dualism of mind and body, which Kant argued to be essential if reason was not to come into conflict with itself. For without this dualism the mind would represent to itself an exhaustive empirical reality within which its own activity could not be located. Yet Kant's dualism cannot be unproblematic if reason itself must be regarded as having a history.

The division between empirical reality and things in themselves was eradicated in different ways by both Hegel and Marx, but in each case with the effect of making human beings, their knowledge structures and their culture, into fully historical beings. Where Hegel removes the division in favor of reason so that the rational becomes the real, Marx removes it in favor of the material dimension of human life, so that ideas and ways of thinking and reasoning arise out of the concrete relations which human beings must sustain with one another in order to provide their own material necessities. In both cases, the thought structures of individuals and societies are essentially historically embedded. They owe their character to their historical location. The same ways of thinking are not open to everyone at every historical period or in every cultural situation.

Both Hegel and Marx continued to think of this history as having a goal, as a progress toward a society in which human fulfillment is possible, even though they had very different conceptions of that goal and of the forces which propel humanity toward it. Both face the problem that the statement of their philosophic positions seems to require them to occupy a standpoint outside history, whereas the positions themselves claim no such standpoint to be possible for individuals. To be rendered self consistent their claims seem to cry out for their efforts to be limited to reflecting on the ideals embodied in the culture of nineteenth century Europe, in which both are situated. But this would not be internally consistent either, for the content of those ideals included the very universalist claims which Hegel and Marx made. The attempt, to find a philosophically coherent expression of the project of progress through reason and through the development of scientific knowledge, gets caught in a conflict between its need for ahistorical foundations (a clean break with the past, the possibility of ignoring the conditioning of past history) and its own historicity, its view of itself as a project with can only be achieved through time.

## 4  Humans as Historical Beings

In a sense this problem was inevitable. It had already been approached early in the eighteenth century by Vico, who took a more direct route because he started from a thorough rejection of Descartes' philosophy. Vico set out by pursuing, more vigorously than Kant, the epistemological implications of the idea that it is through their constructive activities that human beings are able to acquire scientific knowledge. Ultimately this led Vico to a distinctive version of the claim that we can know ourselves better than we know anything in the natural world, but the object of this knowledge was not a self which stands outside history unconditioned by the contingencies of human existence.

Vico's first philosophic publication involved taking Descartes to task for having failed to appreciate the nature of his own achievements in geometry. Descartes proposed clarity and distinctness as the criterion of the truth of his ideas. He derived this criterion from his confidence in what he took to be his knowledge of mathematics, as well as the confidence he felt in his proof of his own existence. This criterion encouraged the conception of the intellect as passive, forced to acknowledge truth by the clarity and distinctness of what was presented to it. But even Descartes acknowledged the possibility that what he took to be clear and distinct was neither correct nor undistorted. To secure his criterion, he needed to establish the existence of a benevolent God.

Geometrical knowledge, Vico insisted, is true not because of its clarity and distinctness, but because geometrical figures are things we construct. It was the similarity of this claim to Kant's doctrine that mathematics gives us (synthetic *a priori*) knowledge "through the construction of concepts," which aroused interest in Vico's thought among followers of Kant over a century later. We can know the objects of mathematics because their only properties are those which our activities put into them. When our constructions make those properties manifest there is no possibility of misperception. Thus Vico says,

> Mathematics are commonly thought to be contemplative sciences and not thought to give proofs from causes; when in fact they alone among all the sciences are the truly operative ones [*operatrici*] and give proofs from causes since, of all the human sciences, they, uniquely, make their way in the likeness of divine science. (*De antiquissimus Italorum sapienta, Opera filosofiche* (p. 77) quoted in Lachterman, 1989, p. 8)

In other words we stand to mathematics as God stands to his creation, our mind has a perfect grasp of its objects because it has made them.

But we do not stand to nature in this cognitively favorable relationship. As Vico saw it Descartes had attempted to understand nature by expressing its principles in geometrical concepts and explaining its phenomena by means of geometrical demonstrations. But while geometry might provide the study of nature with a method of discovering probabilities, it could not provide it with demonstrations. "We demonstrate geometrical things because we make them; if we could demonstrate physical things we would make them" (*Selected Writ-*

*ings*, p. 41). Vico appears here to be claiming in opposition to Descartes that we cannot have knowledge of the natural world because it is not our creation, but because Vico is not taking "knowledge" (*Scienza*) in quite the same sense as Descartes, his confrontation with Descartes is less than perfectly direct. Vico clearly has Descartes in mind when he chides, "Men who do not know the truth (*il vero*) of things endeavour to cling to the certain (*il certo*) in order that, since they are unable to satisfy their intellect with knowledge (*scienza*), their will may at least rest upon consciousness (*coscienza*)" (*Selected Writings*, p. 162). Descartes, of course, hoped to find the truth of things in certainty, but he realized he had to establish the existence of a benevolent God to do so. Vico, as we will see shortly, rejected the possibility of doing this, but his principal complaint is that Descartes treated certainty as a sufficient criterion of *scienza*, when traditionally one could not claim *scienza* (Italian "*scienza*" = Latin "*scientia*" = Greek *epistêmê*) unless one knew why the object of knowledge had to be that way. In other words, Vico, like Kant, was committed to the traditional distinction between knowing that and knowing why, and to treating only the latter as worthy of being called "science" (a body of adequately justified claims to know).

But in his efforts to sustain this distinction Vico went well beyond Kant in the way he pressed the principle that having constructed something places one in a privileged epistemic position with regard to that thing. In this respect Vico differs as much from the tradition, whose distinction he accepts, as he does from Descartes. Vico maintained the thesis (first put forward in the context of engaging Descartes) that "the criterion and rule of the true is to have made it" (*Selected Writings*, p. 55). "In Latin *verum* [the true] and *factum* [what is made] are interchangeable or, in the language of the Schools, convertible terms" (*Selected Writings*, p. 51). This apparently paradoxical thesis arises from identifying truth with the object of *scienza* – in other words there is not truth where there is no grasp of the reason why – and adopting a highly conservative attitude toward what could put a human being in a position fully to know "the why" of anything. Here having made it and being responsible for its properties is, Vico believes, the only guarantee of being able to know "the why" and thus attain *scienza*, which is what we have when we have grasped the truth.

This was not a wholly novel development of the tradition. Vico was building on that part of the tradition which held that to understand anything is to discern that wherein its perfection lies. This includes the natural world and one must not pretend to "know" (in the favored sense equivalent to "understand") anything until one has grasped how it reflects intelligent purpose directed at the good. The revisionary identification of the "true" with the "made" was accompanied in Vico's philosophy by an orthodox (Platonic) identification of the true with the good. "Just as for God the criterion of the true is, in the act of creating, to have communicated goodness to his thoughts – "and God saw that it was good" – so among men the criterion is to have made the truths which we perceive" (*Selected Writings* p. 56). As long as Descartes was read (by no means charitably) as committed to "science" in the traditional sense, the *verum* is *factum* thesis could be pressed not only against the possibility of natural science (physics) but against two other central pillars of Cartesian philosophy. For someone to attempt to demonstrate the existence of God would be not only to undertake the impossible but to proceed with impiety, "For this would be tantamount to making himself the God of God, and denying the God whom he seeks" (*Selected Writings*, p. 65). And the assumption that we know our own minds better than we do the natural world is likewise a serious mistake, "For while the mind perceives itself it does not make itself, and because it does not make itself it does not know the genus or mode by which it perceives itself" (*Selected Writings*, p. 55). Of course Descartes was not claiming to "know" either his own mind or the existence of God in the traditional sense; he was involved in a movement which ended by changing the goal of inquiry from *scienza* to *coscienza*.

Vico's philosophy was not merely a rejection of the philosophy of Descartes; its positive side included an endorsement of experimental natural science and the suggestion that geometrical method was better employed in the design of experiments than in the articulation of general theories (*Selected Writings*, p. 75). Implicit in Vico's approach was an important limitation on human aspirations; our efforts to understand the natural world will lead at best to an understanding of principles which govern what we can do in the natural world, but not to any theory that might claim to represent the natural world as it is in itself (or as God made it), independently of human involvement in it. We can know the world only through our active involvement with it.

This leads to a conception of scientific knowledge and its ground which is the inverse of that proposed by the empiricists, who require total disengagement, or non-interference, before there is any right to claim knowledge. This is because the conceptions of knowledge are different. Where Vico sought knowledge as the form of understanding possessed by a creator, the empiricists sought knowledge of how things are in themselves from the point of view of the universe, not from the point of view of man. These two conceptions can be run together when the point of view of the universe is that of a creator-God. This happens with Descartes, whose disengaged meditations nevertheless made knowledge dependent on his own activity. Vico did not, any more than Bacon, hold that to escape the Idols of the Tribe we must attempt to transcend our humanity altogether.

Vico had worked out and published this much of his philosophy within the first decade of the eighteenth century. After a pause of fifteen years he published the first edition of the *Scienza Nuova*, which contained an important amplification of his position, in that it assigned a privileged status to a certain newly conceived science of "the nature of nations." Two subsequent editions of the *Scienza Nuova*, each a virtual rewriting of the previous edition, refined and broadened what began primarily as an attempt to understand the necessary and universal features of legal institutions. From the outset the sources from which Vico sought the principles of this new body of understanding – viz. common ideas (e.g. providence, eternal and universal justice); institutions of religion, marriage and burial; myths, metaphors, emblems, poetry, language, etc. – collectively pointed to the study of what we now conceive as human culture.

Vico claimed the status of science for this study on the grounds that it is possible for humans to grasp the necessary and universal principles which constitute the causes of human cultural institutions because humans are the authors of those institutions. Here he does not mean that humans are the authors of their own institutions in the sense of having consciously decided to construct them and having then done so according to principles. Rather he means that these institutions are the product of human activity. Participating in human culture does not automatically provide a grasp of its necessary and universal principles. A participant's unreflective rôle in a cultural institution yields only particular experience, and this can form the basis only for that second grade of knowledge, consciousness (*coscienza*), whose object is certainty.

Although Vico acknowledged Hobbes as an important theorist of human society, his thought at this point moves well away from Hobbes. Hobbes treated the acts by which humans make the commonwealth as though they were, or could be, deliberately established conventions. Vico appreciated the circularity in treating human society as established on the basis of interactions (such as reaching an agreement to observe a convention) which presuppose an already constituted human society. Human society for Vico was established by divine providence, which was the term under which he conceived the way that, in interacting with one another, humans modify each other's behavior so as to constitute unreflectively, i.e., without deliberation or intention, a permanent structure of regulated behavior.

Vico's conception of how one attains *scienza* of human society is not easy to grasp because it combines elements which in more familiar accounts of knowledge are supposed to stand in opposition to one another. It does not involve merely placing experience of (participation in) a particular institution under or along side a grasp of abstract laws. Rather the experience has to be linked to an imaginative reconstruction of the earlier forms of institution, out of which the present (participated in) institution developed. It also has to be linked to imaginative constructions and reconstructions of other possible forms of institutions, which might have developed from similar starting points. While there are a number of possible alternative forms, it is clear that Vico believes the number is not unlimited. There are constraints on what is a possible primitive social institution and constraints on what can develop out of a given institution. The hope in Vico's program of being able to generate a science, with universal and necessary explanations, rests on its being able to discover those constraints. But the abstract grasp of these constraints expressed as laws will not constitute Vico's science. The constraints have to be grasped in such a way as to govern the imaginative construction of particular phenomena.

This is not wholly unlike the way in which thought experiments are used in natural science, or the way in which mathematical or physical models are used in attempts to understand particular types of phenomena, such as the behavior of pendulums, interference of waves or complex molecules. These are all cases where understanding is sought through imaginative construction. Commonly these steps are not given any epistemological significance, but are treated as "heuristic," aids to discovery, which are irrelevant to the justification of any knowledge claims which result. Vico, on the contrary, is claiming that the ability to construct, because it reveals "the why" (the cause) is the locus of justifications and is therefore of central epistemological significance.

Thus for Vico the hope of founding a demonstrative science of human institutions rests on being able imaginatively to project our minds into genuinely possible social forms, in which we do not participate and which may indeed not actually exist or exist any longer. Such imaginative projecting informed by knowledge of constraints on possible forms will effect the required demonstrations as the (re)constructions of the social forms, since according to the dictum, "*verum = factum*," "to prove [the true] by means of causes is to effect [it]" (*Selected Writings*, p. 64). Just as geometry cannot demonstrate without the imaginative construction of geometrical objects, Vico's science cannot demonstrate without the imaginative construction of forms of human institutions.

The need for the use of the imagination is so prominent in Vico's work that it is easy to identify his project with later (nineteenth and twentieth century) views of historical method which recommend imaginative projection into the minds – what Bacon would call the private caves or dens – of one's historical subjects. However, Vico's project comes to rest on what we call "imaginative projection" not because he placed any special epistemic value on the individual experience of historical figures, but because of the way he conceived of demonstrations in science and hence in his new science. Demonstrations are based not on projecting into the minds of other individuals, for this could give at most another participant view, another particular experience. What is required is the disciplined, imaginative construction of another society as a possible object of experience.

This requires not a subjective or empathetic projection but in fact a disciplined putting aside of presumptions based on the experience of one's own current situation. We have to put aside the assumption that all people think like we think. From Vico's standpoint it could be argued that Hobbes failed to found a science of human society precisely because he uncritically projected his own mentality – that is his own assumptions, values, expectations, and perceptions of what is possible – onto people in a state of society which afforded no access to those assumptions, values, expectations, and perceptions of what is possible. By doing so he cut himself off from appreciating the different kinds of constraints under which different peoples operate. Vico regarded the key to his conception of a new science to be the realization that primitive humans spoke and thought "poetically;" (see *The New Science*, Book II). That is, he suggests that certain (tendentiously labeled "primitive") cultural forms generate very different ways of thinking, or, as might now be said, give rise to different "mentalities."

Because of the temporal dimension introduced by differentiating between primitive and more developed social forms, Vico called his new science "history." Vico proposed, however, to do more to the concept of history than shift it from a collection of facts to a demonstrative science. The imaginative constructions and reconstructions required for Vico's science of history should do what the constructions of mathematical science manifestly do not, i.e., tell a developmental story. Each nation (i.e., system of institutions) has, to be sure, its own pattern of development. But Vico would not dignify with the term "science" simple narratives which tell of such developments. The narratives have to convey the "whys" and "wherefores" which reveal what are the preconditions, and what are the possible consequences, of a given system of institutions. The temporal dimension of Vico's history implies more than the mere dating of facts.

## 5   Humans as Self-Creators

Vico's significance does not lie in the influence his thought exerted on subsequent generations, for he was largely ignored until well into the nineteenth century. There are, however, at least three enduring strands in his thought. The first is a particularly uncompromising version of the claim that we have no alternative but to understand the world around us in terms of what we are able to make or construct. This means that scientific knowledge is viewed as the kind of understanding of a thing which is associated with knowing how to construct it. This is very different from the conception of knowledge as accurate representation, so that the issue of justification and the criterion of truth play out quite differently in the context of Vico's philosophy. Full justification of a claim to know in this context rests on the disciplined use of the imagination to carry out constructive activity.

The second is the claim that different cultural institutions sustain – and require if they are in turn to be sustained – fundamentally different ways of thinking, fundamentally different "thought styles" or "mentalities." An institution is a structure of customs; customs are shared habits of procedure. One may like Hobbes assume that there is a single core set of shared habits of procedure, variations of which generate different institutions. Or one may realize that habits of procedure not only rest on but create and reinforce expectations and perceptions of what is possible. Expectations and perceptions of what is possible cannot change without changing people's habits and habits cannot change without modifying expectations and perceptions of what is possible. Expectations and perceptions of what is possible are what constitute assumptions, what is taken for granted, and they shape what people will value, what they will reach for if given the opportunity and try to secure in the face of threat. These are what constitute ways of thinking and they are inextricably tied via shared habits to the institutions which constitute a culture.

The third is the claim that human institutions must be understood as phenomena which develop, each stage constrained by previous stages. We may well be able to formulate laws or principles governing these developments, but they will not be such as to make prediction possible. They will be laws of the operation of constraints rather than laws of determination. The first strand in Vico's thought implies that we will be able to grasp these principles only to the extent that they allow us imaginatively to describe (i.e., construct) institutional forms which explain how and why actual forms have the characteristics which they do. The second strand has the consequence that difficulties we face may be the result of our own inability to free our thought from the assumptions and values which are required for participation in our own institutional forms. In other words we may stumble because we have not identified and put aside the Idols of our Caves.

Obviously this enterprise presumes that we can identify and suspend assumptions and values which are conditions of participating in our own institutions. As long as we do not imagine that this has to be done on a wholesale basis, it is not an unreasonable presumption. People moving between cultures and even between different sub-cultures have to adjust their expectations and perceptions of what is possible. It is common enough to undergo the process with a certain amount of reflective awareness and consequently to be able to use information about a culture to imagine what would be involved in the transition to participating in that culture. It is possible to undertake this imaginative exercise in a disciplined way so that one can continue to participate in one's own culture while grasping what it would be to have to live and think in a different framework of shared habits. Clearly this is something which is never done completely, but the benefits of even limited success are an increased self-awareness and access to a much wider range of values and perceptions of what is possible.

The implications of these strands of Vico's philosophy can be either intoxicating, threatening or merely disquieting. Philosophers, whether empiricist or rationalist, who worked within the framework shaped by Descartes assumed that, whether or not it is a part of physical nature, humans have a fixed nature, which includes the cognitive, intellectual functions by which they come to know the world around them. They assumed, moreover, that we have special access to that nature and to those cognitive, intellectual functions. These two assumptions together are necessary presuppositions of the strategy of turning the methods of natural science onto the human mind in an attempt to provide a self-consistent justification of the claim that the methods of science do lead to objective knowledge, whilst at the same time setting the scope and limits of such knowledge. The self-knowledge necessary to be able to claim to have put the Idols aside must not itself be distorted and hence must itself be a product of the method which claims to banish Idols. But this demand of reflexivity proves, as we have seen, to be destabilizing.

If a knowledge system has to include knowledge of itself, sufficient to establish its own reliability, it must be either inconsistent or incomplete (this may, if you like, be thought of as Gödel's first incompleteness theorem rather freely generalized). It follows that one must either abandon the demand that the system conform to familiar standards of rationality (i.e., consistency) or accept that there is scope for development and opt for some kind of historicized view of the system.

For empiricists, this means a particularly stark choice. It appears that the only way to be fully consistent with their empiricism is to give up the foundational, justificatory project of normative epistemology. The only kinds of studies of knowledge which can be conducted are locally applicable empirical studies of belief formation, of the processes which in particular communities lead to the establishment of what is there accorded the authority of knowledge. Such studies would, even when drawing normative conclusions, have to acknowledge that ultimately their conclusions are strictly descriptive of norms which apply in a particular context and carry no authority outside that context. This is the position adopted by advocates (Barnes and Bloor, 1982) of the strong program in the sociology of knowledge. In all self-consistency participants in this program have to acknowledge that the cognitive standards, which they themselves employ, could be the object of such a study. They can advocate that others adopt their position and study the social institutions which generate and legitimate claims to knowledge in a purely descriptive manner, but they cannot claim theirs to be the only legitimate position. It is the only one consistent with their cognitive standards, but these, they must acknowledge, are not universal.

Rationalists can yield on the claim of completeness and accept that there can be no complete foundational epistemology. The forms of judgment and of experience are historically and culturally conditioned. Nevertheless since there are such forms, and knowledge is a product of their imposition, it remains possible to give a locally applicable theoretical account of knowledge using critical methods analogous to Kant's. What cannot be claimed, however, is that the empirical world, as the world of possible experience for human beings generally, is identical to that of the world of experience as represented in, or given through, one particular set of forms. This means that synthetic *a priori* principles have their necessary applicability secured only relative to particular frameworks. Internal recognition of this incompleteness would require acknowledgment that there is no basis for expecting the synthetic *a priori* principles of one framework to be recognized by people operating in another (in other words, cultural relativism)

. . .

Here we get the full impact of the conception of man as self-creating. Individuals are constrained by the society in which they live to act and think in certain ways; there is a framework of customs, laws, and language which set the bounds of what is possible for them to do or think. To this extent all individuals are "made" by others, or are a product of their culture. But as participants in society they can deliberately, by discovering new ways to do things which are picked up by others, change aspects of their culture. With these changes come changes in conceptions of what is and what is not humanly possible.

The idea that there have been fundamentally different "thought styles" or "mentalities" and that these are an integral part of a culture, must necessarily reflect back, first onto our conception of ourselves, and then onto our thoughts about knowledge and the project of epistemology. It is an example of the way in which theories about human beings and their institutions reflect back into views about the status of knowledge and hence of those theories themselves. If Vico (or Hegel or Marx) is right, then we ourselves think in ways which are a product of our cultural and historical embedding. If these frameworks set bounds on what it is possible to think or imagine, and if justification depends on being able to see possibilities and constructively realize them, at least in thought or imagination, then different cultures' views on justification, on the kinds of justification possible for knowledge claims, may be different. And there could be no way to set limits in advance on all possible forms of justification that might be available to human beings in some culture at some time or other.

This means that epistemology, even when it focuses attention on justification rather than discovery, can only be the epistemology appropriate to a particular culture at a particular point in its history, which has to acknowledge the limitations placed on it by historical and cultural location. In other words, tracing the consequences of the view of the intellect as active in its own self-perfection, or more neutrally, formation, we are led inevitably to a developmental conception of humans as historical beings which in the end undermines the project of an epistemology which hopes to ignore the contingencies of historical and/or cultural location.

## 6  Epistemology as Idol Knowledge

We have sought to portray the Baconian reorientation of human knowledge as a contingently conditioned redefinition of a human project. Modern Western culture inherited from the ancient Greeks the idea that the acquisition of knowledge was both integral to living the fulfilled life of a human being and necessary to creating the conditions under which such a life would be possible. But as we have seen the Greek focus was on determining what constitutes the good, (fulfilled) life for a human being and on how to live it. Detailed technical knowledge of the natural world was not an integral part of this project. Bacon's writings reveal that he was conscious both of the extent to which he was drawing on tradition and the extent to which he was redirecting it in a way which marked a decisive break. The connection between knowledge and human fulfillment is retained, but the conception of fulfillment and the route to it is different. Since the reason for which knowledge is to be sought and valued is different, the kind of knowledge sought and valued is also different. It is not contemplative understanding, but the detailed "mechanic's" understanding of how things work and can be made to work that is required.

If the project of science is historically and culturally conditioned, then to remind ourselves of this is to guard against being taken in by an Idol. The conceit, which is internal to (and which indeed has driven) investment in scientific and technological development, is that it is the one route to human progress, a precondition of all others, and one which must be universally acknowledged for its successes. When this is assumed as absolute, when its human origins are forgotten, it becomes an Idol. To put an Idol aside does not necessarily mean rejecting everything that was seen under its distorting influence. This would be a consequence only if one adhered to a strictly representational conception of knowledge, one which is internal, not to science, but to the philosophical theories of knowledge developed to legitimize its project.

Bacon regarded the senses as a source of Idols only to the extent that they were trusted as giving a direct, undistorted view of the material world. To be delivered from their illusion is not to reject them as sources of information, since indeed they are the vehicle of our interaction with the world. It is to recognize that the information they yield must be treated with circumspection, that thought has to be given to the question of exactly where to rely on them, how they can be supplemented and so on. Similarly, much modern science has proved itself through conferring ability to intervene in the material world (it has provided reliable sources of electricity and appliances which use it, for example). To the extent that we value those powers of intervention, we must accord authority to the scientific and technological knowledge which makes them possible. On the other hand, to the extent that the goal, domination of nature, was humanly conceived it may be questioned. Adoption of a modified goal would require reassessment of existing knowledge in the light of its value for contributing to that goal.

The science and technology developed in a Baconian spirit are very much a part of present human reality. To insist that the development of science and technology is a human project is to say that as with any such project our view of it can be expected to change as we proceed to execute it and have to confront the realities, the obstacles, in the way of completing it. Work on these projects also changes us, as we are forced to think in new ways, as we come to live in new ways, made possible or required by the introduction of technology. Our freedoms and constraints change and with them our conceptions of ourselves as human beings. Recognition of this as a human project may serve to remind us that we have a certain responsibility for the science we produce – the scientist is not being dictated to by the world, merely recording its pronouncements. The positivist image of science, with its conceptions of factual objectivity, a standard set by a non-human world, presents science as containing no place either for human values or creative thought. It explicitly sets up an opposition between the scientific and the human as a projection of the opposition between subject and object.

One of the lessons of the history of science in the twentieth century is that what were once taken as scientific certainties, principles not within reach of empirical verification or falsification, may come to be questioned and rejected. When such a change occurs standards and methods of justification also inevitably change. Use of what could once be assumed without justification, Euclidean geometry for example, now needs justifying by reference to the context of use. Thoughts that it would be impossible to entertain within the old framework become thinkable, such as the local warping of space-time by strong gravitational fields. At the empirical level too, new technologies have made whole new kinds of experiments possible. Computers have changed and continue to change the way theories are tested, experiments are done and data collected. These developments are not things which could have been foreseen by nineteenth century physicists. They were not visible, not thinkable. This is the sense in which methods and techniques of justification within science, whether at the theoretical or experimental levels, are context dependent.

But it might be claimed that there are overarching methodological principles governing the practice of the natural sciences, which free them from cultural context dependence and which justify their claim to value neutrality and legitimate their claim to universal authority. This would be the claim that scientific methods have been formed around the sort of strategy suggested by Bacon, the strategy which institutionalizes mechanisms for exposing Idols and the distortions they produce. Theories are discussed and criticized, papers in scientific journals as well as research proposals are subject to peer review, experimental results are published and attempts made to repeat them. Non-repeatable results are treated with extreme suspicion, if not rejected outright. The scientific community is an international community and should therefore be drawing on people from sufficiently varied backgrounds to allow individual and cultural biases to be cancelled out in these processes. Claims which survive and become established knowledge, ought to be neutral and should, by commanding respect within the scientific community, deserve universal respect.

But the standards of peer review are those of the methods and justificatory framework of a particular discipline at a particular time. The only criticisms of a view or theory that can be recognized and thus heard are those that can be articulated within that framework. Similarly, the only claims that will be seriously considered are those that fit into the framework, unless the people suggesting them have already established themselves as pre-eminent in their field. The operation of these kinds of pressures in the development of molecular biology in this century is illustrated by the relative isolation of Barbara McClintock and the subsequent recognition of the value of her work (see Fox Keller, 1983).

The problem with institutions is that, like language, they are resistant to change and can never be merely institutions concerned with ensuring the evaluation of knowledge simply as regards its likely truth or falsity. As currently established, institutions of peer review are also vehicles for funding and for professional power and prestige. These problems are not just human failings which could be eliminated in principle; they are inevitable consequences of knowledge being a source of authority and hence power.

Moreover, the project of modern science carries contradictory tendencies within it. The ideal of openness to pluralistic criticism comes into conflict with the vision of steady progress to a unified truth and claims to scientific authority. In practice criticisms are limited, channelled and deflected. Lapses from the idealized standard of openness to criticism are normal. Dogma is inevitable, since some things must be held fixed in order for problems to be framed and inquiries undertaken. To have any goals at all, is to take some things for granted.

A more detailed understanding of the ways in which knowledge achieves authority status is a necessary part of the self-knowledge, knowledge of present constraints and possibilities, required for any reorientation in the conception of the goals of knowledge and hence of the nature of knowledge. The ideal of openness to pluralistic criticism, unrealizable in day-to-day scientific work, can nevertheless be invoked in service of the project of periodically renegotiating the vision of truth and the nature of its unity.

## 7 Skeptical Strategies

To persuade people to put aside their Idols, you must first shake their faith (the skeptical task) and then convince them that there is something which can take their place. It is necessary to share and build upon their commitment to pursue existing goals, channelling it in a new direction. The exposure of Idols (as Foucault has taught us) is part of the politics of knowledge. But one's purpose might be more, or less, radical than reform. The skeptical stage may be an end in itself, being deployed for conservative or for anarchistic ends. The skeptic persuades us of the status of our Ideas as Idols, as graven images created by human beings, denying them the status of true religion or true knowledge. If we want religions or knowledges, we will have to make do with human-made ones, no one of which can claim moral or cognitive superiority.

One response made in the sixteenth and seventeenth centuries by Roman Catholic theologians to Protestant challenges was to use skeptical arguments to discredit Protestant claims to religious knowledge. They argued that human reason is incapable of being deployed to yield religious knowledge. Individual human beings cannot, by their own efforts, acquire this form of knowledge. Religious knowledge is granted to the chosen few in revelations. For the remainder the important religious attitude is that of faith, acceptance of authority grounded in trust. In this case skepticism served conservative forces in their resistance to change and in their attempt to retain authority.

During the same period humanist scholars were using similar arguments to discredit all traditional authorities on matters of moral and political organization. They argued that since knowledge of any uniquely best moral or political formation is impossible for human beings, they should just get on with using their experience to create what seemed to them to be workable systems of laws, customs and political practices. This served not only as a basis for pluralism, but also as an argument for a separation of Church from State and removal of the Church from secular political power, without disputing its claims to religious authority.

Both of these strategies (and many variations) can be seen in play today with Western technological science substituted for the Catholic Church. Science disputes the cognitive credentials of its critics, encouraging skepticism with respect to their methods and claims. Environmentalists, humanists and feminists seek to limit the scope of the authority of science, examining its methods and arguing that it really cannot claim decisive authority in matters social and environmental.

Philosophy itself has not been immune from this power play. The credentials of epistemology, that branch of philosophy which concerns itself with knowledge and its nature, with knowledge claims and their possible justification, or as Locke put it, with the scope and limits of human understanding, has itself been challenged. If the skeptics are right, if the edifice of science is the most elaborate and most powerful Idol yet, if the whole project of overthrowing Idols in search of true knowledge is bankrupt because finally realized to be not only impossible but also highly dangerous, then the theory of knowledge is the theory of nothing. It must itself have been part of the mystificatory rites of the cult of (scientific) knowledge.

Some of the critics of epistemology, of whom Richard Rorty would be a leading example, take the conception of epistemology as given and urge its total abandonment; philosophy should not concern itself with knowledge, but should restrict itself to the humanistic task of stimulating edifying conversation. We do not advocate this route. It seems to us that it amounts to an abdication of responsibility on behalf of philosophy in an age in which authority rests on high technology and as part of a culture in which the cult of the expert flourishes. Even those opposed to the values they think to be inherent in science and technology, who reckon them to be false Idols, cannot bring about their downfall merely by ceasing to believe whilst continuing the rituals of worship embodied in life in a technologically developed country. So long as knowledge is power and the exercise of the power is prominent in shaping the society and environment in which we live, and so long as we seek to have the sort of understanding of society which is a necessary condition of dissent and political challenge, then it seems to us that there is a rôle for critical reflection on the knowledge process, whatever name one wishes to give it.

Thus we wish to take the reformist route. This involves altering the conception of epistemology rejected by Rorty. It can be admitted that much of what has gone under the heading "epistemology" has played the rôle its critics assign to it without accepting that this is all that epistemology ever has been or could ever be. All the moves discussed above, moves in which Idols are detected and denounced, counter-proposals made and modified, only to be challenged later from other quarters, count for us as part of philosophical discourse on knowledge (epistemology). It is within the theory of knowledge that these arguments take place, arguments involving conceptions of what constitutes knowledge, why it should be pursued, how it can be acquired and by whom. We urge that the epistemology of early and mid-twentieth century analytic philosophy be discarded as a false Idol, and that epistemology be reconnected to the larger and broader tradition of philosophical engagement with the politics of knowledge.

## Works Cited

Aristotle, *The Complete Works of Aristotle*, Jonathan Barnes (ed.), 1984. Princeton: Princeton University Press. [References are by Bekker number.]

Armstrong, David M. 1983: *What is a Law of Nature?* Cambridge: Cambridge University Press.

Bacon, Francis, *The New Organon [Novum Organon]* (1620), Fulton H. Anderson (ed.), 1960, from the translation of Ellis and Spedding, Indianapolis: Bobbs-Merrill.

Descartes, René, *Philosophical Works of Descartes*, trans. Elizabeth Haldane and G. R. T. Ross, 1955. New York: Dover.

Hume, David, *A Treatise of Human Nature* (1734), ed. L. A. Selby-Bigge, 1975. Oxford: Clarendon Press.

——, *Enquiries* (1748), ed. L. A. Selby-Bigge, 1963. Oxford: Clarendon Press.

Kant, Immanuel, *Critique of Pure Reason* (A=1781, B=1787), trans. N. Kemp Smith, 1965. New York: St Martin's Press.

—— *Idea for a Universal History from a Cosmopolitan Point of View* [On History] (1784), trans. L. White Beck, R. E. Anchor, and E. L. Fackenheim, 1963. Indianapolis: Bobbs-Merrill.

Keller, Evelyn Fox, *A Feeling for the Organism: The Life and Work of Barbara McClintock*, 1983. New York: W. H. Freeman.

Lachterman, David Rapport, *The Ethics of Geometry*, 1989. London: Routledge.

Newton, Isaac, *Philosophiae Naturalis Principia Mathematica* (2 vols, 1686), trans. A. Motte, revised by F. Cajori, 1971. Berkeley. University of California Press.

Popper, Karl, *Objective Knowledge*, 1973. Oxford: Clarendon Press.

Vico, Giambattista, *The New Science of Giambattista Vico*, trans. T. G. Bergin and M. H. Fisch, 1970. Ithaca, NY: Cornell University Press.

——, *Selected Writings*, trans. L. Pompa, 1982. Cambridge: Cambridge University Press.

# INDEX

Unger, Rhoda, 294
utilitarianism, 90, 206

verum-factum principle, 427–9
Vico, Giambattista, 426–33
view from nowhere, 125, 128
virtues, intellectual, 207–8

wax analogy, 11–12, 373–4
Weinberg, Stephen, 324
Williams, Michael, 211

Wisan, Winifred, 324
wishful thinking, 103–3
Wittgenstein, Ludwig, 39, 83, 125, 131,
    154, 156, 170, 260, 312
women, *see* gender
Wood, Ledger, 184
Wylie, Alison, 406

Yilmaz, Huseyin, 264
Yourgrau, Palle, 116–18

# Valuable Epistemology Resources

**A GUIDE THROUGH THE THEORY OF KNOWLEDGE**
Second Edition
*Adam Morton*
0-631-20005-3 paperback
0-631-20004-5 hardcover

**AN INTRODUCTION TO EPISTEMOLOGY**
*Charles Landesman*
0-631-20213-7 paperback
0-631-20212-9 hardcover

**EPISTEMOLOGY: the Big Questions**
*Edited by Linda Martín Alcoff*
0-631-20580-2 paperback
0-631-20579-9 hardcover

**A COMPANION TO EPISTEMOLOGY**
*Edited by Jonathan Dancy and Ernest Sosa*
0-631-19258-1 paperback

**INTRODUCTION TO CONTEMPORARY EPISTEMOLOGY**
*Jonathan Dancy*
0-631-13622-3 paperback

**EVIDENCE AND INQUIRY:**
Towards Reconstruction in Epistemology
*Susan Haack*
0-631-19679-X paperback

TO ORDER CALL :
1-800-216-2522 (N. America orders only) or
24-hour freephone on 0500 008205
(UK orders only)

VISIT US ON THE WEB : http://www.blackwellpublishers.co.uk